Ethnic Families in America

PATTERNS AND VARIATIONS

Third Edition

Ethnic Families in America

PATTERNS AND VARIATIONS

Third Edition

Edited by

Charles H. Mindel
Graduate School of Social Work
University of Texas at Arlington
Arlington, Texas

Robert W. Habenstein
Center for Research in Social Behavior
University of Missouri
Columbia, Missouri

Roosevelt Wright, Jr.
Graduate School of Social Work
University of Texas at Arlington
Arlington, Texas

ELSEVIER
New York • Amsterdam • London

In the first edition of this book the chapter on the Italian American family was authored by Francis X. Femminella and Jill S. Quadagno. Dr. Femminella's name was inadvertently omitted from the second edition. The chapter in this third edition does not reflect Dr. Femminella's thinking, which may be found in "Changing Perspectives on Italian American Family Life." This will appear in a forthcoming book by G. Battistella to be published by the Agnelli Foundation/ Center for Migration Studies in New York.

Elsevier Science Publishing Co., Inc.
52 Vanderbilt Avenue, New York, New York 10017

Sole distributors outside the United States and Canada:

Elsevier Science Publishers B.V.
P.O. Box 211, 1000 AE Amsterdam, the Netherlands

Library of Congress Cataloging-in-Publication Data

Ethnic families in America: patterns and variations / edited by
Charles H. Mindel, Robert W. Habenstein, Roosevelt Wright, Jr.—
3rd ed.

p. cm.
Includes index.
ISBN 0-444-01319-9
1. Ethnology—United States. 2. Family—United States.
3. Minorities—United States. 4. United States—Social
conditions—1980- I. Mindel, Charles H. II. Habenstein, Robert
Wesley, 1914- . III. Wright, Roosevelt.
E184.A1E78 1988
305.8'00973—dc 19 88-496 CIP

Current printing (last digit):
10 9 8 7 6 5 4 3 2

Manufactured in the United States of America

Contents

ASIAN ETHNIC MINORITIES

HISTORICALLY SUBJUGATED ETHNIC MINORITIES

SOCIORELIGIOUS ETHNIC MINORITIES

Preface

In the intervening years since the publication of the first and second editions of this book, we have seen interest in the "ethnic" factor continue to increase and grow in American society. Ethnic solidarity among some groups is on the rise, and ethnic conflict both here in the United States and abroad is an almost daily source of news in the mass media. The attachments of heritage, blood, peoplehood, one's own kind, or whatever term chosen, remain highly salient for large numbers of people the world over. They may be dismissed as divisive, primitive, or vestigial by some, but there is no doubt that they exist and will continue to exist for some time to come.

Part of the increase and growth in interest in ethnicity in recent years has been as a response to the widespread attitude that ethnic attachments and ethnic culture should be disposed of so as to enable "ethnics" to more easily assimilate and melt into the larger American society. This "melting pot" metaphor has long been a cornerstone element in American intergroup relations. Recent authors, however, point out that the melting pot has not reflected the actual state of affairs with respect to how ethnic groups are accepted into the mainstream of American society. Today ethnic groups are more likely to reject the negative stereotypical conceptions that were once applied to their groups. They now argue that ethnic culture and ties that exist and persist represent positive and useful modes of existence. Shame, embarrassment, or defensiveness are no longer appropriate responses to the awareness of ethnic differences, but rather pride, self-respect, and a sense of community (a "we" feeling among members) are expected.

In this third edition of *Ethnic Families in America,* the contributing authors have attempted to examine more carefully the distinctions between those things identified as ethnic (i.e., unique cultural traits, sense of community, ethnocentrism, ascribed membership, and territoriality) and those other forces impinging on people's lives such as social class and mobility and other economic matters. We have asked our contributors to distinguish between characteristics or changes in the ethnic family that are ethnocultural and characteristics or changes that are due to social class and mobility trends, and how these two forces have interacted with each other. In addition, we have asked them to address two other important issues: (1) the unique ways that various liberation movements have had an impact on the ethnic family and ethnic identity and, contrariwise, how ethnic families and ethnic identity have affected liberation movements, and (2) the problems associated with the persistence of ethnic diversity in the United States.

Although this edition of *Ethnic Families in America* covers many of the same ethnic minority groups treated in earlier editions, there are several newly included groups and there are some changes in specific ethnic content. In large part, these additions and changes reflect the fact that the social and political climate in the United States has changed dramatically, and we, ourselves, have become wiser in our knowledge and understanding of "ethnics" in this country. There is no doubt that the changed times are reflected at least in the emphasis given to certain ethnic groups in this edition compared with the earlier ones.

In revising this book, we have been heavily influenced by the comments of our colleagues in the field and by the reactions of teachers and students to the content of earlier editions. We would like to thank the many readers who have commented favorably and also those who pointed out the gaps that we have tried to fill in this new edition. If this edition is better, clearer, and more responsive to the field, we owe it to them.

In 1981 we undertook a substantial revision of *Ethnic Families in America* (Mindel and Habenstein). This third edition includes an additional coauthor, Roosevelt Wright, Jr., who did not participate in writing either the first or second edition. We acknowledge his invaluable contribution to this enterprise, and the three of us are responsible for whatever virtues and defects it may have.

A work such as this, on ethnic groups in America, certainly reflects our own academic and scholarly interests, but also in large measure our own personal histories. We, the editors, are products of our own diverse ethnic groups. Our ideas, behavior, and consciousness have been shaped by these ethnic groups, sometimes very consciously, other times on a more subtle level. Most of all, it has been within our own families that we have learned to appreciate the heritage and the contributions of our respective ethnic groups, our "people." We therefore dedicate this work to our families.

Contributors

Melba Sánchez-Ayéndez, Ph.D.
Chairperson, Department of Social Sciences, University of Puerto Rico, Medical Sciences Campus, San Juan, Puerto Rico

Rosina M. Becerra, Ph.D.
Professor and Associate Dean, School of Social Welfare, University of California, Los Angeles, Los Angeles, California

Bruce L. Campbell, Ph.D.
Department of Family Studies and Consumer Sciences, California State University, Los Angeles, Los Angeles, California

Eugene E. Campbell, Ph.D.
Deceased. Professor, Department of History, Brigham Young University, Provo, Utah

Abdo A. Elkholy, Ph.D.
Professor, Department of Sociology, Northern Illinois University, DeKalb, Illinois

Bernard Farber, Ph.D.
Professor, Department of Sociology, Arizona State University, Tempe, Arizona

Robert W. Habenstein, Ph.D.
Professor of Sociology and Research Associate, University Center for Research in Social Behavior, University of Missouri, Columbia, Missouri

Roberto Hernandez, Ph.D.
Senior Associate Professor of Latin American History, Social Science Department, Miami-Dade Community College, Mitchell Wolfson Campus, Miami, Florida

Ellen Somers Horgan, Ph.D.
Research Officer, The Disability Council of N.S.W., Sydney, Australia

Gertrude Enders Huntington, Ph.D.
Visiting Lecturer in Anthropology and Environmental Studies, University of Michigan, Ann Arbor, Michigan

Robert John, Ph.D.
United States Department of the Interior, Bureau of Indian Affairs, Haskell Indian Junior College, Lawrence, Kansas

Harry H. L. Kitano, Ph.D.
Professor of Social Welfare and Sociology, School of Social Welfare, University of California, Los Angeles, Los Angeles, California

George A. Kourvetaris, Ph.D.
Professor, Department of Sociology, Northern Illinois University, DeKalb, Illinois

Bernard Lazerwitz, Ph.D.
Professor, Department of Sociology, Bar-Ilan University, Ramat Gan, Israel

Helena Znaniecka Lopata, Ph.D.
Professor of Sociology and Director of the Center for the Comparative Study of Social Roles, Department of Sociology, Loyola University of Chicago, Chicago, Illinois

Pyong Gap Min, Ph.D.
Associate Professor, Department of Sociology, Queens College, City University of New York, Flushing, New York

Charles H. Mindel, Ph.D.
Professor of Social Work, Graduate School of Social Work, The University of Texas at Arlington, Arlington, Texas

Jill S. Quadagno, Ph.D.
Professor of Sociology and Mildred and Claude Pepper Eminent Scholar in Social Gerontology, Department of Sociology, Florida State University, Tallahassee, Florida

D. Ann Squier, M.A.
Doctoral Candidate, Department of Sociology, University of Kansas, Lawrence, Kansas

Robert Staples, Ph.D.
Professor of Sociology, Department of Social and Behavioral Sciences, University of California Medical Center at San Francisco, San Francisco, California

Jose Szapocznik, Ph.D.
Professor and Director, Spanish Family Guidance Center, Department of Psychiatry, School of Medicine, University of Miami, Miami, Florida

Thanh Van Tran, Ph.D.
Assistant Professor of Social Work, School of Social Work, Boston College, Boston, Massachusetts

Morrison G. Wong, Ph.D.
Associate Professor, Department of Sociology, Texas Christian University, Fort Worth, Texas

Roosevelt Wright, Jr., Ph.D.
Professor of Social Work and Dean, Graduate School of Social Work, The University of Texas at Arlington, Arlington, Texas

CHAPTER ONE

Family Lifestyles of America's Ethnic Minorities: An Introduction

Charles H. Mindel
Robert W. Habenstein
Roosevelt Wright, Jr.

ANALYSIS AND METAPHOR

This is a book about patterned differences in American families—differences based on the national, cultural, religious, and racial identification and membership of groups of people who do not set the dominant style of life or control the privileges and power in any given society. These differences are embedded in what generally are known as "ethnic groups." Ethnicity usually is displayed in the values, attitudes, lifestyles, customs, rituals, and personality types of individuals who identify with particular ethnic groups. If these ethnic identifications and memberships had no other effect on people's lives than to provide interesting variety within a country, sociologists would long since have described their variety and moved on to other matters. However, identification with and membership in an ethnic group has far-reaching effects on both groups and individuals—controlling access to opportunities in life, feelings of well-being, and mastery over the futures of one's children.

Ethnicity and the analysis of ethnic groups have long been topics of discussion in scholarly and popular literature. "Melting pot," the metaphor embodying the notion that immigrants from all over the world somehow fuse together here in America, producing a new and better amalgam that combines the best cultural contributions of each ethnic group, was first coined by Israel Zangwill in a 1906 play of the same name. However, since 1915, when Horace Kallen first introduced the idea of "cultural pluralism," there have been avid discussions about the virtues of becoming "American" while at the same time retaining one's cultural heritage. Still others have claimed that what really exists in America is a highly ethnocentric coercion toward "Anglo conformity," which implies the downgrading and elimination of ethnic culture and the incorporation of the dominant Anglo culture. The element of conflict and the transformation of ethnic groups into politically conscious ethnic minorities are central to this approach.

In recent years, there has been a decline in melting-pot theories of racial and ethnic assimilation, and the notion of American society as a conglomerate of "unmeltable ethnics" existing in a somewhat tenuous societal pluralism has been gaining ground. The "salad bowl" metaphor has found favor in Canada, where pluralism—the willingness of any one group to seek an amicable accord with any other, regardless of hue or creed—has long been an article of national faith (Elkin, 1970; Ishwaran, 1971; Queen and Habenstein, 1974; Wade, 1960). Conflict theory has not yet developed an acceptable figure of speech to characterize American ethnic relations, but "cats in a bag" might not be totally inapplicable.

The concept of assimilation historically has long enjoyed the status of what Gouldner (1970) has called a "domain assumption," carrying with it a kind of value-laden ethnocentricism that presumes superiority on the part of the host culture in all respects and an inferior cultural baggage carried ashore by the newly arrived immigrants. True, "Americanization," the lingual epitome of an earlier twentieth century social movement to detribalize and de-ethnicize the ubiquitous foreign element, has long since left the sociologist's lexicon, although its presence occasionally may be noted in a Fourth of July or Memorial Day public address.

Some of the enthusiasm for denigrating ethnic groups has lost its national appeal. The long-term rise in the standard of living and the disappearance of much physically demanding, toil-ridden work has resulted in fewer "dirty-work" occupations being associated with particular ethnic groups (Fuchs, 1968). The material success of some ethnic groups *qua* ethnic groups—the Chinese, Japanese, Jews, Irish, and, recently, Cubans—has helped explode the myth that ethnics are somehow genetically and culturally best equipped to remain at lower or, at best, middle levels of America's economy.

A more recent and spectacular development in the sociopolitical realm is the impressive growth of the civil rights movement, which has been punctuated by fire storms of political activism and violence and an attendant proliferation of legislation and court rulings aimed directly at eliminating discrimination in all its guises. An expanding black consciousness has for millions of Americans reversed the onus of color: "black" does not "stay back," "brown" is not "down," and "white" is not necessarily "right."

In reviewing these developments of long and short duration, it is evident that recently there has been a growth of ethnic awareness of a different genre than was seen previously in America, whether it expresses itself in the comfort that older ethnic groups can now feel when proclaiming their Old World heritage or in the troubled and troublesome abrasiveness of the long-subjugated ethnic minorities searching for a status yet to be won. Both the achievers and the achieving, it remains to be added, face the universal problem of searching for, finding, and maintaining roots and tradition in the face of the appeals of modernity and homogenized living in the burgeoning mass society.

Although all these contrasting and seemingly contradictory views of American immigrant and minority groups—Anglo conformity, melting pot, and cultural pluralism, or, as sociologists often refer to them, assimilation, amalgamation, and accommodation (Rose, 1974:66)—have taken on a new relevancy today. Only in the last few years have we begun to acquire knowledge about ethnic groups.

Most textbooks on the American family's attempt to meet the challenge of ethnic diversity include examples of one or two distinctive families (Nye and Berardo, 1973; Burgess, Locke, and Thomes, 1963; Kephart, 1972; Cavan, 1969; Reiss, 1971). However, while ethnicity continues to act as an important determinant of behavior for a significant number of people, many scholars and textbook writers have treated ethnicity *en passant,* either as a historical or residual category. It may well be that in the long run ethnic differences will disappear, as Glazer (1954) and others have argued; but as Greeley (1969:21) notes, "Family, land and common cultural heritage have always been terribly important to human beings, and suspicion of anyone who is strange or different seems also deeply rooted in the human experience."

It is the purpose of this book to examine a wide variety of American ethnic groups, probing the historical circumstances that impelled them to come to this country, focusing on the structure and functioning of their family life to determine or, at least, to raise clues about how and why they have been able or unable to maintain an ethnic identification over the generations, and, finally, looking ahead to speculate on what the future has in store for these groups and their constitutive families.

WHAT IS AN ETHNIC GROUP?

What is it to be ethnic? In recent years it often has been suggested that ethnicity is unimportant, that ethnic ties are part of man's primitive past —a past out of which humans have been evolving over many years. As Greeley (1974:10) states:

> In fact the conflicts that have occupied most men over the past two or three decades, those that have led to the most appalling outpourings of blood, have had precious little to do with ideological division. Most of us are unwilling to battle to the death over ideology, but practically all of us it seems are ready to kill each other over noticeable differences of color, language, religious faith, height, food habits, and facial configurations.

Greeley (1974:10) further points out that:

> Thousands have died in seemingly endless battles between two very Semitic people, the Jews and the Arabs. The English and French glare hostilely at each other in Quebec; Christians and Moslems have renewed their ancient conflicts on the island of Mindanao; Turks and Greeks nervously grip their guns on Cyprus; and Celts and Saxons in Ulster have begun to imprison and kill one another with all the cumulative passion of a thousand years' hostility.

More recently, the Persians in Iran and Arabs in Iraq serve as another example of ethnic conflict. It appears that perhaps the collapse of old colonial empires and the rise of nationalism in the post-World War II period have given rise to numerous conflicts at tribal, linguistic, religious, geographical, and cultural levels. The amount of conflict appears to be increasing rather than decreasing.

What all these conflicts seem to share is not "an ideological character" —especially the ideology of modern superpower conflicts, namely economic systems and social class—but a concern in some sense with very basic differences among groups of people, particularly cultural differences. There are concerns reflected in these conflicts that apparently are important to people—matters for which they are willing to fight to the death to defend. Clifford Geertz (1963:109) referred to these ties that people are willing to die for as "primordial attachments":

> By a primordial attachment is meant one that stems from the "givens"—or more precisely, as culture is inevitably involved in such matters the "assured givens"—of social existence: immediate contiguity and kin connection

> mainly, but beyond them, the givenness that stems from being born into a particular religious community, speaking a particular language, or even a dialect of language, and following particular social patterns. These congruities of blood, speech, custom, and so on, are seen to have an ineffable, at times overpowering, coerciveness in and of themselves. One is bound to one's kinsman, one's neighbor, one's fellow believer, *ipso facto,* as a result not merely of one's personal affection, practical necessity, common interest, or incurred obligation, but at least in great part by the virtue of some unaccountable absolute import attributed to the very tie itself. The general strength of such primordial bonds, and the types of them that are important, differ from person to person, from society to society, and from time to time. But for virtually every person, in every society, at almost all times, some attachments seem to flow from a sense of natural—some would say spiritual—affinity than from social interaction.

These attachments, these feelings of belonging to a certain group of people for whatever reason, are a basic feature of the human condition. These ties are called "ethnic ties" and the group of people that one is tied to is an "ethnic group." In this general sense, an ethnic group consists of those who share a unique social and cultural heritage that is passed on from generation to generation.

Gordon (1964), in slightly different terms, sees those who share a feeling of "peoplehood" as an ethnic group. But the sense of peoplehood that characterized most social life in the past centuries has become fragmented and shattered. This, it is suggested, has been occurring for a variety of reasons including, in the last few centuries, massive population increases, the development of large cities, the formation of social classes, and grouping of peoples into progressively larger political units. However, as many other writers have noted, there has been a continuing need for individuals to merge their individual identity with some ancestral group—with "their own kind of people." Gordon proposes that the fragmentation of social life has left competing models for this sense of peoplehood; people are forced to choose among them or somehow to entirely integrate them. In America, the core categories of ethnic identity from which individuals are able to form a sense of peoplehood are race, religion, national origin, or some combination of these categories (Gordon, 1964). It is these categories, emphasizing substantively cultural symbols of consciousness of time, that are used to define the groups included in this book.

Ethnicity in America

In the 1970s, we have seen a growing interest in cultural pluralism, ethnic pluralism, and ethnic differences in the United States. This has not always been the case, and it has been argued by some that the reason why examination of ethnic differences in the scholarly study of man has been lacking has much to do with the dominant assimilationist model of American society. According to this model, ethnic differences, although perhaps useful in the past to preserve the familiar or *gemeinschaft* character of the old country for large numbers of people set adrift in alien America, are not particularly useful today in our more rational and class-oriented society. In addition, the divisive aspects of ethnicity are emphasized and seen as barriers to peaceful coexistence within the American social fabric. The integrative aspects of ethnic ties and culture have been almost entirely neglected. As a result, many individuals with rich ethnic heritages have been encouraged, coerced, and, in other ways, pushed toward giving up their heritage and becoming "Americanized." Stereotypes of the negative aspects and consequences of ethnic culture abound: Italians are corrupt; Poles are ignorant; white ethnics are racists and warmongers; and any number of different ethnic groups are lazy and will not work. These kinds of stereotypes have long been part of the general American culture. The implication is that as soon as one gives up his or her inferior beliefs and ties, and as soon as one leaves this life—this narrow, dull, provincial life—the better the individual will be.

The fact that Americanization is now seen by many as ethnocentric and destructive reflects a major shift. As Greeley (1974:29) states, "Ethnicity is far from being a divisive force in society. It can be viewed as a constructive one, at least it is inevitable." This shift reflects a renewal of ethnic consciousness—a new awareness of distinctive ethnic culture, partly a consciously remembered one and partly a set of inherited customs and beliefs. Ethnics are now allowed to endorse the theme that they "have the right to be different." This new consciousness on the part of ethnic groups reflects the larger changes and upheavals that American society experienced during the 1960s and 1970s, especially the various liberation movements that emerged during this period, most notably the black civil rights movement. These movements tended in their turn to renew the ethnic consciousness of the so-called white ethnics or unmeltable ethnics, as Novak has referred to them, inspiring renewed interest in cultural pluralism and a new sensitivity toward others and their differences. We have seen increases in the personal, conscious self-appropriation of one's own cultural history and a willingness to share in the social and political needs and struggles of groups to which one is personally tied. The reemergence of ethnic feelings and interests has not necessarily meant a return to Old World culture. It does not, as Novak (1973) points out, represent an attempt to "hold back the clock"—instead, it represents a defense of ties that are important to large numbers of individuals in this country.

The reason why these interests are seen as important to defend and, as we have seen in various locales, at times to fight for, is that they are very important to individuals in their daily lives, not a mere nostalgic defense of some useless cultural artifact. There are (and were) many reasons for maintaining ethnic communal ties. Some were primarily useful at the time when members of ethnic groups were early immigrants to this country and other ties continue to be important to this day. The utility of ethnic ties and ethnic groups is in large part the reason for their continued existence. It should be remembered that as Glazer (1973:169) states:

> The immigrants . . . were as much in favor of the melting pot as native American nationals, indeed more so, because they thought the melting pot, if they really succeeded in dissolving into some American mass, would give them access to every position in society; while native American chauvinists trying to monopolize these positions were not nearly so much in favor of so complete a disappearance of the immigrant groups.

In fact, the melting pot never fully succeeded, and large numbers of immigrant groups were forced to maintain ethnic communal ties almost as a matter of self-defense. Glazer and Moynihan (1970), in their work on ethnicity and their analysis of the evolution and persistence of ethnicity, argued that "the adoption of a totally new ethnic identity, by dropping whatever one is to become simply American, is inhibited by strong elements in the social structure of the United States." These inhibitions range from brutal discrimination and prejudice to the "unavailability of a simple 'American' identity" (Glazer and Moynihan, 1970:xxxiii). Most positively seen, ethnic communities provide individuals with congenial associates, help organize experience by personalizing an increasingly impersonal world, and provide opportunities for social mobility and success within an ethnic context (Greeley, 1969).

Glazer and Moynihan also offer some provocative suggestions to explain the increasing importance of ethnicity in recent years. They hypothesize that ethnic identities have replaced occupational identities, particularly working-class occupational identities that have lost much of their glamour in recent years. It is better to be Polish than to be known as a Polish assembly-line worker in a Detroit automobile plant. They also speculate that one's ethnic identity in America largely has become separate from events in the country of origin. Domestic events are more important than international events in evoking feelings of ethnic awareness. They make an important exception for the Jews, a group whose ethnic identification increased dramatically in America with the creation of the state of Israel.

They also suggest, contrary to Greeley and Herberg, that religion, as well as occupation and homeland, has declined as a source of ethnic identification. The reasons, they say, are declining religiosity in general and, among the Catholics, the rather dramatic changes that have overwhelmed the Catholic church in the past decade. Ethnic groups (specifically blacks, Puerto Ricans, Jews, Italians, and Irish) largely have become political, economic, and cultural interest groups (Glazer and Moynihan, 1970:xxxiv–xxxvi). Interethnic relationships, by the same token, become dynamic and tension-laden and carry seeds of potential conflict. The major cities remain the locus of interethnic unrest. One explanation of such conflict, paraphrasing Max Weber, is that cultural relationships that are not power-centered give way to political relations that certainly are.

Minority Groups

Related, of course, but of a different genre is the concept of minority or minority group. "Minority," in the sociological rather than statistical sense, refers to a power or dominance relationship. Those groups that have unequal access to power, that are considered in some way unworthy of equally sharing power, and that are stigmatized in terms of assumed inferior traits or characteristics are minority groups. To be a member of a minority group, therefore, is to share a status relationship, and to act as a minority group member is to express power consciously. To be a member of an ethnic group, on the other hand, is to share a sense of cultural and historical uniqueness, and to act as a member of an ethnic group is to express feelings or call attention to that uniqueness. It should be understood that the same individual at any one moment may act in either capacity. The black student who complains about the student cafeteria food may be expressing (ethnically) a desire for dishes familiar to him from childhood, or he may be expressing (minority) resentment against being denied these foods on the basis of race and race alone.

ETHNICITY AND FAMILY LIFESTYLE

The maintenance of ethnic identification and solidarity ultimately rests on the ability of the family to socialize its members into the ethnic culture and thus to channel and control, perhaps program, future behavior. The manner in which the respective ethnic families carry out this function is referred to as "family lifestyles." Consequently, the distinctive family life-styles that developed as a result of historical and contemporary social processes become the focal concern of this work. Contributors were asked to examine the relationships and characteristics distinctive of ethnic family life; to look to the past for an explanation of historical or genetic significance; to describe the key characteristics of the ethnic family today; and to analyze the changes that have occurred in the family and speculate about what lies ahead.

It bears repeating that the historical experience of the ethnic group, both with respect to when the group arrived on these shores and the conditions under which the members of the group were forced to live, is a vitally important factor in the explanation of the persistence of the ethnic family and the ethnic group. For this reason, each chapter contains an important discussion of the historical background of the respective ethnic groups. In addition to the old-country settings, each contributor was requested to summarize the major characteristics of the family as it previously existed or first appeared in America to more clearly show the subsequent changes and adaptations.

One of the most significant ways an ethnic culture is expressed is through those activities that we identify as family activities. The family historically has been a conservative institution, and those cultural elements concerning family life, if not affected by outside forces, will tend to replace themselves generation after generation (Farber, 1964). Experiences within the family are intense, heavily emotion-laden, and apt to evoke pleasurable or painful memories for most individuals. For example, it is not accidental that in many of the ethnic groups to be discussed here, "eating," particularly eating "ethnic" food, remains a significant part of the ethnic identity. These are activities that occur in a family context. If traditional ethnic values are to be found anywhere, they will be found in the family.

In addition to developing historical context, the contributors were asked to discuss four major areas relevant to ethnic family life in which ethnic culture might either be generated, sustained, or have an impact. First were the demographic characteristics of the ethnic family. How is the ethnic culture specifically expressed in fertility, marriage, and divorce rates? How does the group cope with the cultural matter of intermarriage? Intermarriage can be viewed as an important indicator of assimilation for the ethnic group and ranges in incidence from very low among the black Americans and Amish to relatively high as among the Japanese Americans. Second is the question of the structure of the family, which involves the distribution of status, authority, and responsibility within the nuclear family and the network of kin relationships linking members of the extended family. Most discussions of ethnic family life have focused on this area because many ethnic groups have been characterized as patriarchal, matriarchal, or as having very close-knit extended family relationships. It is in this context that we hear comments about "black matriarchy" or the "Jewish mother." How much is cultural myth or ideology? How much is fact? What has been the effect of the American experience?

In addition to the cultural patterns that define family roles and statuses, rights, and obligations, there are many attributes of an ethnic culture that are mediated through the family. These are cultural values that concern such issues as achievement, style of life, and educational or occupational aspirations. While many historical, economic, and other factors such as discrimination and prejudice have limited the mobility of individuals in many ethnic groups, the possession of a cultural reservoir of motivations and skills has worked to the distinct advantage of many. For others, the lack of this reservoir has worked to their disadvantage. The cultural tradition of the Jews, with its emphasis on literacy and education, has helped them immeasurably from a socioeconomic standpoint. On the other hand, the Poles have only recently begun to emphasize the importance of education to their family members. These cultural distinctions, while existing to some extent outside the family context, are for the most part developed within the family.

Finally, in discussing ethnic family life, it is important to examine the family at different stages of the family life cycle. In this collection of essays, contributors were requested to analyze those aspects of child rearing, adolescence, mate selection, and the place of the elderly in which ethnic culture has had significant influence. The culture of many groups usually specifies what the most desirable end product of the socialization process should be. Whether this product should be a good Mormon or Amishman, the family as the major force of socialization, especially in the critical early years, is the most responsible ethnic institution.

Most of the large-scale immigration to America has ceased, although, as in the case of the Puerto Ricans, the Greek Americans, Arab Americans, and most recently the refugees from Cuba and Indochina, there has been a continuing or sudden large-scale migration to this country. Is it then true, as many writers have suggested, that ethnic differences may very well be on the decline and may be relatively unimportant distinguishing features of individuals in the future? For some, such as black Americans and other racial groups, these differences and the potential for tension and conflict appear destined to continue for some time. For others, such as Greek Americans, Irish Americans, or Polish Americans, these distinctions appear to be disappearing at a somewhat faster rate.

ETHNIC DIVERSITY AS THE CRITERION OF SELECTION

Although not randomly selected, the ethnic families presented in this book were chosen to represent a rather wide spectrum of distinguishable groups, ranging from the less than 100,000 Amish to the 26.5 million black people, whose ethnicity continues to be expressed through identifiable institutions and, significantly, the family. Nevertheless, there *are* large numbers of Americans who find it possible to trace descent to foreign nations and cultures such as Germany, Great Britain, and Canada, yet who retain little, if any, of an Old World cultural identity. Their lifestyles are largely indistinguishable from others of similar socioeconomic classes (except in certain isolated enclaves here and there), and for this reason, they have been excluded from this work.

While the possession of an ethnic heritage that continues to be expressed in a distinctive family lifestyle is the common theme among all groups chosen in this work, the reasons for both the appearance in America (remembering that Native Americans had precedence!) and continued existence as an identifiable ethnic group remain to some extent unique. That groups migrating to America in great numbers in pre- and early-nineteenth century periods were responding to general social, economic, and class-oppressive pressures gave all immigrants of that time a measure of common status. Nevertheless, each has its own distinguishing features, contingencies, and value system to provide significantly different ethnic group life histories, and therefore, each has its own story to be told.

There is some justification, then, for adopting the kaleidoscopic approach and simply jumbling all 17 family groups together without anything more ordered than what can be achieved by an alphabetical arrangement. Conversely, for those more compulsive about systematization, a set of formal ahistorical, all-inclusive categories might be constructed. We have chosen something less abstract through the pragmatically useful grouping of our ethnic families into five substantive categories: (1) European ethnic minorities, (2) Hispanic ethnic minorities, (3) Asian ethnic minorities, (4) historically subjugated ethnic minorities, and (5) socioreligious ethnic minorities.

These categories help sort out the groups, according to several dimensions, but they should in no way be taken as definitive, completely exclusive, or the only way to achieve a useful classification. The most important criterion in the minds of the editors has been that the categories appear to capture a particularly important contingency or group experience that has a continuing influence on its collective fate. In the following paragraphs, we briefly discuss the scheme that we have chosen:

1. European Ethnic Minorities

The four ethnic minorities in this category are the Polish, Irish, Italian, and Greek immigrants who arrived in the late nineteenth and early twentieth centuries. During a period extending roughly from the early 1880s until the outbreak of World War I, almost 25 million European immigrants entered the United States. This influx represents the archetypal immigration to this country, and it is this period that we most often think of when we visualize immigrant life. It is from this wave of European immigration that most of today's non-Protestant white ethnics are descended.

2. Hispanic Ethnic Minorities

The three ethnic minorities in this category are the Mexicans, Cubans, and Puerto Ricans. Unlike other American ethnic groups, Hispanics have entered the United States in a variety of ways. Although Mexicans have come to this country in the nineteenth and twentieth centuries as voluntary immigrants, they retain a heritage of originally having been absorbed into American society as a conquered group. Puerto Ricans, too, are a group not clearly part of either voluntary immigration or conquest. Puerto Rico became a territory of the United States in 1898 following the Spanish American War, and in 1917, the inhabitants of the island were granted American citizenship. The greatest influx of Puerto Ricans to the United States was during the 1950s, when nearly 20 percent of the island's population moved to the mainland.

The movement of Cubans to the United States in the past two decades has been a voluntary immigration. Yet it differs from those of most past groups in that it was initially impelled mainly by political rather than economic motives. The problems that all of these groups have faced include economic integration and social assimilation into American society.

3. Asian Ethnic Minorities

The four ethnic minorities in this category are the Koreans, Chinese, Japanese, and Vietnamese. The Chinese and Japanese American ethnic minorities have been in this country in substantial numbers for 75 to 100 years. The Koreans and Vietnamese, however, are characterized by a sizeable number of recent, as well as a continuing flow of, immigrants. Important questions for the study of all of these groups relate to the effects of time and generation on the cultural heritage but, more particularly, as they directly affect family life. The extent to which assimilation and acculturation has had an impact on ethnic identity and lifestyle remains one of the key problems encountered by these groups of people. In addition, the problems they all have faced include adjusting to a modern business cycle and war-plagued industrialized society and to constant infusion of new representatives from their respective countries of origin.

4. Historically Subjugated Ethnic Minorities

The two groups, blacks and Native Americans, are categorized together because their identity and experience in this country have been the result of or strongly influenced by their respective race. These groups either preceded the arrival of the "Americans" or arrived later and were immediately or later placed in some form of bondage. Enslaved to the land, alienated from it, or bound in a latter-day peonage, blacks and Native Americans have in America the darkest and least savory group life histories from which to build viable ethnic cultures. In both of these groups, it will be noted that the role of the family, whether truncated or extended, becomes crucial for ethnic survival.

5. Socioreligious Ethnic Minorities

The four ethnic minorities in this category are the Amish, the Jews, the Arabs, and the Mormons. They are categorized together because their identity and experience have largely been a result of or strongly influenced, if not dominated, by their respective religions. They all sought in America a place to live that kind of social existence in which religion could continue to be vitally conjoined with all aspects of their life and livelihood.

REFERENCES

Burgess, Ernest, Harvey J. Locke, and Mary M. Thomes. 1963. *The Family* (3rd ed.). New York: American Book.

Cavan, Ruth S. 1969. *The American Family* (4th ed.). New York: Thomas Y. Crowell.

Elkin, Frederick. 1970. *The Family in Canada: An Account of Present Knowledge and Gaps in Knowledge About Canadian Families.* Ottawa: The Vanier Institute of the Family.

Farber, Bernard. 1964. *Family Organization and Interaction.* San Francisco: Chandler.

Fuchs, Victor. 1968. *The Service Economy.* New York: National Bureau of Research. Distributed by Columbia University Press.

Geertz, Clifford. 1963. "The Integrated Revolution," in Clifford Geertz (ed.), *Old Societies and New Societies.* Glencoe, IL: Free Press.

Glazer, Nathan. 1954. "Ethnic Groups in America: From National Culture to Ideology," in Morroe Berger, Theodore Abel, and Charles H. Page (eds.), *Freedom and Control in Modern Society.* New York: Van Nostrand.

———. 1973. "The Issue of Cultural Pluralism in America Today," in Joseph Ryan (ed.), *White Ethnics: Their Life in Working-Class America.* Englewood Cliffs, NJ: Prentice-Hall, pp. 168–177.

Glazer, Nathan, and Daniel P. Moynihan. 1970. *Beyond the Melting Pot* (2nd ed.). Cambridge: MIT Press.

Gordon, Milton. 1964. *Assimilation in American Life.* New York: Oxford University Press.

Gouldner, Alvin. 1970. *The Coming Crisis in Western Sociology.* New York: Basic Books.

Greeley, Andrew M. 1969. *Why Can't They Be Like Us?.* New York: Institute of Human Relations Press.

———. 1974. *Ethnicity in the United States: A Preliminary Reconnaissance.* New York: John Wiley.

Ishwaran, K. (ed.). 1971. *The Canadian Family: A Book of Readings.* Toronto: Holt, Rinehart and Winston of Canada.

Kephart, William M. 1972. *The Family, Society and the Individual* (3rd ed.). Boston: Houghton Mifflin.

Novak, Michael. 1973. "Probing the New Ethnicity," in Joseph Ryan (ed.), *White Ethnics: Their Life in Working-Class America.* Englewood Cliffs, NJ: Prentice-Hall, pp. 158–167.

Nye, F. Ivan, and Felix Berardo. 1973. *The Family: Its Structure and Interaction.* New York: Macmillan.

Queen, Stuart, and Robert W. Habenstein. 1974. *The Family in Various Cultures* (4th ed.). Philadelphia: J. B. Lippincott.

Reiss, Ira. 1971. *The Family System in America.* New York: Holt, Rinehart and Winston.

Rose, Peter I. 1974. *They and We: Racial and Ethnic Relations in the United States* (2nd ed.). New York: Random House.

Wade, Mason (ed.). 1960. *Canadian Dualism.* Toronto: Toronto University Press.

EUROPEAN ETHNIC MINORITIES

CHAPTER TWO

The Polish American Family

Helena Znaniecka Lopata

INTRODUCTION

The main thrust of this chapter is the Polish American family as it exists within the developing and changing Polish ethnic community, called "Polonia" by its residents. This emphasis is different from much of the literature on ethnic groups, which is primarily concerned with individualistic assimilation and acculturation and attempts to determine the factors that impede or facilitate the absorption of peoples into a society. This chapter focuses on certain background characteristics of Old World Polish culture, especially in its peasant variations, and on historical trends in Polonia, which have created a unique ethnic community that persists into the 1980s. The Polish family must be seen in its relation to the continued existence of the Polish American community.

The last of the "early" (prior to the 1920s) immigrants into the United States were the Poles and the Italians. The Poles actually immigrated in three waves. The largest number came between 1880 and 1924, when entrance into America was cut off by new laws. They are known in Polonia, or the Polish American community, as the *stara emigracja,* "old emigration" (the Poles identify the movement as emigration from Poland rather than immigration to another country). The *nowa emigracja,* "new emigration," followed World War II and consisted of people displaced by the Germans or Soviets. The communists who took over Poland after that war did not allow emigration for many years, and only recently has there been a third wave of immigrants, though smaller in number. There is now also a reputedly large number of Poles in America on visitor visas who are working illegally to earn money to improve the situation of families back home.

HISTORICAL BACKGROUND

Families do not live in a vacuum, but within a community and the larger society. Family actions and interactions are patterned by family roles, with obviously idiosyncratic variations growing out of family histories.[1] Family life is embedded in a complex culture, each member holding beliefs, images, expectations, evaluations, and other ideological patterns that concern themselves, other family members, and the world in which they live. The various immigrant waves consisted of quite different people, and the Polish presence in America also included many political émigrés and temporary residents who helped create a very complex community organization. In all, I (Lopata, 1976a) have estimated that approximately a million people identified as Poles or as having been born in Poland came here, and approximately 300,000 left this country during the years between 1899 and 1972. How many and who came, depended on not only the immigration laws of the United States but also the situation in Poland. The country was occupied by three states—Russia, Austria, and Prussia—from 1795 to 1918. The national cultural society, however, retained its identity despite the absence of a unifying political state (for a discussion of these concepts see Znaniecki, 1952).

The Polish immigrants to America came from two separate class subcultures, but they shared the Polish language, the Polish version of Catholicism, and many major cultural complexes. The subcultures actually were variations on the major themes, but the variations basically kept the two groups apart in Poland and in America until recent years. The common themes of the immigrants included beliefs in a national character, a system of status competition, and the willingness and ability to build a complex ethnic Polonian community with horizontal strata and vertical lines of connection (Lopata, 1976b; Thomas and Znaniecki, 1918–1920). One group consisted of the combined, mutually influencing gentry, or small nobility and intelligentsia, and the other group consisted of various levels of the peasantry (Szczepanski, 1970). Urban bourgeois and working-class lifestyles were not highly developed in Poland during the time of the mass emigration (Jawlowska and Mokrzycki, 1978). In the decades when most

[1] I am using here Znaniecki's (1965) definition of a social role as a set of patterned, functionally interdependent, social relations between a social person and a social circle, involving duties and rights.

old emigration families left Poland, "the social cleavage between peasants and *szlachta* (gentry) was absolute and unbridgeable" (Benet, 1951:33). Each group had its own image of the national character, status arenas, and hierarchies—as well as companionate circles of "ethclass" organization and informal association (Gordon, 1964; Lopata, 1976b).

The Poles in Poland undertook many revolts against the occupying forces, which resulted in the migration of political refugees. In addition, the Poles created governments-in-exile in Europe that needed funds and frequently sent representatives to America's Polonias to develop and nurture nationalism among the immigrants. In the interwar years, few immigrants came here, and a fair number of prior settlers in America returned to Poland—although not as many as had originally planned to return once the country was independent, because many had become very comfortable on this side of the ocean.

Although the old emigration was quite heterogeneous, the vast majority belonged to the various subclasses of peasants (Szczepanski, 1970; Thomas and Znaniecki, 1918–1920). At the turn of the century, 34 percent were illiterate. That figure dropped to three percent by 1924. They came from villages and agricultural life-styles, but most settled in urbanized areas and sought jobs in industry. Their memory of Poland was that of the village and a country under foreign domination. After World War II, the American government allowed a large number of Poles (more than 164,000) to enter the United States as displaced persons outside of the quota structure (Lopata, 1976a:13). The new emigration came from a completely different background and much higher level of educational achievement. The country they left had changed considerably over the years since the turn of the twentieth century, when the old emigrants left, as documented by many Polish rural socioligists (Jagiello-Lysiowa, 1976; Kowalski, 1967; Turowski and Szwengrub, 1976).[2] The two immigrant waves were so different that they created a great deal of conflict in the community. The new emigration looked down on the old emigration and its descendents, considering their life-style to be highly Americanized, their use of Polish archaic, and their subculture peasantlike. The old emigration considered the new emigration "uppity," and the new group's presence pushed the early settlers toward greater assimilation. Over time, the more educated descendents of the old emigration joined groups formed by the new, while the new emigration

[2]There are frequent comments in the Polonian press concerning the vast difference in the way most of the *stara emigracja* and the *nowa emigracja* see Poland. It would be interesting to compare family life of former peasants who migrated to Polish cities with that of emigrants to American cities from Poland. Bloch (1976) has done that for families remaining in a smaller community in Poland with their relatives in America.

revitalized established organizations. Despite the differences of emigration waves, social class backgrounds, and generation of residence here, there are certain commonalities among Polish Americans.

Polish American Families: Common Themes

These common themes include belief in a national character, intense interest in status competition, and the willingness to create and participate in a complex ethnic community. In this last characteristic, the Poles are very different than the Italians, as discussed in this book and by Cohler and Lieberman (1979).

NATIONAL CHARACTER. The socialization of children and the interaction among adults in Poland and Polonia were, and apparently still are, based on a strong belief in a national character—admittedly with regional and even community, age, and sex variations.[3] Each believer in the Polish national character affirms its existence, but careful perusal of the literature, including autobiographies, indicates that the content of this alleged character contains only a few common items when expressed by different people (Super, 1939; Szczepanski, 1970).

Szczepanski (1970:167) elucidates some of the components of the ideal national character of the upper classes in his book, *Polish Society:*

> The traditional Polish personality ideal was derived from the culture of the nobility and was composed of such traits as readiness for the defense of the Catholic faith, readiness for the defense of the fatherland, a highly developed sense of personal dignity and honor, a full-blown individualism, an imposing mien, chivalry, intellectual brilliance and dash.

This image contains the moral obligation of members of the Polish national cultural society to develop and perpetuate its culture and to educate potential members into its literary base in an effort to fight denationalization (Lopata, 1976c; Znaniecki, 1952). The obligation to fight the three foreign states that partitioned and ruled the Polish political state for 125 years before World War I resulted in numerous uprisings that failed,

---

[3]Studies of the acculturation of a group of people limited to a few items, such as the use of language and religious celebrations, neglect a very important and more significant aspect of group identity, its feeling and definition of "national character." People who share a belief that they are similar transmit to younger generations this feeling of identity and their whole philosophy of life is incorporated in their child rearing procedures (McCready, 1974). Sandberg (1974) has an extensive set of measures of Polish American ethnicity, but even he does not deal with beliefs about human nature, "Polishness" and child rearing methods.

adding a tragic-romantic element to the upper-class vision of the national character. The intelligentsia's variation on the major theme added a strong intellectual bent—the members of that class saw themselves as "cultured men" familiar with all aspects of the national Polish culture, as well as with the cultures of other nations (Lopata, 1976c; Szczepanski, 1962). This total image was shared by many political émigrés and most of the immigrants to America who had been displaced by World War II. The attempt to nationalize Polish Americans who did not belong to the upper class to gain assistance in the struggle for independence capitalized on this romantic image of the Pole.

Most of the peasants who emigrated prior to World War I did not share the intellectual and nationalistic features in their view of the national character. In fact, they tended to be anti-intellectual, believing that human beings were created for hard physical work. They saw Poles through a mixture of magic-religious prisms—basically as sinful and evil or, at least, weak (Chalasinski, 1946; Finestone, 1964, 1967; Thomas and Znaniecki, 1918-1920). This belief in a basically sinful human nature—the men easily ruled by temper, and both sexes by sexual desire and impulsive, often unwise, action—resulted in relatively harsh methods of socialization of children, different than the patterns evolving in America (Finestone, 1964; Thomas and Znaniecki, 1918-1920).

Despite these major differences between the upper-class and peasant images of the national character, there were many common elements. Super (1939) [quoted by Lopata (1976b:114-115)], who considered himself an objective observer, listed characteristics all Poles felt were common to them:

> A strong emphasis on equality within the two main classes with a strong sense of individualism; tolerance of other groups; religiousity of predominantly Catholic identity; idealism, romanticism; love of the soil; a strong family orientation; hospitality; interest in good food and drink of an international flavor; stress on courtesy, etiquette and manner highly developed and strictly followed.

The anthropologist Benet (1951:216) also pointed to this last characteristic, one that Poles are very conscious of and is apparent in the letters contained in *The Polish Peasant in Europe and America* (Thomas and Znaniecki, 1918-1920):

> The Polish peasant is probably the most polite and well mannered man in Europe. Rural etiquette prescribes certain expressions and even certain dialogues for everyday life and it is not permissible to improvise substitutes.

One persistent theme passed on from generation to generation that is constantly repeated in the Polish and Polonian mass media and among Poles when they talk of themselves is the emphasis on individualism and competitiveness within one's own stratum (Benet, 1951:33):

> Within each class, however, there is an almost fanatical insistence on the equality of individuals. A Pole would rather bow to a foreigner than give authority to one of his own group.[4]

This belief in a basically competitive rather than solidified national group is a basic component of the fabric out of which Polish and Polish American men and women weave their life course.

STATUS COMPETITION. The belief in individualism and competitiveness have evolved and been institutionalized into an elaborate system of status competition that regulates conflict, adds excitement (even joie de vivre), and has contributed to keeping the Polonian community and its families together and internally oriented despite the tendencies toward disorganization and gradual Americanization of the culture (Lopata, 1976b). Concern with and activity on behalf of one's "reputation," or position vis-à-vis other members of the community, underlies much of traditional village and urban life in Poland. The *okolica* (area within which a person's and a family's reputation is contained) can vary from a single

---

[4]There has developed among social scientists an image of peasants, especially those in countries where serfdom was abolished relatively recently, as passive (Brunner, 1929; Cohler and Lieberman, 1979; Schooler, 1976). This image totally ignores the evidence from such work as Thomas and Znaniecki (1918–1920) or the Nobel Prize winning *The Peasants* by Reymont (1925), as well as that of the authors quoted above. Certainly, the Polish peasant was far from passive within his or her *okolica.* The negative image of the Polish immigrant is contained even in sociological literature.

Janowitz (1966:xxiii–xxv) reports in his introduction to a collection of works by W. I. Thomas and from Thomas and Znaniecki's (1918–1920) *The Polish Peasant in Europe and America* that one of the main reasons Thomas became interested in studying the assimilation of Poles was "Polish murder," so labeled by the Chicago police: "Boys and young men who were law-abiding or at least conforming would suddenly, with little provocation and no forethought, engage in violent and explosive fights, including attacks on police officers. . . ." That is hardly a sociological analysis. He further states:

> In the lore about W. I. Thomas that grew up among graduate students at the University of Chicago there was a story of how he came upon the use of letters as a crucial research tool. . . . One morning, while walking down a back alley in the Polish community on the West Side of Chicago, he had to sidestep quickly to avoid some garbage which was being disposed of by the direct means of tossing it out the window. In the garbage which fell at his feet were a number of packets of letters. Since he read Polish he was attracted to their contents, and he started to read a bundle which was arranged serially. In the sequence presented by the letters he saw a rich and rewarding account and in time he was led to pursue the personal document as a research tool.

village to the entire national culture society. In Poland, the *okolica* has expanded in size as villages have become less isolated in recent years and villagers enter other occupations (Dziewicka, 1976; Jagiello-Lysiowa, 1976; Jawlowska and Mokrzycki, 1978; Kowalski, 1967; Slomczynski and Wesolowski, 1978; Turowski and Szwengrub, 1976). Both Poland and the United States have provided not only arenas but also entire systems of status sources and hierarchies (Thomas and Znaniecki, 1918–1920:144; Jawlowska and Mokrzycki, 1978).

Traditionally, the major source of status is property, especially land and buildings. Other means of attaining status include less permanent economic goods, such as farm machinery, animals, products grown or handicrafted, and money earned by family members who gain paid employment. Finally, but also significantly, status evolves from a person's reputation derived from physical appearance, accomplishments, actions, and affiliations. The family is a very important source of status, locating the individual in the community at birth and continuing to contribute to status gain or loss throughout the life course. Spouses and children have a moral obligation to assist in the status-building or maintenance process of the family as a unit and of the individual members. Family members must continue to earn their right to the family's position and cooperative action through their own contributions throughout life. Finestone (1964, 1967) found this family system quite different than that of Italian families, whose right to cooperative membership is acquired at birth and never threatened, even in the face of societally disapproved behavior.

Polish immigrants of all classes brought with them to America this interest in status competition within a self-defined *okolica,* and this characteristic may be one of the major reasons why predictions of complete demoralization and disorganization of the family and the immigrant group as a whole were not fulfilled (Thomas and Znaniecki, 1918–1920). Simultaneously, as a major source of involvement in Polonia, this focus on status competition prevented interest in the community's reputation outside of its social boundaries and the use of more popular, external status symbols. Resources for upward mobility within American society as a whole were not used in the internal status competition if they did not have a traditional Polish base. This is especially true of the schooling of youth instead of immediate employment when legal requirements were met.

POLONIA AS AN ORGANIZED COMMUNITY. Although part of their set of five volumes entitled *The Polish Peasant in Europe and America* is devoted to the organizations of Polonia, Thomas and Znaniecki (1918–1920) did not fully stress the importance of the local and larger community in providing an organized, normative base for individual and family life. Immigrants to America, even if they came from small villages to large urban centers, seldom arrived and lived as isolated beings in a sea of foreigners. Most came to friends, former neighbors, or kinfolk who were already partially established among other Poles (Lopata, 1976a). These people built churches and schools, organized parishes and neighborhoods, and formed a multitude of voluntary organizations—pulling new members into the already existing life. The neighborhoods were woven into local communities in large cities, regional circles, and superterritorial complexes (Lopata, 1976b). During the many decades of its growth, Polonia developed multiple webs of companionate circles and services involving daily contact within local areas—at work, church, stores, and clubhouses. It is into this organized community that immigrants came. They involved themselves through various family members in all levels of community life, creating new groups through schisms or new interests while continuing interaction with kin and neighbors. Thus, the image of a totally disorganized slum with increasingly demoralized and isolated former peasants, as depicted by Thomas and Znaniecki (1918–1920), ignores this fabric of social relations within which the Polish American family carried forth its life course (Suttles, 1968). Undoubtedly, marital and parental conflicts did exist; they were documented in Hamtramck (Wood, 1955), Sunderland (Abel, 1929), and Chicago (Pleck, 1983; Thomas and Znaniecki, 1918–1920), but the families basically survived.

FAMILY LIFE. Families were needed by members for not only involvement in the status competition and maintenance of a social life within the *okolica* but also in everyday existence. Families worked to create a home and a means of having and raising children. Abel (1929:216) explained that the Polish immigrants who settled in the Connecticut Valley were able to buy up the land at astonishing rates:

> The ability of the immigrant to establish himself so quickly and to pay off staggering mortgages in a short time was owing to the cheap labor offered by a numerous family and to the willingness to do hard work, and to his low standard of living.

The neighbors of these immigrants were horrified by this standard of living and the level of child care. The death rate of Polish children was much higher than in neighboring families. Yet, these immigrants and their children (with whom they fought constantly) not only bought land and homes but also built sturdy and sizeable "Polish houses" and parishes.

Life for the immigrants was often very difficult. Parot (1982:165) describes all the problems of families in a Polish American neighborhood in Chicago:

> It was here where young Polish girls were seldom given the opportunity to finish even a grammar-school education; it was here where young Polish girls, out of cultural background or sheer economic necessity, were hustled into any one of several dozen sweatships located in the environs . . . ; it was here where most Polish women "escaped" the exploitation of the shops by settling into rigidly endogamous marriages, which, under the best of circumstances, did little to improve material living standards; it was here, in one of the most degrading tenement districts in all of Chicago, that the Polish working-class female experienced the highest fertility rate of any major ethnic group in the city; it was here where the mortality rate of children born to Polish women exceeded that of any other ethnic group—despite the fact that Chicago had witnessed a declining mortality rate throughout the 1880s and had maintained one of the lowest mortality rates for large cities in the United States in 1900.

Life of the peasant segment of Polonia was described in great detail by Thomas and Znaniecki (1918–1920) in their famous work, *The Polish Peasant in Europe and America.* Unfortunately, many readers assumed that this picture reflected all of Polonia, which it obviously did not or the community would never have developed its institutional and organizational complexity (Breton, 1964).

Thomas and Znaniecki (1918–1920) were pessimistic about the future of Polish peasant families in America. They foresaw a loosening of the ties to the extended families of both the husband and the wife, to the village and the parish, resulting in "hedonistic" and immoral behavior and individuated rather than family-based orientation. They witnessed and documented incidents of wives charging husbands in American courts for nonsupport and parents using the police and the courts in an effort to make their children obey and contribute to the economic welfare of the family. They distinguished the following problems:

> 1. Demoralization of adults: a) economic dependency (on the American welfare system—cases from the archives of United Charities); b) break of the conjugal relation (materials chiefly of the Legal Aid Society): murder (Criminal Court and Coroner's office).
> 2. Demoralization of children (materials from the Juvenile Court): a) vagrancy and dishonesty of boys; b) sexual demoralization of girls.

Their focus on disorganization, arising from their theoretical perspective and the obvious evidence of conflict in some families recorded by the

American agencies, led to a failure to include in *The Polish Peasant in Europe and America* other aspects of Polish American family life.

Several researchers have demonstrated that the predicted dissolution of Polish American families did not take place, at least as far as divorce statistics are concerned. J. L. Thomas (1950), Rooney (1957), Polzin (1973, 1976), and Chrobot (1982) concluded that the main reason high divorce and desertion rates are not true of Polish American families is the strength of their Catholic religion, but there appear to be other binding forces that were not dealt with by Thomas and Znaniecki (1918–1920). I will examine some of these forces and the roles of men and women in the Polish American families throughout the life course, as far as data allow.

While all of the family commotion was going on, the various Polonian communities were developing, expanding, and building their organizational homes. This is true of Chicago (Ozog, 1942), Hamtramck (Wood, 1955), and Buffalo (Obidinski, 1968). In addition, despite their original idea of working hard and saving all the money to return to Poland to buy land (or more land), these people contributed millions of dollars, clothing, and foodstuffs to the Polish fight for independence, Polish care during wars, and rebuilding of the country following wars. Much of that money went to families and home villages, but a considerable amount was sent to the national cultural society at large.

Polonian families were originally diversified by social class, region, and type of community in Poland and they became increasingly diversified as the Polonian communities expanded in America (Golab, 1977). The more educated or affluent immigrants organized an entire range of services and businesses needed by newcomers deprived of the established social institutions that existed in Poland. Geographical and social mobility was possible, one step at a time, because the new environment freed individuals and families from restrictions imposed by past family reputations, regulations, and occupations. Lack of language skills and opportunities for training outside of a limited number of occupations, however, restricted this mobility for many (Duncan and Duncan, 1968; Hutchinson, 1956; Lieberson, 1963; Miaso, 1971). The insularity of the community prevented the use of American contacts, existing lines of mobility, and status symbols. Thus, the community was built with many layers and companionate circles, becoming relatively self-sufficient and opening opportunities for advancement, although mainly within its own boundaries (Breton, 1964). This community changed over time, modifying traditional family patterns and relations. Unfortunately, we do not know how the tensions and conflicts inevitably produced by migration, problems of settlement, and generational gaps were resolved. The community must have cushioned the effects of migration and change, focusing attention away from home problems, but there is insufficient knowledge available about the scars and the strengths of family life in Polonia.

THE MODERN POLISH AMERICAN FAMILY

Roles of Women: Growing Up

Polish culture contained, as does any other culture, many assumptions about the nature and proper roles of women in each major stage of their life course. At the time of the mass migrations, particularly among the peasant classes, many of these assumptions centered around them as sexual objects, actually or potentially. Parents were fearful of girls becoming pregnant before marriage or of developing "loose reputations." Thomas and Znaniecki (1918–1920) devoted an entire section of part 3 of their work (on the disorganization of the immigrant) to the "sexual immorality of girls," equating it with criminal behavior and the vagabondage of boys.[5] Human character being weak, Polish women were expected to be constantly susceptible to sexual advances, even when married. Strict socialization and control throughout life was their traditional lot.

Peasant families expected girls to continue the work of their mothers—learning to keep house, sew, cook, and take care of younger children (Chalasinski, 1946: chap. 12). Formal education was not considered important for them because the knowledge and skills they needed could be learned only at home. Furthermore, the girls, like their brothers, learned to work early in life, contributing what they could to the economic welfare of the family and carrying out tasks around the home and farm (Thomas and Znaniecki, 1918–1920).

Many observers of the Polish American scene reported over the years that this attitude toward women's education was carried over by the peasants to this continent and by parents to their children (Abel, 1929; Obidinski, 1968; Wood, 1955). This does not mean that boys were encouraged to get as much education as possible—only that formal schooling was definitely discouraged for girls. If they had to go to school, the parochial rather than public school system was encouraged since parents wanted

---

[5]Actually, this view of the delinquency of girls is not unique to Polonia. Lerman (1973) points out in "Child Convicts" that the American legal system has built its moral code into definitions of delinquent behavior that allow youths to be punished for behavior legally allowed for adults. "The vast majority of the girls in the Home (The State Home for Girls) today, as in past years, were accused of misbehavior that would not be considered crimes if committed by adults."

their girls to be under the close supervision of nuns (Kusielewicz, 1974; Kuznicki, 1978; Miaso, 1971).

The concern for the morality of Polish American girls extended to their work for pay outside of the home. Nonagricultural families faced a dilemma in that they were very interested in having each member bring in earnings and yet wanted to protect their daughters from temptation and even gossip by keeping them close to home or, at least, under close supervision. Domestic service was a preferred occupation for young women because it provided good training for future home roles.

The result of the undervaluation of education for the women of Polish American families is evident in the types of occupations in which they are and have been found. In 1950, foreign-born Polish women, compared with other foreign-born women, were disproportionately located in such occupations as laborers, factory operatives, and service workers, especially in private service (Hutchinson, 1956:248). Comparatively few Polish women were recorded as clerical workers and professionals. More detailed analyses of job specialization found them disproportionately among charwomen, janitors, sextons, meat cutters, and self-employed managers of wholesale and retail trade. American-born females of Polish parentage were also disproportionately located among operatives and laborers, with few women in farming, either as farmers or farm laborers, or working in white-collar jobs. However, this generation had moved out of service jobs in the private sector. Second-generation Polish American women displayed an even greater occupational concentration than their first-generation counterparts, and more recent figures document a continuing lag in entrance into white-collar occupations, particularly in the professions. Only Spanish and Italian women had lower white-collar employment rates in 1970 (U.S. Bureau of the Census, 1971). These statements do not apply to the women of the new emigration, most of whom entered the country with at least a high school education, many going on to school in America and concentrating in white-collar jobs. Throughout Polish history, the upper classes have maintained themselves through higher education, often using college as a means of ensuring that their daughters have educated, high-income earning husbands. There is recent evidence that Polish American boys and girls have discovered higher education as a major means of upward mobility within American society and that their parents have modified their stance on such schooling (U.S. Bureau of the Census, 1971). One of the reasons Polish parents are becoming increasingly tolerant of the number of years their children, even daughters, spend in school, is that the younger generations appear to have won the struggle for their right to keep the money they earn outside of the home for personal use, so that they no longer contribute to the family economic welfare anyway.

THE ROLE OF WIFE.[6] A frequent component of descriptions of Polish and Polish American families is their allegedly total authoritarian and patriarchal nature. Polzin (1976:109) repeats this imagery as late as 1976: "The pattern of male dominance with corresponding unquestioning obedience by the wife and children belonged to the internalized norms on expected family behavior brought to this country." Yet, there is much evidence that the status of women in agricultural communities is not that of passive subordinates (Radzialowski, 1977). Their influence in the family is determined by their contribution to its welfare (Sanday, 1974). Farm women make a very visible and important economic addition to the family's welfare (Thomas and Znaniecki, 1918–1920:82–83):

> In matters of reciprocal response we find among the Polish peasants the sexes equally dependent upon each other . . . under conditions in which the activities of the women can attain an objective importance more or less equal to those of the man, the greatest social efficiency is attained by a systematic collaboration of men and women in external fields rather than by a division of tasks which limits the women to "home and children."

Bloch (1976:5), contrasting the situation of women in Polish villages and American cities, reinforces this point:

> The source of this equality and partnership between husband and wife can be located in economic nature of the partnership, and particularly in two aspects of village economy. The first of these is the importance of village women to the operation of the house and farm. . . . But even more important than this contribution to subsistence is the strong position of women in terms of the basic wealth of the village—land and buildings.

During times of migration, whether for seasonal work in Europe or America, women on farms or in other economic situations were often left in charge of economic decisions and property maintenance for extended periods of time without their husbands or adult sons (Thomas and Znaniecki, 1918–1920). The pattern of household and family management without the patriarch was not unusual; it had been repeated through centuries of the Crusades, wars, and traveling occupations of men (Origo,

[6]Of course, not all Polish women married, a relatively large number of them going instead into Catholic religious orders. Radzialowski (1975) studied the largest of the Slavic teaching orders, the Felician Sisters, and there were several Polish orders and Polish American nuns in mixed orders.

1956).[7] Emigration, however, introduced two major changes in the roles of married women, especially if they moved across the ocean. First, both the husband and wife deprived themselves of rights of inheritable property, if there was any. Parents usually distributed the property they had inherited and, hopefully, contributed to through their work, to the remaining offspring in Poland. The emigrating children were, in fact, expected to contribute to the family's status by sending money earned in America to Poland to be used for increasing property holdings of relatives. Coming to America with few possessions, the emigrants faced a second major change of life circumstances, resulting in changes of roles and relationships. Both the husband and wife, but especially the wife, were freed from the claims on their residence by the older generation whose home or land it had been before retirement. They were also freed from the daily observation and control by the elders of both families. They were independent of the constant supervision of their behavior found in extended kin village life. At the same time, they were deprived of the support network that exists in stable extended families and neighborhoods (Wrobel, 1979:67–77).

Thomas and Znaniecki (1918–1920:1705) pointed out that "economic ideals, when they exist, contribute, indeed to the maintenance of family life in general, since the immigrant can seldom imagine an economically perfect life without a family." Yet, these sociologists worried about what they considered to be an inevitable "Break of the Conjugal Relation" (chap. 3, vol. 2), mainly because American law "treats him (the husband) and his wife as isolated individuals, not as primary-group members" (pp. 1750–1751):

> The consciousness that she can have her husband arrested any time she wishes on charges of non-support, disorderly conduct or adultery is for the woman an entirely new experience. Though under the old system she had in fact a part in the management of common affairs almost equal to that of the man, yet in cases of explicit disagreement the man had the formal right of coercing her, whereas she could only work by suggestion and persuasion, or appeal to the large family. Now not only can she refuse to be coerced, since the only actual instruments of coercion which the man has left after the disorganization of the large family—use of physical strength and withholding the means of subsistence—are prohibited by law, but she can actually coerce the man into

[7] We have a collection of letters exchanged by my great-grandmother and her husband and sons, as well as two years of her diaries during the Franco-Prussian War, which detail her activities in managing the estate. Wars often removed all adult men from their families and businesses, which were then taken over by the women in addition to their usual labor in the home, on the land, and in whatever other enterprises they were engaged.

> doing what she wants by using any act of violence, drunkenness or economic negligence of his as pretext for warrant. No wonder that she is tempted to use her newly acquired power whenever she quarrels with her husband, and her women friends and acquaintances, moved by sex solidarity, frequently stimulate her to take legal action.

Pleck (1983:98) also reports child and wife battering by immigrant husbands and fathers and that 60 percent of the complaints by wives were made by Poles.

This image of the Polish peasant family in America neglects some of the forces actually present in social relations when physical coercion or economic dependence are removed. Divorce and desertion were negatively evaluated in Polonia, and strong status handicaps occurred from such behavior. In addition, people needed their spouses, in many ways, even when not fully economically dependent on them.

The economic dependence first of Polish and then Polish American wives on their husbands varied considerably. Many women were able to earn substantial incomes by providing services or making goods, even in urban settings. Boarding and rooming houses were kept by many women during the height of immigration, mainly serving men who came over without families and would remain for some time until they made enough money to send for relatives back home (Zand, 1956).

In addition to managing boarding homes for income, many Polish American women cooperated with their husbands in "ma-and-pa" stores, taverns, or restaurants specializing in Polish food. Each Polonian neighborhood had a number of such businesses requiring work from all family members. Seamstresses, beauticians, piano and English teachers, and writers and readers of letters—all these were needed in Polonia and women of the various classes and skills were able to undertake such roles. Such activities were considered appropriate means of contributing to the family's economic status, and some of the services were a source of prestige.

Of lower community approval was employment by wives and mothers outside of the home and its environs, especially among men and, worst of all, among people other than Polish Americans (Wrobel, 1979:76). However, the wish for money was there: initially, to be used to return to Poland and buy land and homes; later, to help people in the homeland; and, always, for material goods for their own use and status and to offset some of the misgivings about the wife's employment away from the home. Interestingly, the employment of the women was seen by the Polonian community and the wider society as an individual choice, and few adjustments were made to help women manage the dual job of working for pay and managing the home and the family.[8]

THE ROLE OF MOTHER. It is possible that the heavy burdens of the job–home combination or of full-time homemaking in a large family have taken their toll in the mother–child relationship. McCready (1974:168–169) uses work by Radzialowski (1974) to support his conclusion drawn from a National Opinion Research Center sample that "the mother did not exert a strong influence in the raising of her children because of the dependence on the extended family in the peasant society." McCready found that mothers of Polish American college graduates of 1961 were not as "salient" as mothers in other ethnic groups, in that they were not mentioned as frequently as were fathers. This was true even of the young women:

> The young Polish women rate themselves high on domestic skills, attractiveness, and sex appeal, indicating that they do espouse the traditional values for women in the society. Their low saliency scores for mother indicate that they have received these values from their fathers rather than emulating their mothers as role models. In other words, they think of themselves as attractive, competent women because their fathers told them they were.

POLISH AMERICAN WOMEN IN THE COMMUNITY. The first- and second-generation Polish American women, unlike the Italians, did not limit their involvement to the home and the family. They were active organizers and participants in voluntary associations and the life of the community. They founded one of the major insurance and financial companies, the Polish Women's Alliance, with branches in many neighborhoods, and a feminist newspaper called *The Voice of Polish Women,* which had "Faith, Enlightenment, Love of the Native Language, Concord, Perseverence" as its motto, and education as its major function aside from economic activity (Radzialowski, 1975:1977). The newspapers and local meetings taught members to be independent and also taught new ways of

---

[8]Caroline Bird (1979) details in *The Two-Paycheck Marriage* the difficulties experienced by American women who return to the labor force after having managed the home full time. Their families usually do not distribute the functions of the role of housewife among all members in adjustment to the woman's occupation outside the home. Sokolowska (1964, 1977) lists extensive resources in Poland developed to help working mothers, because that society, unlike America, ideologically wants such members to be in paid employment and because families really need two breadwinners. However, cultural norms of city life, which assigned to the woman the management of the home, still linger, and husbands reputedly are less than egalitarian in sharing work, unless they are of the youngest married generation.

cooking, cleaning, child care, health, and hygiene (Radzialowski, 1977:196):

> . . . it urged on its members the wisdom of saving for the future, avoiding needless spending, acquiring training and job skills, shunning gambling and excessive use of alcohol and other traits usually subsumed under the misnamed "puritan ethic."

The Polish Women's Alliance had its own doctors, insurance adjusters, teachers, and business leaders. It encouraged mothers to seek higher education for their children. Other organizations for women, branches of superterritorial associations, and even local groups provided opportunities for leadership roles, help in the schooling of children in Polish language and culture, social contact, and activities. Again, this extensive activity at each level of Polonian life negates the image of passive Polish immigrant women [see also Wojniusz (1976)].

THE LATER STAGES OF LIFE. In contrast to the situation that appears to have developed in Poland since World War II, the Polish American working woman does not seem to be able to depend on her mother or mother-in-law to help with the housework or care of the children (Mirowski, 1968; Lobodzinska, 1970, 1974; Piotrowski, 1963; Sokolowska, 1964). Although Polish American widows are more willing to live with a married child, usually a daughter, than are American women of similar age and marital status situations generally, most elderly women who are able to take care of themselves choose to live with only their husband or alone if widowed (Lopata, 1977). They do not undertake household or child care for the younger generations. In this respect they are quite American, in that Polish mothers often help extensively with their children's families (Lobodzinska, 1970, 1974).

American society no longer expects the housing of elderly parents with younger generations, nor the heavy household and child care obligations of older women to their adult children (Lopata, 1971, 1973). The history of the society does not provide an ideological base for such action, mainly because of its disapproval until recent years of the employment of married women who would then require babysitting assistance. In addition, older women are economically independent in many cases, albeit often living on very limited incomes and within narrow life spaces (Chevan and Korson, 1972; Lopata, 1973, 1979). Although often residing in the poorer sections of towns no longer inhabited by Polish Americans, as a result of death of older generations and the upward and outward mobility of younger ones, the older women tend to own their homes. Selling these homes could not bring them sufficient monies to afford moving elsewhere, and their roots and unfamiliarity with life outside of the neighborhood preclude such resettlement. These elderly widows are often strongly involved with one of their children but in an "intimacy at a distance" manner typical of that reported by Rosenmayr and Kockeis (1963) for the elderly in Vienna, Austria [see also Bild and Havighurst (1976) and Siemaszko (1976)].

The social class background of older Polish American women significantly influences their social life space and support systems; the middle- and upper-class women draw on a much wider set of personal and community resources. However, even the lower-class women retain active involvement in voluntary associations, thereby differing from their counterparts in other ethnic and American communities. The lifelong habit of involvement in the community is broken only if friends and familiar neighbors die or move away: the church loses its Polish American parishioners, clubs move out of the area, and the family disperses (Lopata, 1977, 1979; Ozog, 1942; Sanders and Morawska, 1975; Wood, 1955). The consequences of the harshness of life for the immigrant and even the second-generation women is reflected in their health problems and the inability to retain contact with siblings and children living at inconvenient distances (Lopata, 1973, 1979).

There is insufficient evidence on the circumstances of the latter stages of the life course for women of the new emigration to determine how they are different from other Polish women in America at the present time. Their background and the situation in which they entered the United States would lead us to assume that few could bring their older parents over [see also Mostwin (1969, 1971)]. Many ex-combatants and displaced persons came from places other than Poland during and after World War II, and immigration directly from that country has expanded only in recent years. The new emigration is aging, but we know little about this process, because the group numerically is too small to be located through any means but selective sampling. Mostwin (1969, 1971) reports some intergenerational conflict because the parents did not settle in Polonia, and, as a result, the children have Americanized very rapidly. The parents disapprove of some of the actions of younger generations, especially of the girls.

The Roles of Men

The lives of immigrant men also varied considerably according to the resources with which they entered America. The masses of Polish immigrants entering at the turn of the twentieth century were young men who came from a village background and with relatively little education. They obtained jobs in the mines of Pennsylvania, in the steel mills or meat-packing houses of Chicago, on farms in the Connecticut Valley, or in other locations in which knowledge of English and advanced skills in the industrialized or service sectors of the economy were not needed. Boarding at first in Polish homes in the community, they saved money and sent for their wives and children or siblings. Some of the more affluent returned to Poland to stay or to find a wife. Women of Polish background were scarce in America during the early years of Polish immigration. As late as 1920, there were 131 males per 100 females, but the number of males decreased to 116.1 in 1930, 110.4 in 1940, and 101.8 by 1950 (Hutchinson, 1956:19). Men who married daughters of already established families received help in establishing themselves and tended to develop an egalitarian or, at least, not a strongly patriarchal family demeanor, because they did not have their own families to back them up (Zand, 1956). By 1969, 14.5 percent of Polish men were in professional and technical jobs, 15.2 in managerial positions, and another 15 percent in sales or clerical positions (Lopata, 1985:136).

HUSBANDS AND FATHERS. Polish male immigrants worked hard, long hours and often were unable to spend much time with their children. The father's function as the main disciplinarian was the only one known to many children, and his European style of relating to them often created strong conflict. The second generation's young men were reputedly involved in street gang behavior (Thrasher, 1927; Fleis-Fava, 1950). Taft (1936:723) felt obliged to point out to American criminologists that the first generation of Polish immigrants had very low criminal records and that the age distribution of the second-generation males pushed up the rate for the entire immigrant group. Polonia contained a disproportionate number of young men in the "criminally significant" ages. Conflict with the father arose from not only the son's delinquent behavior but also his unwillingness to contribute to the family's social status by turning over his earnings for family use (Thomas and Znaniecki, 1918–1920; Wood, 1955). Thomas and Znaniecki (1918–1920) reported frequent and public disagreement between fathers and their children over economic matters. Finestone (1964, 1967) found that family members would completely ignore members who had been sent to prison for criminal activity. They had to reestablish their relations by promising not to disgrace the family again after they were released. This finding adds weight to the thesis of the importance of the status competition to Polish American families.

Polonia, as an organized community with many mass communication media, also completely ignored problems of juvenile delinquency or criminality. No organization was set up to help the youth or adults in serious trouble and the newspapers did not make mention of it, even in face of American reports. Wood (1955) documents facts of criminal activity never discussed in Polonia except as part of the natural flow of life. Yet, whatever gang fights or other juvenile-delinquent behavior the second generation of Polonian young men were involved in, it seemed to have worked out by the time they reached adulthood, because their criminal record is not high.

The second-generation Polonian men remained organizationally active, although to a lesser extent in ethnic communities than had their parents (Emmons, 1971; Galush, 1975; Obidinski, 1968; Sandberg, 1974). Yet, Polish American men did not experience much intergenerational occupational mobility until after the second generation (Duncan and Duncan, 1968; Greeley and Rossi, 1968; U.S. Bureau of the Census, 1971). Hutchinson (1956:248) found the foreign-born Polish males in service, operative, and laborer jobs in metal industries. Their specific occupations disproportionately included tailors, furriers, cleaners, porters, and self-employed managers. The American-born men of foreign-born parents were employed most frequently as operatives and laborers and less frequently than other groups as professional workers, managers, farmers, service employees, or sales workers. They were even more occupationally concentrated than the second generation of most other foreign-stock Americans. Duncan and Duncan (1968) concluded that the Poles "suffer a modest handicap" in achieving upward mobility from the first job to the current one by American standards. The main reason for this is that sons tended to follow their fathers in the type of job they entered among the Polish Americans more than among other ethnic groups currently in the work force (Duncan and Duncan, 1968:362).

By 1961, Polish American fathers seem to have developed better relations with their children or, at least, with daughters, than prior researchers indicated. As mentioned before, it was the father, not the mother, who was listed as having more influence on the lives of female college graduates (McCready, 1974). McCready (1974:167) seems to uphold the patriarchal image of the Polish American father:

> All the members of the post-migration Polish family exhibited a concern for the well-being of the father, who seemed to have suffered most in the move from village to city. The literature on the Polish family in America describes two types of Polish father. One was the man who had been a strong patriarchal figure in Poland, was unable to maintain that role in the new country, and became a dependent person. Warner reviewed literature that indicated that this type of Polish father eventually became a child to his own children. The

children were his disciplinarians and protectors. The second type was the man who had been a strong patriarchal figure in Poland and was able to maintain that role in this country.

This is a strongly bifurcated picture of the Polish elderly man in America, seen in isolation from other relations and the community. However, Lieberman (1978) also reports high incidence of mental illness and withdrawal into passivity vis-à-vis the rest of the family on the part of men who expected to function as patriarchs in relations with their children but did not have the resources to carry off such relations [see also Trela and Sokolovsky (1979)]. Wrobel (1979:76) found Detroit men "feeling personally inadequate" because of the kind of work they did and their inability to better their "lot in life."

The men of the new emigration, who entered America with more education and occupational skills and mainly settled away from the established Polonia communities, also may have experienced trouble with their offspring as the latter more rapidly absorbed American values, but the problems do not appear to be as severe as those in former peasant families (Mostwin, 1969, 1971). The recorded violence of temper of Polish peasant and lower-class men, especially explosive when combined with alcohol, may easily have been the consequence of frustration over the lack of resources to lead the type of life and relate to others the way they had been socialized to do (Thomas and Znaniecki, 1918–1920; Janowitz, 1966). More educated and less culturally insulated men may have had more resources and more tolerance of the changing behaviors of family members. Second-generation men of either emigration may have engaged in less conflict with their children because of the remembered problems with their fathers. At least, the few studies that focused on intergenerational family relations report less attitudinal and value differences than reported for the first-generation immigrants.

CHANGE AND ADAPTATION

There are many people living in the United States who could be called Polish Americans because their parents, grandparents, or great-grandparents came from Poland, but who have completely obliterated this identification. These people cannot be identified in any way by census-takers or sociologists, especially if they have changed originally Polish-sounding names. Louis Adamic observed the name-changing tendency as early as 1942 in his *What's Your Name?* Several social scientists studied this behavior among "Poles and Polish Americans [who] seem impelled to more changing than any other group" (Kotlarz, 1963:1) [see also Borkowski (1963) and Zagraniczny (1963)]. Kotlarz (1963:1–4) estimated that, of approximately 300,000 Polish Americans living in the Detroit area, approximately 3,000 modified their names annually. The Polonian press occasionally reports that this process has stopped and that some younger members of Polish American families are going back to the original name and its spelling. It is almost impossible to determine the extent of either direction of name change.

There is a second layer of Polish American families whose members have some identification with their ethnic group and belong to some organizations within Polonia, but who otherwise lead ordinary "American" lives. Some studies pick up traces of familial or religious attitudes that harken back to prior generations' culture, but items and complexes vary by family. There are also Poles in America who identify themselves as both Poles and Americans but not as Polish Americans, and tend to have limited involvement in specialized organizations and friendships, but otherwise lead middle- or upper-middle-class lives (Mostwin, 1969, 1971). Both types of this second layer of involvement in Polonian life are really peripheral to it because the community could not depend on these families to maintain itself. A third layer of Polish American families is more involved in the ethnic community activities than the other two, although this varies by age, education, generation, and area (Galush, 1975; Obidinski, 1968; Sandberg, 1974). Some Polish Americans still reside in the heart of the remaining neighborhoods, without speaking English and with restricted lives. Few families controlled by the middle generation are so located. Others live Polonian lives by being involved in superterritorial organizations in which they have informal contact with other leaders, living their ethnicity almost professionally. The families that have such strong ties are usually controlled by second-generation men or women, with occasional involvement and passing of status and ethnicity to the youth. Some of Polonia's life has been taken over by the families of the new emigration.

CONCLUSIONS

The heterogeneity of structure, interaction, and cultural base for Polish American families lies in their original variation when they came to America and in the divergence of paths they followed. The tendency of most social scientists is to focus on the large mass of peasants who migrated before World War I and brought over other family members before the influx was stopped by American legislation. It is they who were studied during their processes of "adjustment" or "disorganization," with frequent reports of interfamilial and intrafamilial conflict. Relations of men and women at all stages of life underwent change, often against the wishes of participants, because such change rarely hits the entire family at the same time. Members who benefited from the village family system had the most to lose when other members refused to follow traditional norms. Yet family members needed each other rather desperately, and the growing community siphoned some of the hurt and conflict by drawing attention to the interfamily status competition. Life in Polonia was very involved and complex, providing many opportunities for individualistic, as well as cooperative, identity and status.

Little is actually known of the processes by which first-generation families worked out the conflicts or, at least, tensions between husband and wife and parent and child. Second-generation children, especially the boys, often expressed their frustrations by moving out into the streets with peers. Most grew up leading "normal" lower- or lower-middle-class lives within or outside of Polonian neighborhoods. The women tended to follow the traditional life course of American urbanites, except that some wives had to work outside of the home for financial reasons, despite community disapproval, and except that, at all class levels, the women were more organizationally active than is generally true of their non-Polish counterparts. The status competition and community life, as well as their control over their own homes in the absence of a tightly controlling male kin line, gave them more independence and power in the family than is usually attributed to women in traditionally patriarchal cultures. Marital conflict appears to have been strong in some families of the old emigration, particularly of the first and early second generations, but it did not result in high divorce rates for a variety of reasons. The older generations of Polish Americans tend to live independently, although there appears to be a certain segment of the male population that suffers psychological problems from the strain of migration and adjustment to life in America.

Upward mobility within Polonia and out of it has been increasing in recent years, enabling children or grandchildren of peasant families to join the Polish Americans who inherited or had earlier built up higher status. Most third- and fourth-generation Polish American families are lost to sociological knowledge, especially when they do not identify with this ethnic group in responses to census and other survey questions. The geographical dispersal of this population and the move to higher education have resulted in a great deal of intermarriage, creating new generations that are less likely to identify with the Polish or Polish American culture or people than is true of people with a single ethnic background. Some of the youth are developing an interest in Poland and its national culture, an interest expressed in a desire to travel to their grandparents' or great-grandparents' homeland and the taking of Polish courses in schools.

REFERENCES

Abel, Theodore. 1929. "Sunderland: A Study of Change in the Group Line of Poles in New England Farming Community," in Edmund De. S. Brunner (ed.), *Immigrant Farmers and Their Children.* Garden City, NY: Doubleday, pp. 213–243.

Adamic, Louis, 1942. *What's Your Name?* New York: Harper and Brothers.

Benet, Sula. 1951. *Song, Dance and Customs of Peasant Poland.* New York: Roy.

Bild, Bernice R., and Robert Havighurst. 1976. "Senior Citizens in Great Cities: The Case of Chicago," special issue of *The Gerontologist,* 16(1) (February), pt. 2.

Bird, Caroline. 1979. *The Two-Paycheck Marriage.* New York: Rawson Wade.

Bloch, Harriet. 1976. "Changing Domestic Roles Among Polish Immigrant Women," *The Anthropological Quarterly,* 49(1) (January):3–10.

Borkowski, Thomas. 1963. "Some Patterns in Polish Surname Changes," *Polish American Studies,* 20(1) (January–June): 14–16.

Breton, Raymond. 1964. "Institutional Completeness of Ethnic Communities and the Personal Relations of Immigrants," *American Journal of Sociology,* 70(2) (September):193–205.

Brunner, Edmund De. S. (ed.). 1929. *Immigrant Farmers and their Children.* Garden City, NY: Doubleday.

Chalasinski, Josef. 1946. *Mlode Pokolenie Chlopow.* Rzym: Wydawnicto Polskiej YMCA Przy APW.

Chevan, A., and H. Korson. 1972. "The Widowed Who Live Alone: An Examination of Social and Demographic Factors," *Social Forces,* 51:45–53.

Chrobot, Leonard F. 1982. "The Pilgrimage From Gemeinschaft to Gessellschaft: Sociological Functions of Religion in the Polish American Community," in Frank Renkiewicz (ed.), *The Polish Presence in Canada and America.* Toronto: Multicultural Society of Ontario, pp. 81–95.

Cohler, Bertram J., and Morton A. Lieberman. 1979. "Personality Change in the Second Half of Life: Findings From a Study of Irish, Italian and Polish-American Men and Women," in Donald E. Gelfand and Alfred J. Kutzik (eds.), *Ethnicity and Aging: Theory, Research and Policy.* New York: Springer, pp. 227–245.

Duncan, Beverly, and Otis Dudley Duncan. 1968. "Minorities and the Process of Stratification," *American Sociological Review,* 33(8) (June):356–364.

Dziewicka, Maria. 1976. "Dual Occupation in Polish Agriculture," in Jan Turowski and Lili Maria Szwengrub (eds.), *Rural Social Change in Poland.* Ossolineum: Polish Academy of Sciences Press, pp. 251–277.

Emmons, Charles F. 1971. "Economic and Political Leadership in Chicago's Polonia: Some Sources of Ethnic Persistence and Mobility." Ph.D. diss., University of Illinois, Circle Campus.

Finestone, Harold. 1964. "A Comparative Study of Reformation and Recidivism Among Italians and Polish Adult Male Criminal Offenders." Ph.D. diss., University of Chicago.

———. 1967. "Reformation and Recidivism Among Italian and Polish Criminal Offenders," *American Journal of Sociology,* 72(6) (May).

Fleis-Fava, S. 1950. "The Relationship of Northwestern University Settlement to the Community." Master's thesis, Department of Sociology, Northwestern University.

Galush, W. T. 1975. "Forming Polonia: A Study of Four Polish-American Communities, 1880–1940." Ph.D. diss., Department of History, University of Minnesota.

Golab, Caroline. 1977. *Immigrant Destinations.* Philadelphia: Temple University Press.

Gordon, Milton. 1964. *Assimilation in American Life.* New York: Oxford University Press.

Greeley, Andrew M., and Peter H. Rossi. 1968. *The Education of Catholic Americans.* Garden City, NY: Doubleday, Anchor Books.

Hutchinson, E. P. 1956. *Immigrants and Their Children: 1850–1950.* New York: John Wiley.

Jagiello-Lysiowa, E. 1976. "Transformation of the Way of Life of the Rural Community," in Jan Turowski and Lili Maria Szwengrub (eds.), *Rural Social Change in Poland.* Warszawa, Ossolineum: Polish Academy of Sciences Press, pp. 123–138.

Janowitz, Morris (ed.). 1966. *W. I. Thomas: On Social Organization and Social Personality.* Chicago: University of Chicago, Phoenix Books.

Jawlowska, Aldona, and Edmund Mokrzycki. 1978. "Styles of Life in Poland: A Viewpoint on Typology," in Polish Sociological Association, *Social Structure: Polish Sociology 1977.* Warszawa, Zaklad Narodowy Imienia Ossolinskich: Wydawnictwo Polskicj Akademii Nauk, pp. 93–107.

Kotlarz, Robcrt J. 1963. "Writings About the Changing of Polish Names in America," *Polish American Studies,* 20(1) (January–June):1–4.

Kowalski, Mieczyslaw. 1967. "Basic Directions of Changes in Rural Life System in Poland," Acta Universitatis Lodziensis, *Zeszyty Naukowe Universytetu Lodzkiego Nauki Ekonomiczne i Socjologiczne,* Seira 3(10):5–29.

Kusielewicz, Eugene. 1974. "On the Condition of Polish Culture in the United States," *The Kosciuszko Foundation Monthly Newsletter,* 29(2) (October):2–6.

Kuznicki, Ellen Marie. 1978. "The Polish American Parochial Schools," in Frank Mocha (ed.), *Poles in America.* Stevens Point, WI: Worzalla.

Lerman, Paul. 1973. "Child Convicts," in Helena Z. Lopata (ed.), *Marriages and Families.* New York: Van Nostrand, pp. 285–294.

Lieberman, Morton A. 1978. "Social and Psychological Determinants of Adaptation," *International Journal of Aging and Human Development,* 9(2).

Lieberson, S. 1963. *Ethnic Patterns in American Cities.* New York: Free Press.

Lobodzinska, Barbara. 1970. *Malzenstwo w Miescie.* Warszawa: Panstwowe Wydawnictwo Naukowe.

———. 1974. *Kodzina w Polsce.* Warszawa: Wudawnictwo Interpress.

Lopata, Helena Znaniecki. 1971. "Living Arrangements of Urban Widows and Their Married Children," *Sociological Focus,* 5(1):41–61.

———. 1973. *Widowhood in an American City.* Cambridge, MA: Schenkman.

———. 1976a. "Polish Immigration to the United States of America: Problems of Estimation and Parameters," *The Polish Review,* 21(4):85–108.

———. 1976b. *Polish Americans: Status Competition in an Ethnic Community.* Englewood Cliffs, NJ: Prentice-Hall.
———. 1976c. "Members of the Intelligentsia as Developers and Disseminators of Cosmopolitan Culture," in Aleksander Gella (ed.), *The Intelligentsia and the Intellectuals.* Beverly Hills, CA: Sage, pp. 59–78.
———. 1977. "Widowhood in Polonia," *Polish American Studies,* 34(2) (Autumn):5–25.
———. 1979. *Women as Widows: Support Systems.* New York: Elsevier.
———. 1985. "The Polish Immigrants and Their Descendants in the American Labor Force," in Winston A. Van Horne and Thomas V. Tonnesen (eds.), *Ethnicity and the Work Force.* Milwaukee, WI: University of Wisconsin System, American Ethnic Studies Coordinating Committee, pp. 124–144.
McCready, William. 1974. "The Persistence of Ethnic Variation in American Families," in Andrew Greeley (ed.), *Ethnicity in the United States.* New York: John Wiley, pp. 156–176.
Miaso, J. 1971. "Z Dziejow Oswiaty Polskiej w Stanach Zjednoczonych," *Problemy Polonii Zajzanichzhej,* 4:19–49.
Mirowski, Wlodzimierz. 1968. *Migracje do Warszawy.* Warszawa: Zaklad Narodowy im Ossolinskich, Wydawnictwo Polskiej Akademii Nauk.
Mostwin, Danuta. 1969. "Post World War II Polish Immigrants in the United States," *Polish American Studies,* 26(2) (Autumn):5–14.
———. 1971. *The Transplanted Family, A Study of Social Adjustment of the Polish Immigrant Family to the United States after the Second World War.* Ann Arbor, MI: University Microfilms.
Obidinski, Eugene. 1968. "Ethnic to Status Group: A Study of Polish Americans in Buffalo." Ph.D. diss., New York: State University of New York Microfilms.
Origo, Iris. 1956. *The Merchant of Prato, Francesco di Marco Datini: 1355–1410.* New York: Knopf.
Ozog, Julius J. 1942. "A Study in Polish Home Ownership in Chicago." Master's thesis, University of Chicago.
Parot, Joseph John. 1982. "The 'Serdeczna Matko' of the Sweatshops: Marital and Family Crises of Immigrant Working-Class Women in Late Nineteenth-Century Chicago," in Frank Renkiewicz (ed.), *The Polish Presence in Canada and America.* Toronto: Multicultural History Society of Ontario, pp. 155–182.
Piotrowski, Jerzy. 1963. *Praca Zawodowa Kobiety a Rodzina.* Warszawa: Ksiazka i Wiedza.
Pleck, Elizabeth. 1983. "The Old World, New Rights, and the Limited Rebellion: Challenges to Traditional Authority in Immigrant Families," in H. Z. Lopata and J. H. Pleck (eds.), *Research in the Interweave of Social Roles: Families and Jobs.* Greenwich, CT: Jai Press, pp. 91–112.
Polzin, Theresita. 1973. *The Polish Americans.* Pulaski, WI: Franciscan Publishers.
———. 1976. "The Polish American Family," *The Polish Review,* 21(3):103–122.
Radzialowski, Thaddeus. 1974. "The View from a Polish Ghetto," *Ethnicity,* 1(2) (July):125–150.
———. 1975. "Reflections on the History of the Felicians," *Polish American Studies,* 32 (Spring):19–28.
———. 1977. "Immigrant Nationalism and Feminism: Glos Polek and the Polish Women's Alliance in America, 1898–1917," *Review Journal of Philosophy and Social Science,* 2(2):183–203.

Reymont, Ladislas. 1925. *The Peasants: Fall, Winter, Spring, Summer.* New York: Knopf.
Rooney, Elizabeth. 1957. "Polish Americans and Family Disorganization," *The American Catholic Sociological Review,* 18 (March): 47–51.
Rosenmayr, Leopold, and E. Kockeis. 1963. "Propositions for a Sociological Theory of Aging and the Family," *International Social Science Journal,* 15:410–426.
Sanday, Peggy R. 1974. "Female Status in the Public Domain," in Z. Rosaldo and L. Lamphere (eds.), *Women, Culture and Society.* Stanford: Stanford University Press, pp. 189–206.
Sandberg, Neil C. 1974. *Ethnic Identity and Assimilation: The Polish American Community.* New York: Praeger.
Sanders, Irwin, and Eva T. Morawska. 1975. *Polish American Community Life: A Survey of Research.* Boston: Boston University, Community Sociology Training Program.
Schooler, Carmi. 1976. "Serfdom's Legacy: An Ethnic Continuum," *American Journal of Sociology,* 81:1265–1285.
Siemaszko, Maria. 1976. "Kin Relations of the Aged: Possible Impact on Social Service Planning." Master's thesis, Loyola University of Chicago.
Slomczynski, Kazimierz, and Wlodzimierz Wesolowski. 1978. "Theoretical Orientation in the Study of Class Structure in Poland, 1945–1975," in Polish Sociological Association, *Social Structure: Polish Sociology 1977.* Warszawa, Zaklad Narodowy Imienia Ossolinskich: Wydawnictwo Polskiej Akademii Nauk, pp. 7–31.
Sokolowska, Magdalena. 1964. *Kobieta Pracujaca.* Warsaw: Wiedza Powszechna.
———. 1977. "Poland: Women's Experience Under Socialism," in Janet Zollinger Giele and Audrey Chapman Smock (eds.), *Women: Roles and Status in Eight Countries.* New York: John Wiley, pp. 347–381.
Super, P. 1939. *The Polish Tradition.* London: Maxlove.
Suttles, Gerald. 1968. *The Social Order of the Slum.* Chicago: University of Chicago Press.
Szczepanski, Jan. 1962. "The Polish Intelligentsia: Past and Present," *World Politics,* 16(3) (April):406–420.
———. 1970. *Polish Society.* New York: Random House.
Taft, D. 1936. "Nationality and Crime," *American Journal of Sociology* (August):1–4, 724–736.
Thomas, John L. 1950. "Marriage Prediction in the Polish Peasant," *American Journal of Sociology,* 55 (May):573–583.
Thomas, William I., and Florian W. Znaniecki. 1918–1920. *The Polish Peasant in Europe and America.* Boston: Richard G. Badger. Reprint. New York: Dover, 1958.
Thrasher, F. M. 1927. *The Gang: The Study of 1,313 Gangs in Chicago.* Chicago: University of Chicago Press.
Trela, James E., and Jay H. Sokolovsky. 1979. "Culture, Ethnicity and Policy for the Aged," in Donald E. Gelfand and Alfred J. Kutzik (eds.), *Ethnicity and Aging: Theory, Research and Policy.* New York: Springer, pp. 117–136.
Turowski, Jan, and Lili Maria Szwengrub (eds.). 1976. *Rural Social Change in Poland.* Warsaw, Ossolineum: Polish Academy of Sciences Press.
U.S. Bureau of the Census. 1971. *Characteristics of the Population by Ethnic*

Origin, November 1969, Current Population Reports, Series P-20. Washington, DC: U.S. Government Printing Office.

Wojniusz, Helen K. 1976. "Ethnicity and Other Variables in the Analysis of Polish American Women," *Polish American Studies,* 39 (Autumn):26–37.

Wood, Arthur Evans. 1955. *Hamtramck: Then and Now.* New York: Bookman Associates.

Wrobel, Paul. 1979. *Our Way: Family, Parish and Neighborhood in a Polish-American Community.* Notre Dame, IN: University of Notre Dame Press.

Zagraniczny, Stanley J. 1963. "Some Reasons of Polish Surname Changes," *Polish American Studies,* 20(1) (January–June):12–14.

Zand, Helen Sankiewicz. 1956. "Polish Family Folkways in the United States," *Polish American Studies,* 13(3–4) (July–December):77–88.

Znaniecki, Florian W. 1952. *Modern Nationalities.* Urbana, IL: University of Illinois Press.

———. 1965. *Social Relations and Social Roles.* San Francisco: Chandler.

CHAPTER THREE

The American Catholic Irish Family

Ellen Somers Horgan

INTRODUCTION

This chapter combines historical research, the sociological eye, and detailed memories of growing up in a Massachusetts Irish parish community to chronicle the dynamics of change and development of new meanings among one of the more successful ethnic groups to come to America. An early arriving group, the Irish immigrants successfully made the shift from living in a disorganized rural setting to that of an adaptive existence in the turbulence of the growing American cities.

In addition to distinctive cultural mannerisms, they brought with them to mid-nineteenth-century America a well-structured variant of the stem family that emphasized familism (a set of beliefs in which the family places its welfare above the idiosyncratic wishes of any one person), matched with a modified, bilateral, extended-kinship system in which consanguineal (blood descent) and sibling relationships were stressed. The role of the church, for most, was central, and parish organization tended to define the limits of the local community. Following World War II, a variety of family life-styles emerged to make being Irish a complex human condition and to make the specification of the typical American Catholic Irish family difficult indeed.

The assimilation of the Irish to American life has been extensive. As a consequence, writing of their family life-styles is not easy, especially considering that the immigration from Ireland to America took place over a period of at least 200 years—and that the heaviest immigration occurred after the middle and throughout the latter decades of the nineteenth century and, at a somewhat reduced rate, on into the twentieth century. Current books and articles on the American Irish, moreover, have concentrated little on the family, and detailed studies of the major cities in which the Irish settled are only now being published. Recent studies indicate that the Irish experience differed depending on the economic opportunity structure, the characteristics of native-born persons in the area, and the nature of the ethnic and racial composition of the urban centers in which the Irish settled (Thernstrom, 1973:220–261). Finally, there are contradictions within the scholarly literature, as well as in more popular works.

People are accustomed to hearing or reading the terms Irish Catholic and Irish American applied to American Catholic Irish, but I have chosen to use the phrase American Catholic Irish in the title and text of this chapter. In explanation, first, when the phrase used for the ethnic identity of the Catholic Irish in this country has the nationality of the group as the adjective and another ethnic identity (American) or a religion (Catholic) as a noun, the emphasis in the term falls not on Irish ethnicity but instead on American or Catholic. Second, despite the many attempts to create a community of Catholics of diverse nationalities, Pan-Catholicism has not often been a popular concept among lay people in this country.

The use of the term American Catholic Irish in no way implies dislike of diversity nor disapproval of aspirations for a pluralistic society in the United States. In fact, I agree with Robert E. Kennedy, Jr. (1976) that the Catholic Irish group is one that demonstrates the success of pluralism. The use of the phrase American Catholic Irish reminds the reader that the ethnicity of the group has roots in Ireland and in its past.

HISTORICAL BACKGROUND

The first notable characteristic of American Irish families is that in matters concerning the history of the immigration and early experiences here, Irish families failed to pass on information much beyond the second generation,[1] except in the case of an important relative or a few startling events. Families, most of whose members were illiterate on arrival, also taught little to their children about the history of Ireland. Yet pride in being Irish, and of so identifying one's self, is characteristic of most American Irish.

[1]The numbering system for generations may be confusing. "First generation" refers to the immigrants; "second generation" to the children of the immigrants; "third generation" to the grandchildren of the immigrants, and so on.

The history of Ireland is complex. The most significant political fact is that Ireland was ruthlessly subjugated by England, which maintained the country as an agricultural colony for its own interest and that of the minority Protestant citizens of Ireland. Declared under the lordship of Henry II (of England) in 1169, the Irish have a turbulent history of battle, rebellion, intrigue, settlement, suffering, terrorism, and pauperism. Independence was attained in 1922: The (now) Republic of Ireland is independent of England and populated heavily by Catholics, whereas Northern Ireland is still tied to the English Parliament and dominated by Protestants. This portion of the chapter will focus on only the socioeconomic and familial contexts in which the emigrants made their decisions to come to this country.

Socioeconomic Background of Irish Migrations

The reasons for the Irish emigration were many,[2] but the interaction of the patterns of rural Irish society with political, economic, and demographic catastrophes were the most important. Briefly, England kept Ireland as a rural colony, taking steps to destroy the beginnings of industrialization. The population increased from approximately 4.5 million in the last half of the eighteenth century to over 8 million by 1845 (Adams, 1932:3–4; Brody, 1974:49). The excess could not be funneled into a growing industrial economy; in fact, urban growth declined from 1851 to 1891 (Kennedy, 1973:156–157). Concomitantly with this large population increase, subdivision of the land became prevalent, facilitated by the widespread use of the potato for subsistence.[3] From 1695 to 1746, Penal Laws were passed that resulted in legal discimination against the Catholic majority, forging in the minds of the Irish a belief that their national identity and religion were one. During the eighteenth and nineteenth centuries, the peasants tried several times but failed to rid themselves of the oppression of both England and the Irish Protestant minority. In addition, famines caused by the infamous potato blights occurred in 1800, 1807, 1816, 1822, 1839, 1845–1848 (the "Great Famine"), 1863, and 1879 (Kennedy, 1973:27). These exacerbated what was already a situation of declining living standards. In

---

[2]For details, see Beckett (1966) for a concise history of Ireland; Adams (1932) for the coalescing of reasons for emigration from 1815 to 1845; and Schrier (1958), Kennedy (1973), and Brody (1974) for short summaries of relevant eighteenth- and nineteenth-century history. Also see Marx and Engels (1970).

[3]The population increase (aided by a decrease in the age of marriage for men) and the subdivision of land occurred when the use of the potato became widespread, but the cause and effect relationships between these changes are disputed by scholars. See Adams (1932:4) and Brody (1974:49–53) for brief discussions of the problem.

the most difficult economic periods, the peasants turned on their landlords and the landlords' agents. These proximate causes for the resulting emigrations were bound up with the ownership and use of land.

LANDLORDISM. By the eighteenth century, most of the land in Ireland was owned by either the gentry or a landlord class, most of whom were Protestant and many of whom lived in England. Another class was made up of small farmers who held long leases and whose holdings were large enough to make a small profit for themselves. These, too, were primarily Protestant. But about 80 or 90 percent of the population, mostly Catholic, were peasants who leased land and raised grain to pay the landlords' rents. During the famines, the blight of the potato led to the near starvation of the peasantry, who dared not eat the grain for fear of eviction.

In the latter half of the eighteenth century, when the cheap, easily raised potato became a staple, peasants began living on smaller amounts of land. Laws favoring landowners encouraged further subdivision of holdings. By the early half of the nineteenth century, subdivision had gone too far, chronic malnourishment was common, and the huts built to house the increased population were inadequate. By the time landlords and peasants realized that land would have to be consolidated, it was too late to halt overpopulation and economic misery, and the peasants stampeded out of Ireland.

STEM-FAMILY CHARACTERISTICS. When peasants attempted to increase their standard of living by increasing the size of their farms, their method was a familial one. Under the Penal Laws, at the death of the owner or tenant, land had to be subdivided so that *all* sons inherited the land equally. When these laws were no longer in force, farmers reverted to a stem-family system of impartible—not to be divided—land holdings, with only one son inheriting the land or, if there were no sons, only one daughter.[4]

[4]Le Play (1871) provided the classic description of the stem family; Zimmerman and Frampton (1935) [reprinted in Farber (1966)] interpret passages from Le Play on types of families. For descriptions of the Irish stem family after it was revived, the reader is referred to Arensberg (copyright 1937, reprinted 1950), Arensberg and Kimball (copyright 1940, reprinted 1968), Messenger (1969), and Brody (1974). For a study of families that migrated from rural Ireland to Dublin, see Humphreys (published in the United States 1966; the field work was done from 1949 to 1951). See Kennedy (1973) for a demographic theory based on the Irish stem family. Glazer and Moynihan (1963:226–229) point out parallels between Irish rural society and the American Irish political machine of New York City. Stein (1971) uses materials from descriptions of the Irish stem family to interpret stressed behavior of young American Irish males. Scheper-Hughes (1979) updates personal dilemmas of stem-family members in Ireland.

Because there was no principle of primogeniture (eldest son inherits) nor ultimogeniture (youngest son inherits), fathers were free to designate among their sons the one who would inherit the land and family home. When the parents retired, the heir married and brought his wife to live in the family home, the young couple establishing themselves as the household heads. The wife brought a dowry, usually comparable in value to the worth of her father-in-law's farm. The dowry was given to her father-in-law, *not* her husband. The patronymic went with the farm. Other children usually had to move out when the heir married. Their father then used the bride's dowry to make provisions for these children, sometimes arranging a marriage for a daughter with a neighbor's son, using the dowry from his daughter-in-law. If a daughter were the heiress, the groom brought money to the bride's father, usually in excess of the dowries paid by brides, but the name of the farm remained that of the bride's father for a generation.

The father and his successor wrote a contract concerning the rights of the retired couple. These often included space for sleeping, the provision of food, land to cultivate, perhaps a cow, depending on the wealth of the farm, and care for the surviving parent when the other died. Fathers understood that the relationship of mother-in-law and daughter-in-law might be strained; the contract specified that if conflict should occur, the parents would be cared for elsewhere.

The two fathers arranged the marriage. The details of the match were often completed within a week. The most important aspect of the arrangements was that the fathers should agree on the value of the groom's father's farm, a decision that affected the size of the bride's dowry. The status of the groom changed from that of boy or lad, to adult when he married.[5]

Several negative consequences arose for family members from this system. The successor was sometimes 40 or possibly 50 years old when the farm was inherited, which resulted in almost-compulsory delayed marriage, with singleness becoming common. Fathers often waited until near retirement before choosing an inheritor, increasing the probability of rivalry among the sons or, if there were no sons, among the daughters. The wife/mother hoped to have a daughter-in-law (or son-in-law) with whom she would get along, yet her interest in harmony within the household might not coincide with the desires of her husband to receive a large dowry from the heir's bride (or a large sum of money from the son-in-law if his daughter were the inheritor). Unless there were only two children in the

[5]Messenger (1969:68) reports that male age grading in Ireland is conceptualized as follows: until age 40, a boy or lad; until age 60, an adult; until age 80, middle-aged; and after that, old-age.

family, there was no structural way in the system for the other children to obtain an inheritance equal to that of the inheritor. There was, however, a strong norm that the father should make some provision for the other children, however unequal this might be.[6] Additionally, the heir and his wife (or the heiress and her husband) were placed in the difficult situation of living with parents; consequently, their marriage was more regulated than those of their siblings (Mattis, 1975).

The major effect of the system, however, was to disperse the unmarried siblings of the inheritor of the land from rural Ireland, a pattern of neolocal residence. At the time of the Great Famine, when land holdings were small and the stem family was being reinstituted, migration to an industrializing nation became an acceptable solution to poverty and overpopulation. Two possible solutions were available for the dispersed siblings: moving to an urban area of Ireland, although economic conditions were little better in the cities, or becoming a landless laborer with no economic security (Kennedy, 1973:154–155).

Counterbalancing the problematic aspects of the system was a positive strength—the development of familism. The father accepted responsibility for the economic welfare of members of the family, and children accepted differential treatment in the interest of family loyalty. All members shared the value that the land or leasehold should remain in the family. Sibling solidarity was a natural outgrowth of familism. And, in fact, both the emigration out of Ireland to this country and the continuing economic stability of the farms from which the emigrants came were supported to a large extent by the savings of siblings and relatives in this country who sent money home even though they were partially destitute themselves (Schrier, 1958:111).

WORK, AUTHORITY, AND THE SEXES. The Irish believed that married women should not go out to work, also a church view. This was reinforced by the belief that a working wife diminishes the status of her husband, that women should stay home and rear children, and that jobs in a marginal economy should go to others. But unmarried daughters were permitted to leave home to go to work. In an economic class with rising material aspirations, some daughters remained single all their lives. Because the maintenance of an acceptable standard of living had become a dominant value in Ireland, more important than marriage and a

---

[6]Mattis (1975) sees the role of the bride as crucial since the other children could not be provided for unless the bride brought the dowry to her father-in-law. She terms the bride the "grand liberator."

family, the numbers of single people increased over time (Kennedy, 1973:159–160).

This increase in single persons was also a function of the low status of women in rural Ireland compared with urban women in America and England. Within the family, the father was dominant. He made decisions, controlled the money, operated the farm, and did no domestic work. The mother, meanwhile, was in charge of all domestic matters, but she was also in charge of the ecological area around the hut (the haggard) and of any animals the family owned. She also did heavy farm work with her husband and sons when needed. Boys worked with their fathers and did no housework; they were treated by their mothers in a warm, supportive manner. Daughters helped their mothers, establishing a no-nonsense quasi-instrumental relationship with them. In the evenings, fathers and sons relaxed, but mothers and daughters worked. The women were also subservient to the men, caring for their needs before their own; for example, they served the fathers and sons first at meals and gave them not only more food but also more nutritious food (Kennedy, 1973:52).

Male domination had serious consequences for women. As early as 1841, men had a higher life expectancy than women in rural areas (Kennedy, 1973:45). After 1870, life expectancy for women in both rural and urban Ireland was only slightly higher than that for men and not as much higher than the same rates for women in America and England (Kennedy, 1973:55). From 1871 until 1940 moreover, age- and sex-specific death rates indicate that more Irish females than males died among children between 5 and 19 years of age (Kennedy, 1973:60). Daughters would have been unaware of these indices, but they were not unaware of their low status vis-à-vis their brothers and their future low status as wives. Daughters left rural Ireland for not only jobs, but also for higher status as women and independence (Kennedy, 1973:7). The uncommonly high number of single women in the Irish immigration may be seen as an early example of feminism.

Migration Periods

There seem to have been three distinct periods in the Irish immigration (Adams, 1932:68):

1. *Colonial Period to 1815.* By 1790, the U.S. Census listed 44,000 Irish immigrants (Adams, 1932:70), with an estimate of about 150,000 people of Irish descent (Shannon, 1963:29). After that, the numbers arriving fluctuated (Adams, 1932:69–70) but were few. Migrating

were small farmers of an economic class above the peasantry (Adams, 1932:34–35). They were young, often single, and mostly Protestants from the north of Ireland, and were of English and Scottish descent.

2. *1815 to the Great Famine of Ireland in 1845–1848.* Although statistics are unreliable for this period,[7] numbers arriving were approximately 50,000 to 60,000 through 1819, approximately 15,000 between 1820 and 1826, approximately 45,000 to 50,000 from 1827 to 1828, and at least 400,000 between 1829 and 1845. The total for the period was probably over one-half million (Adams, 1932).

   The types of immigrants in this transition period changed little at first. Most were small farmers, but others were tradesmen, weavers, spinners, deep-sea fishermen, shopkeepers, domestic servants, and, by 1818 and 1819, a number of peasants from southern Ireland—the first large exodus of Catholic Celts (Adams, 1932:104–111). By 1835, the latter had changed the character of the immigration—50 to 60 percent were Catholics from southern Ireland (Adams, 1932:191–192, 222). Whereas women were about 35 percent of immigrants in the early 1830s, the proportion rose to 48 percent in 1835. More of the latter were married, because it seems that peasants first came as intact families (Adams, 1932:194–195). Single women continued to migrate; those who spoke only Irish increased (Adams, 1932:223).

3. *Immigration After 1845: Great Famine Period.* About 120,000 Irish immigrants arrived in 1845 and 1846. Then, in only eight years, 1847 to 1854, approximately 1.25 million people, mostly Celtic Irish, came (Schrier, 1958:157).

   Those who came in this period were mostly Catholic peasants from southern and western Ireland. From 1850 to 1877, about 66 percent were between the ages of 15 and 35; for the rest of the century, the proportion of those 15 to 35 years of age was never less than 80 percent (Schrier, 1958:4). Except for the early Great Famine years, married immigrants rarely accounted for more than 16 percent (Schrier, 1958:4). After the 1870s, the number of single women increased (Kennedy, 1973:76–85). The immigration of the twentieth century seems to have followed much the same pattern except that more women than men arrived (Ferenczi, 1929:432–443).

---

[7]See Adams (1932:410–428) for a discussion of the difficulties of gathering statistics of immigrant arrivals and the kinds of estimate possible from different sources. The figures are taken from Adams. The writer, however, does not endorse Adams's view of the Irish immigration nor his biased reporting of the Irish poor.

The following is summarized and based on U.S. Census data: From 1821 to 1850, approximately one million Irish entered this country; from 1851 to 1900, about three million arrived (Schrier, 1958:159); and, from 1901 to 1924, 700,000 came (Ferenczi, 1929:432–443). After 1924, the Irish immigration declined.

Social Context of the Lifestyles of the American Catholic Irish

Readers should be aware of the social context in which the Irish settlement and adjustment were embedded.

First, the Irish went to cities and stayed in cities. They congregated in Boston, New York, Jersey City, Philadelphia, Pittsburgh, St. Louis, Chicago, and San Francisco (Wittke, 1956:23–24; Schrier, 1958:6–7). The fact that a rural people became urban is not an anomaly, since the migrants entered as neither intact families nor experienced farmers. They did not, for example, have the technology for horse-drawn methods of farming (Kennedy, 1976:358). They were, instead, the young, single, dispersed children of poor, rural Irish.

Second, the Irish established the Catholic church as a powerful institution in this country. Protestant, native-born people feared and hated the church for both rational and irrational reasons. The church absorbed some of the hatred directed toward the Irish and provided the immigrants and their children a clear personal-salvation theology to help them with life-cycle stressors.

Third, the Irish had startling success, as have other ethnic groups, in building parallel institutions to provide services for their mutual benefit (Handlin, 1941:156–183, Kutzik, 1979:32–65). Kutzik points to these five ways in which the Irish helped each other, including the aged poor: informal aid from kin and neighbors, trade associations (not yet unions), fraternal organizations, creation of their own welfare system through political activities, and homes for the aged, with nuns staffing and priests overseeing (Kutzik, 1979:49–57). These mutual-aid groups and organizations helped the immigrants and protected them from the hurt of exclusion from associations of native-born people, but they also isolated the Irish and impeded rapid acculturation. The Irish, moreover, co-opted urban political machines and major influence centers in the Democratic party, the growing labor movement, the police and fire departments, and civil services in several cities.

Fourth, the Irish changed reference groups. Immigrants first compared themselves to their relatives in Ireland and considered themselves fortunate. Later, they compared themselves with other American Irish, congratulating themselves on success—or else resenting failure. Socially mobile Irish used double comparison groups—other American Irish and native-born people—and were vulnerable to an ambivalence thereby engendered, with the less successful Irish putting the more successful down, and native-born people not accepting them.

Fifth, the work experience of the Irish was harsh. On arrival, they did menial, manual labor, as did most of the second generation. They did pick-and-shovel work, building streets and railroads and were, for instance, the main construction workers on every canal in the north until the Civil War (Adams, 1932:151). In the cities, men were, for example, hod carriers, dock workers, stable hands, street cleaners, waiters, bartenders, and porters. Women were servants, cooks, charwomen, laundresses, and aides to the semiskilled (Wittke, 1956:25). Hours were long, pay was lower than that for native-born people, work was wearying, and employers often unfriendly. The stability of the family was fragile when work was insecure.

Sixth, social class was a factor in the social context of American Catholic Irish lifestyles as has been documented often (Warner and Srole, 1945; Greeley, 1972; Birmingham, 1973; Rose F. Kennedy, 1974). Matza (1966), Thernstrom (1973), and Esslinger (1975) report, however, the slow rise of American Catholic Irish in the class system. The reasons suggested for the slow rise are the following: the pauperization of the Irish before they migrated (Matza); the low level of skill for work on arrival (Thernstrom); the discrimination against them because of their ethnicity, especially their religion (Thernstrom); values learned and perpetuated within the family such as the need for security and lack of interest in risk-taking (Thernstrom); and the large number of people who were economically mobile downward (*skidding* is the term Thernstrom used). This slow upward mobility is a fact of history that tied the American Catholic Irish to their cultural past. Colloquial terms (some are negative labels) have been used for years to describe American Catholic Irish socioeconomic classes. These include "shanty" Irish, "lace curtain" Irish, "venetian blind" Irish, "oriental rug" Irish, and Birmingham's (1973) contribution, "real lace" Irish, used in the title of his book.

Early Adaptation of the American Irish Family

America was ill prepared for the arrival of the Irish. Squalid living conditions existed in all major cities. Those of Boston described by Handlin (1941:93–127) were more than matched, for instance, by the miseries in New York of which McCague wrote (1968:20–27). The immigrants found housing wherever they could: lodging houses; older, larger, subdivided houses; warehouses; shanties (huts); flats; and cellars and attics of old buildings. Sanitation was inadequate or absent, smells deplorable, and the water supply uncertain. Roofs leaked. Walls were damp. Garbage rotted. Privacy was limited. Cleanliness was next to impossible.

Under these conditions, family and community life were often turbulent. Men left for work early and returned late, as did many women; children and young teenagers roamed the streets. In the neighborhoods, pawnbrokers thrived; greengrocers often sold more inexpensive rye whiskey than other items (not exclusively to men); saloons flourished; idle men stood around, hoping for work; fights started easily and spread quickly; prostitution occurred. Handlin (1941) reported that, in Boston, after the Irish came, infant mortality rates rose (p. 199), Irish longevity decreased (p. 199), marriage and fertility rates increased (p. 121), pauperism rose (p. 121), and emotional stress increased (p. 126), as did the rate of illegitimate births (p. 126). Norms of rural family life and social forms such as drinking, argumentation, and visitation lost much of their meaning in a social context of high-density urban living.

In Buffalo, from 1855 to 1875, some carryover of structural elements of the Irish family were found by Mattis (1975). Delayed marriage remained a salient factor in the Irish immigrant community; when both partners were from Ireland, the average age at marriage for males was 35 and for females, 31. The average age for native-born males was 26, and for females, 23. Some Irish, females more so than males, remained single throughout their lives. [For 1950, Heer (1961:236–238) reports that both Irish males and females—immigrants and second-generation people—were more likely to marry late or not at all compared with 12 other ethnic groups and native-born people. These findings are for the end of the Irish immigration.] These patterns in Buffalo may be seen as consistent with the need for the Irish to establish themselves economically before marriage and with the relatively high number of women who came here seeking increased independence. Mattis's finding of more Irish men marrying non-Irish women rather than the reverse pattern is consistent with her finding that some Irish women did not marry at all. [However, by 1920 Irish immigrant men were more likely to have an Ireland-born wife, 71 percent, than Ireland-born women were to have Ireland-born husbands, 61 percent (Carpenter, 1927:234–235).]

HOUSEHOLDS HEADED BY WOMEN. A significant form of adaptation in family organization appeared in the first decades after arrival of the Irish. Mattis (1975) reports that the proportion of households headed by women appeared high—18 percent in 1855, 14 percent in 1865, and 16 percent in 1875. Most of these heads of households were widows, partly a consequence of men marrying women younger than themselves (Mattis, 1975) and partly a consequence of the dangerous occupations of men and their early deaths. As another adaptive aspect, Mattis also notes that *most of the households that expanded to include relatives were headed by women,* a finding noticed in other urbanizing minority groups (Pauw, 1963; Rainwater, 1966; Smith and Biddle, 1975). At the height of the Irish immigration in 1855, families expanded to include parents, siblings, nieces, nephews, and some in-laws. By 1875, the added relatives were mostly grandparents, a finding that might be interpreted as a partial return to the traditional stem family or, more simply, as a reflection of the passage of time during which other relatives found different housing.

Additionally, in both 1855 and 1875, approximately one-fifth or one-fourth of the immigrant households had someone *not* related by blood or marriage living in the house (boarders and *their* relatives). This pattern is one of adaptation to the economic and social exigencies faced by women who headed these households. Women needed the money obtained from rent and assistance with their families. They also provided service for others who had recently immigrated.

THE ESTABLISHED AMERICAN CATHOLIC IRISH FAMILY AND PARISH LIFE: 1920–1950

Over several decades, after the mass immigration and the introduction of further Irish immigrants of a slightly more stable background, the structure, values, and behavior of the Irish stem family combined into an amalgam of the old and new. The immigrant quasi-ghetto neighborhoods in the cities tended to disappear and were replaced by the parish as the unit of community living.[8] Although not a large number were involved, some American Irish families moved as single units into the economically better neighborhoods. The majority, however, remained ethnically and ecologically nucleated, building community and family solidarity around the parish, which was organized by the church. The extensive depiction in the

[8]The use of the parish as a neighborhood unit is common when writing of the American Irish, for the coalescence of residence, church, and parochial school (or public elementary school) within a small geographically closed area was a feature of the Catholic parish that the church administrators wisely fostered in the first half of the twentieth century. The parish as a unit has been used most recently by Greeley (1972) when he described the neighborhood of "Beverly." Farrell's *Studs Lonigan* (1938) also took place in a parish and Curran's novel, *The Parish and the Hill* (1948), contrasts a poor Massachusetts Irish parish with a Yankee neighborhood.

following sections of family life in one Massachusetts parish, represents a form of marshaling ethnographic data through the personalized and extended sociological anecdote as experienced by the writer of this chapter who grew up in the parish described.[9] Apart from the lack of a parochial school, there was little to differentiate this parish from others in Massachusetts.

No justification need be made for the style of reporting, because there are few sociological sources of information about American Irish family life. Novels, biographies, and works on aspects of the American Irish experience other than the family abound, yet none of these provides the kind of sociological information readers may wish to know. The time period of the parish described is approximately 1920 to 1950.

The Parish

The parish was an ecological unit, a community of families and an organized church membership. It was an enclave of American Irish families of the second, third, and sometimes fourth generation living dispersed among native-born people and a few families from other ethnic groups. Church administrators drew boundaries so that families of about the same economic level were included and built the church near the center. Shops were close to the church and included a drugstore, a laundry, two or three proprietor-run grocery stores, a gasoline station, a variety store, a shoe repair shop, a bakery, a liquor store, and a tavern. Some of the stores had delivery service. Many women shopped daily. Three public schools and a park were found in the parish, not always contiguous to the parish center. The parish served during the week as the unit within which social interaction took place.

Controls

The parish was compact enough that some of the children knew almost everyone and at least half the adults knew one another personally and knew more by sight. People with problems and children with handicaps were enveloped in a relatively closed community. Priests were a familiar sight on the streets talking with adults and watching the young. Some men would go the tavern at night although a few might be there all day. Older teenagers and young adult men would gather at the shops in the evenings and teenage girls in groups would find some reason to shop or to visit the church. There were informal cliques among all age groups and, harking back to Ireland, most of these were age and sex graded. The pace of life was not fast. Small talk passed back and forth. Those in need were visited by the priests. Women individually and voluntarily helped other families at times of crisis.

---

[9]Parish people ranged from working class to lower-middle and middle-middle class in the United States system.

Lest this sound like the mythical village, strains should be noted. While small talk kept people informed, it also made family happenings public knowledge quickly, it worked to induce conformity of behavior, and it reaffirmed prevailing attitudes. As a result, new ideas, different values or changes in custom were slow to occur. Constraints on behavior were as much external as internal.

Families were, however, quite private about family matters; children were usually sent outside while family business was discussed. Adult parishioners kept private within the family how they voted, the size of family income, expenditures planned, gossiped-about sexual behavior, the beliefs of those who left the church, public events on which there might be controversy, job changes, and the futures of children. The conversations to which children might listen involved general discussions about politics and politicians, family events being planned, news about relatives, and comments about those persons whose public behavior was not approved.

Church Membership

The parish was an organized church membership. The priests knew every family. The activities of the family revolved around the church calendar as much as the school schedules of children and the work hours of men (and some women). Most religious activities and rituals took place in the church. Mothers were responsible for the religious education of children at home. Boys were expected to serve at mass as altar boys. Girls participated in services on Holy Thursday and Good Friday. Children, if they did not attend parochial school, went to religious instructions on weekday afternoons and were separated into groups by school grade and sex. Catechisms were memorized and lessons listened to, with nuns as the usual teachers. Children were expected to go to confession on Saturday afternoon and, after fasting from midnight, to receive communion on Sunday morning. At the children's mass, the same nuns who taught religious classes supervised and, again, children were seated by school grade and sex. High school students went to religious instruction on a week night, were taught by priests, and, by custom now, segregated themselves by gender.

Families were urged to attend mass on weekdays and to make short visits to the church when close by, although few did. Attendance at Sunday mass and the special holy days was required and those who did not attend committed a mortal sin, serious enough to send one's soul to hell if one died before confessing. Most parishioners attended these masses. Those who aspired to attend mass as a family, as Protestant families attended their services, were disappointed. Priests insisted upon school children attending their own mass, and parents often went individually to separate masses so that the younger children might be attended by the other, if no kin lived nearby to watch the children.

Church and Family

The most important aspect of the church was the underpinning it gave to the structure of the American Irish family and the clear dogma of personal salvation it gave to members. The de facto theology, the beliefs which the laity thought the church taught [Osborne (1969:40) uses this term] was passed from parents to children. The chief points of the doctrine were the following: each individual had an immortal soul; people were born with original sin which could only be removed by Catholic baptism; God was three people, the Trinity—God the Father, God the Son, and God the Holy Spirit—but yet only one; Mary, the mother of Jesus was a virgin and, when she died, her body went to heaven; Jesus became a man to provide an opportunity for people to reach heaven and to create a church that would show people the way to live; the Catholic church was the only true church and adherents of other religions, even if they led exemplary lives, could only go to limbo, a pleasant place but one in which God never appeared; all sins committed in one's lifetime had to be suffered for in purgatory before one's soul went to heaven; the difficulties of life were to be borne as best one could; unequal talents and socioeconomic success or failure were unimportant to God; mortal sins on one's soul at the time of death prevented one from going to purgatory or heaven so that regular confession was necessary; the list of mortal sins was long but included not only those of murder, lying, and theft but also disobedience of parents and others in authority, sinful thoughts, the use of contraceptives, adultery, fornication, abortion, divorce, marriage in a non-Catholic ceremony, suicide, lack of attendance at mass on Sundays or holy days—and others; if one were a good Catholic and died in the grace of God, one went eventually to heaven to be with God forever.[10]

The sinfulness of people was stressed but the way to salvation was clear; follow the teachings of the church; participate in the sacraments and pray—to keep one's faith. Children were admonished to obey their parents, believe in their church and show their faith in such ways as not saying the Protestant end of the Lord's Prayer at school, by blessing themselves before batting in a ballgame or going swimming, and by wearing a "miraculous" medal. When children misbehaved, mothers suggested they confess their sins and, if they raised questions about Catholic beliefs, they talk to the priest. When children, especially girls, were required to do something they found unpleasant, mothers suggested they offer their difficulties to God as a gift.

Father's and Mother's Positions

The church affected family life by supporting the traditional Irish family's way of doing things. When the man lost the tangible sign of the farm as a basis for family cohesion, he did not forfeit his authority and status as head of the family responsible for the economic welfare of all. Because fathers' work hours were long, mothers were in charge of daily domestic activities within the family and some believed they had effective influence. Even so, husbands

[10]The writer wishes to stress that this is the theology as understood by lay people in the parish, circa 1920–1950, to remind readers of the extensive literature created by scholars and philosophers who have astutely interpreted Catholic thought through the centuries, and to note that the Catholic church in the United States has changed extensively since the Second Vatican Council.

made most major decisions alone or perhaps after a brief discussion with their wives. Most importantly the husband was in charge of money and provided a set sum to his wife, usually on a weekly basis. Few children had allowances, including those in high school and even some in college.

Men often decided on the children's occupations and educations and, although the children's abilities were taken into account, their wishes were sometimes ignored. The fathers were deeply involved in decisions about children's marriages but mothers' views were often heard that daughters should be socially mobile by making a good marriage and that marriages for both sons and daughters should be delayed as long as possible, certainly until the young people established themselves economically. In fact, both mothers and fathers emphasized good marriages for their children—in economic terms as well as in terms of the character of the future spouse. This was not spoken about openly.[11] Going steady was discouraged, as was dating a non-Catholic. The father's position was recognized by the expectation that an aspiring groom would ask him for his daughter's hand, not always a ritual matter, for some men were rejected. But, apart from the mother's input concerning marriage, fathers decided when and how the family should move, buy items of furniture, purchase a car, and take a vacation. No matter how quiet, inarticulate, or unassuming the father might have been, nor how kindly he exercised his authority, he made the decisions.

There were, of course, some women who *did* make major family decisions. Some of these had mild husbands who allowed them to do so. There were other women who might not have chosen to head the family, but whose husbands did not through default of character, overuse of alcohol, or desperation in the face of an indomitable woman. These were relatively rare. The more usual case was the gentle, friendly, hardworking husband who quietly headed the family and a competent, industrious but mild wife who accepted her husband's authority. It is unfortunate that the family in Ireland and this country has sometimes been portrayed as dominated by women (Greeley, 1972:110–113; McCready, 1974:164–165), as this view hides the real difficulties of energetic and instrumental American Irish women who accepted a subordinate role within the family. One problem was that some men acted at home in an arbitrary or authoritarian manner.[12]

Women were in charge of domestic activity with some assistance from their husbands, who might take a child for a walk on Sunday, or dry a few dishes, or, more rarely, help prepare a meal. Living in tenements and apartments or rented houses, women no longer were responsible for the haggard, and gardening was not common. Women gained independence in spending the family's money. They also had the responsibility of rearing their sons through the teenage years. They kept up the homes and seldom questioned the family's economic status over which they worried but had little control.

---

[11]See Humphreys (1966) for a discussion of the openness of Dublin families on this issue.
[12]Studs' father is an example (Farrell, 1938).

As in Ireland, single women were free to work. Despite some stigma, expressed by married women, which attached to remaining single, some women chose not to marry, as did some men.[13] Widows, too, went to work but not always full time in a regular job. Some became the itinerant helpers of parish families, helping out when life course events occurred in others' families. Married women usually did not work, either in regular paid jobs or with their husbands, except in small proprietary businesses at busy times of the year. The exceptions to this were women who helped establish the family economically and then stopped [as in Buffalo, see Mattis (1975)] or when their husbands were unemployed during the Great Depression or when the country needed workers during World War II (although, even then, few did). American Irish women behaved very much like their counterparts in Ireland and, out of each cohort of women, some decided to marry and rear a family (having relatively high fertility rates); others delayed marriage or remained single and worked. Widows had little choice. They ran their homes, reared their children, and worked. Widows, although treated deferentially by men, were not usually considered eligible as martial partners. Widowers often married single women, sometimes younger than themselves. Motherhood was considered virtuous; wifehood was rarely mentioned.

CHILDREN

Children in American Catholic Irish homes were treated as children, not small adults. Mothers were firm and moralistic but also kind, sentimental, and active. Children learned to be subordinate, obedient, and respectful. Children were also taught to be respectable—to do the right thing and to be polite. A spoiled, whiny, or bold child was unacceptable to mothers and fathers. Punishment for disobedience of children was external and expressed by parents, parishioners, and priests. Shame and ridicule, appeals to the embarrassment caused one's parents (especially one's mother), and mocking were used interchangeably by all. Success of children, however, was underplayed, was assumed a part of life, and, when told to others, was understated.

Mothers emphasized physical activity for children and often suggested they go outside and play or exercise rather than stay inside the home and read, hang around, or pursue hobbies. Participation in sports was emphasized, especially for boys. Achievement in school was encouraged. Since success in educational and occupational spheres had not been an experience of mothers, they pointed to people they admired in the parish and encouraged children to make something of themselves.

In one area of parenting, fathers stepped in—they taught sons to fight. Mothers disapproved of boys' fighting and hoped their sons would not become

---

[13]Kennedy (1973:152) points out that in Ireland there was little or no stigma attached to remaining single throughout one's life.

involved in neighborhood arguments. Fathers were ambivalent. They, too, did not want their boys to fight but, even more, they did not want their sons to be beaten up or not to stand up for their rights. As a result, many fathers taught their sons to fight; and the boys fought, often over the issue of whether or not they would do so. It was also a part of the youth culture for a boy to be known as a good fighter; girls knew which boys would stand up for their rights and which would not.

Differential treatment by mothers of their sons and daughters continued, as in Ireland. Boys were treated more affectionately than girls. The importance of the boys' work future was stressed while the learning of how to run a household was emphasized for girls. Children knew from an early age that the resources of the family could not provide for all. If their brothers were older or equally talented, or almost so, daughters knew that the resources of the family would go first to their brothers. In the less well-off families, older sons and daughters went to work and younger brothers, and sometimes their sisters, might benefit from the increased status of the family. In the better-off families, the older sons were provided opportunities, the younger waited their turn, and daughters hoped to be helped.

The concept of equal treatment of each child remained subordinate to the concept of providing as best one could for all within the context of limited resources. However different one might consider such familism by today's standards of the enhancement of each individual, there was the advantage that a family in which each looks out for the others has cohesion. Sibling loyalty is not necessary when there are adequate resources but, when they are scarce, some system of allocation *without* rivalry is needed [see Greeley (1972:115–116) on sibling relationships]. Families, who in the usual course of events had a relatively capable father and a responsible mother who was reasonably warm toward her children, were strengthened by the concern of children for one another. When these were absent, difficulties occurred.[14] In the parish, adult siblings kept in touch, assistance was given to one another when needed. All cared for elderly parents but in different ways, depending on their resources—paying bills, shopping, visiting, and having the parents live in their homes.

Sons may have been confused by being the recipients of both affective and instrumental behavior from their mothers in a way in which daughters were not. As long as sons could look forward to being heads of families catered to by their wives and children, major problems were avoided. If daughters could find a husband who would head the family and achieve economic viability, few difficulties occurred. Change the admixture slightly or lessen the priests' support of the traditional family, and some sons would remain bachelors, some would become priests, some would marry a less demanding woman from another ethnic group, and some might simply drink too much. Likewise, some women would remain single, some would become nuns, some would marry but have no children, some would try to dominate their husbands, and some might marry a man from another ethnic group.

---

[14]See Stein (1971) for a discussion of stress reactions among American Irish *male* adolescents.

Kinship among the American Irish follows that of Ireland. Kin were people related by descent (blood) or marriage to whom one owed mutual assistance and among whom some marriages were tabooed. A modified bilateral system prevailed. In Ireland, the kinship bond extended, as an example on the paternal side, from a husband to his father's father's father (great grandparent) and all the kin in the descending generations were kin of the husband (ego); thus, kin on the male side of the family were father's father's brother, and father's father's brother's son and the son of the last. But all possible roots were counted, *female* as well as male, so that the number of consanguineal (blood) kinship *positions* came to 32 in ego's generation of first and second cousins. The church but not the people tabooed marriage with third cousins but dispensations for these marriages were evidently easily obtained. Affinality (kinship by marriage) was limited somewhat, as the spouses of the siblings of one's parents were not considered kin, nor were the spouses of father's and mother's parents' siblings.

The importance of kinship to the Irish cannot be overstated. Although the household in Ireland was both the unit of economic production and of the family (nuclear and husband's parents), farmers needed help from others at times of planting and reaping, especially, and the families needed assistance or support for some events, such as childbirth, illness, or death. The help was given by consanguineal kin who by so doing established a "claim" against the household helped and who could expect that when they were in need the household members they had assisted earlier would reciprocate. Household members were ambivalent about giving and seeking help, however, for household self-sufficiency was a matter of great pride. But knowing that the day would come when the household members could not alone solve some problems, families assisted others and stored up "claims" for the future. For minor matters, the immediate families of the spouses helped one another but, for major crises, the wider extended kindred were on hand.

At marriage, both husband and wife acquired the full consanguineal kindred of the new spouse but only the spouses did so, not their kindred; the wife's parents and the husband's parents, then, did not become kin to one another. After marriage, the immediate families of each spouse were treated by both spouses as if they were consanguineal kin. Members of the immediate family were father-in-law and mother-in-law, brother-in-law and sister-in-law, and son-in-law and daughter-in-law. Again, however, the spouses of one's spouse's siblings (sister-in-law's husband, brother-in-law's wife) were not included as kin although there were often warm relationships between them. The extended kin of one's spouse were less important than the immediate ones, but in times of need mutual help was given, and on ritual occasions kin ties operated more extensively.

In the Massachusetts parish, the immediate families of both husband and wife were the close kin: For the couple, these included the four parents, siblings of both spouses (brothers-in-law and sisters-in-law), and the children of the siblings (nephews and nieces). For the children of the couple, the relatives were grandparents, aunts and uncles, and cousins. And, although from the viewpoint of one's parents, spouse's siblings' spouses were ambiguously treated, children used the American system and made no such distinction between aunts and uncles in terminology or gift-giving but did know which of these aunts and uncles were relatives by descent and which by marriage. In most matters, kinship relations took place between members of immediate families and more distant relatives attended weddings, wakes, and funerals. When godparents were chosen, one usually came from the father's side of the family and one from the mother's, symbolizing the bilaterality of the kin system.

Rituals and Rites of Passage

Marriages in the parish took place at a mass before noon and usually on a Saturday so relatives and friends could attend. They ranged from the simple with only immediate families present, to formal with several bridesmaids and ushers. Festivities included a meal before which toasts were made, and sometimes dancing after the meal. Because of the expense, the custom arose of sending invitations of two types: one for the church service only and one which also included the reception. Families followed closely the usual American strictures about which family paid for various expenses of the wedding. Those marrying non-Catholics usually had a private service, not always in the parish. The non-Catholic was asked to take instructions in which the tenets of the church were learned and signed a contract with the priest present in which it was agreed that the children of the couple would be reared as Catholics. Almost as often, the non-Catholic was urged to convert to Catholicism. Couples were often engaged for a year or more in order to get to know one another and, as importantly, to get to know one another's families. The wait also permitted the young couple to save money to furnish their home. Premarital sex was absolutely forbidden and so serious was the situation of a pregnant bride that the marriage took place in great haste, often outside the parish, and usually without announcement from the altar.

The American Irish wake is somewhat unusual. In the parish the family waked the dead person at home after the body had been prepared at a funeral home. The body was raised up in a casket with the upper half of the body showing, a rosary entwined in the hands. Flowers were banked around the casket. Usually for one or two afternoons and two evenings the family was home to meet friends and relatives. The rosary was said around ten o'clock. There was sherry or red wine for the women, whiskey for the men, and food for all. The women often stayed in the living room or parlor with the casket, and the men moved to the kitchen. Much of the talk was of happy or humorous events concerning the dead person and the reminiscing helped families to mourn publicly and without embarrassment. Drunkenness and raucous joking were not as common as alleged; the usual case was that a few women had a little too much sherry or a few men had too much rye. Two male relatives often stayed up all night in the room with the body. For the religious services, the funeral home took over and brought the body in a hearse and the family in limousines to the church for the funeral mass. Burial was at a Catholic cemetery. Afterward all returned to the family home for a luncheon. Very young children did not attend wakes but by their teen years children in the family were expected to attend. The cars in the funeral procession were assigned by degree of closeness of the kin relationship or of friendship and of children by birth order. Many persons made contributions for masses to the church for the deceased relative or friend. Cremation was taboo. For people who committed suicide or who were apostates, there were no public services and their graves were located in unblessed land in the cemetery.

Baptisms were less ritualized and usually celebrated with a party at the parents' home. The infant was taken to the church by the godparents for baptism by the priest who usually performed the ceremony on a Sunday afternoon. Children were given one saint's name. But the naming was deemed less important than the sacrament that removed original sin. Guests usually brought small gifts for the baby, sometimes money to start a savings account. Being a godparent carried with it the responsibility to see that the child was not only reared as a Catholic but also remained so until marriage.

The American Catholic Irish family, then, adapted to conditions in this country and succeeded in creating strong, loyal family units. Entering as the least experienced of the immigrant groups who arrived about the same time historically, they moved slowly into solid working-class jobs and the lower levels of bureaucracies, while some became upper-middle-class professionals and others successful owners of companies (Birmingham, 1973) or corporation executives. The family of the parish exists in an attenuated degree in enclaves in several of our large cities today. Others who were more successful have made the exodus to the suburbs, bringing with them many of the attitudes of the parish. The children who grew up in the parish are the parents of today's young adults and teenagers. Some of these young people may go on to complete integration in this country, not knowing much about their Irish ancestors.

THE MODERN AMERICAN CATHOLIC IRISH FAMILY: CHANGE AND ADAPTATION

If one assumes a 30-year period for a generation, then the young people today are the fifth generation descended from the Great Famine immigrants and the fourth generation descended from those who entered this country in the 1870s. Some immigrants arrived later, of course, and there are some young people today whose grandparents came from Ireland but few compared to the total population descended from Irish immigrants. To write about the new generations in general terms is difficult, since there is little data on family life-styles of American Irish of different generations and differing social classes with the exception of the now outdated Warner and Srole work (1945), Thernstrom's study (1973), and Esslinger's book (1975). There are, however, a few types that may be briefly described.[15]

The Enclaved American Catholic Irish Families

There are those who remain in enclaves in our large cities or in nearby suburbs and work in blue-collar jobs or in the lower echelons of government and business bureaucracies. This group still lives in parishes but now side-by-side with those from other ethnic groups. The family is still highly important, as is their religion. The father has a tendency to make decisions for the family, but the participation of wives and children has increased significantly. Intergenerational mobility aspirations are slightly less than in preceding generations. Married women are more likely to work to maintain the economic viability of the family, and the number of permanently single women has declined. While home ownership remains important, education of children is stressed equally. Some of the children attend parochial schools; some go to Catholic colleges. The views of the Catholic church are heard equally with those of the secular society. The group identifies itself as Irish, usually votes Democratic, and sometimes ignores the beliefs of their church, especially regarding use of contraceptives, although some young people believe contraception introduces an unnatural aspect to sexual behavior. Delayed marriage is a matter of the past, since both spouses work; women often work before the last child enters school. Marriage to non-Catholics is more common. Family schedules are less organized by the church now, while church schedules are more flexible.

Most have become members of working-class America but retain Irish identification. Structural differences in families have disappeared, but many of the characteristics of the group have not. These include the lesser amount of overt affection, the favoritism toward sons, the attitudes of male authority, the preference for action, the use of alcohol to increase sociability, the obligations of families to care for one another, and the gathering of family members for rituals and holidays.

Although this group has not risen high economically, its members form an important part of our industrial society. They also remain a slightly controversial group in our national life. The issue of separation of church

---

[15]The types described here are not Weberian ideal types and cannot be, because the criteria distinguishing them are too many and the data on which to construct them too few. In fact, the difficulties encountered in trying to present even a few types leads the writer to commend Nancy Scheper-Hughes on her proposed study in Massachusetts of American Catholic Irish families.

and state, for example, is seen not as one of civil liberties but as one of unfair taxation, especially in regard to education. Some are resistant to alternate life-styles for families.

They are loyal to this country and patriotic. When convinced that an activity is for the country's good, they are enthusiastic. When they believe that they are being wronged by government action, they will feistily resist. One need only recall the vehemence of opposition from South Boston Irish to bussed racial integration of the school system to underscore the importance of their neighborhoods.

Middle-Class American Catholic Irish Families

Among those who have risen economically, there is diversity of life-styles. A few types emerge. *First,* out of the strength of parish families, in which fathers and mothers stressed economic and educational advancement, and in which the children grew up during the Great Depression and the strains of World War II, have come professional and business men and women whose life-styles vary little from those of other successful urbanites and suburbanites. Many have degrees from private Protestant colleges, from state universities, and from Catholic colleges. They are integrated into American life, live in neighborhoods of professional and business families, understand well the philosophical underpinnings of the country, and have close friends among many groups.

Their orientations are to their organizations, companies, professions, and communities first—their church and neighborhood, second. The new Catholic church does not surprise them. They sometimes complain about the poor quality of parochial schools, which they help maintain, but which their children often do not attend. Although not living and interacting with many Irish people on a daily basis, they nevertheless identify themselves as Irish, they seem not to accept the Pan-Catholic attitudes of the church, and they note the ethnic backgrounds of those with whom they work. They are also identified as Irish by others.

This group is mixed with respect to political party affiliation—perhaps more of the lawyers and teachers remaining Democrats and more of the bankers, physicians, and business men and women becoming Republicans. There is little favoritism of sons over daughters. Their children appear less interested in striving for achievement or excellence in professions and business; some are downwardly mobile. Affection within the family is open, especially by mothers. Some of the women work after marriage; others return to work when the last child enters school.

Second, there is a subgroup of successful middle-class American Catholic

Irish families begun in the 1950s and early 1960s, in the era of togetherness, who have had five, six, seven, or more children *by choice*. Mothers are affectionate, worry little about their matter-of-fact child-rearing styles, and identify positively with *traditional* American Catholic Irish families. The men are likely to be preoccupied with their work. They take small part in the rearing of children, expressing most concern when it is time to choose colleges for and with the children, although they insist on the best available precollege education for them, and, having succeeded themselves, worry little about an improvement in the economic welfare of their children.

Third, there is a group among American Irish middle-class people who maintain close ties to the Catholic church but in a new way. Many of these were educated in parochial schools and Catholic colleges. They orient their family life around the church, and they bring the church into their homes, celebrating church holidays with family rituals or days of special significance for the family with religious rituals. As expected, they are active in churches, both with formal councils and groups, and with informal groups that join together in members' homes to discuss issues, perhaps adding a semiritualistic aspect by sharing wine and bread. Some are active in the ecumenical movement.

The comfort of this third group of middle-class American Irish as Catholics and their serious concern with religion seem paradoxical when they state that many of the tenets of the Catholic church are not applicable to their lives. Many are in favor of abortion, sterilization, the use of contraceptives, and vasectomy. Others think the celibacy of priests is not necessary. Some think women should be priests. Divorce is considered an alternative to stressed marriages. The Bible is read and interpreted by themselves. Many participate in communion and in the weekly mass when in a spiritual mood. Many talk of situation ethics regardless of any universal system of morality. Some have little understanding of more traditional Catholics, seem not to know the meaning of heresy, and find it difficult to understand why anyone would be an apostate, now or in the past. At issue, however, is whether they can transmit their religious loyalty to their children.

The family life of this third group of middle-class American Catholic Irish is one of togetherness. There usually are two or three children; women do not work until the children enter school, although some obtain college or professional degrees while rearing their children. Men work hard but are more integrated into family life than other American Catholic Irish men. Children are reared with a mixture of American flexibility overlaid with learning of complex family rules. Some fathers in these families are less successful economically than those in the first and second middle-class groups.

Other American Irish

Many American Catholic Irish do not fit the types described. There are those who are third, fourth, or fifth generation married to members of other American ethnic groups—some of whom were educated in Catholic colleges, some not—whose Pan-Catholicism seems more important than their ethnicity: some live in mixed ethnic enclaves, some in surburbia. There are second-, third-, fourth-, and fifth-generation American Catholic Irish at all class levels who married descendents of native-born people, who have children who do not know of their Irish ethnic past. There are those who drifted away from Catholicism and the Irish parish without much concern; their descendents have little knowledge of their ethnic heritage. There are apostates from the Catholic church. Of these, some have joined other religious groups; others, who are not religious, term themselves renegades, apostates, agnostics, or atheists. There remain people of second-, third-, and fourth-generation American Catholic Irish who remained single or who married late and had no children. There are many American Catholic Irish in the Midwest and West, and some in the South, who were not reared in ethnic parishes, have little identification with the Irish, and are unfamiliar with the ethnic rivalries of their compatriots. Yet there are others in the Midwest and West, and a few in the South, who were reared in Irish enclaves and who share much with their northeastern counterparts.

Issues of Serious Concern to the American Catholic Irish Family

As an ethnic group, the American Catholic Irish find issues that are problematic for their family life. Particularly difficult are those concerning care of the elderly, marital disruption, feminism, and divisiveness within the Catholic church.

THE ELDERLY. Among American Catholic Irish, care of older adults is an issue. As in the colonial United States (Fischer, 1978), older males in Ireland controlled the family and the land, constructing a legacy of ambivalent response and wary distrust among the children. Stivers (1976:51–74) writes that male noninheritors of the farms in Ireland joined with their nephews in an avunculate, often symbolized by joining one another in drinking behavior. In this country, the pattern varied in that the male family head was away working while the woman reared children, including the sons, for a longer time period than in Ireland. Sibling loyality, familism, and the strength of both parents led to behavior in the United States in which kin cared for older adults. Some older siblings lived with one another. Today, some middle-aged children prefer expanding families to include older adults, other prefer care within a long-term care residence managed by Catholic orders, and still others prefer use of public or private long-term care settings.

Acceptance of Medicaid funds is difficult for some—not for others. Sons and daughters both share concern for older adults, although their functions sometimes differ, men more often being instrumental and daughters affective. Care for older nuns, brothers, priests, and monks has been resolved by some orders establishing their own long-term care residences. Not quite ready to relinquish the familial system of care and yet not always able to pay the costs of in-home and community-based services and residences, American Catholic Irish remain ambivalent and behave diversely concerning older adults.

MARITAL DISRUPTION. Problematic issues for Catholic Irish are those of marital status and of parenting after separation, divorce, or desertion. In many urban areas there are groups of single Catholics, largely made up of divorced people, but which sometimes include widows, widowers, and people single by choice. Of those divorced, separated, or deserted, many seek annulments of their former marriages so that they may remarry within their religion. Joint custody of children is sometimes sought by those divorced. Single parenting and stepparenting are common among separated and divorced people and among widows and widowers. Remarriage is relatively common—sometimes within the Catholic church, and sometimes without. Men often marry younger women, thus creating a cohort of women who find a dwindling group of same-aged men to marry. (Norms remain that proscribe women marrying younger men.) Postmarital sexual behavior without the bond of marriage has increased, as has the number of people living together without formalizing the relationship. Problematic for single American Catholic Irish people is the link between their behavior, proscribed by their religion, and maintenance of membership in their church. Celibacy is not welcomed by many, nor are homosexuality, lesbianism, and bisexuality.[16] While some masturbate, this solution is also not a permanent nor satisfying one for many.

---

[16]Heterosexual orientation has been the norm among American Catholic Irish. This does not imply, however, that sexual behavior of individuals has usually followed the norm nor that there is an absence of bisexual, lesbian, and homosexual behavior among American Catholic Irish.

FEMINISM. Another issue for the American Catholic Irish is the place of feminism in their lives. Although strong, directed women have always been a part of the group, authority in the family in both Ireland and this country remained with men. With the reemergence of feminism, several issues have arisen that have yet to be resolved—the three most controversial being passage of the Equal Rights Amendment (ERA), equality of women with men in decision making within all areas of family life, *and* choice concerning whether or not to have children and/or choice concerning the timing and the number of children. Catholic Irish women are in many ways prepared to respond to these issues in terms of the history of the group. Yet the close link of the Catholic church with national identity has juxtaposed the issues in a way that makes it difficult for women in the group to ally with one another to gain equality. There would be little controversy over the ERA among the Catholic Irish, for example, were not the issue of choice regarding contraception and abortion a serious concern of the Catholic church, and egalitarianism within the family would not remain problematic were women socialized within the family and within the Catholic church to take an active stance about control of their bodies. However, in the present situation, where the three issues are intertwined with concepts of sin and with calls to become or remain traditional wives and mothers, it is difficult for women to differentiate their roles as women, Catholics, workers, wives, mothers, citizens, and quite fallible people.[17] As a result, the ERA, equality within the family, and choice regarding family planning remain divisive with Catholic Irish families.

DIVISIVENESS WITHIN THE CATHOLIC CHURCH. A final issue of concern for the Catholic Irish is the Catholic church itself. Many nuns, priests, brothers, and monks have left their orders with sorrow. Participation in the ecumenical movement is somewhat ambivalent, particularly after the papal visit in 1980 and after the papal notice for withdrawal from political office by those with priestly, sisterly, and brotherly callings. Feminists within the Catholic church and within the orders of sisters find their activities proscribed to more traditional behavior than now expressed, and their hopes for equality within the church may not be met. The tightening of rules about the ritual aspects of religion has led to some dismay. Calls for noncelibacy of priests (on principle and on grounds of assistance in the

[17]Mary Daly (1968, reprinted 1975; 1973; 1975; 1978), who is distinctively American Catholic Irish, has presented an ideological background or metaethics for radical feminism that illustrates the dilemmas of choice for American Catholic Irish women as well as for women of all groups nationally and internationally.

recruitment of priests) continue, although the same calls have not been made for orders of sisters. At issue for Catholic Irish in this country is the response of those affected by divisiveness within the Catholic community, functionaries and laypeople alike who hold alternate realities to those officially held by the Catholic church. Alienation from one's traditional religion is more than difficult.

Conclusion

For every family characteristic described, some Catholic Irish person will find his or her experiences at variance with those depicted. Yet, there are some cultural and structural tendencies that came from the stem family in Ireland and the established families in the United States that remain.

Despite numerous exceptions, American Irish families are still predominantly Catholic. Fathers remain heads of families, but egalitarian spouseship is rapidly increasing. Mothers continue to work at home and, now, with full-time paid jobs. Familism is still prevalent; sibling loyalty continues. Extended kinship gatherings still occur. Children receive sensible rearing. Loyalty to the family unit, even with separated and divorced parents, is emphasized. Enthusiasm for feminism has increased.

American Catholic Irish are still very much concerned with the economic welfare of the total family unit. Men and women appear to work for achieved status. Entry to active, rather than contemplative, occupations remains the norm. Many still seek secure jobs. Catholic Irish women appear to maintain resistance to the concept of work being more important than family. Interest in politics is little abated. Higher education is valued. Parents now exercise considerably less authority over the marriages of children. Sexual behavior—premarital, marital, postmarital, and nonmarital—now more closely matches that of other people in this country. Other tendencies have diminished.

American Catholic Irish families retain characteristics that differ from other groups—a striking example of cultural pluralism. It would be facile, then, to predict full structural and cultural integration in the future, particularly in view of the new ethnic assertiveness. If economic conditions turn downward and the gap widens between those who are economically successful and those who are not, ethnic competitiveness might increase. Such an eventuality would be tragic, because the American Catholic Irish have tried to transmit to their descendents a belief in the ability of those with differing backgrounds to live in peace with one another in this country.

REFERENCES

Adams, William Forbes. 1932. *Ireland and Irish Emigration to the New World, from 1815 to the Famine.* New Haven: Yale University Press.

Arensberg, Conrad M. 1950. *The Irish Countryman: An Anthropological Study.* New York: Peter Smith.

Arensberg, Conrad M., and Solon T. Kimball. 1968. *Family and Community in Ireland.* Cambridge: Harvard University Press. Original copyright, 1940.

Beckett, J. C. 1966. *The Making of Modern Ireland, 1603–1923.* New York: Knopf.

Birmingham, Stephen. 1973. *Real Lace: America's Irish Rich.* New York: Harper & Row.

Brody, Hugh. 1974. *Inishkillane: Change and Decline in the West of Ireland.* New York: Schocken.

Carpenter, Niles. 1927. *Immigrants and Their Children, 1920.* Census Monographs 7. Washington, DC: U.S. Government Printing Office.

Curran, Mary Doyle. 1948. *The Parish and the Hill.* Boston: Houghton Mifflin.

Daly, Mary. 1968. *The Church and the Second Sex.* New York: Harper & Row.

———. 1973. *Beyond God the Father: Toward a Philosophy of Women's Liberation.* Boston: Beacon Press.

———. 1975. *The Church and the Second Sex: With a New Feminist Postchristian Introduction by the Author.* New York: Harper & Row.

———. 1978. *Gyn/Ecology: The Metaethics of Radical Feminism.* Boston: Beacon Press.

Esslinger, Dean R. 1975. *Immigrants and the City: Ethnicity and Mobility in a Nineteenth Century Midwestern City.* Port Washington, NY: Kennikat.

Farber, Bernard (ed.). 1966. *Kinship and Family Organization.* New York: John Wiley.

Farrell, James T. 1938. *Studs Lonigan: A Trilogy Containing Young Lonigan, The Young Manhood of Studs Lonigan and Judgment Day.* New York: Random House.

Ferenczi, Imre. 1929. *International Migrations.* Vol. 1. "Statistics." Compiled on Behalf of the International Labour Office, Geneva. With Introduction and Notes. Edited on Behalf of the National Bureau of Economic Research by Walter F. Willcox. New York: National Bureau of Economic Research, Inc.

Fischer, David Hackett. 1978. *Growing Old In America: The Bland-Lee Lectures Delivered at Clark University, Expanded Edition.* New York: Oxford University Press.

Glazer, Nathan, and Daniel P. Moynihan. 1963. *Beyond the Melting Pot.* Cambridge: MIT Press.

Greeley, Andrew M. 1972. *That Most Distressful Nation: The Taming of the American Irish.* Chicago: Quadrangle.

Handlin, Oscar. 1941. *Boston's Immigrants, 1790–1865: A Study in Acculturation.* Cambridge: Harvard University Press.

Heer, David M. 1961. "The Marital Status of Second-Generation Americans," *American Sociological Review,* 26(2):233–241.

Humphreys, Alexander J. 1966. *New Dubliners: Urbanization and the Irish Family.* New York: Fordham University Press.

Kennedy, Robert E., Jr. 1973. *The Irish: Emigration, Marriage, and Fertility.* Berkeley: University of California Press.

———. 1976. "Irish Americans: A Successful Case of Pluralism," in Anthony Gary Dworkin and Rosalind J. Dworkin (eds.), *The Minority Report: An Introduction to Racial, Ethnic, and Gender Relations.* New York: Praeger, pp. 353–372.

Kennedy, Rose Fitzgerald. 1974. *Times to Remember.* Garden City, NY: Doubleday.

Kutzik, Alfred J. 1979. "American Social Provision for the Aged: An Historical Perspective," in Donald E. Gelfand and Alfred J. Kutzik (eds.), *Ethnicity and Aging: Theory, Research, and Policy.* New York: Springer, pp. 32–65.

Le Play, Frederic. 1871. *L'Organisation de la famille selon le vrai modèle signalé par l'histoire de toutes les races et de tous les temps.* Paris: Tequi.

Marx, Karl, and Frederick Engels. 1970. *Ireland and the Irish Question: A Collection of Writings by Karl Marx and Frederick Engels.* New York: New World Paperbacks. (This is a relatively recent organization of the writings of Marx and Engels which has been "gleaned from handwritten notes and fragments" (p. 15) taken from the "Introduction" by L. I. Golman (Moscow).)

Mattis, Mary Catherine. 1975. "The Irish Family in Buffalo, New York, 1855–1875: A Socio-Historical Analysis." Ph.D. diss., Washington University.

Matza, David. 1966. "The Disreputable Poor," in Reinhard Bendix and Seymour Martin Lipset (eds.), *Class, Status and Power: Social Stratification in Comparative Perspective* (2nd ed.). New York: Free Press, pp. 289–302.

McCague, James. 1968. *The Second Rebellion: The Story of the New York City Draft Riots of 1863.* New York: Dial Press.

McCready, William C. 1974. "The Persistence of Ethnic Variation in American Families," in Andrew M. Greeley, *Ethnicity in the United States: A Preliminary Reconnaissance.* New York: Wiley, pp. 156–176.

Messenger, John C. 1969. *Inis Beag: Isle of Ireland.* New York: Holt, Rinehart and Winston.

Osborne, William A. 1969. "The Church as a Social Organization: A Sociological Analysis," in Philip Gleason (ed.), *Contemporary Catholicism in the United States.* Notre Dame, IN: University of Notre Dame Press, pp. 33–50.

Pauw, B. A. 1963. *The Second Generation: A Study of the Family Among Urbanized Bantu in East London.* Cape Town: Oxford University Press.

Rainwater, Lee. 1966. "Crucible of Identity: The Negro Lower-Class Family," *Daedalus: The Negro American—2,* 95(1):172–216.

Scheper-Hughes, Nancy. 1979. *Saints, Scholars, and Schizophrenics: Mental Illness in Rural Ireland.* Berkeley: University of California Press.

Schrier, Arnold. 1958. *Ireland and the American Emigration 1850–1900.* Minneapolis: University of Minnesota Press.

Shannon, William V. 1963. *The American Irish.* New York: Macmillan.

Smith, Hazel M., and Ellen H. Biddle. 1975. *Look Forward, Not Back: Aborigines in Metropolitan Brisbane 1965–1966.* Canberra: Australian National University Press.

Stein, Rita F. 1971. *Disturbed Youth and Ethnic Family Patterns.* Albany: State University of New York Press.

Stivers, Richard. 1976. *A Hair of the Dog: Irish Drinking and American Stereotype.* University Park: Pennsylvania State University Press.

Thernstrom, Stephen. 1973. *The Other Bostonians: Poverty and Progress in the American Metropolis, 1880–1970.* Cambridge: Harvard University Press.

Warner, William Lloyd, and Leo Srole. 1945. *The Social Systems of American Ethnic Groups.* New Haven: Yale University Press.

Wittke, Carl. 1956. *The Irish in America.* Baton Rouge: Louisiana State University Press.

Zimmerman, Carle C., and Merle E. Frampton, 1935. *Family and Society.* Princeton: Van Nostrand.

CHAPTER FOUR

The Greek American Family

George A. Kourvetaris

SOCIOHISTORICAL BACKGROUND

Before undertaking an analysis of the Greek American family, I shall attempt to briefly delineate the sociohistorical context of these families in the United States. Greeks along with other immigrant groups from southeastern and central Europe made up the "late immigrants" vis-à-vis the "early immigrants" from countries of northwestern Europe. Most European immigration to the United States has almost ceased. Greek immigration, excluding the interwar years, has continued up to the 1970s, especially during the 1950s and 1960s. However, by the mid-1970s even Greek immigration to the United States had dramatically declined. In fact, there is now more repatriation of Greeks to Greece than migration of Greeks to other countries.

In the recent past, continued Greek immigration gave the larger Greek American community a graduated scale of ethnicity and continual doses of "Greek cultural transfusion." At one extreme of the continuum, one could find all those Greeks who were totally "Americanized," whereas at the other extreme, one could find those who hardly spoke a word of English. It is only proper that one can differentiate between the "early" Greek immigrants, who came prior to the 1920s, and the "late" Greek immigrants, who came in the 1950s and the 1960s. Although no exact figure for either group is known, a reasonable combined estimate of the present population is somewhere between 2 million and 2.5 million Greek-born and Greek-descended Americans.[1]

---

[1]The Greek embassy estimates the Greek American population to be 2,000,000 while the Greek Archdiocese estimates it to be about 3,000,000. The 1980 U.S. census reports that *(continued)*

The overwhelming majority of the early Greek immigrants were working class and came from Peloponnesos in southern Greece. It has been reported that early Greek immigrants, as a rule, were poor, had limited education and skills, came primarily from agricultural communities, and consisted of young males (Fairchild, 1911:3, 35; Xenides, 1922:81; Saloutos, 1964; Moskos, 1980). Included in this group were a small number of Greek school teachers, priests, journalists, and other professionals who became the apostles of the ideals and values of Greek society. Like most southern European immigrants, particularly Italians, early Greek immigrants did not come as families because they did not expect to stay in the United States. They intended to better their finances and return to their homeland. Despite their working-class and rural origins, the early Greek immigrants had a middle-class work ethic. They were industrious, independent, and thrifty. They had a sense of determination and cultural pride coupled with a sense of ethnic consciousness and community.

In addition to the majority of early Greek immigrants to the United States from the southern regions of Greece, especially from the rocky, mountainous peninsula of Peloponnesos, others came from different parts of Greece or from the islands. Still other Greeks came from parts of Asia Minor (modern Turkey) when nearly 1.5 million Greeks were uprooted during the 1920s. Immigration to the United States was looked on as a way toward social and economic mobility, particularly for the farming and lower classes. In the past, immigration has also served as a solution to the unemployment problem of Greece.

By contrast, the late Greek immigrants were more educated and did not come exclusively from small agricultural communities; many came as families, sponsored by friends and relatives among the early immigrants. Included in this group were a substantial number of students and professionals[2] who came to the United States either to practice their profession or to pursue an education in American institutions of higher learning. The education of the late Greeks, however, should not be exaggerated. By and

---

(continued)
most foreign-born Greeks, estimated at 210,998 persons, live in urban and suburban areas. Insofar as selected ancestry groups of U.S. population, the U.S. census reports Greek ancestry at about 615,882, most of them found in the northeastern and north central regions. Moskos (1982) estimates that there were about 1,250,000 Greek Americans in 1980 distributed among first, second, third, and fourth generations.

[2]In a study of the "Greek Brain Drain," I found that Greece is among the few countries that lose a considerable number of their talented and professional people annually (Kourvetaris, 1973). For example, in the decade between 1962 and 1971, Greece lost to America alone 4,517 of professional, technical, and kindred people; 4.4% of the total members of professional occupations admitted to America in the same decade were Greek.

large, late Greek immigrants followed the same occupational patterns as their predecessors, becoming restaurant owners, stock brokers, realtors, tavern operators, and grocers. Early and late Greeks were overrepresented in the service industry.

As a rule, both groups brought with them a lifestyle that was folk-oriented, ethnocentric, familistic, and traditional. Their provincial and traditional ways of life were a carryover from the village subculture in Greece and still are maintained in the United States as they were in the early years of immigrant life. One finds a proliferation of small, ethnic village fraternal societies in urban America that reflect the values and traditions of agricultural communities and regions in Greece. The purpose of these *gemeinschaft*-type societies was and still continues to be ethnic and benevolent in nature: to maintain the group's ideals and raise funds for their respective communities in the homeland. These village subcultures were transplanted to the New World and enabled the immigrant to keep in touch with the home community, find solace and relief from urban life, and facilitate the transition and adjustment to the larger American society. The subcultures also reflected the regional diversity, localism, and individualism of the Greeks in Greece proper, which was maintained in the United States even beyond the immigrant generation.

Unlike the old, northwestern European immigrants, who generally settled in small towns and rural areas, most late southeastern European immigrants, including the Greeks, settled in large cities, where opportunities for employment and entrepreneurial activities were greater and ethnic communities flourished. These ethnic communities became the marketplace in which intraethnic, informal, social, cultural, religious, family, and business transactions took place.

From the very beginning, the early Greek immigrant was ambivalent about his permanent settlement in the New World. His original intention was to amass his fortune and return to his place of birth. Because of indecisiveness, the scarcity of Greek women, job insecurity, and the problems of social adjustment and acceptance in the host society, the Greek male was reluctant to commit himself to marriage and raising a family. While he was physically in America, he was sentimentally and emotionally in his land of birth. (This is also somewhat true of the late Greek immigrants.) Although a substantial number of early Greek immigrants returned to Greece, the vast majority remained in America.[3] Only when the

---

[3]Somewhat similar patterns of repatriation are followed by the late Greek immigrants. Since the early 1970s, a number of new Greek immigrants have returned to their homeland.

(continued)

Greek male felt reasonably secure in his job or business did he decide to settle down, get married, and have a family. Under those circumstances, he found it difficult to return to his native Greece. In fact, for many immigrants, marriage and family were the turning point that not only provided them with a feeling of permanence in America, but also made it more difficult, if not unthinkable, for them to return to Greece (Saloutos, 1964:85).

During the late immigration, feelings of xenophobia in America, cultivated by a prejudiced press, raised questions about the contamination and lowering of standards of the Anglo-Saxon culture, or the *Herrenvolk,* by the so-called unassimilated and inferior stocks of southeastern European immigrants. In fact, in 1924, Congress enacted a racist and discriminatory law based on a quota system and drawn on the 1870 U.S. Census, sharply limiting the number of southeastern Europeans entering America. Prior to the 1900s, few Greeks and other southern Europeans came to the United States. The 1924 law, which was the official United States immigration and naturalization policy until 1965, conspicuously favored immigrants from countries of northwestern Europe (Simpson and Yinger, 1972:121). Thus, like other late immigrants, Greeks encountered problems of social discrimination. Omaha and Salt Lake City were two extreme examples of cities where many riots and strikes occurred, in which some immigrants, including Greeks, were killed (Saloutos, 1964; Papanikolas, 1970; Moskos, 1980). However, the tough beginnings, coupled with problems of adjustment and ehtnic prejudice, galvanized the character of the early Greek immigrants and made them more determined to master and overcome their lowly social and economic origins. Despite the success and *embourgeoisement* of thousands of Greeks, thousands of others did not make it in America.[4]

Despite considerable differences between the early and late Greek immigrants and between generations, a number of students of Greek culture (McNeil, 1978; Sanders, 1962; Capanidou Lauquier, 1961; Scourby, 1984) maintain that family and religion seem to be the two social institutions

---

(continued)
The extent of repatriation is not known. However, as a result of inflation, Greek–American relations over the Cyprus and Aegean issues (the American foreign policy in this area has politically alienated and angered many Greeks), the higher standard of living, and the general socioeconomic and political improvements in Greece, many Greeks have been convinced to return. The Greek government has also encouraged repatriation, especially among the more skilled and technically trained Greeks. [See Terlexis, 1979.]

[4]For the *embourgeoisement,* success, and struggle of Greeks in America, see Moskos (1980). The book is a second-generation view of Greeks and Greek Americans. It somewhat exaggerates the success and *embourgeoisement* thesis and underemphasizes the failure and problems. Moskos draws primarily from English writings and not from Greek sources written by the Greek immigrants.

largely responsible for preserving the traditions, values, and ideals of modern Greek culture among the Greeks of the diaspora. The importance of religion and family to Greek immigrants set them, and other late immigrant groups, apart from the early northwestern European immigrant groups. Despite their importance to the early Greek immigrants, these very institutions have been challenged by the younger Greek American generations and indeed some of the late Greek immigrants. Ideally, every Greek ethnic community in the United States was a spiritual community. A Greek church signified the existence of an ethnic colony and that every Greek was potentially a member of the church. The admonition of Athenogoras, archbishop of the Greek Orthodox church in the Americas and later the patriarch of Constantinople, that the Greeks of the United States should unite around the church was clearly in effect in the 1920s and the early 1930s.

In reality, however, and despite a considerable number of Greek Orthodox churches in the United States (about 499 according to the Greek Orthodox Archdiocese of North and South America's *Yearbook* published in 1986), only a small number of Greek Americans are sustaining, dues-paying members (not more than 10–15 percent), and even fewer are actively interested in church affairs. Furthermore, while Greek communities and churches were established early in the present century, 1922 marked the beginning of the organized ecclesiastical life of the Greek Orthodox Archdiocese of the Americas (which includes the United States, Canada, and South America). The average Greek, both in Greece proper and in the United States, does not perceive the church or religion in institutional/organizational terms. A parish priest is closer to the Greek immigrant than the bishop, archbishop, and patriarch, or the clergy in the hierarchical and administrative structure of the Greek Orthodox church. A Greek church is a personalized, extended family system of relationships interwoven with such events of the life cycle as births, baptisms, weddings, deaths, and religious and national holidays.

During the 1920s, the church, following the political developments in Greece proper, was divided along two political lines: the Royalists (supporters of the king) and the Venizelists (supporters of a Greek republic). Although this cleavage is no longer present in the church, it has nevertheless been replaced by cleavages along generational lines (first versus second generation, early versus late Greek immigrants); differences between social classes, or what Milton Gordon calls "ethclass"[5] subcultures (self-em-

[5]By "ethclass," Gordon (1964) meant that primary-group relationships tend to be generated within one's social-class segment of one's ethnic group. He speaks of the intersection between ethnicity and behavioral-class similarities.

ployed versus employed, educated versus uneducated, professionals versus small businessmen); and divisions concerning national and ethnic (Greekness, language) versus orthodox (religious) forms of cultural and ethnic identification. Most churches are bilingual and run by small businessmen and more conservative Greeks. As the first generation or the immigrants die out, the Greek church becomes more and more Americanized. This means that the Greek language is replaced by English and the Greek Orthodox traditions become less stringent. Greek Orthodox becomes an organizational religious identity alongside Catholic, Protestant, and other religious identities in the United States.

When the Greek Orthodox church was formally organized in 1922, a group of early Greek immigrants met in Atlanta, Georgia, and established the American Hellenic Educational Progressive Association (AHEPA). Its original purpose was to combat ethnic prejudice and discrimination, including the activities of the Ku Klux Klan; later its scope was broadened to include educational, social, political, cultural, and benevolent activities. It endorsed a policy of "Americanization" and urged all its members to become American citizens. Although AHEPA is a secular organization, it maintains close ties with the Greek Orthodox church in America and has become the formal link between the Greek and larger American communities. Despite a proliferation of Greek American federations and ethnic associations (more than 163 in the United States, not including the village fraternal societies), AHEPA is by far the largest Greek American organization, with an estimated membership of between 20,000 and 25,000 members in America. Other national associations are the United Hellenic American Congress (UHAC), which has its headquarters in Chicago. Its president is Andrew Athens, a Chicago-based industrialist and close associate of Archbishop Iakovos, the primate of the Greek Orthodox church in the Americas. This organization is active in cultural, ethnic, and political issues affecting Greece, Cyprus, and the Greeks of the United States.

The American Hellenic Institute and Public Affairs Committee, and KRIKOS are two additional organizations. The former is a Washington-based Greek American political action committee. Since its inception twelve years ago, its main objective has been to monitor legislation in the U.S. Congress and activities in the executive branch concerning foreign issues affecting Greece and Cyprus. KRIKOS is a professional and cultural link with Greece. Its main purpose is to mobilize professional and cultural resources among Greek Americans and friends of Greece, to assist Greece in any way possible for its social, economic, and scientific development. KRIKOS also draws from the larger Greek American professional community and tries to maintain and foster professional ties and exchanges with Greek professionals in Greece.

Greeks established other ethnic institutions, schools, professional societies, and mass media (including over 140 ethnic radio and TV stations). Among these are approximately 18 religious radio programs in the United States and Canada; 41 newspapers and magazines, both religious and secular, in the United States and Canada; and the Greek Orthodox parochial school system of approximately 25 Greek American daily elementary and high schools and many more part-time Greek language afternoon classes conducted in Greek parishes, usually after American public school. There are also a number of private Greek language schools (Greek Orthodox Archdiocese of North and South America, 1986:156–167). Usually, most of these ethnic institutions are managed by late Greek immigrants and patronized by those who are active in church affairs or other ethnic organizations. The ethnic press is often the spokesman of the businessmen, the nouveaux riches of the larger Greek American community.

Three types of Greek American communities can be discerned at the present time: a predominantly post–World War II Greek community made up of late Greek immigrants and their families, a mixed Greek American community of early and late Greek immigrants and their progenies, and a Greek American community made up of second- and third-generation American-born Greeks. The first two are by and large ethnic urban communities. Their members are characterized by working- and lower-middle-class life-styles, with a substantial number engaged in small service-oriented establishments, particularly restaurants and taverns, and lower-level white-collar occupations. Most Greeks of the first two groups reside in proximity to their parishes. The third group, which is increasingly a suburban Greek American community, is characterized primarily by middle- and upper-middle-class life-styles, and its members are professionals and businessmen. The latter increasingly follow the patterns and life-styles of the tripartite Catholic, Protestant, and Jewish suburban ethnoreligious groups. Although most Greek churches are bilingual, in the third type of Greek community, English is gradually but steadily replacing Greek, and the priests are, by and large, American-born, second- and third-generation Greeks. While most Greek Orthodox priests are American-born, the bishops of the Greek Orthodox church are Greek or foreign, including Archbishop Iakovos. There are about 10 dioceses in the Americas. Each diocese is administered by a bishop. The archdiocese, the administration of the Greek Orthodox church in the Americas, is located in New York. The chairman of the archdiocese is Archbishop Iakovos. Other members include the synod of bishops, representing the 10 dioceses, and four bishop assistants to the archbishop. More recently, the chancellor of the Greek diocese of Chicago, an American-born clergyman, was elevated to auxiliary bishop (Greek Orthodox Archdiocese of North and South America, 1986:48–50). In the last analysis, language has become the differentiating issue between first- and second-generation Greeks. Greek language is valued mostly by the late Greek immigrants, while the second generation tends to value an increasingly Americanized church. The remainder of this chapter is devoted to an analysis of the Modern Greek American Family in three successive generations.

THE MODERN GREEK AMERICAN FAMILY

First-Generation Greek Family

The first-generation Greek family includes both the early Greek immigrants (1900–1920s) and late Greek immigrants (1950s to the present). In analyzing the ethnic patterns of the first-generation Greek family, one should keep in mind the sociocultural and economic antecedents in Greece proper and those in the United States at the time of both early and late Greek immigration.[6]

Coming from agricultural communities in which a large and extended kinship family system was more conducive to an agrarian economy, the first-generation Greek family in America wanted to follow patterns similar to those in rural Greece. However, for many reasons, this did not always work out. First, the socioeconomic conditions of the immigrants and the problems of adjustment and hardships they encountered did not permit them to replicate the Greek village patterns of extended families. Second, the presence of many siblings in the immigrants' family of orientation in Greece forced them to migrate in the first place. Immigrants, therefore, wanted to see their children succeed and projected their own unfulfilled aspirations onto them. The smaller the family unit the more economic resources could be used for each child's benefit. Third, the immigrants had

---

[6]Similarly, when one refers to the late first-generation Greek family's lifestyle, one must consider the changes both in Greece proper and those in America at the time of late and present Greek immigration. On the contemporary Athenian urban family, for example, see studies by Safilios-Rothschild (1965, 1967a, 1967b, 1969a, 1969b, 1971–1972) whose repertoire of topics is extensive and includes, among others, research on fertility and marital satisfaction; social class and family; deviance and mental illness; morality, courtship, and love in Greek folklore, and sex roles. Also see the study by Vassiliou and Vassiliou (1966) on social attitudes, stereotypes, and mental health in the Greek family.

On the rural and semi-urban Greek family see studies by Lambiri-Dimaki (1965) on dowry and the impact of industrial employment on the position of women in a Greek country town. Also, see studies by Friedl (1962) on dowry, kinship, and the position of women in rural Greece. In addition, Bardis (1955, 1956, 1957), Campbell (1964), and Sanders (1962, 1967) have also written on various aspects of the rural Greek family.

many obligations and promises to fulfill in their home communities such as to provide for their sisters' or nieces' dowries,[7] or to pay their fathers' debts. In fact, many never married for this reason. Fourth, most early immigrants were males with no firm decision to settle in the United States. Finally, the immigrants had to support their own families in the United States and having extended families was more difficult. Despite all this, a number of early and late first-generation Greek immigrants had large families.

As previously noted, early Greeks did not come together as family units: primarily young males migrated. Vlachos maintains that "very few females crossed the Atlantic Ocean in the early years of Greek immigration and their small percentage increased significantly only after 1923" [quoted in Kardaras (1977)]. The scarcity of first-generation women forced a substantial number of Greek males to marry non-Greek women (Mistaras, 1950). There is some evidence to suggest that those Greek Americans (especially women) who married non-Greek spouses follow the Greek Orthodox faith and traditions. This was true of early and late Greek immigrants. One can observe similar patterns in subsequent generations of Greeks in the United States. These exogamous marriages were neither encouraged nor accepted by the more enthnocentric Greeks. Thus, the more tradition-bound the Greek male was, the more strongly he needed a mate of his own nationality and religion. Many of the early Greek males returned to Greece in search of a bride. Some had prospective brides arranged and vouched for by relatives and friends waiting for them in Greece, or they simply arranged a marriage through an exchange of photographs (Saloutos, 1964:85). The arranged marriage should be understood in the context of the Greek kinship system, in which mate selection was an affair that went beyond the immediate parties concerned. It was also a matter of economics, because many early immigrants could not afford to travel to Greece in search of a

---

[7]The dowry system was an extension of the arranged marriage system whereby the bride's family had to provide their future son-in-law a negotiated amount of cash or property in exchange for marrying their daughter. The dowry system has long been a part of the economic stratification and social status systems in general, which view marriage as a vehicle of class mobility or immobility for the parties concerned and favors the higher socioeconomic classes. For example, the higher the socioeconomic class or social status of the groom, the greater the amount of expected dowry. In the past, the dowry system has brought tragedy to many poor families in Greece, particularly to those with large numbers of girls. Since 1975, by law, the institution of dowry has been abolished. However, in many parts of Greece it is still practiced on a voluntary and informal basis. While in the United States the institutionalized form of dowry as practiced in Greece in the past was discontinued among Greeks, nevertheless, vestiges of this practice continue to exist in informal ways in terms of gifts and elaborate wedding ceremonies provided by the bride's parents. The dowry system was more prevalent in the rural and southern parts of Greece.

bride. Furthermore, many of the prospective grooms had known their brides' families prior to coming to the United States.

In the past, the arranged marriage *(proxenio)* was more prevalent in the rural Greek family. At present, it is less often practiced. More and more, mate selection is left to the individual. Sanders (1967:8) distinguished three major types of marital selection in agricultural communities: marriage arranged by parents, marriage with parental consent, and marriage by the future couple themselves. The *proxenio* highlights the importance of marriage and of the family as an enduring, interdependent social institution. Marriage was to be taken seriously. It was not simply the union of two independent individuals, but was and still is considered a fundamental union of two families. In the past, romantic love was not a prerequisite in the arranged Greek marriage, but romantic love and physical attraction today play a more decisive role. The institution of the dowry system also played its part in the arranged marriage and mate selection.

In the past, marriage and family ties were viewed as permanent responsibilities. First-generation Greeks would take care of their parents. At present, the situation has changed. There is an erosion of the family ties. Tensions developed between generations, and the young live a divided life between two societies. Today's generation rejects old traditions. Marriage and motherhood are not the only option for women. Mutual attraction and companionship are more important in marriage. In the 1975 Greek Constitution, Article 4, paragraph 2 states that "Greek men and women have the same obligations and rights." No longer is the man the sole head of the household—both husband and wife decide on family matters. In many respects, the patterns of the rural Greek family were continued in the urban United States, but they had to be adjusted to the existing conditions and could not be exactly replicated.

Another important dimension of family organization involves the structural differences in sex roles and decision-making processes traditionally vested in different family statuses and occupied by different members of the immediate family. Thus, one can speak of father versus mother, male versus female, and husband versus wife relationships and sex roles. The majority of fiction and nonfiction writers (Bardis, 1955, 1956; Safilios-Rothschild, 1967b; Vlachos, 1968; Saloutos, 1964; Petrakis, 1966; Chamales, 1959; Stephanides, 1972; Koty, 1958; Lambiri-Dimaki, 1965; Capanidou Lauquier, 1961) have suggested that the early Greek family both in America and Greece was a male-dominated, patriarchal, and close-knit social unit. In most of these writings, the Greek father is portrayed as an imposing figure whose authority over the other family members, particularly the wife, was absolute. The Greek wife was depicted as a submissive and powerless creature whose major role was homemaking and catering to the rest of the family. Scourby (1984:130) also argues that the "overall image that emerges of Greek women through the eyes of novelist, therapist, the ethnographer, and the social scientist is that of good wife, good mother, and good housekeeper whose needs are always subservient to those of her husband and children." This image of the Greek family's authority and sex roles was a carryover from Greece; however, it was not unique to the Greeks. However, one can argue that these sex roles were contingent on the socioeconomic conditions and prevailing ethos in male–female relationships in the United States and Europe.

That there is an "ideal" and "real" dimension culturally and socially prescribed for every sex role and family member is well documented. However, one finds the tendency among students of the sociology of marriage and the family to describe normative/ideal patterns of sex-role differentiation as empirical/real facts. Most studies tend to de-emphasize the conflict and pathology of the Greek marriage and the family. With the exception of some studies conducted by Safilios-Rothschild (1967b, 1969a, 1969b) and those conducted by Friedl (1967) and Campbell (1964) in Greece proper, no systematic studies have been conducted on the sex-role differentiation and authority relationships in the Greek family at the level of role performance and conflict in the United States. The Greek woman's role was confined primarily to the private domain—including the home, church, and religious ritual—not to the public domain.

A more realistic analysis of role differentiation in the Greek family would entail a network of complementary roles rather than strict differentiation on the basis of widely held beliefs of male-dominated (instrumental) versus female-subordinate (expressive) roles. In other words, a Greek husband or father usually could simultaneously assume both expressive and instrumental roles whenever the primary-group (family) interests were served and family contingencies demanded it. The early Greek immigrant father was, as a rule, older than his wife. Most first-generation Greek men took an active role in the household chores, including shopping and cooking. Some of these roles were learned in restaurants, in the old country, or when the immigrant men who came alone to the United States had to improvise to save money.

Ideally, the father was the head and authority figure of the family unit, and he expected respect and cooperation from his wife and children. In reality, however, his authority was contingent on his ability to prove himself and be a good provider for his family, a compassionate husband, and an understanding father. Masculinity alone, based on arbitrary exercise of authority without considerations of fairness, family unity, and common good, could not sustain the first-generation immigrant family. The Greek father was as compassionate and good-natured as the Greek mother, particularly in times of adversity and life crises. While he primarily was a provider for the entire family and had to work incredibly long hours outside the home, he helped whenever he could in the household chores, and in the discipline and socialization of his children. These norms have changed more and more in the contemporary Greek family in Greece proper and the late Greek immigrant family. Greek women work outside the home and men do more chores in the house. This is in line with the American urban family.

The discrepancy between the "ideal" and "real" aspects of husband–wife and mother–father roles is also evident if one examines what Friedl (1967) and Campbell (1964) refer to as the "public" versus "private" domains of behavior in the rural family in Greece. In the public and social sphere, both husbands and wives put on a facade and behave according to the prevailing societal cultural norms. These norms depict Greek husbands and fathers as though they were the true masters and dominant figures within the family unit. The wives and mothers, however, are expected to behave in a modest and submissive manner, particularly in public places when their husbands are present. However, in a more private family setting, men and women change considerably and behave more naturally. What seems to the outsider to be the unequivocal dominance exercised by the husband over the wife is in reality not so in more informal family settings. In some instances, the Greek wife and mother was the most dominant figure in the Greek immigrant family. Her presence and influence was felt in not only the family but also in larger ethnic community affairs. As a rule, early first-generation women did not work outside the home, and this gave them more time to run the household.

To an immigrant husband who left his parents at a young age, his wife was more than the sociological sex-role partner. She was the wife, the adviser, the partner, the companion, and the homemaker. She also assisted her husband in the business and the family decision making. Wives and mothers usually exercised their influence indirectly in the family decision making through the process of socialization of the children, because the Greek father had to work long hours away from the home. Children were attached to the mother, not the father, particularly in the formative years of immigrant life. Later, it was the mother who had to approve or disapprove of her daughter's marriage, and then she would convince her husband. Furthermore, it has been reported by Tavuchis (1972) that among his "respondents and a large unknown proportion of second-generation Greek Americans, the father emerges as a shadowy, distant figure throughout childhood and adolescence but his sociological presence was always felt. . . ." In addition, the relatively higher status and freedom enjoyed by Greek American women vis-à-vis Greek women in Greece benefited the Greek American women more than the men.

Greek immigrant women have played an important role in not only the family but also the church and Greek American community in general. Moskos (1980:27) argues that the arrival of Greek women greatly contributed to the cohesion of the Greek American family and, indeed, the Greek American community and the church at large. As a rule, early immigrant women—married and unmarried—did not work outside the house. This contrasts sharply with post-World War II Greek immigrant women who, by and large, work outside the house—either in the family restaurant or in some other capacity as seamstresses, beauticians, and factory workers.

As a rule, early Greek immigrant brides were younger than their husbands and became widows at a younger age. In addition to being mothers, they assumed other family roles, including heads of families, fathers, business women, and matchmakers. The late Greek immigrant brides were not that different in age than their prospective husbands.

As in the American family in general, one of the primary functions of the Greek family is procreation. A family without children was, and still is, thought to be incomplete. It is not by accident that the formal ideology of the Greek Orthodox church (and other religions for that matter) encourages procreation within a marital context. The birth of a child is an affair of not only the family, but also the church. Motherhood is highly esteemed in the Greek Orthodox religion. Those couples who have children are looked on by the church as fortunate and blessed. Doumanis (1983), in her study of mothering among 24 rural and Athenian Greek working-class mothers who did not work outside the home, found that motherhood still has been the only means by which a woman can achieve full adult status in Greek society. Mothering, she observed, is a more individual and alienating experience in the modern Greek metropolis than in the collectivistic and emotionally supportive village setting.

Childless couples, especially the husband, were, and still are, made uncomfortable in the Greek community. Not having children created suspicion, and impinged on the Greek male image. In many instances, the childless immigrant family or the old bachelor uncle would support a nephew or niece, but adoption of Greek or non-Greek children was not an accepted practice.

It has been reported (Stephanides, 1972; Tavuchis, 1968) that first-generation Greek parents tended to overprotect their children, even to the extent of wanting to find marriage partners for them. This should be interpreted in the context of the traditional ideal norms of a family and kinship system. In most instances, this was part of the arranged marriage practice in Greece that continued in the immigrant family. Parents underwent personal sacrifices for their children and therefore expected their children to meet their high expectations even after they reached maturity. Ideally, first-generation Greek parents worked and strived to give their children happiness, love, and material comforts. Parents regulated and guided their children's behavior to a certain point. In return, children were expected to respect their parents, develop a sense of responsibility and self-reliance, and become a credit to their family unit and the larger ethnic and American communities. Like their immigrant parents, the children had a minimum of leisure time. They were exposed to the vicissitudes of life at a tender age and were socialized to postpone their immediate gratifications for a future goal. For a majority of the Greek parents, that goal was to see their children happily married, maintain certain ethnic traditions, and move up on the social ladder through the avenues of education, business, and commerce outside the Greek ethnic community.

In general, the Greek immigrant family was adult- rather than child-centered. The child had to learn to respect his or her parents and the elderly. It has also been reported (Vlachos, 1968; Capanidou Lauquier, 1961) that there was a differential preference for boys in the immigrant family. One can argue however that this preferential treatment was not as pronounced in the United States as it was in Greece because of the following:

1. There was no dowry system in the United States as such, other than the usual gifts from relatives or friends of the couple;
2. Girls incorporated the Greek traditional norms and ideals more readily than boys;
3. Girls were more attached to their parents, particularly to the mother; and
4. Above all, it was the daughter, not the son, who would look after her elderly parents, even after she was married.

Despite the similarities, however, the experiences of the early and late first-generation Greek families had the following differences, which created many conflicts between them and their progenies:

1. In contrast to the earlier immigrants, the later immigrants arrived when there was a more equal number of males and females in their age groups.
2. In contrast to the earlier immigrants, the later first-generation Greek

women (both married and unmarried), particularly from blue-collar and working classes, are gainfully employed outside the household.
3. Late Greek immigrant families more frequently visit Greece than early Greek immigrant families, due to the availability of cheap charter flights.
4. The late Greek immigrants are less integrated in the Greek ethnic (church) community than are the second- and third-generation (children of the early arrivals).
5. In contrast to the earlier immigrant families, the later Greek immigrant families tend to be more educated, more diverse in social-class background, less religious, less conservative, more materially and exogamy oriented, more likely to divorce, less traditional, more business oriented, and more ethnically oriented through Greek language and nationality identification rather than orthodox religious identification.

Some of these differences and conflicts stem from generational, age, class, regional, and cultural differences in general. Despite many contrasts between the two groups of the first-generation Greek family, both groups share the Protestant work ethic, strong ethnic family ties, the drive to compete for material success, and ethnic pride.

Sex roles are rapidly changing in Greece toward a more egalitarian or shared familial and occupational responsibility between men and women. The position of women has been improved. For the first time, rural Greek women, including wives, recently received some form of social security after reaching 60 years of age. The 1976–1982 family law bill reflects the gradual liberalization of the traditional sex roles that gave men authority over women. According to the new law, both spouses have equal rights and responsibilities. No longer is a woman's role restricted to the domestic domain and the man's to the public domain. Women can pursue their own interests. Schooling is more coeducational. These changes in sex roles have been going on in American marriages and families for more than 20 years. One would expect that the first-generation late Greek immigrant family is not immune to these changes occurring in both Greece and the United States.

Second-Generation Greek Family

The second-generation Greek family is that social unit in which both parents are American-born of Greek extraction or mixed parenthood (one parent Greek from Greece and the other either non-Greek or American-born Greek). As in other ethnic groups, the second-generation Greek family is a transitional family. Children are born and raised in two social worlds or subcultures. One is particularistic, with an ethnic subculture made up of the Greek immigrant parents and relatives, immigrant priests, school teachers, Greek religious and national holidays, and Greek peers. These agents of socialization transmitted similar experiences and attempted to socialize the children to traditional norms and values of the Greek subculture. The other is a more universalistic world made up of American public schools, non-Greek peers and friends, and institutional norms and values of the dominant society and culture. The second generation emerges as a product of a Greek subculture on the one hand, and an American culture and society on the other—a sociocultural hybrid with a dual identity. Identity crises and generational conflicts are common phenomena of the second generation.

In many respects, members of the second generation share similar experiences and life-styles with their immigrant parents throughout their formative and adolescent years. However, pressures from within and outside the family unit make them somewhat ambivalent and marginal. They are torn between two ways of life. The emphasis on family ties, the Greek language, and the Greek church shaped their attitudes and behavior (Saloutos, 1964:311). These early attitudes and behaviors changed, however, as the children came of age, went to public schools, began to work, moved away from the original settlement, were married, and started a family. However, it must be pointed out that the influence of the first-generation (immigrant) family on the second generation was not uniform in all Greek American families throughout the United States. For example, in small towns and communities where fewer Greeks were found, the process of assimilation and convergence (including intermarriage) with the rest of the population was greater than in larger cities with larger numbers of Greek ethnic communities. Furthermore, ethnic identity in the first generation was looked on as a process and a continuum rather than as a structure. Not all Greek American families shared symmetrical ethnic family experiences in the United States.

Three types of family life-styles seem to be prevalent in second-generation Greeks (Vlachos, 1968:150–151). From a somewhat different perspective, these family life-styles appear to be phases along a continuum of assimilation and acculturation. The first type of life-style represents a complete abandonment of the traditional Greek way of life. A substantial number in this group Anglicized their names and moved away from the Greek community; some changed their religion; and many minimized their interaction with their foreign-born parents and relatives. This group was more concerned with social status and acceptance by their peers and other Americans.

They were not interested in maintaining their Greek nationality and incorporating the ideals and norms of Greek culture as perceived and represented by their parents and relatives in the United States. Their intent was to assimilate the values and norms of American culture as soon as possible. In many respects, this type of second-generation family passed for an American family, and it was rather atypical. It was more prevalent in small towns and suburbs with dispersed Greek ethnic populations.

A second type of life-style of the second-generation Greek family illustrates "cultural atavism," an inward retrogressive orientation and identification with what were perceived to be, by second-generation Greeks, ethnic Greek life-styles. Ideally, this type of family was economically, culturally, socially, and psychologically tied to the Greek community and its ethnic institutions, and was usually working class or blue collar. Many of these families were found close to Greek immigrant colonies and could be described as "stable" or downwardly mobile working-class ethnic families.

A third type of second-generation Greek family was marginal at the structural, cultural, and sociopsychological levels. Norms and values were of a "hybrid" nature. Social interaction and networks of social relationships were neither genuinely American nor Greek. The family was likely to move out of the original settlement, and its members were less likely to engage in primary-group interaction with members of the first-generation Greeks outside the immediate intergenerational kinship group. In most instances, this type of family accommodated living between two worlds by taking what it considered the best of each. This family appeared to be more representative of the majority of the second-generation Greeks, a contention supported by the existing literature on the second-generation Greek Americans.

In addition to these three types, there is perhaps a fourth in which ethnicity and class intersect, what Gordon referred to as "ethclass." In a study of ethclass (Kourvetaris and Dobratz, 1976), it was found that second- and third-generation Greek Americans follow ethclass rather than ethnicity or class alone in patterns of interpersonal and primary relations, including marriage. Thus, if a second-generation Greek American marries within his or her ethnic group (religious), the tendency is to also marry within his or her social class in the Greek American community. This type of ethclass marriage is also prevalent in the first generation. It is more characteristic, however, in the second-generation Greek American family.

As in other ethnic groups, second-generation Greeks had certain advantages over the first generation. First, they did not have to start from scratch as their parents did. Second, they grew up in a fairly close-knit Greek family in which rudiments of Greek ethnic subculture were transmitted to them, particularly those pertaining to courtship, marriage, language, religion, and respect for mother, father, and the elderly. Third, the values of aspiration, hard work, and the Greek *philotimo* (love for honor), were implanted in them by their parents. Achievement and success were a credit to not only their immediate families and kin but also the entire Greek community. It is within this frame of reference that the organization of the second-generation Greek family emerged in the United States. Although first- and second-generation families actually shared many of these advantages, they markedly contributed to the mobility of the second generation.

Several writers (Saloutos, 1964; Sanders, 1962, 1967; Friedl, 1962; Vlachos, 1968) have reported that Greeks traditionally display a high degree of family cohesion and extended kinship relationships within and across generational lines. It has also been reported (Rosen, 1959; Handlin and Handlin, 1956; Kourvetaris, 1971a, 1971b; Tavuchis, 1972; Chock, 1969; Moskos, 1980) that this intergenerational kinship system is coupled with a strong ideological commitment to social mobility and achievement in the American social structure. Tavuchis (1972), in his study of 50 second-generation male family heads, found an elaborate system of kinship and ethnic ties, coupled with strong intergenerational patterns of vertical class mobility.

Unlike other social scientists, particularly family sciologists who have lamented the weakening of kinship bonds and the demise of family as a viable institution, Tavuchis found no evidence of family disintegration among the second-generation Greeks. In fact, Tavuchis argues that the stronger the kinship ties, the more highly mobile its members were found to be: "Differential class mobility was not found to be a detriment to close ties with parents, siblings, and affines. . . ." Tavuchis (1972:296–297) mentions five mechanisms that, in his judgment, prevented potential strains: a strong commitment to kinship values, a close propinquity to relatives, extraclass criteria of ranking, identification with successful kinsmen, and gross status differences neutralizing invidious distinctions. However, in a more recent conference on Greek American family organization sponsored by the Greek Orthodox Ladies Philoptochos Society,[8] the participants lamented the erosion of family ties, the rejection of traditions, the

[8]A charitable, benevolent, and sociocultural organization, which is attached to the Greek Orthodox Archdiocese with its national headquarters in New York and organized locally in most Greek Orthodox parishes in the Americas.

increasing divorce rate in the Greek American family, and the loss of faith among the young Greek Americans.

Although Tavuchis's finding is not unique among Greek Americans (Jewish Americans display similar patterns), it is somewhat contrary to the prevailing notion among sociologists who believe that extended kinship relationships are a detriment to intergenerational social mobility. More recently, a somewhat similar finding has been reported by Kardaras (1977), who found no relationship between different types of modernity (marital, sexual, and educational) and structural and psychological assimilation. The second generation was found to be conservative or traditional in one dimension and modern in another. Somewhat surprisingly, the higher the social class among the second generation the greater the tendency to espouse a more traditional (conservative) view in sex roles.

The structure of authority relations is a source of tension in Greek family life. The assertive or overconfident Greek woman is seen as a threat to the authority of the father. The long absence of the first-generation father from the home made it difficult for the son to identify with him. According to Scourby (1984:128), the father's absence enabled the son to identify not with his individuality and self-reliance but, inaccurately, with his authoritarianism alone. The son's exposure to the equalitarian model in the United States only magnified the father's authoritarianism and thus created a conflict between dependency and independence.

Themes of stress and cultural conflict between the first and second generations are found in a number of novels written by second-generation writers. *Going Naked in the World* is a moving account of the frustrations that Tom Chamales encountered as a member of a traditional authoritarian family of the 1940s. Elia Kazan's *The Arrangement* portrays a Greek American with an unyielding father. In *Lion at My Heart,* Harry Mark Petrakis describes the painful conflict between the patriarchal father and his sons and the subsequent despair and disillusionment experienced by the father [mentioned in Scourby (1984)]. Although fictional accounts provide us with insights to human and family relationships, they are not a substitute for a sociological analysis of intergenerational and family conflicts.

Three trends of authority relations seem to be prevalent in the emerging literature on the second-generation Greek American family:

1. The "quasi-patriarchal" model, or a trend toward lessening the patriarchal orientation in which ultimate authority in decision making no longer is exercised by the father (Tavuchis, 1972);
2. The "equalitarian" model in which the father shares his status and

authority with his wife (Capanidou Lauquier, 1961:225; Kardaras, 1977); and

3. The "patriarchal" model (Vlachos, 1969:162) in which the father is still the ultimate authority with final responsibility for providing for his family and for the discipline of his children, partly because that is a father's duty and partly because he is a man and men are economic providers (Chock, 1969:38).

Sex roles of the siblings are also viewed in normative terms by most writers, not in actual role performances. For example, the traditional Greek cultural norms and ideals of filial piety and respect for one's parents and the elderly persist in the second-generation Greek American family. Unlike the case of the first generation, the father is not perceived as a fearful and distant person, but the father–son relationship is one of mutual understanding and respect (Tavuchis, 1972; Chock, 1969; Capanidou Lauquier, 1961; Moskos, 1980). According to Chock, "Greek children are expected to love their parents, to respect them and to assume some care for them if they need it in their old age." Despite the respect between the first and second generations, as a rule second-generation Greeks do not live in the same household with their parents and in-laws. More and more immigrant generations (especially widows) live alone or are placed in homes for the aged. The immigrant family, particularly the father, has a sense of pride that does not accept living with one's children, especially not a son-in-law. This is even more true of the second-generation family in a mixed marriage.

As in the first generation, both parents in the second generation share in the responsibility for the care, education, and well-being of their children. The second generation tends to have fewer children than the first generation. However, many second-generation parents tend to spoil their children. Second-generation Greek women are inclined to take a greater interest in the Greek Orthodox church and religion rather than in the Greek language schools. Scourby (1984:131) argues that women more than men identified themselves as "Greek Orthodox" or "Greek American," reaffirming their positive response to the church. They are also less critical of the church. As in the first generation, second-generation families show respect for their parents and the elderly. Grandparents (*papa* and *yiayia*) are important figures in the Greek American family.

Recently, as a result of the women's liberation movement, many sex roles in the second generation have changed. Safilios-Rothschild, Constantakos, and Kardaras (1976) and Kardaras (1977) have found that both husbands and wives in the upper-class second-generation families in the

Detroit metropolitan area share somewhat similar views on marriage and the family. Thus, both husbands and wives are against a double standard for sexual matters, disapprove of infidelity and extramarital relations, and approve of divorce on grounds of brutality. They also believe that they should have the right to both initiate and refuse sexual activity. Although we do not know the extent to which these findings are uniform among all second-generation Greek American families, one can suggest that ethclass and generation are more important variables in explaining ethnic family patterns than ethnicity, class, or generation taken singly.

Greek Americans, regardless of generation, tend to be conservative on civil rights and economic issues. Moskos (1980) contends that "the conservatism of the Greek Americans is an attitude of mind rather than a body of ideas—a distaste for confrontation politics and a suspicion of collective action for social improvement." Greek Americans, Moskos argues, "search not for a better world, but for a better life." The conservative ethos of Greek Americans reflects the individualistic orientations of the Greek entrepreneur, the influence of the Greek Orthodox church, emphasis on the cohesiveness of the family, and the rural origins of the early Greek immigrants, the majority of whom came from the southern part of Greece (Peloponnesos). One can also conclude that second-generation Greek American families more often tend to be churchgoers on Sunday than first-generation families (especially the late Greek immigrants). In short, Greek American families maintain an ethnic identification through their membership in the Greek Orthodox church and such ethnically oriented organizations as AHEPA.

Third-Generation Greek Family

The third-generation family consists of grandchildren of the first generation or the children of the second-generation Greek family in America. This group also includes the offspring of intermarriages of second-generation couples. By the third generation, there is a significant decrease in Greek ethnic identification (as measured by language and Greek family norms), but some vestiges of ethnic social behavior remain, particularly those pertaining to politics (Humphrey and Brock, 1972), Greek religion, and Dionysian aspects of modern Greek culture (Kourvetaris, 1971c).

As a rule, members of the third generation have incorporated the values, attitudes, and norms of the American middle- and upper-middle-class subcultures. Social class and life-style are more important to them than ethnicity and religion. Despite the lack of empirical studies, both education and professional achievement seem to be highly valued among members of the third generation. In an empirical and comparative study of six ethnic groups, it was found (Rosen, 1959:47–60) that a high level of aspiration and achievement exists among members of third-generation Greeks. Rosen argued that white Protestants, Jews, and Greeks stand out as being more individualistic, activistic, and future-oriented than Italians, blacks, and French Canadians.

Unlike the first and second generations, members of the third generation are not preoccupied with ethnic prejudice and discrimination. Viewing their world this way, they can afford to be proud of their ancestry. However, they consider themselves primarily American and only symbolically manifest an interest in and liking for Greek food, music, and dancing. This Dionysian cultural atavism in things Greek was stimulated by the new influx of Greek immigrants following World War II and the popular movies *Zorba the Greek* and *Never on Sunday,* whose theme songs became worldwide favorites. Furthermore, the marriage of Jacqueline Kennedy to Aristotle Onassis, the Nixon–Agnew ticket in 1968 and 1972, the resurgence of ethnic studies and programs, and summer excursions to Greece have further awakened their interest in modern Greek ethnicity and ethnic culture. In addition, the new influx of post–World War II Greek immigrants brought a new awareness of Greek ethnic identity. However, one finds little or no interest among members of the third generation in maintaining the ethnic institutional aspects of Greek culture, such as language, family traditions, and endogamous marriage—with the exception of the Americanized form of the Greek Orthodox church.

It has been argued by some Greek American writers that the new influx of Greeks following World War II would retard the Americanization and assimilation processes of the third generation. However, American-born Greeks (even post–World War II Greeks who have been in America for a longer period of time) do not usually associate with the newcomers. This is primarily because dating within one's own group has a constraining influence. Greek American women are no different from other American women—especially when they date non-Greeks. When Greek American women date Greek American men, they tend to be more serious about marriage, especially if they are members of the same community. There is also a matter of availability of both sexes of the same ethnic group in a college population. In general, the more ethnically oriented the Greek man or woman, the greater the tendency to date someone with similar ethnic background. Furthermore, the more assimilated the Greek, the less likely he or she is to place importance on dating other Greek Americans. This is also true in terms of ethnic endogamous patterns of marriage.

If ethnicity (nationality) is the single most important characteristic in the first generation and religion in the second generation, it appears that an awareness of social class characterizes the third generation (Kourvetaris, 1971a, 1971b). Thus, the oncoming third generation brings a concomitant decline in ethnoreligious concerns and an increasing emphasis on the importance of social class as a factor in marriage. However, those who maintain their ethnic (nationality/religiosity) identification tend to date and marry within their class segment of their ethnic group (ethclass). In a recent study, Safilios-Rothschild, Constantakos, and Kardaras (1976), found ethnic generation and class to be the most differentiating variables between traditional Greek culture and third-generation Greek Americans. Thus, the higher the social class, the more removed a Greek American woman is from her Greek cultural heritage and sex-role restrictions. As a rule, the third generation is a college-oriented generation. It is a status- and class-conscious generation rather than an ethnic-conscious generation.

At the same time, while intermarriage in the first and second generations was not an accepted norm in the Greek American family, by the third generation it is not only accepted but, in some Greek American communities, it is the norm rather than the exception. It has been estimated that one in five Greeks entered a mixed marriage by 1926 [Saloutos (1973), quoted in Moskos (1980)]. By the 1960s, intermarriages accounted for three out of ten church marriages and by the mid-1970s, it was about half (Moskos, 1980:73). In some communities it is even higher. In the vital statistics kept by the Registry Department of the Greek Orthodox Archdiocese of North and South America (1986:102–103), there is a steady increase of mixed marriages. Although there was an equal number of mixed marriages and marriages between Greek Orthodox men and women until 1979, there were more mixed marriages than orthodox marriages from 1980 to 1984. In some areas, mixed marriages reached a ratio of two (mixed) to one (Greek ethnic). Even the archbishop, in a speech delivered recently to the Academy of Athens, acknowledged that intermarriage is inevitable, and in some communities has reached 65 percent and higher.

By the same token, we find an increase in the divorce rate among Greek American families. Although divorce was rare in the first generation, the third generation matches the divorce pattern of the American family in general. In 1980, the Greek Orthodox Philoptohos Society (a charitable and benevolent Greek Orthodox institution) held a conference in San Francisco on the Greek Orthodox family. The conference dealt with a number of changing realities and issues (including divorce, abortion, sex roles, cults, and ethnic and religious identity) faced by Greek American families in the 1980s. They reported an increased number of divorces and mixed marriages.

Scourby (1984) argues that traditional role expectations continue to be the norm across generations, particularly with respect to their attitudes toward the institutional Greek Orthodox church, ethnic identity, sex roles, and intermarriage. In her study of 76 Greek-born students drawn from three generations of college students from four colleges of the New York metropolitan area, Scourby (1984) found the following:

1. Women of all three generations were more favorable toward traditional adherence to the ethnic church than men;
2. Men showed a weaker attachment to their ethnic identity, were more likely to favor exogamy, and displayed a more assimilative attitude for getting ahead in American society; and
3. American-born students perceived the church as the locus of identity in a pluralist society, whereas the first generation identified nationalism with religion.

CHANGE AND ADAPTATION

The movement from the life-styles of the early first-generation Greek family to those of the third generation is accompanied by an attenuation of the Old World family ideals and norms (as exemplified in the first-generation Greek family) and new values more symmetrical with those of the American middle-class family (as exemplified in the third-generation Greek family). "Greekness" (nationality) as a form of ethnic identification in the first generation gave way to orthodoxy (religion) in the second generation, which in turn gave way to class life-styles (behavioral identification) by the third generation. A recent study by professors Constantinou and Harvey (1985) of a Greek community in Akron, Ohio, found a two-dimensional structure underlying Greek American ethnicity. One they call *externalities* (that which pulls the Greek American toward the place of origin), and the other they call *internalities* (that which binds Greek Americans together as a community). Although they found a variation across generations, use of the Greek language is definitely on the decrease. They found the first generation to be the most cohesive, tending to identify with the ancestral home, especially insofar as preserving the Greek language goes, whereas the second generation was found to be the least cohesive of the three, because of its transitional nature—it had a split identity. The third generation was found to be less cohesive than the first but showed signs of ethnic revival. The authors concluded that no single factor is adequate to define ethnic identity. They examined 17 ethnically related factors including Greek language, Greek cooking, church membership, family, the Greek press, and endogamy as the most important dimensions of ethnic identity. It is my suggestion that by the third generation, the "Greekness" of the first generation has been transformed into "philhellenism" (friend of Greece). This generational transformation might be genuinely conceptualized as roughly following five processes or phases of acculturation initially suggested in part by Park (1950): initial contact, conflict, accommodation, assimilation, and pluralist phases.

The Initial Contact Phase

In the first decades of Greek immigrant life in America, the organization of the Old World family was still fairly intact. As a result of pressures from within and outside the family structure, the Old World ideal was challenged. One of the most salient factors was the physical/ecological separation from the parental and kinship system and village subculture in Greece. The urgency of the immigrant's physical survival and sociopsychological adjustment to a different sociocultural and urban ecological environment was real. The separation of work and residence, and the exposure of the immigrant's children to the life-styles of the American community and public schools, which in many ways meant ethnic prejudice and discrimination against those ethnic groups and families, were contributing factors that made the first generation culturally different from the dominant Anglo-Saxon group. All these made the first-generation immigrant family extremely ethnocentric and highly cohesive, as in the Old World. In this phase of initial contact, the immigrant family was socially and culturally insulated in the Greek colony and did not seriously feel the pressures of American society. Despite its many problems, the first-generation Greek family was stabilized by its strong desire to return to Greece. It drew social and psychological support from the family unit, the family and kinship system, the church, and the Greek community in general. However, this initial phase gave way to both the conflict and accommodation phases with the coming of the second generation.

The Conflict Phase

With the oncoming second generation, the highly ethnocentric, traditional, and folk-oriented outlook of the first-generation subculture was challenged. Although cultural conflict between parents and children was not inevitable, in many instances it did take place. Out of this generational conflict, three major subtypes of first-generation Greeks emerged: the ethnic subculturalists (pluralists), the social assimilationists, and the convergent types (in some respects ethnic pluralists and in other respects social assimilationists).

The ethnic subculturalists (pluralists) were faced with major difficulties in carrying out their intent to socialize their children in Greek ways of life. These difficulties and their fear of losing control over their children were intensified when the children came into contact with the larger American society, particularly when they entered public schools, began working and dating, and came of marital age. The Greek immigrants' exaggerated fear of losing control over their children was further aggravated by the Greek Orthodox church and the family kinfolk. Furthermore, it stemmed from the inability of the immigrant parents to more readily adjust to the subtler, nonmaterial aspects of American culture and thus be able to understand their children. This group, usually found in cities with large Greek colonies, proved unyielding. They insisted on preserving their ethnic institutions, particularly those pertaining to religion, language, endogamous marriage, and a close-knit family. They attempted to convince their children of the mystique of the Greek ancestry, warned them against the dangers of intermarriage, and made an effort to instill in them a sense of ethnic consciousness and peoplehood. According to Papajohn and Spiegel [quoted in Moskos (1980:94)], clinical studies of mentally disturbed second-generation Greek American children indicated that these children came from families in which an extremely traditionalist Greek form of childrearing was attempted. In fact, those immigrant parents who were more open to American influences were more successful in passing down Greek ethnicity than those who tried to entirely resist all American encroachment.

Dunkas and Nikelly (1978), in their study of 60 maladjusted first-generation Greek women who had recently immigrated, found that Greek married women were more attached to their mothers than their husbands, which the authors called the "Persephone Syndrome." The dependency bond remains between the mother and the daughter. The Greek female, compared with the Greek male, is especially vulnerable to this "dependency hang-up." According to Scourby (1984:135), as a result of the dependency of the daughter on the mother, the daughter is incapable of developing her own self-identity: "The mother keeps her daughter's ego confounded with her own." In Scourby's words, "The ego-boundary weakness compels the daughter to define herself in terms of others, a pattern in keeping with the relational system that has characterized Greek family life." According to her, both the Greek subculture and American culture tend to reinforce these daughter–mother dependency roles. The dependent daughter, when she is married, becomes the dependent wife and then the dependent mother, and the cycle continues.

The social assimilationists (also known as environmentalists) believed that their children must grow up as Americans but wanted them to retain membership in the Greek Orthodox church, maintain their Greek name, and learn some of the Greek language (Saloutos, 1964:312). This group felt that the assimilation process could not be stopped but only temporarily delayed. They were more realistic, experienced less conflict with their children, and were more aware that powerful social and cultural forces operate in the American social structure and culture that exert an unprecedented influence on their children, pulling them toward Anglo conformity and Americanization. This assimilation process has been challenged by the ethnic resurgence of the 1960s and early 1970s. This is especially true among Greek-born, post–World War II immigrants, students, and professionals. The lack of support in American foreign policy for the Greek-Cypriot position in Cyprus has alienated many Greeks and Greek Americans. Cyprus became the catalyst for ethnic solidarity and consciousness, especially for new first-generation Greek immigrants and some second-generation Greek Americans (especially Greek American politicians who expect financial contributions and support from Greek businessmen).

The social assimilationist process began approximately during the second decade that the first-generation family lived in America, especially when the first-generation immigrant family abandoned its intent to return to Greece. It was during this period that both the organizational structure of the Orthodox church and AHEPA, by far the largest ethnic association, launched an all-out effort to organize the Greeks in America, facilitate the transition and Americanization processes, and maintain the ethnic institutions of church and family, which in many ways became complementary to each other. Nationality gradually was giving way to religion, particularly during the 1920s, when Greeks, along with other southern and eastern European immigrants, were targets of prejudice and discrimination. Second-generation Greeks were discovering that to be of Greek ancestry did not necessarily indicate particularly high social status. This phase gave way to the new realization that religious identity was preferable to ethnic or national identity, and a new intergenerational relationship emerged. Whereas the first generation perceived religion and ethnicity as inseparable, the second and subsequent generations saw them more and more as independent phenomena.

Much of the first generation, especially those more educated (both early and late immigrants), followed a mixed approach that was a compromise between the two polar opposites. This was compatible with the pluralist ideology of ethnic groups that replaced the Americanization and assimilation models. This trend started in the 1940s but was more evident in the

1950s and 1960s with the influx of new immigrants. Also, the ethnic resurgence of the 1960s gave a new impetus to ethnic consciousness in American society. The defeat of the Italian forces by the Greeks in October 1940 gave a shot in the arm to the second-generation Greeks in America, and new ethnic pride and consciousness flourished. This pride, along with the rise of a professional and commercial class of second-generation Greeks and the arrival of post–World War II Greeks, contributed to a new status for Greeks in America. It must be stressed that conflict between the first and second generations was always present, but both groups worked out a modus vivendi and followed a pattern of accommodation.

The Accommodation Phase

An effort was made to broaden the base for continued and meaningful interaction between the two generations (Tavuchis, 1972). On the one hand, the first generation realized that they had to modify the Old World family life-styles for the sake of retaining the affection of their children and maintaining the unity of the family. On the other hand, the second generation came to the realization that complete repudiation of the parents' way of life would hurt their parents and leave them isolated. Both generations searched for points of compatibility, mutual levels of tolerance, complementarity of lifestyles, individuality, and family unity.

This period of accommodation between first- and second-generation family units led to a more stable form of family relationships. The parents came to realize that life in the United States was to be permanent. They also recognized that social and economic status and success could come to their offspring as the latter became more and more socialized into the Anglo-American culture. A parallel effort was made on the part of the second generation to resocialize their parents to their own generational values and life-styles. The interdependence of the parents and children gave way to the dependence of parents (especially those whose English was not proficient enough) on their children as interpreters and informants on the American scene. This dependence led to the conscious and unconscious willingness on the part of the parents to sacrifice certain norms and ideals of the Old World family for the sake of their own happiness and that of their children. Finally, it was a matter of realism and convenience.

As the first generation was dying out, the conflict and accommodation phases between the first and second generations gave impetus to new forms of social and generational change. By the late 1950s and 1960s, the coming of the third-generation Greek American was caught between an ongoing process of assimilation and *embourgeoisement* and an ethnic resurgence spearheaded by blacks and later by Chicanos. Added to these ethnic movements was the new Greek immigration of the mid-1960s and early 1970s, which brought a new cultural transfusion and a new ethnicity to Greek Americans. It is my contention that neither the rise of ethnic/racial consciousness in the United States nor the late Greek immigration arrested the Americanization of the third-generation Greek Americans. By the late 1950s and early 1960s, second- and third-generation Greeks had by and large joined the lower-middle-, middle-, and the upper-middle-class life-styles. While ethnicity had been present all along, it was giving way to class and ethclass life-styles and patterns of behavior.

Third- and later-generation Greek Americans, hedonistic as most American youth, mostly retained the Dionysian aspects of the Greek culture, but, with a few exceptions, had very little knowledge and understanding of the contemporary nonmaterial or Apollonian aspects of the Greek culture. Greek cuisine, dancing, and music were more appealing to them than the abstract and remote notions of *philotimo* (honor and generosity), *philoxenia* (hospitality), Greekness (ethnicity), nationality, the Greek language, literature, family traditions, history, and other like concepts. The Greek American youth, like American youth in general, were disenchanted with the institutional forms of religion. The Greek American youth complained that they could not understand the almost mystical and highly ritualistic practice of Orthodox Christianity. Many turned to more socially minded religions or were converted through intermarriage to other religions.

Assimilation or Pluralism?

By the third generation, the Greek American family's life-style becomes more and more symmetrical with that of the larger American middle-class family. This, however, does not mean that all vestiges of ethnic subcultural life-styles are lost. The Greek American maintains some of his or her unique ethnic features. For example, Greek names, the Orthodox religion, ethnic food, holidays, trips to Greece, some intergenerational family ties, and to some extent, some endogamous marriages remain. Assimilation, a multidimensional process itself, does not have to be complete. It has been suggested (Kourvetaris, 1971c) that Greek Americans maintain their ethnic identity through their religion. As the subsequent generations of Greek Americans grow remote from the original generation, emphasis on Greek nationality and language is replaced by religion for those who support the organization of the Greek Orthodox church in the United States. The Greek American family life-style is both assimilative and pluralistic. It is a blending, but not necessarily a perfect or equal blending, of two cultures.

One can tentatively suggest that as one moves away from the first generation to the second and subsequent generations, there is an increasing rate of intermarriage (this include interethnic, interreligious, and interclass marriages). The first generation tends to be the most endogamous, the third the least, and the second in-between. By the third generation, intermarriage is more likely to follow class lines. Ethnicity, defined in most cases by nationality, religion, language, or a combination of the three, declines as one moves from the first generation to the second and subsequent generations (Kourvetaris, 1984).

The gradual transformation from the Greek rural, traditional (first-generation immigrant) family to the Greek American urban middle class is somewhat coterminous with those changes brought about by urbanization and internal migration processes in Greece proper. Since the 1920s, and especially the 1940s, these processes have been accelerated. By the third generation, even Greeks in Greece have changed family life-styles and mores from those found in the traditional rural family to those more symmetrical with the contemporary middle-class, urban Athenian family. The differences lie in linguistic, national, and cultural areas, but the values and norms are similar to Greek American ones. In short, unless Greek immigration continues, the Greek family in America by the third and subsequent generations will mostly retain the organizational and institutional aspects of Greek American subculture, particularly religion, family, and the success ethic, but not the more subtle aspects of Greek culture and ethnicity. The generational family ties will be attenuated, but Greeks will not lose respect for those institutions that sustained them throughout their long history.

In conclusion, the Greek American family is moving away more and more from the ethnic patterns of the Old World, and becoming more of a homegrown phenomenon. It is undergoing the same changes as the American middle-class family at large. The divorce rate and pathology of the American family also have affected the Greek American family. The divorce rate, unheard of in the first-generation immigrant family, has become a common occurrence by the second and third generations. Parental respect, family traditions, and cooperation among the members of the family unit, all typical of the first generation, have been undermined by the decline of the father's authority. The erosion of family solidarity and the growing individualism within American families have also affected the Greek American family. Extrafamily agencies and organizations, including state laws, have taken over many family functions. Consumerism reigns supreme. The American family, including the Greek American, feels the pressures and demands of a consumerist psychology that has challenged the stability and cohesiveness of the Greek American family.

REFERENCES

Bardis, Panos. 1955. "The Changing Family in Modern Greece," *Sociology and Social Research,* 40 (October):19–23.

———. 1956. "Main Features of the Greek Family During the Early Twentieth Century," *Alpha Kappa Delta,* 26 (Winter, November): 17–21.

———. 1957. "Influences on the Modern Greek Family," *Social Science,* 32 (June): 155–158.

Campbell, J. K. 1964. *Honor, Family, and Patronage.* Oxford: Clarendon Press.

Capanidou Lauquier, H. 1961. "Cultural Change Among Three Generations of Greeks," *American Catholic Review* (now *Sociological Analysis*), 22 (Fall):223–232.

Chamales, Tom T. 1959. *Go Naked in the World.* New York: Scribner.

Chock, P. Phyllis. 1969. "Greek-American Ethnicity." Ph.D. diss., Department of Anthroplogy, University of Chicago.

Constantinou, Stavros T., and Milton E. Harvey. 1985. "Basic Dimensional Structure and Intergenerational Differences in Greek American Ethnicity," *Sociology and Social Research,* 69(2) (January):241–246.

Doumanis, Mariella. 1983. *Mothering in Greece: From Collectivism to Individualism.* London: Academic Press Passim.

Dunkas, Nicholas, and Arthur G. Nikelly. 1978. "The Persephone Syndrome," *Social Psychiatry,* 7:211–216.

Fairchild, H. P. 1911. *Greek Immigration to the United States.* New Haven: Yale University Press.

Friedl, Ernestine. 1962. *Vasilika: A Village in Modern Greece.* New York: Holt.

———. 1967. "The Position of Women: Appearance and Reality," *Anthropological Quarterly,* 40 (July):97–108.

Gordon, Milton. 1964. *Assimilation in American Life: The Role of Race, Religion and National Origin.* New York: Oxford University Press.

Greek Orthodox Archdiocese of North and South America. 1986. *Yearbook.* New York: Graphic Arts Laboratory, pp. 102–103, 156–167.

Handlin, F. Oscar, and Mary F. Handlin. 1956. "Ethnic Factors in Social Mobility," *Explorations in Entrepreneurial History,* 9 (October):4–5.

Humphrey, R. Craig, and Helen T. Brock. 1972. "Assimilation, Ethnicity, and Voting Behavior Among Greek-Americans in a Metropolitan Area." Paper presented at the annual meeting of the Southern Sociological Society, New Orleans, April 5–8.

Kardaras, Basil P. 1977. "A Study of the Marital and Familial Options of the Second Generation Greek-Americans in the Detroit Metropolitan Area." Master's thesis, Department of Sociology, Wayne State Uiversity.

Kazan, Elia. 1968. *The Arrangement.* New York: Avon Books.

Koty, John. 1958. "Greece," in Arnold M. Rose (ed.), *The Institutions of Advanced Societies.* Minneapolis: University of Minnesota Press, pp. 330–383.

Kourvetaris, George A. 1971a. *First and Second Generation Greeks in Chicago.* Athens, Greece: National Center of Social Research.

———. 1971b. "First and Second Generation Greeks in Chicago: An Inquiry Into Their Stratification and Mobility Patterns," *International Review of Sociology* (now *International Review of Modern Sociology*), 1 (March):37–47.

———. 1971c. "Patterns of Generational Subculture and Intermarriage of the Greeks in the United States," *International Journal of Sociology of the Family,* 1 (May):34–48.

———. 1973. "Brain Drain and International Migration of Scientists: The Case of Greece," *Epitheoris Koinonikon Erevnon (Review of Social Research),* nos. 15–16.

Kourvetaris, George A., and Betty A. Dobratz. 1976. "An Empirical Test of Gordon's Ethclass Hypothesis Among Three Ethnoreligious Groups," *Sociology and Social Research,* 61 (October):39–53.

Lambiri-Dimaki, Ioanna. 1965. *Social Change in a Greek Country Town.* Athens, Greece: Center of Planning and Economic Research.

McNeill, William. 1978. *The Metamorphosis of Greece Since WWII.* Chicago: University of Chicago Press.

Mistaras, Evangeline. 1950. "A Study of First and Second Generation Greek Outmarriages in Chicago." Master's thesis, Department of Sociology, University of Chicago.

Moskos, Charles C., Jr. 1980. *Greek Americans: Struggle and Success.* Englewood Cliffs, NJ: Prentice-Hall.

———. 1982. "Greek American Studies," in Harry J. Psomiades and Alice Scourby (eds.), *The Greek American Community in Transition.* New York: Pella Publishing Co., pp. 17–19.

Papanikolas, Z. Helen. 1970. *Toil and Rage in a New Land: The Greek Immigrants in Utah.* Salt Lake City: Utah State Historical Society.

Park, Robert E. 1950. *Race and Culture.* Glencoe, IL: The Free Press.

Petrakis, Harry Mark. 1959. *Lion at My Heart.* Boston: Little, Brown, An Atlantic Monthly Press Book.

———. 1966. *A Dream of Kings.* New York: McKay.

Rosen, Bernard. 1959. "Race, Ethnicity, and the Achievement Syndrome," *American Sociological Review,* 24 (February):47–60.

Safilios-Rothschild, Constantina. 1965. "Mortality, Courtship, and Love in Greek Folklore," *Southern Folklore Quarterly,* 29 (December):297–308.

———. 1967a. "Class Position and Success Stereotypes in Greek and American Cultures," *Social Forces,* 45 (March):374–383.

———. 1967b. "A Comparison of Power Structure and Marital Satisfaction in Urban Greek and French Families," *Journal of Marriage and the Family,* 29 (May):345–352.

———. 1969a. "Patterns of Familial Power and Influence," *Sociological Focus,* 2 (Spring):7–19.

———. 1969b. "Family Sociology or Wives' Family Sociology? A Cross-Cultural Examination of Decision-Making," *Journal of Marriage and the Family,* 31(May):290–301.

———. 1971–1972. "The Options of Greek Men and Women," *Sociological Focus,* 5 (Winter):71–83.

Safilios-Rothschild, Constantina, Chrysie Constantakos, and Basil P. Kardaras. 1976. "The Greek-American Woman." Paper presented at the Greek Experience in America Symposium, at the University of Chicago, October 29–31.

Saloutos, Theodore. 1964. *The Greeks in the United States.* Cambridge: Harvard University Press.

———. 1973. *They Remember America.* Berkeley and Los Angeles: University of California Press.
Sanders, Irwin. 1962. *Rainbow in the Rock: The People of Rural Greece.* Cambridge: Harvard University Press.
———. 1967. "Greek Society in Transition," *Balkan Studies,* 8:317–332.
Scourby, Alice. 1984. *The Greek-Americans.* Boston: Twayne Publishers, pp. 133–151.
Simpson, George, and J. Milton Yinger. 1972. *Racial and Cultural Minorities: An Analysis of Prejudice and Discrimination* (4th ed.). New York: Harper and Row.
Stephanides, C. Marios. 1972. "Educational Background, Personality Characteristics, and Value Attitudes Towards Education and Other Ethnic Groups Among the Greeks in Detroit." Ph.D. diss., Department of Sociology, Wayne State University.
Tavuchis, Nicholas. 1968. "An Exploratory Study of Kinship and Mobility Among Second Generation Greek-Americans." Ph.D. diss., Department of Political Science, Columbia University.
———. 1972. *Family and Mobility Among Greek-Americans.* Athens, Greece: National Center of Social Research.
Terlexis, Pantazis. 1979. "Metanastefsi Kai Epanapatrismos: 1 Prosklisi to 1980" (Immigration and Repatriation), *Review of Social Sciences* (in Greek) (July–September).
Vassiliou, George, and Vasso Vassiliou. 1966. "A Transactional Approach to Mental Health." Contribution to the International Research Conference on Evaluation of Community Mental Health Programs of N.I.M.H.
Vlachos, C. Evangelos. 1968. *The Assimilation of Greeks in the United States.* Athens, Greece: National Center of Social Research.
———. 1969. *Modern Greek Society: Continuity and Change.* Special Monograph Series no. 1, Department of Sociology and Anthropology, Colorado State University.
Xenides, J. P. 1922. *The Greeks in America.* New York: George H. Doran.

CHAPTER FIVE

The Italian American Family

D. Ann Squier
Jill S. Quadagno

INTRODUCTION

The central debate among those studying the Italian American family has focused on the significance of ethnic identity in maintaining family ties. One group of scholars argues that Italian Americans possess unique traits that emphasize the significance of familism and that the pressures of cultural assimilation are unlikely to reduce the importance of this value (Greeley, 1974:22; Kantrowitz, 1973). Another group argues that most of the traits that have been ascribed to Italian Americans are components of working-class culture and that upper mobility will eliminate these supposedly distinguishing characteristics (Gans, 1962; Gordon, 1964; Lopreato, 1970). There is no simple way to resolve these issues. This chapter will explore the various dimensions of the impact of ethnic identity on the Italian American family.

HISTORICAL BACKGROUND

Traditional Family Structure

Italian immigrants to the United States brought with them a family structure that was different in many ways not only from American society, but also from other European cultures. The main group of Italian immigrants in the United States came from the Mezzogiorno in southern Italy. Within Mezzogiorno culture, families, not individuals, held the central place in society as the only truly valued social group. Nuclear households were prominent but, because of strong filial obligations, individuals were expected to subordinate their needs to those of the family. Family members included the household, the extended family, and even the extended family of one's spouse (Alba, 1985).

Italian households often contained extended kin rather than solely the conjugal family. This contrasted with the pattern in western Europe in general, in which the small, conjugal-family household predominated (Wrigley, 1977:78). Particularly among sharecropper families, in which the labor of many people enhanced the entire family's economic situation, married brothers shared a common household with their families. Three-generation households, including aged parents, were likely to be found at the end of the life cycle, when widowed parents move into the home of their married children and grandchildren (Kertzer, 1978:341).

Family solidarity was the basic code of family life, encompassing the parents, grandparents, aunts, uncles, cousins, and godparents (Covello, 1967:149). The strength of the norm of solidarity meant that the disgrace of one member of the family affected everyone. Thus, a disobedient child was the concern of not only the parents, but also the extended kin. Within the family, a complex system of rules regulated both an individual's relations and responsibilities to the members of his or her family and his or her posture to the outside world.

The concept of obligation was a distinctive aspect of family solidarity. The family council, headed by the *capo di famiglia*, usually the father, made decisions about such diverse matters as the education of a child, a cousin's dowry, or the funeral expenses of an aunt (Covello, 1967:151). A person in need of credit would apply first to family members and only if no help were forthcoming would he or she then turn to *stranieri* ("outsiders").

Although the Italian family has often been perceived as patriarchal, there were many limitations on patriarchal authority. First, because the southern Italian *famiglia* ("family") embraced many marriage units, the decision about who was the head of the extended family was not reached without rivalry among several aspirants. Although authority was usually conferred on the oldest married male family member, this was not always the case. Thus, in a general sense, the oldest Italian male was neither the sole nor absolute authority. The fact that a system of orthodox patriarchy was not adhered to can be seen in the limitations on leadership that prevailed. As long as a man was the main provider, his leadership was not questioned. However, old age or feebleness definitely terminated his role as the representative of family tradition. Similarly, if he became a widower, he retained his leadership only if one of his sons were not married. As soon as a son, preferably the oldest, married, the son assumed the leadership role of his widowed father (Covello, 1967:154). The father retained respect, but there was no longer blind obedience.

A second limitation on male dominance was the power and authority of the Italian mother. An important indicator of this was the fact that the wife had the right to possess property and dispose of it without her husband's consent (Covello, 1967:206). The dowry was an economic weapon that she retained until her death and, at her death, went either to her children or, if childless, back to her own blood relatives. Another source of power for the peasant woman was the fact that she often contributed economically to the family by working part time in the fields. Thus, the husband did not provide the sole support of the family. In addition, cultural tradition granted a prestige to the mother that contradicted her assumed subservience to her husband (Covello, 1967:213). The major kinship ties were with the female relatives, and the nurturing of children was performed by the mother and her female relatives. The mother was the center of the family in a society where nonfamilial relationships were secondary. In a world where the family status was judged not by the occupation of the father but by the signs of family well-being that emanated from the household, the mother played an important role in securing that status.

Traditional Ethnic Culture

The Italian family system formed the basis of the perpetuation of a set of beliefs and values that affected all areas of social life including work, education, and definitions of social status.

The necessity of family ties was of singular importance. One's personal identity was derived from family, and family membership was essential in terms of defining one's place in society. The most shameful condition was to be without a family (Gambino, 1974:31). A man who violated the family code was an outcast from not only his family but also the larger society. He could only become a day laborer, and even in this, he was the last hired. For a woman without a family, the only options were to become a beggar or a prostitute. However, loyal kin were rewarded by always having a place within the family. The aged were cared for in the family and "no one went to poorhouses, orphanages, or other institutions of charity in the Mezzogiorno except those few unfortunates without any family intimates" (Gambino, 1974:29).

The strength of familial ties also affected the attitude of the *contadino* ("peasant") toward work: "Work is regarded as moral training for the young. And among adults, it is regarded as a matter of pride. To work is to show evidence that one has become a man or a woman, a full member of the family" (Gambino, 1974:80). Thus work was not defined as abstract but as tangible—something that could be shown to others as a "visible" result of an individual's skills and efforts. The disdain for intangibles was also related to the *contadino*'s attitude toward education.

Although the ideal of the *contadino* was to cultivate children who were *ben educato* ("well-educated"), the translation of this phrase is deceptive. Being educated referred not to formal schooling but to education in proper behavior. "*Ben educato* meant raised with the core of one's personality woven of those values and attitudes, habits and skills that perpetuated *l'ordine della famiglia*, and thus one was attuned to the welfare of the family" (Gambino, 1974:225). In this sense, formal schooling was antithetical to proper training for manhood or womanhood, involving the influence of *stranieri* who might interfere with *la via vecchia* ("the old ways"), as well as with keeping young people from the more important lessons they might learn from work.

THE MODERN ITALIAN AMERICAN FAMILY

Demographic and Ecological Factors

Although people tend to associate Italian immigration with the late nineteenth and early twentieth centuries, the immigration of Italians to the United States has actually been a continuing process, beginning much earlier and continuing to the present time. Four different periods of exodus can be identified, each having somewhat distinctive characteristics.

In the eighteenth and nineteenth centuries, small numbers of northern Italians came to the United States. These immigrants were scarcely visible in the population and did not identify themselves with the masses of southern Italians who came later. The 1870s were the starting date of the migratory flow from southern Italy, which increased rapidly during the next 50 years until the outbreak of World War I (Velikonja, 1977:68). In 1860, there were only 9,231 Italians in the United States; by 1904, there were 741,986 (Castiglione, 1974:53). The crest of the immigrant wave was between 1901 and 1914, when the yearly average totaled 616,000 (Gallo, 1974:25).

In this heaviest immigration period, young healthy men were the typical immigrants, with few elderly and even fewer female arrivals. Pushed by economic necessity, many men, both single and married but traveling alone, came to the United States with the idea of going back to Italy as soon as possible. The United States represented a source of work and income for them that would support their families, who during the trying times, by necessity, remained at home. This kind of emigration was not only acceptable but also encouraged in Italy. Although the exact number is unknown, Caroli (1973) has shown that of the millions who left Italy to come to the United States, 1.5 million returned home during the years from 1900 to 1914. Thus, there was substantial return migration. The wandering of these men was permitted by the economic and political leadership of the United States as long as the need for cheap labor outpaced the demands of the ever-growing native xenophobia.

Gradually, migration chains formed as families followed the men to specific sites, assisting each other in the adjustment to the new environment. This second generation of immigrants became more assimilated into American culture and changed the perception of Italian ethnic identity. As Alba (1985:56) explains, "The awareness of a very different set of cultural standards in the surrounding society, of which it was more a part than its parents, weakened its loyalty to Mezzogiorno culture." Thus, ethnic identification extended beyond the village to include people from the same province, sharing a dialect and practicing similar customs. This expansion of ethnic identity included all persons with an Italian surname and heritage. As the boundary of ethnicity grew, new and different social and cultural characteristics became identified as Italian American. This broader scope of ethnicity included many traits of the mainstream culture of the United States (Tricarico, 1985). Until 1925, the number of men remained three times greater than that of women as a result of return migration (Meloni, 1977:7).

In 1926, strict immigration quotas based on national origin were imposed by the United States government, and the flow of immigrants decreased to a trickle. The Immigration Act of 1965 substituted the national origin quotas for a new set of preferences, helping new immigrants join close relatives who were already residents of the United States (Velikonja, 1975:191).

Since 1967, an average of 23,000 Italian immigrants have come to the United States annually (Gallo, 1974:45). Recently arrived immigrants are quite different from the peasants who entered the North American continent at the turn of the century. More exposure to the modern world has lessened their isolation in the old country, and they are more likely to be well educated, having been specifically selected for certain occupations and professions that would not replace indigenous workers. Although more familiar with the modern world, these new arrivals also help to strengthen and maintain the traditions and customs of *la via vecchia.*

RESIDENTIAL MOBILITY AND KINSHIP TIES. In arguing for pluralism or assimilation, a key indicator used by both sides has been residential segregation—that is, to what extent do ethnic groups, regardless of social class, remain ethnically segregated, and how lasting are these patterns of residential segregation?

Several studies have examined residential segregation among Italian Americans. From the very beginning of their immigration, Italians settled in what have been called "Little Italies," and these ethnic communities tended to be concentrated along the eastern seaboard, particularly in New York and the major cities of Rhode Island, Connecticut, Massachusetts, and New Jersey (Lieberson, 1963:79; Lopreato, 1970:41). Americans of Italian descent make up more than one-sixth of the population of New York City (Gallo, 1974:25). To a large extent, these general patterns of residential settlement have been maintained (Abramson, 1973:29; Lopreato, 1970:53). According to the 1960 census, nearly 70 percent of Italian Americans are concentrated in the northeastern portion of the United States.

Although general patterns of residential segregation have been maintained, a more significant indicator of ethnic pluralism is the maintenance of neighborhoods. There is evidence to suggest that, for Italians, the meaning of "neighborhood" transcends the physical characteristics of housing. Italians imbue neighborhoods with a special significance that creates, in effect, an atmosphere of extended families. In an early study of the Italian North End of Boston, Firey (1947) found that second-generation Italians were more inclined to move to the suburbs than the older, first-generation Italians. He interpreted this to mean that they were seeking identification with American cultural patterns (Firey, 1947:200–209).

Years later, when assimilationist theories were being challenged, Glazer and Moynihan (1963:187) noted that, "While the Jewish map of New York City in 1920 bears almost no relation to that in 1961, the Italian districts, though weakened in some cases and strengthened in others, are still in large measure where they were." They also noted two trends among second- and third-generation Italians. One trend was a tendency to refurbish old neighborhoods, so that social mobility did not necessarily mean moving to suburbs. They also noted that when Italians did move, it was often a two-generation process, with both children and parents moving to suburban neighborhoods together. Glazer and Moynihan's findings were confirmed by a detailed analysis of residential segregation by ethnicity in

New York City based on 1960 census data (Kantrowitz, 1973). Kantrowitz (1973:7) concludes, "that ethnic segregation . . . has declined little over a generation."

The meaning of the maintenance of ethnic neighborhoods, particularly for Italian Americans, has been investigated in a comprehensive study of ethnicity from the National Opinion Research Center (NORC) (Greeley, 1971). Greeley (1971:77) found that, "Of all the ethnic groups, Italians most often live in the same neighborhood as their parents and siblings and visit them every week." Further, he notes that, "When the same data are sorted out according to social class and the physical distance that separates the respondents from parents and relatives, Italians are still the most likely to visit both their parents and their siblings." Greeley (1971:78) concludes that among Italians, "ethnic differences seem to persist even when different social classes are examined separately." Similar data were reported by Abramson (1970). Studying ethnic communities in four Connecticut cities, Abramson found that more than 50 percent of Italians and eastern Europeans had friends and relatives in the immediate neighborhood, as compared with 10–15 percent for Jews, German Catholics, and other Americans of northern-European and British descent.

Extending the analysis to visiting patterns as well as residential propinquity, Gallo (1974:86) found that, although first-generation Italians tended to live in closer proximity to kin than the second and third generation, the younger Italian Americans visited relatives and were in turn visited more frequently. Gallo (1974:86) concluded that, "the second and third generation respondents became increasingly active outside the family as they acculturate to urban values, but at the same time retain family contacts. The extended family plays a greater role for the second and third generation respondents than for those of the first." Similar findings were reported by Goering (1971), who found that third-generation Italians were more likely to think of themselves ethnically than first- or second-generation Italians and concluded that ethnic awareness may be increasing.

In contrast to these findings, Lopreato's research on Italians in New Haven, Connecticut, indicates that middle-class Italians visit relatives only slightly more frequently than the general population, whereas working-class Italians visit twice as frequently. Lopreato (1970:51) concludes that "These findings seem to indicate that to a considerable extent the working class still adheres to old world habits and practices. The Italian-American middle-class, on the other hand, is for all practical purposes indistinguishable from the American middle class as a whole."

Drawing data from household surveys in Rhode Island, Kobrin and Goldscheider (1978) compared four Catholic ethnic groups with Protestants and Jews on several issues. In regard to the issue of residential concentration, they found, like Lopreato, that it was affected by social class. Working-class Italians were more likely than middle-class Italian Americans to reside in ethnically cohesive neighborhoods.

Obviously, the relationship between social class and ethnicity is complex, and the final answer has not been provided. It seems unlikely that the upward social mobility of third- and fourth-generation Italians will lead to complete assimilation. Part of the problem stems from the fact that, although studies of the relationship between the family system and ethnicity include a comparison by social class, many generalize their findings to the entire population. Thus, it becomes difficult to determine whether behaviors are indeed a function of ethnicity or related to social class. Yancey, Erickson, and Juliani (1985:186) critique this monolithic treatment of ethnic groups, claiming that researchers have not paid enough attention to differences that exist within an ethnic group. Examination of the internal structure of the group would facilitate the identification of conditions that produce ethnicity and ethnically related behavior. Instead, evidence indicates that they will continue to maintain a distinct ethnic identity.

FAMILY SIZE AND FERTILITY. Although impoverished Italian immigrant women had exceptionally large families, their second-generation daughters completely reversed this pattern. As reported by Rosenwaike (1973:272), the 1910 census showed that women of Italian parentage constituted 4.9 percent of the female population in Boston between the ages of 15 and 44 and accounted for 15.3 percent of the births for that city. Data from New York indicate a similar pattern. First-generation immigrant women generally had more children than other Americans, but those from Italy had exceptionally more. This changed drastically with the second generation. Rosenwaike (1973:275) concludes that "Obviously very strong assimilationist pressures had been at work, for not only did the second generation Italian-American women, on the average, have fewer than half the children of the immigrant generation; they curtailed their childbearing to a level below that of Americans of native parentage."

Certainly, assimilationist pressure is one possible explanation for this intergenerational difference in fertility. However, Gambino (1974:163–164) offers an alternative explanation of this same phenomenon:

> Large families were found in the *Mezzogiorno* not because the *contadini* confused womanhood with high fertility. Nor did they have large families to satisfy any religious views. They had large families for two reasons. First, they lacked effective birth control technology. Second, a large number of children

> was an asset to a family in the economic system of old southern Italy. . . . Italian-American women of the second generation had means of birth control available to them. They were free to exercise only the traditional criterion regarding children—the economic well-being of the family . . . they had children in proportion to their family incomes in America, where economic realities punished families with many children. They and their husbands decided it was better for the family to limit its number of children. And they did so.

Thus, according to Gambino, it was not assimilationist pressures that caused second-generation women to limit their family size, but a continuing tradition of primary concern for family well-being.

The birth rate for third-generation Italians still appears to be decreasing. In a study of three generations of Italians in New York City, Russo (1970:207) found definite generational variation in family size, with third-generation Italians reporting the fewest number of children. In response to the question, "How many children do you have?", 42.2 percent of third-generation Italians reported two or less. In contrast, among first-generation Italians, 54.7 percent came from families of five or more children. This trend is apparent despite the fact that most Italians are Catholic. In fact, in a national survey, Ryder and Westoff (1971) reported that Italian Catholics were most likely of all Catholic ethnic groups to use contraception other than the rhythm method. Thus, it would appear that the stereotype of the Italian woman burdened by large numbers of children as a result of religious convictions is certainly not typical of the average second- or third-generation Italian woman.

ENDOGAMY. Rates of intermarriage are useful indicators of social amalgamation and the disposition to lose ethnic identification. Endogamy among Italian Americans has been the subject of several studies, dealing in various ways with each of the immigrant waves.

In one study, Kennedy (1952) investigated intermarriage among seven ethnic groups in New Haven, Connecticut, for the period 1870–1950, she found that, after Jews, Italians had the highest in-groups marriage rate of the seven ethnic groups considered. However, the rate of in-group marriage showed a decrease from first-generation to second-generation Italians. In 1900, 97.9 percent of Italian marriages were strictly endogamous, like most newly arrived ethnic groups. By 1950, this rate had fallen to 76.7, a sizable decrease but still high compared to other ethnic groups.

More recently, Abramson (1973) studied endogamy among nine Catholic ethnic groups using data from the NORC that sampled the entire white Catholic population of the United States between the ages of 23 and 57. He found that Italians were the only ethnic group of those arriving prior to 1920 that still showed relatively high rates of endogamy. Sixty-six percent of Italian Catholics in his sample were endogamous, compared with 50 percent or less for the Polish, Lithuanian, eastern European, German, Irish, and English groups. The only groups with higher rates of in-group marriage were the Spanish-speaking Catholics and the French Canadians. However, these results were tempered by several factors. Among those factors influencing rates of intermarriage was geographic location. Those Italians living in the middle Atlantic states with high concentrations of Italians had very low rates of intermarriage (only 27 percent), but this increased to 49 percent in the north central portion of the United States, where Italians are relatively few in number. Even more significant were the different rates of intermarriage when age was used as a control. Whereas only 27 percent of Abramson's sample of Italian Americans between the ages of 40 and 50 married non-Italians, 42 percent of those between 20 and 30 intermarried. He also found level of education to have an effect on endogamy, with those completing high school having much higher rates of intermarriage than those without a high school diploma. This indicates that education is a powerful influence on assimilation and that rates of intermarriage for Italians may continue to increase as they obtain college degrees and are increasingly exposed to individuals of other ethnic backgrounds.

These findings were basically confirmed and further refined by Alba (1976), who used the same data to determine whether there was a generational effect on rates of intermarriage. He found that rates of intermarriage increased in each generation, although they remained lower for Italians than for most other groups. Alba (1976:1039) concluded that "the most obvious finding . . . is the universality of a trend toward increasing social assimilation."

Finally, in the extensive study of ethnic pluralism in American life (previously discussed in regard to residential concentration), Kobrin and Goldschneider (1978) found that Italians of all age groups were more likely than Irish, French Canadians, and Portuguese to have a spouse of the same ethnic origin, although this was less true of younger than older Italians. Kobrin and Goldscheider's (1978:230) conclusions about the meaning of ethnicity in American life disagree sharply with those of Alba:

> Overall, ethnic homogamy has declined as the most important distinguishing feature of ethnic groups. Ethnicity in America is much less based on marriage within narrowly defined ethnic communities and the role of the intermarried is apparently being redefined in such a way as to allow for the ethnic community identification . . . These convergences and growing homogeneity among

ethnic communities in marriage patterns do not necessarily imply similarities and uniformities. That these marriage differences reflect more than class and cohort variations among ethnic groups suggests that specific ethnic structural and cultural determinants are operating.

DIVORCE. Marriage was essential for the southern Italian as a source of social identity, and family stability still seems to be relatively intact. According to the 1973 census report on ethnicity (U.S. Bureau of the Census, 1973), "There were 2.6 million families in March 1972 whose head was of Italian origin. Most of these families were composed of husband–wife families, eighty-seven percent, and only about ten percent were families with a female head." This was the smallest percentage of 11 major ethnic groups for women between the ages of 15 and 44.

The stability of the Italian family is reflected in the low divorce rates for Italian Americans. According to the U.S. Bureau of the Census (1973) only approximately 3 percent of all Italian Americans are divorced, and the divorce rate for younger Italians is not significantly higher than for those over 45 years of age. In a comprehensive study of ethnicity in the United States using data based on seven NORC surveys, Greeley (1974:46) found that Italian American Catholics had the second-lowest divorce rate (only 2 percent) of all ethnic groups. The only group with a lower divorce rate was Irish American Catholics (1.8 percent). Similar findings were reported by Kobrin and Goldscheider (1978:40), who found that Italians and Irish were least likely of all Catholic ethnic groups to not only divorce but also to remarry if they did terminate their first marriage. Although the effects of religion cannot be discounted, the relatively weaker ties of the Italians to the Catholic church indicate that family influence is certainly playing some role in maintaining a low divorce rate. This can be illustrated by the fact that other Catholic groups that have stronger ties to the Catholic church have higher divorce rates. For example, Polish, Slavic, and French Catholics all have divorce rates of more than 4 percent, and Spanish-speaking Catholics have a divorce rate of 6.6 percent. Thus, Catholicism cannot be the only explanatory factor for the low divorce rate among Italian Americans. Strong familism is certainly a critical variable.

SOCIAL CLASS. The Italians came to this country basically illiterate and with few skills to offer, except a willingness to work. The significance attached to work and the disdain of the *contadino* for the value of education, as previously described, was carried over into their life in American society by resistance to the educational institutions. This conflict was very conspicuous in the early part of the twentieth century, when Italian children were perceived as "problems" in the school system (Covello, 1967:284). Second-generation Italian children were more likely than other children to be truant, late, and involved in disciplinary infractions (Covello, 1967:285). According to Covello (1967:288–296), there were many aspects of southern Italian cultural patterns that contributed to resistance to education. First, there was a fear on the part of the parents of the indoctrination of alien concepts that might destroy family unity. This fear was compounded by the belief that all necessary skills could be learned in the home or through apprenticeships. Second, there was an economic aspect to the conflict. The southern Italian peasant was accustomed to economic contributions to the household from children as young as 12 years of age. The idea of adolescents remaining in school throughout their teenage years was perceived by the first generation as enforced idleness of no clear benefit (Covello, 1967:289). Girls, in particular, were actively discouraged from attending school, an attitude that put them in direct conflict with compulsory education laws.

This antagonism toward formal education expressed by first-generation Italians has had long-range repercussions. In terms of level of education, the Italians have ranked behind other ethnic groups that came to the United States at approximately the same time. According to a U.S. census report based on 1972 data, the greatest difference between Italian Americans over the age of 35 and those under 35 was in the percentage of graduations from high school. As shown in Table 1, although only 31.9 percent of those over 35 graduated from high school, 51.1 percent of the younger Italians finished high school—an increase of almost 20 percent. Similarly, whereas only 16.5 percent of those under 35 years of age graduated from college (a relatively low figure), this still represents a marked increase over the 6 percent of college graduates over 35 years of age.

These specific beliefs regarding the value of formal education are part of a more general orientation toward life. Several studies have attempted to measure these beliefs and assess their impact on social mobility. An early study by Rosen (1959) found that Italian Americans placed relatively low value on independence and achievement training and had relatively low aspirations in terms of expectations for education and occupational choice. In a more recent study of adult males, Featherman (1971) found that Italian and Mexican Catholics expressed a high "materialistic orientation" toward work, regarding work as instrumentally valuable in achieving other goals rather than as intrinsically satisfying. However, Featherman cautions against using adult motivation as an explanatory variable for ethnic group achievement differentials and suggests that motivation to complete school might be the key intervening variable. Finally, in a study of college seniors,

TABLE 1

Years of School Completed by Italian Americans by Age

AGE	ELEMENTARY			HIGH SCHOOL		COLLEGE		MEDIAN SCHOOL YEARS (%)
	0–4 (%)	5–7 (%)	8 (%)	1–3 (%)	4 (%)	1–3 (%)	4 OR MORE (%)	
25–34	0.9	2.4	3.3	13.0	51.1	12.3	16.5	12.6
35 and over	8.7	10.5	17.0	19.7	31.9	6.1	6.0	11.1

SOURCE: U. S. Bureau of the Census (1973).

Gottlieb and Sibbison (1974) asked students to explain their reasons for attending college. Both male and female Italian American students rated job training as a more important reason than more abstract reasons such as seeking knowledge.

One visible outcome of these attitudes is that Italians largely went into blue-collar work, a pattern that has begun to change only within the third generation. Table 2 compares the employment patterns of first- and second-generation Italian men from the 1950 census and all men from the 1972 census. There was very little change between the first and second generations, with men of both generations largely employed in blue-collar work as either craftsmen or operatives. As Meloni (1977:10) explains, "As many as two-thirds of the second generation have remained common labourers like their fathers. The gap between the first and second generation is still smaller for Italian-Americans than for any other major European ethnic group in America." By the third generation, a significant shift toward white-collar work accompanied by an increase in the ranks of professionals can be seen. However, much of social mobility that has occurred has been in the television industry, newspaper reporting, and sports (Meloni, 1977:10). This can probably be attributed to the lesser role of education in occupational mobility among Italians. Unlike many other ethnic groups, upward mobility among Italians has not necessarily been correlated with higher educational levels (Kobrin and Goldscheider, 1978:32).

TABLE 2

Employment Patterns of Three Generations of Italian American Males

	FIRST-GENERATION MALES (%) 1950	SECOND-GENERATION MALES (%) 1950	ALL ITALIAN MALES (%)[a] 1972
Professional	3	6	13
Managerial	13	10	14
Clerical and sales	6	17	15
Craftsmen	24	22	22
Operatives	24	29	16
Laborers	14	9	9
Service workers	14	6	10
Private household workers	0	0	0

SOURCES: Gambino (1974:83); U. S. Bureau of the Census (1973).

[a]The census report did not differentiate by place of birth but by ethnic identification, thus all three generations are included in this figure.

In analyzing the work history of Italian women, some research has centered on the expected conflict between work and family life. A study of Italian immigrants in Buffalo, New York, in the early part of the twentieth century discovered that, although most Italian women were employed, their employment was limited to certain types of work (Yans-McLaughlin, 1977). Specifically, they were likely to work as seasonal laborers for fruit- and vegetable-processing companies. In contrast to Polish immigrants, they rejected domestic labor, which would take them out of the Italian community and into other people's homes. I interpret this pattern of work choice as being compatible with the family orientation of the immigrant, because it allowed the family to continue as the basic productive unit. It was a situation that minimized family strain by permitting mother and child to work together. As Yans-McLaughlin (1977:189) notes, "While 90 percent of the American-born children came to the canneries as independent workers, all the Italian youngsters worked and travelled with their parents. This suggests the foreign parents' willingness to relinquish economic and familial control over their young." In addition, seasonal work was not an assault on male pride, because the women were not working more steadily than their frequently unemployed husbands. Thus, they could contribute to the family income, while minimizing the sex-role conflicts. Further, as a community activity, field work permitted more strict familial and sexual control over women than domestic work.

More recently, the work patterns of Italian women have been similar to those of Italian American men. As shown in Table 3, first-generation Italian women were most likely to be operatives. The second generation

TABLE 3

Employment Patterns of Three Generations of Italian American Females

	FIRST-GENERATION FEMALES (%) 1950	SECOND-GENERATION FEMALES (%) 1950	ALL ITALIAN FEMALES (%) 1972
Professional	2	5	12
Managerial	4	2	6
Clerical and sales	8	40	46
Craftsmen	2	2	1
Operatives	77	44	18
Laborers	0	0	1
Service Workers	4	4	15
Private household workers	1	0	2

SOURCE: Gambino (1974:84); U. S. Bureau of the Census (1973).

shifted to clerical work, as did most women during the expansion of this sector of the labor force after World War II. Even so, a relatively high percentage of women remained operatives compared with most other women, who were more likely to be service workers. Further, Italian women are least likely of all ethnic groups except the Spanish to be professionals; although, like the men, they did show a significant increase in this category by 1972. Because professional occupations require extensive schooling and a stronger career orientation, which might interfere with family life, both these factors probably have worked as impediments to the upward occupational mobility of Italian women.

Roles in the Nuclear Family

Although the southern Italian family has been termed patriarchal, the limitations of this description have already been discussed. All authority did not reside with the father, largely because of the social and emotional leadership roles of the Italian mother, which gave her considerable power and influence in her family's affairs. However, her power, like the father's, was circumscribed, and there was a distinct separation of roles for men and women. This division of labor was largely maintained by the first-generation immigrant to the United States, and even in the second generation, there are indications that remnants of fictitious patriarchy remain. As one second-generation mother (and grandmother) describes her marriage, "The most important thing is, that a man wants to be head of the family, so he could be, but in a roundabout way, I get my own way. So he's the boss, but I get my way if I know how to work it. . . . But you have to work very hard to make a successful marriage. You have to be a saint sometimes."

Several writers have explored this theme, comparing attitudes toward familial roles of first- and second-generation Italians. One study (Ware, 1935) found quite different beliefs between those over 35 years of age and those under 35 in regard to the interpretation of familial roles. Ware (1935:193) found that 64 percent of younger Italians compared with 35 percent of the older group disagreed with the statement, "the husband's authority should be supreme." Eighty-six percent of the younger group compared with 58 percent of the older group did not think large families were a blessing. Finally, 54 percent of the younger group compared with 31 percent of the older group disagreed that a child should sacrifice his personal ambition for the welfare of the family group.

In a comprehensive study examining changes between the southern Italian peasant and first- and second-generation Italian Americans, Campisi (1948) found major changes. He described the southern Italian peasant as patriarchal, the first generation as fictitiously patriarchal, and the second generation as democratic with the father sharing high status with the mother and children. He found little in-group solidarity among second-generation Italians and a general weakening of Italian culture, which was no longer transmitted by the family but by the larger society.

Both Ware (1935) and Campisi (1948) performed their studies at a time when researchers believed that assimilation was inevitable, and thus both studies concentrated on differences between generations. Other more recent studies have found more cultural continuity than was originally believed to exist. In a descriptive study of an urban Italian neighborhood, Gans (1962) found that, although some of the outward manifestations of Italian culture had disappeared, many traditional patterns remained. One specific manifestation was what Gans termed the "segregated conjugal pattern," in which husbands and wives had distinctly separate roles, duties, and obligations and turned to kin of the same sex for advice and companionship so that the society essentially was sexually segregated. According to Gans (1962:52):

> The segregated conjugal pattern is closely associated with the extended family, for the functions that are not performed by husband and wife for each other are handled by other members of the extended family. In a society where male and female roles are sharply distinguished, the man quickly learns that, on many occasions, his brother is a better source of advice and counsel than his wife.

Although Gans's findings have been criticized for being applicable to only second-generation, working-class Italians, not suburban, college-educated Italian Americans (Lopreato, 1970), some more recent empirical studies indicate that even among upwardly mobile individuals, traditional patterns remain. In a survey of graduating college seniors in five schools in Pennsylvania, Gottlieb and Sibbison (1974:49) found that Italian Catholic students were more likely to have a traditional view of sex roles than any other ethnic group, including the Irish, Jews, Poles, and blacks. They also found that Italian women were less traditional than the men and even more so than the other ethnic groups.

Similar findings were reported by Greeley (1974:157), who attempted to determine "whether ethnic heritage continues to have an influence on the relationships within the contemporary American family despite the process of assimilation and homogenization that was the American context of the immigrant family."

In measuring the source of identification for third-generation Italians,

Greeley (1974:162) found that the males found their father to be their primary source of identification, whereas the females were most likely to identify with their mothers. The identification with the mother was stronger for Italian females than for any other group except blacks. However, Italian females tended to reject traditional roles for women and not consider domestic skills important. In contrast, Italian men's acceptance of the traditional role for women was particularly high.

Pursuing the issue of generational change in a study of three generations of Italian Americans, Gallo (1974:84) found increasing egalitarianism with each succeeding generation. Although the father still maintained his primary status within the family in the first generation, 80 percent of the second-generation respondents asserted that there was shared decision making among all family members and that discipline was shared between mother and father. This trend was increased among third-generation respondents, who reported democratic decision making within the family and the family performing primarily affectional functions.

Modern Italian American marriages still appear to be more traditional when compared with the norm of American marriages today. The cultural ideal of the modern American marriage, according to Johnson (1985), is romantic love, companionship, and emotional support. In contrast, Italian American marriages are more likely to be characterized by sex-role differentiation and an emphasis on instrumental, not emotional, functions. This varies by social class, however, because working-class marriages function with the greatest degree of sex segregation, hierarchy, and lack of emphasis on emotional concerns. The closely bound social network of the working class, including relatives and friends, maintains a greater segregation of sex roles but enables emotional needs to be satisfied by network members other than the spouse.

Socialization of Children

The first generation of Italians who came to the United States and settled in insulated communities were able to resist encroachments of American culture in their own lives, but the beliefs and customs they valued were more difficult to instill in their second-generation children. The second-generation Italians were unable to maintain the same degree of isolation. They were socialized by not only their parents but also American institutions, particularly the school system, and what they were taught at home frequently conflicted with what they learned at school.

One solution to generational conflict used by many young Italian men was to identify with peers rather than parents or school, which made friends an important source of socialization. In Gans's (1962:38) study of Italians in the West End of Boston, he describes the significance of the peer group:

> Before or soon after they start going to school, boys and girls form cliques or gangs. In these cliques, which are sexually segregated, they play together and learn the lore of childhood. The clique influence is so strong, in fact, that both parents and school officials complain that their values have difficulty competing with those being taught in the peer group. The sexually segregated clique maintains its hold on the individual until late adolescence or early adulthood.

Among the concerns of the male adolescent peer groups were self-control, independence, and a competitive sort of display involving games of skill, verbal bantering, and conspicuous consumption related to clothes or cars (Gans, 1962:38).

In Gans's study, the actual responsibility for childrearing belonged to the mother, with formal discipline provided by the father (Gans, 1962:59). He found the West End family to be adult-centered in the sense that the household was run to satisfy adult wishes first. Children were expected to act like adults and not interfere with adult activities. By the age of seven, girls were expected to assist their mothers, and boys were given more freedom to roam (Gans, 1962:56). Punishment tended to be physical but intermingled with verbal and physical signs of affection.

In a recent study, 76 families in which both spouses were Italian American were interviewed, and their responses were compared with those of families in nonhomogamous marriages. Distinctive patterns of childrearing among the Italians were identified. Specifically, the Italian mother was found to exhibit a high level of nurturing. As Johnson (1978:38) reports:

> Her total devotion to her children in material and emotional support, caresses, food-giving, and in fact, supportive extension of herself makes her an indispensible figure in her children's lives. Her love for her children has few contingencies, and other than diffuse expectations for respect and sociability, she has few strings attached to it.

A second distinguishing feature was the manner in which discipline as a means of social control was used (Johnson, 1978:38):

> In Italian-American families, discipline is frequently used, and it is physical, swift and directed at the external locus of control (rather than appeals to the child's conscience). . . . Italian parents value love and affection between themselves and their children. Love, enjoyable for its own sake, is also employed to manage and control the behaviors of their children.

According to the author, this use of both punishment and love as mechanisms of social control cements family solidarity while discouraging autonomy and independence.

The Extended Family

Researchers have described the ethos of familism as characteristic of the southern Italian family. The concept of familism refers to the domination of the kinship group over other forms of social organization (Gallo, 1974:87). Because of this domination, interaction with nonfamily members was limited, and in southern Italy, few moral sanctions existed outside the immediate family. One indicator of familism is the number of friendships formed outside the immediate family group. In a study of first- and second-generation Italian Americans, Palisi (1966:175) found that first-generation Italians were likely to have fewer friends outside the family and belong to fewer formal organizations than the second generation. However, the extent of participation in family affairs was still stronger for the second-generation Italians. He concluded that "individuals in the second-generation are likely to be more assimilated, and more outgoing and have more opportunities to make friends than do first-generation persons. Thus, they make friends fairly easily. But, they also retain some of the old world patterns of family participation" (Palisi, 1966:175).

Another indicator of familism is the strength of sibling relationships. One extensive analysis of modern Italian American families (Johnson, 1982) examined sibling solidarity by ethnicity and social class. Between 1974 and 1977, Johnson interviewed three family subgroups: in-group married Italian Americans, out-group married Italian Americans, and a Protestant, non-Italian control group. The subjects were of comparable ages and stages in the family cycle and geographically stable, which enabled a comparison by ethnicity, religion, and social class of sibling relationships of middle-aged persons in solid marriages.

The availability of relatives often is considered a primary factor affecting kinship interaction. To test this claim, Johnson (1982:160) compared the ethnic subgroups by the number of relatives living within the city. The in-group married Italian Americans were more likely to have siblings living within the city and more relatives in geographic proximity. This finding supports the proposition that Italian Americans establish and maintain households near their closest kin.

Daily or weekly contact of Italian Americans with siblings was found to be quite high. The proportion of in-group married Italians having daily contact with siblings (63 percent) was twice as high as out-group married

Italians (32 percent) and was five times greater than the Protestant group (12 percent) (Johnson, 1982:161). The frequency of interaction also varied by sex, with fewer husbands than wives in all three subgroups reporting daily contact with siblings. Still, the in-group married Italian American men maintained the highest frequency of contact among the males.

When analyzed on the basis of social class, working-class families had the most frequent interactions with siblings. Class differences were large among the out-group married and Protestant families, but the in-group married families showed little social-class variation, maintaining higher frequency of sibling contact than the other subgroups. Thus, Johnson's findings support the argument that intermarriage rather than social class accounts for the variation in sibling solidarity.

Johnson attributes the high degree of sibling solidarity among in-group married Italians to the organization of immigrant families. The emphasis on parental respect and authority minimized conflict among children, and the employment of both parents led them to focus their attention on the children as a group rather than on any individual child. Immigrant families were often part of an active, extended family system living near enough to allow frequent contact. This contact enhanced surrogate parenting and diluted strong, emotional relationships between parents and children.

Sibling solidarity served many important functions in Italian American families. Siblings provided physical care, supervision, education, and an amelioration of the family's power structure and parental distraction. The sibling mutuality and interdependence established during the childhood years continued into adulthood as the result of close geographical proximity and the set pattern of "sociability and mutual aid" (Johnson, 1982:164).

The strength of extended family ties also results in exceptional nurturing and support for aged family members. In comparing data on family interaction of Italian American elderly with a national sample, Johnson (1978:36) found that the Italian elderly were more likely to be integrated into a family system, have a larger number of surviving children, and be in more frequent contact with their children and that the widowed were less likely to live alone. Further, the younger, married Italian families were four times more likely than non-Italians to endorse without reservation the thought of an elderly parent living with them (Johnson, 1978:37). They were also decidedly more likely than non-Italians to reject outright the choice of a nursing home as a last resort for an incapacitated parent. Johnson (1978:39) concluded that, because Italian families are more likely to spend leisure time with relatives than friends, they viewed their obligation to aged parents as a natural outcome of the family cycle. Because the family operates as a source of nurturing that fulfills the dependency needs of all its members, the onset of dependency of an elderly member is merely an extension of a lifetime pattern.

Another study (Tricarico, 1984) examined three generations of Italian Americans residing in the southern Greenwich Village. Tricarico (1984:x) employed an in-depth and extensive collection of historical, census, demographic, geneological, economic, and participant observation data to discover the social and filial characteristics of the elderly Italian Americans residing in Greenwich Village.

The elderly in Tricarico's sample had lived in this neighborhood for most, if not all, of their lives. Although characterized by low incomes, the survival skills secured during years of economic hardship left the immigrants and their children with low expectations and a desire for continued independence. The elderly tried to provide their own economic support and live alone rather than with their children or any other family members.

A major determinant of neighborhood status for these elderly was filial obligation to care for an aging parent (Tricarico, 1984:86). Their children usually resided nearby and were available for assistance when advanced age and poor health lessened the parents' ability to maintain total independence and care for themselves. Although family care was clearly a filial obligation, it was often a source of considerable strain on the entire family network. The primary burden of care fell on the child, married or not, who was the last to remain in the neighborhood. This was usually the daughter who lived geographically closest to her parents or in-laws. Children who lived further away remained in close contact with parents by telephone but did not assist with the physical care.

In the previously cited study of in-group married Italian Americans, out-group married Italian Americans, and Protestant non-Italians, Johnson (1985:10) also analyzed "how variations in values on independence are translated into ongoing relationships between generations in a family: the elderly parents, their middle-aged offspring and the adolescent children." With ethnicity as the independent variable, Johnson (1985:11) asked the question, "Does the family system of this subculture (Italian-American) resolve the dependence-independence dilemma differently from the (dominant) American pattern?"

In this analysis, the three ethnic subgroups were compared in terms of network connections, filial relationships, kinship solidarity, marital relations, and the socialization process. All these categories were expected to vary by ethnic group, as well as be significantly influenced by geographical and social mobility, intermarriage, and the transmission of values throughout the developmental cycle of the family.

The sample was composed of nuclear households, each maintaining economic independence from the kinship network. Few had an elderly parent or any other relative residing in the household—only the married couple and their non-adult children. However, elderly parents, siblings, and other relatives often lived in geographical proximity and reported very cohesive bonds throughout the network. Thus Johnson (1985:66) concluded that "although the structure is inclined to be nuclear, the family can readily incorporate members of the extended group into its functions."

Geographic mobility had little effect on the life situation of the 65-years-old and older sample of in-group married Italian Americans, because 97 percent had at least one child living in proximity (Johnson, 1985:146). These elderly reported frequent interaction with their children and a rewarding and satisfying grandparent role. Strong family ties compensated for role losses and helped avoid progressive withdrawal from social interaction.

Social activity and degree of social isolation did not vary by sex, but there was a difference between the "old, old" (75 years of age and over) and the "young, old" (65–74 years). Many of the young, old were born in the United States and had led an active social life involving many contacts outside the family, as well as a kinship network that grew larger with each generation. The growing social network also eased the compensation of role losses, including widowhood. Fluency in English was greater with the young, old and allowed for an easier integration into family activities and American culture.

This study verified the existence of a strong filial bond between middle-aged children and their elderly parents. The norms of the in-group married Italian Americans' subculture still holds the family in a position of centrality, establishes a familial hierarchy with parents at the top, and prescribes that parents are given respect, gratitude, and love. Johnson found that this subgroup was most likely to include their elderly parents in their social activities and households and would never consider placing them in a nursing home.

CHANGE AND ADAPTATION

Two perspectives characterize present debates regarding the maintenance of ethnic identity. One perspective emphasizes the class-based nature of ethnic traits; the other stresses the uniqueness of Italian ethnicity that will perpetuate a sense of identity among third- and fourth-generation Italian Americans.

According to the class-based view, the problems experienced by Italian

Americans and the issues raised about them are expressed in ethnic terms that are produced by the life experiences of the working and lower-middle classes (Tricarico, 1985:80). The focus on the family, which characterizes the lower classes, includes values incompatible with the individualism and consumerism emphasized by the general cultural pattern in the United States.

The family networks of the Italian Americans, dispersed in individual households, have become increasingly mobile. This movement and the resulting transformation of kinship relations is likely to continue as Italian Americans become more integrated with the American middle class. The neo-localism of modern-day Italian American households has changed the family network. Kin are no longer neighbors, and great differences have arisen in income, education, and occupation among members of a family system, causing segregation and isolation of family households (Tricarico, 1984). As Tricarico (1984:89) explains, Italian American households have "become increasingly neospatial and heterogeneous, having implications for the greater authority of the nuclear unit." This new lifestyle places great pressure on the solidarity of the family network and continues to exist as more married children become absorbed in occupations, homes, and the performance of familial functions as an independent unit.

Similarly, a 1975 study in the Bridgeport, Connecticut, metropolitan area of persons of Italian descent found a continuity in close ties among all kin members, with a decline in the closeness of later generations and among those with higher educational and/or occupational levels. Social class had little effect on the closeness of relations within the nuclear family, but higher social class was associated with a diminishment of positive attitudes toward relatives outside the household. The middle-class Italian Americans placed a stronger emphasis on individualism, relying on friends to play the roles once filled by their large family network. From this study, Crispino (1980) concluded that close family ties are likely to continue among nuclear family members, but mobility concerns will exceed the extended family in importance, leaving only infrequent occasions for direct involvement in the family network to strengthen the ties.

The traditional assumption about cultural assimilation is the "straight-line" theory, which assumes a decline in ethnicity with each successive generation of a cultural group as it confronts the focal culture and its standardizing influences. The straight-line theory, confined to an upwardly mobile society, claims that both social and economic mobility have a positive correlation to acculturation and assimilation. In other words, ethnicity is a property of the working class and disappears as second and third generations of immigrants ascend to the middle class.

Tricarico (1985) cites studies that present straight-line assimilation as incompatible with Italian American ethnicity. The low prestige assigned to immigrants caused them to reject their Italian ethnicity and culture. However, these studies have uncovered new definitions of the relationship to their ethnicity by third- and fourth-generation Italian Americans. The broader social acceptance of cultural diversity has enabled these later generations to have an ethnic identification and expression combined with a mainstream identity and culture.

One problem with recent studies of white ethnicity is that they have only classified persons into ethnic categories and have failed to measure the strength of ethnic commitments. The result has been a lack of empirical data to support the many claims of the resurgence of ethnicity among certain groups of whites in the United States. To fill in this gap, Roche (1984:27) employed the attitudinal ethnicity scale to measure the "degree of attachment to the cultural, national and religious aspects of ethnicity." A large sample of suburban Italian Americans were interviewed to "discover the extent to which individuals in the same ethnic category are committed to the group" (Roche, 1984:28).

The sample was drawn from two suburbs of Providence, Rhode Island, one predominantly Italian American and the other ethnically mixed. Roche employed Sandberg's group cohesiveness scale, comprised of 30 statements, to measure respondents' attitudes toward several aspects of their ethnic groups, including three subscales centered on culture, nationalism, and religion.

Roche found a drop in ethnicity on all measures with each consecutive generation. None of his data supported claims of third-generation growth in ethnicity. Instead, measures of the scale supported the straight-line theory that movement away from ethnicity and assimilation into the mainstream accompanies each generation.

Many variables affected the degree of ethnicity. Age was positively related to ethnicity, with stronger levels of commitment found among the elderly and weaker levels among younger people. A strong, negative association was found between education and ethnicity. The highest levels of ethnicity were found among those with the fewest years of schooling, and ethnicity decreased as the number of years in school increased. Occupational status was also negatively related to ethnicity, because it declined in the white-collar portion of the sample.

The concept of symbolic ethnicity was developed by Gans (1984), who argues that ethnicity has become increasingly peripheral to the lives of many upwardly mobile members of ethnic groups. Members of ethnic groups adapt their ethnic identity to their current social position by selecting a few symbolic elements of their cultural heritage that do not affect their social interaction with others of a variety of ethnic backgrounds. This practice is explained in detail by Alba (1985:173):

> Symbolic ethnicity is vastly different from the ethnicity of the past, which was a taken-for-granted part of everyday life, communal and at the same time imposed on the individual by the very fact of being born into the group. The ethnicity that survives in the melting pot is private and voluntary . . . the ethnicity of white Americans has moved from the status of an irrevocable fact of birth to an ingredient of lifestyle.

The mobility of white ethnic groups has enabled them to maintain ethnic sentiments and diversity to an extent beyond that allowed their lower-class counterparts. Still, this ethnicity is American enough, in both behaviors and values, not to be perceived as threatening or divisive of the mainstream culture in the United States today.

As a result of the upward mobility of white ethnic groups, including Italian Americans, the ethnic role played by those reaching the middle classes is no longer ascriptive, but a voluntary role assumed with other social roles. Ethnicity, for these classes, has become an expressive rather than intrumental function in their lives (Gans, 1984). Ethnic identity has lost its focus in culture and organization and, in turn, its relevance to social behavior and family structure and has become a component of social–psychological identity for the individual, not the group.

REFERENCES

Abramson, Harold J. 1970. "Ethnic Pluralism in the Central City." Storrs, CT: University of Connecticut.

———. 1973. *Ethnic Diversity in Catholic America.* New York: John Wiley.

Alba, Richard D. 1976. "Social Assimilation Among American Catholic National Origin Groups," *American Sociological Review,* 41 (December):1030–1046.

———. 1985. *Italian Americans.* Englewood Cliffs, NJ: Prentice-Hall.

Campisi, Paul. 1948. "Ethnic Family Patterns: The Italian Family in the United States," *American Journal of Sociology,* 53 (May):443–449.

Carlyle, Margaret. 1962. *The Awakening of Southern Italy.* London: Oxford University Press.

Caroli, Betty Boyd. 1973. *Italian Repatriation from the United States, 1900–1914.* New York: Center for Migration Studies.

Castiglione, G. E. Di Palma. 1974. "Italian Immigration into the United States, 1901–1904," in F. Cordasco and E. Bucchioni (eds.), *The Italians: Social Background of an American Group.* Clifton, NJ: Augustus M. Kelley, pp. 53–73.

Chapman, C. G. 1971. *Milocca: A Sicilian Village.* Cambridge, MA: Schenkman.

Child, Irwin L. 1943. *Italian or American? The Second Generation in Conflict*. New Haven: Yale University Press.
Covello, Leonard. 1967. *The Social Background of the Italo–American School Child*. Leiden, The Netherlands: E. J. Brill.
Dore, Grazia. 1968. "Some Social and Historical Aspects of Italian Emigration to America," *Journal of Social History*, 2(Winter):95–122.
Featherman, David L. 1971. "The Socioeconomic Achievement of White Religo-ethnic Groups," *American Sociological Review*, 36(April):207–222.
Feldstein, Stanley, and Lawrence Costello. 1974. *The Ordeal of Assimilation*. Garden City, NY: Anchor Books.
Femminella, Francis X. 1961. "The Impact of Italian Migration and American Catholicism," *The American Catholic Sociological Review*, 22(Fall):233–241.
Firey, Walter. 1947. *Land Use in Central Boston*. Cambridge, MA: Harvard University Press.
Foerster, Robert L. 1919. *The Italian Emigration of Our Times*. Cambridge, MA: Harvard University Press.
Gallo, Patrick J. 1974. *Ethnic Alienation: The Italian Americans*. Rutherford, NJ: Fairleigh Dickinson University Press.
Gambino, Richard. 1974. *Blood of My Blood*. New York: Doubleday.
Gans, Herbert H. 1962. *The Urban Villagers*. Glencoe, IL: Free Press.
———. 1985. "Symbolic ethnicity: The future of ethnic groups and cultures in America," in N. R. Yetman (ed.), *Majority and Minority* (4th ed.). Boston: Allyn and Bacon, pp. 429–442.
Glazer, Nathan, and Daniel P. Moynihan. 1963. *Beyond the Melting Pot*. Cambridge, MA: MIT Press.
Goering, John. 1971. "The Emergence of Ethnic Interests: A Case of Serendipity," *Social Forces*, 50(March):379–384.
Gordon, Milton. 1964. *Assimilation in American Life*. New York: Oxford University Press.
Gottlieb, David, and Virginia Sibbison. 1974. "Ethnicity and Religiosity: Some Selective Explorations Among College Seniors," *International Migration Review*, 8(Spring):43–58.
Greeley, Andrew M. 1971. *Why Can't They Be Like Us*? New York: John Wiley.
———. 1974. *Ethnicity in the United States*. New York: John Wiley.
Hansen, Marcus Lee. 1958. "The Third Generation: Search for Continuity," in H. D. Stein and R. A. Cloward (eds.), *Social Perspectives on Behavior*. New York: Free Press, pp. 139–144.
Johnson, Colleen Leahy. 1978. "Family Support Systems of Elderly Italian Americans," *Journal of Minority Aging*, 3–4(August–June):34–41.
———. 1982. "Sibling Solidarity: Its Origins and Functioning in Italian-American Families," *Journal of Marriage and the Family*, 44(1):155–167.
———. 1985. *Growing Up and Growing Old in Italian-American Families*. New Brunswick, NJ: Rutgers University Press.
Kantrowitz, Nathan. 1973. *Ethnic and Racial Segregation in the New York Metropolis*. New York: Praeger.
Kennedy, Ruby Jo Reeves. 1952. "Single or Triple Melting Pot? Intermarriage in New Haven, 1870–1950," *American Journal of Sociology*, 58(July):56–59.
Kertzer, David I. 1978. "European Peasant Household Structure: Some Implica-

tions From a Nineteenth Century Italian Community," *Journal of Family History*, 3:333–349.
Kluckholn, Florence R., and Fred L. Strodtbeck. 1961. *Variations in Value Orientations*. Evanston, IL: Row, Peterson and Co.
Kobrin, Frances E., and Calvin Goldscheider. 1978. *The Ethnic Factor in Family Structure and Mobility*. Cambridge, MA: Ballinger.
Lieberson, Stanley. 1963. *Ethnic Patterns in an American City*. New York: Free Press.
Lopreato, Joseph. 1970. *Italian Americans*. New York: Random House.
———. 1976. *Peasants No More*. San Francisco: Chandler.
Meloni, Alberto. 1977. *Italian Americans: A Study Guide and Source Book*. San Francisco: R and R Research Associates.
Palisi, Bartolomeo. 1966. "Patterns of Social Participation in a Two Generation Sample of Italian Americans," *Sociological Quarterly*, 7(Spring):167–178.
Roche, John P. 1984. "Social Factors Affecting Cultural, National and Religious Ethnicity: A Study of Suburban Italian-Americans," *Ethnic Groups*, 6:27–45.
Rosen, Bernard C. 1959. "Race, Ethnicity and the Achievement Syndrome," *American Sociological Review*, 24(February):47–60.
Rosenwaike, Ira. 1973. "Two Generations of Italians in America: Their Fertility Experience," *International Migration Review*, 7(Fall):271–280.
Russo, Nicholas J. 1970. "Three Generations of Italians in New York City: Their Religious Acculturation," in Sylvano M. Tomasi and Madeline H. Engel (eds.), *The Italian Experience in the United States*. New York: Center for Migration Studies, pp. 195–213.
Ryder, Norman B., and Charles F. Westoff. 1971. *Reproduction in the United States, 1965*. Princeton: Princeton University Press.
Spiegel, J. 1972. *Transactions: The Interplay Between Individual, Family and Society*. New York: Science House.
Tomasi, Lydio F. 1972. *The Italian American Family: The Southern Italian Family's Process of Adjustment to an Urban America*. New York: Center for Migration Studies.
Tomasi, Sylvano M. 1970. "The Ethnic Church and the Integration of Italian Immigrants in the United States," in Sylvano M. Tomasi and Madeline H. Engel (eds.), *The Italian Experience in the United States*. New York: Center for Migration Studies, pp. 163–193.
Tricarico, Donald. 1984. *The Italians of Greenwich Village*. New York: Center for Migration Studies.
———. 1985. "The 'New' Italian-American Ethnicity," *Journal of Ethnic Studies*, 12(3):75–93.
U. S. Bureau of the Census. 1973. *Population Characteristics: Characteristics of the Population by Ethnic Origin*. Series P-20, no. 249, April. Washington, DC: U. S. Government Printing Office.
Vecoli, Rudolph J. 1969. "Prelates and Peasants," *Journal of Social History*, 2(Spring):217–268.
———. 1974. "The Italian Americans," *The Center Magazine*, 7(July/August):31–43.
Velikonja, Joseph. 1970. "Italian Immigrants in the United States in the Sixties," in Sylvano M. Tomasi and Madeline H. Engel (eds.), *The Italian Experience in the United States*. New York: Center for Migration Studies, pp. 23–39.

———. 1975. "The Identity and Functional Networks of the Italian Immigrant," in Francesco Cordasco (ed.), *Studies in Italian American Social History.* Totowa, NJ: Rowman and Littlefield, pp. 182–198.

———. 1977. "Territorial Spread of the Italians in the U.S." in S. M. Tomasi (ed.), *Perspectives in Italian Immigration and Ethnicity.* New York: Center for Migration Studies, pp. 67–79.

Ware, Caroline F. 1935. *Greenwich Village.* New York: Harper and Row.

Wrigley, E. Anthony. 1977. "Reflections on the History of the Family," Daedalus, (Spring):71–86.

Yancey, William L., Eugene P. Erickson, and Richard N. Juliani. 1985. "Emergent Ethnicity: A Review and Reformation," in N. R. Yetman (ed.), *Majority and Minority,* (4th ed.). Boston: Allyn and Bacon, pp. 185–194.

Yans-McLaughlin, Virginia. 1977. *Family and Community, Italian Immigrants in Buffalo, 1880–1930.* Ithaca: Cornell University Press.

HISPANIC ETHNIC MINORITIES

CHAPTER SIX

The Mexican American Family

Rosina M. Becerra

HISTORICAL BACKGROUND

The history of the Mexican American people predates by many years the incorporation of the Southwest into the United States. Native to the Southwest, the Mexican American people have a history marked by conflict and colonization, first by the Spanish and then by the Anglo Americans. This early history, perhaps especially because of the proximity of the southwestern states to the Mexican border, has left a legacy of conflict that is present today between Mexican Americans and Anglo Americans. The present position of Mexican Americans as a people, their family life, and the effects of their position on their family life can best be understood through a brief review of their histories as Mexicans and North Americans.

Spanish Colonization

The period of Spanish colonization began in the sixteenth century and lasted until 1821, when Mexico achieved independence from Spain. The first Spanish settlements in southwestern North America were in what is now known as New Mexico, where 25 missions were established between 1598 and 1630. Beginning in 1769, missions were established in California, and a few were established in the areas of Texas and Arizona. The mission system helped to incorporate the Catholic church into the region (McWilliams, 1968).

Because the Spanish *conquistadores* (conquerors) were all men, they intermarried with the Mexicans and indigenous Indians. This mixed heritage of the Spanish, Mexicans, and Indians remains predominant among today's Mexican Americans. The Spanish heritage, language, and numerous other contributions, which were modified by time and the indigenous cultures of the Indians and Mexicans, constitutes the foundation of the unique Mexican American culture, as noted by McWilliams (1968:34):

> Beyond all doubt the culture of the Southwest was a trinity: a whole consisting of three intricately interwoven, interpenetrated, thoroughly fused elements. To attempt to unravel any single strand from this pattern and label it 'Spanish' is, therefore, to do a serious injustice to the Mexicans and Indians through whom, and only through whom, Spanish cultural influences survived the region.

Anglo-Mexican Conflicts

The history of the Southwest during the nineteenth century is basically a history of conflict between the United States and Mexico. The Mexican government had opened the area of Texas to settlers under the condition that they pledge allegiance to Mexico and agree to become Catholics. The Anglo American settlers (mostly United States citizens), however, resisted these conditions. At the same time, Mexicans of the territory resisted the Anglo American colonization through various forms of rebellion. Through the political process, Anglo Americans of the territory were able to pass laws favoring their minority group, and Mexicans were stripped of what little wealth they had and relegated to the lowest social and economic classes. Often, a small group of wealthier Mexicans collaborated with the Anglo Americans to maintain their own positions in the new order (Acuna, 1981).

Rebellions between the Anglo Americans and the Mexican government occurred throughout the territory of Texas between 1821 and 1848, setting the stage for the conquest of the rest of the Southwest. Until this time, the Southwest had been relatively isolated. The development of the railroad system ended the isolation of the Southwest from the rest of the country and brought larger numbers of Anglo Americans to the region (Acuna, 1981).

In 1832, Stephen Austin went to Mexico City to press for lifting the restrictions on Anglo American immigration and for separate statehood. "Anglos in Texas saw separation from Mexico and eventual union with the United States as the most profitable political arrangement because the colonists had developed a strong economic trade arrangement with the United States" (Acuna, 1981:7). By 1835, 5,000 Mexicans resided in the Texas territory, and the Anglo American population had risen to 30,000. A full-scale rebellion escalated, and the Anglo Americans in Texas (with some Mexican supporters) declared war on Mexico. To squelch this rebellion, General Santa Anna led an army of approximately 6,000 men from the interior of Mexico. He arrived in San Antonio, Texas, in February 1836, when 187 Texans took refuge in a former mission, the Alamo. Although the Texans lost the battle, much mythology grew around the struggle and continues today. The cry "Remember the Alamo" prompted aid from the United States to assist the Texans, most of whom were United States citizens (Acuna, 1981).

Later in 1836, Sam Houston defeated Santa Anna at the Battle of San Jacinto. This defeat ended the era of the Texas revolution, or Texas's war for independence, and Texas became a United States territory. The Texas victory paved the way for the Mexican-American War.

Although some Mexicans had fought on the side of the Texans, the development of the Republic of Texas and the negative feelings generated about Mexico increased the already existing schism with the Texan Mexicans. Fear of continued domination by Mexico prompted the annexation of Texas by the United States in December 1845. This act severed United States diplomatic relations with Mexico.

The Mexican-American War (1846-1848) terminated with the Treaty of Guadalupe Hidalgo, in which Mexico accepted the Rio Grande River as the Texas border and ceded territory in the Southwest to the United States for $15 million. The ceded territory incorporated the present-day states of California, New Mexico, and Nevada and parts of Colorado, Arizona, and Utah. Thus began the occupation of conquered territory (Acuna, 1981).

In 1850, 13,300 persons of Mexican origin resided in the United States, and by 1880, this figure was 68,400 (Jaffe, Cullen, and Boswell, 1980). In the intervening 30 years, the Southwest was, for the most part, an isolated, self-contained area that was culturally and economically removed from the rest of the United States. Most of the major movement between Mexico and the United States concentrated at the borders.

Immigration

Between 1880 and 1910, the southwestern United States experienced rapid economic development and commercialization of agriculture. Mexican labor was highly sought by United States mining, railroad, and agricultural interests (Reisler, 1976). During these three decades, the population of Mexican origin grew threefold as Mexican immigrants gravitated toward the region's growing demands for low-wage labor. In 1910, the U.S. Census recorded 220,000 Mexican-born persons and 162,000 persons of Mexican parentage living in the United States (Jaffe, Cullen, and Boswell, 1980). The railroads played a crucial role in the expanding Mexican immigration, because they were a rapid and relatively easy means of transportation from central Mexico and a principal source of employment during the late nineteenth and early twentieth centuries. In 1909, 17 percent of the work-force of the nine largest western railroads were Mexican workers (Reisler, 1976).

Between 1910 and 1930, the Mexican population in the United States continued to grow rapidly. By 1930, the population of Mexican origin (i.e., those of Mexican birth or parentage) exceeded one million persons (Jaffe, Cullen, and Boswell, 1980). Emigration from Mexico continued to be spurred by a strong demand for labor, heightened by the entry of the United States into World War I. The 1910 Mexican Revolution and the Cristero Rebellion (1926–1929) in Mexico also served to heighten Mexican migration to the United States (Massey, 1982).

The 1930s were a period of widespread domestic unemployment, and the demand for unskilled labor decreased. Anti-Mexican feeling swept through the Southwest, resulting in mass repatriations. Between 1929 and 1935, more than 415,000 Mexicans were forcibly expelled from the United States (some of them were American citizens). Another 85,000 left "voluntarily" (Hoffman, 1974). As a result, between 1930 and 1940, the Mexican population dramatically declined, and 41 percent of Mexican-born persons actually returned to Mexico (Jaffe, Cullen, and Boswell, 1980).

The United States again began to experience labor shortages in the Southwest during World War II. In the Southwest, agricultural interests sought and obtained government cooperation in the recruitment and importation of Mexican workers for agricultural labor. In 1942, the United States entered into an agreement with Mexico that arranged for the importation of Mexican workers into the United States for periods not to exceed six months. Although the Bracero Program was originally conceived as a temporary wartime measure, agricultural growers pressured the governments to both extend and expand this program throughout the 1950s. The program ended in 1964, following growing opposition by organized labor. During the 22 years of its operation, the Bracero Program had recruited over 4 million workers, and at its height, over 400,000 workers were entering the United States annually (Reichert and Massey, 1980).

After the Bracero Program phased out, Mexican workers continued to enter the United States legally and illegally. Between 1940 and 1970, the Mexican population nearly doubled from 377,000 to 746,000 (Reichert and Massey, 1980; Jaffe, Cullen, and Boswell, 1980).

During the 1970s, Mexican immigration became more of a self-feeding phenomenon because of the years of active recruitment by United States businesses. Legal and illegal migration, high fertility rates, and social and economic conditions in Mexico combined to produce a 64 percent increase in the population of Mexican origin between 1970 and 1979. In 1979, the number of persons of Mexican origin was estimated at 7.3 million (Massey, 1981; Pachon and Moore, 1981). Today, 8.7 million persons of Mexican origin or descent inhabit the United States. This figure represents 60 percent of the total Hispanic population. The majority of the Mexican American population (86 percent) reside in the five southwestern states of Arizona, California, Colorado, New Mexico, and Texas. In 1970, Mexican Americans constituted 2.7 percent of the total population of the United States. In 1986, they were 3.9 percent of the total United States population and secured their place as one of the fastest-growing ethnic groups in the United States (U. S. Bureau of the Census, 1985).

The Chicano Movement

The mid-1960s gave rise not only to the civil rights and black movements but also the Chicano movement.[1] During this era of the New Frontier and the War on Poverty, the growing ferment of Chicano youth focused on inequities in educational opportunities, the high rate of unemployment and low-wage occupational opportunities, and the general poverty status of the Mexican American population. This generation of Chicano activists pressed for the rights they had been guaranteed by the United States Constitution, as well as for the many rights guaranteed historically by the numerous treaties with Mexico. This movement had the effect of generating a new pride in the Spanish, Mexican, and Indian heritage, and it also gave rise to many Mexican American organizations that continue to press for equal rights in all arenas of the society (Acuna, 1981).

With the growth of the Chicano population and the legacy of the Chicano movement, mainstream political power emerged in the late 1970s and early 1980s. Because of the sheer numbers of Mexican Americans now residing throughout the United States, with major concentrations in both the Southwest and the Midwest, Mexican Americans are becoming a politi-

[1]"Chicano" was a term that emerged in the middle to late 1960s to denote a politically aware and politically active individual of Mexican American descent. There are numerous explanations of the origin of the term, but there does not seem to be *one* explanation that is embraced by all. It still continues to represent the same meaning, but it is primarily a self-identifier used by younger rather than older cohorts of Mexican Americans.

cal force to be reckoned with. This developing political strength may prove to empower the Mexican American with a stronger voice and base in the future society of the United States (Acuna, 1981).

THE MEXICAN AMERICAN FAMILY IN HISTORICAL PERSPECTIVE

Mexican American families consist largely of individuals who are descended from or who are themselves unskilled immigrants who come to the United States to work in low-wage sectors of the southwestern economy (McWilliams, 1968; Grebler, Moore, and Guzman, 1970). Unlike the members of some other Hispanic groups, very few Mexicans entered the United States as professional people.

Because of the Southwest's geographic proximity to Mexico and its demand for low-wage labor, the Mexican population is highly concentrated in the southwestern states. In fact, in 1979, 76 percent of Mexican Americans lived in one of two states: California or Texas (Pachon and Moore, 1981). From 1870 through 1980, these two states have always been home to between 70 percent and 80 percent of the Mexicans in the United States (Jaffe, Cullen, and Boswell, 1980). During most of their time in the Southwest, Mexicans have been the victims of prejudice and discrimination, varying in intensity from time to time and place to place but always present (Grebler, Guzman, and Moore, 1970; Hoffman, 1974; Estrada et al., 1981).

Because of their long history of settlement in the United States and continuous emigration from Mexico, the Mexican American population is far more generationally diverse than other Hispanic groups. In 1970, 16 percent were first-generation immigrants (i.e., foreign born), 34 percent were second generation, and 50 percent were third or later generations (Jaffe, Cullen, and Boswell, 1980). The generational diversity of the Mexican American people implies a corresponding diversity of social and economic statuses within the population.

What makes the situation of the Mexican American any different than that of other immigrating groups, who with the passage of time have been acculturated into mainstream America? Although change and, presumably, acculturation are taking place, Mexican Americans have more continuous interaction with first-generation immigrants and proximity to their original homeland. First-generation community members constantly reinforce traditional values. The rate and direction of acculturative change are thus greatly influenced and cause some cultural values to remain unchanged. The proximity of Mexico to the United States, regardless of the amount of flow back and forth, reinforces the familial ties—and the family values—that span the two countries (Becerra, 1983).

Heterogeneity and Homogeneity

Because family socialization takes root in the economic and political forces of society, the history of the Mexican American family must be anchored in the context of the American economy (Saragoza, 1983). Mexican Americans are a highly heterogeneous population. An important factor accounting for this variability is history. Mexican groups in the United States have different histories of immigration and settlement. Some trace their roots to the Spanish and Mexican settlers who first settled the Southwest before the arrival of the pilgrims, whereas others are immigrants or children of immigrants who began to arrive in large numbers by the beginning of the twentieth century (Martinez, 1985). Saragoza (1983) points out that this history supports the fundamental cultural variation and social differentiation among Mexican American families. Crucial factors are variability across region (including Mexico) and changes over time. Mexican American families in different historical periods have adapted differently to economic and political forces, and family socialization patterns have responded differently to societal pressures (Baca-Zinn, 1983).

The traditional structure of the Mexican family grew out of the socioeconomic needs dictated by the agrarian and craft economies of Mexico. For the traditional Mexican, the word *familia* ("family") meant an extended, multigenerational group of persons, among whom specific social roles were ascribed. By dividing functions and responsibilities among different generations of family members, the family was able to perform all the economic and social support chores necessary for survival in the relatively spartan life circumstances of the rural Mexican environment. Mutual support, sustenance, and interaction among family members during both work and leisure hours dominated the lives of persons in these traditional Mexican families (Becerra, 1983).

After the conquest of the Southwest, Mexican families who remained or moved to the United States out of necessity tended to work and live in ethnically homogeneous settings. Minimally influenced by Anglo American culture, these communities supported the maintenance of Mexican familial structures as they might have been practiced in rural Mexico. The male took the role of authority figure and head of the household, and the female took the role of childbearer and nurturer (Sanchez, 1974). This family form was a response to particular economic and political forces, as are all family forms, that resulted in the Mexican American family carrying both these ideals and values and the need for modification under the new economic and political circumstances in the United States.

Traditional Family Structure

Much has been written about the traditional structure of Mexican American families. Depending on the author, these structures appear rigid, cold, and unstable on one end of the continuum or warm, nurturing, and cohesive on the other end. The three main characteristics of the Mexican American family that are addressed by these polar views are the following: (1) male dominance, (2) rigid sex and age grading so that "the older order the younger, and the men the women", and, (3) a strong familial orientation (Mirande, 1985:152).

MALE DOMINANCE. Of all the popular stereotypes surrounding the Mexican American family, none has become so much a part of American usage as the concept of *machismo.* Machismo is often equated with male dominance. Male dominance is the designation of the father as the head of the household, the major decision maker, and the absolute power holder in the Mexican American family. In his absence, this power position reverts to the oldest son. All members of the household are expected to carry out the orders of the male head.

The concept of machismo has various interpretations. For many, machismo is equated with excessive aggression, little regard for women, and sexual prowess. The macho demands complete allegiance, respect, and obedience from his wife and children. Madsen (1973:20) states that "ideally the Latin male acknowledges only the authority of his father and God. In case of conflict between these two sources, he should side with his father."

In contrast, genuine machismo is characterized by true bravery, or valor, courage, generosity, and a respect for others. The machismo role encourages protection of and provision for the family members, the use of fair and just authority, and respect for the role of wife and children (Mirande, 1985).

Although male dominance is a Mexican American cultural entity, as well as a structural component, its counterpart, the self-sacrificing, virtuous, and passive female, is no more true than the selfish, sexually irresponsible, and aggressive male. In fact, since 1848, many men have, for economic reasons, had to leave the family home to search for work, leaving the woman behind to head the household. Mexican American history is full of examples of women who have deviated from the submissive role.

The ideals encompassed in the patriarchal tradition were often contradicted by the circumstances of day-to-day life. The types of jobs available to Mexican American men kept them away from their families for long periods of time working as teamsters, wagon drivers, miners, and farm workers. Over time, more and more women who were heads of households (even temporarily) were forced into the job market, further changing the expected roles of women (Griswold del Castillo, 1984).

Partriarchal values did not disappear under the impact of economic and political changes. Mexican American men continued to expect women to be submissive, but in this respect, they were no different from other men. Family life became a mixture of the old and new values regarding paternal authority and the proper role of women. Increasing poverty and economic insecurity intensified the pressures on Mexican American nuclear families and led to increased matriarchy and more working, single mothers. As a result, the ideology of patriarchy found less confirmation in everyday life. As a system of values and beliefs, however, the ideology of patriarchy continues to exist (Griswold del Castillo, 1985:39).

SEX AND AGE GRADING. Complementing the concept of male dominance is the concept of sex and age subordination, which holds that females are subordinate to males and the young to the old. In this schema, females are viewed as submissive, naive, and somewhat childlike. Elders are viewed as wise, knowledgeable, and deserving of respect.

To some degree, these designations were derived from division of labor. Women as childbearers and childrearers did not perform the so-called more physically difficult jobs and therefore needed to be more protected by the man. If the women needed protection, the man took the role of overseeing the family. Nonetheless, the power of the male was more apparent than real. Respect for the breadwinner and protector rather than dominance was more key to the family. Roles within the familial network were stressed so that the constellation of the minisystem operated to the betterment of the individual and the familial system (Mirande, 1985).

In the isolated rural areas where many of the Mexican American families lived, the coordination of role expectations facilitated survival on the frontier. Each person behaviorally and institutionally carried out those roles that would ensure family survival.

The female child learned the roles and skills of wife and mother early, because she would carry them out both in the absence of the mother and as a future wife and mother. The eldest female child was expected to oversee the younger children so that the mother could carry out her tasks in the upkeep of the family. The eldest male, after puberty, had authority over the younger children as well as his elder sisters, because he would take on the responsibility for the family in his father's absence and for his own family as a future father.

The older family members, after they physically could no longer work, assumed the role of assuring family continuity. They were the religious teachers, family historians, nurturers of small children, and transmitters and guardians of accumulated wisdom. Their accumulated wisdom and numerous years of labor for the family was repaid by the respect given to them for their years (Becerra, 1983).

Thus, although particular role expectations are based on gender and age, and these dictate relationships and interactions, these roles were originally developed in response to a means for family maintainance and survival.

FAMILISTIC ORIENTATION. The Mexican American family form was a result of a style that was brought from Mexico, modified in the United States, and adapted to fit a pattern of survival in the isolated, rural areas of the Southwest. Because of this history, there is an assumption that the Mexican family and the Mexican American family are isomorphic, allowing one to evaluate the Mexican American family from knowledge of the Mexican family, which is, in fact, fallacious (Montiel, 1970). However, the importance of the familial unit continues as a major characteristic among Mexican Americans to this day.

The familistic orientation continues because the family is viewed as a warm and nurturing institution for most Mexican Americans. It is a stable structure, in which the individual's place is clearly established and secure (Mirande, 1985). The family, as Murrillo (1971:99) indicates, offers "emotional security and sense of belonging to its members," and offers support throughout the individual's lifetime. The family is a major support system, a unit to which the individual may turn for help when in stress or in other types of need. Key to the family system is the value of sharing and cooperation.

Extended kinship ties assume a prominent place within the Mexican American culture. The extended family may include godparents and/or very close friends. Studies show that Mexican families tend to live near relatives and close friends, have frequent interaction with family members, and exchange a wide range of goods and services that include babysitting, temporary housing, personal advice, nursing during times of illness, and emotional support (Muller et al., 1985:67).

In sum, numerous studies (Ramirez 1980; Ramirez and Arce, 1981) demonstrate that familial solidarity among Mexican Americans is not just a stereotypical ideal, but a real phenomenon. Although expressed differently today because of changing cultural values and socioeconomic pressures, the pattern of a strong familistic orientation continues. It appears that Mexican Americans continue to have more cohesive family support systems than other groups (Griswold del Castillo, 1984).

THE CONTEMPORARY MEXICAN AMERICAN FAMILY

Sociodemographic Trends

The Hispanic population of the Southwest is 86 percent Mexican in origin. Sixty percent of all Hispanics living in the United States are of Mexican origin. Despite the stereotype of Mexicans as rural farm workers, 85 percent of all Mexican Americans reside in major metropolitan areas, usually in the major cities (Sullivan, 1985). In fact, only 4.6 percent of Mexican American people work as farm workers.

A significant fact about the Mexican American population is its young median age. The median age in 1985 of the Mexican American population was 23.3 years compared with the non-Hispanic population median age of 31.9. With respect to the percentage of males, 51.1 percent of Mexican Americans are males compared with a male population of 48.5 percent for the entire United States population. Because of their proximity to the Mexican border, Mexican men may come to the United States to seek work and leave their spouses behind in Mexico. This could account for the slightly higher number of Mexican American males than females (U. S. Bureau of the Census, 1983).

With respect to median family income, Mexican American families had a median income of $19,184 in 1985, compared with $26,433 for all United States families and $26,951 for white, non-Hispanic families. Among Hispanic families, Mexican American families have the lowest median income, except Puerto Rican families, who received $12,371 (U. S. Bureau of the Census, 1985).

Mexican American families are significantly larger than all other ethnic or racial families. The mean number of persons in Mexican American families is 4.15, compared with 3.88 persons in all Hispanic families and 3.23 persons in all United States families. Thus, the larger Mexican American family must be supported by a family income that is smaller than that of most other groups. Furthermore, almost one out of five Mexican American families have six or more members, compared with one out of 20 for all United States families that have six or more. This rate is also higher than for all Hispanic families (13.7 percent) (U. S. Bureau of the Census, 1985).

Twenty-four percent of Mexican American families are below the poverty level, compared with 10.7 percent of white, non-Hispanic families (U. S. Bureau of the Census, 1985). As expected, the highest percentage of Mexican American families in poverty are female-headed households (43.8 percent), but this figure is the lowest of all Hispanic populations and is also lower than that for blacks. The percentage of female-headed households in poverty among whites is 32.7 percent, and the figure is 34.5 percent for the entire United States family population (U. S. Bureau of the Census, 1983).

With regard to occupational status, Mexican Americans are far more concentrated in blue-collar jobs (48.9 percent) than in white-collar jobs (29.2 percent). Compared with other Hispanics, Mexican Americans are least likely to be found in white-collar jobs. The greatest proportion (21.5 percent) are employed as operatives or as clerical and kindred workers (14.6 percent) (U. S. Bureau of Labor Statistics, 1981). With respect to employment, except for blacks and Puerto Ricans, Mexican Americans have the highest unemployment rates (11.9 percent) of any other group in the United States. This rate is highest for males (12.5 percent) (U. S. Bureau of the Census, 1985).

With regard to education, Mexican Americans have the lowest median school years completed of any other group in the United States. They complete an average of 10.2 years, compared with 12.6 years for the total population (U. S. Bureau of the Census, 1985). This figure is 11.5 years for all Hispanic groups. Mexican Americans are the most likely to have completed less than five years of education (17.1 percent), compared with the next lowest group, Puerto Ricans (12.8 percent). In part, this can be explained by the high rate of people who emigrated from Mexico looking for unskilled labor. As a result, and compounded by the elevated high-school dropout rate among Mexican Americans in the United States, only 37.6 percent of Mexican Americans 25 years old and over have completed high school, compared with 51.2 percent for blacks and 69.6 percent for white non-Hispanics (Sullivan, 1985).

Thus, today's modal Mexican American family can be characterized as having a disproportionate percentage of members in low socioeconomic status. They have lower incomes that support larger families. In part, these lower incomes are a result of higher levels of unemployment and lower-paying jobs, which are partially explained by low educational attainment, which in turn creates a high proportion of families in poverty. Still, this is not the entire story. Like trends for all groups, these socioeconomic trends do not reflect the diversity of the population, especially that proportion of the Chicano population who fare better than others. If the median family income is $19,184 per year, 50 percent of the population members earn more than $19,184. Any discussion of the sociodemographic trends for the Mexican American family must be considered within the context of a specific time period by region, overall economic trends, and migration patterns.

Fertility

Table 1 shows the fertility rates in 1980 for various ethnic and racial groups. The data show that Mexican Americans have the highest fertility rates compared with all other groups. In fact, Mexican American fertility is significantly higher for every age group—73 percent higher than the total population in the 15–24 age group, 43 percent higher than the total population in the 25–34 age group, and 38 percent higher in the 35–44 age group. Compared with blacks and whites in the three age groups, Mexican Americans are 1.5 percent, 13.3 percent, and 14.5 percent higher, respectively. Compared with whites, the differences are even more dramatic. In the same three age groups for whites, Mexican Americans have 109 percent, 52 percent, and 45 percent higher fertility rates.

The 1980 fertility data, compared with 1970 data, show a 10 percent decrease in the total population's fertility rate among older women 35–44 years old. Mexican Americans in this age group have decreased approximately 5 percent, whereas both blacks and whites have each increased approximately 2 percent in this age group. The overall fertility rate among

TABLE 1
Children Born to Women Ages 15–44, by Race and Ethnicity: 1980

	CHILDREN BORN PER 1000 WOMEN		
GROUP	AGES 15–24	AGES 25–34	AGES 35–44
SPANISH ORIGIN	475	1922	3202
Mexican	528	2105	3646
Puerto Rican	548	1986	3202
Cuban	192	1189	2033
Other Spanish	337	1567	2640
WHITE	262	1383	2523
BLACK	540	1858	3184
ASIAN	211	1219	2256
TOTAL POPULATION	317	1476	2639

SOURCE: U. S. Bureau of the Census. 1983. *General Social and Economic Characteristics: United States Summary.* Washington, DC: U. S. Government Printing Office. Table 166.

Mexican women aged 15–44, however, continued to be higher than for all other groups. Mexican women tend to begin childbearing at younger ages and to have more children than other Hispanic or non-Hispanic women. In 1982, for example, 19 percent of Mexican American births were to women under 20 years of age, compared with 14 percent for non-Hispanic women. Finally, 19 percent of births to Mexican women were fourth or higher order in 1982, compared with 9 percent of births to non-Hispanic women (7.6 percent for whites, 14.6 percent for blacks) (National Center on Health Statistics, 1982).

In short, Mexican American families tend to be larger. As previously noted, Mexican American families average 4.15 persons, compared with 3.23 for the total population. Furthermore, 71 percent of all Mexican families have children under 18 years of age residing in the home, compared with white non-Hispanic families, who report only 48.9 percent having children under 18 living in the home. Moreover, Mexican families are twice as likely to have small children under age six (40.3 percent), compared with white, non-Hispanic families (20.5 percent).

In a study by Becerra (1981) on Mexican American adolescents aged 13–19, the data show that the fertility rate for Mexican adolescents is twice that for Anglo American girls. The data show, however, a lower rate of use of contraceptives among Mexican American adolescents. The use of contraceptives seems to be linked to levels of acculturation, sex-education information, educational levels of the parents, and general peer-group networks. These data are not unlike those found by Bean et al. (1984) in their study on the generational differences among Mexican Americans. On the other hand, Fisher and Marcum (1984) suggest that higher fertility rates seem to be associated with stronger ties, measured by ethnic integration, to the ethnic culture.

What may account for the higher fertility and birth rates among Mexican Americans has been pondered by many researchers. The question of whether the explanations are cultural or structural or both continues to be debated with some evidence on both sides.

Marriage and Divorce

Marriage patterns among Mexican Americans are similar to those of other groups. Among those individuals ages 15 and over, 59.6 percent of Mexican Americans are married, compared with 59.2 percent for the total United States population. Interestingly, the percentage of never-married Mexican Americans is larger than that for persons of non-Hispanic origin (31 percent compared with 25.8 percent). This could be accounted for by the large proportion of younger persons in the Mexican American population (U. S. Bureau of Census, 1983).

Mexican Americans have a divorce rate of 5.4 percent, the lowest rate of all groups, compared with the United States population average of 7.2 percent (U. S. Bureau of Census, 1983).

With respect to family stability among Mexican American families, 75.7 percent are headed by married couples, compared with 52 percent for Puerto Rican families, 80.9 percent for non-Hispanic families, and 80.3 percent for the total population. Furthermore, 18.6 percent of Mexican American families are female-headed households, compared with a high of 44 percent for Puerto Rican families and a low of 16 percent for Cuban families. Interestingly, of male-headed (no wife present) families, Mexican males are more likely (5.8 percent) to take on the single parent role than any other group (compared with 3.6 percent for the entire population of the United States). Thus, Mexican families generally appear to be stable, two-parent families with a relatively lower rate of divorce than other ethnic families. The men seem to take over the household more often when there is no mother present.

Assimilation and Intermarriage

Assimilation is a multidimensional process in which ethnic groups begin to blend into a total community. One major dimension in this process is structural integration (Yinger, 1985). Considering the structural dimension, Yinger (1985:32) defines integration as the "degree to which members of a group are distributed across the full range of associations, and regions of a society in a pattern similar to that of the population as a whole." According to this definition, Mexican Americans are only moderately assimilated. As previously noted, they are beginning to be a political strength, a voting bloc sought after, and a strong enough constituency to promote and elect their own politicians (e.g., nine of the 13 Hispanics in the House of Representatives are Mexican Americans). In this arena, it appears that this political force will continue to increase.

In other areas, however, considerable inequities prevail. Economically, Mexican American family income is still only 73 percent of the median income for all United States families, Mexican American unemployment rates are 60 percent higher than for non-Hispanic whites, and Mexican Americans continue to be concentrated in blue-collar jobs and underrepresented in white-collar jobs. Educationally, only approximately two out of five Mexican Americans complete high school. Although there has been some progress in these areas, as indicated by the higher proportion represented in colleges and universities, greater numbers in white-collar jobs, and increased incomes, the gains are only moderate.

Intermarriage is often considered one major measure of integration, reflective of the degree of other assimilative processes (Yinger, 1985). Intermarriage in this context usually means marriage between a Mexican American and an Anglo American. Murguia (1982) has compiled one of the most extensive studies on Mexican American intermarriage. His findings suggest that among the three most populous southwestern states (which have high concentrations of Mexican Americans), the intermarriage rates range from 9–27 percent in Texas, from 27–39 percent in New Mexico, and from 51–55 percent in California. Intermarriage rates are greatly influenced by the forces that influence integration. As educational levels increase, residential segregation decreases, and social-class mobility increases with decreases in discrimination, intermarriage should probably increase accordingly. Furthermore, as the Mexican American socioeconomic profile moves closer to the socioeconomic profile of the population as a whole, the assimilation process should move accordingly.

CHANGE AND ADAPTATION

Today's Mexican American family is a unique culture in American society in that it is fully characterized by neither the Mexican culture nor the American culture—it maintains elements of both. The Mexican family has been modified by the social and economic pressures of American life, yet the proximity of the Mexican border provides a continual influex of Mexican nationals that serve to maintain the familial and emotional ties to Mexico and to enhance the Mexican cultural values.

One key element encouraging change has been the increased movement of families from rural to urban life. Today, 85 percent of all Mexican American families reside in the urban centers of the southwestern and midwestern United States. This factor has had a profound impact on the familial structure. Although a familial orientation remains, Mexican American families today are less likely to be composed of extended kin residing in the same household than to be residing nearby, which still facilitates more frequent interaction. The supportive family system is much more characterized by voluntary interaction than by the necessity for economic survival that characterized the rural environment of their forefathers.

Because of the various patterns of immigration, there exists much heterogenity among the Mexican American population. Mexican American families span the continuum of acculturation and assimilation, depending on the conditions of their immigration, length of time in the United States, and their sense of relatedness to Mexico.

Since the advent of the Chicano movement, Mexican American families have increasingly become more involved in the political process. For example, Los Angeles, the home of the largest concentration of persons of Mexican origin outside of Mexico City, have shown their political strength by electing the first Mexican American state senator to the California legislature, the first Mexican American female assemblywoman, the first Mexican American city councilman in many years (California's Ed Roybal was the first), several other state assemblymen, and another member of the House of Representatives. This show of political strength is becoming more apparent throughout the nation.

Although there continues to be a disproportionate number of Mexican American families in the lower socioeconomic levels, there has been increasing social and economic mobility, as characterized by a growing number of Mexican American students in colleges and universities, an increase in Mexican Americans in professional and managerial positions, and a stronger Mexican voice in all aspects of society.

As has been true of all women in society, more Mexican American women are entering the labor force. There are greater numbers entering professions and participating more fully in various walks of life.

These factors come together to continually modify the Mexican American family by changing roles and expectations of all family members. As more opportunities emerge, social forces affect family life, and responses to an economic and political structure occur, the Mexican American family will continue to change and adapt to the forces around them. However, although the traditional Mexican American family has changed and will continue to change, there will continue to be a family form among Mexican Americans that fuses the culture of its roots and that of its American homeland.

REFERENCES

Acuna, R. 1981. *Occupied America: A History of Chicanos* (2nd ed.). New York: Harper and Row.

Baca-Zinn, M. 1983. "Ongoing Questions in the Study of Chicano Families," in A. Valdez, A. Camarillo, and T. Almaguer (eds.), *The State of Chicano Research on Family, Labor, and Migration.* Stanford, CA: Stanford Center for Chicano Research.

Bean, F. D., R. M. Cullen, E. H. Stephen, and C. G. Swicegood. 1984. "Generational Differences in Fertility among Mexican Americans: Implications for Assessing the Effects of Immigration," *Social Science Quarterly,* 65(June):573–582.

Becerra, R. M. 1983. "The Mexican American: Aging in a Changing Culture," in R. L. McNeeley and J. L. Colen (eds.), *Aging in Minority Groups.* Beverly Hills: Sage Publications, pp. 108–118.

Becerra, R. M., G. Sabagh, and D. de Anda. 1981. *Sexual Behavior among Mexican-American Adolescents.* Office of Adolescent Pregnancy, DHHS.

Estrada, L. F., F. C. Garcia, R. F. Macias, and L. Maldonado. 1981. "Chicanos in the United States: A History of Exploitation and Resistance," *Daedalus,* 110:103–131.

Fischer, N. A., and J. P. Marcum. 1984. "Ethnic Integration, Socioeconomic Status and Fertility Among Mexican Americans," *Social Science Quarterly,* 65(June):583–593.

Grebler, L., J. W. Moore, and R. C. Guzman. 1970. *The Mexican American People.* New York: Free Press.

Griswold del Castillo, R. 1984. *La Familia: Chicano Families in the Urban Southwest, 1848 to the Present.* Notre Dame: University of Notre Dame Press.

Hoffman, A. 1974. *Unwanted Mexican Americans in the Great Depression.* Tucson: University of Arizona Press.

Jaffe, A. J., R. M. Cullen, and T. D. Boswell. 1980. *The Changing Demography of Spanish Americans.* New York: Academic Press.

Madsen, W. 1973. *The Mexican-Americans of South Texas* (2nd ed.). New York: Holt, Rinehart, and Winston.

Martinez, M. A. 1985. "Towards a Model of Socialization for Hispanic Identity: The Case of Mexican Americans," in P. San Juan Cafferty and W. C. McCready (eds.), *Hispanics in the United States: A New Social Agenda.* New Brunswick, NJ: Transaction Books, pp. 63–85.

Massey, D. S. 1981. "Dimensions of the New Immigration to the United States and the Prospects for Assimilation," *Annual Review of Sociology,* 7:57–85.

———. 1982. *The Demographic and Economic Position of Hispanics in the United States: 1980.* Report to the National Commission on Employment Policy. College Park, MD: University of Maryland.

McWilliams, C. 1968. *North From Mexico.* New York: Greenwood Press.

Mirande, A. 1985. *The Chicano Experience: An Alternative Perspective.* Notre Dame: University of Notre Dame Press.

Montiel, M. 1970. "The Social Science Myth of the Mexican-American Family," *El Grito: A Journal of Contemporary Mexican-American Thought,* 3(Summer):56–63.

Muller, T., et al. 1985. *The Fourth Wave: California's Newest Immigrants.* Washington, DC: Urban Institute Press.

Murguia, E. 1982. *Chicano Intermarriage: A Theoretical and Empirical Study.* San Antonio, TX: Trinity University Press.

Murrillo, N. 1971. "The Mexican-American Family," in N. N. Wagner and M. J. Haug (eds.), *Chicanos: Social and Psychological Perspectives.* St. Louis: C. V. Mosby, pp. 97–108.

National Center on Health Statistics. 1985. *Births of Hispanic Parentage, 1982.* Washington, DC.

Pachon, H. P., and J. W. Moore. 1981. "Mexican Americans," *Annals, American Academy of Political and Social Science,* 454:111–124.

Ramirez, O. 1980. "Extended Family Support and Mental Health Status among Mexicans in Detroit," *La Red,* 28 (May).
Ramirez, O., and C. Arce. 1981. 'The Contemporary Chicano Family: An Empirically Based Review," in A. Barton, Jr. (ed.), New York: Praeger.
Reichert, J. S., and D. S. Massey. 1980. "History and Trends in U. S. Bound Migration from a Mexican Town," *International Migration Review,* 14:479–591.
Reisler, M. 1976. *By the Sweat of Their Brow: Mexican Immigrant Labor in the United States, 1900–1940.* New York: Greenwood Press.
Sanchez, P. 1974. "The Spanish Heritage Elderly," in E. P. Stanford (ed.), San Diego: Campanile Press.
Saragoza, A. M. 1983. "The Conceptualization of the History of the Chicano Family," in A. Valdez, A. Camarillo, and T. Almaguer (eds.), *The State of Chicano Research on Family, Labor, and Migration.* Stanford, CA: Stanford Center for Chicano Research.
Sullivan, T. A. 1985. "A Demographic Portrait," in P. San Juan Cafferty and W. C. McCready (eds.), *Hispanics in the United States: A New Social Agenda.* New Brunswick, NJ: Transaction Books, pp. 7–32.
U. S. Bureau of the Census. 1983. *General Social and Economic Characteristics: United States Summary.* Washington, DC: U. S. Government Printing Office, 1985.
———. 1985. "Persons of Spanish Origin in the United States: March 1985," *Current Population Reports.* Series P-20, no. 403. Washington, DC: U. S. Government Printing Office.
U. S. Bureau of Labor Statistics. 1981. *Employment and Earnings,* 28(1), Washington, DC: U. S. Government Printing Office.
Yinger, J. M. 1985. "Assimilation in the United States: The Mexican Americans," in W. Conner (ed.), *Mexican Americans in Comparative Perspective.* Washington, DC: Urban Institute Press, pp. 30–55.

CHAPTER SEVEN

The Cuban American Family

Jose Szapocznik
Roberto Hernandez

HISTORICAL BACKGROUND

Given the scope of this chapter, it would have been an almost impossible task to provide the reader with a truly comprehensive review of Cuba's historical past. The existing literature on this topic is quite extensive. Instead, our goal has been to explore some of the most salient developments of Cuban history that have helped shape the island's sociocultural, economic, and political evolution. More specifically, our intention is to explore the historical development of the Cuban national character, its influence on the Cuban family structure, and the transformation that both have undergone in American society.

It is generally recognized that the history of Cuba and the Cuban people has been markedly influenced by Spain, the United States, and, more recently, since 1959, by the Soviet Union. What is not so generally recognized is the influence that West African cultures such as the Yoruba have played in the development of the Cuban national character, attitudes, and traditional value systems. It is in the midst of the historical interplay of these foreign influences that Cuba's social, political, and economic institutions have evolved and continue to evolve.

Among these influences, Spain seems to have had the greatest impact on the shaping of the Cuban value system and institutions. In both cases, no doubt, Spain's traditional emphasis on a highly personalistic approach to the definition, distribution, and use of power and authority is evidenced at public levels of social, political, and economic interaction. However, within the family, conventional Cuban values are highly structural and hierarchical.

Cuba remained under Spanish control from 1511 to 1898, making the island one of Spain's first and last colonies in the New World. Both Puerto Rico and Cuba remained the only two colonies that Spain managed to keep in the New World after 1825, when it lost virtually all of its empire in America. The fact that Spain had only Cuba and Puerto Rico left to control after losing the vast empire proved to be both beneficial and detrimental to Cuba's historical evolution.

It was beneficial because it contributed to Cuba's economic growth. Although sugar cane had originally been introduced to Cuba during the first half of the sixteenth century, the sugar industry in Cuba did not gain importance until after 1800. This phenomenon was largely a result of two factors: first, the mechanization of sugar production during the early stages of the industrial revolution and, second, the emphasis that Spain placed on Cuba's rapid economic development following the demise of the empire in America in 1825. Cuba's sugar industry, in fact, became Spain's main source of income after all else was virtually lost in America.

Spanish control was detrimental precisely because the strategies that Spain used to develop Cuba's sugar industry had a lasting impact on the shaping of Cuba's social and political future. For one thing, Spain doubled its former control of the island's social, economic, and political institutions. Virtually every government post was filled with *peninsulares* ("individuals born in Spain") who were directly appointed by the crown. Every position from captain-general to the major decision-making posts in Havana were held by Spaniards who directly answered to Madrid. With the exception of a few enlightened or benevolent captain-generals, the rest of the Spanish governors of Cuba during the nineteenth century directed their policies to favor what were perceived as Spain's economic and political interests in Madrid. Spain's interests were, therefore, on more than one occasion, in direct opposition to the interests of a growing and cohesive *criollo* ("national") class of landowners. This class of Cuban sugar barons became the chief source of political opposition to Spain's control of the island's destiny.

During the nineteenth century, most of the leaders of the various *autonomista* and *independentista* movements against Spain came from these prominent families of sugar planters. It was during this century of economic growth, as well as political turmoil and social imbalances, that the Cuban national character was born and, with it, an almost inbred mistrust of government. These were times in which the central government in Madrid attempted or pretended to try to satisfy the demands of the Cuban planter class and a growing, native Cuban *inteligencia*. Among their most pressing demands were a free voice in Cuba's decision-making processes and, above all, in the selection of foreign markets for sugar. Spain's refusal to even compromise with the Cubans' demands generated among Cubans a lack of confidence in government and a mistrust of public officials and their intentions. In such a society, therefore, where there were few, if any, links of trust and cooperation between government and people, there could be no faith in social institutions but, in keeping with the personalistic tradition, only in individuals. This eventually served to retard the evolution of Cuba's social, political, and economic institutions toward a more open and egalitarian system, particularly after Cuba attained independence in 1898.

Historical events in the nineteenth century contributed to not only the validation of the traditional approach toward a personalistic style but also the reenforcement of the need to maintain an authoritarian tradition in the family structure. Prior to independence from Spain in 1898 and, most assuredly, throughout the pre-revolutionary era, the average Cuban's sense of national identity, security, and emotional stability were established primarily through the family system and various other patterns of inter-family relationships. The Cuban national character that was formed throughout the nineteenth century and matured into the twentieth was marked by very little trust or faith in social institutions except the carefully elaborated and maintained system of personal loyalties within the family structure. In this sense, the Cuban experience was not much different than that of Cuba's Latin American counterparts.

In addition to the Spanish contributions to the formation of the Cuban national character, West Africa had a highly significant role in the molding of Cuban values and attitudes. The labor demands created by the *ingenio azucarero* led to the massive importation of African slaves. It has been estimated that approximately one million slaves were transported to Cuba during the island's three and one-half centuries of slave trading. The vast majority, however, arrived during the last 100 years of this period to fulfill the increasing needs of the booming sugar industry. According to a census of Cuba's population conducted in 1846, the total slave population was 660,000, with an additional 220,000 free blacks and mulattoes. The white population, on the other hand, amounted to 565,000. After the decline of the slave trade following the enactment of the Emancipation Law of 1880, the demand for cheap labor was met by the importation of indentured servants from China, the arrival of a few thousand Indians from Mexico's Yucatán Peninsula, and the continued Spanish immigration, largely from economically depressed southern Spain and the Canary Islands. After the blacks, the Chinese came to constitute Cuba's most important ethnic minority in the twentieth century.

The impact of African cultures on the development of Cuban history and social institutions has been carefully studied by well-known and highly respected Cuban scholars such Lydia Cabrera (1972) and Mercedes Sandoval (1977), leading experts on Afro–Cuban culture and history.

Black African religions, folklore, and music have come to form an integral part of Cuba's national character and contemporary historical themes. Blacks have figured prominently among Cuban poets and other literary figures, patriots, musicians, and composers. Black identity and culture have been turned into cherished symbols of the Cuban cultural heritage. The Cuban female mulatto (*mulata*), for example, has become a symbol of not necessarily a primitive sensuality but an exalted archetype of Cuban female beauty. Similarly, the love and affection that black mothers display toward their children have also become a major theme in Cuban literature and a symbol of motherly love in the Cuban family structure. Cubans, for example, normally use such expressions as *mi negro* ("my black one") and *Que pasa mulato*? ("How goes it, mulatto?") to manifest comradeship and familiar affection and love. However, it is in the area of religion that Africa had the greatest impact on Cuban culture. The religious cult known as *Santeria* in pre-Castro Cuba and the United States represents a syncretism of traditional Spanish Catholic and Yoruban African religious value systems. Like the Catholic religious tradition, Santeria tends to promote and reenforce strong traditional family ties among Cubans. Members of a pantheon of virgins,[1] demigods, and saints interact as part of a large family unit, much like the way in which members of the Catholic church's "Sacred Family" interact with each other and provide role models in the traditional Christian family system. Such role models are particularly predominant in Catholic societies such as Cuba, where the mothers and wives act as benevolent intermediaries between the children and the fathers and husbands, similar to the Virgin Mary counterpart within the "Sacred Family".

Castro's Communist revolution began to dramatically change the social, political, and economic fabric of Cuban society. The Cuban family, which

---

[1] Virgins all have the same root, the Virgin Mary, with local adaptations such as Virgen de Regla of Black African heritage; Virgen de la Caridad, the Patroness of Cuba, who synthesized Cuba's ethnic composition and is depicted surrounded by a white, a black, and an Indian. The most prominent of all African demigods are Chango and Obatala, who are miracle workers by virtue of their own powers. Saints, on the other hand, perform miracles by virtue of the grace of God. One of the most popular Cuban saints (not a Roman Catholic Church ordained saint) is Saint Lazarus.

was always sensitive to environmental forces, found itself in the midst of this socioeconomic and political conflict. Family members became identified with the various political factions, and as a result, some families were cemented together by their common political beliefs, whereas others were torn apart by divergent loyalties.

The families that arrived in the United States seeking refuge from Castro's Cuba are representatives of both of these phenomena. Some families transplanted themselves to America with their entire extended family network intact, with a strong sense of achievement and success in having protected the family network. Others, on the other hand, felt wounded by the fragmentation brought about by the political schism.

The family plays a pivotal role in determining patterns of immigration to the United States. In the earliest stages, parents of children, adolescents, and young adults left the island in an effort to secure freedom for their offspring, as well as to protect the integrity of the nuclear family, which was under siege by the Marxist regime. Subsequent stages through the 1960s and 1970s were driven by family reunification efforts.

History of Cuban Immigration to the United States

Geographical proximity, as well as historical and political ties, has made Florida a logical place of refuge for Cubans seeking to escape their Communist-controlled island. As a Spanish colony during the seventeenth and eighteenth centuries, Florida was, at times, placed under the political jurisdiction of the Spanish governor-general in La Habana. Thus, political, cultural, and economic bonds were always strong between Florida and Cuba, and it seems natural that Cubans sought refuge in Florida from periodic political and economic woes for more than a century.

As early as 1870, approximately 5,000 Cuban immigrants arrived in the United States. In the 1850s, Cuban immigrant families established significant enclaves in Key West and Tampa, Florida, as laborers in the growing tobacco industry of South Florida.

In the turbulent years of 1928–1933, during the dictatorship of President Gerardo Machado, a number of Cuban professionals, politicians, and members of a growing, middle-class opposition to the Machado regime sought temporary exile in Miami and other parts of the United States. Then, during the years immediately following World War II, with the beginning of economic expansion in Florida, many Cubans invested in real estate, paving the way for an image of Cubans as a successful immigrant group.

The turning point in the history of Cuban immigration to the United

States took place on January 1, 1959, with the arrival of the Marxist-oriented revolution led by the charismatic Fidel Castro. Prior to this time, there reportedly was a small community of approximately 30,000 Cubans residing in the United States. Subsequent waves of Cuban immigration to the United States can be divided into six stages, detailed in Table 1.

By 1986, the Cuban population in the United States was estimated at approximately 1 million. As shown in Table 1, as the immigration progressed, the demographic composition of the refugee population increasingly reflected the population profile of pre-revolutionary Cuba. It is noteworthy that the third, fourth, and fifth stages were driven by the family reunification process. The most recent immigration stage, however, was comprised of a large number of single men who came without their families. It is therefore not surprising that these men have remained less integrated into American society and express a strong desire to return to Cuba (Portes and Clark, 1987). Portes and Clark interpret the desire of these men to return as the only available alternative to be reunited with their families.

THE MODERN CUBAN AMERICAN FAMILY

The traditional Cuban family had already begun its transition from extended to nuclear family prior to the massive migration that began in 1959. The nuclear family is tightly knit but allows for the inclusion of relatives and *padrinos* ("godparents") within the nuclear family structure. Cubans have a strong preference for lineal or hierarchical family relations and thus, conventionally at least, parents expect absolute obedience from their children, and husbands expect the same from their wives (Szapocznik et al., 1978).

The economic success of the Cuban American immigrant is widely recognized. What is not widely acknowledged, however, is the role that the family has played in this development. Whereas women in pre-Castro Cuba were not fully integrated into the labor market, Cuban women who arrived in the United States were, in many instances, the first to be employed and thereby became contributors to the families' economic well-being. As the wife's resource contribution to the family became greater through her employment, her power to make decisions also increased while that of the husband declined. As a result, the traditional, patriarchal family structure of Cuban Americans began to change and brought about a disruption of family functioning, particularly during the 1970s. The younger families of the 1980s are usually comprised of husband and wife teams that grew up in the United States and thus are less likely to find the greater equality in decision making among the spouses disruptive. As a

TABLE 1

Estimates of Cuban Arrivals, 1959–1980

IMMIGRATION STAGES	MANNER OF TRANSPORTATION	ESTIMATE 1	ESTIMATE 2
FIRST STAGE			
Early departures (Castro's takeover January 1, 1959–October 22, 1962)	Commercial flights from Havana	248,070[a]	153,534[b]
SECOND STAGE			
Postmissile crisis (October 22, 1962–September 28, 1965)	No direct transportation; small boats, and rafts; escapees	55,916[a]	29,962[b]
THIRD STAGE			
Freedom flights (family reunification projects September 28, 1965–April 6, 1973)	U. S. airlift	297,318[a]	268,040[b]

FOURTH STAGE			
Third country arrivals (April 6, 1973–September 1978)	Commercial flights from Spain, Mexico, and Jamaica	38,903[a] (January 1972/December 1974)	17,899[b]
FIFTH STAGE			
Ex-political prisoners, family, and other arrivals (October 1978–April 1980)	Flights from Cuba; small boats and rafts	10,000[d]	21,839[b]
SIXTH STAGE			
Mariel boatlift (April 22, 1980–September 27, 1980)	Boatlift to Key West from Mariel Harbor	124,789[c]	124,789[c]
TOTALS		774,996	616,063

SOURCE: McCoy, C. B. and D. H. Gonzalez. 1985. "Cuban Immigration and Mariel Immigrants." In J. Szapocznik, R. Cohen, and R. E. Hernandez (eds.), *Coping With Adolescent Refugees*. New York: Praeger, p. 25.

[a] Juan Clark, 1975

[b] Cuban Refugee Program Registration

[c] Office of Refugee Resettlement Records Cuban–Haitian Task Force

[d] Guillermo Martinez, the *Miami Herald*, 1981

result, young Cuban American families are less male-dominated today, and the roles of husbands and wives are less segregated than in the traditional Latin American family that typified Cuba before 1959 (Boswell and Curtis, 1983).

Biculturalism and Bilingualism

With ethnic minorities and immigrant groups, much debate has centered around such topics as acculturation, assimilation, and adjustment. Typically, acculturation has been a one-dimensional process that usually is restricted to an accommodation of the host culture on the part of a migrant group (Szapocznik et al., 1978). The Cuban experience, however, has not conformed to this pattern. Cuban Americans have learned, adapted, and adjusted to the host, or mainstream, culture. They have also, however, had a deep impact on the surrounding community. Cubans have undergone a process of biculturation. This three-dimensional biculturation process consists of, first, the usual linear process of accommodating the host culture (i.e., acculturation), a second dimension in which the characteristics of the original Cuban culture are retained or relinquished, and a third dimension by which both Cuban and American characteristics are syncretized.

According to the Bicultural Involvement Model of Szapocznik and his colleagues (Szapocznik and Kurtines, 1979; Szapocznik, Kurtines, and Fernandez, 1980; Szapocznik et al., 1984), individuals in bicultural contexts tend to become biculturated. In biculturation, the individual and the family develop the flexibility to successfully interact with the surrounding host culture (which, in this case, is mainstream America) and simultaneously retain the skills and abilities to successfully interact within the culture of origin (in this case Cuban American). Families themselves become a social laboratory within which biculturation is learned. This occurs because Cuban adolescents tend to become Americanized while their Cuban parents tend to adhere more closely to their Cuban roots. From the conflict that ensues from these differences in acculturation, each generation is forced to learn to come to terms with the other generation's cultural preference. In the process, parents learn how to remain loyal to their ethnic background while becoming skilled in interacting with their youngsters' Americanized values and behaviors, and vice versa.

How Did Miami Become a Bicultural Community?

Historically, Cubans arrived in the United States at a most propitious time for minorities. The long struggle for civil rights carried out in American society under the leadership of Dr. Martin Luther King, Jr., paved the way for a more egalitarian recognition of ethnic minorities such as the Cuban American. Under these circumstances and with the advantages of the social, economic, and political know-how of the first waves of immigrants, Cubans were able to make a significant inroad into the greater Miami economy and, later, into communities in New Jersey, such as West New York and Elizabeth. These original inroads were expanded, particularly in greater Miami, to embrace key aspects of the area's social, cultural, and political arenas. This is important because these accomplishments have contributed to increase the leverage for bicultural negotiation at all levels: individual, family, and community.

As so often has happened in history, out of the need for cultural "trading partners," Cubans sought their fellow Latin Americans from throughout the hemisphere. These trading partners share a common language and cultural heritage. What initially began as a short-term experiment while awaiting the liberation of Cuba developed into a major economic bonanza for not only the Cubans but also all of greater Miami. As a result, Miami became an economic and a cultural magnet for Latin Americans. These links with Latin America, both cultural and economic, are precisely what accounts for the continuously increasing strength of Hispanic culture in greater Miami and a strength that bolstered Hispanic culture to the level of a co-culture in greater Miami, thereby fostering the establishment of true bicultural environment.

CHANGE AND ADAPTATION

There have been benefits and great enrichment in the restructuring process that made possible the establishment of a bicultural community. However, to achieve these gains, several obstacles had to be overcome. The family was at the center of these conflicts.

This process of adaptation and adjustment resulted in the disruption of the traditional, closely knit family. This, in turn, led to various psychological disorders in family members including such behavioral problems as drug abuse among youths and heightened rates of depression in the parents (Szapocznik et al., 1978; Szapocznik, 1977). As youngsters became Americanized more quickly than their parents, intergenerational acculturational differences developed that precipitated or exacerbated family intergenerational conflict (Szapocznik and Truss, 1978). Figure 1 illustrates the process of the development of these intrafamily differences.

In these cases, the typical patterns of interaction in these families became disorganized. The parents became alienated from their highly Americanized children. The children, in turn, experienced alienation from their

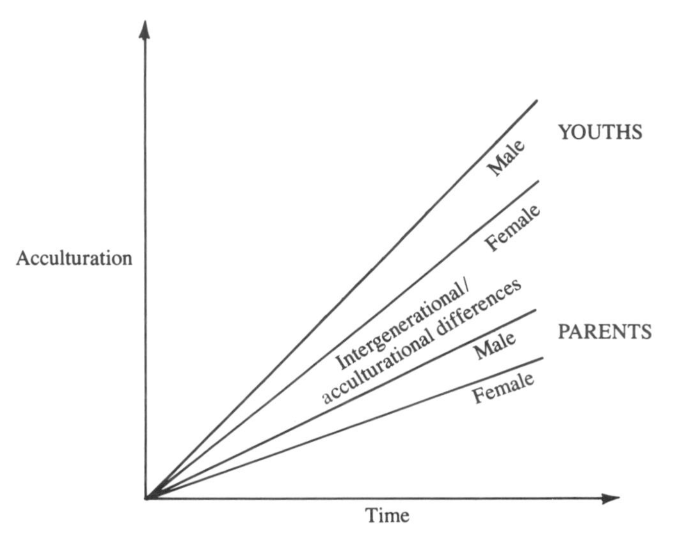

FIGURE 1 The Development of Intergenerational/Acculturational Differences in Nuclear Families as a Function of Time. Reproduced from J. Szapocznik, M. A. Scopetta, W. Kurtines, and M. A. Aranalde. 1978. "Theory and Measurement of Acculturation," *Interamerican Journal of Psychology*, 12:113–130.

less acculturated parents. In an effort to cope with these differences, stifling patterns of over involvement arose, impeding the natural process of family development and individual growth. The parents attempted to restrict the process of acculturation in their children and, instead, succeeded in further alienating the children from family interactions and values of the Cuban culture. As a consequence of this struggle, the parents' authority was invalidated.

Whether in the family or larger society, individuals living in bicultural environments, such as the families described above, develop psychological/psychosocial problems when they remain or become monocultural. Individuals who live in a bicultural context (such as an Americanized youth or parent who strongly adheres to his or her Cuban culture) must learn to interact successfully with both cultures. Those who "underacculturate" (fail to learn how to or do not want to interact with the American context) or "overacculturate" (reject the skills necessary to interact with the Cuban culture) do not have the flexibility necessary to cope with their entire cultural milieu. This type of imbalance is dysfunctional, within both the family and the community.

In families whose members are characterized by cultural differences, the typical intergenerational differences found within families of adolescents are exacerbated by these cultural differences. Such differences are most severe when they are additive. This additive effect is the case of a typical

Cuban American family with an adolescent in the area of greater Miami. In this case, the adolescent's normal striving for independence combines with the adolescent's powerful acculturation to the American cultural value of individualism. The parents' normal tendency to preserve family integrity, on the other hand, combines with the parents' tenacious adherance to the Hispanic cultural values of strong family cohesion and parental control. The combination of the intergenerational and cultural differences add together to produce an exacerbated intergenerational/cultural gap within the family that results in an intensified family conflict. As Figure 2 below illustrates, the normal intergenerational conflict within families (family integrity vs. independence), intrinsically gives rise to value differences that tend to promote conflict. When these intergenerational differences are added to differences in cultural value orientation (parental family control vs. individualism), the intergenerational/cultural gap widens and the potential for serious conflict increases considerably.

Szapocznik and Kurtines (1979) and Szapocznik, Kurtines, and Fernandez (1980) argue that to avoid the detrimental effects of adaptation to a new culture, individuals living in bicultural communities—or families, for that matter—must become bicultural themselves. The process of becoming bicultural involves learning communication and negotiation skills in two different cultural contexts, each with a separate set of rules.

FIGURE 2 The Additive Effects of Integenerational and Acculturational Differences in Cuban American Families. Reproduced from J. Szapocznik et al. 1984. "Bicultural Effectiveness Traïning: A Treatment Intervention for Enhancing Intercultural Adjustment," *Hispanic Journal of Behavioral Sciences*, 6(4) (December): 328.

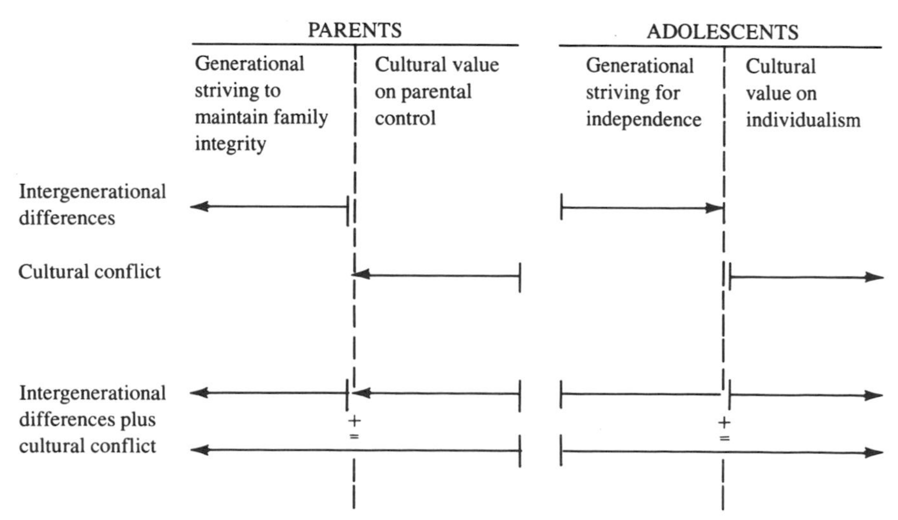

At present, it seems as though recent changes in the social, cultural, and political environments will have a beneficial impact on the future adjustment of the Cuban American family. Both social institutions and the general culture have become more supportive of traditional family values, as well as of Cuban ethnic identity.

Hence, youngsters are growing into a milieu that is less hostile and more accommodating to the Cuban American family. For these reasons, we venture to predict that the cultural/generational gap that has plagued the Cuban family during the last 25 years is less likely to be a source of conflict during the coming decade.

REFERENCES

Boswell, T. D., and J. R. Curtis. 1983. *The Cuban-American Experience, Culture, Images, and Perspectives.* Totowa, NJ: Rowman and Allanheld.

Cabrera, L. 1972. *Cuentos Negroes de Cuba.* Madrid, Spain: Ramos Art Graf.

McCoy, C. B., and D. H. Gonzalez. 1985. "Cuban Immigration and Mariel Immigrants," in J. Szapocznik, R. C. Cohen, and R. Hernandez (eds.), *Coping With Adolescent Refugees.* New York: Praeger.

Portes, A., and J. M. Clark. 1987. *Mariel Refugees: Six Years After.* Technical Report. Baltimore: Johns Hopkins University.

Sandoval, M. 1977. "Santeria: Afrocuban Concepts of Disease and its Treatment," *Journal of Operational Psychiatry,* 8(2):52–65.

Szapocznik, J. 1977. *Role Conflict Resolution in Cuban Mothers.* Technical Report. Miami, FL: University of Miami Spanish Family Guidance Center.

Szapocznik, J., and W. Kurtines. 1979. "Acculturation, Biculturalism and Adjustment Among Cuban Americans," in A. Padilla (ed.), *Psychological Dimensions on the Acculturation Process: Theory, Models, and Some New Findings.* Boulder, CO: Westview.

Szapocznik, J., W. Kurtines, and T. Fernandez. 1980. "Bicultural Involvement and Adjustment in Hispanic American Youths," *International Journal of Intercultural Relations,* 4:353–366.

Szapocznik, J., D. Santisteban, W. M. Kurtines, A. Perez-Vidal, and O. Hervis. 1984. "Bicultural Effectiveness Training: A Treatment Intervention for Enhancing Intercultural Adjustment," *Hispanic Journal of Behavioral Sciences,* 6(4) (December):317–344.

Szapocznik, J., M. A. Scopetta, M. A. Aranalde, and W. Kurtines. 1978. "Cuban Value Structure: Clinical Implications," *Journal of Consulting and Clinical Psychology,* 46(5):961–970.

Szapocznik, J., M. A. Scopetta, W. Kurtines, and M. A. Aranalde. 1978. "Theory and Measurement of Acculturation," *Interamerican Journal of Psychology,* 12:113–130.

Szapocznik, J., and C. Truss. 1978. "Intergenerational Sources of Role Conflict in Cuban Mothers," in M. Montiel (ed.), *Hispanic Families.* Washington, DC: COSSHMO.

CHAPTER EIGHT

The Puerto Rican American Family

Melba Sánchez-Ayéndez

HISTORICAL BACKGROUND

Puerto Rican culture has traditionally been understood as developing from the interaction between the Spanish conquerors, Taíno Indians, and black African slaves, with the Hispanic colonial traits predominating. The crystallization of this national culture is assumed to have occurred during the nineteenth century. The United States' domination of this Caribbean island from 1898 to the present has also left its mark on contemporary Puerto Rican social, political, and economic institutions.

In 1898, as a result of the Spanish-American War treaty, Puerto Rico became a possession of the United States. This brought radical changes to the social and economic structure of the island. Through the Foraker Act of 1900, Puerto Rico became integrated into the economic system of the United States by the establishment of free trade between the two nations, the inclusion of Puerto Rican production under the United States tariff system and cabotage laws, and the inclusion of the island in the country's monetary system. Under the Jones Act of 1917, Puerto Ricans were granted United States citizenship.

The first four decades of domination by the United States were characterized by an emphasis on agricultural production of export crops, especially sugar cane. Coffee production, although growing in value in the world market, suffered a decrease because it was excluded from the United States market, which favored sugar exports. This, in conjunction with tight credit restrictions, weakened the position of small- and medium-sized coffee plantation owners, many of whom were forced to sell their lands (History Task Force, 1979). It also led to an expansion and concentration of land controlled by absentee United States corporations. The development of monopoly capital in the sugar industry brought about the collapse of existing pre-capitalist relations of production and the formation of a rural proletariat (History Task Force, 1979). Furthermore, it led to an exodus of the unemployed labor force from the mountainous inland areas (where coffee production was concentrated) to coastal sugar-cane fields and urban tobacco factories.

From 1928 and 1940, the Puerto Rican economy suffered the devastating effects of the world depression. The negative consequences of an export economy based on a few products were felt as the world market rapidly contracted and prices dropped during the recession years. After 1935, sugar production declined, and the manufacturing sector began to contract.

From 1899 to 1940, the population of the island doubled from a total of 953,243 inhabitants to 1,869,255. At the beginning of the 1940s, a majority of the population still lived in rural areas. Almost 45 percent of the labor force was employed in the agricultural sector; more than 50 percent of agricultural workers were involved in sugar cultivation (History Task Force, 1979). During this time, manufacturing absorbed 20 percent of the work force. Male employment in this sector was concentrated in the food industry; female employment was concentrated in the tobacco industry, needlework, and related tasks performed in the house. Women outnumbered men as factory laborers in both rural and urban areas. Between 1941 and 1942, unemployment increased from 99,100 to 237,000 individuals (History Task Force, 1979).

As a solution to the serious economic crisis, the government implemented a program of industrialization in the early 1940s and throughout the 1960s that was to transform the economy of the island from agrarian to industrial. The majority of the new firms were branch plants of United States companies that exported their finished products to the mainland. During this period, manufacturing, construction, and commerce comprised a rising share of the gross national product. Nonetheless, the number of employed workers during the years from 1945 to 1960 remained almost unaltered (History Task Force, 1979). Agriculture was not rehabilitated during this period, and its growth, compared with other economic sectors, was minimal. The mechanization of agriculture brought a substantial decrease in the proportion of the work force employed in farming.

Since 1968, the pattern of industrialization on the island changed. The manufacturing sector shifted toward petrochemical, chemical, and pharmaceutical industries, relying more heavily on capital investment than labor. The smaller number of available jobs required specialized skills. Manufacturing has remained the most important productive sector, while agriculture has dramatically declined. Today, the government is the largest employer on Puerto Rico, followed by the commercial and manufacturing sectors.

The Puerto Rican Migration

The immigration of a large sector of the Puerto Rican working class to the United States must be viewed within a historical context and linked to the political-economic relationship between the two countries. These relations served to facilitate the migration of Puerto Ricans, because, as United States citizens, they were able to travel to the mainland without the restrictions imposed on other immigrant groups.

In 1920, approximately 12,000 Puerto Ricans were reported to be living in the United States, dispersed throughout the 48 states (History Task Force, 1979). During the depression years, the migration declined, and between 1930 and 1934, approximately 20 percent of the Puerto Rican population in the United States returned to the island (Vázquez Calzada, 1979). By 1944, the number of those who had left the island increased to 90,000 (López, 1974).

After World War II, in the early years of the industrialization period, there was a massive immigration of Puerto Ricans to the United States. A series of factors, including rapid population growth on the 3,435 square-mile island, high rates of unemployment, the prospect of higher wages, and the demand of United States corporate interests for cheap labor in the services, agriculture, and garment industry sectors, accounted for the large numbers of immigrants to the mainland.

Efforts were made by the insular and mainland governments to cooperate in the migration of workers to the United States. For the Puerto Rican government, the migration was a way of dealing with a "surplus" unemployed population, particularly rural farm workers; whereas, for the United States, the migration was a source of cheap, unskilled labor (Leavitt, 1974; López, 1974). Reduced air fares, seasonal farm worker contracts between Puerto Rican government agencies and United States corporations, and a propaganda campaign about prospective jobs and higher wages resulted.[1]

---

[1]Even Mayor Wagner of New York went to Puerto Rico to inform the people of the availability of jobs in the city (*New York Times*, 1954).

Immigration data show that during the 1940s, an average of 18,700 Puerto Ricans immigrated to the United States annually (López, 1974). During the 1950s, the average number of immigrants increased to 41,200 annually, and decreased during the 1960s to approximately 14,500 annually. The 1950s were the years of the massive migration; migration during the 1960s was of an erratic nature (Vázquez Calzada, 1978). At the beginning of the 1960s, approximately 900,000 Puerto Ricans were living in the United States (López, 1974). In 1970, the number increased to 1,429,396 (U. S. Bureau of the Census, 1980), despite the fact that during the second half of the 1960s and throughout the 1970s more than a quarter million Puerto Ricans returned to the island (Vázquez Calzada, 1978). The 1980 census counted a total of 2,013,945 Puerto Ricans living throughout the United States (U. S. Bureau of the Census, 1980).

Prior to World War II—the period of corporate agriculture in Puerto Rico—the migrants tended to be skilled and semi-skilled urban workers (Leavitt, 1974). A great majority of those who migrated after World War II were unskilled rural farm workers who were unable to become incorporated into the labor force during the industrialization period. Abroad, some became employed in unskilled farm labor, and a majority in semi-skilled blue-collar and service work (Sandis, 1975; U. S. Department of Labor, 1974). For most of those who left the island, migration meant occupational downward mobility despite an increase in earnings (Friedlander, 1965; Sandis, 1975).

The migration was selective in terms of age—70 percent of those who left were between 15 and 39 years of age—but not in terms of sex (Vázquez Calzada, 1979). The migrants established themselves in urban areas of the United States, particularly in New York, where 95 percent of those who left the island during the 1950s settled (History Task Force, 1979).

An important dynamic of the Puerto Rican migration is the constant ebb and flow of the migrant population between their country of origin and the United States, which is a direct consequence of the political relationship between the two countries. Another trend is return migration. During the second half of the 1960s and throughout the 1970s, more than a quarter million Puerto Ricans returned to the island. The majority of returning migrants in the 1970s were in the age groups 12–28 and 55 and over (Vázquez Calzada, 1983).

Cultural Description of the Group

THE FAMILY. In speaking of the traditional Puerto Rican family, one must realize that cultural traits are subject to variation by socioeconomic status, area of residence, and even racial or age group. Furthermore, the notion of a traditional family is mostly an idealized version, although one that allows for a starting point from which to make comparisons.

Traditionally and prior to the 1960s, the Puerto Rican family was described as an extended family. Today, a modified extended family predominates on the island—particularly in the urban centers—with the primary responsibility for childrearing vested in the nuclear family (Mintz, 1966; Safa, 1974; Seda Bonilla, 1958; Steward, 1956). Although husbands have been the traditional source of family authority, most of the decisions concerning childrearing are made by the mothers (Bryce-Laporte, 1970; Landy, 1959; Safa, 1974; Seda Bonilla, 1972; Steward, 1956).

FAMILY INTERDEPENDENCE. Kinship bonds among Puerto Ricans are strong, and interaction among kin is frequent. The kinship group is a source of strength and support, especially for rural and working-class families (Buitrago,1973; Bryce-Laporte, 1970; Lewis, 1963; Mizio, 1974; Safa, 1964, 1974). The family plays the primary supportive role in the lives of its members and is characterized by strong norms of reciprocity. These norms emphasize interdependence among the various family members, particularly those in the immediate kinship group. The interdependence framework conceptualizes individuals as unable to do everything or do everything well and, therefore, in need of others for assistance (Bastida, 1979:70–71). Within this value orientation, individualism and self-reliance assume different meanings than those prevailing in the United States. Puerto Rican grandparents have often helped and continue to help in childrearing. Adult children are expected to provide support for their parents in later years, and institutionalization of the elderly is not widely accepted (Rivera Medina, 1978).

Components of the extended kinship system are the ritual form of *compadrazgo* (co-parenthood) and the practice of *hijos de crianza* (informal adoption of children).

FICTIVE KIN. Among Puerto Ricans, godparents are selected for different occasions but most frequently for the baptism of children (Fitzpatrick, 1971:81–82; Mizio, 1974;77). *Compadrazgo* has different social meanings. It is a form of affirming deep friendship and establishing social and economic rights and duties in symmetrical and asymmetrical relations. The important thing, though, is that the co-parent is expected to participate in the responsibilities of the extended-kin network.

The cultural practice of informal adoption of children is more common during family crises such as economic hardship and death of parents. *Hijos de crianza* are treated by their adoptive parents as though they were their own (Mizio, 1974:77; Padilla, 1958:131; Sánchez-Ayéndez, 1984:157–159). The status of *hijos de crianza* within the household is like that of the other children of their parents. Even when no legal adoption is involved, *hijos de crianza* know that the family and home of the adoptive parents is their own. The adoptive parents (*padres de crianza*) can be but are not necessarily related to real parents by kinship or friendship ties.

MALE AND FEMALE ROLES. From early childhood, individuals are socialized to a double standard about gender and an interaction pattern of male dominance (Buitrago, 1973; Landy, 1959; Nieves Falcón, 1972; Safa, 1974). The prevailing conceptualization of women derives from the notion of *marianismo* (Stevens, 1973). *Marianismo* uses the Virgin Mary as a role model. Therefore, motherhood is perceived as a woman's primary role despite her other roles. It is through motherhood that a woman realizes herself and achieves her greatest satisfactions in life. Patience and forbearance are qualities inherent in *marianismo*. The woman's world revolves around the household and her children, even when she works outside the home. This has led to a perception of women as having a central role in the household, whereas men are seen as having a marginal role (Leavitt, 1974). Women are "of the home" (*de la casa*), whereas men belong "to the street" (*de la calle*) and are considered the primary providers.

Men are conceptualized as having authority over women. Often, the concept of maleness in the Puerto Rican culture has been defined exclusively as *machismo* and, thus, associated with the need to prove virility by the conquest of women, sexual aggressiveness, dominance over women, and a belligerent attitude when confronted by male peers. The concept of maleness, however, involves more than *machismo* (Seda Bonilla, 1958; Wells, 1972). It also refers to being the primary provider and protector of the family. In addition, it involves the notion of *respeto* ("respect"): a man must be brave if necessary but also respectful of others.

INTERPERSONAL RELATIONS. For Puerto Ricans, the basis for all relationships is *respeto*, which involves a recognition of the inherent value of the human being (*dignidad*), not merely his or her accomplishments (Lauria, 1964; Leavitt, 1974:46,67; Sánchez-Ayéndez, 1984:188–190). Lauria (1964) stresses that *respeto* refers to the notion of "generalized deference" in all social interactions, as well as to a variety of deferential acts or rituals relevant to particular kinds of social relations. Even in asymmetrical power relations, those in an inferior position expect a certain ceremonial deference from their superiors. Furthermore, kin relationships, or those characterized by familiarity (*confianza*), do not preclude formality in the form of specific rituals of deference.

Puerto Rican cultural tradition emphasizes personal relations. Face-to-face relationships are considered important. These relationships are dependent on the value of *personalismo*: the notion that what is important is the singularity of each human being. It is believed that this quality can be observed only in a direct interaction, whether it is a political, economic, or social relation. Puerto Ricans traditionally have preferred to deal with others in terms of a network of personal relationships and do not have the same trust in formal organizations.

Despite Puerto Ricans' preference for associating with others and their belief in establishing warm interpersonal relationships, as a group they stress individuality more than collectivity and are careful in establishing personal relations with individuals outside their kinship group.

Some social scientists (Mintz, 1966:394–395; Wells, 1972:35) stress that the reason for this cautiousness is fear of being used by others. Alternatively, the development of cautiousness may be the result of the familial support network. Because most individual needs are met inside the family, there has been little necessity to establish numerous interpersonal relations with persons other than kin. Nonetheless, this does not imply that cooperativeness is unvalued or performed unwillingly under certain circumstances. Furthermore, once familiarity develops with those other than kin, obligations and patterns of support similar to those existing in the modified extended family become the norm (Sánchez-Ayéndez, 1984:163–166).

LANGUAGE AND RELIGION. The language spoken in Puerto Rico is Spanish, with a few borrowings from the Taíno and African groups. Knowledge of English is more common among the upper and professional classes and in the San Juan metropolitan area. Return migrants who have spent most of their formative years in the United States and the mainland-born and raised children of Puerto Rican migrants also speak English more frequently. Yet, Spanish has great resiliency among most people.

For Puerto Ricans, the Spanish language is their major source of ethnic identity. The roots for this identification stem from the particular political relationship between the United States and Puerto Rico. Puerto Rico is neither a federal state nor independent. For political purposes, this territorial possession has been called a commonwealth. Steward (1956) has stressed that the Spanish language became a source of identity for Puerto Ricans only when the United States imposed English as the official language in the educational system, a practice that was discontinued some decades ago.

Although Puerto Rico is a predominantly Catholic society, its Catholicism is unorthodox. It is mixed with personalistic saint worship and spiritualism. Different religious ideologies of the supernatural overlap and interact, yet this is not perceived as contradictory but as helpful in a better understanding of supernatural forces. Spiritualism attracts many Puerto Ricans who feel that it does not conflict with more orthodox religious practices. It is a set of beliefs found throughout different socioeconomic strata (Saaverdra de Roca, 1970). Protestantism, however, is more prevalent among the middle class than the upper and lower classes. Some revivalist sects (Baptists, Pentecostals, and Jehovah's Witnesses) have been attracting a significant number of people in the lower socioeconomic strata, especially during the last 15 years.

The Ethnic Community and Its Experience During the Early Period of Residence in the United States

The Puerto Rican migrants who came to the United States during the two decades after World War II, when the island began to industralize and agriculture declined, were mostly unemployed, rural farm workers. They had much to gain from the opportunities for unskilled laborers on the mainland that followed the war period. This was not a middle-class migration: their level of education was not high,[2] and their job skills were limited. Given these characteristics, the Puerto Rican migrants were faced by limited job prospects and dealt with problems of underemployment, unemployment, low income, and substandard housing. A majority had never lived in cities or large towns. Because most migrated to New York City, another source of stress derived from becoming accustomed to life in the impersonal metropolis.

Another difficulty faced by Puerto Rican immigrants was racial discrimination. A conceptualization of this ethnic group as non-white has permeated their status as a minority group in the United States. It stems from the wide array of variations in color among Puerto Ricans, which are the result of intermarriage among Spaniards, Taíno Indians, and black Africans. Although racial discrimination prevails in Puerto Rico, those in the lower and middle social stratas are accustomed to variations in color among family members (Betances, 1972; Seda Bonilla, 1966). Intermarriage on the island is scarce among the upper classes, which still adhere to a color criteria to socially classify individuals.

The racial classification of people in the United States is two-sided: white

---

[2]Nonetheless, as a group they exhibited higher levels of education than those who stayed on the island (Vázquez Calzada, 1979).

or non-white, regardless of appearance. For Puerto Ricans, physical appearance is the basis for racial classification, and they recognize, broadly, three categories—white, black, and intermediate (Leavitt, 1974; Seda Bonilla, 1966). Most non-white, mulatto Puerto Ricans place themselves in the intermediate category, which conveys a higher criteria of social stratification than black. However, in the United States, all Puerto Ricans are ascribed a mixed racial ancestry that automatically places them within the lower stratification criteria. The historical experience of the Puerto Ricans in the United States has been that of an ethnic collectivity and a racial minority. Although faced with the additional stigma of speaking Spanish, the discrimination to which they have been subjected involves not only the notion that they belong to a different cultural tradition from that generally conceived of as North American but also racial bias.

What must be kept in mind when trying to understand the process of the adaptation of Puerto Rican immigrants is that, although willing to migrate to improve their living conditions, they have been a group whose migration was actively enforced by both the Puerto Rican government and United States industries. Furthermore, this was a migration of United States citizens. However, once they arrived in the mainland United States, they were perceived as foreigners and non-whites and faced discrimination in such areas as housing and jobs. Likewise, their children faced educational problems that were complicated by language difficulties.

THE MODERN PUERTO RICAN FAMILY

Demographic Description

According to the 1980 census, the 2,013,945 Puerto Ricans living in the United States account for 14 percent of the total Hispanic population (U. S. Bureau of the Census, 1982). Puerto Ricans are the largest Hispanic group in the northeastern part of the country; 74 percent of the total population of Puerto Ricans live in the Northeast.

There have been changes in the geographical distribution of the Puerto Rican population during the last two decades. They have shifted from New York—the state with the largest concentration, and where 95 percent of those who left the island during the 1950s settled—to other industrial centers in the northeastern and north central areas of the United States (U. S. Bureau of the Census, 1982). The 1980 census reported almost 1 million Puerto Rican living in New York. The next largest concentrations were found in New Jersey (244,000) and Illinois (129,000). California, Connecticut, Florida, Massachusetts, and Pennsylvania follow with more than 75,000 Puerto Ricans in each. The Puerto Rican population is concentrated in metropolitan areas, predominantly in the inner-city areas.

New York City, Newark, Hartford, Chicago, Boston, Philadelphia, and Miami are some of the cities in which large nuclei of the Puerto Rican population are located (U. S. Bureau of the Census, 1981).

The Puerto Rican population in the United States, according to the 1980 census, is a relatively young group with a median age of 22.3 years (U. S. Bureau of the Census, 1980). It represents a much younger population than its Cuban counterpart (37.7 years of age) and a slightly older one than Mexican Americans (21.9 years of age). Thirty-four percent of the Puerto Rican population is under 15 years of age, and only 3.4 percent are 65 years of age and older. The percentage of Puerto Ricans 65 years old and over on the island is 8 percent (Carnivali and Vázquez Calzada, 1985), a fact that stresses the young age composition of this ethnic group in the United States, and one that is interlinked with job availability for a young age group and the ability to return to the homeland.

ECONOMIC CHARACTERISTICS. During 1979, the annual median family income for Puerto Ricans in the United States was $9,855, reflecting lower median incomes than Mexican Americans and Cubans, who earned $15,171 and $17,538, respectively (U. S. Bureau of the Census, 1981). The annual median income for all families in the United States during that year was $19,661. Puerto Ricans as a group are more seriously affected by low income levels than the other two large Hispanic groups and the United States population as a whole. Fifty-one percent of all Puerto Rican families on the mainland during 1979 had annual incomes of less than $10,000.

Almost one-third (30 percent) of the employed Puerto Ricans 16 years old and over in 1980 were working as operatives, including transportation jobs (U. S. Bureau of the Census, 1981). Clerical and service workers accounted for the other two major occupations (19 percent each), followed by craft workers (10 percent). The underrepresentation of this ethnic group in professional and white-collar occupations and the large number of Puerto Rican blue-collar and service workers demonstrate the group's disadvantaged position within the occupational structure of the United States. This could be the result of lack of education and occupational training but could also be the result of practices stemming from ethnic discrimination.

FERTILITY AND MARRIAGE. Evidence concerning fertility shows that the birth rate for the Puerto Rican population in the United States is 20.3 children for every 1,000 women, compared with 14.2 for Anglo Americans and 22.9 for black Americans (U. S. Bureau of the Census, 1980). Puerto Ricans occupy an intermediate position in terms of birth rates, between their Mexican American and Cuban counterparts, who exhibit rates of 26.6 and 9.6, respectively.

The average size of the Puerto Rican family is 3.73 persons. Almost three-fourths (71 percent) of all Puerto Rican families in the United States have children who are under 18 years of age, a percentage similar to Mexican Americans (70 percent) but very different from Cubans (17 percent). Thirty-seven percent of Puerto Rican families have children who are under six years of age.

Patterns of marital status show that 46 percent of married Puerto Ricans among persons 15 years of age and older have a spouse present (U. S. Bureau of the Census, 1980), which is lower than that for Mexican Americans (56 percent) and Cubans (58 percent). More Puerto Ricans (8 percent) than their other two Hispanic counterparts are separated from their spouse. At the same time, the lowest proportion of widowed persons (4 percent) occurs among the Puerto Ricans. When marital status is analyzed by sex for those 15 years of age and older, as shown in Table 1, more Puerto Rican women (9 percent) than men (5.1 percent) are divorced; 4.9 percent of men and 11 percent of women are separated from their spouse.

Of the three largest Hispanic groups in the United States, Puerto Ricans

TABLE 1

Persons of Hispanic Origin in the United States, by Marital Status: 1980

MARITAL STATUS	PUERTO RICANS (%)	MEXICANS (%)	CUBANS (%)
PERSONS 15 YEARS OF AGE AND OVER			
Single	35.2	1.5	25.1
Married	45.8	55.8	58.1
Separated	8.1	3.1	2.7
Widowed	3.8	4.2	6.7
Divorced	7.1	5.4	7.4
MALES 15 YEARS OF AGE AND OVER			
Single	39.8	35.6	28.3
Married	48.8	56.1	62.2
Separated	4.9	2.3	2.3
Widowed	1.4	1.6	2.0
Divorced	5.1	4.4	5.2
FEMALES 15 YEARS OF AGE AND OVER			
Single	31.1	27.3	22.3
Married	43.0	55.6	54.5
Separated	11.0	3.8	3.0
Widowed	5.9	6.8	10.9
Divorced	9.0	6.5	9.3

SOURCE: U. S. Bureau of the Census. 1980. "Census of Population: 1980," *General Population Characteristics*. PC80-1-131, table 98.

have the largest number of separated persons. This high distribution among females has a bearing on the high percentage of Puerto Rican women under 18 years of age who are heads of household and do not live with their husbands (42.6 percent). For their Cuban and Mexican counterparts, the distribution—15.3 percent and 15.8 percent, respectively—is much lower (León-López, 1985).

Puerto Rican women tend to be less educated, have less income, and have more children out of wedlock than Mexican American and Cuban women (Lowe, 1984). They also exhibit higher rates of marital separation and of being heads of household. The average number of completed years of schooling for Puerto Rican women is 9.3, compared with 10.4 for Mexican Americans, 12.1 for Cubans, and 12.7 for Anglo Americans. Puerto Rican women have a higher percentage of children born out of wedlock (46.3 percent) than the other two Hispanic groups (20.3 percent for Mexican Americans and 10.1 percent for Cubans). Thirty five percent of all Puerto Rican families have a woman as head of the household. In 81 percent of female-headed households, there are children under 18 years of age. The proportion of female-headed households with children under six years of age is 40 percent. All this points to the perpetuation of poverty among this ethnic group as a whole, despite the fact that a small percentage are moving upward in the job structure and that an increasing number of the Puerto Rican migrants since the late 1970s have become professionals in such fields as engineering, medicine, and law.

INTERMARRIAGE. According to Fitzpatrick (1976), from 1949 to 1969 there has been a significant increase in the rate of out-group marriage among second-generation Puerto Ricans in New York. Data on other geographic areas where Puerto Ricans have concentrated since the early 1970s are nonexistent. The Fitzpatrick study stresses that the increase in the rate of out-group marriage among Puerto Ricans between 1949 and 1959 is similar to that of all immigrants in New York City in the years from 1908 to 1912. It concludes that if intermarriage is accepted as an index of assimilation, Puerto Ricans are moving as rapidly toward assimilation as all immigrant groups during the years 1908 to 1912. The lack of available data on Puerto Ricans outside New York City precludes arriving at the same generalization for the population as a whole.

Family Structure

The diversity of household composition among Puerto Ricans is interlinked with variations in ecological setting and the need to cope in different economic and social circumstances. For an overall description, using a modification of Fitzpatrick's typology (1971), four types of familial household structures can be identified among this ethnic group.

1. *Modified extended family.* This group includes families with frequent interaction and strong interdependence patterns among two and three generations and other kin members—natural or ritual—outside the direct line of descent. Grandparents, children, and grandchildren may dwell under the same roof or have separate but relatively nearby households. Frequent visiting (at least once a week) or telephoning are the norm. The familial supportive system is rapidly mobilized during emergencies and crises.
2. *The nuclear family.* This group includes families comprised of the conjugal unit of father, mother, and children, with weak bonds to the modified extended family. Generally, they do not have close relatives living nearby.
3. *Father, mother, their children, and children of another union or unions of husband or wife.*
4. *Single-parent families.* Statistical evidence shows that such groups are more common among low-income females. Safa (1974:39–41) has stressed that female-headed households in urban Puerto Rico tend to occur in middle or late adulthood, when nuclear family structures have been ruptured by the death of the husband, divorce, separation, or desertion. Young, female heads of household are more common among the mainland Puerto Rican population (Lowe, 1984).

The primary problem with describing households according to structural typologies is that patterns of interaction are overlooked, and consequently, important features of familial lifestyles go unnoticed. For instance, to classify a household as a single-parent family is to overlook that this type of arrangement can very well be part of the modified extended-family pattern. Yet, it is important to acknowledge variations in family structure that can lead to variations in adaptation to social and economic circumstances despite culturally shared meanings and styles.

Most of the existing literature on Puerto Rican families in the United States focuses on New York City immigrants. Little is known about variations among Puerto Ricans regarding such variables as gender, generation, age, income, education, age at arrival, length of residence in the United States, and ethnic composition of the neighborhood. No comparable data exist for Puerto Rican communities in such major urban centers as Chicago and New York City nor those in much smaller urban centers such as Hartford, Connecticut, and Holyoke, Massachusetts. Despite the lack of systematic comparative statistics, the few available published documents indicate that Puerto Ricans outside New York City are worse off in terms of average income and unemployment than their New York City counterparts (U. S. Bureau of the Census, 1975).

Many Puerto Ricans have a considerable number of relatives and friends within easy social contact, and they can rely on their informal supportive networks for confronting economic, social, health, and emotional problems (Mattei, 1983; Nazario, 1986; Sánchez-Ayéndez, 1984; Vázquez de Nuttall, 1979). However, this is more common in the inner-city ethnic neighborhoods than in public housing projects. Historically, the immigrants have concentrated in areas of the city or a particular geographical location where members of their family or friends from their hometown are located. This has eased adaptation to life in a country different than the country of origin, as well as served as a buffer against a hostile host society. However, the random placement of families in public housing projects tends to separate kin and close friends and undermine prevailing informal networks of support without contributing to the creation of new supportive networks among those living in these projects.

Some aspects of the traditional Puerto Rican family have already been discussed in relation to the cultural description of the group. In examining certain cultural features characteristic of contemporary Puerto Rican families on the mainland, it should be noted that although variations based on social-class differences exist among Puerto Ricans in the United States, they have not been studied systematically. As stated before, a brain-drain migration of young Puerto Rican professionals has been a tendency during the last 10 years. Like all Puerto Ricans, they are faced with discrimination and misconceptualization in their adjustment to life in the United States. However, their higher levels of education, occupational status, and knowledge of English and, in many cases, their light skin can make adaptation easier and enable them opportunities for different lifestyle possibilities. It seems obvious that they are likely not to reside in the low-income housing project or ethnic enclave but in more mixed or predominantly Anglo American, middle-class neighborhoods. They probably are more likely than their low-income counterparts to interact socially with Anglo Americans. The following section centers on low-income Puerto Ricans because there are no available studies about the adaptation and the lifestyle consequences of professionals with higher socioeconomic position.

FAMILY VALUES AND RELATIONSHIPS. The modified extended family (Litwak and Szeleny, 1969) continues to be the primary support system for first- and second-generation Puerto Ricans in the United States. Despite social changes and adaptation to life in a culturally different society, Puerto Rican families are still characterized by strong norms of reciprocity among the various family members, particularly those in the immediate family.

Family interdependence is conceptualized as positive. Individuals expect and ask for assistance from those in their networks, without any derogatory implications for self-esteem. Interdependence does not conflict with individual self-reliance and independence; it co-exists with them and assumes priority in a hierarchy of values. It is not based on mutual-giving or reciprocal-exchange relationships. The prevailing reciprocity norms are not predicated on strictly equal exchanges (Carrasquillo, 1982:150–152; Sánchez-Ayéndez, 1984:171).

Family unity is another theme underlying the conceptualization that Puerto Ricans have of ideal family relations of familism. Family unity refers to the desirability of close and intimate kin ties. Family members should try to get along well and, despite dispersal, keep in touch frequently. Celebration of holidays and special occasions—happy or sad—are seen as opportunities for kin to be together and strengthen family ties. Funerals draw large numbers of relatives together. Trips to and from Puerto Rico are common, even among those with meager resources, at the death of close relatives.

The value of family unity is also evident in the attitude about the desirability of frequent interaction with kin members. Visits and telephone calls are interpreted by family members as a caring attitude that cements family unity and are more common among women than men. As part of their female role, interrelated with the domestic domain, women are conceptualized as responsible for establishing the bases for good relationships among family members. The creation and maintenance of family unity among offspring is considered a female responsibility. Good relations with consanguineal and affinal kin are also envisioned to be the wife's concern. They are conceptualized as relations between the wife's and other women's domestic units. To fulfill their familial role, many women rely on telephoning and visiting.

There is a continuum of degrees of responsibility in the practice of family unity and the obligation for assistance among those in the kin group. More is expected of consanguineal than affinal kin. Among the consanguine, expectations of familial unity and support are greater among those in the inner circle: parents and children, followed by grandchildren. Siblings and their families, as well as those who form part of the fictive kin, follow in this continuum. Such factors as health, gender, personality, compatibility within a specific relationship, and geographical distance also influence the position in this continuum.

Despite the prevalence of family unity and interdependence among Puerto Ricans in the mainland, changes are occurring in traditional attitudes about family relations. In a study of 100 Puerto Rican families in New York City, Colleran (1984) found that first- and second-generation Puerto Ricans realized and regretted the loss of family unity and closeness taking place among their people. They felt that Puerto Ricans residing in the city were less generous and more disrespectful in family relations and were less concerned about family members than those in Puerto Rico. Most believed that the changes occurring were not for the better. Colleran observes that there has been a statistically significant decline in the value of familism among the younger Puerto Ricans in New York and stresses that despite the economic advantages of migration, Puerto Ricans are aware that something valuable is being lost in the adaptation to life in New York.

One cultural pattern mediated through the family is *respeto*. Many first-generation Puerto Ricans feel that deferential acts relevant to respect are undergoing change (Colleran, 1984; Sánchez-Ayéndez, 1984:188–190) and that the degree of formality necessary in certain personal relations is decreasing. However, despite changes occurring in Puerto Rican families, ritualized acts of deference prevail within the familial networks. They are generally bestowed on elder adults and parents. Respect among Puerto Ricans is strongly related to age hierarchy: increased status as one ages. Respect for elders is contingent on their status as older adults, not on their functions and power in familial and community structures. Respect for parents stems from their conceptualization as adults and figures of authority within the household.

HUSBAND AND WIFE ROLES. Despite changes in the husband and wife roles related to more sharing in decision making and female autonomy (Cooney et al., 1982; Leavitt, 1974:194–199, Fitzpatrick, 1971:94–95), a strict dichotomy between the sexes is prevalent. Although it is easier for Puerto Rican women than men to get jobs in urban centers and attain economic independence through work or welfare assistance, women still are primarily conceptualized as responsible for the domestic realm, whereas men are visualized as the main providers. They are also assigned a status subordinate to men. Although most decisions concerning the household are made by the woman without intervention by her husband, the pre-eminence of male authority in husband–wife relations is the norm. Women are still conceptualized as patient and, to a large degree, forbearing in their relations with men. Patience and forbearance are not to be confused with passivity or total submissiveness (Sánchez-Ayéndez, 1984:146–149).

The high unemployment rate of Puerto Rican men in the United States poses a threat to their undisputed authority. When supplementary income is provided by the wife or welfare assistance or when the man is unable to earn money, male authority within the familial context, based on his role as the primary provider, decreases. In many cases, his reaction results in increased acts of *machismo* as a mechanism for dealing with the loss of status and power (Mizio, 1974), which, in turn, the economically independent female is unwilling to tolerate.

Puerto Rican women brought up in New York are perceived by their male counterparts as demanding a more egalitarian sex-role pattern (Leavitt, 1974:198–199). They want their husbands to become more involved in household chores and childrearing and believe that husband and wife should share family problems and recreational activities. However, the New York-raised Puerto Rican men often adhere to the traditional values about female and male roles despite accepting that their wives work outside the home and contribute economically to the maintenance of the household. A conflict between values and expectations is bound to arise, which accounts for the rates of divorce and separation among Puerto Ricans on the mainland.

FICTIVE KIN. Fictive kin are part of the modified extended-family group. In a previous section, the cultural practices of *hijos de crianza* and *compadrazgo* were explained. The practice of informal adoption still exists among Puerto Ricans in the United States. However, adaptation to life in a culturally different society and modifications in the legal system are affecting this tradition. Many of those Puerto Ricans who might consider informally adopting a child opt for legal adoption to avoid emotional suffering and legal consequences in the future. Co-parenthood is still invested with a symbolic bond and retains some of its reciprocity norms within the family context. Yet, family dispersal and the incorporation of women into the labor force are factors affecting the nature of the *compadrazgo* relationship.

A particular group of friends also form part of the kinship networks of Puerto Ricans. The phrase "my friend who is like family" (*como de la familia*) is used on some occasions to distinguish specific friends from others. The obligations to this group of friends and the support expected from them are similar to those in the modified extended family.[3] Relationships with "friends who are like family" are characterized by more familiarity than those with other friends, particularly in the case of elders.

[3]Their functions in the supportive network of migrant Puerto Ricans have been explained by Nazario (1986) and Sánchez-Ayéndez (1984:163–166, 223–226).

Within this special group of friends, individuals are assigned priority according to the designated specific relationship among those involved. For example, a person might refer to someone as "my friend who is like my cousin" or "my friend who is like my sister." The interdependence pattern characteristics of the sister-like relationship involve more assistance and obligations than those arising from the cousin-like relationship. The stronger bonds on which this particular relationship is based ensue from the evaluation that certain friends are engaging in a particular dynamic of interdependence relevant only to family members. This valorization entails that only a few friends will be considered part of the fictive-kin network.

Different Stages of the Life Cycle

Childrearing practices among Puerto Rican immigrants tend to perpetuate, although with modifications, the double standard of conduct between the sexes (Leavitt 1974:200–204). The modesty training of girls begins during early childhood and continues through adolescence. Overt expressions of affection are more common with girls than boys. Mothers, on the whole, tend to be more warm and playful with children than fathers and interact more frequently with daughters than sons (Weissman, 1966:82).

Children are rarely consulted on matters that directly affect them or informed of the reasons for a specific action pertaining to them. They are envisioned as passive creatures who are molded entirely by their parents. Good behavior is taken for granted, whereas reasons for punishment are seldom offered. Physical punishment is more frequent among families with the least mobility and status (Leavitt 1974:202–203).

A study of low-income Puerto Ricans in New York revealed that Puerto Rican parents tended to be person-oriented (*personalismo*) and unconcerned with time (Chess, 1967). These cultural patterns, along with familism and *respeto*, are transmitted by the family to mainland-born and -raised Puerto Ricans. Education for many Puerto Ricans on the mainland is conceived as a means of social mobility but not as an end in itself. They believe that education allows individuals to attain better paying jobs and ascend the social ladder. Work is seen as necessary for survival but unvaluable in itself.

Children's marriages do not mean that the middle-aged or elderly couple is left alone. Frequent visits by adult children and the prevalence of family interdependence contribute to the "empty nest" not being a characteristic stage in the life cycle of older Puerto Ricans. This is further reinforced by the eagerly awaited arrival of grandchildren, and the active role that grandmothers play in child care. In fact, many older Puerto Rican women have migrated to help their adult children raise their families. Studies of elderly Puerto Ricans demonstrate that adult children are the primary source of assistance to their aged parents and that older Puerto Ricans—particularly women—play functional roles in providing their families with assistance and remain integrated within the familial structure (Cantor, 1979; Carrasquillo, 1982; Sánchez-Ayéndez, 1984, 1986).

CHANGE AND ADAPTATION

During the past decade, Puerto Ricans have migrated out of New York City to smaller, urban northeastern communities. The rapid migration to these smaller urban centers is indicative of their search for a better economic situation. However, these urban centers cannot meet the rapidly growing demand of this ethnic group for jobs of low skill level.

Unlike other immigrant groups, the proximity to their homeland and the relative ease of return encourage many Puerto Ricans to search on the island for the strength and support needed to adapt. This ease of return has given the Puerto Rican migration its distinctive ebb-and-flow characteristic. The fact that a large percentage of return migrants are 55 years old and over could indicate a passive resistance to the adaptation process. Nevertheless, young return migrants who have spent their formative years on the mainland often complain about the difficulties of adjusting to life in their homeland. They are perceived as "too Americanized", unfamiliar with island ways, and lacking proficiency in Spanish and are labeled *Niuyoricans* (New York Ricans).

Most of those Puerto Ricans born and/or raised in the United States rely less on Spanish as the means of communication among peers and siblings than those born and/or raised on the island (Colleran, 1984; Cooney et al., 1982; Rogler, Cooney, and Ortiz, 1980). They have greater proficiency in English than Spanish. The younger the person is on arrival, the greater the likelihood of use of English as the principal language. The children of Puerto Rican immigrants hold a more activist approach to life and describe themselves as more aggressive and less humble than their parents (Colleran, 1984). Although some parents express their concern regarding this attitudinal and behavioral change, many agree that it is necessary in order to survive in the United States.

However, despite these changes, younger generations cling to their identification as Puerto Ricans. Second- and third-generation Puerto Ricans do not identify themselves as exclusively American (Rogler, Cooney, and Ortiz, 1980), a fact that points out a trend toward biculturalism instead of complete assimilation. This is even more prevalent in the contemporary ethnic enclave, because it promotes ethnic cohesiveness and solidarity among its residents. Children living in ethnic neighborhoods are likely to speak and understand Spanish better than those living in housing projects with fewer Puerto Ricans.

During the last decade, Puerto Ricans, as a group, have become more politically active. National organizations, such as the Puerto Rican National Coalition, and community-based agencies, such as Inquilinos Boricuas en Acción in Boston and La Casa de Puerto Rico in Hartford, have been defending the rights of Puerto Ricans and promoting grass-roots movements among Puerto Rican communities on the mainland to improve the socioeconomic condition of their people. They are defining their interests as Puerto Ricans, assessing their resources, and stressing the necessity for community-based action. Much remains to be done, but such organization at the national and local levels can bring forth needed changes related to housing and health problems and improve educational and training opportunities to raise the current conditions of the majority of Puerto Rican families on the mainland.

The value of family interdependence and social relations within the ethnic neighborhood have eased the adaptation of low-income Puerto Rican families to the United States, as well as served as a buffer against racial discrimination. Strong, supportive familial and community networks are characteristic of economically deprived minorities. In this respect, social-class and cultural factors have fostered the development of strong patterns of familial interdependence among low-income Puerto Ricans. To underscore the importance of cultural factors in the functions and dynamics of Puerto Rican informal supportive networks is to ignore that the desirability of family interdependence and unity, *personalismo*, and *respeto* are prevalent shared meanings among Puerto Ricans on the island. Despite social and economic changes that have altered patterns of interaction, Puerto Ricans on both the mainland and the island share their commonality of meanings through which they define and interpret their social reality.

To state that changes in familial and community structure that are inherent to adaptation to life in another country have drastically altered the system of meanings of Puerto Rican immigrants is an oversimplification of their situation. Like many immigrant groups, they indisputably have had to undergo modifications in the course of their adaptation to life in the host country. But, unlike other immigrant groups, consciousness of their United States citizenship, the proximity to their homeland, the ease of return, and the close contacts maintained with relatives and friends on the island have provided for a continuity of certain shared meanings, particularly family interdependence. This continuity has proven to be their best resource in adapting to their circumstances and dealing with racial discrimination. Changes in structural and demographic features and changes in cultural meanings do not necessarily go hand in hand.

REFERENCES

Bastida, Elena. 1979. "Family Integration and Adjustment to Aging Among Hispanic American Elderly." Ph.D. diss., University of Kansas.

Bryce-Laporte, Roy S. 1970. "Urban Relocation and Family Adaptation in Puerto Rico," in William Mangin (ed.), *Peasants in Cities: Readings in the Anthropology of Urbanization.* Boston: Houghton Mifflin.

Buitrago, Carlos. 1973. *Esperanza: An Ethnographic Study of a Peasant Community in Puerto Rico.* Tucson: University of Arizona Press.

Cantor, Marjorie H. 1979. "The Informal Support System of New York's Inner City Elderly: Is Ethnicity a Factor?" in Donald L. Gelfand and Alfred J. Kutzik (eds.), *Ethnicity and Aging.* New York: Springer.

Carnivali, Judith and José L. Vázquez Calzada. 1985. *Perfil Sociodemográfico de la Población de Edad Avanzada de Puerto Rico.* San Juan, Puerto Rico: Universidad de Puerto Rico.

Carrasquillo, Héctor A. 1982. "Perceived Social Reciprocity and Self-Esteem Among Elderly Barrio Antillean Hispanics and Their Familial Informal Networks." Ph.D. diss., Syracuse University.

Chess, Stella. 1967. "Social Class and Child Rearing Practices." Unpublished manuscript.

Colleran, Kevin. 1984. "Acculturation in Puerto Rican Families in New York City." Research Bulletin, Hispanic Research Center. New York: Fordham University, 7:2–7.

Cooney, Rosemary Santana, et al., 1982. "Decision Making in Intergenerational Puerto Rican Families," *Journal of Marriage and the Family,* (August):621–631.

Fitzpatrick, Joseph. 1971. *Puerto Rican Americans.* Englewood Cliffs, NJ: Prentice-Hall.

———. 1976. "The Puerto Rican Family," in Charles H. Mindel and Robert W. Habenstein (eds.), *Ethnic Families in America.* New York: Elsevier.

Friedlander, Stanley. 1965. *Labor, Migration and Economic Growth.* Cambridge, MA: MIT Press.

History Task Force, Centro de Estudios Puertorriqueños. 1979. *Labor Migration Under Capitalism: The Puerto Rican Experience.* New York: Monthly Press.

Landy, David. 1959. *Tropical Childhood.* Chapel Hill, NC: University of North Carolina Press.

Lauria, Anthony J. 1964. "Respeto, Relajo and Interpersonal Relations in Puerto Rico," *Anthropological Quarterly,* 37:53–67.

Leavitt, Ruby Rohrlich. 1974. *The Puerto Ricans: Cultural Change and Language Deviance.* Tucson: University of Arizona Press.

León-López, Luz E. 1985. *La Población de Descendencia Hispana en los Estados Unidos.* San Juan, Puerto Rico: Universidad de Puerto Rico.
Lewis, Gordon K. 1963. *Puerto Rico: Freedom and Power in the Caribbean.* New York: Monthly Review Press.
López, Adalberto. 1974. "The Puerto Rican Diaspora," in Adalberto López and James F. Petras (eds.), *Puerto Rico and Puerto Ricans.* Cambridge, MA: Schenkman.
Lowe, Karen. 1984. "Ven Triste Cuadro de Mujeres Boricuas en los Estados Unidos," *El Mundo,* 19 de septiembre, p. 9-A.
Mattei, María de Lourdes. 1983. "Women's Autonomy and Social Networks in a Puerto Rican Community." Ph.D. diss., University of Massachusetts at Amherst.
Mintz, Sidney W. 1966. "Puerto Rico: An Essay in the Definition of a National Culture," in *Selected Background Papers, Prepared for the United States–Puerto Rico Commission on the Status of Puerto Rico.* San Juan, Puerto Rico: Commonwealth of Puerto Rico.
Mizio, Emelicia. 1974. "Impact of External Systems on the Puerto Rican Family," *Social Casework,* 55:76–83.
Nazario, Teresa. 1986. "Social Support Networks of Migrant Puerto Rican Women." Ph.D. diss., Boston University.
New York Times. 1954. "Mayor Wagner in Puerto Rico," June 21, section 1, p. 17.
Nieves Falcón, Luis. 1972. "El Niño Puertorriqueño: Bases Empíricas para Entender su Comportamiento," in Luis Nieves Falcón (ed.), *Diagnóstico de Puerto Rico.* Río Piedras, Puerto Rico: Editorial Edil.
Padilla, Elena. 1958. *Up From Puerto Rico.* New York: Columbia University Press.
Rivera Medina, Eduardo. 1978. "Los Escolares y el Entendimiento de las Personas de Mayor Edad," in Wenceslao Serra Deliz (ed.), *La Problemática de los Envejecientes en Puerto Rico.* Río Piedras, Puerto Rico: Universidad de Puerto Rico.
Rogler, Lloyd H., Rosemary Santana Cooney, and Vilma Ortiz. 1980. "Intergenerational Change in Ethnic Identity in the Puerto Rican Family," *International Migration Review,* 14:193–214.
Saavedra de Roca, Angelina. 1970. *El Espiritismo como Religión.* Río Piedras, Puerto Rico: Universidad de Puerto Rico.
Safa, Helen I. 1964. "From Shanty Town to Public Housing: A Comparison of Family Structure in Two Urban Neighborhoods in Puerto Rico," *Caribbean Studies,* 4:3–12.
———. 1974. "The Urban Poor of Puerto Rico." New York: Holt, Rinehart, and Winston.
Sánchez-Ayéndez, Melba. 1984. "Puerto Rican Elderly Women: Aging in an Ethnic Minority Group in the United States." Ph.D. diss., University of Massachusetts at Amherst.
———. 1986. "Puerto Rican Elderly Woman: Shared Meanings and Informal Supportive Networks," in Johnetta B. Cole (ed.), *All American Women: Lines that Divide, Ties that Bind.* New York: Free Press.
Sandis, Eva E. 1975. "Characteristics of Puerto Rican Migrants To, From, the United States," in Francesco Cordasco and Eugene Bucchioni (eds.), *The Puerto Rican Experience.* New York: Littlefield, Adams.
Seda Bonilla, Edwin. 1958. "Normative Patterns of the Puerto Rican Family in Various Situational Contexts." Ph.D. diss., Columbia University.

———. 1966. "Social Structure and Race Relations," in S. W. Webster (ed.), *Knowing the Disadvantaged.* San Francisco: Chandler.

Stevens, Evelyn P. 1973. "Marianismo: The Other Face of Machismo in Latin America," in Ann Pescatello (ed.), *Female and Male in Latin America.* Pittsburgh: University of Pittsburgh Press.

Steward, Julian H., ed. 1956. *The People of Puerto Rico.* Urbana, IL: University of Illinois Press.

U. S. Bureau of the Census. 1975. "Persons of Spanish Origin in the United States," *Current Population Reports.* Series P-20, no. 361. Washington, DC: U. S. Government Printing Office.

———. 1980. "U. S. Census of Population: 1980." *General Population Characteristics.* Series PC 80-1-B. Washington, DC: U. S. Government Printing Office.

———. 1982. "U. S. Census of Population: 1980." *Persons of Spanish Origin by State.* Supplementary Report. Washington, DC: U. S. Government Printing Office.

U. S. Department of Labor. 1974. "The New York Puerto Ricans: Patterns of Work Experience," in Adalberto López and James F. Petras (eds.), *Puerto Rico and Puerto Ricans.* Cambridge, MA: Schenkman.

Vázquez Calzada, José L. 1978. "La Población de Puerto Rico y su Trayectoria Histórica." San Juan, Puerto Rico: Universidad de Puerto Rico.

———. 1979. "Demographic Aspects of Migration," in *Migration Under Capitalism: The Puerto Rican Experience.* New York: Monthly Review Press.

———. 1983. "Estimaciones Realizadas sobre Migración." Unpublished statistical estimates.

Vázquez de Nuttall, Enna. 1979. "The Support System and Coping Patterns of Female Puerto Rican Single Parents," *Journal of Non-white Concerns,* 7:128–139.

Weissman, Julius. 1966. "An Exploratory Study of Communication Patterns of Lower-Class Negro and Puerto Rican Mothers and Pre-School Children." Ph.D. diss., Columbia University.

Wells, Henry. 1972. *La Modernización de Puerto Rico.* Río Piedras, Puerto Rico: Editorial Universitaria.

ASIAN ETHNIC MINORITIES

CHAPTER NINE

The Korean American Family

Pyong Gap Min

INTRODUCTION

The current Korean community in the United States is largely the product of the Immigration Act of 1965. The Korean American population in 1970 was less than 100,000, but more than 400,000 Koreans have been admitted to this country as legal immigrants since 1970. As a result, the Korean population in this country has increased to more than 800,000. Because recent Korean immigrants are the vast majority of the Korean American population, this chapter focuses on recent Korean immigrant families.

The number of Korean immigrants has increased so rapidly during recent years that there is a paucity of literature and data on Korean immigrants. This is especially true of the family system of Korean immigrants. Only a few studies on Korean immigrant families have been published. Accordingly, it is impossible to write a comprehensive report on Korean immigrant families dealing with different aspects of family structure and family life, which is the main objective of this chapter. I will depend on personal observations and impressions when data on particular aspects of Korean immigrant families are not available. To present Korean immigrant families effectively, data on Korean immigrant families will be compared with those on Korean families in Korea and those on American native families. Before describing and analyzing Korean immigrant families, an overview is provided on the history of Korean immigration to this country, the traditional Korean culture in general, and the family system in particular. This historical background may be more important in understanding Korean immigrant families than the family system of any other ethnic group included in this book, because recent immigrants are believed to constitute a greater percentage of the Korean American population than any other ethnic population.

HISTORICAL BACKGROUND

Korean Immigration to the United States

THE PIONEER PERIOD. The official immigration of Koreans to the United States started during the period 1903–1905, when 7,226 Koreans came to Hawaii to work on sugar plantations. The economic difficulty in Korea at the turn of the century was the major factor pushing the pioneer immigration of Koreans. The famine in 1901 and the nation-wide starvation in ensuing years led the Korean government to loosen its tight emigration policy. The pioneer Korean immigrants came to Hawaii as free laborers and were allowed to stay in the United States permanently. However, most of them wanted to return to Korea as soon as they earned enough money or when the Japanese annexation of Korea came to an end. The first wave of Korean immigrants consisted primarily of male adults, the majority of whom were farmers. A great many of them were Christians who came from the northern provinces of Korea, and the majority attended church after immigration (Choy, 1979:77).

THE INTERMEDIATE PERIOD. The Korean immigration to Hawaii came to an end in April 1905, when the Korean government was almost forced by the Japanese government to stop sending immigrants.[1] Between 1906 and 1924, only approximately 2,000 Koreans are estimated to have come to Hawaii and the West Coast (Choy, 1979:78; Houchins and Houchins, 1974). Korean "picture brides" constituted the majority of Korean immigrants during this period. Also during this period, more than 2,000 of the pioneer immigrants moved from Hawaii to the West Coast, mostly to San Francisco, to work on rice farms or railroad construction.

---

[1]In 1902, there were more than 30,000 Japanese immigrants in Hawaii, constituting approximately three-fourths of the total sugar cane workers in the islands. Plantation owners in Hawaii began recruiting Korean workers to create a more even racial balance among workers. As the Korean workers increased on the farms, Japanese workers asked their government to influence the Korean government to stop sending Korean immigrants to Hawaii. With the Treaty of Protectorate in 1905, the Japanese government intervened in the Korean government by sending its administrators on financial and foreign affairs to Korea and thus forced the Korean government to stop emigration.

With the implementation of the national-origins quota system in 1924, the immigration of Koreans almost came to an end. The immigration of Koreans resumed in the 1950s as the United States government became deeply involved in Korea with the outbreak of the Korean War. The Korean War brides were one primary group that immigrated to this country in the 1950s. Orphans constituted another major group. The marriage of United States military personnel to Korean girls and the adoption of Korean orphans by American citizens, which started during the Korean War, have continued until today.

THE NEW IMMIGRATION. The Immigration Act of 1965 abolished discriminatory quotas based on national origins and allowed the admission of immigrants to the United States on the basis of their skills required in the American labor market and their close relations to those already here. The passage of the immigration act has led to an influx of new Asian immigrants, especially Koreans. As shown in Table 1, approximately 30,000 Koreans have been admitted annually to this country as legal immigrants since 1970. Koreans are the third largest immigrant group following Mexicans and Filipinos who immigrated to the United States

TABLE 1
Korean Immigrants to the United States 1970–1982

YEAR	TOTAL IMMIGRANTS TO THE UNITED STATES	TOTAL ASIAN IMMIGRANTS	TOTAL KOREAN IMMIGRANTS
1970	373,326	94,883	9,314
1971	370,478	103,461	14,297
1972	384,685	121,058	18,876
1973	400,063	124,160	22,930
1974	394,861	130,662	28,028
1975	386,194	132,469	28,362
1976	398,615	149,881	30,803
1977	462,315	157,759	30,917
1978	601,442	249,776	29,288
1979	460,348	189,293	29,248
1980	530,639	236,097	32,320
1981	596,600	264,343	32,663
1982	594,131	313,291	31,724
Total	5,953,697	2,267,133	338,770

SOURCE: Derived from Annual Reports of the Immigration and Naturalization Service (1970–1982).

over the last 15 years. In the early 1970s, occupational immigrants, a great percentage of whom were medical professionals, and their nuclear family members constituted the majority of Korean immigrants. However, a revision of the immigration act in 1976, following the economic recession in the United States, has led to a drastic reduction of occupational immigrants. Since the later 1970s, many Korean immigrants have become naturalized citizens, and thus they have been able to invite their non-nuclear relatives, elderly parents, and siblings. Thus, the vast majority of Korean immigrants admitted over the last 10 years have come to this country not by virtue of their skills required in the American job market, but by virtue of their relationships to those already here. Better economic opportunity in the United States is the major pulling factor for the current immigration of Koreans. Better opportunity for children's education and political and social insecurity in South Korea are the other important factors that precipitated the massive immigration of Koreans to this country (Hurh and Kim; 1984; Kim, 1981; Min, 1984c).

The 1980 census estimated the Korean population to be 354,593 (U. S. Bureau of the Census, 1983a:50). The Korean American population in 1980 was five times larger than that in 1970. The Korean Ambassador to the United States and Korean community leaders in New York and other major Korean centers claimed that Koreans were greatly undercounted in the 1980 census, suggesting that the Korean population in the United States in 1981 was over 600,000 (*Choong Ang Daily*, Sept. 11, 1981). Taking into account the 100,000 Korean residents who lived in this country before 1970, the more than 450,000 Koreans who have immigrated since 1970, the Korean children born in this country since 1970, the illegal residents, students, and temporary visitors, the number of Korean residents in this country probably is more than 800,000 as of January 1986.

Social Characteristics of Recent Korean Immigrants

There are significant class differences, as well as ethnic differences, in family system, and thus it is important in understanding the family characteristics of recent Korean immigrants to overview their class background. The old immigrants consisted largely of uneducated and unskilled workers. In sharp contrast, however, the new Asian immigrants are of a higher social class, with a heavy concentration in educated professionals and technicians. Recent Korean immigrants, like other Asian immigrants, are characterized by high educational and pre-immigration occupational levels. Table 2 compares Korean immigrants with other groups in educational level as reported in the 1980 census. Although Korean immigrants

TABLE 2
Comparison of Korean Immigrants with other Groups in Education

	KOREAN IMMIGRANTS	KOREAN GENERAL POPULATION	AMERICAN NATIVES	CHINESE IMMIGRANTS	FILIPINO IMMIGRANTS	INDIAN IMMIGRANTS
% of persons 25 years old and over with high school education	77.4	26.0	67.7	59.7	77.1	87.2
% of persons 25 years old and over with four years of college education	31.6	6.8	16.3	27.6	47.9	63.1

SOURCE: U. S. Bureau of the Census (1984:12). Korean National Bureau of Statistics (1983a).

compare unfavorably in educational level with Filipino and Indian immigrants, they surpass native-born Americans by approximately two times in the percentage of the population that has received a college education. Case studies of Korean immigrants also indicate the white-collar, professional background of recent Korean immigrants. According to one survey, 80 percent of the Koreans in New York were engaged in white-collar and professional occupations at the time of departure from Korea (Kim, 1981:41). The majority of Korean male adults were medical professionals, managers for large private companies, teachers, and government officials.

The special characteristics of Korean immigrants are also reflected in their urban background. One survey (Kim, 1978b:181) found that almost 90 percent of the Korean respondents in Chicago came from urban areas and that more than 60 percent had grown up in cities with a population over 1 million. In contrast, 48 percent of the Korean population is in urban areas (Korean National Bureau of Statistics, 1980a:149). Recent Korean immigrants are also largely Protestant. Protestantism is a minority religion in South Korea, representing about 16 percent of the total population (Choong Ang Daily, May 21, 1981). However, studies of Korean immigrants suggest that more than 50 percent of Korean adult immigrants were affiliated with Protestant churches in Korea (Hurh, Kim, and Kim, 1979:24; Kim, 1978b:179). Quite naturally, a greater proportion of Korean Protestants than other Koreans chose to immigrate to this country because of similarities in values associated with Protestantism.

Settlement Patterns and Community Organization

As expected, a large percentage of Korean immigrants (43.4 percent) live in the western region of the country, and approximately 30 percent are located in California (U. S. Bureau of the Census, 1983b:125). The rest of the Korean population is evenly scattered throughout other parts of the country. Los Angeles is the largest Korean center, with a population of more than 200,000, followed by New York and Chicago. These are the three largest metropolitan cities in this country. This reflects the tendency of Korean immigrants to settle in large metropolitan cities.

Most immigrants in the nineteenth century concentrated in ethnic ghettoes located near central business districts, and their second- and third-generation descendants moved to suburban areas as they achieved cultural and economic mobility. With the exception of "Koreatown" in Los Angeles, however, Korean immigrants do not maintain geographically segregated ethnic communities. Researchers (Hurh and Kim, 1984; Kim, 1981; Yu, 1983) have indicated that Korean immigrants are widely dispersed throughout the metropolitan areas and that they have a high level of suburban residence. The 1980 census (U. S. Bureau of the Census, 1983b:50), for example, shows that 46.4 percent of the Korean American population is in suburban areas, compared with 33.8 percent of the white American population. Although recent immigrants constitute the vast majority of the Korean American population, the Korean ethnic group shows the highest level of suburban residence of all ethnic groups.

Although Korean immigrants have not formed territorial enclaves, they maintain nonterritorial ethnic communities by intensifying organization-centered community activities (Kim, 1981). An overwhelming majority of Korean immigrants (approximately 90 percent) are affiliated with one or more ethnic organizations and maintain informal friendship networks with kin members and ethnic friends. One noteworthy characteristic in this regard is that recent Korean immigrants, unlike earlier Asian immigrants, maintain neither the kin- nor the locale-based system of community organization. Instead, they establish ethnic associations along occupational lines, religious denominations, differences in leisure activities, and other differences in the present environment. Kim (1981), for example, in his study of the Korean community in New York, indicates that ethnic churches and various professional and recreational associations constitute the backbone of social activities for Korean immigrants. As was the case for many earlier white immigrants, Korean ethnic churches are the center for grass-roots community activities. Many non-Christians attend the ethnic church because the latter performs all kinds of secular functions, including immigration orientation for Korean immigrants.

Most Korean communities have established a community-wide formal association with an elected president and other staff members. Such comprehensive Korean associations organize recreational activities for all Korean immigrants and serve as a voice for Korean immigrants in their relationship with the larger society. However, unlike the central organization in traditional Chinatowns, the Korean association does not have firm control over the activities of community members. This observation is supported by the fact that many Korean communities in New York, San Francisco, and other cities, unable to settle internal disputes, took them to American courts (Choy, 1979:234; Kim, 1981). Kim (1981:185) indicates that having no centralized ethnic organization or leadership to integrate, coordinate, and direct the various community activities is one of the major characteristics of the Korean ethnic community in New York.

The Economic and Occupational Adjustment of Recent Korean Immigrants

Despite their high educational levels, most Korean immigrants have serious difficulty speaking English. As a result of this language difficulty and other disadvantages in the American labor market, most Korean immigrants cannot achieve the same white-collar and professional occupational levels in this country that they held in Korea. Thus, underemployment has been indicated as one of the major problems in Korean immigrants' occupational adjustment (Hurh, Kim, and Kim, 1979:72–73; Kim and Wong, 1977; Min, 1984c). We previously indicated that more than 90 percent of Korean adult immigrants were engaged in white-collar occupations in Korea. However, the 1980 census (U. S. Bureau of the Census, 1984:12) indicates that 47 percent of Korean immigrant workers are in white-collar occupational categories. This means that a significant number of Korean white-collar immigrants have switched to blue-collar occupations. In many cases, college-educated Korean immigrants work as factory laborers, janitors, and gas-station attendants.

Unable to find white-collar occupations, a large number of Korean immigrants turn to small business, and this has become an important research issue in the area of race and ethnic minorities during recent years. The census report (U. S. Bureau of the Census, 1984:12) shows that 12.2 percent of recent Korean immigrant workers (those who immigrated between 1970 and 1980) are self-employed, compared with 6.8 percent of native-born American workers. The Korean group records the highest self-employment rate among 17 recent immigrant groups classified in the 1980 census. Case studies of Korean communities (Bonacich, Light, and Wong, 1976, 1980; Kim, 1981; Light, 1980; Min, 1984b, 1984c, 1987b; Min and Jaret, 1985) show that 25–30 percent of Korean households own at least one business. In addition to their labor-market disadvantages, Korean immigrants' mobility orientation has been found to be an important reason for their decision to start a business (Min, 1984c). Such labor-intensive trade and service businesses as grocery/liquor stores, green groceries, dry cleaners, and fast food restaurants are major lines of business that Korean immigrants pursue (Kim, 1981; Min, 1984c). A large number of Korean immigrants are also engaged in wholesale and retail trade dealing in imported Korean items such as wigs, handbags, jewelry, and clothing. Most Korean business owners start their businesses with the savings of their earnings made in this country, and approximately one-fourth use the money brought from Korea as start-up capital (Kim and Hurh, 1985a; Min, 1987). A typical Korean business is a small family business usually operated by the husband and wife and, in some cases, with the additional help of adult children.

The Traditional Korean Culture and Family System

Korea is a peninsula extending northwest to Manchuria and southeast to nearly the southern islands of Japan. Historically, the Chinese cultural influence spread southward to Korea and then to Japan. Thus, Chinese culture came to have greater effects on Korea than on Japan, although Japan was under the strong cultural influence of China. In fact, until very recently, the one dominating feature of Korean culture was the impact of Chinese civilization, especially through Confucianism. At the turn of the century, three Asian superpowers—Japan, China, and Russia—struggled for political control over Korea. When Japan won the war against Russia in 1905, it established a hegemony on the Korean peninsula. Korea was under Japanese colonial rule for 36 years until the end of World War II. Because of this historical event, there is still a strong anti-Japanese feeling in Korea, although South Korea normalized diplomatic relations with Japan in 1965. Since the end of World War II, Korea has been politically divided into two halves: South Korea under the influence of the United States and North Korea under the influence of Russia and China. Since the outbreak of the Korean War in 1950, South Korea has maintained close political and military connections with the United States. The United States had cultural influence on Korea through Protestant missionaries even before the Korean War. It was American missionaries that first established modern schools in Korea in the beginning of the twentieth century. The Korean War and close political, economic, and military connections between South Korea and the United States in ensuing years have accelerated the American cultural influence in South Korea.

The Chinese Confucian cultural tradition had such great effects in Korea that it is almost impossible to understand the Korean traditional culture in general and the family system in particular without understanding the influence of Chinese Confucianism. Concerned mainly with the life in this world rather than the other world, Confucius provided many important principles according to which he advised individuals to behave for harmonious social relations. Five categories of interpersonal relations form the basis of his teachings concerning the duties and obligations of each individual. These relations are between (1) parents and children, (2) king and people, (3) husband and wife, (4) older (brother) and younger (brother), and (5) friends. The significance of Confucianism for the Korean family system is clear because three of these five cardinal relations involve the family.

Confucius taught that parents and children should maintain a mutual attitude of benevolence. However, Confucianism, as applied to the Korean family system and social life, demanded children's one-sided obedience to and respect for parents and other adult members. Children were required to not only pay the highest respect for parents throughout their lives but also fulfill some important obligations to them. The first son was supposed to cohabit with parents even after marriage, providing them with financial support and care. Moreover, filial piety was extended after the death of a parent in the form of ancestor worship. Sons observe ritual mourning for three years after a parent dies, and younger generations of sons show worshipful veneration to their ancestors.

Confucianism emphasized a clear role differentiation between the husband and wife, and this principle helped to establish an extreme form of patriarchy in Korea. In the traditional Korean society, the husband was considered the primary breadwinner and decision-maker in the family and exercised authority over his wife and children. The wife was expected to obey her husband, devotedly serve him and his family members, including in-laws, and perpetuate her husband's family lineage by producing children. The wife was eliminated from decision making in all important family affairs, including the education of children. The husband, his parents, and other male relatives participated in decision making.

In the traditional Korean society based on patrilineage and patriarchy, sons were considered more valuable and given more power than daughters. The first son very often attended important family meetings to which his mother was not allowed. The interpersonal relations between brothers and sisters were regulated by the Confucian ideology that put emphasis on age. Older brothers or sisters were allowed to exercise a moderate level of authority over younger brothers or sisters. Because of this emphasis on age, sibling rivalry was not frequent in the traditional Korean family. Age was important for not only sibling relations but also interpersonal relations in general. People were expected to be polite and respectful to other people with whom they interacted when they were younger than the others even by a few years.

Another major effect of Confucianism on Korean society is the adoption in the tenth century of the civil service examination originally devised in China. The system, which was intended to bring men of intelligence and ability into government regardless of social position, annually gave examinations based on Chinese literature and Confucian classics. Those who passed the examination were offered high government positions that gave great power and economic rewards. Koreans put great emphasis on education as the main avenue for social mobility because, historically, the civil service examination provided the only efficient outlet for upward social mobility. Until very recently, most parents in South Korea gave children private instruction after school by hiring tutors or sending children to private institutions. Because this private instruction was a major financial burden to many parents, the government made a law several years ago banning all kinds of private instruction.

KOREAN IMMIGRANT FAMILIES

Size and Composition of Households

The first five rows of Table 3 provide data on family size and composition of households for three groups: (1) Koreans in Korea, (2) Korean immigrants, and (3) Americans. The mean number of persons per household for Korean immigrants is 3.63, compared with 4.62 for Koreans in Korea and 2.73 for Americans. As expected, Korean immigrants maintain a smaller family (household) than the general Korean population but a larger family than Americans. The difference in household size between Korean immigrants and Americans can be explained by two factors. First, most American adult children live separately from parents after graduation from high school, but Korean immigrant children live with parents until marriage. Although Korean immigrant families have a lower fertility rate than Americans (see the last row of Table 3), they have on average a greater number of children (1.88 children per Korean family, compared with 1.35 children per American family). Less than 4 percent of Korean immigrant households are single-person households, compared with 22 percent for American households. Korean immigrants have a smaller percentage of single-person households mainly because a high number of unmarried Korean adult children live with their parents. Second, Korean immigrant households include a larger number of non-nuclear members than American households. One out of two or three Korean immigrant households has one non-nuclear member, whereas one out of five or six American households has such a member. Approximately 17 percent of Korean immigrant families are of the extended type, compared with 8 percent of American families (see Table 3). More than half of Korean immigrant extended families include one or more parents (Hong, 1982:110). Many Korean immigrants also include brothers, sisters, and other relatives (see the following section on kin ties and care of the elderly).

TABLE 3

Two-Way Comparison of Korean immigrants in Family Characteristics

	KOREAN IMMIGRANTS	KOREANS IN KOREA	AMERICAN NATIVES
Number of persons per household	3.48	4.63	2.73
Number of children per family	1.88	—	1.35
Number of non-nuclear members per household	0.41	—	0.18
Proportion of single-person households	3.6[a]	4.8	21.9[b]
Proportion of extended families	16.9[c]	23.1	8.3[d]
Number of divorcees per 1,000 persons 15 years and over	15.0 (male) 36.8 (female)	3.6 (male) 6.2 (female)	53.7 (male) 72.6 (female)
% of female-headed households with no husband present	9.6	9.7	13.9
% of married-couple families	86.0	—	82.7 (U. S. total)
% of females in the labor force	53.5 (16 years old and over)	28.8 (14 years old and over)	50.5
% of married women in the labor force	56.0 (Korean Americans)	18.8	49.2 (U.S. total)
Number of children ever born per 1,000 women 35-44 years old	2097	4036	2652

SOURCE: Data on Korean immigrants and American natives are based on U. S. Bureau of the Census. (1983a, 1983b, and 1984) unless the source is footnoted separately. Data on Koreans in Korea are based on Korean National Bureau of Statistics (1980a, 1980b, 1983a, 1983b, 1983c, and 1984).

[a]Hong (1982).

[b]U.S. Bureau of the Census (1976).

[c]Hong (1982).

[d]Tienda and Angel (1982).

Marital Stability

Table 3 also provides data on marital stability for the three groups. As expected, Korean immigrants show a much lower divorce rate than Americans. However, recent Korean immigrants show a five to six times higher divorce rate than the general Korean population. Three major factors explain this great difference in divorce rate between recent Korean immigrants (those who came here between 1970 and 1980) and Koreans in Korea. First, residence in this country for several years has led to a change in Koreans' attitudes toward divorce. In Korea, many people continue unhappy marital relations because custom discourages divorce. In this country, however, divorce is not considered to be deviant behavior, and thus exposure to this liberal cultural milieu leads many Korean immigrants to more easily make a decision to divorce than in Korea. Second, many young Korean immigrants unable to find spouses here bring spouses from Korea, and these couples seem to have a higher divorce rate than other Korean immigrant couples. Young Koreans usually stay one month in Korea to find a partner, which is not long enough for each partner to know enough about the personality and family background of the other partner. Third and most importantly, a high divorce rate of Korean brides married to American soldiers also contributes to Korean immigrants' higher divorce rate than the general Korean population. In both Korea and the Korean community in the United States, divorced women outnumber divorced men by approximately two to one (see Table 3). Although the larger number of divorced women than divorced men in Korea primarily is the result of the tendency of female divorcees not to remarry because of cultural constraints, the larger number of divorced women in the Korean American community actually reflects a higher divorce rate for female Korean immigrants than male immigrants. Since the Korean War, many American soldiers stationed in South Korea have brought home Korean wives, and a higher percentage of these interracial marriages have terminated in divorce (see the section on intermarriage).

Going back to Table 3, 9.6 percent of Korean immigrant families are headed by females compared with 13.9 percent of American families. Korean immigrants' lower divorce rate and the tendency of elderly Koreans not to emigrate contribute to a lower level of female-headed households for Korean immigrants. There is no significant difference in the proportion of female-headed Korean immigrant families to female-headed Korean families in Korea (see Table 3). This is because Korean immigrants have a higher divorce rate but a lower percentage of widowed women than the general Korean population. A higher percentage of Korean immigrant families (86 percent) than American families (83 percent) are married-couple families. All three indicators (divorce rate, percentage of female-headed families, and percentage of married-couple families) suggest that Korean immigrant families are more stable than white American families, which are known to be more stable than families of other minority groups. In addition to the factors previously discussed, the current immigration law, which respects family unity, has helped Korean immigrants maintain stable families. The situation of recent Korean immigrants contrasts with that of an overwhelming majority of pre-war Asian immigrants who could not bring their family members.

Conjugal Role Differentiation

Although a high level of urbanization and industrialization has led to great changes in the traditional family system in South Korea during recent years, the traditional family ideology of conjugal role differentiation has not been significantly modified. In Korea, the wife is still expected to stay home as a full-time homemaker, while the husband's role is limited to earning a living (Choi, 1977:6; Kim and Hurh, 1983). Both role expectations and employment discrimination discourage married women from participating in the labor market. Table 3 indicates that 30 percent of Korean females 14 years old and over in cities are in the labor force but that the labor force participation rate of married women in this group is only 19 percent. This means that many women stop their careers after marriage to fulfill their roles as full-time housekeepers.

The immigration of Koreans to this country has led to many changes in the traditional Korean family system, but the most noteworthy change is the radical increase in the female labor-force participation rate. The 1980 census indicates that 54 percent of Korean immigrant females 16 years old and over and 56 percent of Korean married women are in the labor force (see Table 3). The Korean immigrant group shows a slightly higher rate of female labor force participation than Americans and a much higher rate than the general Korean population. There is a radical difference between Korean immigrants and the general Korean population, especially in the percentage of married women in the labor force. The proportion of Korean immigrant married women in the labor force to married women in the labor force in Korea is approximately three times greater. Three factors contribute to this radical increase in the larger number of Korean married women in the labor force in the United States. First, Korean immigrants have a number of disadvantages in the American labor market, and in most cases, both the husband and wife need to work to economically survive or achieve faster economic mobility.[2] The wife's work is necessary for economic survival, especially for self-employed families. Second, in dollar values, Korean immigrants earn approximately seven times more in

---

[2]In the 1979 study of Korean immigrants in Los Angeles (Hurh and Kim, 1984:125), 46 percent of the two-income families reported that their annual family income was $25,000 or more, whereas only 32 percent of the one-income families indicated an income of this level.

this country than they could in Korea, and this wage difference attracts many Korean married women to participate in the labor market. Third, residence in this country has led to a change in Korean immigrants' attitude toward the traditional sex-role ideology, and this is closely related to the two previously mentioned factors. The advantage of dual-career families for economic mobility and the importance of Korean women for the Korean immigrant-family economy have led many Korean immigrants to discard the traditional view that the husband should be the only or primary breadwinner.

Has this increase in the Korean wife's economic role in this country led to a decrease in her homemaker's role and the increase in household tasks being performed by the husband? A series of studies by Kim and Hurh (Hurh and Kim, 1984, Ch. 4; Kim and Hurh, 1983, 1984, 1985b; Kim, Kim, and Hurh, 1979) are useful in answering this question. Using two sample groups in Chicago and one sample group in Los Angeles, the authors tried to determine whether the Korean immigrant wife's participation in the labor market has led to a significant modification of the traditional sex-role differentiation in the performance and expectations of household tasks. Their findings indicate that the Korean wife's employment or self-employment generally has not reduced her homemaker's role. The working wife predominantly performs four household tasks: grocery shopping, house cleaning, laundry, and dishwashing, unless she is helped by children and kin members. Only in two other household tasks, managing the family budget and disposal of garbage, is the Korean husband substantially involved. The expectations of both the husband and wife about who is to primarily perform each household task are consistent with the actual role performance. Based on these findings, Kim and Hurh conclude that the traditional ideology of conjugal-role differentiation persists in the Korean immigrant community[3] and that double roles give the Korean immigrant working wives role pressure and role conflicts.

Conjugal Power

Despite several controversies involved in conjugal power research, most family sociologists currently seem to agree with Rodman (1967, 1972) that conjugal power derives from the interaction of comparative resources of

[3]The traditional ideology that the wife should be the only or the main homemaker still persists in the Korean American community, as Hurh and Kim claim (1984). However, as indicated above, most Korean immigrants seem to reject the traditional view that the husband should be the only or the main breadwinner.

the husband and wife and cultural or subcultural expectations of power distribution. An overwhelming majority of Korean adult immigrants spent the first 20 or more years of their lives in Korea, where the husband exercised much greater power than the wife (Lee, 1975; Rhim, 1978). However, the majority of Korean immigrant women make a significant contribution to the family economy by participating in the labor market as employed or self-employed workers. If the above theoretical view is accurate, then we can expect Korean immigrant women to exercise greater power than their counterparts in Korea but less power than their American counterparts.

Because no comparative study has been done, one cannot draw a conclusion on this hypothesis. However, one study (Hong, 1982) based on a sample group of 65 Korean immigrants in Los Angeles suggests that Korean immigrant couples are less egalitarian than American couples in terms of decision making on important family affairs. Analyzing the responses to 12 family-power issues, Hong reported that 22 percent of the Korean couples are characterized by the husband-dominant pattern of decision making, 71 percent by the egalitarian, and 8 percent by the wife-dominant. The author compared these findings with those derived from a similar study in 1964 based on a sample of white, married couples in Los Angeles. The respective figures for the 1964 American sample were 9 percent for the husband-dominant, 86 percent for the egalitarian, and 5 percent for the wife-dominant. Pointing out that there has been a great change in conjugal relations in this country since 1964 in the direction of a more egalitarian pattern, Hong suggested that the difference between Korean immigrant and American couples in conjugal power would be much greater if a more recent sample of Korean immigrants in Los Angeles were available for comparison. My personal observations of Korean immigrant couples strongly suggest that Korean husbands exercise much greater power than American husbands.

Fertility

The last row in Table 3 provides information about fertility. The number of children ever born for 1,000 Korean immigrant women 35 to 44 years old is 2,097. The respective figures for the general Korean population and native-born Americans are 4,036 and 2,652, respectively. This means that a Korean immigrant woman who has passed childbearing age has on the average two children, compared with approximately four children for a Korean woman in Korea and 2.5 children for a native-born American woman. That Korean immigrant women have a lower fertility rate than the general Korean population is to be expected, but the fact that the

Korean immigrant group shows a significantly lower fertility rate than even the general American population is surprising.

Two major factors explain the low fertility rate of Korean immigrants. First, a low fertility rate is largely the result of selective immigration. As previously discussed, Korean immigrants are a select group in many characteristics. Yet, two aspects of their selective nature seem to be useful in understanding their low fertility rate. One is selectivity in their socioeconomic background. Korean immigrants largely represent the highly educated, middle-class segment of the Korean population, and middle-class people generally have a lower fertility rate than lower-class people. The other is selectivity in their motivations. All immigrants are self-selected in that more progressive, economically aggressive, and achievement-oriented people choose to leave their native countries for life in an alien environment (Chiswick, 1982). Korean immigrants as a group have a higher level of aspiration for economic success and social mobility than the Korean middle-class people in general, and this mobility orientation has negative influence on fertility. Second, the adjustment difficulty Korean immigrants have serves as a restrictive force to fertility. Approximately one-third of Korean women 35 to 44 years old are believed to have given birth to their children in this country. The majority of these women participated in the labor market. The cost and difficulty of child care and other adjustment problems may have discouraged them from deciding to have more than two children.

Mate Selection Patterns

The majority of the Korean young people in this country who have married during recent years reached marital age immigrated here as children accompanied by parents. These Korean-born and American-raised children are very often referred to as "1.5-generation" Koreans. The parents of these young Koreans are in their fifties and early sixties. Quite naturally, they are strongly opposed to intergroup marriage. In one survey, (Hurh and Kim, 1984:80), for example, only 22 percent of the Korean respondents approved of the Korean–white interracial marriage. The mean age of these respondents was approximately 40 years, and an even smaller number of the Koreans in their fifties and sixties would approve interracial marriage. Although young Koreans are more tolerant of out-group marriage than their parents, most feel that they would be more compatible with Korean partners because they spent their early years in Korea. This observation is supported by a survey (Song, 1982:146) in which 66 percent of the Korean college respondents in Los Angeles selected Koreans as preferable spouses. Thus, the intermarriage rate of recent Korean immigrants is likely to be low unless other structural factors force Korean immigrants to find their spouses outside the group (see the following section on intergroup marriage).

Korean immigrants can either find Korean spouses in this country or bring them from Korea. The number of Korean brides and grooms who find their Korean spouses in this country differs depending upon community size and other factors. A 1986 survey (Min, 1987a) shows that approximately 34 percent of the Koreans in Los Angeles who married during the previous five years brought their spouses from Korea. Koreans in smaller Korean communities have more difficulty finding their spouses in this country than those in Los Angeles or New York. Thus, the majority of young Koreans in smaller Korean communities seem to marry Koreans in Korea. In addition to the difficulty of finding Korean partners in this country, the popularity of Korean immigrants as prospective spouses in Korea encourages many Korean immigrants to visit Korea for marriage. Taking advantage of their status as United States immigrants, they can usually find better partners in Korea in terms of education and family background than in this country.

Not only community size but also sex ratio and sex differences in norms about conjugal relations have influence on the mate-selection patterns of Korean immigrants. Females outnumber males by 58 to 42 for Korean Americans as a whole, and the sex-ratio imbalance is much greater for those at marital ages (20 to 29 years old) with females constituting 68 percent of the Korean American population in that age category (U. S. Bureau of the Census, 1983b:50). This indicates that Korean female immigrants have more difficulty finding Korean spouses in this country than Korean male immigrants. Furthermore, the difficulty of Korean women in finding Korean spouses in this country becomes greater because of the tendency of many Korean male immigrants to consider Korean women in Korea who accept the traditional conjugal norms as more desirable spouses than American-raised Korean women.

Under these conditions, Korean immigrant women have to meet their needs by bringing Korean spouses from Korea or choosing out-group spouses. Most of the Korean females who cannot or do not choose Korean spouses in this country take the latter alternative (choose out-group spouses) rather than the former. It is not difficult to understand why this is the case. The Korean female immigrants who finished high school or college in this country have been greatly influenced by more egalitarian American conjugal relations. Thus, most of the Korean women who cannot find Korean spouses in this country prefer white American men to Korean men in Korea, and many Korean women prefer white American men to even Korean male immigrants (see the next section). Many of the Korean women whose parents strongly oppose out-group marriage are forced into choosing their spouses in Korea, but this odd marriage between Americanized Korean brides and Korean-raised grooms seem to involve more marital conflicts than the marriage in the opposite combination. This hypothesis is based on my personal observations and from reading ethnic newspaper articles. The relationship between marital patterns and marital conflicts (or marital satisfaction) is a good research topic for the future.

Intergroup Marriage

To present Korean intergroup marriage effectively, three Korean groups are analyzed separately: (1) Korean Americans in Hawaii, (2) Korean war brides, and (3) recent Korean immigrants.

INTERMARRIAGE IN HAWAII. The oldest Korean community in the United States was established in Hawaii when approximately 7,200 Koreans came to the islands between 1903 and 1905. The pioneer immigrants and their descendants in Hawaii were isolated from the rest of the Korean population because, until very recently, there had been no significant migration of Koreans to the earlier Korean bachelor immigrants. The absence of chain migrations, the ethnic enclave, a small group size, and high assimilation orientation led to a high intermarriage rate for Korean descendants in Hawaii. Harvey and Chung (1980) reported that during the period between 1960 and 1968, 80 percent of Korean brides and grooms in Hawaii married out-group members, compared with 40 percent of out-group marriage for other ethnic groups. The authors indicated that the out-group marrying Korean females tended to prefer white grooms and the out-group marrying Korean males chose more Japanese than white females. Again, this pattern is primarily the result of the difference between Korean men and women in norms concerning conjugal relations. American-born Korean women want to maintain more egalitarian conjugal relations and thus consider white men preferable to Asian men as spouses. The out-group marrying Korean men, however, feel more comfortable with the traditional conjugal relations than with those practiced by the majority of white Americans and thus prefer Asian to white brides.

KOREAN WAR BRIDES. Since the outbreak of the Korean War in 1950, tens of thousands of United States servicemen have annually stayed in South Korea, and many of them have brought home Korean brides. The immigration report (U. S. Immigration and Naturalization Service, 1952–1982) shows that more than 40,000 Korean brides came here as spouses of American citizens. An overwhelming majority of these brides were married to servicemen stationed in South Korea. A high percentage of these marriages are known to have ended in divorce (Kim, 1972, 1978a; Ratliff, Moon, and Bonacci, 1978), although no statistics concerning the divorce rate of these intermarriages are currently available. It is not difficult to understand why these interracial marriages are more unstable than other forms of Korean–American interracial marriage. Most of these marriages were formed under special circumstances without going through the formal procedures of dating, courtship, and marriage. The majority of these marriages started with cohabitations between American servicemen seeking sex and companionship and Korean women seeking monetary rewards (Ratliff, Moon, and Bonacci, 1978). Moreover, both Korean brides and American servicemen involved in interracial marriage generally represent the segment of low socioeconomic status in each country, and this socioeconomic background is a factor for marital instability. In addition, Korean–American cultural differences and objection to the marriage by the parents of both parties significantly contribute to marital and familial conflicts. Most Korean war brides received little education, and thus they have greater difficulty learning English and American customs than other Korean immigrants. The language barrier and unfamiliarity with American customs lead many Korean brides to feel a sense of isolation from their children, husbands, and other family members who are monolingual (Kim, 1978b). The Korean cultural norm of female subordination and lack of resources gives many Korean brides little power in conjugal relations, and this power imbalance makes them vulnerable to physical violence and abuse by American husbands. Korean ethnic newspapers are replete with stories of family violence and wife abuse that Korean war brides suffered.

INTERMARRIAGE OF RECENT KOREAN IMMIGRANTS. As previously noted, the marked sex-ratio imbalance makes it difficult for Korean women to find Korean spouses in this country and that Americanized Korean women are unwilling to seek a prospective spouse in Korea. This suggests that a higher percentage of Korean women than men choose out-group members as spouses. This expectation is supported by a study in Los Angeles. Kitano and Chai (1982) examined the out-group marriage rate of Korean immigrants in Los Angeles using marriage-license applications for the years 1975, 1977, and 1979. Their data show that out-group marriages accounted for 30 percent of total Korean marriages in Los Angeles during the three years and that female out-group marriages constituted 73 percent of total Korean out-group marriages. Moreover, as noted in the previous section, a significant number of Koreans in Los Angeles found their spouses and had weddings in Korea. These in-group marriages were not included in the Los Angeles County marriage statistics. Thus, the actual out-group marriage rate of Koreans in Los Angeles during the three years may have been lower than 30 percent, although the out-group marriage rate in smaller Korean communities may have reached this figure.

Kitano and his associates (Kitano et al., 1984) compared three Asian groups in Los Angeles and found the Korean group to have the lowest out-group marriage rate and the Japanese to have the highest rate. The low out-group marriage rate of the Korean group relative to the other two Asian groups seems to be primarily the result of a relatively greater number of Korean immigrants. Kitano and Chai (1982) also indicated that 27 percent of Korean out-group marriages were to persons with Japanese and Chinese surnames and the other 73 percent to non-Asians, the vast majority of whom are presumed to have been whites. As each Korean community grows in population size and achieves sex-ratio balance in the future, most young Koreans may be able to choose Korean spouses in this country. However, despite these structural changes, the out-group marriage rate of Korean Americans is likely to increase as more and more Americanized second-generation Koreans reach marital age.

Socialization of Children

It is difficult to generalize about Korean immigrants' child-socialization practices, because there are significant in-group differences. Generalizations about the degree to which Korean children are permitted freedom are especially difficult to make. Older Korean parents whose children were born and raised in Korea for several years are more authoritarian than younger Korean immigrants. Many of these Korean parents have conflicts with their children in high school or college who have been exposed to a more liberal educational environment in the American school. Most of the younger Korean immigrants whose children were born and raised in this country are similar to American middle-class parents in adopting the democratic method of socialization, which emphasizes mutual respect between parents and children. They seem to do so mainly because they do not expect their children to accept traditional socialization practices. There are also significant class differences in Korean immigrants' childrearing practices. Korean immigrants with higher education, especially those who received college education in the United States, adopt more of the American, liberal childrearing practices.

Despite these in-group differences, Korean immigrant parents as a group significantly differ from American middle-class parents in child socialization. Korean immigrants seem to use negative reinforcement (punishment) more often than American middle-class parents. Moreover, Korean immigrant parents do not give monetary rewards for positive reinforcement as often as American middle-class parents. Another major difference in socialization practices between Korean immigrant families and American middle-class families relates to relative social status of the aged. Under the influence of the Confucian cultural tradition, the elderly still enjoy a considerable degree of respect in South Korea. Korean immigrant parents put more emphasis than American middle-class parents on teaching children to show respect for the elderly. In Korea, children are expected to use different vocabularies and gestures in their interaction with adult members than those used in their interactions with peers. Complaining that their children do not learn the proper norms in interactions with adults in the American schools, most Korean immigrant parents try to teach some of these norms at home.

There are also significant differences between Korean immigrant and American middle-class parents in gender-role socialization. Of course, Korean immigrant parents are stricter than American parents in teaching different social roles to boys and girls. Because the majority of Korean married women are in the labor force, children need to help their mothers with cooking and other household tasks in many Korean immigrant families. However, it is very rare to see Korean boys cooking and dishwashing, whereas most Korean girls in dual-career households take the role of housemaid. This is partly the result of gender-role socialization at home. Few Korean immigrant mothers would like to ask their boys to help them with cooking and dishwashing. Korean parents' teaching of gender roles based on sex stereotypes is also seen in their children's extracurricular activities. Table 4 shows the results of a survey concerning Korean chil-

TABLE 4
Korean Children's Extracurricular Activities

BOYS (%)		GIRLS (%)	
Sports	54	Piano lessons	69
Piano lessons	17	Violin lessons	9
Art lessons	8	Art lessons	6
Other music	5	Other music	5
Violin	4	Ballet	3
Other	12	Other	10

SOURCE: "A Survey of Korean Immigrants' Economic and Cultural Activities," *Korean People* 2 (January 1986:29–30).

dren's extracurricular activities. The data were based on responses to a questionnaire by 600 Korean women in Los Angeles who participated in a cooking class. The majority of Korean boys (54 percent) are involved in some kind of sport as an extracurricular activity, whereas only 17 percent of them take piano lessons. In sharp contrast, 69 percent of Korean girls receive piano lessons, and there is no sports category for girls. Although softball has become a very popular sport for girls in this country, one rarely sees a Korean girl playing softball. Most Korean parents discourage their girls from engaging in any sport that involves much action. Instead, they encourage girls to learn talents in music and art.

The most noteworthy feature of Korean immigrants' child socialization probably is the high mobility orientation and aspiration for children's education. As previously noted, Koreans have historically had great faith in education as the major avenue for social mobility. Recent Korean immigrants as a group are more progressive and more mobility-oriented than the general Korean population. Thus, Korean immigrant parents seem to put much more emphasis on children's education and mobility than native-born American parents. Because it is very expensive to send children to college in Korea, many Koreans chose to immigrate to this country to give their children better opportunities for education (Hurh, Kim, and Kim, 1979; Kim, 1978b:189; Min, 1987b). The Korean group, according to the 1980 census, shows the highest level of suburban residence of all ethnic groups (see the section on settlement patterns). This seems to reflect Koreans' eagerness to buy houses in affluent suburban areas where they can send their children to good public schools. Many Koreans also send their children to private schools to better prepare them for good colleges. Moreover, many Korean medical doctors and businessmen hire tutors to help their high school children study after school. In large Korean communities such as Los Angeles and New York, several private institutions have been established to provide Korean high school students with English, math, and SAT classes. Thus, they have re-established the Korean custom that was prohibited by law in South Korea. Parents' excessive demands for a high level of scholastic achievement seem to be stressful for many Korean American children.

Kin Ties and Care of the Elderly

One of the main characteristics of the Immigration Act of 1965 is its emphasis on family unity. Under the current immigration law, immigrants who become naturalized citizens after five years of residence in this country can bring over not only their spouses and children but also elderly parents and siblings. As previously noted, occupational immigrants and their nuclear family members constituted the majority of Korean immigrants in the early 1970s. However, as more and more Korean immigrants have become naturalized citizens since the late 1970s, they have been able to invite their elderly parents and siblings for permanent residence in this country. Thus, the majority of Korean immigrants admitted during recent years came as relatives of Korean naturalized citizens. This means that most Korean immigrant families have relatives in this country. For example, almost all (96 percent) of the sample of 116 Koreans in Atlanta reported having one or more non-nuclear kin member living with them or elsewhere in this country (Min, 1984a). In another survey (Hurh and Kim, 1984:90), three-fourths of the Korean sample in Los Angeles said that they had one or more kin members living in Los Angeles. The majority of Korean immigrants' kin members are their siblings.

Kin ties among Korean immigrants seem to take three different forms during the three stages of immigration: the pre-immigration stage, adjustment stage, and the settlement stage (Min, 1984a). During the pre-immigration period, prior immigrants help their relatives to immigrate to this country by applying for citizenship and then processing applications for permanent visas for their relatives. They also give prospective immigrants useful information and advice for employment in and successful adjustment to this country. In the second stage, prior immigrants help their relatives with immigration orientation. When asked who helped them with immigration orientation, more than half (52 percent) of the Korean respondents in Atlanta indicated relatives as the source of help, and 28 percent chose Korean friends (Min, 1984a). New arrivals usually stay at their brothers' or sisters' home for one week to three months during immigration orientation. Single persons cohabit with their brothers or sisters for a longer period of time, and many women live with them until they get married. In the third stage, the patterns of mutual assistance develop among Korean immigrant relatives. The Atlanta case study (Min, 1984a) indicates that for both financial and nonfinancial problems, Korean relatives were found to be a more important source of help than Korean friends. Korean immigrants also maintain active social interactions with their kin members. In the Los Angeles Korean community study (Hurh and Kim, 1984:90), for example, approximately half of the respondents reported contacting their kin members at least once a week. Association with kin members seems to be essential for Korean immigrants in coping with the alienation deriving from their residence in a foreign environment.

Many Korean elderly people are reluctant to immigrate to this country because of language and other adjustment problems. Thus, Korean immigrants 65 years old and over constitute only 2.6 percent of total recent Korean immigrants (U. S. Bureau of the Census, 1984:12), whereas the elderly people in this age category constitute 3.9 percent of the general Korean population (Korean National Bureau of Statistics, 1984:41). The vast majority of Korean elderly people in this country were invited by their adult children who had become naturalized citizens, and few Korean occupational immigrants have reached the age of retirement. Nearly all Korean elderly people in South Korea live with adult children, usually with the first son. The pattern of shared residence of parents and adult children seems to have changed in the Korean American community as more and more Korean elderly parents live apart from their children. One study conducted in New York (Koh and Bell, 1987) shows that 19 percent of Korean elderly people live alone and that another 25 percent live with a spouse. Living apart from children is more likely in a large Korean center such as New York, where many Korean elderly people live in the same apartment complex for the purpose of friendship and sociability. It is, however, very difficult in a smaller Korean community where there are few Korean elders. Thus, the proportion of Korean elderly people living apart from children seems to be smaller in smaller Korean communities.

Korean elderly immigrants do not maintain the same level of authority and status as they had in Korea. Experience is the primary source of authority and power for elderly people in most societies. However, the age-related experience of Korean elderly immigrants is not useful to their children's adjustment in a foreign environment. Thus, adult children generally make decisions on important family affairs without consulting cohabiting elderly parents. Moreover, American-born grandchildren do not show as much respect for elderly Koreans in speaking and other manners as the children in Korea usually do; although, as previously indicated, their parents try to teach them the proper norms involved in dealing with elderly people. Another major problem faced by most Korean elderly people is the lack of the opportunity for meaningful social interactions. The social interaction of Korean elderly people is largely limited to family and kin members and other Korean elderly people. Many Korean elderly people complain that they have too little time to talk with their cohabiting adult children who work long hours outside the home. Moreover, because most Korean elderly people cannot drive, they depend entirely on their adult children for companionship with kin members and friends. Large Korean centers have a few places where Korean older people meet together every day, but Korean elderly people in small Korean communities have no such places except the ethnic church. Thus, they are confined to home except on Sundays, when they attend church.

CHANGE AND ADAPTATION

The economic adaptation of immigrants has far-reaching effects on all phases of their immigrant life, including family life. A great many recent Korean immigrants make occupational adjustment through small businesses because they cannot find white-collar occupations commensurate to their education and ability. Accordingly, to adequately understand the changes and adaptations made in Korean immigrants' life patterns, the effects of their concentration in small businesses must be analyzed. The effects in the three following areas deserve special attention in this chapter: (1) changes in family life, (2) intergroup conflicts, and (3) ethnic solidarity.

Changes in Family Life

Immigrant groups usually show a high female labor-force participation rate because of immigrants' labor-market disadvantages and mobility orientation. A very high percentage of Korean female immigrants are in the labor force primarily because a large number of Korean families are engaged in labor-intensive small businesses such as small grocery stores, green groceries, and fast food services. To survive in a small business that involves long hours of work and small profit margins, both the Korean husband and the wife need to stay in the store. Thus, many Korean women, who played only the role of the homemaker in Korea, work full time outside the home in this country. The wife's help in the store is so essential to small business success that her economic role is accepted as natural in the Korean community. Korean immigrants' occupational adjustment in small business therefore has led to a significant modification of the traditional marital-role differentiation.

Korean immigrants' concentration in small business has not merely increased their female labor-force participation; it has also strengthened conjugal ties. To survive in a small business, the husband and wife need to work together and share drudgery and hardship. This, in turn, further reinforces conjugal ties. In Korea, many housewives wait for their husbands until late at night while the latter eat and drink outside the home with their friends after work. Korean business families in this country usually do not have this problem because the husband and wife stay together in the store during most work hours. Usually, the wife controls the cash register and the husband takes care of total management of the store. Their involvement in a small business leads the husband and wife to realize that their cooperation is essential to their economic survival. The money a Korean family makes out of its business belongs not to the individual worker but to the entire family and is mostly reinvested for the expansion of the family business. Although the family business deprives the Korean working woman of any independent source of earnings (Kim and Hurh, 1984), it strengthens the family as an economic unit.

Intergroup Conflicts and Ethnic Solidarity

The operation of small business puts Korean immigrants in a position to compete and conflict with other ethnic group members. Although Korean businessmen come into conflict with several different classes of out-group members (Kim, 1978), their conflict with two groups is worthy of special attention. First, Korean small businessmen conflict with white suppliers. Kim's study of the Korean community in New York (Kim, 1981) documents conflicts that Korean businessmen have with white wholesalers. According to Kim, Korean green grocers in New York encountered discrimination in pricing and the allocation of parking services by Jewish and Italian wholesalers at the Hunts Market. A series of discriminatory practices led Korean businessmen to stage a massive demonstration in the spring of 1977.

More serious conflicts, however, have arisen between Korean ghetto businessmen and black ghetto residents. Korean small businesses concentrate in crime-ridden downtown and minority areas where white businessmen are unwilling to invest (Min, 1984b; Kim, 1978; Bonacich, Light, and Wong, 1976, 1980). Thus, recent Korean immigrants take the role of a middleman minority distributing corporate products to minority members. The middleman minority role makes Korean merchants vulnerable to the violent reactions of minority customers. In New York, Los Angeles, and other cities, there have been many anti-Korean campaigns by black residents and leaders in the forms of murder, arson, boycotts, and press attacks. Black customers have complained that (1) Korean ghetto merchants are prejudiced against blacks, (2) they do not employ enough black workers, and (3) they are unwilling to contribute money for black neighbors. Korean community and business leaders in many cities have invited black community leaders, politicians, and ministers to explore the possibility of moderating interracial conflicts. Despite these efforts, the Korean–black interracial conflicts may be inevitable as long as a large number of Korean immigrants own and operate small businesses in black communities.

Historically, factionalism has dominated Korean politics, and the Korean community in the United States is known to have suffered from internal conflicts (Choy, 1979:234; Gardner, 1977; Kim, 1981:116, 117,

132). However, Korean immigrants' business-related conflicts with other ethnic members during recent years have enhanced ethnic ties. The murder of Korean businessmen and boycott of Korean-owned stores by minority customers have made Korean merchants aware of their common fate in this country. Korean community leaders and ethnic newspapers very often identify attacks on Korean merchants as attacks on the Korean community as a whole. Thus, Korean ghetto businesses have occasioned not only Korean business owners but also nonbusiness Korean immigrants to think about their common fate and marginal status in this country. The Korean Grocers' Association in Atlanta was established in 1983 to take concerted action against monopoly prices by wholesalers, especially Jewish wholesalers (Min, 1987). Korean grocers have negotiated through their organization with suppliers over prices of some grocery items, and they have been moderately successful in their efforts to protect common interests. In other Korean communities, similar trade organizations have been established to protect common interests against suppliers and customers, the vast majority of whom are out-group members. Without the threat to their economic survival from the outside world, Koreans would not resort to these kinds of collectivistic methods.

Projection of Future Changes in the Korean American Family System

Despite Korean immigrants' efforts to teach their children Korean customs and values, American-born Korean children seem to be making an almost complete cultural assimilation to the American mainstream. Thus, when these second-generation Koreans are married and move into the labor market, Korean American families will undergo significant changes. Second-generation Korean families are likely to modify the practices of male dominance and conjugal-role differentiation to the extent that they will maintain conjugal relations that are almost as egalitarian as those in white middle-class families. They will also substantially reduce parents' authority over children; most current Korean immigrant families do not give the first son the authority over their younger brothers and younger sisters. More and more of those Korean immigrants who came to this country in their fifties will reach retirement age in the near future. These Korean immigrants, unlike those who came here after retirement, are able to live independently of their children. Moreover, many of them are aware of the convenience of living independently. Therefore, the rate of Korean elderly people's cohabitation with adult children is expected to decline drastically in the near future.

REFERENCES

Bonacich, Edna, Ivan Light, and Charles Choy Wong. 1976. "Small Business among Korean Immigrants in Los Angeles," in Emma Gee (ed.), *Counterpoint: Perspective on Asian America.* Los Angeles: University of California, pp. 437–449.

———. "Korean Immigrants: Small Business in Los Angeles," in Roy Simon Bryce-Laporte (ed.), *Sourcebook on the New Immigration.* New Brunswick, New Jersey: Transaction Books, pp. 167–184.

Chiswick, Barry R. 1982. "The Economic Progress of Immigrants: Some Universal Patterns," in Barry R. Chiswick (ed.), *The Gateway: U.S. Immigration Issue and Policies.* Washington, DC: American Enterprise Institute for Public Policy Research, pp. 119–158.

Choong Ang Daily. 1981. May 21 and September 11.

Choi, Jai-Seuk. 1977. "Family System," *Korea Journal,* 17:4–14.

Choy, Bong Youn. 1979. *Koreans in America.* Chicago: Nelson Hall.

Gardner, Arthur. 1977. "Notes on the Availability of Materials for the Study of Korean Immigrants in the United States," in Hyung-chan Kim (ed.), *The Korean Diaspora.* Santa Barbara: ABC Clio Press, pp. 247–258.

Harvey, Young Sook, and Soon-Hyung Chung. 1980. "The Koreans," in John McDermott et al. (eds.), *People and Cultures of Hawaii.* Honolulu: University of Hawaii Press, pp. 135–154.

Hong, Lawrence K. 1982. "The Korean Family in Los Angeles," in Eui-Young Yu et al. (eds.), *Koreans in Los Angeles.* Los Angeles: California State University, pp. 99–132.

Houchins, Lee, and Chang-Su Houchins. 1974. "The Korean Experience in America, 1983–1924," *Pacific Historical Review,* 43:548–575.

Hurh, Won Moo, Kwang Chung Kim, and Hei Chu Kim. 1979. *Assimilation Patterns of Immigrants in the U.S.: A Case Study of Korean Immigrants in the Chicago Area.* Washington, DC: University Press of America.

Hurh, Won Moo, and Kwang Chung Kim. 1984. *Korean Immigrants in North America: Structural Analysis of Ethnic Confinement and Adhesive Adaptation.* Madison: Fairleigh Dickinson University Press.

Kim, Bok-Lim. 1972. "Casework with Japanese and Korean Wives of Americans," *Social Casework,* 53:273–279.

———. 1978a. "Pioneers in Intermarriage: Korean Women in the United States," in Harold Hakwon Sunoo and Dong Soo Kim (eds.), *Korean Women in Struggle for Humanization.* The Association of Korean Christian Scholars in North America, pp. 59–96.

———. 1978b. *The Asian Americans: Changing Patterns, Changing Needs.* New Jersey: The Association of Korean Christian Scholars in North America.

Kim, David, and Charles Choy Wong. 1977. "Business Development in Koreatowns," in Hyung-Chan Kim (ed.), *The Korean Diaspora.* Santa Barbara, CA: ABC Clio Press, pp. 229–245.

Kim, Illsoo. 1981. *New Urban Immigrants: The Korean Community in New York.* Princeton, NJ: Princeton University Press.

Kim, Kwang Chung. 1978. "Intra- and Inter-Ethnic Group Conflicts: The Case of Korean Small Business in the United States," in Harold Hakwon Sunoo and

Dong Soo Kim (eds.), *Korean Women in a Struggle for Humanization.* Tennessee: Association of Korean Christian Scholars in North America, pp. 201–232.

Kim, Kwang Chung, and Won Moo Hurh. 1983. "Employment of Korean Immigrant Wives and Division of Household Tasks." Unpublished manuscript, Macomb, IL: Western Illinois University.

———. 1984. "The Wives of Korean Small Businessmen in the U.S.: Business Development and Family Roles." Paper presented at the Annual Meeting of the American Sociological Association, San Antonio, TX.

———. 1985a. "Ethnic Resources Utilization of Korean Immigrant Enterprise in the Chicago Minority Area." Forthcoming in *International Migration Review.*

———. 1985b. "Immigration Experiences of Korean Wives in the U.S.: The Burden of Double Roles." Paper presented at the Annual Meeting of the National Council on Family Relations, Dallas, TX.

Kim, Kwang Chung, Hei Chu Kim, and Won Moo Hurh. 1979. "Division of Household Tasks in Korean Immigrant Families in the United States," *International Journal of Sociology of Family,* 9:161–175.

Kitano, Harry, and Lynn Kyung Chai. 1982. "Korean Interracial Marriage," *Marriage and Family Review,* 5:75–89.

Kitano, Harry, Wai-Tsang, Lynn Chai, and Herbert Hatanaka. 1984. "Asian American Interracial Marriage," *Journal of Marriage and the Family,* 46:179–190.

Koh, James Y., and William G. Bell. 1987. "Korean Elders in the United States: Intergenerational Relations and Living Arrangements," *The Gerontologist,* 27:66–71.

Korean National Bureau of Statistics. 1980a. *Social Indicators in Korea.* Seoul, Korea: Economic Planning Board of the Korean Government.

———. 1980b. *Annual Report on the Economically Active Population Survey.* Seoul, Korea: Economic Planning Board of the Korean Government.

———. 1983a. "Compete Enumeration," in *1980 Population and Housing Census Report.* Vol. 1. Seoul, Korea: Economic Planning Board of the Korean Government.

———. 1983b. "Fertility," in *1980 Population and Housing Census Report.* Vol. 2. Seoul, Korea: Economic Planning Board of the Korean Government.

———. 1983c. "Economic Activity," in *1980 Population and Housing Census Report.* Vol. 2. Seoul, Korea: Economic Planning Board of the Korean Government.

———. 1984. *Korean Statistical Year Book.* Vol. 31. Seoul, Korea: Economic Planning Board of the Korean Government.

Lee, Don Chang. 1975. *Acculturation of Korean Residents in Georgia.* San Francisco: R & E Research.

Light, Ivan. 1980. "Asian Enterprise in North America: Chinese, Japanese, and Koreans in Small Business," in Scott Cummings (ed.), *Self-Help in Urban America: Patterns of Minority Business Enterprise.* New York: Kenikart, pp. 33–57.

Min, Pyong Gap. 1984a. "An Exploratory Study of Kin Ties among Korean Immigrant Families in Altanta," *Journal of Comparative Family Studies,* 15:75–86.

———. 1984b. "A Structural Analysis of Korean Business in the United States," *Ethnic Groups,* 6:1–25.

———. 1984c. "From White-Collar Occupations to Small Business: Korean Immigrants' Occupational Adjustment," *Sociological Quarterly,* 25:333–352.

———. 1987a. "Korean Immigrants' Marital Patterns and Marital Adjustment." Paper presented at the Annual Meeting of the American Sociological Association, Chicago, IL.

———. 1987b. *Ethnic Business Enterprise: A Case Study of Korean Small Business in Atlanta.* Forthcoming. New York: The Center for Migration Studies.

Min, Pyong Gap, and Charles Jaret. 1985. "Ethnic Business Enterprise: The Case of Korean Small Business in Atlanta," Sociology and Social Research, 69:412–435.

Ratliff, Bascom W., Harriett Faye Moon, and Gwendolyn A. Bonacci. 1978. "Intercultural Marriage: The Korean American Experience," *Social Casework,* 59:221–226.

Rhim, Soon Man. 1978. "The Status of Women in Traditional Korean Society," in Harold Kakwon Sunoo and Dong Soo Kim (eds.), *Korean Women in a Struggle for Humanization,* Tennessee: Association of Korean Christian Scholars in North America.

Rodman, H. 1967. "Marital Power in France, Greece, Yugoslavia and the United States: A Cross-sectional Discussion," *Journal of Marriage and the Family,* 29:320–324.

———. 1972. "Marital Power and the Theory of 'Resources in Cultural Context'," *Journal of Comparative Family Studies,* 3:50–67.

Song, Johng Doo. 1982. "Korean College Students in Los Angeles: Basic Characteristics," in Eui-Young Yu et al. (eds.), *Koreans in Los Angeles.* Los Angeles: California State University, pp. 133–153.

Tienda, Marta and Ronald Angel. 1982. "Headship and Household Comparison among Blacks, Hispanics, and Other Whites," *Social Forces,* 61:508–531.

U. S. Bureau of the Census. 1976. *Current Population Reports.* Series p-20, no. 291. *Household and Family Characteristics: March 1975.* Washington, DC: U. S. Government Printing Office.

———. 1983a. "General Population Characteristics," in *1980 Census of Population.* Vol. 1: Part 1: "United States Summary." Washington, DC: U. S. Government Printing Office.

———. 1983b. "General Social and Economic Characteristics," in *1980 Census of Population.* Vol. 1: Washington, DC: U. S. Government Printing Office.

———. 1984. "Detailed Population Characteristics," in *1980 Census of Population.* Vol. 1. "United States Summary." Washington, DC: U. S. Government Printing Office.

U. S. Immigration and Naturalization Service. 1952–1982. *Annual Reports.* Washington, DC: U. S. Government Printing Office.

Yu, Eui-Young. 1983. "Korean Communities in America: Past, Present, and Future." *Amerasia Journal,* 10:23–52.

CHAPTER TEN

The Chinese American Family

Morrison G. Wong

INTRODUCTION

The Chinese have been residing in the United States in significant numbers for over 130 years. In 1980, approximately 812,178 Chinese lived in the United States (U. S. Department of Commerce, 1983). By 1985, the Chinese population was estimated to have increased by approximately 33 percent to approximately 1,079,400 Chinese (Gardner, Robey, and Smith, 1985), and is expected to continue to increase, barring any major immigration reform. Although they comprise less than half of 1 percent of the total United States population, the Chinese are the largest of the various Asian groups in the United States. Despite their lengthy residence and their numbers, a review of the literature on the Chinese American family suggests that theories on their family life are almost nonexistent and empirical studies are sparse and lacking. With the exception of a few early studies (Hayner and Reynolds, 1937; Lee, 1956; Schwartz, 1951), it is only within the last two decades that there has been a proliferation of research on the Chinese American family (Glenn, 1983; Huang, 1981; Lyman, 1968), their intermarriage rate (Barnett, 1963; Beaudry, 1971; Burma, 1963; Kitano and Yeung, 1982; Sung, 1987; Wong, 1988; Yuan, 1980), or their childrearing practices (Sollenberger, 1968). This paucity of literature on the Chinese American family may be the result of such factors as their small numbers and geographical concentration in major cities on the West and East Coasts. The underrepresentation of Chinese among social scientists—

to develop theories and carry out research on the Chinese family and life-styles—may be another factor. Lastly, the perception that the Chinese American family is not a "problem" in American society but, instead, bears a close resemblance to the white middle-class model—a hardworking, conforming, cohesive family that is the carrier of a traditional culture—may be another reason for the dearth of research (Staples and Mirande, 1980; Sue and Kitano, 1973). For the most part, past and present research on the Chinese American family has focused on the traditional Chinese cultural values and how they are manifested and modified in the Chinese family in America (Glenn, 1983). In general, the portrayal of the Chinese American family includes such favorable characteristics as (1) a stable family unit, as indicated by low rates of divorce and illegitimacy (Huang, 1981); (2) close ties between generations, as shown by the low rates of juvenile delinquency (Sollenberger, 1968); (3) economic self-sufficiency, as demonstrated by the avoidance of welfare dependency (Light, 1972); and, (4) conservatism, as expressed by the retention of the Chinese language and customs (Braun and Chao, 1978). This chapter will review, evaluate, extend, and synthesize the literature on the Chinese family in the United States.

Before beginning the discussion, two issues on the Chinese American family need to be addressed. First, there is no typical Chinese family, just as there is no typical American family. The family variations within the culture are as wide as between cultures (Kitano, 1985:223). Hence, it would be a gross simplification and inaccuracy to single out one Chinese family form as representative of all Chinese American families. Instead, a more profitable approach to a greater understanding of the formation, development, and modification of the Chinese American family is to look at the different types of Chinese families that have existed and still exist in the United States, realizing that even these are ideal types. Second, although the major emphasis of past research on the Chinese American family has focused on cultural factors, it should be noted that the Chinese American family is a product of the complex interaction between structural factors (i.e., social, legal, political, and economic) and cultural factors. Moreover, because both structural and cultural factors are constantly undergoing change, the Chinese American family may be best viewed not as a static entity, but as one also undergoing constant changes and adaptations. Knowledge and awareness of the effects these various structural and cultural factors have had on the Chinese family will result in a greater understanding of the changes and adaptations the Chinese American family has undergone and will continue to undergo. It is within this framework that the Chinese family in the United States will be analyzed.

The discussion of the formation and evolution of the Chinese American family in the United States will be presented within the context of five historical periods, with the understanding that there is considerable overlap between historical periods and family types. They are (1) the traditional Chinese family before their arrival in the United States; (2) the "mutilated" or "split household" Chinese family between 1850 and 1920; (3) the small producer Chinese family between 1920 and 1943; (4) normalization of the Chinese family between 1943 and 1965; and (5) the ghetto and the professional Chinese family from 1965 to the present. Lastly, the changes and adaptations of the modern Chinese family in the United States will be discussed.

THE TRADITIONAL CHINESE FAMILY

The Chinese American family, both past and present, has its foundation in the traditional family structure of China, which remained unchanged for many centuries and encompassed a much broader connotation than the Western ideal consisting of only the conjugal unit of father, mother, and children. The traditional Chinese family also includes the extended kinship groups and clan members (Sung, 1967:152).

There were many distinctive characteristics of the traditional family in China. First, the traditional Chinese family was patriarchal. Roles were clearly defined, with males, particularly the father and eldest son, having the most dominant roles (Hsu, 1971a). Authority passed from the father to the eldest son, whose authority and decisions were absolute. Females, relegated to a subordinate position in the traditional Chinese family, were expected to please and obey their fathers and, if married, were subordinate to not only their husbands but also their husbands' parents (Kitano, 1985: 223–224).

A second characteristic of the traditional Chinese family was that it was patrilocal; that is, the married couple lived with the husband's parents. According to this ideal, the grandparents, their unmarried children, their married sons, together with their wives and children, all lived in one household. Because of patrilocal residence, daughters were considered less valuable and important than sons in the Chinese family. Parents felt that daughters were being reared at their expense for the benefit of another family or clan (Sung, 1967:152). In some cases, particularly if the family was extremely poor, infanticide of the female child was practiced.

Because of its patrilocal residence pattern, the traditional family in China was also an extended family in which many generations and their offspring lived under one roof. Ideally, the more generations living under the same roof, the more prestigious the family. Besides the prestige factor, the extended family structure of the Chinese family provided another important function. In an agriculturally based economy, there was an urgent need for many workers to cultivate and till the land and harvest the crops. A nuclear family would be at a disadvantage in this economy. The extended family system was a much more suitable arrangement, providing the family with the much needed additional laborers, as well as providing the members of the extended family with some degree of economic security.

According to the Chinese system of patrilineal descent, the household property and land were to be divided equally among the sons, either at the father's death or the marriage of the youngest son. However, in exchange for the property and land, the sons were expected to reciprocate by sharing equally in the responsibility for the care and support of their parents in their old age (Fei, 1939; Hsu, 1971b; Ikels, 1985; Nee and Wong, 1985).

Ancestor worship was greatly emphasized in the traditional family in China. It was believed that a Chinese male could achieve some sense of immortality only if his family line was continued (i.e., if he bore sons). In fact, one of the greatest sins that a man could commit was to die without having any sons to carry on the family line and perform the ancestor worship ritual of burning incense at his grave. As a consequence, an intense desire to have sons, and as many sons as possible, existed among the Chinese. Ancestor worship reflected the strength and importance of lineage solidarity, providing a link between the past and present (Hsu, 1971b).

Filial piety was a highly cherished value in the traditional Chinese family. Briefly, filial piety is a set of moral principles, taught at a very young age and reinforced throughout one's life, of mutual respect to those of equal status and reverence toward the dominant leader and one's elders. Duty, obligation, importance of the family name, service, and self-sacrifice to the elders, all essential elements of filial piety, characterized the Chinese family relations (Hsu, 1971a; Kung, 1962:206).

As in many other agrarian-based societies, marriage was a family concern, not a private matter between a couple in love. In fact, love was not a prerequisite for marriage and was highly discouraged. Because the bride lived with the husband's parents (in the patrilocal residence), the parents felt that they should have an important voice in the decision about who would live with them. The arranged marriage, another characteristic of the traditional Chinese family, is a classic case of not leaving important decisions to the impetuous young. In many cases, the son did not know who the bride was until after the wedding ceremony when the bride unveiled her face (Fong, 1968).

These characteristics, as well as Chinese customs and family norms, resulted in the domestic and international migration patterns in which the males left for economic opportunities, even to working distant lands for extended periods of time, while the wife and children remained in the home of the husband's parents in the village (Lyman, 1968; Nee and Wong, 1985).

In sum, many scholars have concluded that because of the strong traditional bonds of the family, the Chinese peasants during this period may be characterized as "familist": lacking any sense of a developed national identity and valuing the family first and foremost (Fei, 1939; Johnson, 1962). The Chinese family entailed much more than a family in the Western sense. It was a link to a much larger chain of extended kinship and clan members, bringing large numbers of people together with a common bond, whether real or imagined, and promoting a sense of solidarity, security, and belonging (Freedman, 1961–1962; Liu, 1959; Yang, 1959).

THE "MUTILATED," OR "SPLIT HOUSEHOLD," CHINESE FAMILY (1850–1920)

Although there were Chinese residing in the United States as early as 1785, the discovery of gold in California and the political and economic instability of China provided the major impetus to the immigration of a significant number of Chinese to the United States in the early 1850s (Chinn, Lai, and Choy, 1969:7; Hirschman and Wong, 1981; Lai and Choy, 1971:22). The Chinese practice and custom of expecting the emigrating men to leave their wives and children behind in China had three major consequences. First, it guaranteed that the emigrating sons would continue to send back remittance to their parents to support them in old age (Glick, 1980). Second, it instilled in the emigrating Chinese a sojourner rather than immigrant orientation. Hence, the single male or the husband who left his wife in China looked on his stay in the United States as temporary and evaluated American society primarily in terms of its economic opportunities. They sought to make and accumulate as much money as possible as quickly as possible to pay off debts and hoped to rejoin their family in China with a much higher status (Barth, 1964:157; Lyman, 1968; Siu, 1952). Third, it ensured a continual bond to the family and the village on the part of the emigrating men (Nee and Wong, 1985).

From their arrival in the 1850s until the 1920s, the overwhelming majority of the early Chinese immigrants were men. More than half of the arriving men were single, and those who were not often were separated from their wives and condemned to live a good portion of their lives as bachelors in Chinese communities scattered throughout the United States (Coolidge, 1909; Kingston, 1981; Lyman, 1968, 1977; Nee and Nee, 1973; Siu, 1952; Weiss, 1974). As a consequence, the majority of the early Chinese immigrants did not lead normal family lives. In fact, one can hardly speak of Chinese family life during this period because there were so few Chinese women (Glenn, 1983; Lyman, 1968; Nee and Nee, 1973; Sung, 1967).

Table 1 presents the sex ratio of the Chinese in the United States from 1860 to 1980. A glance at the table shows the tremendous imbalance in the sex ratio among the Chinese. From 1860 to 1890, the sex ratio fluctuated from 1,284 to 2,679 Chinese men per 100 Chinese women. After 1900, the imbalance among the Chinese began to decline. However, in 1920 and 1930, when an American-born Chinese population began to emerge, the sex ratio was still highly imbalanced. Without a significant number of Chinese women, the formation of Chinese families was greatly hindered.

The view of emigration solely as a temporary economic proposition,

TABLE 1

Chinese Population in the United States, by Sex, Sex Ratio, Percentage Foreign Born, and Percentage under 14 Years of Age: 1860–1980.

YEAR	TOTAL	MALE	FEMALE	SEX RATIO	FOREIGN BORN (%)	UNDER 14 YEARS OF AGE (%)
1860	34,933	33,149	1,784	1,858	—	
1870	63,199	58,633	4,566	1,284	99.8	
1880	105,465	100,686	4,779	2,106	99.0	
1890	107,475	103,607	3,868	2,679	99.3	
1900	89,863	85,341	4,522	1,887	90.7	3.4
1910	71,531	66,856	4,675	1,430	79.3	—
1920	61,639	53,891	7,748	696	69.9	12.0
1930	74,954	59,802	15,152	395	58.8	20.4
1940	77,504	57,389	20,115	286	48.1	21.1
1950	117,140	76,725	40,415	190	47.0	23.3
1960	236,084	135,430	100,654	135	39.5	33.0
1970	431,583	226,733	204,850	111	46.9	26.6
1980	812,178	410,936	401,246	102	63.3	21.1
1985	1,079,700*					

SOURCES: Gardner et al. (1985), Glenn (1983:38), Lyman (1970a:79), U.S. Department of Commerce (1983).

Note: *Estimated by Gardner et al. (1985).

coupled with the Chinese practice of leaving the wife and children in China, resulted in a bizarre family structure among these early Chinese immigrants. In these "mutilated" families (Sung, 1967), or "split household" families (Glenn, 1983), the married Chinese male in the United States was physically separated from his wife and children in China. The economic, or production, function of the family was carried out by the Chinese male living in the United States, whereas other family functions, such as socialization of the young, were carried out by the wife and other relatives in the home village in China. In essence, many Chinese men in the United States were family men without the presence of a wife or family members. Obviously, this family form was not preferred but was tolerated because many Chinese males looked on their stay in the United States as temporary.

Racial and ethnic antagonism, coupled with white xenophobia against the early Chinese immigrants, culminated in the passage of the Chinese Exclusion Act of 1882. This act, the first national act that excluded a particular nationality group from immigrating, barred Chinese laborers and their relatives from entering the United States. However, Chinese officials, students, tourists, merchants, and relatives of merchants and citizens were exempt from this exclusion. Although Chinese custom prevented most women from joining their husbands, the Chinese Exclusion Act erected an official barrier to their coming. Because a Chinese wife was accorded the status of her husband, Chinese merchants were allowed to bring their wives from China with them. However, wives of Chinese laborers were denied entry into the United States by the same law that excluded their husbands (Kung 1962:101; Lyman 1974:87). The shortage of women among the Chinese immigrants in the United States might have been mitigated if the Chinese had had the opportunity to intermarry with the white population. However, the mutual peculiarities of dress, language, customs, and diet, the physical and racial distinctiveness, the mutually exclusive associations, and the enforcement of antimiscegenation laws restricted the amount of intimate contact and interaction between the two groups, precluding any possibility of romantic involvement. As a consequence, Chinese laborers, faced with an unfavorable sex ratio, forbidden as noncitizens from bringing their wives, and prevented by laws in most western states from marrying whites, had three options regarding their marital status: return permanently to China; if single, stay in the United States as bachelors; or, if married, remain separated from families except for occasional visits (Glenn, 1983). Thus, for many Chinese immigrants, the establishment of a family in America was a near impossibility.

The 1888 Scott Act further exacerbated the plight of many Chinese laborers, stipulating that they would be barred re-entry into the United States if they left. Those Chinese laborers who wished to stay in the United States could look toward a future of only loneliness and isolation (Kung, 1962:101).

Table 2 shows the number of Chinese immigrants to the United States by time period. From this table, one can note the dramatic impact these two acts had on Chinese immigration. In the years preceding the Chinese Exclusion Act, there was a continual and dramatic increase in Chinese immigration, reaching its peak of 123,201 Chinese immigrants in the decade of the 1870s. However, after the passage of this act, Chinese immigration declined precipitously. Only 10,242 Chinese immigrated to the United States in the 1880s and 14,799 Chinese in the 1890s. With the restrictions placed on Chinese entering the United States and without the establishment of families in America, there was little incentive for these

TABLE 2

Chinese Immigrants[a] to the United States: 1820–1981.

YEARS	NUMBER OF IMMIGRANTS
1820–1850	43
1851–1860	41,397
1861–1870	64,301
1871–1880	123,201
1881–1890	61,711[b]
1891–1900	14,799
1901–1910	20,605
1911–1920	21,278
1921–1930	29,907
1931–1940	4,928
1941–1950	16,709[d]
1951–1960	9,657[e]
1961–1970	34,764[f]
1971–1981	150,129

SOURCES: U. S. Department of Commerce (1975), U. S. Department of Justice (1981).

[a]Beginning in 1957, includes Taiwan.

[b]In 1881 and 1882, before the Chinese Exclusion Act, 51,469 Chinese immigrated to the United States.

[c]Before the Immigration Act of 1924, from 1921 to 1924, 20,393 Chinese entered the United States.

[d]After various immigration and refugee policies were passed, about 15,341 Chinese immigrants entered the United States (1946–1950).

[e]The McCarran-Walter Immigration Act was passed in 1952.

[f]The 1965 Immigration Act was passed.

early Chinese immigrants to invest in acquiring the social and cultural skills necessary to integrate or blend into American society (Siu, 1952).

Although immigration laws excluded the majority of Chinese from entering the United States, it did allow entry of relatives of United States citizens of Chinese ancestry. When the 1906 San Francisco earthquake and fire destroyed not only most of Chinatown and much of San Francisco but also most of the municipal records (including Chinese immigration and citizenship records), this provided a loophole by which the Chinese could immigrate to the United States. The "slot racket" or "paper son" form of immigration developed. Chinese residents would claim American birth, and the authorities were powerless to disprove their contention. American-born Chinese, actual or claimed, would then visit China, report the birth of a son, and thereby create an entry slot. Years later, the slot could be used by a relative, or the birth papers could be sold to someone wanting to immigrate. The purchaser, called a "paper son," simply assumed the name and identity of the alleged son. Under the terms of this type of immigration, the Chinese in America developed a long-term pattern of sojourning — "come today, stay tomorrow" (Glenn, 1983; Kung, 1962; Lyman, 1974; Sung, 1967).

A limited number of Chinese women immigrated to the United States in the latter part of the nineteenth century (see Table 1). Those women who immigrated between 1850 and 1882 were either prostitutes or wives of the small group of Chinese merchants (Lyman, 1977:69; Nee and Wong, 1985). Hirata (1979) suggests that Chinese prostitution was an important element in the maintenance of the "split household" family by helping men avoid long-term relationships with women in the United States and ensuring that the bulk of their meager earnings would continue to support the family in China. From 1882 to 1924, a period of restricted immigration, the few Chinese women who immigrated to America were usually married to merchants or those who could assume the legal status of merchants (Lyman, 1968).

For those few Chinese men who were fortunate enough to have resident wives in the United States, the old patriarchal Chinese family system continued. Values of the Old Country were stressed. The husband was expected to be obeyed by the wife. She was kept in seclusion by her husband, seldom ventured forth alone in the Chinese community, and almost never ventured beyond the community into white America. Obedience and filial piety to the patriarch was a prime virtue and was often exhibited by children long after maturity. Parental control even extended to matters of courtship and mate selection. Marriages were always arranged, either by relatives living in China or between or with relatives in other Chinatowns in the United States (Hsu, 1971a; Kung, 1962; Lee, 1960; Lyman, 1968; Weiss, 1970, 1974:32–33). Men were expected to accept jobs under the direction or sponsorship of one's father or male relatives to provide economic support of the parental household (either in China or the United States) and to take care of the parents in their old age (Ikels, 1985).

In sum, Chinese custom and tradition, the sojourner orientation of the Chinese immigrants, and the imbalanced sex ratio all had profound consequences for the personal, social, and family life of the early Chinese in the United States. One consequence was the formation of the "mutilated," or "split household," family structure and the subsequent perpetuation of this Chinese family type by various racist and exclusionist immigration laws. Another consequence was that only a small number of Chinese immigrant families was established in America during this early period. The emergence and maturation of a substantial second-generation Chinese American population was delayed for almost 70 to 80 years after the initial arrival of the Chinese immigrants.

THE SMALL PRODUCER CHINESE FAMILY (1920–1943)

Despite the numerous obstacles to family formation, by the 1920s and 1930s, a sizeable second-generation Chinese population was becoming increasingly evident in the major Chinatowns in the United States. These early Chinese families consisted primarily of small entrepreneurs or former laborers who were able to accumulate enough capital to start their own business, either alone or with partners. They were involved in such enterprises as laundries, restaurants, mom and pop grocery stores, and other small shops. The change in immigration status from laborer to merchant was of no small consequence for the Chinese. It allowed the new merchants to return to China and bring over their wives and children (Glenn, 1983; Nee and Wong, 1985). This is evident in the slight increase in Chinese immigration after the 1891–1900 period (see Table 2). From 1920 to 1950, the percentage of Chinese born in the United States grew from 30 percent to a little over 50 percent of the total Chinese population in the United States. However, the sex ratio still remained highly imbalanced (see Table 1).

Two types of Chinese families tended to predominate during this period. The first type, which was already discussed, was the "mutilated," or "split household," family. Chinese tradition was certainly one barrier keeping Chinese families separated. Another barrier was the discriminatory features of the Immigration Act of 1924. This act made it impossible for

American citizens of Chinese ancestry to send for their wives and families. Even Chinese merchants, who previously were able to bring their wives to the United States, were denied this privilege. This law was later changed in 1930 to allow wives of Chinese merchants, as well as Chinese wives who were married to American citizens before 1924, to immigrate to the United States (Chinn, Lai, and Choy, 1969:24). The "mutilated" family remained one of the predominant forms of family life among the Chinese in the United States until the end of World War II, when more liberal immigration legislation was passed (Sung, 1967:156).

Another type of Chinese family, the small producer family, emerged during this period. This family type consisted of the immigrant and first-generation American-born family functioning as a productive unit (Glenn, 1983). All family members, including the children, worked in the small family business, usually within the ethnic economy. The business was profitable only because it was labor intensive, and family members put in extremely long hours (Mark and Chih, 1982:66).

The small producer family had four distinctive characteristics. First, there was a lack of any clear demarcation between work and family life. Second, the family was a self-contained unit in terms of production and consumption. Third, although all family members participated in the family enterprise, there was a division of labor according to age and gender, with gradations of responsibility according to capacity and experience. Fourth, there was an emphasis on the collectivity over the individual (Glenn, 1983).

Children undertook a great deal of responsibility and gained considerable status at a very early age in the small producer family. Because of their knowledge of English was superior to that of their immigrant parents, children played a crucial role in carrying out the daily business and domestic affairs of the family. Acting as mediators between their immigrant parents and the outside society, they performed such tasks as reading and translating documents and business contracts, filling out bank slips, and negotiating with customers (Kingston, 1976; Lowe, 1943; Nee and Nee, 1973; Wong, 1950).

Wives in the small producer Chinese family had much higher status compared with their traditional Chinese counterparts. As a result of limited immigration, the small producer family tended to be nuclear in form. Consequently, wives did not have to contend with in-laws. Moreover, being more-or-less equal producers in the family business enabled Chinese wives to improve their position in the family and attain considerable autonomy and equality.

The traditional Chinese family system lived in the minds of the older

Chinese during this period. The Chinese American family was patriarchal, with the oldest living male theoretically being the master of the household. In actual practice, however, the opinion of the mother of the oldest living male carried considerable weight in major family decisions. In relations between parents and children, the old-fashioned Chinese father occupied the seat of authority and expected to be obeyed. The practice of deferring to the wishes of the elders was strengthened by the difficulty of the children in finding employment outside of Chinatown, making them economically dependent on the older members of the family and clan. Patrilocal residence was still practiced among the Chinese in America during this period. The Chinese family conformed to traditional sex roles. A good husband was expected to be a good provider who earned the money but also spent it. A good, traditional Chinese wife in America was expected to spend very little money and rear as many children as possible—preferably sons (Hayner and Reynolds, 1937). However, there was considerable variation in this pattern. If the wife was born and educated in this country, her position in the family approximated the American pattern. Likewise, American-born Chinese children who were educated in American schools developed attitudes very similar to those of native-born children of European immigrant parents and other native-born Americans.

In sum, the shortage of Chinese women and various racist immigration policies resulted in the "mutilated," or "split household," family continuing to be a predominant family form among the Chinese in America from the 1920s to the 1940s. Another type of Chinese family that emerged during this period was the small producer family. A distinguishing characteristic of this sizeable second-generation Chinese American family was that the Chinese children divided their time between growing up as active participants in the small family enterprise serving the ethnic community and trying to get ahead in school. Despite the emergence of this new Chinese family form, the cultural link between the Chinese family in the United States and the traditional family in China was maintained. However, a gradual weakening of this link was in progress as the family members became more acculturated into American society.

THE NORMALIZATION OF THE CHINESE FAMILY (1943–1965)

The racist and exclusionist immigration policies during the early tenure of the Chinese in America played a major role in the resultant shortage of Chinese women in the United States and in the delay in the emergence of a second-generation Chinese population in the United States. However, it was the liberalization and reforms of immigration policies during and after World War II that were instrumental in partially rectifying past discrimination against the Chinese, which slowly led to the development and normalization of family life among the Chinese in the United States. In 1943, the Chinese Exclusion Act of 1882 was repealed, making Chinese immigrants, many of whom had been living in the United States for decades, eligible for citizenship. In recognition of China's position as an ally of the United States in World War II, a token quota of 105 persons per year was set for Chinese immigration. Although small, the quota did open the door to further immigration and had an impact on the future formation of Chinese families in the United States. In 1945, the War Brides Act was passed, allowing approximately 6,000 Chinese women to enter the United States as brides of men in the United States military. In 1946 an amendment to this law put Chinese wives and children of United States citizens on a nonquota basis. The Displaced Persons Act of 1948 gave permanent resident status to 3,465 Chinese visitors, seamen, and students who were stranded here because of the Chinese civil war. This same year saw the California antimiscegenation law declared unconstitutional. In 1952, the McCarran–Walter Act was passed, eliminating race as a bar to immigration and giving preferences to relatives (Chen, 1980: 211–213; Lee, 1956; Li, 1977a). The Refugee Relief Act of 1953 allowed 2,777 Chinese into the United States as refugees of the Chinese civil war. A presidential directive issued in 1962 permitted refugees from mainland China to enter the United States as parolees from Hong Kong. By 1966, approximately 15,000 refugees had entered under this provision. During the period from 1943 to the repeal of the quota law in 1965, Chinese immigration was overwhelmingly female, approximately nine females for every one male. Most of these women were alien wives of citizens admitted as nonquota immigrants (Simpson and Yinger, 1965:350–351; Sung, 1977; Yuan, 1966).

Although many of the Chinese male immigrants remained bachelors or separated from their wives during most of their lives in the United States, the liberalization of immigration policies after World War II enabled many "mutilated," or "split household," families to be reunited. Reform in immigration policies also encouraged Chinese men to return to Hong Kong in droves to find wives. The quest for a bride generally conformed to the age-old pattern of getting their family elders to find a mate for them through a go-between or matchmaker (Sung, 1967:156–157). The courtship was usually instantaneous, and complete strangers often married after knowing each other for as little as one week. These trans-Pacific marriages were characterized by a wide disparity in age—men in their 30s and 40s marrying women between 18 and 22 years old—and level of education.

Tremendous differences also existed in the cultural upbringing between the partners—older, traditional men marrying younger, more modern women (Kitano, 1985:225; Sung, 1967:162). After their wedding, these newlyweds returned to the United States to ghetto conditions and a life of hardship in the urban Chinatowns of the West Coast. Despite the stress, strain, and cultural shock, these Chinese families usually remained intact. However, Sung (1967:162) argues that the relatively low divorce rate among the Chinese is the result of marital discord and unhappiness generally being turned inward on the self, which may be reflected in a higher suicide rate rather than in divorce statistics. She found that the suicide rate among the Chinese in San Francisco was four times higher than for the city as a whole and that predominantly women committed suicide.

For those Chinese families in which both spouses were native-born Americans, the family pattern approximated the American form consisting of the husband, wife, and children and, occasionally, elderly parents. The parent–child relationship may be characterized as being situated somewhere between the strict formality of the traditional Chinese family and the high degree of permissiveness of the American (white) family (Sung, 1967:162, 176).

The stranded Chinese who were displaced by the Chinese civil war in 1948 had family backgrounds strikingly different than the other Chinese in the United States. They were well-educated, having attended teacher-training institutions and colleges in China and having received post-graduate education in the United States. Selection of a spouse was based more on individual preferences and love rather than the traditional reliance on or the decision of elders or matchmakers. These former students settled in the suburbs near the universities and research facilities where they ultimately found employment (Ikels, 1985).

The size of the Chinese families in the United States during this period was much larger than the general American population. One study found that Chinese families in New York's Chinatown had an average of 4.4 children, compared with 2.9 children for white families (Liu, 1950). This difference may be the result of the Chinese value that a man's stature rose in direct proportion to the number of sons he sired and that women gained status by producing sons. It may also result partly from generational differences. Kwoh (1947) observed that if both parents were born in China, the median number of children in the family was 6.2; if both were American born, the median number was 3.2 children. Taken together, the average Chinese family had 5.5 children. As the Chinese became more Americanized and acculturated, the number of children in the Chinese family declined.

There are several general characteristics of the Chinese family during this period that hold regardless of the nativity or generational status. First, filial piety, or loyal devotion to one's parents, was still highly stressed, although in varying degrees. No matter how old a child was or how exalted his social position, the son's first obligation was to his parents.

Second, Chinese children were taught the concept of "face" at a very early age. If the children did something wrong, it was not just a personal matter between themselves and their conscience: they also brought dishonor and shame to their family, family name, and loved ones.

Related to the concept of "face" was the fact that the Chinese went to great lengths to keep their "dirty linen" within the family walls. This may account for their infrequent use of social agencies at such times and the common perceptions or misconceptions that the Chinese take care of their own and that the Chinese family is relatively problem-free.

In sum, the liberalization of immigration policies after World War II slowly led to the normalization and formation of the Chinese families in the United States. As the Chinese families became more acculturated to American society, their family patterns began to closely resemble those of their American counterparts.

THE GHETTO AND THE PROFESSIONAL CHINESE FAMILY (1965 TO THE PRESENT)

The Immigration Act of 1965 has had a profound influence on the family life of Chinese in America. With its emphasis on family reunification, this act abolished the national-origins quota system of 1952 and granted each country a quota of 20,000 immigrants per year. Since 1968, when the law went into effect, approximately 22,000 Chinese have immigrated to the United States through Hong Kong each year (Wong, 1985, 1986; Wong and Hirschman, 1983) (see Table 2). Unlike the pre-1965 immigrants, who came over as individuals, most of the new Chinese immigrants are coming over as family groups—typically husband, wife, and unmarried children (Hong, 1976). A family chain pattern of migration has developed (Li, 1977b; Sung, 1977; Wong and Hirschman, 1983). Initially, many of these new immigrants usually settled in or near Chinatown so that they could trade in Chinese-speaking stores, use bilingual services, and find employment (Glenn, 1983).

Before discussing the characteristics of the various types of modern Chinese families, it may be informative to first briefly discuss some of the general social, demographic, economic, and family characteristics of the Chinese in the United States. A glance at Table 3 shows that although in

1980 there was a slightly greater proportion of males to females in the Chinese population, the Chinese sex ratio was much more balanced than in previous decades. The Chinese were more highly urbanized and younger than the white population. As a consequence of renewed immigration, approximately two-thirds of the Chinese population is foreign born.

Interestingly, Chinese women had a lower fertility rate for every age category than their white counterparts. However, the average number of persons in Chinese families was higher than for white families. This apparent contradiction may be partially explained by the tendency of many adult sons and daughters of Chinese ancestry to live with their parents until they marry and/or the presence of extended family members, such as the elderly grandparents. It may also be partially explained by a slightly greater proportion of Chinese families consisting of married couples with children living with them than white families.

The slightly higher labor-force participation rate of the Chinese compared with the white population was accounted for by the greater labor-force participation of Chinese women. There was basically no difference between the Chinese and white population in terms of class of worker: although, interestingly, a slightly higher percentage of whites than Chinese were self-employed. Occupationally, approximately 30 percent of the white and Chinese population was involved in technical occupations. The Chinese were overrepresented in managerial, professional, and service occupations, a distribution that is partly a reflection of nativity status. With the exceptions of the overrepresentation of the white population in agriculture, mining, and construction and the much greater overrepresentation of Chinese in retail trade, the industrial distribution of these two groups were roughly the same. A greater proportion of Chinese than white families had multiple workers, which may partly explain their higher family income, approximately $2,000 higher than white families. However, at the other end of the income continuum, Chinese families were more likely to have family incomes below poverty level. Approximately 25 percent of all Chinese families lived in poverty. This finding suggests that many Chinese families barely make ends meet. For many of these families, even if members work, they are involved in the secondary labor market or enclave economy, barely making enough to survive.

The present-day Chinese American family can be divided into two major types. The first type is the "ghetto or Chinatown Chinese" (Huang, 1981), or "dual worker family" (Glenn, 1983). This family type consists of the new immigrant Chinese family living in or near Chinatowns in the major metropolitan areas of this country. Approximately half of the immigrants may be classified as working class, being employed as service

TABLE 3

Demographic, Social, Economic, and Family Characteristics of the White and Chinese Population in the United States: 1980

CHARACTERISTICS	WHITE (%)	CHINESE (%)
SEX		
Males	49	51
Females	51	49
Sex ratio (males/females)	94.9	102.4
RESIDENCE		
Urban	71	97
Rural	29	3
AGE		
0–14	21	21
15–34	34	41
35–64	32	31
65+	12	7
Median	31.3	29.6
NATIVITY STATUS		
U. S. born	95	37
Foreign born	5	63
FERTILITY		
Women 15–44 years per 1000	1358	1020
Women 15–24 years per 1000	269	82
Women 25–34 years per 1000	1404	939
Women 35–44 years per 1000	2544	2233
PERSONS PER FAMILY		
Average number of persons	3.19	3.64
FAMILY TYPE, BY PRESENCE OF CHILDREN		
Total families		
with natural children under 18 years old	71	83
Married couples (percentage of total)	(86)	(87)
with natural children under 18 years old	71	89
Female heads of household (percentage of total)	(11)	(8)
with natural children under 18 years old	73	53
Persons under 18 years old living with two parents	83	88
LABOR FORCE STATUS		
In the labor force (16 or more years old)	62	66
Male	76	74
Female	49	58
CLASS OF WORKER		
Private	74	76
Government	16	16
Self-employed	10	8

TABLE 3—*Continued*

CHARACTERISTICS	WHITE (%)	CHINESE (%)
OCCUPATION		
Managerial and professional	24	33
Technical, sales, and administrative support	31	30
Service	12	19
Farm	3	0
Crafts	13	6
Operatives and laborers	17	13
INDUSTRY		
Agriculture, mining, and construction	10	3
Manufacturing	22	20
Transportation and communication	7	5
Wholesale trade	5	3
Retail trade	17	27
Banking and insurance	6	7
Business and repair	4	4
Service	3	4
Entertainment	1	1
Professional	20	21
Public administration	5	5
WORKERS IN FAMILY		
Total families		
0	12	7
1	33	27
2	42	47
3 or more	12	19
Married Couples		
0	11	6
1	30	26
2	45	49
3	13	19
FAMILY INCOME		
Median	$20,835	$22,559
Mean	$24,166	$26,600
POVERTY STATUS OF FAMILY		
Below poverty level	7.0	10.5
Below 125% poverty level	10.3	14.8

SOURCES: Gardner et al. (1985), U. S. Department of Commerce (1983).

workers, operatives, craftsmen, or laborers (Nee and Nee, 1973). Both husband and wife seek employment in the secondary labor market or enclave economy, in the labor-intensive, low-capital service and small manufacturing sectors, such as the tourist shops, restaurants, and garment sweatshops (Light and Wong, 1975; Wong, 1980a, 1983; Wong and Hirschman, 1983). Husbands and wives are more-or-less coequal breadwinners in the family. However, unlike the small producer family, there tends to be a complete segregation of work and family life. Parents and children are separated for most of the day. Moreover, it is not uncommon for parents to spend very little time with each other because of different jobs and job schedules—one parent having a regular shift (i.e., sweatshop), and the other parent having the swing shift (i.e., restaurant)—or with their children. The parents' fatigue, the long hours of separation, and the lack of common experience can undermine communication between the parents and their children. Chen (1980:227–228) vividly describes the life-style of these new immigrants:

> Penetrate, if you can, into the crowded tenements, and you will find families of four, five, and six living, working, playing, and sleeping in a single room. Pots, pans, and food must be taken to a community kitchen shared with other families. Privacy is a sometime thing. These facts speak for themselves: for all its gaiety, good humor, and indomitable spirit, this area suffers from widespread poverty, high unemployment, substandard and overcrowded housing, inferior public services and facilities, and resulting grave health problems.

The latest influx of new Chinese immigrants has helped preserve some of the old traditional ways. Parental authority, especially the father's, is more absolute, and the extended family, if present, plays a much more significant role than typically found in middle-class Chinese or white families (Schaffer, 1984:350).

The second type of Chinese family is the middle-class, white-collar, or professional Chinese American family that moved away from Chinatown into the surrounding urban areas and suburbs. These immigrant or American-born Chinese are more modern and cosmopolitan in orientation and view themselves as more American than Chinese (Huang, 1981; Kitano, 1985:224; Weiss, 1970, 1977). Highly educated, the parents, one if not both, probably have college degrees and are involved in professional or white-collar occupations. Their relatively high socioeconomic status and degree of acculturation to American society allow these Chinese to live fairly comfortable lives in the suburbs (Kuo, 1970; Yuan, 1963, 1966). However, there is a tendency for these Chinese to re-establish a Chinese community in the suburbs (Lyman, 1974:149). The Chinese family in this situation may be structurally termed "semiextended." Although grandparents may prefer to establish their own household, many prefer to live in the same building, block, or neighborhood as their children (Huang, 1981:123).

The modern Chinese family, whether dual worker or middle class, has more conservative views in regard to sexual values, a lower fertility rate, fewer out-of-wedlock births, and more conservative or traditional attitudes toward the role of women than the white population (Braun and Chao, 1978; Monahan, 1977). Moreover, divorce is a rarity among the Chinese (Huang, 1981:122; Schaffer, 1984:351). It is not uncommon for unhappy Chinese couples to remain together for fear of public opinion, social disgrace, and social ostracism. However, among the younger generation brought up to believe in the American ideal of romantic love and personal happiness in marriage, the incidence of divorce has increased. The economic position of the husband and wife as co-breadwinners and/or their high socioeconomic position lends itself to a mutual sharing of responsibility and authority in the decision making of most aspects of family life (Sollenberger, 1968), although the wife usually assumes the role of helper rather than equal partner (Huang, 1981).

In regard to childrearing, researchers (Huang, 1981; Sollenberger, 1968; Sung, 1967:165, 168–169) have observed that the father maintains his authority and respect in the Chinese family by means of a certain amount of emotional distance. The mother does not interact with the children but commands and decides what is best for them, and the children are expected to obey. Although Chinese parents may be more indulgent with their young children than parents of the white American culture, discipline is much more strict than that which the typical American child receives (Petersen, 1978). Punishment is immediate and generally involves withdrawal from the social life of the family or the deprivation of special privileges or objects rather than physical punishment. As the child grows older, overt expressions of physical and emotional affection exhibited among family members, whether between the husband and wife or between the parents and children, are withdrawn. Many Chinese children have never seen their parents kiss or hug each other nor are they expected to kiss or hug their parents (Huang, 1981:126). Moreover, the public display of affection is considered in poor taste by many Chinese. Independence and maturity are stressed at a very young age. The child is expected to behave as an adult. Aggressive behavior on the part of the young and sibling rivalry is not tolerated and is highly discouraged (Sollenberger, 1968). Moreover, older children are expected to be directly or indirectly involved in the socialization of their younger siblings—serving as role models of adult behavior. Huang (1981:124–125) notes that, in general, Chinese children are brought up in the midst of adults, not only their parents but also members of the extended family. As a consequence, they learn at a very early age socially approved patterns of behavior and also what others think of them. Instead of individual guilt governing their behavior (as is true of their white counterparts), the sense of face, or shame, to themselves and to their family acts as a major form of social control.

Education is highly valued in the Chinese family, and Chinese parents will undergo extreme financial sacrifice and hardship so that their children can receive as much education as possible. This value on education may stem from numerous factors: the parents' traditional Confucian respect for learning; the realization that education is an avenue by which their children will gain security and lead a better life then they have; the social status that the parents receive in the Chinese community if they have a college-educated or professional child; and, the demographic and high socioeconomic characteristics of the Chinese (Hirschman and Wong, 1986; Wong, 1980b). Education does not stop with the typical American school curriculum. Fearing a loss of Chinese heritage, many Chinese parents feel that their children should be instilled with knowledge about Chinese culture, traditions, customs, history, and language. As a consequence, many native-born and foreign-born Chinese children attend Chinese language school after American school or during the weekends (Fong, 1968).

The strength of the bond between Chinese parents and their children has been the subject of much research and discussion. It is believed that Chinese children show greater concern and devotion toward their elders than average American (white) children. A common stereotype of the Chinese family is that because of the Confucian ethic of filial piety, Chinese children will take care of their elderly parents. The exact strength of this bond compared with other ethnic groups and the validity of this stereotype of the Chinese family is an empirical question for which limited data are available. However, studies do suggest that family members are the primary source of assistance for the elderly Chinese and that assistance from social service agencies and professional persons is almost nonexistent. Cheng (1978) found that approximately 68 percent of the elderly Chinese in San Diego, California, would first turn to a family member (their children) if any difficulty arose. Hirata (1975) found that approximately 90 percent of both native- and foreign-born Chinese youths and their parents overwhelmingly indicated that they believed children should support their aged parents. Chinese children felt a strong sense of guilt and shame over what they considered inappropriate care for elderly parents, such as the placement of their elderly parents in nursing homes (Kalish and Moriwaki,

1973). Part of this may be because of their sense of filial responsibility or their knowledge that the lack of facility with the English language on the part of their parents may result in problems of adjustment, mistreatment, inadequate care, and a sense of isolation and alienation in nursing homes (Wong, 1984).

In sum, the modern Chinese family can be categorized into two different types. As a result of the Immigration Act of 1965 and its emphasis on family reunification, many new Chinese immigrants are arriving at the shores of the United States and settling in Chinatowns scattered throughout the United States. This form of Chinese family life has been called the "ghetto or Chinatown Chinese," or the "dual worker family." Another form of the modern Chinese family is the white-collar or professional Chinese family, which, because of its higher socioeconomic status and degree of acculturation, has moved to the suburbs and is gradually integrating into the American mainstream.

CHANGE AND ADAPTATION

The Chinese family in the United States has undergone tremendous changes and adaptations during its 130 years in the United States—from the "mutilated," or "split household," family to the small producer family to the trans-Pacific marriage pattern to the present-day Chinese American family structure consisting of the "ghetto or Chinatown Chinese," or "dual worker family," and the professional Chinese American family. Many of these changes and adaptations were the result of complex interactions between cultural and structural factors. During the latter half of the 1980s and beyond, the Chinese family will probably continue to change, modify, adapt, and reorganize according to the ebbs and flows of societal forces and the constraints and expansion of opportunities in American society.

The Chinese family is intensely involved in the process of urban sociocultural changes and acculturation resulting in a divergence from traditional practices. One indicator of this process is the geographic dispersion of the Chinese away from the Chinatown areas and into the metropolitan areas and the suburbs. As Chinese children attend American schools and develop friendships with white American children, become more competent in English than in Chinese—in essence, as they become more acculturated—they will probably tend to view themselves as more American than Chinese. Consequently, they will gradually drift away from the older generation. With their high degree of acculturation, the younger Chinese Americans will probably face a clash of generations, identity conflicts, and a lack of ethnic cohesion (Fong, 1965, 1968).

Another indicator of the acculturation of the Chinese family is the recent dramatic increase in the incidence of interracial marriages, particularly with whites, among the younger generation (Barnett, 1963; Burma, 1963; Simpson and Yinger, 1965; Staples and Mirande, 1980; Weiss, 1970; Wong, 1988). Currently, approximately 33 percent of all marriages among the Chinese are intermarriages (Wong, 1988). Other trends in intermarriage include a strong inverse relationship between age and the proportion of those who intermarry (Yuan, 1980), more Chinese women than Chinese men intermarrying (Barnett, 1963; Hsu, 1971a; Wong, 1988; Yuan, 1980), and a strong positive relationship between generational status and incidence of intermarriage (Kitano and Yeung, 1982). Numerous explanations for these trends have been suggested: (1) dissatisfaction with the more traditional Chinese male's limited attitudes toward women by more acculturated Chinese women (Braun and Chao, 1978); (2) the inability of Chinese American males to relate positively to Chinese–white social/sexual situations (Weiss, 1970); (3) occupational, housing, social mobility, and acculturation of the Chinese, especially by generation (approximately 73.5 percent of the third-generation Chinese American females outmarry) (Kitano and Yeung, 1982); (4) changes in the attitudes of the Chinese, as well as the dominant group (Kitano and Yeung, 1982; Wong, 1988); and (5) the social-class position of the Chinese and the increasing dispersal of Chinese away from the Chinatown ghetto (Huang, 1981; Wong, 1988). Whatever the reason, there is no question that there has been a dramatic increase in the incidence of intermarriage among the Chinese in recent years. One ramification that this increase in interracial marriages will have for the Chinese family is the further acculturation of the Chinese into American society and, hence, hopefully their greater acceptance on the part of the dominant group. However, intermarriage is not without its costs. A loss of ethnic tradition, heritage, and a distinct sense of Chinese identity resulting in "symbolic ethnicity" (Gans, 1979) and intergenerational strain and conflict between the Chinese parents and their interracially married children are but some of the costs. The continued tremendous influx of Chinese immigrants into the United States will probably result in an increase in the incidence of intermarriage among the Chinese over the long run (Wong, 1988).

One last issue indirectly involving the Chinese family deserves discussion. One of the most popular cultural explanations for the low rate of juvenile delinquency among the Chinese, which involves the traditional values of the Chinese family, its emphasis on face and filial piety, and the concerns of the collective group rather than the individual, is that the Chinese community, not only the family, acts as a major agent of social control on the child (Hayner and Reynolds, 1937; Kung, 1962:207; Sung, 1976). Although this cultural explanation may be partially correct, a structural explanation may provide additional insight. The near absence of established Chinese families in the United States until around the 1920s and 1930s resulted in very few Chinese children. This absence may have contributed more to the low rate of juvenile delinquency than the traditional values of the Chinese family (Lyman, 1974:113). Recently, there has been an increase in the rates of juvenile delinquency and gang violence among the Chinese (Fong, 1968; Lee, 1952; Lyman, 1970b; Sung, 1967). Although this increase may be partially explained by the absence of a close-knit family life (Nee and Nee, 1973), structural factors such as the high percentage of new Chinese immigrants who arrived as adolescents and encountered difficulty in language, school, and seeking employment, the relaxation of immigration restrictions, and attempts by Chinese American youths to alleviate the ghetto conditions in Chinatowns may also be partly responsible (Glenn, 1983; Lyman, 1970b:101). Although this issue will probably never be resolved, the complex interaction between cultural and structural factors deserve attention in future research.

Change and adaptation were important elements in the formation and development of the Chinese family in the United States, and it is probably safe to say that they will continue to play important roles in the future. Although some people may regard the Chinese family as breaking down or undergoing social disorganization, as evidenced by the increase in acculturation, interracial marriages, and juvenile delinquency rates (Fong, 1968; Sung, 1967:185–186), one can view the recent changes and adaptations in the Chinese family as essential elements of the greater process of modification and reorganization that has been occurring for the past 130 years and will continue to occur in the foreseeable future. The present-day Chinese family in the United States is much different than the Chinese families of the past. With the continued increase in Chinese immigration to the United States and the further acculturation of the Chinese population to American society, the Chinese American family of the future will probably continue to successfully evolve, develop, and adapt from its present-day form.

REFERENCES

Barnett, Larry D. 1963. "Interracial Marriage in California," *Marriage and Family Living,* 25:4:425–427.

Barth, Gunther. 1964. *Bitter Strength: A History of the Chinese in the United States, 1850–1870.* Cambridge: Harvard University Press.

Beaudry, James A. 1971. "Some Observations on Chinese Intermarriage in the

United States," *International Journal of Sociology and the Family,* 1(May):59–68.

Braun, J. and H. Chao. 1978. "Attitudes Toward Women: A Comparison of Asian-Born Chinese and American Caucasians," *Psychology of Women Quarterly,* 2(Spring):195–201.

Burma, John H. 1952. "Research Note on the Measurement of Interracial Marriage," *American Journal of Sociology,* 57:587–589.

———. 1963. "Interethnic Marriages in Los Angeles, 1948–1959," *Social Forces,* 42(December):156–165.

Chen, Jack. 1980. *The Chinese of America.* San Francisco: Harper and Row.

Cheng, Eva. 1978. *The Elder Chinese.* San Diego, CA: Campanile Press.

Chinn, Thomas, H. Mark Lai, and Philip Choy. 1969. *A History of the Chinese in California: A Syllabus.* San Francisco: Chinese Historical Society of America.

Coolidge, Mary. 1909. *Chinese Immigration.* New York: Henry Holt.

Fei, H. T. 1939. *Peasant Life in China: A Field Study of Country Life in the Yangtze Valley.* London: Routledge and Kegan Paul.

Fong, Stanley, L. M. 1965. "Assimilation of Chinese in America: Changes in Orientation and Social Perception," *American Journal of Sociology,* 71:3:265–273.

———. 1968. "Identity Conflict of Chinese Adolescents in San Francisco," in Eugene B. Brody (ed.), *Minority Group Adolescents in the United States.* Baltimore, MD: Williams and Wilkins, pp. 111–132.

Gardner, Robert W., Bryant Robey, and Peter C. Smith. 1985. "Asian Americans: Growth, Change, and Diversity," *Population Bulletin.* Vol. 4, no. 14. Washington, DC: Population Reference Bureau.

Gans, Herbert J. 1979. "Symbolic Ethnicity: The Future of Ethnic Groups and Cultures in America," *Ethnic and Racial Studies,* 2:1:1–20.

Glenn, Evelyn Nakano. 1983. "Split Household, Small Producer and Dual Wage Earner: An Analysis of Chinese-American Family Strategies," *Journal of Marriage and the Family,* 45:1:35–46.

Glick, Clarence E. 1980. *Sojourners and Settlers: Chinese Migrants in Hawaii.* Honolulu: University of Hawaii Press.

Hayner, Norman S. and Charles N. Reynolds. 1937. "Chinese Family Life in America," *American Sociological Review,* 22:5:630–637.

Hirata, Lucie Cheng. 1975. "Youth, Parents, and Teachers in Chinatown: A Triadic Framework of Minority Socialization," *Urban Education,* 10:3:279–296.

———. 1979. "Free, Indentured, Enslaved: Chinese Prostitutes in Nineteenth-Century America," *Signs,* 5(Autumn):3–29.

Hirschman, Charles and Morrison G. Wong. 1981. "Trends in Socioeconomic Achievement among Immigrant and Native-Born Asian-Americans, 1960–1976," *Sociological Quarterly,* 22:495–513.

———. 1986. "The Extraordinary Educational Attainment of Asian-Americans: A Search for Historical Evidence and Explanations," *Social Forces,* 65:1–27.

Hong, Lawrence K. 1976. "Recent Immigrants in the Chinese-American Community: Issues of Adaptations and Impacts," *International Migration Review,* 10:509–514.

Hsu, Francis L. K. 1970. *Americans and Chinese.* Garden City, NY: Doubleday Natural History Press.

———. 1971a. *The Challenge of the American Dream: The Chinese in the United States.* Belmont, CA: Wadsworth.

———. 1971b. *Under the Ancestors' Shadow: Chinese Culture and Personality.* Stanford, CA: Standford University Press.

Huang, Lucy Jen. 1981. "The Chinese American Family," in Charles Mindel and Robert Habenstein (eds.), *Ethnic Families in America.* New York: Elsevier, pp. 115–141.

Ikels, Charlotte. 1985. "Parental Perspectives on the Significance of Marriage," *Journal of Marriage and the Family,* 47:2:253–264.

Johnson, C. 1962. *Peasant Nationalism and Communist Power: The Emergence of Revolutionary China.* Stanford, CA: Stanford University Press.

Kalish, Richard A. and Sharon Moriwaki. 1973. "The World of the Elderly Asian American," *Journal of Social Issues,* 29:2:187–209.

Kingston, Maxine Hong. 1976. *Woman Warrior.* New York: Knopf.

———. 1981. *China Men.* New York: Ballantine.

Kitano, Harry H. L. 1985. *Race Relations.* Englewood Cliffs, NJ: Prentice-Hall.

Kitano, Harry H. L. and Wai-Tsang Yeung. 1982. "Chinese Interracial Marriage," *Marriage and Family Review,* 5:1:35–48.

Kung, S. W. 1962. *Chinese in American Life: Some Aspects of Their History, Status, Problems, and Contributions.* Seattle: University of Washington Press.

Kuo, Chia-Ling. 1970. "The Chinese on Long Island—A Pilot Study," *Phylon,* 31:3:280–289.

Kwoh, Beullah Ong. 1947. "The Occupational Status of American-Born Chinese Male College Graduates," *American Journal of Sociology,* 53:192–200.

Lai, H. Mark and Philip P. Choy. 1971. *Outlines History of the Chinese in America.* San Francisco: Chinese-American Studies Planning Group.

Lee, Rose Hum. 1952. "Delinquent, Neglected, and Dependent Chinese Boys and Girls of the San Francisco Bay Region," *Journal of Social Psychology,* 26(August):15–34.

———. 1956. "The Recent Immigrant Chinese Families of the San Francisco–Oakland Area," *Marriage and Family Living,* 18(February):14–24.

———. 1960. *The Chinese in the United States.* Hong Kong, China: Hong Kong University Press.

Li, Peter S. 1977a. "Fictive Kinship, Conjugal Tie, and Kinship Chain Among Chinese Immigrants in the United States," *Journal of Comparative Family Studies,* 8:1(Spring):47–63.

———. 1977b. "Occupational Achievement and Kinship Assistance Among Chinese Immigrants in Chicago," *Sociological Quarterly,* 18:4:478–489.

Light, Ivan H. 1972. *Ethnic Enterprise in America.* Berkeley, CA: University of California Press.

Light, Ivan H. and Charles Choy Wong. 1975. "Protest or Work: Dilemmas of the Tourist Industry in American Chinatowns," *American Journal of Sociology,* 80:1342–1368.

Liu, Ching Ho. 1950. "The Influence of Cultural Background on the Moral Judgment of Children," Ph.D. diss., Columbia University.

Liu, Hui-chen Wang. 1959. *The Traditional Chinese Clan Rules.* Locust Valley, NY: J. J. Augustin.

Lowe, Pardee. 1943. *Father and Glorious Descent.* Boston: Little, Brown.

Lyman, Stanford M. 1968. "Marriage and the Family Among Chinese Immigrants to America, 1850–1960," *Phylon,* 29:4:321–330.
———. 1970a. "Social Demography of the Chinese and Japanese in the U.S. of America," in Stanford M. Lyman (ed.), *The Asian in the West.* Las Vegas: Western Studies Center, pp. 65–80.
———. 1970b. "Red Guard on Grant Avenue: The Rise of Youthful Rebellion in Chinatown," in Stanford M. Lyman (ed.), *The Asian in the West.* Las Vegas: Western Studies Center, pp. 99–118.
———. 1974. *Chinese Americans.* New York: Random House.
———. 1977. *The Asian in North America.* Santa Barbara, CA: Clio Press.
Mark, Diane Mei Lin and Ginger Chih. 1982. *A Place Called Chinese America.* Washington, DC: Organization of Chinese Americans.
Monahan, T. 1977. "Illegitimacy by Race and Mixture of Race," *International Journal of Sociology and the Family,* 7(January–June):45–54.
Nee, Victor and Brett Nee. 1973. *Longtime Californ': A Study of an American Chinatown.* New York: Pantheon.
Nee, Victor and Herbert Y. Wong. 1985. "Asian American Socioeconomic Achievement: The Strength of the Family Bond," *Sociological Perspectives,* 28:3:281–306.
Petersen, William. 1978. "Chinese Americans and Japanese Americans," in Thomas Sowell (ed.), *Essays and Data on American Ethnic Groups.* Washington, DC: Urban Institute Press, pp. 65–106.
Schaffer, Richard T. 1984. *Racial and Ethnic Groups.* Boston: Little, Brown.
Schwartz, Shepard. 1951. "Mate Selection Among New York City's Chinese Males, 1931–1938," *American Journal of Sociology,* 56:562–568.
Simpson, George E. and J. Milton Yinger. 1965. *Racial and Cultural Minorities.* New York: Harper and Row.
Siu, Paul. 1952. "The Sojourner," *American Journal of Sociology,* 58:34–44.
Sollenberger, Richard T. 1968. "Chinese-American Child-Rearing Practices and Juvenile Delinquency," *Journal of Social Psychology,* 74(February):13–23.
Staples, Robert and Alfredo Mirande. 1980. "Racial and Cultural Variations among American Families: A Decennial Review of the Literature on Minority Families," *Journal of Marriage and the Family,* 42:4:887–903.
Sue, Stanley and Harry Kitano. 1973. "Asian American Sterotypes," *Journal of Social Issues,* 29(Spring):83–98.
Sue, Stanley, and Derald W. Sue. 1971. "Chinese American Personality and Mental Health," in Amy Tachiki et al. (eds.), *Roots: An Asian-American Reader.* Los Angeles: Continental Graphics, pp. 72–81.
Sung, Betty Lee. 1967. *Mountain of Gold.* New York: Macmillan.
———. 1977. "Changing Chinese," *Society,* 14:6:44–99.
———. 1987. "Intermarriage Among the Chinese in New York City," in *Chinese America: History and Perspectives 1987.* San Francisco: Chinese Historical Society of America, pp. 101–118.
U. S. Bureau of the Census. 1983. "Characteristics of the Population," *General Social and Economic Characteristics: U. S. Summary.* PC80-1-C1. Washington, DC: U. S. Government Printing Office.
U. S. Department of Commerce. 1975. Bureau of the Census. Historical Statistics of the United States. Washington, DC: U. S. Government Printing Office.

U. S. Department of Justice. 1981. *Statistical Yearbook of the Immigration and Naturalization Service.* Washington, DC: U. S. Government Printing Office.

Weiss, Melford S. 1970. "Selective Acculturation and the Dating Process: The Patterning of Chinese-Caucasian Interracial Dating," *Journal of Marriage and the Family,* 32(May):273–278.

———. 1974. *Valley City: A Chinese Community in America.* Cambridge: Schenkman.

———. 1977. "The Research Experience in a Chinese American Community," *Journal of Social Issues,* 33:4:120–132.

Willmott, W. E. 1964. "Chinese Clan Associations in Vancouver," *Man,* 49:33–36.

Wong, Jade Snow. 1950. *Fifth Chinese Daughter.* New York: Harper and Brothers.

Wong, Morrison G. 1980a. "Changes in Socioeconomic Achievement of the Chinese Male Population in the United States from 1960 to 1970," *International Migration Review,* 14:511–524.

———. 1980b. "Model Students?: Teachers' Perceptions and Expectations of their Asian and White Students," *Sociology of Education,* 53:236–246.

———. 1983. "Chinese Sweatshops in the United States: A Look at Garment Industry," in Ida H. Simpson and Richard L. Simpson (eds.), *Research in the Sociology of Work: Volume II.* Greenwich, CT: JAI Press, pp. 3, 7–79.

———. 1984. "Economic Survival: The Case of Asian-American Elderly," *Sociological Perspective,* 27:2:197–217.

———. 1985. "Post-1965 Immigrants: Demographic and Socioeconomic Profile," in Lionel A. Maldonado and Joan W. Moore (eds.), *Urban Ethnicity: New Immigrants and Old Minorities.* Urban Affairs Annual Review. Vol. 29. Beverly Hills, CA: Sage, pp. 51–71.

———. 1986. "Post-1965 Asian Immigrants: Where Do They Come From, Where Are They Now, and Where Are They Going," in Rita J. Simon (ed.), *The Annals of the American Academy of Political and Social Science.* Vol. 487. Beverly Hills, CA: Sage, pp. 150–168.

———. 1988. "A Look at Intermarriage Among the Chinese in the United States in 1980." Paper presented at the Conference on Racial and Ethnic Relations in the 1990s, Texas A&M University.

Wong, Morrison G. and Charles Hirschman. 1983. "The New Asian Immigrants," in William McCready (ed.), *Culture, Ethnicity and Identity: Current Issues in Research.* New York: Academic Press, pp. 381–403.

Yang, C. K. 1959. *The Chinese Family in the Communist Revolution.* Cambridge: Technology Press.

Yuan, D. Y. 1963. "Voluntary Segregation: A Study of New Chinatown," *Phylon,* 24:3:255–265.

———. 1966. "Chinatown and Beyond: The Chinese Population in Metropolitan New York," *Phylon,* 27:4:321–332.

———. 1980. "Significant Demographic Characteristics of Chinese Who Intermarry in the United States," *California Sociologist,* 3:2:184–197.

CHAPTER ELEVEN

The Japanese American Family

Harry H. L. Kitano

INTRODUCTION

By the latter part of the twentieth century, the typical Japanese family was more likely to be Sansei (third generation) than the more familiar Issei (first generation) or Nisei (second generation). The newer generations reflect an increased heterogeneity, brought about by such factors as mobility, acculturation, and living in a more open American society. In this sense, the Issei were relatively more homogeneous in terms of demographic profile, geographic distribution, and exposure to American society than the Nisei, who in turn were more similar to the Issei in attitudes and life-styles than to the present day Sansei.

The use of generation groups for description is relevant to Japanese Americans because such groups connote common experiences and similar exposures and life-styles. Although recognizing that many differences will remain within generations, the immigration patterns of the Issei lend themselves to a generational framework. Japanese immigration started in the later part of the nineteenth century and was terminated in 1924. Therefore, the original Issei survivors are now in the 80 years old and older category, their American-born Nisei children are upwards of 50 years of age, and the third-generation Sansei make up the bulk of the young adult population. It would appear to be fruitless to carry the generational framework further than the Sansei, so the *Sansei* is also used when referring to the fourth, or Yonsei, and subsequent generations.

A current picture of the Japanese Americans, based on the 1985 census, shows that in 1985, there were an estimated 766,300 Japanese residents. Their median age was 31 years for males and 35.9 for females. The average of 2.7 persons per household was identical to that of white households, and the 912 children born per 1000 women was the lowest of all identified groups in the United States (Population Reference Bureau, 1985). Other Asian groups, especially Chinese, Filipinos, and Koreans, have grown rapidly in number during the last 20 years as a result of immigration; the Japanese immigration rates have been negligible. For example, in 1970, they were the most numerous Asian American group, but at the present time, their numbers fall below the more than 1 million Chinese and Filipino residents.

Further data from the census indicated that for the employed males, the two most common occupational categories were technical, sales, and administrative support (32 percent) and managerial and professional specialty occupations (29 percent). The most popular female occupations included technical sales (46 percent), administrative support occupations, including clerical (32 percent), and managerial and professional (23 percent). The mean annual household income was $25,923; the mean annual family income was $30,527, which ranked the Japanese highest among all the Asian groups. The percentage of Japanese families falling below the poverty level was 4.2 percent, which was the lowest figure for all of the Asian groups.

The purpose of this chapter is to trace the changes in the Japanese American family through an analysis of the various Japanese generations and their adaptations to life in America.

HISTORICAL BACKGROUND

In 1885, the first official immigration of Japanese was to Hawaii, which was then a United States territory. Prior to that time, Japanese had emigrated, but without the official sanction of the Japanese government. The majority of immigrants were single, young men with a sojourner orientation. Most applied for immigration as contract laborers, which meant that after a specified period of working on the plantations, they would return to their homeland. Like many immigrants of this period, they came with minimal English language skills, had little knowledge of the American culture, and faced hardship, prejudice, and discrimination. Yet, despite the difficult times, many chose to remain in Hawaii, and by 1920, there were more than 109,000 Japanese residing in Hawaii.

Immigration to the mainland, especially to the West Coast, began in the 1890s. Again, the group faced racist barriers. Job opportunities were restricted to domestic services, hard labor, and to unskilled positions. Many turned to agriculture, where capital, education, and special training were not required. They retained a sojourner orientation with the hope of making enough money to retire in the home country. The notion of marriage, family life, children, and upward mobility appeared to be unrealistic dreams. Most came with the hope of making money and returning to Japan, but there were also others who had emigrated with the hope of more permanent residence in the new country.

The Issei were products of the Meiji period in Japan (1868–1912), although there is also evidence of the influence of the Tokugawa era (1603–1868). It is difficult to generalize about the degree of internalization of the values of these various eras, except that the Issei were exposed to certain ways of looking at family life, such as a hierarchical family structure with the husband at the top and preferences for male heirs, appropriate role behavior dependent on age, status, and sex, and the importance of obligation, duty, and loyalty. Individual desires were submerged for group and familial priorities, and therefore arranged marriages were common, as was deference to parental prescriptions. Loyalty to larger units than the family, such as the country, were also considered desirable virtues, and as a result, one appropriate generalization would be that the Issei were exposed to a culture that placed high value on a group and family orientation in which prescribed roles for males and females were clearly drawn and individualistic attitudes and behaviors at variance with stated role prescriptions were discouraged.

Central to the family system was the *ie* ("family, household, house"), the primary unit of social organization. As a legal and political organization, it was based on Confucian political principles, which emphasized that stable families ensured a stable society. The *ie* continued over time and was deemed of greater importance than the individuals constituting the unit; individual interests and goals were secondary to the larger unit. It was a composite of the concrete and abstract, the material and the spiritual, and included such elements as family name, occupation, property, tradition, family altar, graveyard, and codes of expected behavior (Wagatsuma, 1977).

Because the continuation of the *ie* was of utmost importance to the family's future, marriage and the selection of prospective mates was a serious matter and involved the entire family. The social, psychological, and physical background of prospective mates and their families were carefully scrutinized before final arrangements were made. Marriages were made for the purpose of producing an heir and the continuation of the *ie;*

marriage for love was considered immoral because it placed individual interest above that of the *ie*. The continuation of the unit was considered to be of such importance that adoption of a daughter, husband, or husband and wife was practiced when there were no offspring.

The moral and legal duty of continuing the *ie* was vested in the household head (*kacho*) who, as eldest son and heir to the property rights, had the obligation of securing a stable environment for its members and providing arrangements for marriage, occupation, food, and living comforts. The jurisdiction of his authority encompassed final decisions in matters concerning marriage, choice of occupation, place of residency, and expulsion from the family for each member of the *ie*.

Dedication of one's life for the advancement and good reputation of the *ie* was an obligation. Respect, obedience, and filial piety to parents and ancestors were highly emphasized along with observance of rank order within the family structure. Generally, respect was required from persons of lower rank to those of higher rank, from younger member to older member, from children to parents, and from wife to husband (Wagatsuma, 1977).

What are being described are "ideal models," in the sense that these ideals were deemed to be the ways that people should behave. Most Issei were exposed to these prescriptions, but it would be fallacious to assume that all behaved in this idealized fashion.

THE JAPANESE IN AMERICA

The Issei

Most of the original Issei immigrants are deceased or living in retirement. Depending on circumstances, some are living with their children, others are in retirement and nursing homes, and still others have been relegated to independent living arrangements, often of marginal quality. Perhaps the most fortunate are the Issei living with understanding families or in senior-citizen housing projects such as the Little Tokyo Towers in Los Angeles. Here they can enjoy ethnic foods, ethnic ambiance, and familiar surroundings that enhance the quality of their lives during their remaining years. The least fortunate are those without family or friends, with minimal income, and forced to live in unfamiliar surroundings.

Initial Issei immigration did not involve intact family units. The majority were young men who arrived in this country with the intention of returning. Miyamoto (1939) describes the early period as the frontier era, which took place from the 1890s to the Gentleman's Agreement in 1907, which limited the immigration of Japanese laborers. Family life started after this period.

Strong (1934) described the initial immigrants as ambitious and intelligent and having the equivalent of an eighth-grade education. They left a nation that was changing from a feudalistic system to an urban, industrialized economy. The reasons behind the migration included better educational and economic opportunities, escape from conscription in the Japanese armed services and unstable home conditions, and a variety of personal reasons. Issei came to Hawaii as contract laborers, which meant that it was a temporary migration, although many opted to stay after their contract period expired.

The Issei came after the "Chinese problem" had been resolved. Racial antagonism had been faced by the Chinese migrants (also made up of single, young male laborers) from the time of their immigration in 1849. In 1882, Congress passed the Chinese Exclusion Act, which forbade the entry of Chinese into the United States. The anti-Chinese feelings were soon transferred to the Japanese, and a variety of laws were passed to limit Japanese participation in the mainstream of American society. The Issei could not become citizens; they could not marry Caucasians or own land and were limited in terms of where they could live, the kinds of jobs they could have, and the types of social and recreational opportunities available to them.

The Issei found employment in occupations that called for hard work, little capital, and minimal use of English. They worked on the railroads, in canneries, and in the logging, mining, and fishing industries. The most popular jobs lay in agriculture, where an individual had some chance for mobility. He could start as an ordinary laborer, move towards share tenancy and cash leasing, and then possibly purchase the land outright and start his own small farm. However, California and other states thwarted this route by passing alien land laws, which prohibited the Issei and other Asian immigrants from owning their own land.

The decision to remain in the United States and start family life probably was difficult. American women were unavailable for a variety of reasons, including antimiscegenation laws, cultural differences, and segregated living conditions. The future was clouded with racism and limited social and occupational opportunities in the American mainstream.

The Issei turned to Japan for their future wives and were assisted by family, relatives, and friends. This practice was not that unusual for them; the American style of falling in love on an individual basis was not a part of their socialization. One interesting practice was that of "picture brides," whereby an exchange of photographs constituted a part of the marital procedure. However, many other variables were also included in making the arrangements, and it would be incorrect to assume that the marriage was between total strangers. The number of such arrangements is difficult to assess, nevertheless these marriages must have been stable because the official number of divorces, 1.6 percent, was very low.

However, the official rates of divorce may have hidden problems of marital instability. Yanagisako (1985:34) found in her interviews with Issei that there were stories of women leaving their husbands to live with other men, some leaving their spouses and moving to other cities, while still others were reputed to have become prostitutes. The imbalanced sex ratio created conditions for wife stealing.

There is evidence that much of the immigration on a more permanent basis involved parents and siblings. Modell (1971) reports that a high percentage of Issei who emigrated after the Gentleman's Agreement of 1907 involved relatives. Fathers might encourage sons to emigrate, and brothers might encourage siblings to emigrate, suggesting that the picture of lonely, isolated individuals trying to make it by themselves was not a common one.

As a consequence, Issei family life and marriages were from the beginning a continuity of family life in Japan. Family and kin were intimately involved in all stages of the marriage; it was the rare Issei who married without the approval of parents. The expectation of living in a foreign country did not remove Issei marriages from kinship and locality ties in Japan (Yanagisako; 1985).

Miyamoto (1939) emphasizes four aspects of the Issei family system. The first was the conception of society as one large family in which family norms were reinforced by the ethnic community. Numerous Issei organizations provided support, enabling the family not to exist in isolation. Secondly, the organization of the family was in patriarchal terms, which emphasized male dominance. The third factor was that of primogeniture and adoption as the system of family inheritance, ensuring that property and power flowed to the eldest sons. Finally, there was a high degree of importance attached to family customs on such occasions as marriage, birth, and death. Picnics, anniversaries, and holidays, whether Japanese or American, were celebrated. These celebrations were important in breaking the monotony of the long, hard work days.

The Issei generally understood that their own participation in the American mainstream would be limited, but high hopes were placed on their American-born Nisei children. They saw the Nisei as American citizens with the advantage of an American education, even though they must have realized that race and national origin remained as barriers to equal participation for all persons of Japanese ancestry, whether citizens or not. Issei often thought of themselves as a sacrificial generation; their own lives were to be secondary to the advancement of their children. The phrase *kodomo no tame ni* ("for the sake of the children") (Ogawa, 1978) was a common one, and it was a familiar sight to see parents in old clothes buying newer clothes for their children and the larger and choicer portions of food going to their sons, with leftovers for the mother.

Their life was one of hardship but not total deprivation. Daniels (1985) indicates that although the depression of the 1930s affected most Americans, the Japanese community was less affected by the collapse of the American economy. The types of jobs—in agriculture, especially, and in small businesses in insulated ethnic communities—protected many from poverty and dependence on public welfare. A Los Angeles County supervisor counted only 25 welfare cases in a Japanese population of 37,000. There were leadership positions in ethnic organizations, and entertainment from Japan brought moments of nostalgia and joy. Festive occasions were eagerly anticipated and celebrated; the entire family enjoyed the community picnics, and even solemn occasions such as deaths and funerals brought large groups together. The most visible arena of success for the Issei family lay in their children. A high value was placed on education, and the picture of Nisei children entering and competing in the public schools was a source of pride in not only the ethnic family but also the entire community, especially because the children generally did well.

A college degree for the Nisei was viewed, perhaps unrealistically, as the ticket to success. Thus, the picture prior to December 7, 1941, was one of a Japanese community dominated by the Issei. Like most immigrant groups before them, they maintained many of the ways brought over from the old country. They fashioned their version of a Japanese American community, reinforced by the hostility of the surrounding world. Few Issei participated in the mainstream; most could survive in the environs of their own family and the ethnic ghettos. There were ethnic professionals and organizations for business, professional, and recreational activities; an active ethnic press, and ethnic service organizations and food stores. In most ways, Issei could survive with only a limited command of English, minimal interaction with the larger community, and an adherence to the ways they brought over from Japan. Conservative traditions were more likely to survive in rural, isolated areas with few of the influences of the American culture and among Issei women, whose primary duty was to remain at home and raise children.

The Wartime Evacuation (1942–1945): Camp Life

The Japanese attack on Pearl Harbor brought about drastic changes in the family and community. In summary, the more than 110,000 Japanese, residing in the Pacific states were relocated to isolated sites in California,

Arizona, Idaho, Utah, Wyoming, Colorado, and Arkansas. The camps were surrounded by barbed wire, armed guards, and guard towers. Freedom to move was restricted, and life was totally controlled by the United States government.

The camp environment created living conditions "unlike the ancestral Japanese culture, the composite culture of the ethnic enclaves, and the culture of the *hakujin* (white) society (Broom and Kitsuse, 1956:25)." Evacuees learned how to live by official directives, how to respond to announcements, and the importance of adjusting to the whims of government-appointed white administrators. Priority was given to daily routines; long-term planning was deemed fruitless. Much of this camp culture was peculiar to the incarceration and had little or no transfer value to outside life. Broom and Kitsuse (1956) noted that it was easy to recognize the consequences of this period on those Nisei who spent their early school years in the camps when compared with peers who had spent their adolescent years in a freer society.

The Issei were strongly influenced by their forced detention. Association with other Issei tended to reinforce conservative cultural tendencies. However, this was not a return to the old Japanese forms brought over from Japan, because most of these forms were too far away in terms of time and experience. The conservative movement was toward a Japanese American subculture incorporating influences from Japan but modified through life in America. For most Issei, the influences of Japan were still stronger, especially for those who had previously lived in rural areas isolated from the American mainstream.

Families were housed in one room units in modified barracks. There was little privacy; family quarrels, crying children, and almost all noise could be heard throughout the units. Community mess halls, lavatories, showers, and washrooms meant adjusting to communal living. Mess hall food was served cafeteria style and discouraged family dining, hampering the important socialization ritual of family mealtimes.

Recreational and leisure activities were programmed for individuals and peer groups, limiting family participation. Issei parents lost economic and social control over their children. The minimum wage for employment ($16 to $19 per month) meant that parents and children who worked were making the same wages. The maintenance of family solidarity and integration became primarily dependent on affectional ties, and in many Issei-run families, these bonds were weak. Issei controls over their Nisei children were therefore weakened by cutting the ties of economic dependence and a strengthening of peer group socialization.

Mothers with newborn babies faced special problems. Sanitary facilities for their babies were limited. The sterilization of bottles, the availability of formulas, the washing of diapers, and the ability to find clean space for children to crawl were constant, additional stresses.

Families living where there were strong affectional roles were less likely to be vulnerable to the various crises that occurred during internment. Various demands were made on families—answering loyalty questionnaires requesting leave from camp, and finally, deciding where to relocate and settle after the closing of the camps. More information regarding the camps can be found in Irons (1983), Daniels (1971), Weglyn (1976), and others.

The Nisei Family

The Nisei generation is now entering the late-adult and senior-citizen years and facing questions concerning health, aging, and problems of retirement. Their age span is broad; some Nisei are in their 80s, whereas younger Nisei may be in their 50s. They are products of a variety of influences; their Issei parents, Japanese American peers, other minorities, and the American mainstream. Older Nisei are closer than the younger to Issei norms. They are apt to be more fluent in Japanese and enjoy songs and television programs sent from Japan. Some Nisei, called the Kibei, were sent to live in Japan in the 1930s and were exposed to the values of the Japan of that period.

An interview reported by Strong (1934:2) of a college-educated Nisei gives a flavor of life in the depression years:

> Our community is not self sufficient. We can't stand off and live our own lives. We've got to find a place in the American society to survive. And yet, no matter what our qualifications may be, evidently the only place we are wanted is in positions that no American would care to fill—menial positions as house-servants, gardeners, vegetable peddlers, continually 'yes, ma'ming.

A source of strength for the Nisei during this period lay in their families and the ethnic community. Brothers, sisters, and peers were more helpful than Issei parents; they knew the language and the culture, and had faced similar problems. The Nisei developed such organizations as the Japanese American Citizen's League (JACL), founded in the 1930s as a civil-rights organization. There were leagues for basketball, baseball, and football; social activities enhanced in-group cohesion. Denied access to the mainstream, the Nisei practiced such American-type activities as participating in dating, outings, retreats, conferences, and dances within their own group. It was a structurally pluralistic community but, culturally, closer to American than Issei life-styles.

Conflicts between the Issei and Nisei were common. The Issei felt that the Nisei were turning away from their parents and the ancestral culture, that their Americanization was too fast, and that their search for independence ignored family needs and obligations. The second generation felt that the first wished to exert too much control over their lives and that the old ways were inappropriate in the modern world.

CAMP LIFE. The concentration camps had a differential impact on the Nisei, just as on the Issei. Age, marital state, previous education, and occupation affected individual and family life. Older Nisei generally suffered more than those of high-school age. For many Nisei, living among Japanese Americans meant that the racial variable was not the most relevant one in competing for the limited occupational opportunities in the camps. They could become firemen, policemen, and managers—positions generally denied to them in the outside world.

Social life in the concentration camps for the Nisei was in typical American activities. Youngsters danced to the recorded music of the big bands of Glen Miller, Tommy Dorsey, and Harry James; held hands, and dreamed of the opposite sex. The Issei preferred old Japanese songs, organized poetry groups, and more traditional Japanese cultural activities.

Nisei independence was enhanced. There were opportunities to leave the camps with governmental clearance or to volunteer for the United States Army. Many took advantage of these offers and, for the first time, experienced life away from the ethnic ghettos. Life in Chicago, New York, Cleveland, and Minneapolis was different than life in the Little Tokyos and Little Osakas of Los Angeles and San Francisco.

The post-war period saw considerable progress for the Nisei. Job opportunities were more open, and higher education began to pay off. The tuition-free campuses of the University of California had large numbers of Nisei enrollees. Although there remained more subtle forms of discrimination, especially in administrative and decision-making positions, Nisei began to participate in occupations more congruent with their training and education.

Models of Marriage

A number of differences can be seen in the lives of the Issei and the Nisei, but nowhere can these divergences be more clearly seen than in their different views on marriage. Differences between the Issei and Nisei models of marriage were summarized by Yanagisako (1985). Issei marriages, built on the model from Japan, were characterized by the following:

1. Absence of choice in the selection of spouse
2. Interaction based on obligation
3. Strong involvement in other family relationships
4. Priority of filial bond over conjugal bond
5. Male dominance
6. Rigid division of labor by sex
7. Emotional restraint, with emphasis on compassion, respect, and consideration
8. Stability
9. Little verbal communication between spouses

Nisei views of marriage, following American models, provide contrasts on all levels. There is freedom of choice of the spouse, the concept of romantic love, relative freedom from other family relationships, priority placed on the conjugal bond over filial bonds, greater equality of the sexes, more flexibility in sex roles, high emotional intensity, with emphasis on sexual, romantic attractions, and greater instability and verbal communication between spouses (Yanagisako:1985:122).

Both Issei and Nisei respondents agreed that there were these differences between the generations but did not agree on the comparative value and desirability of the different models. For example, some Issei reacted negatively to the instability of American marriages but incorporated some of the dimensions of equality, just as some Nisei spoke of the need for a degree of duty and commitment in a marital relationship. It was rare to find Issei who subscribed to all features of the Japanese model, just as it was difficult to find Nisei who identified with all features of the American way. Both generations achieved a synthesis of the two models but not in any even, symmetrical fashion, making simple generalizations concerning how the Nisei way followed the Issei way not entirely accurate.

Nisei families thus represent a variety of models. There are those who carry on some of the conservative traditions of the Issei families and those who are closer to American family norms. Such variables as degree of isolation, availability of alternative models, structure of the family and community, and the receptiveness of the dominant, Caucasian community interact in a number of ways to affect Nisei family life. Variables within the family, such as affective ties, bonding patterns, the effectiveness of socialization procedures, allocation of roles, and personalities, are other variables that determine family types.

In summary, the Nisei family was shaped by Issei influences and exposure to the American culture. Values, attitudes, and behaviors were reinforced by the ethnic community with its many organizations. Discrimination, especially during the pre–World War II era ending with a forced evacuation, shaped a Japanese American identity based on visibility and the problems associated with being identified as a Japanese. The evacuation changed the dependency ties of the group with the Issei and paved the way for a much more independent existence. Nisei with college degrees saw occupational opportunities more congruent with their training, and the era of equal opportunity and affirmative action beginning in the 1970s saw further advancement for qualified Nisei. The one resource denied to the Nisei was that of grandparents; there were no older persons to provide wisdom, solace, advice, and continuity with the ethnic past.

One of the unstated but constant concerns of the Nisei is that an event similar to the wartime evacuation should not happen again. However, for a long period after the event, many Nisei remained silent concerning the violation of their civil liberties; instead, they concentrated on re-establishing themselves in financially secure positions, with the hope that economic gain would somehow take care of most problems.

Nisei families continue many of the practices learned from their Issei predecessors. Family gatherings involving extended family and kinship ties are common; such celebrations as weddings and funerals remain important events. Such organizations as the JACL provide a resource for community participation, although one visible change relates to the sites of their biannual conventions. In the early days, they were held in ethnic community buildings located in the heart of the ghetto. Now, they are held at big-name convention hotels in Hawaii, Chicago, and Los Angeles, with invitations to bring the entire family to enjoy a luxury vacation. The expectations of upward mobility and greater participation in the American mainstream have been passed on to the Sansei.

The Sansei

The Sansei and younger generations of Japanese born in the United States are products of their Japanese background and exposure to the American world. The extent of their integration with the various influences varies with the area of residence, expectations, power of the ethnic enclave, and the socialization practices of the family. One appropriate hypothesis would be that there are probably higher percentage of American models in Sansei than Issei and Nisei views of marriage and family life. For example, if we compare Issei and Nisei attitudes on marriage, Sansei reactions would be more congruent with American expectations. They would feel that there should be no parental interference with marriage, and choices would not have to be restricted to those of Japanese ancestry. Freedom of choice has significantly affected the rates of Sansei marriage to non-Japanese (Kitano, 1984). In 1979, Japanese American out-group marriage rates were over 60 percent, primarily as a result of Sansei marital preferences.

Table 1 shows the out-group marriage rates of Japanese Americans in Los Angeles County for selected years limited to those in which studies and statistics were available.

Out-group marriage rates were defined as any marriage involving one Japanese American partner and one partner who was not a member of the ethnic group. Interracial marriage would be a marriage in which one of the partners is non-Asian.

It can be seen that there have been sharp increases in the number of marriages between Japanese Americans and non-Japanese, starting with a low of 2 percent in 1924 and up to the 60 percent level in the 1970s. It should also be noticed that the marriages prior to 1958 were illegal, but as far as we know, none of the individuals involved were ever arrested or prosecuted. Our general impression is that the majority of out-group marriages were to whites (Kitano et al., 1984).

The data on intermarriage are important because they are symptomatic of the present changes in the American society. Japanese American out-group marriage, from our perspective, includes attitudinal and behavioral changes, on the part of both the dominant and ethnic community. The changes also include those embedded in history, such as immigration laws and other legislation, and it is the mixture of better opportunities, the breakdown of ethnic ghettos, the mobility of Nisei families, and changes in

TABLE 1
Out-group Marriage Rates for Japanese Americans in Selected Years for Los Angeles County

YEAR	OUTMARRIAGE RATE (%)
1979	61
1977	63
1975	55
1972	49
1971	47
1958	23
1950	11
1924	2

family control that lead to out-group marriage. For example, historical changes include the elimination of antimiscegenation laws and immigration restrictions; dominant community changes include more opportunities for equal status interaction; and ethnic community and family changes include the lessening of social controls over the marital choices of their children. Then, there is the rapid acculturation of the third and fourth generation, including the emphasis on love. It is the interaction of all these above factors that provides an explanation of the current state of marital choice in the ethnic community. One can also hypothesize that in areas where there are few Japanese Americans, the percentage of out-group marriages should be higher. Because Los Angeles has one of the largest Japanese American communities, the rate of out-group marriage should be higher in almost every other section of the country.

Sansei follow the American model of love as the most important variable in marriage and are less prone to become enmeshed in family obligations and relationships, although some interracial married couples felt that the Japanese partner in the marriage clung more closely to the family than the Caucasian partner. Sansei couples give priority to the husband–wife relationship over kinship ties, and the instances of male dominance, at least on the verbal level, appear to have changed to egalitarian models. However, it is interesting to note that in our studies of interracial marriage, one of the reasons given by Asian American women for marrying non-Asians is that of being placed in traditional female roles by Asian men (Kitano, 1984).

The division of labor by sex is not rigidly defined, although there remains a general tendency to view the male as having primary responsibility for concerns outside the home and the female for tasks within the household. However, because many Sansei families include working wives, the differences continue to be blurred. There still remains a degree of emotional and verbal restraint on the part of Sansei families when compared with middle-class Caucasians; although, when compared with Issei and Nisei norms, the Sansei appear to be completely open. There is little empirical evidence concerning the stability of Sansei marriages; it is my observation that separation and divorce are becoming much more common.

Individual Sansei growing up in different families show the diversity of Sansei life. One UCLA student describes her growing up in Gardena, a Los Angeles suburb, which has a large Japanese population. She grew up surrounded by Japanese culture; she practices *enryo* ("behavioral restraint") and loves Japanese food, and her family celebrates the New Year in traditional Japanese fashion. She dresses in a Japanese *yukata* and *zori* ("kimono" and "slippers") for *obon* festivals, can speak Japanese, and avoids such American teen-age fashions as designer jeans.

The family helps one other at home; her two sisters and younger brother help with preparing dinner, washing dishes, and cleaning the house. There is much verbal communication but very little overt expression such as hugging and kissing. Her Nisei mother is described as old fashioned, and so the thought of a woman asking a man for a date is taboo. She admits that she is the most "Japanized" of the family and that the influences of the Issei and Nisei culture have less effect on her siblings (Taguma, 1985).

Another Sansei student describes a different life-style. She grew up in an all white area of San Diego, and her only contact with the ethnic community was through attendance at an ethnic church. She went through her high-school years with no thought of being different; she felt at home with her friends, who were primarily Caucasian. Culture shock for her was attending UCLA, where she found a large Asian population, including an Asian sorority, which she eventually joined. She had not been subjected to racism and had never been called a "Jap." Her parents had told her that it would be nice if she married a Japanese American but that happiness was of more importance than marrying within the group. Her older sister had married a Caucasian and was very happy with her choice. She feels close to her mother; (her father is a little more distant), but they have family gatherings. She feels different from the "Gardena girls," who have a distinctive style that includes their Japanese language, hair, dress, and makeup. The Gardena girls are characterized by participating in all-Asian volleyball leagues, sororities, and ethnic church activities and having a network of friends who are mostly Asian.

Her boyfriend, who is of Japanese ancestry, grew up with other Japanese Americans. He feels uncomfortable with Caucasians and believes that women are more readily accepted in interracial situations. He participates in the all-Japanese athletic leagues. One reason for his preference for ethnic peers is that he does not have to prove himself to them.

Another male of her acquaintance grew up in a rural community with all Caucasian families. He has joined a UCLA fraternity (Nisei were not readily accepted into the fraternity system) and has friends of both Japanese and Caucasian backgrounds. He feels that growing up in a predominantly Caucasian community has made him comfortable with his choice of friends (Amano, 1985).

Certain expectations have characterized Issei, Nisei, and Sansei families. Good grades, discipline, concern about what others think, and not standing out in any deviant fashion remain part of the culture. Sansei tend to choose "safe" college majors, preferring a professional education (e.g., medicine, pharmacy, engineering, education, and law), in which the chances of employment are high. There are Sansei yuppies—trips abroad, ski clubs, and individual vacations—who have life-styles that were not an integral part of the lives of the previous generations.

A survey of Asian Americans in fraternities and sororities, which included 143 Sansei, primarily women, revealed the following picture. The vast majority of these students had close relationships with their parents, positive feelings about their grandparents, and did not feel competitive with their siblings. They felt that they worked hard for their grades, and most of them held part-time and summer jobs while attending school. They were active in high-school activities but less so in college. The majority did not participate in the drug and alcohol culture and felt more comfortable with Asian than Caucasian friends. They were financially dependent on their parents; a high percentage received assistance from parents in purchasing a car. They were comfortable with their ethnic background and had few problems with their ethnic identity (Takahashi, 1985).

The issue of ethnic identity remains an important one. There is a preference for identifying one's self as Japanese American (Arakawa, 1984), although the content of that identity may be different among generations. It may be closer to what Gans (1979) has termed a "symbolic ethnicity." Sansei identity may include such diverse activities as attending ethnic festivals, eating ethnic foods, and seeing a Japanese movie, but it would not necessarily include studying and learning about Japan, its culture and its language, or becoming deeply involved in ethnic-group activities and giving high priority to ethnic-group concerns. They have instead become more like the descendants of other immigrant families, changing from a primarily ethnic to an American perspective. Even the factor of racial visibility, once considered an impassable barrier to life in the mainstream, has apparently been modified, although there are constant reminders that anti-Japanese sentiments have not disappeared. Japanese Americans, even of the third and fourth generations, are often mistaken for Japanese from Japan, and such comments as "My, you speak good English," and "You people make such wonderful automobiles," serves as a reminder that they are still categorized as foreigners by some Americans. These incidents and other erroneous perceptions were a part of the thinking that lead to the evacuation of World War II.

In summary, we have traced the generational lines of the major Japanese American groups. There are other Japanese in America, including newly arrived immigrants, Japanese businessmen and their families, students, and the ubiquitous tourists. Their numbers are small, but the one common denominator is that of visibility, resulting in, at one time or another, all Japanese residing in America having been mistaken for natives of Japan.

In terms of the family, the following characteristics are important:

1. There is a continuity from the first to the second and to the succeeding generations. Visibility is the most important ingredient in shaping the continuity.
2. Certain cultural styles have also been retained. They include *enryo,* preference for ethnic peers, close family ties, ethnic celebrations, and high educational expectations. The retention of and changes in various cultural elements vary by families in terms of size, socialization, area of residence, influence of the ethnic community, and contact with the dominant community.
3. The most dramatic change in Japanese American families is that of out-group marriage. Sansei out-group marriage rates of over 60 percent may mean the eventual demise of a monolithic ethnic community. The increase in out-group marriage rates is the result of the breakup of the ghetto, loss of family control over marital choices, changes in the law, and more liberal attitudes toward interracial unions on the behalf of both the ethnic and majority communities.
4. Most Sansei families are similar to American models. However, there are some three-generation households, ensuring that the old ways are not completely forgotten.
5. Although the future of Japanese American families appears to be bright, the tendency of Americans to equate Japanese Americans and Japanese from Japan suggests that the relationship between the two countries remains an unknown and unpredictable factor. Hostility toward Japan has, in the past, had an effect on the treatment of Japanese Americans and similar events may occur in the future.

REFERENCES

Amano, Karen. 1985. "Interracial Marriages: A Comparative Analysis of Views of Japanese Americans." Unpublished manuscript, University of California at Los Angeles.

Arakawa, Kathie. 1984. "The Background and Ethnic Identity of Japanese Americans." Unpublished manuscript, University of California at Los Angeles.

Broom, Leonard and John Kitsuse. 1956. *The Managed Casualty.* Los Angeles: University of California Press.

Daniels, Roger. 1972. *Concentration Camps, USA: Japanese Americans and World War II.* New York: Holt, Rinehart and Winston.

———. 1985. "Japanese America, 1930–1941: An Ethnic Community in the Great Depression," *Journal of the West* (October) 35–49.

Gans, Herbert J. 1979. "Symbolic Ethnicity: The Future of Ethnic Groups and Cultures in America," *Ethnic and Racial Studies,* 2 (January) 1-20.
Irons, Peter. 1983. *Justice at War.* New York: Oxford University Press.
Kitano, Harry H., Wai-tsang Yeung, Lynn Chai, and Herb Hatanaka. 1984. "Asian American Interracial Marriage," *Journal of Marriage and the Family,* 46 (February) 179-190.
Miyamoto, Frank. 1939. *Social Solidarity among the Japanese in Seattle.* Seattle: University of Washington Press.
Modell, John. 1971. "Tradition and Opportunity: The Japanese Immigrant in America." *Pacific History Review,* 40(2):163-82.
Ogawa, Dennis M. and Glen Grant. 1978. *Kodomo No Tame Ni—for the Sake of the Children: The Japanese American Experience in Hawaii.* Honolulu: University of Hawaii Press.
Population Reference Bureau. 1985. "Asian Americans: Growth, Change and Diversity," *Population Bulletin.* Washington, DC: U. S. Government Printing Office.
Strong, Edward K. 1934. *The Second Generation Japanese Problem.* Stanford: Stanford University Press.
Taguma, Joy. 1985. "What Gardena Means to Me." Unpublished manuscript, University of California at Los Angeles.
Takahashi, Linda. 1985. "Studying the Sansei Generation." Unpublished manuscript, University of California at Los Angeles.
Wagatsuma, Hiroshi. 1977. "Some Aspects of the Contemporary Japanese Family: Once Confucian, Now Fatherless?" *Daedalus,* 106(2):181-210.
Weglyn, Michi. 1976. *Years of Infamy.* New York: Morrow.
Yanagisako, Sylvia J. 1985. *Transforming the Past.* Stanford: Stanford University Press.

CHAPTER TWELVE

The Vietnamese American Family

Thanh Van Tran

INTRODUCTION

The influx of Indochinese refugees into American society since 1975 has become a matter of interest for social scientists and professionals in the area of human services. A recent statistical report of Asian Americans revealed that more than 600,000 Vietnamese currently are living in almost every state and territory of the United States (Gardner, Robey, and Smith, 1985). Also, a considerable amount of research has already begun focusing on patterns of occupational adaptation and psychological problems of Southeast Asian refugees, especially the Vietnamese refugees (Montero, 1979; Starr, 1981; Benjamin, Tran, and Benjamin, 1983). As yet, there seems to be very little research or literature concerning the Vietnamese family in the United States.

The family is a fundamental social institution in every human society. It then follows that to understand the culture of a group or a society, one needs to understand the structure, the evolution, and functions of the family in such a group or society. With this in mind, this chapter will attempt to provide a comprehensive review of the Vietnamese family in American society. It will focus on the following areas:

1. The historical background of Vietnamese society;
2. The influx of Vietnamese into America and their current status;
3. The traditional Vietnamese family in the context of history and culture;

4. The present-day Vietnamese family in the United States; and
5. The processes of adaptation of the Vietnamese family in America.

HISTORICAL BACKGROUND

A well-known national legend of the Vietnamese people is that they are children of the dragons and grandchildren of the fairies. According to this ancient legend, the son of the first Vietnamese king of the *Xich Qui* kingdom, *Lac Long Quan,* whose mother was a daughter of the dragons, married *Au Co,* who was a daughter of the fairies. *Au Co* gave birth to 100 eggs that became 100 sons. Then, *Lac Long Quan* decided to separate from his wife, *Au Co.* He told her that they could not live together as a family because his origin was of the dragons and hers the fairies. They agreed to split their family; he took 50 sons and moved to the seashore, and she took 50 sons and moved to the mountains. *Lac Long Quan* later made his first son the king of *Van Lang,* and he became the ancestor of the Vietnamese people (Dao, 1961; Do, 1962). This legend could be interpreted as the symbol of the first Vietnamese family conflict. Actually, there are different theories about the origin of the Vietnamese people. Some believe that the Vietnamese originated from China; others think the Vietnamese have Melanesian and Indonesian origins (Pham, 1960; Nguyen, 1967). Hinton (1985:91) suggests:

> From their physical appearance, the Vietnamese appear to have a common ancestry with the Malays, Indonesians and Polynesians of Southern Asia, but there is a definite Mongolian element also present.

No matter what their origin, Vietnamese settled their country thousands of years ago. Nguyen (1967:2) notes:

> The first traces of human life on Vietnam's territory date back to about the end of the Tertiary period and consist of pieces of stone either left in their natural shapes and serving as rudimentary tools or worked into pointed spears or sharp blades.

The Vietnamese have developed their own culture and national identity over thousands of years. They have their own language and social institutions including family, religion, education, economy, and political systems. Historically, Vietnamese people have been continuously subjected to the domination, colonization, and invasion of outside forces, such as 1,000 years of Chinese domination and 100 years of French colonization. In addition, they also have been torn apart by political conflicts within the nation itself (Nguyen, 1967; Marr, 1981). At the end of the French colonization, Vietnamese started fighting each other. The country was divided into North and South Vietnam. The civil war between the North and South ended in 1975. In 1978, Vietnam invaded Cambodia. Here they started another war (Hinton, 1985). More than 1 million Vietnamese have fled their country seeking asylum in the West since 1975.

In terms of the population size, in 1985 Vietnam had an estimated population of 55,610,000, with the annual rate of population growth at 2.4 percent. Currently, Vietnam is one of the poorest countries on earth and is, in fact, a simple agrarian society with a per capita income about $170 (Swearer, 1984; Hinton, 1985). There are several ethnic groups that make up the total population of Vietnam. These ethnic groups are the Vietnamese, Muong, Thai, Meo, Khmer, Man, Cham, Chinese, and mountain tribes. Vietnamese make up 90 percent of the total population (U. S. Department of State, 1984, Hinton, 1985). Ethnic minority groups in Vietnam have their own languages and cultures (Kunstadter, 1967; Hickey, 1982). In regard to religion, Vietnamese society has been a tolerant society. There are several religions in Vietnam such as Confucianism, Buddhism, Taoism, Christianity (Roman Catholicism and Protestantism), *Hoa Hao, Cao Dai,* Animism, and Islam. There is no national religion in Vietnam. There have been times when Confucianism and Buddhism were considered the main national religions, but people were not forced to belong to any religion. Buddhism has the largest number of adherents because many Vietnamese tend to claim they are Buddhist if they do not belong to any particular religion.

Over the millenia, Vietnam has changed her name several times. The word Vietnam was chosen under the last Dynasty of Vietnam, which was the *Nguyen* Dynasty, the last kingdom of modern Vietnam (Pham, 1960). In the prehistoric period, Vietnamese society was a matriarchal tribal society in which the mother was the head of the family. Later, Vietnam developed a simple feudal society in which the king was the head of the country. Under the king, there were chiefs of tribes, and in each tribe, there were different family clans with a head of the clan called *Truong Toc.* In the feudal period, Vietnamese society was dominated by the male, who was also the head of Vietnamese family.

During 1,000 years of Chinese domination of Vietnam, the Chinese significantly influenced Vietnamese culture. However, most Vietnamese and Western historians agree that Vietnamese culture, while containing many similarities to Chinese culture, has managed to preserve its own unique national characteristics and identity (Dao, 1961; Do, 1962). The ability to preserve their unique identity under different external influences was determined by their will to fight against the invaders. Taylor (1983:xviii) explains that "no theme is more consistent in Vietnam history than the theme of resistance to foreign aggression." With such a long history, Vietnamese society accumulated many traditions that have been passed down from generation to generation.

Traditional Vietnamese Society

Pham (1960) and some other historians agree that traditional Vietnamese society following the prehistoric period was similar in many ways to traditional Chinese society. Fishing and growing rice were the two main occupations. The king occupied the highest social position. He was considered as the *Thien Tu* ("son of God") and had absolute power. In the family, the head of a family also had absolute power. Traditionally, there were four common social classes:

1. Scholars, or people who were educated and from which class came those who were appointed by the king to hold different positions in the government;
2. Peasant farmers, who provided food for themselves and others;
3. Craftsmen; and
4. Salesmen or businessmen.

Scholars were the most respected social class in the society. This social group had access to governmental positions, and in this manner, they could potentially help their entire village. Farmers were the second-highest ranking class in society because they provided food, and in an agrarian society, producing food was a matter of the utmost importance. The importance of farmers was expressed in an old Vietnamese saying translated into English by Do (1962:138):

> The scholar ranks first, and then the peasant; but when the rice fails and men run wildly about, then the peasant comes first, and the scholar second.

The craftsmen and businessmen were not as well respected as the scholars and farmers. These people did not produce and provide food. They also could not hold governmental positions, and therefore, they had fewer privileges and less respect than scholars and farmers.

In traditional Vietnamese society, the village was considered next in importance to one's family. Nguyen (1967:16) describes a traditional Vietnamese village as "a group of patriarchal families whose members shared the same family name." More than that, a Vietnamese village was the place in the past where most Vietnamese were born, grew up, got married, built their houses, and died. A Vietnamese village can be understood in the sense of the German term *gemeinschaft* (Tonnies, 1957) in which the village members have a very close relationship with each other. However, because of several wars in Vietnam, many traditional villages were either destroyed or abandoned. Recently, after the civil war ended in 1975, 1 million Vietnamese again had to leave their villages, but this time they also left their homeland.

THE INFLUX OF VIETNAMESE TO AMERICA

On April 30, 1975, when the South Vietnamese government collapsed, more than 100,000 Vietnamese escaped from South Vietnam to avoid persecution by the North Vietnamese communists.

South Vietnamese soldiers, government officials, businessmen, religious leaders, students, fishermen, and people from every social class in South Vietnam risked their lives for a new, unknown homeland. The American government quickly responded to the Vietnamese refugee crisis by ordering the American Navy in the Pacific to rescue Vietnamese refugees (Montero, 1979).

Refugee centers were established to receive and process the first group of Vietnamese refugees arriving in America, although more than one half of the American people believed that Vietnamese refugees should not be allowed to enter or remain in the United States (Newsweek, 1975). Schaefer (1979:122) describes the American perception of Vietnamese refugees in 1975:

> In almost all segments of the population—the college educated, the rich, the poor, Blacks, Protestants, and Catholics—only the minority favored permitting the South Vietnamese to live in the country. Only the young, those under thirty, seemed to favor settlement but even a third of that group rejected the idea. Rejection was greatest among the working class, where almost two-thirds opposed accepting South Vietnamese.

Despite this strong rejection of the public against the settlement of Vietnamese refugees, the United States government felt a moral obligation to receive Vietnamese refugees. The influx of Vietnamese refugees has continued from 1975 to the present. Nguyen (1985) identifies four types of Vietnamese refugees in the United States:

1. The first wave refugees, who left South Vietnam at the end of the war in 1975 and who tend to be more educated than the later groups;
2. The second-wave refugees, who are also called "boat people" and left Vietnam during the 1978–1979 period, when the Vietnamese Communist government tried to eliminate the Chinese business community and forced them to leave the country. Thousands of ethnic Chinese Vietnamese and, also, Vietnamese who falsified their ethnic identification as Chinese left Vietnam;
3. The escapees, who either organized their trips by way of boats to Thailand, Malaysia, Singapore, and Japan or by walking across the borders of Laos and Cambodia to Thailand; and
4. The orderly departees, who emigrated in 1979 after the Vietnamese Communist government agreed with the United Nations High Commissioner for Refugees to allow Vietnamese to join their immediate relatives such as parents, spouses, children, and siblings abroad. In addition, the United States government also accepted its former employees from Vietnam. The orderly departures are officially allowed to leave Vietnam to join their relatives abroad.

The United States was not the only nation that gave political asylum to Vietnamese refugees. More than a dozen nations in the world responded kindly to the problem. Vietnamese refugees, as most newly arrived ethnic immigrant groups have done, have concentrated and built their communities in specific areas of the country. Thus, despite the United States government's initial resettlement policy that attempted to disperse Indochinese refugees throughout the country, another migration occurred within the Vietnamese refugee population soon after their settlement in the United States. After their initial settlement, many Vietnamese started moving to California, Texas, and areas with a higher concentration of Vietnamese. Table 1 shows the distribution of the Southeast Asian refugee population in 14 states that have a significantly high number of Southeast Asian refugees.

California has the largest number of Southeast Asian refugees. For many Vietnamese in America, California is the capital in exile of Vietnam. Vietnamese in California control the Vietnamese market in America. They publish Vietnamese books and produce Vietnamese video movies, music, and food for the Vietnamese in the United States and throughout the world.

In general, the first-wave Vietnamese refugees who arrived in the United States in 1975 were well-educated and have successfully adapted to American society. Many of the later groups of Vietnamese refugees came from a

TABLE 1
Distribution of Southeast Asian Refugees in 14 States and Others

STATE	NUMBER	PERCENT
California	285,100	40.1
Texas	51,300	7.2
Washington	32,600	4.6
New York	24,800	3.5
Pennsylvania	23,900	3.4
Illinois	23,400	3.3
Minnesota	22,600	3.2
Virginia	21,000	3.0
Massachusetts	19,300	2.7
Oregon	17,200	2.4
Louisiana	13,500	1.9
Florida	11,500	1.6
Colorado	10,700	1.5
Wisconsin	10,300	1.4
Others	143,800	20.2
TOTAL	711,000	100.0

SOURCE: U. S. Department of Health and Human Services, *The Report to Congress: Refugee Resettlement Program* (1985).

low socioeconomic status in Vietnam, and they tend to experience more socioeconomic problems than their predecessors (Strand & Jones, 1985).

To understand the Vietnamese American family, one needs to have a clear idea of the traditional Vietnamese family. There is no doubt that the present-day Vietnamese family in the United States is the product of traditional family in traditional Vietnamese society.

THE TRADITIONAL VIETNAMESE FAMILY

Toan Anh (1969), a well-known Vietnamese scholar of Vietnamese tradition and culture, notes that a Vietnamese person usually cares about his or her family more than himself or herself. In traditional Vietnamese society, the family was the center of an individual's life and activities. The word "family" in Vietnamese means a social entity that consists of all an individual's relatives, not just one's father, mother, and siblings. This means an extended rather than nuclear family. The traditional Vietnamese family was modeled after the traditional Chinese family in terms of its ethical and moral structure (Pham, 1960; Toan Anh, 1969; Vuong, 1980; Che, 1979).

The teachings of Confucius clearly defined the power, position, and relationship of each member of a family. There were certain fundamental characteristics of the traditional family, such as the domination by sex hierarchy (father–son relationship), by the age hierarchy (elderly have more power), the center of loyalty, and the cult of ancestor worship. An individual was expected to be loyal to his or her family and obey and respect elders. Parents were required to raise and educate their children. Children were required to take care of their parents when they became old or sick and to worship their parents when they passed away.

Vietnamese Kinship System

The Vietnamese kinship system is a patrilineal system, or a male-oriented kinship model (Hickey, 1964; Luong, 1984). The term for the kinship system in the Vietnamese language is *Ho*. This is an extended family system that includes both the living and the dead members. The *Ho* is the combination of small families, (*Nha*) of different generations. There are two types of *Ho*: *Ho Noi* and *Ho Ngoai*. The *Ho Noi* is comprised of all relatives on the father's side, and the *Ho Ngoai* is comprised of all relatives on the mother's side. Members of *Ho Noi* are prohibited to marry each other. Members of the third generation of the *Ho Ngoai* are allowed to marry each other. Spencer (1945:286) in his classic study, describes the Vietnamese kinship system:

> The kinship system of the Annamese (Vietnamese) is bifurcate collateral in that it distinguishes paternal and maternal aunts and uncles from one another as well as from the parents.

Very little has been written about the Vietnamese kinship system. Some available anthropological studies examine only the structural pattern of the kinship system (Spencer, 1945; Benedict, 1947; Luong, 1984). As a result, there is a lack of studies concerning the evolution, relationship, and function of the kinship system in terms of individual Vietnamese life situations.

To better understand the traditional Vietnamese family, it is necessary to study the role and function of each member within the family unit.

The Head of the Family and the Father

In a traditional Vietnamese extended family, the head of the family was called *Truong Toc*. The *Truong Toc* was the oldest male who had responsibilities in maintaining the patrimonial land, ancestral graves, and the worship of the common ancestors. He made decisions about matters related to and interfered in the lives of the extended family.

The heads of the traditional Vietnamese nuclear family (*Gia Truong*) were the grandparents, if they were alive. At the death of the grandparents, the father became the head of the family, and the eldest son would take over this position at the death of the father. Traditionally, the head of the family had absolute power over the members of his family. Toan Anh (1969) notes that the role of the head of the family was similar to the role of the King. Nguyen (1967:15) explains this further:

> At the top of each family, the *paterfamilias* or *gia-truong* exercised an absolute authority over his wife and children. He had full power to act and command. He was invested with rights prevailing over those of the other members of the family.

The head of the family had responsibilities to not only the living members of the family but also those who passed away. His obligations were to take care of the living and to worship the spirits of the dead. Under traditional law, the head of the family also had legal responsibilities for all members of the family. The law punished the father for failing to prevent his children or other members of the family from committing crimes (Whitfield, 1976).

The Mother and the Wife

Vietnamese women, like Chinese women, in traditional society (Toan Anh, 1969; Che, 1979) had no power and fewer privileges than Vietnamese men. A Vietnamese woman was expected to obey her father when she was single and her husband after she got married and to live with her eldest son when she became a widow. Morally, she was not expected to marry again after her husband died.

After her marriage, a Vietnamese woman was expected to live with her husband's parents until her husband was ready to have his own house, obey them absolutely, and serve and care for them. Her husband had the right to punish her if he thought that she did something wrong. She could be repudiated by her husband under seven conditions: (1) she disobeyed her husband's parents, (2) she could not have children, (3) she committed adultery, (4) she was overly jealous, (5) she had an incurable disease, (6) she was garrulous, and (7) she stole (Toan Anh, 1969). There were three conditions under which a husband was not permitted to divorce his wife: (1) she had been in mourning for her husbands' relatives for three years, (2) she and her husband became rich after the marriage (they were both poor before their marriage), and (3) no one would take care of her after her husband divorced her (Phan, 1975). A woman could not leave or separate from her husband; this was a crime. The only areas in which husband and wife had equal rights were properties and debts.

In many traditional villages, polygamy was common before the 1959 Family Bill was passed by the National Assembly of South Vietnamese government. This bill made both polygamy and concubinage illegal (Hickey, 1964). Under the polygamy practice, the first wife in a family had more power than her followers. The first wife could decide to find another wife for her husband if she felt that he needed one. There were some common features of the practice of polygamy: it often occurred among the rich; in families in which the first wife could not have children, especially sons; and in families that needed more people to work on the farm.

As a woman and a wife, a Vietnamese woman had very limited rights. She had to accept control by the men in her life: father, husband, and son. Vietnamese women in traditional society began to gain some power when they became mothers. A mother held the second rank in power in a family after the father. She could expect her children to obey and respect her and managed her family in the absence of her husband. Many Vietnamese mothers raised and managed their families while their husbands were in battle. Vietnam has experienced so many wars and revolutions in its history that, as a result, Vietnamese women had no choice but to take care of their families and to play the role of the head of the family.

Children

The teachings of Confucius required children to obey and respect their parents. Children's piety for their parents was regarded as the most important moral obligation of children while their parents are alive and also after they died (Phan, 1975). Vietnamese children had to live with their parents until they married and had their own house (Toan Anh, 1969). Vietnamese children were expected to contribute to the family economy but own nothing. When they were old enough, they were required to work and bring home their wages and salaries. The parents were supposed to provide for all of the children's needs.

SOCIALIZATION. The socialization process of Vietnamese children took place in everyday life situations. The teachings of Confucius gave the father the most responsibility in socializing a child. One of the traditional principles of the role of the father was that of *Duong bat giao, phu chi qua,* which means that failing to raise a child appropriately was the mistake of the father. However, society tended to blame the mother for the child's misconduct or deviant behavior. An old Vietnamese saying, *con hu tai me,* means that a child was spoiled by the mother (Toan Anh, 1969). The mother tended to take her children with her to visit the neighbors and attend religious or social ceremonies to teach them how to deal with different people and how to behave in different social situations. Socialization of a boy was dependent on the father when the boy reached six or seven years old. The mother continued to socialize her daughter as long as the daughter was single. In general, the children learned to develop their social conduct by participating in the family's everyday activities and by observing the parents' and older siblings' behaviors in different social situations. Parents and the older siblings were expected to set good examples for their children and younger siblings. Life experiences were passed down from grandparents to parents, from parents to older siblings and from older to younger siblings.

SIBLINGS. In traditional Vietnamese family hierarchy, older people had more power than younger people. The eldest son in the family (*Anh Ca*) was expected to have more responsibility in taking care of the family after the death of his father. There is an old Vietnamese saying (*quyen huynh the phu*) that "the older brother has the same power as the father in the absence of the father." The older sister also had more power than her younger brothers and sisters. Siblings of the same parents are called *Dong Bao* ("having the same skin.") On the other hand, siblings of the same father but different mothers were called *Di Bao* ("having different skin"). Siblings were expected to express mutual affection and protection for each other. There is an old Vietnamese saying (*la lanh dum la rach*) that "brothers and sisters must protect each other." When one was in trouble, the others were obligated to help. Vietnamese siblings were expected to share everything they had with each other while they lived under the same roof. However, boys had more educational advantages than girls. Vietnamese parents thought about their son's education before their daughter's. In traditional Vietnamese society, only boys could go to school. Girls were expected only to become housewives and therefore did not need a formal education.

Marriage

The ultimate goal of marriage in traditional Vietnamese society was to bear children (Toan Anh, 1965). In traditional Vietnamese society, boys were allowed to marry at 16 years of age and girls at 13. However, most

Vietnamese male students did not marry until they completed their education. Traditionally, after a student's graduation, his parents looked for a wife for him. According to the teachings of Confucius, marriage is a ceremony that allows a man to continue his family clan by having new children (Dao, 1961). Parents chose the marriage partner for their children. There is an old Vietnamese saying (*lay vo ken tong, lay chong ken giong*) that "one needs to know the origin of the man or woman whom one would marry." It was also assumed that only parents had the proper knowledge to choose a wife or a husband for their children. Boys and girls were not allowed to date or choose their own mate. Marriage was one of the most important events in a Vietnamese person's life. Traditionally, the marriage ceremony was complicated and colorful, encompassing five different traditional ceremonial events in the celebration (Toan Anh, 1965). The first ceremony was *le ban tin*; this ceremony was held after the parents and the son found the right girl in the village. The parents asked the *Ba Mai* ("matchmaker woman") who knew the young woman's family to deliver a message concerning their desire to marry her to their son. The *Ba Mai* also observed the reaction of the young woman's family about the proposal and reported it to the young man's parents. The second ceremony, *le cham ngo,* was held after the young woman's parents accepted the proposal of the young man's parents. This ceremony allowed the young man and his parents to take a good look at the young woman and her family. The third ceremony, *le an giam,* allowed the young man's parents to send someone with gifts to the girl's family to ask for her birth certificate. The fourth ceremony, *le an hoi,* allowed both families to officially announce the engagement of their children. Between *le an hoi* and the wedding ceremony, the young man had to practice *Seu,* which means that he had to bring gifts to the girl's parents in March, May, August, and October. Each of these months is the beginning of a season; therefore, the man had to bring gifts according to each season. These gifts were the local agricultural products. Besides the *Seu,* the man was required to bring gifts to the young woman's house for special religious or social ceremonies such as the *Tet* ("new year's day"). In many traditional villages, the young man had to work for the woman's family for certain periods of time. This practice was called *O Re.* During the *O Re,* the man was expected to work very hard and do anything that the girl's family wanted. Finally, came the wedding ceremony (*Le Than Nghinh,* or *Le Hon Nhan*) in which the man's family came to bring the new daughter-in-law home. This was the most important ceremony, complicated and costly. The entire village, including relatives and guests from the bride's family, was invited to the ceremony, and all expenses were paid by the groom's family.

In general, after the marriage ceremony, the young couple lived with the husband's family. The new daughter-in-law had to completely adjust and adapt to her husband's parents. She was expected to obey her husband's parents and to do everything to please them. The couple would live with the husband's parents until they were able to build their own house or could afford to live independently. Today, the marriage ceremonies have become simpler. Most of the time, people practice only three ceremonies: *Le Cham Ngo* ("the first meeting ceremony between the man's family and the woman's family"); *Le An Hoi* ("engagement ceremony"); and *Le Cuoi* ("wedding ceremony").

MARRIAGE TO FOREIGNERS. Vietnam was under the domination of China for 1,000 years, followed by a 100-year period of French colonization and 20 years of the influence of the United States and the Soviet Union during the period of the Vietnam War. Even so, marriage with a foreigner has been considered a traditional taboo. Toan Anh (1969) notes that there is more concern about women who marry foreigners than about men who do so. General public opinion has been negative toward women who marry foreigners. These women are called *Lu Me,* which indicates a group of women who marry foreigners. If a Vietnamese woman marries a Frenchman, people call her *Me Tay,* and if she marries an American she is called *Me My.* The word *Me* encodes an unfavorably stereotyped symbol for all Vietnamese women who marry foreigners, no matter who their husbands are. Traditionally, Vietnamese women were expected to marry men in the same village. There is an old Vietnamese saying (*lay cho trong lang hon lay nguoi sang thien ha*) that "a woman would rather marry the poorest man in her own village than the richest man in another village." This traditional attitude may have significant influence on the Vietnamese attitude toward women who marry foreigners.

THE VIETNAMESE FAMILY IN AMERICA

Background

One of the significant values of the Vietnamese family is the mutual caring or concern among its members; the saying *mot giot mau dao hon ao nuoc la* ("one drop of blood is much more precious than a pond full of water") means that one should always value one's relatives no matter who they are. Vuong (1976:21–22) describes the Vietnamese family prior to arrival in the United States:

> It is a mini-commune where its members live and share together, a maternity center where children are born . . . a funeral home where funeral rituals are performed, a religious place where the family altar is set up to revere ancestors

> or observe rituals, . . . a welfare center where assistance and social security services are rendered, a nursing home where the elderly are taken good care of, an educational institution where family and formal education is provided, a bank where money is available, . . . and a place where all members share the joys, the sadness, the enjoyments, the suffering of life.

A Vietnamese person can always depend on family or relatives in time of need, and it is a moral obligation to support one's family and relatives. The responsibilities of an individual Vietnamese person to his or her family are the same no matter how far this person may live from his or her family. Haines, Rutherford, and Thomas (1981), who have studied the Vietnamese refugee family and community structure in the United States, note that:

> Family, for the Vietnamese, can be a very extended group. Many refugees, when asked about other members of their family, stressed those remaining in Vietnam, in France and on the west coast of the United States.

It seems to be true among all Asian American groups that the family is the most important part of their life. As Bell (1985:30) notes, "All the various explanations of the Asian Americans' success tend to fall into one category: self-sufficiency. The first element of this self-sufficiency is family." As a matter of fact, Vietnamese feel more responsible for their family's well-being than their own. They tend to be proud of the family rather than the self. In the present situation, Vietnamese need their family more than ever. The existence and support of family are important for a refugee's physical and psychological well-being in a host society.

Household Size and Composition

Recently, Gardner, Robey and Smith (1985) note that the 1980 census revealed that the average number of persons in a Vietnamese household was 4.4. In addition, among the Vietnamese population in the United States, 55 percent of the households were composed of head of household, spouse, children, and relatives (extended family). Thirty-eight percent were nuclear families, and 7 percent were combination of family members and nonrelatives living in the house. Compared with other Asian American groups such as Chinese, Japanese, Filipinos, Koreans, and Asian Indians, Vietnamese had the highest percentage (55 percent) of extended families.

The size of a Vietnamese family in the United States ranged from one person to 18 or more (Montero, 1979). Table 2 presents the picture of the Vietnamese family's size in the United States.

These statistics, however, do not tell us whether these families were complete or whether some members remained in Vietnam. It appears that

TABLE 2
Distribution of Vietnamese by Family Size (N = 1,570)

SIZE OF FAMILY	NUMBER	PERCENTAGE
1	96	6.1
2	137	8.7
3–5	533	33.9
6–8	508	32.4
9–11	196	12.5
12–14	62	3.9
15–17	24	1.5
18 or more people	7	0.4

SOURCE: Montero (1979:107).

there are at least four different Vietnamese family patterns in the United States:

1. The complete Vietnamese nuclear family with husband, wife, and children.
2. The incomplete Vietnamese extended family with a nuclear family, grandparents, and some relatives living together in the United States.
3. The broken Vietnamese family with father or mother and some children in the United States and the rest of the family in Vietnam or having died on their way to freedom.
4. The one person family that consists of a Vietnamese person who arrived in the United States by himself or herself and left behind husband or wife, children, or parents in Vietnam.

In general, the Southeast Asian refugee population, including the Vietnamese, is a young population. The Vietnamese population will increase rapidly in the near future because of "the large numbers of Vietnamese in or about to enter the prime childbearing ages of the twenties and early thirties" (Gardner, Robey, and Smith, 1985:16). The median age of the Vietnamese population was 21.5—20.6 years for males and 22.7 years for females. In terms of sex distribution, 56 percent of Southeast Asian refugees are male, and 44 percent are female. The male–female sex ratio is 107.6:100, which means for every 100 females, there are 107.6 males among the Vietnamese in the United States. The reason for the male domination in terms of sex ratio among the Vietnamese is that it has been easier for men to flee the country than for women.

According to Gardner, Robey, and Smith (1985), the Vietnamese are the only Asian group with a high percentage (14.2 percent) of households headed by women. It is obvious that many Vietnamese wives left their husbands in Vietnam; these husbands could be prisoners in Communist re-education camps in Vietnam or killed during the war. Also there are only 74.1 percent of Vietnamese children under 18 years of age living with two parents; this figure was lower than for whites (82.9 percent) and all other major Asian American groups.

The war and the relocation of Vietnamese people to the United States significantly influenced their family structure. Many left behind most of their family or could bring only a few members with them.

Family Values

Many of the traditional values of the Vietnamese family are still held by the majority of those now in America. However, the American economic system tends to force some changes in Vietnamese family values. For example, Vietnamese children are becoming more economically independent. Many young Vietnamese are now able to work and bring home wages and salaries. As a matter of fact, in 1979 88.0 percent of male and 84.4 percent of female Vietnamese between the ages of 16 to 24 years were employed (Montero, 1979). Traditionally, the majority of this group would be nonproductive members of their families. If they were students, they would have to depend on their parents for financial support. In addition, many Vietnamese parents are aware of the fact that their children know more about America and Americans than they do; therefore, young Vietnamese are now allowed more freedom. Parents also no longer require their children to live with them until they get married as they did in Vietnam. Also, many young Vietnamese, because of their job and career situations, have to move away from home to work in another city or state. With communication and transportation technology available, the young Vietnamese are changing their attitudes toward dating and marriage. Boys and girls are allowed to go to parties at night without parental supervision.

Family members are still expected to help each other. However, there are some changes in the roles of family members as a result of external influences from the new sociocultural environment.

The Vietnamese American Father

Many Vietnamese refugee fathers spent their lives as soldiers in Vietnam. Their entire professional careers involved military service with perhaps one or two weeks annual vacation with their family. A majority of them never played the roles of full-time father or head of the family. They depended on their wives to take care of the family and raise the children. As a result, the Vietnamese father in America has had to learn how to adjust to American society and also to being a full-time father and husband. He has also had to learn to accept the fact that he has no absolute power over his family. His wife, likewise, is now able to get a job and bring home money. His children are living in a different culture; they think and act differently, and he finds that his use of the types of punishment that he could have used in Vietnam to correct or discipline his children is not always acceptable.

The Vietnamese American Woman

Vietnamese women in the United States have a significantly higher fertility rate than all major groups of Asian American women such as Chinese, Japanese, Filipino, Korean, and Asian Indian women. Vietnamese women's fertility rate is similar to that of Hispanic and black women. There have been 1,785 Vietnamese children born per 1,000 Vietnamese women aged 15–44. It is interesting to note that educational levels had a significant influence on fertility in that Vietnamese women with higher levels of education tended to have fewer children. This inverse correlation was also true among the general United States population and major ethnic groups. Vietnamese women in America are also in a process of transition. They are being forced, out of economic necessity, to enter the job market. As a result, they are gaining increased status and power in the family because of the contributions they make to the family income.

The U. S. Department of Health and Human Services (1981) reported that 87.2 percent of Vietnamese men worked 35 or more hours per week, compared with 81.6 percent for Vietnamese women. However, Vietnamese women are still expected to be good wives and mothers and take care of their children, husbands, and homes. In many Vietnamese families, even though both husband and wife work full time, the wife is expected to cook, clean the house, and take care of the children. The husband is still the dominant authority figure in the Vietnamese family. For example, in the Nguyen family, Mrs. Nguyen is employed by a local sewing factory, where she works 40 hours per week and often works overtime. Her husband, Mr. Nguyen, is a machinist employed by a local factory. He also works 40 hours per week. The couple have four children who are all of school age. Every morning, Mrs. Nguyen gets up early to cook breakfast (her husband only eats Vietnamese food) and prepares lunches for the children, her husband, and herself. In the evening, Mrs. Nguyen hurries home to cook dinner. When she has to work overtime, her oldest daughter, a 16 year old, prepares dinner for the family. Mr. Nguyen never knows what is going on in the kitchen, but he would become angry if dinner were not ready at 7:00 P.M. Mrs. Nguyen takes care of all domestic affairs, including controlling and planning the family budget. During the weekend, Mr. Nguyen spends most of his time working with the Vietnamese Catholic community (attending meetings or other social activities) while his wife stays home and cleans the house or works in the garden. Gradually, domestic labor has become more equally divided among younger Vietnamese couples than older couples.

Marriage

Vietnamese parents in America no longer make all decisions regarding their children's marriages. The relocation from Vietnam to America destroyed many traditional ceremonies that were part of the marriage celebration. Vietnamese young people are more economically independent from their parents and more self-sufficient. They have more freedom to make decisions on all matters relating to their marriage. Parents and older members of the family still exercise important influence over their children's marriages, but their influence is not absolute. Most Vietnamese parents still expect their children to marry other Vietnamese rather than people of another race, and interracial marriage is still an uncommon practice among Vietnamese Americans. In regard to the traditional goal of marriage, many young Vietnamese in America, unlike their parents, do not see bearing children as the ultimate goal of marriage. For example, birth control methods are becoming more widely used by many young Vietnamese, and this is affecting family size. However, young Catholic Vietnamese are still influenced by the teachings of their church regarding birth control. In fact, the Catholic church and priest have significant influence on Vietnamese Catholic's lives. In Vietnam, before and during the civil war, a Catholic priest was the most powerful person in a Catholic village or town. The combination of Catholic teaching and Vietnamese culture, which emphasizes that the ultimate goal of one's marriage is to bear children, seems to affect young Vietnamese Catholics in the United States. However, more and more young Vietnamese are venturing into a new era of sexual freedom, and premarital sexual activities are increasingly common among young people. The size of families among young couples also tends to be smaller. As a matter of fact, many young couples are realizing that it is costly to have children in America and that their new standard of living does not allow them to have as many children as they might like to have. The new economic environment has changed traditional values and practices pertaining to marriage among the younger generation of Vietnamese.

Socialization of Young Vietnamese Americans

Young Vietnamese have less opportunity to interact with other young Vietnamese than do young white Americans. In a state or city with a high concentration of Vietnamese, the opportunity to interact with other Vietnamese naturally is greater. In addition, unlike the children of many previous immigrant groups arriving in America in earlier years, Vietnamese children quickly learn about America and Americans through a daily diet of television. Many Vietnamese parents are too busy working and have little time to teach their children the Vietnamese language and culture. In some Vietnamese families, the children communicate with each other in English and with their parents in Vietnamese. Vietnamese children are learning to become Americans on their own. Their parents, in most situations, do not have enough knowledge about American culture to help their children. As a result, many young Vietnamese tend to experience conflict between their parents' culture and the culture they learn from school and television. Also, the communication gap between parents and children in the Vietnamese family is becoming wider. Vietnamese children are also experiencing the conflicts between their Vietnamese and American identities. Stonequist (1961) explains this phenomenon with the concept of "the marginal man." A "marginal person" stands on the edges of two cultures. This person is torn between the differences between both cultures. A marginal man cannot make up his mind to choose what culture is right for him: his parent's culture or the culture of the host society. Even so, when a marginal man attempts to assimilate to his host culture, he would experience rejection from members of the dominant group.

CHANGE AND ADAPTATION

The Vietnamese family in America is in the process of change and adaptation as a result of the new sociocultural environment. Knoll (1982:188) reports some of the observations and concerns of a Vietnamese community leader and the head of a Vietnamese family about the nature of family in the United States:

> Back in Vietnam the family is something precious for us—father, mother, children. But in coming here, we saw that the family here is too loose. The father works in one place, the mother works in another and they don't see each

other at all. Sometimes the father works in the morning and the mother works in the afternoon and the children go to school. When they get home, they hardly see each other at all. We try to keep our family together as long as possible.

The above observations and concerns have become the reality for many Vietnamese families in the United States. Like it or not, Vietnamese couples have no choice but to accept the fact that they must work in different places during different shifts and rarely see each other during the week. Their children are growing up by themselves with less and less influence from the parents.

Economic Adaptation

In terms of the economic adjustment of Vietnamese refugees in the United States, Gardner, Robey, and Smith (1985) note that the 1980 census revealed 35.1 percent of Vietnamese families living below the poverty level, compared with 7.0 percent for whites, 26.1 percent for blacks, and 21.3 percent for Hispanics. Caplan, Whitmore, and Bui (1985) conducted a national survey on the economic self-sufficiency of Indochinese refugees and found that household composition was one of the significant predictors of poverty. Their data revealed that nuclear and extended families were the two household groups with the highest percentage of those living below the poverty level. Households with unrelated, single people living together tended to be significantly better off than all other household types in terms of economic self-sufficiency. In general the average income of Vietnamese families was lower than the average family income of other groups in American society. The economic adjustment of Southeast Asians as a whole and Vietnamese refugees in particular depends on their ability to speak and understand the English language (Montero, 1979). The findings of the 1985 study on the economic adjustment of Southeast Asian Americans by the U. S. Department of Health and Human Services show that, first of all, the ability to speak and understand the English language determines the rates of both labor participation and unemployment of Southeast Asian refugees. Table 3 shows the relationship of English competence and the economic adjustment of Southeast Asian refugees.

Although the majority of Vietnamese Americans are still at the bottom of the American economy, they have continuously improved their economic self-sufficiency over the last decade.

There is no doubt that in order to survive in America, the Vietnamese family must change and adapt to its new sociocultural environment. Using

TABLE 3

English Language Ability and Economic Adjustment of Southeast Asian Refugees (1984)

ABILITY TO SPEAK AND UNDERSTAND ENGLISH (%)	LABOR FORCE PARTICIPATION (%)	UNEMPLOYMENT (%)	AVERAGE WEEKLY WAGES ($)
Not at all	19.6	32.3	193.93
A little	55.3	18.5	197.14
Well	63.3	9.1	224.20
Fluently	64.4	4.4	275.19

SOURCE: U. S. Department of Health and Human Services, *Refugee Resettlement Program: Report to the Congress* (1985:94).

Maslow's hierarchy of needs theory, one can assume that the Vietnamese family now spends most of its energy in meeting its economic needs. As a result, many Vietnamese families may not be able to preserve their traditional values. Change and adaptation are always painful processes for any immigrant group in a host society. The change and adaptation of the Vietnamese family in America may produce negative effects, such as the communication gap, problems of isolation among elderly Vietnamese, and marital conflicts.

Communication Gap

Many Vietnamese parents are similar to first-generation Japanese American parents (Issei) in believing that if their children learned English and adopted Western customs, they would be respected American citizens. Unfortunately, in the extreme, some young Vietnamese tend to favor English over Vietnamese and quietly rebell against their parent's culture as many Nisei (second-generation Japanese American) did (Knoll, 1982:62–63). In some Vietnamese families, children prefer to speak English rather than Vietnamese and prefer to eat hamburgers or hot dogs rather than traditional Vietnamese food. Communication between the elders and the youngsters in a family has become wider and wider. The older Vietnamese try to hang onto their traditional culture and values, whereas the youngsters are quickly learning the new culture and adopting new values—American values. Worse, some Vietnamese parents cannot understand the new culture and the values that their children are adopting at school and at home through television. As a result, many Vietnamese parents are losing their authority in educating their children. They cannot understand their children and do not know how to communicate with them. Their children have become Americanized too quickly and too soon. In the long run, Americanization of Vietnamese children may have negative effects. As Gardner, Robey, and Smith (1985:39) suggest:

> [I]n the past, Americanization has involved the absorption of values relating to schooling and work which encourage both individual success and national productivity. But the Americanization of Asian immigrants may have the opposite effect—reducing their exceptionally high level of dedication to learn and work.

In many Vietnamese families, traditional values still have some influence on the members, but if the lack of communication between parents and children persists, many of these values will disappear in the near future.

The Elderly Vietnamese

The elderly Vietnamese are isolated from not only American society but also their own family members. Most of the elderly Vietnamese are unable to speak English and cannot drive. They spend most of their lives at home alone. Although they are living with their children, there is rarely an opportunity to talk to them because of the amount of time they spend working outside the home in America. Their grandchildren prefer to speak English rather than Vietnamese, and when they are at home, they spend most of their time in front of the television. Elderly Vietnamese lost the respect they would have had in Vietnam, where their age status would allow them to pass down their knowledge to the younger generation. In America, their knowledge becomes useless. There is no doubt that elderly Vietnamese are experiencing tremendous loneliness and homesickness in the United States. In most Vietnamese communities in the United States, the church and Buddhist temples are the only places for elderly Vietnamese to socialize. In small communities, the elderly Vietnamese are completely cut off from the outside world.

Marital Conflicts

Vietnamese husbands and wives most likely will experience more role conflicts and role ambiguity in their marital relationship. In many Vietnamese families, as mentioned previously, the husband rarely stayed home because he was a soldier. Now, he has the role of a husband and father who assumes more responsibilities in everyday family life. At the same time, he has to deal with his wife, who now is a competitor with him in the outside world—the job market. He realizes that he is not the only breadwinner in the family. As a result, the divorce rate probably will increase because Vietnamese women are now free from their traditional social obligations.

CONCLUSION

Ten years is a short period of time in which to evaluate the process of adaptation of Vietnamese refugees in American society. Inevitably, the Vietnamese family will have to change in order to survive. The critical issues are the direction in which the Vietnamese family should change and the degree to which it should adapt to American culture. Many Vietnamese community leaders and parents are concerned about the future of young Vietnamese Americans. Efforts have been made in many Vietnamese communities to teach Vietnamese language to Vietnamese children in hopes of the younger Vietnamese preserving their traditional values and ethnic identity. An ideal Vietnamese American family would be one that could adopt American culture to survive but still preserve its traditional Vietnamese values and ethnic identity.

REFERENCES

Bell, D. A. 1985. "The Triumph of Asian-Americans," *The New Republic* (July 15 and 22) 30.

Benjamin, R., T. V. Tran, and M. Benjamin. 1983. "Alienation Among Vietnamese Students in American Society," *Free Inquiry in Creative Sociology,* 5:32–34.

Benedict, P. K. 1947. "An Analysis of Annamese Kinship Terms," *Southwestern Journal of Anthropology,* 3:371–392.

Caplan, N., J. K. Whitmore, and Q. L. Bui. 1985. *Southeast Asian Refugee Self-Sufficiency Study.* Ann Arbor, MI: Institute for Social Research.

Che, W. 1979. *The Modern Chinese Family.* Palo Alto, CA: R & E Research Associates.

Dao, D. A. 1961. *Vietnam Van-hoa Su Cuong* "History of Vietnamese Culture." Saigon, Vietnam: Nha Xuat Ban Bon Phong.

Do, M. V. 1962. *Vietnam: Where East & West Meet.* Rome, Italy: Edizioni.

Gardner, R. W., B. Robey, and P. C. Smith. 1985. "Asian Americans: Growth, Change, and Diversity," *Population Bulletin,* 40:1–44.

Haines, D., D. Rutherford, and P. Thomas. 1981. "Family and Community Among Vietnamese Refugees," *International Migration Review,* 15:310–319.

Hickey, G. C. 1964. *Village in Vietnam.* New Haven: Yale University Press.

———. 1982. *Free in the Forest: Ethnohistory of the Vietnamese Central Highlands 1954–1976.* New Haven: Yale University Press.

Hinton, H. C. 1985. *East Asia and the Western Pacific 1985.* Washington, DC: Skye-Post Publications.

Knoll, T. 1982. *Becoming Americans.* Portland: Coast to Coast Books.

Kunstadter, P. (ed.). 1967. *Southeast Asian Tribes, Minorities, and Nation, Volume II*. Princeton: Princeton University Press.
Luong, H. V. 1984. "'Brother' and 'Uncle': An analysis of rules, structures contradictions, and meaning in Vietnamese kinship," *American Anthropologist*, 86:290–315.
Marr, D. G. 1981. *Vietnamese Tradition on Trial, 1920–1945*. Berkeley: University of California Press.
Montero, D. 1979. *Vietnamese Americans: Patterns of Resettlement and Socioeconomic Adaptation in the United States*. Boulder, CO: Westview Press.
Newsweek. 1975. "The New Americans" (May 12) 132–141.
Nguyen, H. M. 1985. "Vietnamese," in D. W. Haines (ed.), *Refugees in the United States: A Reference Hand Book*. Westport, CT: Greenwood.
Nguyen, K. K. 1967. *An Introduction to Vietnamese Culture*. Tokyo, Japan: Centre for East Asian Cultural Studies.
Pham, S. V. 1960. *Viet su toan thu: Tu thuong co den hien Dai* ("Vietnamese history: From ancient time to the present day"). Saigon, Vietnam: Thu Lam An Quan.
Phan, B. K. 1975. *Viet-Nam Phong Tuc (Vietnamese Traditions)*. Paris, France: École Française D'Extrême-Orient.
Schaefer, R. T. 1979. *Racial and Ethnic Groups*. Boston: Little, Brown.
Spencer, R. F. 1945. "The Annamese Kinship System," *Southwestern Journal of Anthropology*, 1:284–310.
Starr, P. D. 1981. "Troubled Waters: Vietnamese Fisherfolk on America's Gulf Coast," *International Migration Review*, 15:226–238.
Stonequist, E. B. 1961. *The Marginal Man*. New York: Russel & Russell.
Strand, P. J., and W. Jones, Jr. 1985. *Indochinese Refugees in America: Problems of Adaptation and Assimilation*. Durham, NC: Duke University Press.
Swearer, D. K. 1984. *Southeast Asia*. Guilford, CT: Dushkin Publishing Group.
Taylor, K. W. 1983. *The Birth of Vietnam*. Berkeley, CA: University of California Press.
Toan Anh. 1965. *Nep Cu: Con nguoi Vietnam* ("The old way: vietnamese people"). Saigon, Vietnam: Dai Nam.
———. 1969. *Phong Tuc Viet-Nam: Tu ban than den gia dinh* ("Vietnamese customs, from individual to family"). Saigon, Vietnam: Dai Nam.
Tonnies, F. 1957. *Community and Society*. New York: Harper Torchbook.
U. S. Department of Health and Human Services. 1985. *Refugees Resettlement Program, Report to the Congress*. Washington, DC: U. S. Government Printing Office.
U. S. Department of State. 1984. *Vietnam: Background Notes*. Washington, DC: U. S. Government Printing Office.
Vuong, G. T. 1976. *Getting to Know Vietnamese and Their Culture*. New York: Ungar.
Whitfield, D. J. 1976. *Historical and Cultural Dictionary of Vietnam*. Metuchen, NJ: Scarecrow Press.

HISTORICALLY SUBJUGATED ETHNIC MINORITIES

CHAPTER THIRTEEN

The Black American Family

Robert Staples

INTRODUCTION

As the United States' largest visible minority, the black population has been the subject of extensive study by behavioral scientists. Its family life has been of particular concern because of the unique character of this group, as a result of a history that is uncharacteristic of other ethnic groups. There are four cultural traits of the black group that distinguish it from other immigrants to the United States: (1) blacks came from a country with norms and values that were dissimilar to the American way of life; (2) they were from many different tribes, each with its own language, culture, and traditions; (3) in the beginning, they came without women; and, most importantly, (4) they came in bondage (Billingsley, 1968).

The study of black family life has, historically, been problem-oriented. Whereas the study of white families has been biased toward the middle-class family, the reverse has been true in the investigation of black family patterns. Until relatively recently, almost all studies of black family life have concentrated on the lower-income strata of the group, ignoring middle-class families and even stable, poor black families. Moreover, the deviation of black families from middle-class norms has resulted in them being defined as pathological. Such labels ignore the possibility that although a group's family forms may not fit into the normative model, it may instead have its own functional organization that meets the needs of the group (Billingsley, 1970).

One purpose of this description of black family life-style is to demonstrate how it has changed in the decade of the 1970s. Additionally, the forces that black families encounter, which create the existence of large numbers of "problem" families, must be carefully examined. Out of this systematic analysis of black family adaptations may come a new understanding of the black family in contemporary American society.

HISTORICAL BACKGROUND

The Preslavery Period

There are several historical periods of interest in the evaluation of black family life in the United States. One era is the precolonial period of the African continent from which the black American population originated. The basis of African family life was the kinship group, which was bound together by blood ties, common interests, and mutual functions. Within each village, there were elaborate legal codes and court systems that regulated the marital and family behavior of individual members (Brown and Forde, 1967).

The Slave Family

In attempting to accurately describe the family life of slaves, one must sift through a conflicting array of opinions on the subject. Reliable empirical facts are few, and speculation has been rampant in the absence of data. Certain aspects of the slave's family life are undisputed. Slaves were not allowed to enter into binding contractual relationships. Because marriage is basically a legal relationship that imposes obligations on both parties and exacts penalties for the violation of those obligations, there was no legal basis for any marriage between two individuals in bondage. Slave marriages were regulated at the discretion of the slaveowners. As a result, some marriages were initiated by slaveowners and just as easily dissolved (Genovese, 1975).

Hence, there were numerous cases in which the slaveowner ordered slave women to marry men of his choosing after they reached the age of puberty. The slave owners preferred marriages between slaves on the same plantation, because the primary reason for slave unions was the breeding of children who would become future slaves. Children born to a slave woman on a different plantation were looked on by the slaveholder as wasting his man's seed. Yet, many slaves who were allowed to get married preferred women from a neighboring plantation. This allowed them to avoid witnessing the many assaults on slave women that occurred. Sometimes, the matter was resolved by the sale of one of the slaves to the other owner (Blassingame, 1972).

Historians are divided on the question of how many slave families were involuntarily separated from each other by their owners. Despite the slaveholder's commitment to keeping the slave families intact, the intervening events of a slaveholder's death, his bankruptcy, or lack of capital made the forceable sale of some slave's spouse or child inevitable. In instances where the slavemaster was indifferent to the fate of slave families, he would still keep them together simply to enforce plantation discipline. A married slave who was concerned about his wife and children, it was believed, was less inclined to rebel or escape than would an unmarried slave. Whatever their reasoning, the few available records show that slaveowners did not separate a majority of the slave couples (Blassingame, 1972).

This does not mean that the slave family had a great deal of stability. Although there are examples of some slave families living together for 40 years or more, the majority of slave unions were dissolved by personal choice, death, or the sale of one partner by the master. Although individual families may not have remained together for long periods of time, the institution of the family was an important asset in the perilous era of slavery. Despite the prevalent theories about the destruction of the family under slavery, it was one of the most important survival mechanisms for African people held in bondage (Blassingame, 1972; Fogel and Engerman, 1974).

In the slave quarters, black families did exist as functioning institutions and as models for others. The slave narratives provide us with some indication of the importance of family relations under slavery. It was in the family that the slave received affection, companionship, love, and empathy with his sufferings under this peculiar institution. Through the family, he learned how to avoid punishment, cooperate with his fellow slaves, and retain some semblance of his self-esteem. The socialization of the slave child was another important function for the slave parents. They could cushion the shock of bondage for him, inculcate in him values different than those the masters attempted to teach him, and represent another frame of reference for his self-esteem besides the master (Abzug, 1971).

Much has been written about the elimination of the male's traditional functions under the slave system. It is true that he was often relegated to working in the fields and siring children rather than providing economic maintenance or physical protection for his family, but the father's role was not as insignificant as presumed. It was the male slave's inability to protect his wife from the physical and sexual abuse of the master that most pained him. As a matter of survival, few tried, because the consequences were often fatal. However, it is significant that tales of their intervention occur frequently in the slave narratives. There is one story of a slave who could no longer tolerate the humiliation of his wife's sexual abuse before his eyes by the master. The slave choked him to death with the knowledge that it also meant his own death. He said he knew it would mean his death, but he was unafraid of death, so he killed him (Abzug, 1971:29).

One aspect of black family life frequently ignored during the slave era is the free black family. This group, which numbered about one-half million, was primarily composed of the descendants of the original black indentured servants and the mulatto offspring of slaveholders. For this minority of black families, the assimilation and acculturation process was, relatively, less difficult. They imitated the white world as closely as possible. Because they had opportunities for education, owning property, and skilled occupations, their family life was quite stable. Some of them even owned slaves, although the majority of black slaveholders were former slaves who had purchased their wives or children. It is among this group that the early black middle-class was formed (Frazier, 1932).

After Emancipation

There has been a prevailing notion that the experience of slavery weakened the value of marriage as an institution among black Americans. Yet, the slaves married in record numbers when the right to the freedom to marry was created by governmental decree. A legal marriage was a status symbol, and weddings were events of great gaiety. In a careful examination of census data and marriage licenses for the period after 1860, Gutman, (1976) found that the typical household was a simple nuclear family headed by an adult male. Further evidence that black people were successful in forming a dual-parent family structure is the data that show that 90 percent of all black children were born in wedlock by the year 1917.

The strong family orientation of the recently emancipated slaves has been observed by many students of the reconstruction era. One newspaper reported a black group's petition to the state of North Carolina asking for the right "to work with the assurance of good faith and fair treatment, to educate their children, to sanctify the family relation, to reunite scattered families, and to provide for the orphan and infirm" (Abzug, 1971:34). Children were of special value to the freed slaves, whose memories were fresh with the history of their offspring being sold away.

It was during the late nineteenth century that the strong role of women emerged. Men preferred their wives to remain at home, because a working woman was considered a mark of slavery. However, during the period, which has been described as the most explicitly racist era of American history (Miller, 1966), black men found it very difficult to obtain jobs and, in some instances, found work only as strikebreakers. Thus, the official organ of the African Methodist Episcopal church exhorted black families to teach their daughters not to avoid work, because many of them would marry men that would not make on the average more than 75 cents per day (Abzug, 1971:39). In 1900, approximately 41 percent of black women were in the labor force, compared with 16 percent of white women (Logan, 1965).

What was important, then, was not whether the husband or wife worked, but the family's will to survive in an era when blacks were systematically deprived of educational and work opportunities. Despite these obstacles, black families achieved a level of stability based on role integration. Men shared equally in the rearing of children; women participated in the defense of the family. As Nobles (1972) comments, a system in which the family disintegrates because of the loss of one member would be in opposition to the traditional principles of unity that defined the African family. These principles were to be tested during the period of the great black migration from the rural areas of the South to the cities of the North.

The rise of black illegitimately born children and female-headed households are concomitants of twentieth century urban ghettos. Drastic increases in these phenomena strongly indicate that the condition of many lower-class black families is a function of the economic contingencies of industrial America. Unlike the European immigrants before them, blacks were disadvantaged by the hard lines of northern segregation along racial lines. Furthermore, families in cities are more vulnerable to disruptions from the traumatizing experiences of urbanization, the reduction of family functions, and the loss of extended family supports.

In the transition from Africa to the American continent, there can be no doubt that African culture was not retained in any pure form. Blacks lacked the autonomy to maintain their cultural traditions under the severe pressures to take on American standards of behavior. Yet, there are surviving Africanisms that are reflected in black speech patterns, esthetics, folklore, and religion. They have preserved aspects of their old culture that have a direct relevance to their new lives. Out of the common experiences they have shared, a new culture has been forged that is uniquely black American. The elements of that culture are still to be found in their family life.

Among the principal variables that undergird family life are education, employment, and income. Looking at the 1980 census, one can find some absolute progress in certain areas for black families, little change in their status vis-à-vis white families, and the general problems of poverty and unemployment unchanged overall for many black families. In education, for example, the percentage of blacks graduating from high school increased slightly, but blacks were still more likely than whites to be high-school dropouts. The median number of school years completed by black Americans over 24 years of age was 12.0, in contrast to 12.3 for white Americans (U. S. Bureau of the Census, 1983).

There are two important aspects of the education situation to consider in assessing its relevance to blacks. First, black women tend to be slightly more educated than black men at all levels. In the past decade, the educational level of white men increased to reach the average of white women, whereas black men continued to lag behind black women (U. S. Bureau of the Census, 1983). Hence, an increase in the educational level of the black population will not automatically mean a rise in income or employment opportunities. The fact that much of that increase in education belongs to black women reduces the mobility level for blacks because black women, even educated ones, tend to be concentrated in lower-paying jobs than black men. Another significant factor is the sexual discrimination that women in our society face in the labor force (Bianchi, 1981; Collier and Williams, 1982).

The second important aspect of education is that it does not have the same utility for blacks as it does for whites. Although the incomes of black college graduates and whites who have completed only elementary school are no longer the same, the equal educational achievements of blacks and whites still are not reflected in income levels. The 1980 census reveals that blacks are still paid less for comparable work than whites. These figures lend substance to the argument by Jencks et al. (1972) that education alone will not equalize the income distribution of blacks and whites. In fact, the relative unemployment gap between blacks and whites increases with education. Although both blacks and whites incur difficulties because of a low level of education, college-educated whites face fewer barriers to their career aspirations. In analyzing the unemployment rate of black college graduates, they were unemployed as frequently as white males who had not graduated from high school (U. S. Civil Rights Commission, 1982).

During the past decade, the yearly median family income for blacks decreased at a faster rate than the median income for the population as a whole. Black family income is only 56 percent of white family income. The annual median income for white families in 1981 was $23,520, and for black families only $14,460. Even these figures are misleading because they do not show that black family incomes must be used to support more family members and that their family income is more often derived from the employment of both the husband and the wife. Also, according to the Labor Department, the majority of the female-headed black families are not earning the $9,284 a year needed to maintain themselves at a non-poverty standard of living (U. S. Bureau of the Census, 1983).

Furthermore, more than one-third of the nation's black population is still officially living in poverty. Approximately one-fourth of them are receiving public assistance. The comparable figures for whites were 10 percent and 4 percent. More than 70 percent of these black families living in poverty are headed by women. Approximately 41 percent of all black children are members of these families who exist on an income of less than $7,510 a year. Less than 15 percent of white children live in households that are officially defined as poor (U. S. Bureau of the Census, 1983).

The unemployment rate for blacks in 1982 was at its highest level since 1945. Overall, 18.9 percent of blacks were officially unemployed, compared with 8.6 percent for whites. In the years 1972–1982, black unemployment increased from 10.3 percent to 18.9 percent. Furthermore, this increase in unemployment during that 10-year period was highest among married black men who were the primary breadwinners in their household. Just as significant is the unemployment rate of black male teenagers. Approximately 50 percent of that group was unemployed, compared with 20.4 percent of white male teenagers. The highest unemployment rates in the country are among black male teenagers in low-income areas of central cities. Their unemployment rate is approximately 65 percent and has risen as high as 75 percent (U. S. Bureau of the Census, 1983).

What the recent census figures indicate is that the decade of the 1970s saw little significant change in the socioeconomic status of black families. An increase in educational achievements has produced little in economic benefits for most blacks. Based on the rate of progress in integrating blacks in the labor force in the past decade, it will take 9.3 years to equalize the participation of blacks in low-paying office and clerical jobs and a period of 90 years before black professionals approximate the proportion of blacks in the population (Staples, 1982).

Changing Patterns of Black Family Life

Recent years have brought about significant changes in the marital and family patterns of many Americans. Americans have witnessed an era of greater sexual permissiveness, alternate family life-styles, increased divorce rates, and reductions in the fertility rate. Some of these changes have also occurred among black families and have implications for any public policy developed to strengthen black family life.

The sexual revolution has arrived, and blacks are very much a part of it (Staples, 1981). By the age of 19, black women were twice as likely as white women to have engaged in intercourse. Although the percentage for white females was lower, they were engaging in premarital coitus more often and with a larger number of sexual partners. However, a larger number of sexually active black females were not using reliable contraceptives, and 41 percent had been, or were, pregnant (Zelnik and Kantner, 1977).

One result of this increased premarital sexual activity among blacks is the large number of black children born out of wedlock. More than one-half of every 1,000 black births were illegitimate in the year 1980. Moreover, the rate was higher in this period for blacks than in the most recent earlier periods. The racial differences in illegitimacy rates also narrowed in the last 20 years (U. S. Bureau of the Census, 1983). One reason for the continued racial differential is the greater use by white women of low-cost abortions. In one study, 26 percent of pregnant black women received an abortion, compared with 41 percent of white women (Cummings, 1983). In all probability, the black out-of-wedlock birth rate will continue to increase as a higher percentage of black children are born to teenage mothers.

When blacks choose to get married, the same economic and cultural forces that are undermining marital stability in the general population are operative. In the last decade, the annual divorce rate has risen 120 percent. For white women under the age of 30, the chances are nearly two out of four that their marriage will end in divorce. Among black women, their chances are two out of three. In 1981, 30 percent of married black women were separated or divorced, compared with 14 percent for white women. The divorce rate of middle-class blacks is lower, because the more money that a family makes and the higher their educational achievements, the greater are their chances for a stable marriage (U. S. Bureau of the Census, 1983).

A combination of the aforementioned factors has increased the percentage of black households headed by women. The percentage of female-headed families among blacks increased 130 percent in the last decade, from 21 percent to 47 percent. One-third of these female household heads worked and had a median annual income of only $7,510 in 1981. The percentage of black children living with both parents declined in the last decade, and currently, only 42 percent of children in black families are residing with both parents. It is apparently the increasing pressures of discrimination, urban living, and poverty that cause black fathers to leave their homes or never marry. At the income level of $20,000 and over, the percentage of black families headed by a man is similar to that for white families (U. S. Bureau of the Census, 1983).

The fertility rate of black women is hardly a factor in the increase of female-headed households among blacks. Between 1970 and 1980, the total birth rate for black women decreased sharply. The fertility rate of black women (2.3 children per black woman) is still higher than the 1.7 birth rate for white women. However, the average number of total births expected by young black wives (2.6) and young white wives (2.4) are very similar. As more black women acquire middle-class status or access to birth control and abortion, one can expect racial differentials in fertility to narrow (U. S. Bureau of the Census, 1983). The birth rate of college-educated black women is actually lower than their white counterparts.

This statistical picture of marital and family patterns among blacks indicates a continued trend toward attenuated nuclear families caused by the general changes in the society and the effects of the disadvantaged economic position of large numbers of black people. An enlightened public policy would address itself to the needs of those families rather than attempt to mold black families into idealized middle-class models, which no longer mean much, even for the white middle class. What is needed is a government policy that is devoid of middle-class puritanism, the protestant ethic, and male-chauvinist concepts about family leadership.

Sex Roles

In recent years the issue of sex roles and their definition has received much attention. Although the debate has centered on the issue of female subordination and male dominance and privilege, blacks have considerably different problems in terms of their sex-role identities. They must first overcome certain disabilities based on racial membership—not gender affiliation. However, that does not mean that sex-role identities within the black community do not carry with them advantages and disadvantages. In many ways they do, but instead of fighting over the question of who is the poorest of the poor, blacks must contend with the plaguing problem of an unemployment rate that is as high as 45 percent among black men. Factors correlating to that central problem are the declining life-expectancy rate of black men and rises in drug abuse, suicide, crime, and educational failures. These facts do not warrant much support for a movement to equalize the condition of men and women in the black community (Staples, 1982).

Along with the economic conditions that impinge on their role performance, black men are saddled with a number of stereotypes that label them as irresponsible, criminalistic, hypersexual, and lacking in masculine traits. Some of these stereotypes become self-fulfilling prophecies because the dominant society is structured in a way that prevents many black men from achieving the goals of manhood. At the same time, the notion of the castrated black male is largely a myth. Although mainstream culture has deprived many black men of the economic wherewithal for normal, masculine functions, most function in a way that gains the respect of their mates, children, and community.

Along with all the dynamic changes occurring in American society are slow but perceptible alterations in the role of black women. The implications of these changes are profound in light of the fact that they are central figures in the family life of black people. Historically, the black woman has been a bulwark of strength in the black community. From the time of slavery onward, she has resisted the destructive forces that she has encountered in American society. During the period of slavery, she fought and survived the attacks on her dignity by the slave system, relinquished the passive role ascribed to members of her gender to ensure the survival of her people, and tolerated the culturally induced irresponsibility of her man in recognition of this country's relentless attempts to castrate him.

Too often, the only result of her sacrifices and sufferings have been the invidious and inaccurate labeling of her as a matriarch, a figure deserving respect but not love. The objective reality of the black woman in America is that she occupies the lowest rung of the socioeconomic ladder of all sex–race groups and has the least prestige. The double burden of gender and race has put her in the category of a super-oppressed entity. Considering the opprobrium to which she is subjected, one would expect her to be well-represented in the women's liberation movement. Yet, that movement remains primarily white and middle class. This is in part the result of the class-bound character of the women's movement—it being middle class whereas most black women are poor or working class. Their low profile in that movement also stems from the fact that many of the objectives of white feminists relate to psychological and cultural factors such as language and sexist behavior whereas the black woman's concerns are economic.

There is a common ground on which blacks and women can and do meet—on such issues as equal pay for equal work, child care facilities, and female parity in the work force. Instead of joining the predominantly white, middle-class women's movement, many black women have formed their own organizations such as the Welfare Rights Organization, Black Women Organized for Action, and the Black Feminist Alliance. There is little question that there is a heightened awareness among black women of the problems they face based on their sex-role membership alone. Whether the struggle of black women for equal rights will come into conflict with the movement for black liberation remains to be seen. It is fairly clear that black women must be freed from both the disabilities of race and sex.

Male–Female Relationships

Relationships between black men and women have had a peculiar evolution. Unlike the white family, which was a patriarchy and sustained by the economic dependence of women, the black dyad has been characterized by more equalitarian roles and economic parity in North America. The system of slavery did not permit black males to assume the superordinate role in the family constellation because the female was not economically dependent on him. Hence, relationships between the sexes were ordered along social–psychological factors rather than economic compulsion to marry and remain married. This fact, in part, explains the unique trajectory of black male–female relationships.

Finding and keeping a mate is complicated by a number of social–psychological factors, as well as structural restraints. Social structure and individual attitudes interface to make male–female relationships ephemeral rather than permanent. The imbalance in the sex ratio will continue to deny large numbers of black women a comparable mate. Furthermore, there are only a limited number of ways to deal with that irreversible fact of life. At the same time, there exists a pool of black males who are available to this group of women, and the tension between them builds barriers to communicating and mating. This is a complex problem, and there is no easy solution. Although there are some black men who are threatened by the successful black woman, further investigation reveals other underlying forces. Men are torn between the need for security and the desire for freedom, the quest for a special person to call their own and the temptation of sexual variety. They see marriage as a way of establishing roots but are seduced by the enticement of all the attractive, possibly "better" women in their midst.

Given the advantage he has as a male in a sexist society and a high prestige in short supply in the black community, there is little incentive for him to undertake the actions needed to meet the needs of women. The women who feel that their emotional needs are not being met begin to recoil and adopt their own agenda based on a conception of self-interest. Some recognition must be made of the changing relations between men and women. The old exchange of feminine sexual appeal for male financial support is in a declining state. Women, increasingly, are able to define their own status and are economically independent. What they seek now is the satisfaction of emotional needs, not an economic cushion. Whereas men must confront this new reality, women must realize that emotional needs can be taken care of by men in all social classes. Although a similar education and income can mean greater compatibility in values and interests, it is no guarantee of compatibility nor of personal happiness. Common needs, interests, and values are more a function of gender than class.

One should not be deluded by the ostensible reluctance of many black single adults to enter the conjugal state. When a person has not been able to develop a lasting, permanent relationship with a member of the opposite sex, he or she must play it off and make the best of whatever it is they have at the moment. Although the industrial and urban revolution has made the single life more a viable way of life, it has also made the need for belonging more imperative. The tensions of work and the impersonality of the city have created a need to escape the depersonalization by retreating into some sort of an intimate sanctum. This is especially imperative for blacks in the middle class who have their selfhood tested daily by a racist society and who must often work and live in isolation. In modern society, individuals are required to depend on each other for permanence and stability, which is a function previously served by a large familial and social network.

It is the fear that even marriage no longer provides that permanence and stability that causes people to enter and exit their relationships quickly. It is the fear of failure that comes from failure. Until black single adults develop a tenacity to work as hard at a relationship as they did at their schooling and jobs, we will continue to see this vicious cycle repeated again and again. Marriage and the family continue to be the most important buffer for blacks against racism and depersonalization. When one looks at the strongest predictors of happiness in America, it is inevitably such social factors as marriage, family, friends, and children. Across the board, married people tend to be happier than those who are unmarried. The best confirmation of this fact is that most people who divorce eventually remarry. Before anyone can find happiness in a marriage, they must form a strong basis for marriage. It is that task that continues to perplex black single adults.

There is a growing trend toward single life among American blacks. A majority of black women over the age of 18 years are no longer married and living with a spouse (Staples, 1981). Although the institutional decimation of black males is the primary factor in this unprecedented number of singles, other sociocultural forces have an impact on the relationships between black men and women. Among them are the changes in black institutions and values. Franklin (1984) traces the conflict between black men and women to incompatible role enactments by the two sexes. The societal prescription that women are to be passive and men dominant is counteracted by black women who resist black men's dominance and black men who wish to be accorded the superior male role but cannot fulfill the economic provider role, which supports the dominance of men in American society.

HUSBANDS AND WIVES. Marriages are very fragile today. Fewer people are getting married, and the divorce rate in the United States is at an all-time high. There are many forces responsible for this changing pattern including changing attitudes and laws on divorce, changing and conflicting definitions of sex roles and their functions in the family, economic problems, and personality conflicts. Although divorce is on the rise and its increase cuts across racial and class lines, it is still more pronounced among blacks. Only one out of every three black couples will remain married longer than 10 years.

It is not easy to pinpoint unique causes of black marital dissolution because they are very similar those of their white counterparts. In some cases, it is the severity of the problems they face. Economic problems are a major factor in marital conflict and there are three times as many blacks as whites with incomes below the poverty level. The tensions blacks experience in coping with the pervasive incidents of racism often have their ramifications in the marital arena. One peculiar problem blacks face is the imbalanced sex ratio, which places many women in competition for the available males. Too often, the males they compete for are not available, and this places serious pressure on the marriages of many blacks.

At the same time, many blacks are involved in a functional marriage at any given point in time. Many adult blacks are married and have positive and loving relationships with their spouses. Unfortunately, practically no research exists on marital adjustment and satisfaction among blacks. What little research does exist indicates that black wives are generally less satisfied with their marriages than white wives. However, the source of their dissatisfaction is often associated with the problems of poverty and racism.

The last decade witnessed a significant increase in interracial dating and marriage. Among the reasons for this change in black–white dating and marriage was the desegregation of the public school system, the work force, and other social settings. In those integrated settings, blacks and whites met as equals, which facilitated homogenous mating. There were, of course, other factors such as the liberation of many white youth from parental control and the racist values they conveyed to them.

Not only has the incidence of interracial relations increased but their character has changed as well. Over 25 years ago, the most typical interracial pairing was a black male and a white female with the male partner generally being of a higher status. This pattern was so common that social theorists even developed a theory of racial hypergamy. In essence, it was assumed that the higher-status black male was exchanging his socioeconomic status for the privilege of marrying a woman who belonged to a racial group that was considered superior to all members of the black race. Contemporary interracial relations are much more likely to involve people with similar educational background and occupational status.

Although no research studies have yet yielded any data on the subject, there appears to be a change in interracial unions toward a decline in black male/white female couples and an increase in black female/white male pairings. Several factors seem to account for this modification of the typical pattern. Many black women are gravitating toward white men because of the shortage of black men and disenchantment with those they do have access to. In a similar vein, some white men are dissatisfied with white women and their increasing vociferous demands for sex-role parity. At the same time, there is a slight but noticeable decrease in black male/white female unions. One possible reason is that it is no longer as fashionable as it was a few years ago. Also, much of their attraction to each other was based on the historical lack of access to each other and the stereotype of black men as superstuds and white women as forbidden fruit. Once they had had extensive interaction, the myths exploded and the attraction consequently diminished (Poussaint, 1983).

We should be fairly clear that there are relatively normal reasons for interracial attractions and matings. At the same time, it would be naive to assume that special factors are not behind them in a society that is stratified by race. Given the persistence of racism as a very pervasive force, many interracial marriages face rough sledding. In addition to the normal problems of working out a satisfactory marital relationship, interracial couples must cope with social ostracism and isolation. One recent phenomenon is the increasing hostility toward such unions by the black community, which has forced some interracial couples into a marginal existence. Such pressures cause the interracial-marriage rate to remain at a very low level. Less than 5 percent of all marriages involving a black person are interracial (Poussaint, 1983).

Childhood and Childrearing

One of the most popular images of black women is that of "Mammy," the devoted, affectionate nursemaids of white children who belonged to their slavemaster or employer. This motherly image of black women probably has some basis in fact. Motherhood has historically been an important role for black women, even more meaningful than their role as wives (Bell, 1971). In the colonial period of Africa, missionaries often observed and reported the unusual devotion of the African mother to her child. The slave mother also developed a deep love for, and impenetrable bond to, her children (Ladner, 1971). It would appear that the bond between the black mother and her child is deeply rooted in the African heritage and philosophy that places a special value on children because they represent the continuity of life (Brown and Forde, 1967).

Many studies have conveyed a negative image of the black mother because she does not conform to middle-class modes of childrearing. Yet, black mothers have fulfilled the function of socializing their children into the multiple roles they must perform in this society. They prepare them to take on not only the appropriate sex and age roles but also a racial role. Children must be socialized to deal with the prosaic realities of white racism that they will encounter daily. Black females are encouraged to be independent rather than passive individuals because many of them will carry family and economic responsibilities alone (Iscoe et al., 1964). Taking on adult responsibilities is something many black children learn early. They may be given the care of a younger sibling, and some will have to find work while still in the adolescent stage. The strong character structure of black children was noted by child psychiatrist Robert Coles (1964) who observed their comportment under the pressure of school integration in the South during a very volatile era.

The black mother's childrearing techniques are geared to prepare her children for a kind of existence that is alien to middle-class white youngsters. Moreover, many white middle-class socialization patterns may not be that desirable for the psychological growth of the black child. The casual upbringing of black children may produce a much healthier personality than the status anxieties associated with some rigid middle-class childrearing practices (Green, 1946). Using threats of the withdrawal of love if the child fails to measure up to the parent's standards is much more common among white parents than black parents of any class stratum. One result of the black child's anxiety-free upbringing is a strong closeness to his parents (Nolle, 1972; Scanzoni, 1971).

Although black parents are more likely to use physical rather than verbal punishment to enforce discipline than white parents, this technique is often buttressed by the love they express for their children. Moreover, as Billingsley (1969:567) has noted, "even among the lowest social classes in the Black community, families give the children better care than is generally recognized, and often the care is better than that given by white families in similar social circumstances." One indication of the decline in this attitude is found in the statistics, which show that child abuse has become more common in black families than in white families (Gil, 1971). Some of the racial differences can be attributed to reporting bias, but much of it reflects the effect of poverty and racism on black parent–child relationships.

The most undesirable aspect of the black child's life is reputed to be the absence of a positive male figure (Moynihan, 1965; Rainwater, 1966). A plethora of studies have found that the black child has low self-esteem because of his "blackness" and the fact that many children grow up in homes without a male role model. A number of studies have emerged that are in opposition to the theories of low self-esteem among blacks. In reviewing the literature on black self-esteem, some have concluded that much of it is invalid, and others have concluded that blacks are less likely to suffer from low self-esteem because of such countervailing influences as religion, reference groups, group identification, and positive experiences in the extended family (Staples, 1976:82–84).

Problems in child development are alleged to be a function of the father's absence or ineffectiveness. There has yet to be found a direct relationship between the father's absence and child maladaption (Hare, 1975; Rubin, 1974). In part, the black child continues to have male role models among the male kinsmen in his extended family network, and the mother generally regards her children's father as a friend of the family who she can recruit for help rather than as a father failing his parental duties. However, one must be careful not to overromanticize the single-parent family as a totally functional model. They are the poorest families in the United States and are overrepresented among the society's failures in education, crime, and mental health.

The ineffective black father has been assumed to be pervasive among black families. Much of the more recent literature suggests that black fathers have warm, nurturing relationships with their children and play a vital role in their children's psychology and social development (Lewis, 1975; Scanzoni, 1971). How well they carry out the paternal role may be contingent on the economic resources available to them. Hence, we find better patterns of parenting among middle-class black fathers who have the economic and educational resources, and, consequently, participate more in child care, are more child-oriented, and view their role as different from the mother's (Cazanave, 1979; Daneal, 1975). As far as the male child's sexual identity is concerned, Benjamin (1971) discovered that black male youth had a better conception of the male role when their father had one or more years of college education, indicating a strong relationship between the opportunity to play a role and the actual playing of that role.

The Aged

As a result of the declining fertility rate among blacks, the elderly represent a larger percentage of the total black population than in previous times. By 1979, blacks over the age of 65 years constituted 8 percent of the black population, in contrast to half the corresponding percentage in 1910. Increasingly, the black elderly population is disproportionately female. As a result of the growing gap in mortality rates between black men and women, widowhood occurs at an earlier age for black than white women. For example, during the years 1939–1941, there was only a difference of two years in the life-expectancy rate of black men and women. As of 1979, that gap had widened to 12 years (U. S. Bureau of the Census, 1983). Based on his calculations from 1975 fertility and mortality data, Sutton (1977) estimated that the chances of becoming a widow among married black women prior to age 65 are nearly one out of two. Those who become widows could expect to have a tenure of nine years in that status before their 65th birthday. Their chances of remarriage are undermined by the extremely low sex ratio among blacks 65 years of age and over. For every 100 black females in that age category, there were only 72 males in 1976 (U. S. Bureau of the Census, 1983).

Compounding the problems of early widowhood among the black elderly is the lingering problem of poverty. Approximately 36 percent of the black elderly were poor in 1977, compared with only 12 percent of elderly whites. Moreover, while the percentage of poor elderly decreased from 13 percent to 12 percent between 1975–1977, the number of poor black persons 65 years of age and over increased by 110,000 during the same period, maintaining the same percentage in poverty in 1975. One result of this overwhelming poverty is that a much larger percentage of elderly black wives continue to work after reaching the age of 65 years than their white counterparts (U. S. Bureau of the Census, 1983).

Despite their poverty, the extended-kin network manages to buttress the problems attendant to aging among its elderly members. When Hutchinson (1974) compared black and white low-income elderly, his results indicated that blacks and whites were identical in their expectations for the future, feelings of loneliness, amount of worrying, perception of others, and general life satisfaction. Moreover, the black elderly were more likely to describe themselves as being happier. One of the reasons the black elderly do not experience previous adjustment problems with growing old is that they continue to play a vital role in the extended family. Very few, for instance, are taken into the households of younger relatives. Only 4 percent of black families have relatives 65 years of age and over living with them. Instead, young black children often are taken into the households of elderly relatives, usually a grandmother. This process of informal adoption is so common that half of all black families headed by elderly women have dependent children, not their own, living with them (Hill, 1977).

CHANGE AND ADAPTATION

The last 30 years have culminated in the gradual disintegration of the black nuclear family. Changes in the black family structure are in tune with the changes in American families. A number of social forces account for the increase in the number of single adults, out-of-wedlock births, divorces, and single-parent households. As women have become economically and psychologically independent of men, they have chosen to remain single or leave marriages they regarded as not satisfying their needs. Simultaneously, the growing independence of women and the sexual revolution of the 1960s and 1970s have allowed many men to flee from the responsibility attendant to the husband and father roles (Ehrenreich, 1983).

Although these sociocultura' forces have an impact on the marriage and family patterns of many Americans, they are more pronounced among blacks because of one critical etiological agent: the institutional decimation of black males. As an Urban League report concluded, "the attrition of Black males . . . from conception through adulthood finally results in an insufficient number of men who are willing and able to provide support for women and children in a family setting" (Williams, 1984). Thus, many black women are denied a real choice between monogamous marriage or single life. Most do choose to bear and raise children because that is deemed better than being single, childless, and locked into dead-end, low-paying jobs. Although many would prefer a monogamous marriage, that is no longer possible for the majority of black women. The same forces that drive many black men out of social institutions also propel them out of the family.

Those forces have their genesis in the educational system. Black women are more educated than black men at all levels except the doctoral level. This, again, is in the overall direction of change in American society. White men have also been losing ground to white women in educational achievements. The reasons for the ascendency of women in the school system are unclear. Some speculate that because teachers are disproportionately female, the behaviors tolerated and most encouraged are those that are more natural for girls (Hale, 1983). The higher educational level of black women endows them with educational credentials and skills that make them more competitive in the job market. The changing nature of the economy has placed women at an advantage. While the industrial sector has been declining, the service and high-technology sectors of the economy have been expanding. Black women are more highly concentrated in the expanding sector of the economy whereas black men are overrepresented in the shrinking industrial jobs.

One consequence of the aforementioned factors is the attrition of black men in the labor force. According to a study by Joe and Yu (1984) almost 46 percent of the black men of working age were not in the labor force. As a rule, unemployed males are not good marriage prospects. The percentage of black women heading families alone in 1982 (42 percent) corresponds closely to the percentage of black males not in the labor force. Along with the number of black males not gainfully employed is the imbalance in the sex ratio, especially in the marriageable age ranges (18–35 years). Guttentag and Secord (1983) have shown that imbalanced sex ratios have certain predictable consequences for relationships between men and women. They give rise to higher rates of single adults, divorce, out-of-wedlock births, and female-headed households in different historical epochs and across different societies. Another analysis by Jackson (1971) revealed that among blacks, the percentage of female-headed households increases as the supply of males decreases. On the other hand, the percentage of female-headed households decreases when the supply of black males increases.

The crisis of the black family is, in reality, the crisis of the black male and his inability to carry out the normative responsibilities of husband and father in the nuclear family. The family's disintegration is only a symptom of the larger problem, that problem being the institutional decimation of black males. One should be clear that the institutional decimation of black males represents the legacy of institutional racism. The implications of this problem extend beyond the family. A majority of black children live in one-parent households today, and the median income available to those families is less than $7,500 per year. Although many children rise out of poor families to become successful adults, the odds are against them. Large numbers of them, especially the males, will follow their biological fathers to an early grave, prison, and the ranks of the unemployed. Only by resolving the problems of the black male can we restore the black family to its rightful place in our lives. The future of the race may be at stake.

REFERENCES

Abzug, Robert H. 1971. "The Black Family During Reconstruction," in Nathan Huggins, et al. (eds.), *Key Issue in the Afro-American Experience.* New York: Harcourt, Brace and Jovanovich, 26–39.

Adams, Bert N. 1970. "Isolation, Function and Beyond: American Kinship in the 1960s," *Journal of Marriage and the Family,* 32(November):575–598.

Bell, Robert. 1971. "The Relative Importance of Mother and Wife Roles Among Negro Lower-Class Women," in *The Black Family: Essays and Studies.* Belmont, CA: Wadsworth, 248–256.

Benjamin, R. 1971. *Factors Related to Conceptions of the Black Male Familial Role by Black Male Youth.* Mississippi State University Sociological-Anthropological Press Series.

Bianchi, Suzanne. 1981. *Household Composition and Racial Inequality.* New Brunswick, NJ: Rutgers University Press.

Billingsley, Andrew. 1968. *Black Families in White America.* Englewood Cliffs, NJ: Prentice-Hall.

———. 1969. "Family Functioning in the Low-Income Black Community," *Social Casework,* 50(December):563–572.

———. 1970. "Black Families and White Social Science," *Journal of Social Issues,* 26(November):127–142.

Blassingame, John. 1972. *The Slave Community.* New York: Oxford University Press.

Brown, A. R. Radcliffe, and Darryle Forde. 1967. *African Systems of Kinship and Marriage.* New York: Oxford University Press.

Brown, Prudence, et al. 1977. "Sex Role Attitudes and Psychological Outcomes for Black and White Women Experiencing Marital Dissolution," *Journal of Marriage and the Family,* 39(August):549–562.

Cazanave, Noel. 1979a. "Middle-Income Black Fathers: An Analysis of the Provider Role," *The Family Coordinator,* 28(November).

———. 1979b. "Social Structure and Personal Choice in Intimacy, Marriage and Family Alternative Lifestyle Research," *Alternative Life Styles,* 2(August):331–358.

Chavis, William M., and Gladys Lyles. 1975. "Divorce Among Educated Black Women." *Journal of the National Medical Association,* 67(March):128–134.

Clayton, Richard R., and Harwin L. Voss. 1977. "Shacking: Cohabitation in the 1970s," *Journal of Marriage and the Family,* 39(May):273–284.

Coles, Robert. 1964. "Children and Racial Demonstrations," *The American Scholar,* 34(Winter):78–92.

Collier, Betty, and Louis Williams. 1982. "The Economic Status of the Black Male: A Myth Exploded," *Journal of Black Studies,* 12(June):487–498.

Cummings, Judith. 1983. "Breakup of Black Family Imperils Gains of Decades," *New York Times* (November 20):1–2.

Daneal, Jealean Evelyn. 1975. "A Definition of Fatherhood as Expressed by Black Fathers." Ph.D. diss., University of Pittsburgh.

Davis, George. 1977. *Black Love.* Garden City, NY: Doubleday.

Ehrenreich, Barbara. 1983. *The Hearts of Men: American Dreams and the Flight from Commitment.* Garden City, NY: Doubleday.

Fogel, William, and Stanley Engerman. 1974. *Time on the Cross.* Boston: Little, Brown.

Franklin, Clyde W. 1984. "Black Male-Female Conflict: Individually Caused and Culturally Nurtured," *Journal of Black Studies,* 15(December):139–154.

Frazier, E. Franklin. 1932. *The Free Negro Family.* Nashville, TN: Fisk University Press.

Genovese, Eugene. 1975. *Roll, Jordan, Roll.* New York: Pantheon.

Gil, David. 1971. Violence Against Children. *Journal of Marriage and the Family,* 33(November):637–648.
Green, Arnold. 1946. "The Middle-Class Male Child and Neurosis," *American Sociological Review,* 11(February):31–41.
Gutman, Herbert. 1976. *The Black Family in Slavery and Freedom, 1750–1925.* New York: Pantheon.
Guttentag, Marcia, and Paul Secord. 1983. *Too Many Women: The Sex Ratio Question.* Beverly Hills, CA: Sage.
Hale, Janice. 1983. *Black Children.* Provo, UT: Brigham Young University Press.
Hare, Bruce R. 1975. "Relationship of Social Background to the Dimensions of Self-Concept." Ph.D. diss., University of Chicago.
Hays, William and Charles Mindel. 1973. "Extended Kinship Relations in Black and White Families," *Journal of Marriage and the Family,* 35(February).
Hill, Robert. 1977. *Informal Adoption Among Black Families.* Washington, DC: National Urban League Research Department.
Hill, Robert B., and Lawrence Shackleford. 1975. "The Black Extended Family Revisited," *Urban League Review,* 1(Fall):18–24.
Hutchinson, Iran. 1974. "Life Satisfaction of Lower Income Black and White Elderly." Paper presented at the National Council on Family Relations Meeting, St. Louis, MO.
Iscoe, Ira, Martha Williams, and Jerry Harvey. 1964. "Age, Intelligence and Sex as Variables in the Conformity Behavior of Negro and White Children," *Child Development,* 35:451–460.
Jackson, Jacqueline. 1971. "But Where Are the Men?" *The Black Scholar,* 4(December):34–41.
———. 1972. "Comparative Life Styles and Family and Friend Relationships Among Older Black Women," *The Family Coordinator,* 21(October):477–486.
Jencks, Christopher. 1972. *Inequality: A Re-Assessment of the Effect of Family and Schooling in America.* New York: Basic Books.
Joe, Tom, and Peter Yu. 1984. *The "Flip-Side" of Black Families Headed by Women; The Economic Status of Black Men.* Washington, DC: The Center for the Study of Social Policy.
Ladner, Joyce. 1971. *Tomorrow: The Black Woman.* Garden City, NY: Doubleday.
Lewis, Diane R. 1975. "The Black Family: Socialization and Sex Roles," *Phylon,* 36(Fall):221–237.
Logan, Rayford. 1965. *The Betrayal of the Negro.* New York: Collier.
Miller, Elizabeth. 1966. *The Negro in America: A Bibliography.* Cambridge: Harvard University Press.
Moynihan, Daniel Patrick, 1965. "Employment, Income, and the Ordeal of the Negro Family," *Daedalus,* 94(Fall):745–770.
Nobles, Wade. 1972. "African Root and American Fruit: The Black Family," *Journal of Social and Behavioral Sciences,* 20(Spring):52–64.
———. 1973. "Psychological Research and the Black Self-Concept: A Critical Review," *Journal of Social Issues,* 29(Winter):11–31.
Nolle, David. 1972. "Changes in Black Sons and Daughters: A Panel Analysis of Black Adolescent's Orientation Toward Their Parents," *Journal of Marriage and the Family,* 34(August):443–447.

Peters, Marie, and Cecile de Ford. 1978. "The Solo Mother" in R. Staples (ed.), *The Black Family: Essays and Studies* (2nd ed.), Belmont, CA: Wadsworth, pp. 192–200.

Poussaint, Alvin. 1983. "Black Men–White Women: An Update," *Ebony,* 38(August):124–131.

Rubin, Roger H. 1974. "Adult Male Absence and the Self-Attitudes of Black Children," *Child Study Journal,* 4:33–44.

Scanzoni, John. 1971. *The Black Family in Modern Society.* Boston: Allyn and Bacon.

Schulz, David. 1969. "Variations in the Father Role in Complete Families of the Negro Lower-Class," *Social Science Quarterly,* 49(December):651–659.

Scott, Joseph W. 1976. "Polygamy: A Futuristic Family Arrangement for African-Americans," *Black Books Bulletin,* 4(Summer).

Smith, Marie. 1978. "Black Female's Perceptions on the Black Male Shortage." Master's thesis, Howard University.

Staples, Robert. 1976. *Introduction to Black Sociology.* New York: McGraw-Hill.

———. 1978. *The Black Family: Essays and Studies, Volume 2.* Belmont, CA: Wadsworth.

———. 1978a. "Race and Masculinity: The Black Man's Dual Dilemma," *Journal of Social Issues,* 34(Winter):169–183.

———. 1979. "Beyond the Black Family: The Trend Toward Singlehood," *Western Journal of Black Studies,* 3(Fall):150–157.

———. 1981. *The World of Black Singles: Changing Patterns of Male/Female Relations.* Westport, CT: Greenwood Press.

———. 1982. *Black Masculinity: The Black Male's Role in American Society.* San Francisco: Black Scholar Press.

Sutton, Gordon F. 1977. "Measuring the Effects of Race Differentials in Mortality upon Surviving Family Members," *Demography,* 14(November):419–429.

U. S. Bureau of the Census. 1983. *America's Black Population, 1970 to 1982: A Statistical View, July 1983.* Series P10/POP83. Washington, DC: U. S. Government Printing Office.

U. S. Civil Rights Commission. 1982. *Unemployment and Underemployment Among Blacks, Hispanics and Women.* Washington, DC: U. S. Government Printing Office.

Williams, Juan. 1984. "Black Male's Problems Linked to Family Crises," *The Washington Post,* August 1, p. A-6.

Zelnick, Melvin, and John Kantner. 1977. "Sexual and Contraceptive Experience of Young Unmarried Women in the United States, 1976 and 1971," *Family Planning Perspectives,* 9(May/June):55–59.

CHAPTER FOURTEEN

The Native American Family

Robert John

HISTORICAL BACKGROUND

As the indigenous people of the Western Hemisphere, Native Americans[1] have a long and rich historical past. Depending on the source one consults, it has been estimated that at the period of contact, there were anywhere from 1 million (Kroeber, 1939) to as many as 18 million (Dobyns, 1983) Native Americans living north of what is now Mexico. The diversity of this population is an overriding characteristic, reflected by a high degree of linguistic and cultural variation. At the time of contact with European cultures, there were approximately 300 languages spoken. Few scholars, however, have attempted to estimate the number of separate groupings, or tribes, that existed, and no accurate estimate is possible.

Because the number of groups was large, attempts to summarize the cultural practices and reduce the cultural complexity to a few cultural types has occupied anthropological attention for most of the last century. Toward this end, modern anthropologists have divided North America into 10 to 12 different cultural areas. However, this division is based largely on material artifacts and the modes of subsistence in a given geographical

[1]I use the terms Native American, Indian, and American Indian interchangeably throughout this chapter to denote all aboriginal people, whether American Indian, Eskimo, or Aleut. According to 1980 Census figures (United States Department of Commerce, 1984:14) American Indians comprise ninety-six percent of the native American population, three percent are Eskimos and one percent are Aleut.

area rather than social organization or a people's way of life including their family relationships.

The task of reducing Native American societies to relatively few cultural types has been made more difficult because diverse family practices existed within not only each culture area but also each group, and as a result, a wide variety of family practices were common and accepted. In fact, according to Harold Driver (1969:222) "almost all of the principal variants" of marriage and family practices can be found among American Indian groups. Those practices found among American Indians include bride price, bride wealth, bride service, and dowry; arranged marriage and betrothal; interfamily exchange marriage and adoptive marriage; bride abduction and elopement; cross-cousin and parallel cousin marriage; patrilocal, matrilocal, neolocal, avunculocal, and bilocal residence patterns; patrilineal, matrilineal, bilateral inheritance and descent; infanticide; primogeniture; monogamy, polygyny and temporary polyandry; premarital and extramarital sexual relations; divorce; temporary marriage; trial marriage; wife lending; spouse exchange; sororate and levirate marriage; couvade; adoption; patriarchy, and matriarchy.

Obviously, one can conclude that the degree of diversity within Native American populations has been greatly reduced since first contact, largely because of the extermination of many groups through the introduction of European pathogens including smallpox, measles, chickenpox, influenza, scarlet fever, malaria, typhus, typhoid fever, diphtheria, and other diseases. An indication of the degree of impact can be recognized in the fact that nearly one-half of the aboriginal languages are now extinct, and within the United States, there are only approximately 300 federally recognized American Indian groups. It has been estimated (Porter, 1983) that there are another 100 "nonrecognized" tribes, mainly in the eastern states and California, from which the federal government withholds benefits. Although many of these tribes are in the process of petitioning to be recognized, the inescapable fact is the dramatic reduction of Native American population and peoples since sustained contact with European cultures began.

Within the last century, attempts to force acculturation to Anglo-European practices has resulted in the further reduction of the range and diversity of American Indian family practices. Among the influences with the greatest impact on Native American family practices, certainly, the intrusive nature of education, missionary activities, federal policies to force individual landholding, expropriation of their land base, economic exigencies on reservations, intermarriage, and federal government inducements to relocate to urban areas have all played a major role in bringing about change. More recently, the overwhelming influence of American popular culture on Native American youth has also contributed to a convergence of Native American values and practices with the Anglo–European mainstream. Despite nearly 500 years of destructive contact with Anglo–European cultures, important differences in family practices persist among Native Americans.

MODERN NATIVE AMERICAN FAMILIES

Academic research on the status and needs of Native American families has lagged far behind research on other minority families. One need only contrast the amount of information available about other minority groups, much less middle-class whites, to realize the relative paucity of information on Native American families. Indeed, the difference is easily seen when one looks at the model of family life believed to describe the two groups and the theoretical concepts used to explain current Native American family practices.

Coming out of the isolated nuclear family debate that dominated family studies during the post–World War II era, the modified extended family model has been established as characteristic of white family life since 1965. However, studies of Native American family life have not achieved a similar level of understanding. If any model of Native American family life is offered at all it is the extended family model, a family form that has never been universally practiced by American Indians (Driver, 1969). This model is largely the legacy of anthropological studies that have shaped our concepts of Native American family life until now.

Indeed, if one looks at works on family life published during the post–World War II period, one must conclude that Native Americans were the exclusive concern of anthropologists. On the few occasions when sociologists did include discussions of Native American families, they simply provided summary statements gleaned from anthropological works rather than their own research.

Coming out of this intellectual heritage, compared with the family structure of white Americans, the opposite presumption was thought to characterize the family life of Native Americans. As examples of cultures that were not fully modernized, family life was presumed to approximate forms typical of primitive societies (see Queen and Adams, 1952).[2] It is true that

---

[2]An interesting reflection, and perhaps a sign of academic irrelevance in shaping social policy during the 1950s, is the divergence between how academics and politicians viewed Native Americans. While academics continued to treat Native Americans as examples of "primitive" societies the federal government was busy terminating Indian groups because of a belief that many groups were already, and all groups should and would be, assimilated into the American cultural mainstream.

the existence of extended family structures among many Native American groups was well-documented in the anthropological literature, but very little of that literature was of recent origin, having been written during the prolific era of ethnographic studies that ended with the Great Depression. This situation of viewing Native Americans as living in an unchanging "ethnographic present" began to alter during the late 1960s when researchers began to study Native Americans from other perspectives and with other research questions in mind.

During this decade, the rapid pace of change within American society that had taken place since World War II was apparent among Native American cultures, too, and scholars adopted a generalized version of acculturation theory to explain changes that were evident in Native American family practices. These two characterizations of Native American family life derived from anthropological studies—that extended families are the norm and families can be classified according to degree of acculturation—persist today as the twin themes of Native American family studies.

Even though studies of various aspects of Native American family life have increased during the last 15 years, these studies do little to clarify precisely what is occurring within Native American families as a whole.[3] This however, has not deterred gratuitous characterizations of Native American family life based on the presumed existence of extended families that integrate all generations into a cohesive Native American family along with general acknowledgment of importance of culture change in modifying family practices. This viewpoint is particularly evident in the literature on Native American aging. For example, according to a December 1979 staff report to the Federal Council on the Aging (U. S. Department of Health and Human Services, 1979:32):

> Various statements . . . as well as documented reports, attest to the strong traditional bond existing between the Indian family and their older members. Older Indians continue to play an important role in the extended American Indian families. However, according to the National Indian Council on Aging, the increasing acculturation of young American Indians has caused the natural

[3]Although I am pointing out the inadequacies of what is known about Native American family life, our ignorance about Native Americans is general. As Manson and Pambrun (1979:89) note "a thorough review of the social and health sciences literature indicates that only eighteen publications even remotely examine the psychosocial dimensions of the elderly Indian life experience." After reviewing this literature, these authors conclude that the literature "is severely limited" (Manson and Pambrun, 1979:90). Bell, Kasschau and Zellman (1978:185) bluntly state that "the literature . . . on Indians, and elderly Indians in particular, is not of very high quality."

support network to erode at a rapid pace. It is important to note that there are still insufficient data to draw definite conclusions.

The contradictory nature of this statement should be evident. Despite allusions to statements and documented reports that attest to the strength of family ties, no sources were cited. The most reliable portion of this statement suggests the opposite: that family integration is, in fact, declining, leading to the disruption of the familial support network.

Majorie Schweitzer (1983:173) also acknowledges the tension between continuity and change in Native American family life:

> The most important social structure which operates within the Indian community remains that of the family. It is the family which provides the framework in which the elderly Indian occupies roles which constitute the most important area of power and prestige for old people. Part of that power is economic, attained through land holdings and lease monies. If prestige accrues in any context just for the sake of being old it is in the family.[4]

In one of the few studies to challenge the prevailing consensus, Manson and Pambrun (1979:92) question whether the common view of elders' position in Native American family and community life is a stereotype:

> The popular image of Indian elders places them in their children's homes, caring for young, respected in turn, and totally dependent upon these circumstances for a sense of self-worth and fulfillment. Communities presumably provide social and psychological support by seeking their counsel and apprenticing members to them to preserve rare skills and valued knowledge. The relevant literature is dated, limited theoretically as well as substantively, and provides no insight into this image.

---

[4]It is important to recognize that the family life of Native Americans may be the residual institution of their societies that has been most resistant to change. Other institutions, notably their political, economic, educational, even their religious institutions, were decimated long ago having been changed through violent or legal force. However, I question her assessment that land holding and lease money is an important source of economic power. Schweitzer suggests that because of lifelong employment problems many Native Americans do not qualify for Social Security. Her own study was based on participant observation and she offers no figures to support her contention that this is prevalent. Even if this were true, most would be entitled to Supplemental Security Income, which currently guarantees $325 per month. Even this minimal income far surpasses the income most Indians receive from leases (Goodman, 1985), given that many of these holdings have become so fractionalized that federal legislation, through the Indian Land Consolidation Act of 1978, has sought to consolidate landholdings.

As Manson and Pambrun recognize, we have no definitive research to give a measure of certainty to our knowledge of the status of Native American families or how Native American families are changing.

Typology

Among the researchers who discuss Native American family life, although squarely within the parameters of the consensus perspective, Red Horse et al. (1978) offer a typology of "three distinct family patterns" among urban Chippewas, which they label "traditional," "bi-cultural," and "pan-traditional." Although each of these family types differs from the others in terms of the degree of acculturation, including language used in the household, religious affiliation, value system, recreational and cultural activities, *all three* are characterized as having an extended family network. Elsewhere, Red Horse (1980a:466) claims that despite the differences between these three family patterns, "many cultural features remain constant: family structure, incorporation and relational bonding, and Indian preference in social behavior." Red Horse et al. (1978:69) make the extreme claim that "extended family networks represent a universal pattern among American Indian nations."

Although this statement was generally true of most Native American groups in the past, it is not unequivocally true of the present. Perhaps the reason Red Horse adopts this position is explained by another essay (Red Horse, 1980b) in which he reveals how loosely he defines the term "extended family network." In this article, Red Horse delineates four structural patterns of family life typical of each of four settings: 1) small reservation communities, 2) "interstate" extended families, 3) families in urban areas that include kin and non-kin as extended family members, and 4) families in large metropolitan areas that "appear highly influenced through informal incorporation of non-kin" who assume family roles. The problem with the claim that extended families are a universal feature of each of these environments is that Red Horse is imprecise about the nature of these extended family relationships, especially whether face-to-face interaction or affective bonding is the key to their extension. Guillemin (1975:142) flatly states that "face-to-face interaction is more desirable than letters and telephone calls" in maintaining reassuring and meaningful contact with family members.

Much, therefore, depends on the answer to this question of the types of contact necessary to consider a family an extended one: if affective bonding is all that is required, then the white middle-class family would be counted as an extended family too. The problem with Red Horse's analysis is that he seems to compare the Native American family with the *isolated* nuclear family model that has been abandoned as an adequate conceptualization of white family life. Naturally, this error of comparing Native American families with a nonexistent, isolated nuclear family typical of whites does not mean that his general characterization is wrong; namely, that Native American families are more firmly based on *interdependence* than Anglo–American families.

Indeed, there is a good deal of evidence to support this somewhat more modest conclusion. For instance, Stanton Tefft (1967:148) found that Shoshone and Arapahoe youth "place many more job restrictions on themselves than whites by refusing to seek jobs for which they are qualified very far from the reservation." Claudia Lewis (1970:164) also found a similar self-imposed limitation among the Salish in the mid-1950s. In addition, Gary Witherspoon (1975) provides ample detail of the interdependence of traditional Navajo family economic activities and kinship expectations. Interdependence also extends to childrearing activities. Robert Ryan (1981:28) characterizes childrearing in traditional American Indian families as a "total family process" in which a number of relatives, rather than just the parents, provide guidance and instruction, although he states that it is being less utilized today.

Red Horse, too, provides support for this conclusion in revealing a difference between Indian and Anglo-American intergenerational family relations. Red Horse (1980a:464) contends that "eventual retirement, with self-responsibility apart from the mainstream of family, serves as a life goal in a nuclear model. Ego identity in extended family models, however, is satisfied through interdependent roles enacted in a family context."[5]

Other research also adheres to a typology of Native American families constructed on an acculturation framework. Based on field work conducted on the reservation of a band of coastal Salish in the mid-1950s, Claudia Lewis (1970) advanced a tripartite model of family life very similar to the one suggested by Red Horse. Lewis categorized Salish families as following the "old Indian ways," "between old and new," or as following "new ways" based on an assessment of the degree of acculturation derived from family life-styles and values. The characteristics that distinguished the group following the "old Indian ways" included extended family households, use of Indian language, participation in tribal religious practices, low educational attainment and little value placed on education, a communal family economy with minimal participation in wage labor, little and toler-

---

[5]For example, see Troll (1978), Ward (1978), Cantor (1980), Powers, Keith, and Goudy (1981), or Mercier and Powers (1984:335) on the normative value Anglos place on independence. In fact, Bultena et al. (1971) found that moving into a nursing home was preferable to moving in with relatives. Few American Indian elders would feel the same way.

ant supervision of children, and the importance of grandparents in child-rearing. At the other extreme, families following "new ways" were characterized by nuclear family households, high educational attainment and value on education, more material possessions, steady employment in wage labor, Christian religion, more contact with whites, strict supervision of children, and intermarriage outside tribal boundaries. Despite these differences, Lewis does make clear that this more acculturated group has not severed all participation in traditional Native American cultural practices and rejects the influence of intermarriage as a special determinant of style of family life, largely because a great deal of "admixture" with whites had occurred before tribal genealogical rolls were made.

Wagner (1976:218), however, claims that "intermarriage is an independent primary measure of assimilation." In other words, rather than being a cause of assimilation, intermarriage reflects the degree of assimilation that has already taken place. Based on a sample of 17 urban Indian women, Wagner constructed a typology that, like the others, is divided into three categories based on degree of acculturation. She identifies these as the following (Wagner, 1976:219):

> Tradition-oriented (those who adhere to traditional values, including a de-emphasis of material possessions, and seek to preserve or revitalize their culture); . . . Transitional (those who identify with their ancestral group but evidence more of the values of the dominant culture . . .); and . . . American middle-class (those whose cultural identification is with the dominant society but who identify themselves as Indians.

All in the traditional group had married other Indians, maintained strong ties with their family, reservation, and tribe, adhered to values that were distinctly Indian, and had social lives centered around other Indians. Degree of Indian blood, however, was not found to be a factor in acculturation or intermarriage. The factors that were most significant in acculturation were the presence of a white father or grandfather, "an Indian parent who deliberately chose to abandon his cultural heritage," as well as white school teachers, schoolmates, and clergy. Having a white husband represented another "potent maximizing agent."

Miller (1979), on the basis of a longitudinal study of 120 American Indian families in the San Francisco Bay Area, has constructed the most sophisticated typology of Native American modes of adaptation based on the degree to which the families she studied exhibit Indian or white values and behaviors. She identified the four groups as the following (Miller, 1979:479):

> Traditional, in which the person clings to Indian values and behaviors; Transitional, where the individual adapts to white means and ends . . . ; Bicultural, in which the person is able to hold onto Indian values and means and is also able to adapt to white ends without considering them the primary value structure; and Marginal, whose individuals are anomic in both worlds.

Miller quantified the incidence of each of these types. Thirty-nine percent of the families she studied were classified as "transitional," 23 percent "bicultural," 22 percent "traditional," and 16 percent "marginal." Miller considered the "bicultural" family to be the one most well-adjusted to contemporary demands because they are able to balance Native American and white values and behaviors, thus maintaining a sense of identity and operating equally well in both worlds. In contrast, the "marginal" family has lost their cultural roots without having found anything to replace them. Miller maintained that they were maladapted in both worlds and experience the greatest number of problems. On the other hand, the "traditional" group provided a supportive environment for their children but made only a marginal adaptation to city life, and the "transitional" group was in the process of becoming fully assimilated into the cultural mainstream but at the expense of an Indian identity.

Price (1981, 1976) also characterizes Native American families in terms of acculturation. In these essays, Price summarizes the wide variety of family practices that existed among Native American tribes prior to contact with Europeans. His theme is that, although the diversity has been greatly reduced, there is still a variety of family practices among Native Americans. These practices vary from tribe to tribe and within specific tribes according to the degree of acculturation they have experienced. Although Price (1976:257) recognized that "specific tribal identities are almost universally stronger and more important than identity as a native American," he attributed this convergence of family practices to the growth of a pan-Indian ethnic identity originating in the major urban areas that was in the process of creating a new ethnic group in American society. He summarized the general changes in American Indian family life in the following manner (Price, 1976:268):

> We have . . . examined the process of convergent *social adaptation* through acculturation. In family life we have seen this in the increasingly predominant pattern of the monogamous, bilateral, patrilineal-biased, nuclear family. However, there appear to be some residual differences in family life between even urbanized American Indians and the majority society. Indian families seem to

be less child centered and have less emphasis on such things as toilet training, cleanliness, punctuality, competition, and worldly achievement.[6]

It is important to note that Price based his conclusion on anthropological accounts of only four North American Indian groups.[7] Note, too, that most of his comments concern the socialization process of children rather than other periods of the life course that are of equal importance if we are to more fully understand family life among Native Americans.

Other scholars provide somewhat different representations of American Indian family life. Dukepoo (1980), in a study of 62 Indian elders over 54 years old residing in the county of San Diego, California, documented urban and rural differences in the support networks of elderly Native Americans. Dukepoo concluded that reservation life was more family-centered than was urban life among the Indian elders he studied. According to Dukepoo (1980:19), elders living on reservations were more likely to have relatives (including siblings, children, grand- or great-grandchildren) living in their "immediate neighborhoods." This greater availability and proximity of kin among reservation elders resulted in a difference in their support network. As Dukepoo (1980:31) noted, the "reservation sample relied either solely or primarily on the family member(s) in time of need, the urban Indian indicated that in addition to family and friends there was reliance on formal agencies to meet their needs." My own research (John, 1986) has confirmed this finding of rural and urban differences for a nationwide sample of Indians over 45 years of age.

Whether or under what conditions this generalization of urban and rural differences in the nature of extended family networks holds true is yet to be firmly established. Steele (1972) alludes to the existence of extended family households among urban Potawatomi residing approximately 30 miles from their tribal reservation. Based on her findings, Miller (1979) concludes that proximity to their home of origin is an important factor associated with extended family households in the San Francisco Bay Area. Williams (1980) claims that family extension exists among non-reservation residing Oklahoma Native Americans in terms of a social network charac-

---

[6]Price does not explain what he means by "less child centered." In its most obvious sense because of higher fertility, Indian families are *more* child centered than Anglo families. Indeed, Bock (1964) acknowledges "the Indians' love of children" as a factor supporting high rates of illegitimacy among reservation Micmac.

[7]Price chose these particular groups because they illustrated a range of acculturation patterns. However, there are currently around 300 federally recognized Indian tribes. This makes generalization to Native Americans as a whole particularly questionable, something other authors (Levy, 1967; Red Horse et al. 1978; Red Horse, 1980b, 1982a; Murdock and Schwartz, 1978) have done on the basis of studies of, at most, only a few groups.

terized by residential propinquity. Schweitzer (1983), in a similar study of aging among the Oto-Missouri and Ioway of rural Oklahoma, identifies an extended network of residentially proximate kin that provides support to elders.

In contrast to these studies, Miller (1979) concluded the opposite: compared with reservation residents, the extended family system was not available among urban Native Americans in the San Francisco Bay Area. Indeed, Miller (1979:458) stated the following:

> Adjustment from the complexity and interdependency of extended family life on or near the reservation to the constriction of an isolated nuclear, or conjugal, family life in a city is possibly the most difficult adjustment the recently urbanized Native American must make.

Metcalf (1979) also found that among Native Americans in the San Francisco Bay Area that urbanization has disrupted extended family supports resulting in child abuse and neglect, and Red Horse (1982) found that absence of extended family supports was associated with premarital pregnancy among Native American adolescents in Minneapolis. In other studies, Oakland and Kane (1973) discovered that the absence of extended family support was linked to child neglect on the Navajo reservation, and Fox (1960) suggested that psychological disturbances may be associated with the absence of extended family structures and the support they provide.

Given this contradictory evidence, one is tempted to agree with Staples and Mirande (1980:168) that there "is no such institution as a Native American family. There are only tribes, and family structure and values will differ from tribe to tribe." Although this has always been true, as the recent feminist reconceptualization of family studies has shown, there is no such institution as "the family" among other groups in the United States either. Further, Staples and Mirande's statement may be more a reflection of the lack of academic knowledge about and interest in Native American families than a conclusion based on a sufficient number of research findings.

As one can see, the way in which particular researchers define and measure family extension is a crucial consideration. The two basic measures of family extension are household composition and residential propinquity. Both Red Horse et al. (1978) and Williams (1980) argue persuasively that the household is an inappropriate measure of family extension among Native Americans. According to Red Horse et al. (1978:68), compared with the definition of an extended family as a household containing three generations (in other words, the stereotypical, "classical" extended family):

> American Indian family networks . . . are structurally open and assume a village-type characteristic. Their extension is inclusive of several households representing significant relatives along both vertical and horizontal lines.

In a later essay, Red Horse (1980a:463) described this pattern as most common in small reservation communities. Accordingly, the best measure of family extension is an *effective or functioning* support network based on interaction and proximity of residence (see Sussman, 1959, 1965; Klatzky, 1972; Wilkening, Guerrero, and Ginsberg, 1972; Gibson, 1972; Powers, Keith, and Goudy, 1981). If we are to refine our model of Native American family life, studies of Native American family networks are essential in order to advance our understanding of contemporary Native American families.

Without a doubt, Guillemin (1975) has written the best account of contemporary family networks among a group of Native Americans. Her qualitative research on the Micmac of the Canadian maritime provinces and Boston provides the most complete portrait of the operation of what Red Horse characterized as "interstate extended families." She describes the network processes she witnessed that link Micmac family members and their friends within a highly mobile but tribally based "community" grounded in the ethic of sharing resources, which extends over much of New England. Her book is valuable also because of the range of issues that she addresses.

Despite this very rich portrait of Micmac extended family operation, Guillemin (1975:246ff) does describe a group of Micmac, which she characterized as few in number, that lives outside or, at best, on the margins of Micmac community life. These urban "spin-offs" include people who have married outside the tribe, elders, people with tuberculosis, heart disease, or drinking problems, vagrants, as well as another group of families who live in neighborhoods where few Indians reside and restrict their extended family and peer group contacts more in line with family patterns of the cultural mainstream.

Sociodemographic Characteristics

Currently, the American Indian population is, and should continue for some time to be, the fastest growing and youngest subpopulation in the United States. According to the 1980 census (U. S. Department of Commerce, 1984), between 1970 and 1980, the American Indian population increased by 72 percent from 827,268 to 1,420,400. In large part, this is the result of a change in census enumeration procedures to the use of self-identification to classify the race of the respondent. However, natural increases and greater efforts to accurately count the Native American population are also responsible for the dramatic increase within the decade. In addition to the 1.4 million people who are considered Native Americans in this chapter, another 6.7 million people claimed to be of partial Native American ancestry (U. S. Congress, 1986).

Census results reveal that Native Americans are the most rural of any ethnic group in the United States. One-half of all Native Americans reside in non-metropolitan areas, another 21 percent live in central cities, and the remaining 29 percent live in metropolitan areas outside central cities. However, only 24 percent of Native Americans actually live on one of the 278 recognized reservations. Another 8 percent live in the historic reservation areas of Oklahoma, 3 percent live in the 209 Alaska Native villages, and 2 percent on other tribal trust lands. The remaining 13 percent live in rural areas adjacent to recognized Indian reservations (United States Department of Commerce, 1984). Seventy-seven percent of all American Indians live west of the Mississippi River, with four states (California, Oklahoma, Arizona, and New Mexico) each having more than 100,000 Native Americans, together accounting for 44 percent of the total.

FERTILITY. The median age of the American Indian population is substantially lower than the general population (U. S. Department of Commerce, 1984). More to the point, the median age of American Indian females (23.5 years) is more than seven years less than the median age of the general population (31.2 years), and the median age of American Indian females residing on federally recognized reservations is even lower (20.3 years). The significance of this difference is that a substantially higher percentage of American Indian women are in their prime childbearing years. Indeed, findings for the period 1980–1982 (U. S. Congress, 1986) for the 32 states with Indian reservations reveal that fertility is highest among Native American women between 20–24 years old, followed by the 25–29 age group, with the 15–19 age group having the next highest fertility rate (although roughly half that of 20–24 year olds), followed by 30–34 year olds.

Despite somewhat lower fertility rates among teenage Native American women, this evidence documents that a substantial amount of American Indian fertility is attributable to adolescent childbearing. In fact, a little over 32 percent of all births during 1980–1982 were to women in the

15–19 age group (U. S. Congress, 1986:76). In many cases, these births are to unwed mothers. Indeed, Haynes (1977) found that unwed, teenage Arapahoe and Shoshone girls between 15–19 years old were 37 percent of the females who did not practice contraception on the Wind River Reservation.

The full extent of premarital pregnancy among American Indians, however, is not known. The limited evidence that does exist suggests that it is relatively common because no stigma is attached to having a child whether a woman is married or not. Bock (1964:144) characterizes the attitude toward illegitimacy among reservation Micmac in Canada as "matter-of-fact and tolerant," although he stresses that legitimacy is still considered the norm by the community, as it had been prior to contact with European cultures. His study of illegitimacy from 1860–1960 on this Micmac reservation found a 20 percent incidence of illegitimacy throughout the period.

More recent figures compiled by New Mexico and South Dakota, ranked fourth and eighth in Native American population, show that 47 and 62 percent, respectively, of all Indian births are to unmarried Indian women (U. S. Congress, 1986). Indeed, Guillemin (1975:219) found that a "pattern of pregnancy and the birth of the eldest child out of wedlock followed by a marriage to a man who was not necessarily the father of that first child" had been prevalent among the Micmac for some time. Guillemin (1975:226) explains this pattern by noting that among the Micmac "a woman's ability to have children is a mark of her strength and value and there is really no one to shame her for having had a child out of wedlock." The interdependent nature of Native American families makes it possible to absorb an event like this without travail.

During the twentieth century, fertility among American Indians has declined, although American Indian fertility is still higher than it is in the general population. A study by Sweet (1974), compared the fertility of *married* women under age 40 for seven racial, or ethnic, groups for the two periods 1957–1960 and 1967–1970. Sweet maintained the adequacy of his measure of fertility even though he acknowledged that it may not be a fully accurate estimation of fertility among groups such as Native Americans, that have high infant and child mortality or among groups that have children who do not live with their mother. Taking into consideration that Native American fertility was underestimated for these reasons, Sweet (1974:105) found that the "fertility rates for American Indians, who started the period with the highest fertility of all groups considered . . . , declined most rapidly (by 44 percent). In 1957–1960 American Indian fertility was 67 percent higher than urban white rates, but by the 1967–1970 period, American Indian fertility was only 27 percent above that of urban whites."

There is contradictory and inconclusive evidence about how fertility is associated with urban or rural residence. Liberty (1975) and Liberty, Scaglion, and Hughey (1976) studied urban and reservation differences in fertility among the Seminole of Florida and the Omaha of Nebraska. Among the Seminole, Liberty, Scaglion, and Hughey (1976) found urban and rural differences in fertility, something that was not found among the Omaha. In another study, Kunitz (1974) found significant differences between reservation Navajo and Hopi fertility during the twentieth century. During this period, Navajo fertility remained relatively high, and their population increased steadily, whereas Hopi fertility declined dramatically within one generation after World War II. Furthermore, in contrast to evidence that links urbanization with lower fertility, Kunitz discovered that fertility was higher among non-reservation Hopi living in three border towns in Arizona than it was among Hopi living on the reservation, although he was at a loss to explain why.

BIRTH CONTROL AND CONTRACEPTION. Liberty and her associates (1976) also explored Seminole and Omaha attitudes toward abortion. Although approval of abortion was generally higher among the urban residents of both tribes and fewer urban women were undecided on their attitude toward abortion given a particular situation in which an abortion may be contemplated, women in both reservation and urban environments held similar opinions with few exceptions. Both urban and reservation women disapproved of abortion simply because the couple could not afford another child, did not want another child, or because the woman was not married. The majority of Omaha women in both reservation and urban environments and urban Seminole women approved of abortion if the pregnancy seriously endangered the health of the mother, if there were good reasons to believe the child would be deformed, or if the woman had been raped. Reservation Seminole women also approved of abortion if the mother's health was seriously endangered but were less certain that fetal deformity or rape were adequate justifications, although opinion on these last two issues was equally divided, with a large percentage of the women being undecided.

This study of attitudes toward abortion is complemented by a study of the use of surgical procedures to avoid childbearing among the Navajo and Hopi. Consistent with the attitudes expressed in the two studies just discussed, Kunitz and Slocumb (1976) found that the incidence of induced abortions among Navajo and Hopi women is lower than it is for the general population of Arizona and New Mexico. Overall, there is almost no difference between the two tribes in the rate of induced abortions. However, induced abortions vary greatly by age group. Navajo women make relatively uniform use of induced abortion regardless of their age whereas induced abortions among the Hopi increase with the woman's age. Hopi women between the ages of 40–49 have the highest rate of induced abortions (approximately 5.5 times the overall rate among Navajo and Hopi women in general).

FEMALE HEADED HOUSEHOLDS. There are also significant differences between Navajo and Hopi women in their use of sterilization procedures through hysterectomies and bilateral tubal ligations. Hopi rates of hysterectomies are nearly four times greater than among the Navajo, and bilateral tubal ligations among the Hopi are approximately 1.5 times more prevalent than among Navajos. In addition, Hopi women are more likely to undergo sterilization through tubal ligation during their prime child-bearing years (between the ages of 20–34 years).[8] Compared with the use of sterilization procedures among women, Kunitz and Slocumb (1976:9) found that "vasectomies are virtually never done on Hopi and Navajo men." Regardless of whether men share concern about contraception, pregnancy, and childbearing, this evidence strongly suggests that females bear the brunt of the responsibility to avoid pregnancy and childbearing.

One major change in Native American family life is documented in the 1980 census, which reports a 28 percent increase in the incidence of American Indian families maintained by women between 1970 and 1980 from 18 percent to 23 percent of *all* American Indian families (U. S. Department of Commerce, 1984). Even more alarming, Miller (1979) found that one-third of the families she studied in the San Francisco Bay area were headed by women, suggesting that female-headed families may be more common in urban areas.

An increase in female-headed families has occurred in the general population as well, but the rate for Native Americans exceeds the rate for the rest of the population by 9 percent. This appears to be a new adaptation to

---

[8]The current incidence of sterilization among Native American women is not known. Kunitz and Slocumb acknowledge the controversy that has arisen over the use of sterilization procedures on American Indian females stating that there "has been considerable feeling on the part of some individuals that the Indian Health Service has engaged in unethical practices in some areas by performing sterilization procedures without informed consent or after exerting undue pressure on patients." Indeed, these authors report that over 90% of bilateral tubal ligations are performed on postpartum patients, and that females are far less likely to undergo the operation at other times. This leads to the possible conclusion that females may be more willing to agree to sterilization while the painful experience of childbirth is fresh in their memory and make a decision that they will later regret. Haynes (1977) found that this controversy was associated with a reluctance to utilize contraceptives among Arapahoe and Shoshone females.

American society. Although a number of authors, past and present, have commented that marriage and divorce among Native American groups has always been more casual (Guillemin, 1975; Christopherson, 1981) and not fraught with guilt, recriminations, trauma, or adverse effects on extended family life including affinal relations (Heinrich, 1972), this elevated rate of female-headed families does not appear to be a continuation or legacy of traditional cultural practices because remarriage, except by elders, was common for both men and women in the past. Naturally, this increase in female-headed families has been at the expense of other family forms. Between 1970 and 1980, the percentage of married couple families among American Indians decreased by 6 percent to 71 percent of families. Separate figures on marital status are available for reservations and the rural, historic areas of Oklahoma.[9]

Marital Status of Native Americans over Fifteen Years Old (1980)

	RESERVATIONS		HISTORIC OKLAHOMA	
	MALES	FEMALES	MALES	FEMALES
Single	40.6	33.4	30.5	21.3
Married				
Spouse Present	42.4	39.7	54.8	50.2
Spouse Absent	5.9	5.9	3.7	3.3
Separated	2.4	3.5	1.5	2.9
Widowed	3.3	10.2	3.0	13.5
Divorced	5.4	7.3	6.5	8.8
Number	100,955	107,627	36,042	40,250

INCOME AND FAMILY LIFE. Median family income of American Indian families ($13,678) in 1979 was more than $6,000 per year less than the median family income of the general population (U. S. Department of Commerce, 1984), at which time over one-fourth of all American Indians were living in poverty.[10] Although this does represent a decline in the percentage of American Indians living in poverty compared with 1970, when 38 percent met the official conditions, American Indians are still more than twice as likely to be impoverished as the general population.

[9]This information on marital status (U. S. Department of Commerce, 1986) covers approximately one-third of the Native American population as a whole. The figures are for Native Americans residing in rural settings on "identified" reservations and the historic areas of Oklahoma (excluding urban areas).

[10]Government poverty figures underestimate the extent of poverty in the United States. See Olson (1982:57ff) for a discussion of how poverty is defined in the United States.

Several authors (Guillemin, 1975; Miller, 1979) explain that the accumulation of resources is difficult for Native Americans, in part because of the nature of their work experience, but also because of the ethic of sharing with others within the family network.

Although poverty affects a significant percentage of the Native American population in general, a more somber picture emerges if one looks only at those Native Americans living on identified reservations. Poverty, even according to official figures, is pervasive. According to the U. S. Department of Commerce (1986:560), 41 percent of reservation families with a Native American head of household or spouse live in poverty. The poverty rate for unrelated individuals, an indication of poverty among people who live alone, was 59 percent, and 57 percent for female-headed households with no husband present. These female-headed families are impoverished despite the fact that a majority of these women are in the labor force according to the 1980 census. Indeed, 60 percent of Indian female heads of household were in the labor force in 1979, and 74 percent of working American Indian women with no husband present had children under 18 years old in the home (U. S. Department of Commerce, 1986). Detailed income figures are available for reservations and the rural, historic areas of Oklahoma.

Income of Households with Native American Householder or Spouse (1980)

	IDENTIFIED RESERVATIONS	HISTORIC OKLAHOMA
Under $5,000	30.8	25.2
$5,000–9,999	22.9	24.8
$10,000–14,999	17.0	18.0
$15,000–19,999	11.7	12.5
Over $20,000	17.6	19.5

As income figures suggest, unemployment among Native Americans is another pervasive problem that has a direct impact on family life. The 1980 census reports that unemployment among American Indians was 13 percent. Undoubtedly, this figure, like those for poverty rates of the Indian population as a whole, is an underrepresentation of the extent of this social problem because a disproportionate number of American Indians would not be counted as unemployed because there is little point in actively seeking work in environments like Indian reservations where few employment opportunities exist.

The Bureau of Indian Affairs (BIA) also estimates employment rates, although only for those Indians "living on or adjacent to reservations." The BIA figure is probably a more accurate assessment of the extent of unemployment among the rural Indian population because their figures include everyone who is unemployed (i.e., the potential labor force) in addition to the standard Labor Department definition of people who are not employed but are "actively seeking work." Using either of these methods of calculating unemployment gives a very different picture than the 1980 census. According to the BIA (January 1985), 49 percent of the potential labor force or, alternately, 39 percent of those who were actively seeking work were unemployed. Miller (1979:461) corroborates the pervasive unemployment among the urban families she studied, one-half of which were not earning a living in the labor market.

The effects of employment or unemployment on Native American family life have not been adequately studied. Bock (1964) found that periods of unemployment were associated with high rates of premarital pregnancy among the Micmac between 1860–1960. More recently, Oakland and Kane (1973) studied the relationship between working mothers and child neglect among the Navajo. They were interested in discovering whether the growth in women's participation in wage labor was linked to child neglect, as popular opinion at a local Indian Health Service Unit maintained. Oakland and Kane (1973:849) concluded that "child neglect was not found to be closely related to the mother's age, education, [or] employment, but the significant factors appeared to be marital status and size of family." These researchers found that mothers of the neglected children were significantly more likely not to be married (single, widowed, or divorced) or come from smaller families in which extended family support was insufficient. In their discussion, they reported that 90 percent of working mothers left their children in the care of relatives and only 10 percent utilized a babysitter or nursery, an arrangement that Miller (1979) claimed Native Americans do not like because they feel it divides the family. Oakland and Kane (1973:852) concluded from their research that "close and extended family ties remained intact" even when mothers secured wage labor, although extended family supports were not universally available.

Another study of the effects of labor force participation among the Navajo (Henderson, 1979) found differences in family life between skilled and unskilled blue-collar workers. Although Henderson (1979:69) stressed that these were only "tendencies," he found that in "general, skilled workers are younger, better educated, have more off-reservation experience, higher incomes, steadier employment records, live more frequently in single household camps and maintain more limited kinship obligations." From the standpoint of the Navajo kinship system (Witherspoon,

1975), the skilled workers studied by Henderson do not participate as fully as unskilled workers in these extended family communal ventures. Skilled workers reveal such nuclear family features as neolocal residence, less proximity to kin, less economic support of kin, formalized giving to kin they do support, and usually support of only a narrow range of relatives (generally parents and siblings). Despite these similarities to family practices of Anglo American skilled workers, Henderson (1979:77) denied that this reflected that these workers were becoming acculturated, stating that there is something "distinctively 'Navajo' about the way in which Navajo skilled blue collar workers live.

Witherspoon also corroborates the impact of wage labor on Navajo subsistence residential units in one area of the large Navajo reserve. Witherspoon documents that neolocal residence patterns are now typical among the under-forty generation and that there was little neolocal residence before wage labor became an option. Change has occurred, but like Henderson, Witherspoon emphasizes the Navajo-like character of these adaptations. According to Witherspoon (1975:78):

> [T]he traditional subsistence residential units are continuing to function much the way they have for a long time. At least half of the younger people, however, are not living in these units but are supporting themselves in other ways . . . . Thus, the new economic and residence patterns are not destroying the old patterns; they are just supplementing them.

Witherspoon also illustrates the important difference between household composition and residential proximity as measures of Native American family life. Witherspoon found that 64 percent of the subsistence residential units were composed of three or more generations. However, household composition was overwhelmingly nuclear. Seventy-eight percent of the households were two-generation households, 13 percent were three-generation households, and 9 percent contained one generation.

INTERMARRIAGE. Intermarriage has also changed Native American family life. Although less than 1 percent of marriages in the United States in 1970 were between individuals from different racial groups, American Indians were the least likely of six races studied (Clayton, 1978) to practice racial endogamy. Sixty-one percent of American Indian men and 64 percent of American Indian women were married to another American Indian in 1970. The remainder were married to a person of a different race. This relatively high incidence of intermarriage is reflected in the fact that overall, American Indians were involved in 27 percent of all interracial marriages in 1970.

Based on Clayton's findings, the most prevalent interracial union, constituting 13.7 percent of interracial marriages, is a white husband and American Indian wife. An American Indian husband married to a white wife comprises another 12.2 percent of all interracial marriages. Compared with intermarriage with whites, black and American Indian intermarriage is far less common, which is consistent with some findings by Feagin and Anderson (1973) at an all Indian high school that prejudice against blacks was expressed by a majority of these students despite extremely limited contacts with them. Nonetheless, black and American Indian unions constitute approximately 6 percent of all interracial couples. A black husband and American Indian wife couple is most common (3.7 percent of all interracial marriages), and an Indian husband and black wife combination comprises 2 percent of all interracial marriages.

Figures available from the 1980 census (U. S. Congress, 1986:74) reveal that intermarriage has increased in the last decade by nearly 20 percent or that approximately 50 percent of married Native Americans are married to someone from another race. However, there are significant differences between urban Indians and Indians living on reservations or in rural areas. Urban Native American racial endogamy is much lower than it is among Native Americans residing on identified reservations or among Native Americans residing in the historic areas of Oklahoma. Nearly 80 percent of married Native Americans over 15 years old residing on identified reservations are married to another Native American, and in the rural, historic areas of Oklahoma, racial endogamy is approximately 50 percent (U. S. Department of Commerce, 1986). In addition, within each of these three settings there are almost no differences in the marital practices of males and females.

Socialization

For the most part, research on the Native American life course during the last 20 years has focused on the extremes of the life cycle: childhood and old age. A good deal of attention (Fanshel, 1972; Brieland, 1973; Garcia, 1973; Slaughter, 1976; Blanchard and Unger, 1977; Byler, 1977; Unger, 1977; Edwards, 1978; Ishisaka, 1978; Red Horse et al., 1978; Fischler, 1980; Blanchard and Barsh, 1980; Red Horse, 1982a) was devoted to the subject of the state's intervention into Native American family life through the routine placement or adoption of Indian children into non-Indian families.

Claiming that this policy contributed to the further destruction of Native American cultures by disrupting the socialization process whereby children learned tribal values and customs, this debate and attendant political efforts were particularly intense in the mid-1970s and led to the enactment of the Indian Child Welfare Act of 1978 (Pub. L. No. 95–608). This legislation limited the right of the states to intervene in Native American family life by giving tribes the right to protect the welfare of Indian children as an aspect of tribal sovereignty and self-determination. Under the authorization provided by this legislation (Pipestem, 1981), many tribes have established tribal agencies and judicial procedures to oversee the placement of Indian children within the tribe (preferably with a family member). As a consequence, the child's tribe now has legal jurisdiction in these cases and placement of Indian children in non-Indian homes has been greatly reduced. Pipestem (1981:60) states that the preponderance of cases in which the Indian Child Welfare Act has protected children are in circumstances of "neglect, what we call dependent and neglected cases, where there is a substantial amount of chemical abuse by the parents."

Another line of research on childhood focused on the socialization process in Native American cultures (Underhill, 1942; Boggs, 1956; Williams, 1958; Downs, 1964; Tefft, 1968; Schlegel, 1973; Lefley, 1974, 1976; Guillemin, 1975; Miller, 1979; Lewis, 1981; Ryan, 1981). According to Downs (1964:69) the socialization process among the Navajo operates on the principle of "the inviolability of the individual." I would interject that to some interpreters this would appear to be permissive. Downs maintains that the system operates by "light discipline, by persuasion, ridicule, or shaming in opposition to corporal punishment or coercion." Ron Lewis (1981:104) states that the lack of corporal punishment is attributable to the respect that is "at the very center of a person's relationship with all others starting with the childs' relationship to the family." Supernatural sanctions (Williams, 1958; Lefley, 1976; Ryan, 1981) are also used to control behavior.

Underhill (1942), Boggs, (1956), Williams (1958), Guillemin (1975) and Miller (1979) stress that much of the socialization process among Native Americans is nonverbal, with communication by stern looks, or simply ignoring inappropriate behavior. In addition, children are supposed to learn by observing others (by example), are expected to share with others, to not make unreasonable or selfish demands, to show deference to everyone older than themselves, to take responsibility for themselves and others in the family, and contribute to the group from an early age.

Stanton Tefft (1968) investigated changes in the socialization practices and values of the Wind River Shoshone and found what amounts to a generation gap between people over 50 years old and younger people. According to Tefft, the values of older Shoshone were more "Indian-oriented" than the values of their adult children. Tefft (1968:331) found that among people over 50 years old "Collateral, Past, Subjugation-to-Nature, and Being Orientations predominated . . . while Individual, Future, Over-Nature, and Doing Orientations predominated" among their children. He attributed this difference to a shift in the agents of socialization that have had the greatest influence on the formation of values of each of these generations. Respondents in the oldest generation identified their parents and grandparents as most influential in their lives, whereas their children mentioned representatives of white institutions (white school mates, teachers, church leaders, or neighbors).

Tefft concludes that socialization practices have changed from "cohesive and structured" households characterized by high-dominance/high-support parent–child relations in which the older generation grew up to "loosely structured" households with low-dominance/low-support parent–child relations of the younger generations. My own research (John, 1985:305ff) among Prairie Band Potawatomi elders confirms, at least, the perception of similar changes in childrearing practices as well as values and behaviors of younger generations. A composite portrait of these changes can be summarized as follows: Back when these elders were growing up, the family was much closer, more organized and protective, combined discipline with permissiveness better than today, and had the advantage of having parents (particularly the mother) around the home.

Lefley (1974, 1976) studied the effects of the socialization process on self-esteem among the Seminole and Miccosukee tribes of Florida. These two tribes were chosen because they are closely related and represent more- and less-acculturated groups, respectively. Lefley wished to determine the effects of acculturation on a child's self-esteem, which she defined as "a sense of identity, worthiness, and self-acceptance as a human being" (Lefley, 1976:387). She posited that members of the less-acculturated Miccosukee tribe would have higher self-esteem because greater cultural integrity would provide a higher level of social integration that would be more conducive to the development of psychological health.

Results confirmed her hypothesis. In fact, both mothers and children in the less-acculturated Miccosukee tribe had significantly higher self-esteem. However, some in-group differences were also evident. Girls were significantly higher in self-esteem and perceived parental love in both tribes. In addition, Lefley found that boys' self-concept was significantly correlated with perceived parental love, whereas girls' self-concept was positively correlated with their mothers' self-concept.

The basic idea advanced by Lefley's research is the destructive impact that acculturation has on self-esteem and the unfortunate prognosis that the intrusive agents of socialization in American culture will further increase the likelihood that younger members of relatively traditional groups will experience lowered self-concepts. Miller (1981) also views a number of these agents of socialization as powerful and insensitive forces shaping American Indian family life. In a study of the effects of one such institution, Metcalf (1976) concludes that religious and federal boarding schools undermine self-esteem, as well as the maternal behaviors among Navajo women in adulthood. Metcalf states (1976:543) that "a disruptive school experience had significant detrimental effects on the women's measured levels of commitment to the maternal role, their attitudes toward their children and family life, and their sense of competence as mothers." This, in turn, negatively affected their children's self-esteem.

Adolescence

Another stage of the life course, adolescence, is much in evidence among Native Americans. Christopherson (1981) states that adolescence has arrived on the largest and, in many ways, most traditional of the reservations. Christopherson (1981:105–106) points to "alcohol, glue and gasoline sniffing, venereal disease, and a variety of delinquent behaviors" as evidence of adolescence among the Navajo. However, he did not estimate the prevalence of these behaviors and they probably represent the extremes of adolescent behavior and are probably more common among young males. Unfortunately, it is these extreme behaviors that receive attention. According to Dinges, Trimble, and Hollenbeck (1979:259), "there has been a major emphasis on social problems and behavioral difficulties associated with Indian adolescence. Suicide, alcoholism, academic failure, and generally poor psychosocial adjustment have been quite heavily researched." This emphasis on social problems and deviant behavior has skewed our perceptions of Native American youth.

Marriage

Christopherson (1981:106), quoting a study by the Office of Indian Education, characterizes gender differences among the Navajo that I believe are common among Native Americans in general. There is a tendency among females to settle down at an early age, whereas "males . . . do not reflect qualities of sociological adulthood until their very late 20s or early 30s. Until then, males typically defer marriage, maintain their peer-group orientations, and have very little job stability" (see Guillemin, 1975 also). This is undoubtedly related to the scarcity of employment opportunities on reservations as much as any other factor. When young Indians do settle down, as in American society in general, mate selection is based on romantic love, subject to the informal pressures that tend to result in relatively high levels of homogamy (especially on reservations).

Despite this similarity, there are attitudinal differences between Native American and other youth toward marital practices. Edington and Hays (1978) conducted a comparative study of the differences in family size and marriage age expectation and aspiration of Anglo American, Mexican American, and American Indian youth living in rural New Mexico. They found that Native American youth wanted more children (2.90 on average) and expected to have more children (3.05 on average) than Anglo American (2.30 and 2.49 on average, respectively) or Mexican American (2.71 and 2.87 on average, respectively) youth. In addition, the age at which American Indian youth wanted to marry (23.4 years on average) and expected to marry (23.2 years on average) was higher than the responses from the other two groups. On balance, however, Edington and Hays concluded that Native American youth were less certain of their desires and expectations regarding marriage and procreation because of a higher rate of non-response than Anglo American or Mexican American youth.

The middle period of the life-cycle has received much less attention. Very little is known about husband–wife interaction among Native Americans. Only one such study (Strodtbeck, 1951) compared ten Navajo, Texan, and Mormon couples on how they interacted during decision making and whose opinion prevailed when asked to characterize families in their community. Strodtbeck hypothesized that Navajo women, because of their economic power and independence gained through the control of property, would win in more of the decisions than either Texan or Mormon women. This hypothesis was confirmed by his study. Strodtbeck also discovered that the character of the dyadic interaction was very different among the Navajo couples. According to Strodtbeck (1951:473), Navajos had a tendency to minimize analysis:

> Navajos gave *opinion, evaluation, and analysis* acts during the solution of their differences only one-half as frequently as the Mormon and the Texan group. As a result they required on the average fewer acts per decision (8 in contrast with 30 for the other groups) and the reasoning and persuasion in their protocols seemed extremely sketchy. They did not emphasize the arguments that might bear upon the issue, they tended to reiterate their choices and implore the other person to 'go with them:' 'go together,' or simply consent. This is in marked contrast with the other couples who appeared to feel that they had to give a reasoned argument to show that they were logically convinced, even when they were giving in to the other person.

Without commenting directly on this study by Strodtbeck, Witherspoon (1975:98) corroborates the relative lack of verbal interaction during the decision-making process among Navajos. Because of the emphasis on unity, cooperation, and consensus in Navajo family life, when important decisions need to be made:

> [F]eelings, attitudes, and decisions are sensed rather than verbally expressed. Serious matters are seldom dealt with at the level of speech, and important decisions are seldom discussed. Decisions are felt and sensed before they reach a verbalized conclusion.

According to Witherspoon, family members think over the situation until one of them "has the sense of the group" and then offers a suggestion to the group that either resolves the issue or results in further deliberations. Because the Navajo live and work together closely, over the years they "learn to communicate with each other without the use of language."

This nonverbal approach extends to other tribes as well as other areas of family life. Quoting one of her informants, the first strength of Indian families identified by Miller (1979:457) was that "[r]elatives 'help without being asked. It's just our way'." Elders, too, do not feel that they should have to ask for assistance but that family members, tribal officials, and social service workers should be able to sense their needs and respond to them.

Guillemin (1975:94) provides a reasonable explanation for the nonverbal capabilities of American Indians when she characterizes the socialization process of Micmac children. "Micmac children learn by observation and are not subjected in the family to intense verbal instruction. Younger children are expected to imitate their older siblings in the basics of eating, toilet training, and general physical dexterity without individual instruction. . . ." Williams (1958) and Underhill (1965) also document this approach among the Papago.

Sex Roles and Gender Differences

Little is known about gender roles among Native Americans. Coming from cultures that traditionally had very rigid gender roles, contemporary Native Americans have modified their gender-role behaviors toward the androgenous norms of American society as a whole. However, this point should not be overdrawn. Based on a small sample from Los Angeles, Price (1981) characterized the primary emotional concerns of women largely as expressive and men as instrumental. Price found that women were more concerned with kinfolk, family, marriage, and sexual relations, and men were more concerned with employment, money, success, and material matters. Guillemin (1975) characterized other aspects of gender roles including same-sex confidants and peer groups.

Another issue concerning gender roles is role change. The few scholars who have studied this issue differ on whether men's or women's roles have changed the most. Some observers of the Navajo (Witherspoon, 1975; Christopherson, 1981) suggest that men's gender roles have changed more than women's because women continue to exercise economic power in subsistence residential units that have been the basis of the Navajo tribal economy for over a century. Kendall Blanchard (1975), however, maintains the opposite for the Navajo, and Burt Aginsky and Ethel Aginsky (1947) describe a complete role reversal among the Pomo from a "man-authoritarian culture to a woman-authoritarian culture."

Blanchard claims that Protestant sects have afforded women new sex roles and statuses to compensate for the loss of roles and prestige that have accompanied economic change. Blanchard found that Navajo women who had joined either of the Protestant churches on the Ramah Reservation had twice the formal education, were twice as likely to work outside the home, were more likely to have lived and worked off the reservation, were more likely to live in a neolocal situation and in smaller households and have fewer children, and were less likely to honor traditional social obligations than their more traditional counterparts. On balance, however, I would have to conclude that men have experienced the greatest role change.

Elders

Another body of recent research on the life course has investigated the other end of the life cycle. Grounded in a structural–functional theoretical framework, the earliest studies of American Indian elders focused on the roles held by elders in the economic, political, familial, religious, and educational institutions of so-called primitive societies. The general finding of these studies was the greater the number and the more important the roles held by elders, the higher their status was.

The earliest work dealing with these issues (Simmons, 1945; see also Simmons, 1960) greatly influenced subsequent research by academics well into the 1970s. Indeed, the only other scholarly work prior to the 1970s is Levy's (1967) functionalist analysis that covered much of the same ground as Simmons. In the most valuable portion of his essay Levy did, however, focus on the destruction of traditional social relations among the Navajo that had altered the position of the aged by reducing or eliminating the "functions" they performed.

Although Munsell (1972), Williams (1980), Amoss (1981), and Schweitzer (1983) have continued this line of inquiry, research inspired by a functionalist framework is now studied by a declining number of social scientists. The central question, whether social status is the result of cultural knowledge (Amoss, 1981), material contributions, or both (Williams, 1980; Schweitzer, 1983) has been dropped by those most active in studying Native American elders in favor of more practical investigations, the goal of which is to improve the quality of life of Native American elders.

For the most part, this social policy research has investigated the current status, service needs, and service use of Native American elders (Bell, Kaschau, and Zellman, 1978; Murdock and Schwartz, 1978; Manson and Pambrun, 1978; National Tribal Chairmen's Association, 1978; Rogers and Gallion, 1978; Curley, 1979; National Indian Council on Aging, 1979, 1981a, 1981b, 1983; Dukepoo, 1980; Edwards, Edwards and Daines, 1980; John, 1980; Edwards, 1983; Red Horse, 1982b). The general findings are that Native Americans are disadvantaged in old age compared with the general population. However, there are significant differences between urban and reservation aging American Indians in their current status, need for services, and the mix of support they receive from formal and informal sources.

Based on my own research on a nationwide sample of Indian elders over the age of 45 (John, 1986), it is possible to characterize the current status of urban and reservation differences. Without a doubt, the deprivation experienced by aging reservation Indians is substantially greater than among urban Indians. In general, the reservation group is poorer, has greater financial concerns, supports more people on their income, has fewer social contacts, has somewhat lower life satisfaction, and is in poorer health.

In addition, there are also major differences between urban and reservation aging American Indians in their need for services as well as the mix of support they receive from formal and informal sources. As is true of the general population, the greatest service needs for both groups are for nonpersonal (i.e., housework, shopping, transportation) rather than personal (i.e., bathing, dressing, eating) assistance. The four primary activities of daily living for which both urban and reservation groups need ongoing assistance are help with housework, transportation, using the telephone, and going shopping, and the foremost unfulfilled need of both groups is for information and referral assistance. However, the levels of need are substantially greater on reservations.

Sources of assistance also differ between urban and reservation environments. Compared with urban Indians, family members are more salient as *direct* and *sole* service providers to reservation residents. In addition, family members of reservation residents are more likely than their urban counterparts to share service responsibility with formal sources of support. In contrast, urban residents rely more on formal social services to meet their needs. Despite these differences, family is important in providing services for both reservation and urban Indians, although the relative demands on the family network are greater on reservations.

Family and Kinship Network

The issue of the existence and extent of the family support network is important during all periods of the life course. Among Native Americans, the absence of family support has been linked to child abuse and neglect (Oakland and Kane, 1973; Metcalf, 1979), adolescent pregnancy (Red Horse, 1982), psychological disturbances (Fox, 1960), and problems adapting to urban life (Miller, 1979; Metcalf, 1979). As is true of other minorities (U. S. Department of Health and Human Services, 1979; National Indian Council on Aging, 1981b), Native Americans, in general, have very low formal service utilization.

In addition to its role as a direct service provider, recent scholarship suggests that the Native American family network may be an important source of indirect assistance, as well. That is, the family network is also instrumental in facilitating formal service use by family members.[11]

According to Murdock and Schwartz (1978), the availability of and contact with family members is an important factor in both the perception of needs and the use of services. In fact, they claim that "family structure is clearly related to objective indicators of need: the smaller the family unit, the greater its financial and housing needs" (Murdock and Schwartz, 1978:476–77). Murdock and Schwartz (1978:480–481) conclude that "children may assist elderly persons by both creating greater awareness of the needs for and availability of services, and in directly obtaining the required services."

Although they state their conclusion in a tentative manner, they suggest that "extended families serve to increase the mechanisms for service usage

---

[11]Colen (1982) maintains that information dissemination, crisis intervention, and broker activities with formal agencies are a common feature of the natural helping networks of minority-group elders. Miller (1979) states that eighty-one percent of her respondents from the San Francisco Bay Area report receiving assistance from family members in emergency situations such as illness or financial distress.

as well as the sources of information concerning services" (1978:481). Or further, that "levels of use as well as awareness . . . appear to be increased by living in a couple or in an extended family setting" (Murdock and Schwartz, 1978:479).[12] In their view, family members are not only the primary caregivers within the support network but also may serve an indispensable mediator role between family members and alien service bureaucracies. Whether as direct provider or intermediary, then, the existence of an extended family network is no less crucial now compared with the not-so-distant past when they were the sole source of support of Indian family members.

Another of the important features of American Indian families in which extended family relationships are present is the special nature of the grandparent–grandchild relationship (Tefft, 1968; Lewis, 1981; Ryan, 1981) and the importance of grandparents (particularly the grandmother) in the family network. Indeed, the grandmother is the center of family life, and she holds the family together. Given the tendency to begin childbearing at a very early age, it is common for a woman to be a grandmother by the time she is 40 and often by the time she is in her mid-30s.[13] Although motherhood is an important transition in the life course marking the status of becoming a woman, grandmotherhood is an important transition because of the additional family responsibilities a woman assumes. Women who have children while they are teenagers frequently have little inclination or preparation for motherhood and some irresponsibility is anticipated and tolerated (Metcalf, 1979), as long as it does not endanger the well-being of the child. Generally, the girl looks to her mother for assistance and training and frequently passes a great deal of responsibility for the care of the child to her mother. In fact, on occasion, the grandmother takes over rearing one or more grandchildren because she or other family members feel that the child is not being raised properly or the parent(s) decide that it would benefit the child (Howell, 1970; Guillemin, 1975; Miller, 1979). A child may also go to live with a family member who needs help that the child can provide or who would like to have a child around

[12]Murdock and Schwartz are right to emphasize the important intermediary role of family members in service utilization. However, my research (John, 1986) suggests that this role is more important on reservations than it is in urban environments, primarily because of smaller households and fewer intact marriages. This does not contradict their findings since their study was of reservation Sioux. It does question the generalizability of their findings to urban environments. However, even on reservations, the role of family members as direct service providers is more important than their mediator role.

[13]This is very different than the pattern found in the general population since the mean age at which Americans in general become grandparents is the mid-fifties (Brody, 1978:25).

(Underhill, 1965). It is also not unusual for a child to ask to live with grandparents, a request that is honored if not a manifest impossibility.

CHANGE AND ADAPTATION

Among the industrialized nations, the United States is one of the few without a formal family policy. Moroney succinctly characterized the existing bias evident in social policy in the United States, a bias that is attributable to precisely the prevailing ideology and social interests arising from the concrete social location of most politicians and social planners. According to Moroney (1980:33–34):

> [M]ost social policies are oriented to individuals and not to families. Furthermore, when the object of the policy is the family, invariably it defines the family as nuclear. To shift policy development so that the modified extended family is explicitly included would require a major reorientation. . . . If successful, such a reorientation could result in policies that set out to maximize available resources, the natural resources of the family, and the resources of the social welfare system. Such an approach begins with a search for ways to support families by complementing what they are already doing—intervening directly and indirectly, but not interfering.

Without doubt, pressures to modify Native American family life in the direction of the patterns of the cultural mainstream will continue. By and large, the greatest influence on Native American families will be the same as it is for Americans as a whole. The capitalist political economy sets the conditions of employment and indirectly shapes the family structure and relationships within it for the ever-increasing number of people who wish to pursue American-style success. Generally, such success can be achieved only at the sacrifice of family life.

The United States asks everyone to make a mutually exclusive choice: dedicate yourself to your work or your family. Although this statement may continue a controversy within family sociology because it denies the ideological but mythical belief that American culture is family-oriented, the sad truth is that family structures in the United States are fragile, temporary and shrinking in size and importance. Any number of social trends attest to the truth of this statement: rising divorce, the institutionalization of cohabitation and single living, prenuptial agreements, the dramatic increase in the number of female-headed families, the escalation of women's labor-force participation, the economic pressures that encourage dual-wage-earner families, the increasing number of people of all ages who live alone, the rise of voluntary childlessness, and the delay of marriage and childbearing. I should make it clear that my intent in listing these trends is not for the purpose of making any invidious comparison with other family practices, past or present, nor to make any moral judgment on these practices. They are symptomatic and do reveal something about our political economy and culture.

Indeed, each of these trends can be explained as a rational response to the political economy and American culture. Children, from a strictly economically rational viewpoint, are unalloyed economic liabilities for an entire lifetime. Economically rational behavior dictates delaying childbearing, having only one or, at most, two children or not having children at all. Working women and dual-wage-earner families have become a necessary response to the steady decline in the standard of living in the United States that has occurred over the last 15 years. Concomitant development of a focus on self and immediate gratification (whether these are labeled narcissism or hedonism), so promoted by commodified, prepackaged American mass culture, is consistent with most of these trends. I raise these issues not to call for sacrifice or devotion to some presumed duty but to recognize these family trends as the most likely response and consequence of living in American society and the fact that government policy fails to adequately mitigate the negative influences that the political economy has on family life.

The impact of the political economy on family life is most clearly evident in the dire financial position of most female-headed families, and the fact that the impoverished in our society are disproportionately children, women, minorities, and elders. The lack of an adequate family policy (or even the idea that one is needed) means that structural changes in the American economy are ostensibly dealt with through public exhortations that plenty of jobs exist and go unfilled and through cutbacks in public financial, housing, and food support in the face of growing poverty, hunger, and homelessness in the United States. Likewise, the consequences of decisions made in corporate boardrooms to shut down operations or move them to another state or country are evaluated in terms of the large costs that families must ultimately absorb.

Despite the fact that Native American families are not immune to the larger, social structural forces in operation in the United States, I believe that Native American families continue to exhibit a unique character attributable to longstanding cultural differences from American culture as a whole. Indeed, Native Americans continue to exhibit a great deal of cultural diversity and divergence from the American cultural mainstream.

Culture change has occurred as the result of contact with whites but not to the degree that some observers would have us believe. The recognition by several researchers that even when Native American family practices have a *formal* resemblance to Anglo–European practices that there is something distinctively Native American in the way in which that practice is experienced should make academics circumspect in their use of an acculturation paradigm to explain family change among Native Americans. The rebirth of Native American cultural pride and the concomitant invigoration of tribal entities, clearly a direct outgrowth of the red power movement of the 1960s, have protected substantial numbers of Native Americans from acculturation and assimilation.

However, it is true that Native American elders are more exclusively "Indian-oriented" than middle or younger generations. Among the middle and younger generations, the best description of their value orientations would be "bicultural;" having knowledge of two different cultural worlds and being able to operate in either one. Family practices have also changed. Although extended families remain the cultural ideal among Native Americans, in reality, extended families are not universal, and within families that exhibit extended family characteristics, there are prodigal sons and daughters who have moved outside the sphere of routine, extended family operations. Nonetheless, it is true that Native American families are based more on interdependence and consanguineous ties compared with the independent and conjugal emphasis within Anglo American society.

The extent to which Native Americans adopt, resist, or adapt in modified form the family practices of the cultural mainstream depends on a number of factors. Certainly, some groups will have an advantage over others in retaining the cultural grounding of their tribal family practices. Among these, tribes that maintain or expand their land base (i.e., their cultural community) will have an advantage over tribes that do not have a community locus. Similarly, the largest groups will fare better than small ones in preserving their cultural heritage and unique family practices. Furthermore, tribes that succeed in building a tribal economy capable of sustaining their cultural community will have an advantage over tribes with weak and dependent economies. In addition, groups that maintain tribal spiritual practices and teach their children the tribal language will fare better than other groups.

However, the forces of change and cultural homogenization at work in American society as a whole will also have an effect on Native Americans. In addition to the American political economy, a number of other factors will pressure Native Americans toward practices of the cultural mainstream. American popular culture, education grounded in Anglo–European intellectual ways of knowledge, institutions or social movements (such as Christian churches or the women's movement) that consciously or unwittingly undermine Native American values and practices, racial exogamy, and urbanization present a challenge to Native Americans. How Native Americans respond to these external pressures remains to be seen, but their history of cultural resilience suggests that they will be able to absorb them and adapt their family practices to meet their own cultural needs.

REFERENCES

Aginsky, Burt W. and Ethel G. Aginsky. 1947. "A Resultant of Intercultural Relations," *Social Forces,* 26:84-87.

Amoss, Pamela T. 1981. "Cultural Centrality and Prestige for the Elderly: The Coast Salish Case," in Christine L. Fry (ed.), *Dimensions: Aging, Culture and Health.* New York: Praeger, pp. 47-63.

Bell, Duran, Patricia Kasschau, and Gail Zellman. 1978. "Service Delivery to American Indian Elderly," in *The Indian Elder, A Forgotten American.* Albuquerque, NM: National Indian Council on Aging, pp. 185-198.

Blanchard, E. L. and Steven Unger. 1977. "Destruction of American-Indian Families," *Social Casework,* 58(5):312-314.

Blanchard, Evelyn Lance, and Russel Lawrence Barsh. 1980. "What is Best for Tribal Children? A Response to Fischler," *Social Work,* 25(5):350-357.

Blanchard, Kendall. 1975. "Changing Sex Roles and Protestantism Among the Navajo Women in Ramah," *Journal for the Scientific Study of Religion* 14:43-50.

Bock, Philip K. 1964. "Patterns of Illegitimacy on a Canadian Indian Reserve: 1860-1960," *Journal of Marriage and the Family,* 26(2):142-148.

Boggs, Stephen T. 1956. "An Interactional Study of Ojibwa Socialization," *American Sociological Review,* 21:191-198.

Brieland, D. 1973. "Far From Reservation—Transracial Adoption of American Indian Children," *Social Service Review,* 47(2):310-311.

Brody, Elaine. 1978. "The Aging of the Family," *The Annals of the American Academy,* 438:13-26.

Bultena, Gordon L. et al. 1971. "Life After 70 in Iowa," *Sociology Report,* 95.

Bureau of Indian Affairs. 1985. *Indian Service Population and Labor Force Estimates.* January. Washington, DC: U. S. Government Printing Office.

Byler, W. 1977. "Removing Children—Destruction of American-Indian Families," *Civil Rights Digest,* 9(4):19-27.

Cantor, Majorie H. 1980. "The Informal Support System: Its Relevance in the Lives of the Elderly," in Edgar F. Borgatta and Neil G. McCluskey (eds.), *Aging and Society: Current Research and Policy Perspectives.* Beverly Hills, CA: Sage, pp. 131-144.

Christopherson, Victor A. 1981. "The Rural Navajo Family," in Raymond T. Coward and William M. Smith, Jr. (eds.), *The Family in Rural Society.* Boulder, CO: Westview Press, pp. 105-111.

Clayton, Richard R. 1978. *The Family, Marriage, and Social Change* (2nd ed.). Lexington, MA: D. C. Heath.

Colen, John N. 1982. "Using Natural Helping Networks in Social Service Delivery Systems," in Ron C. Manuel (ed.), *Minority Aging: Sociological and Social Psychological Issues.* Westport, CT: Greenwood Press, pp. 179–183.

Curley, Larry. 1979. "Title VI of the Older Americans Act, 'Grants to Indian Tribes'," in E. Percil Stanford (ed.), *Minority Aging Research: Old Issues—New Approaches.* San Diego, CA: San Diego State University, pp. 223–226.

Dinges, Norman G., Joseph E. Trimble, and Albert R. Hollenbeck. 1979. "American Indian Adolescent Socialization: A Review of the Literature," *Journal of Adolescence,* 2:259–296.

Dobyns, Henry F. 1983. *Their Number Become Thinned: Native American Population Dynamics in Eastern North America.* Knoxville, TN: University of Tennessee Press.

Downs, James F. 1964. *Animal Husbandry in Navajo Society and Culture.* Berkeley: University of California Press.

Driver, Harold E. 1969. *Indians of North America* (2nd ed.). Chicago: University of Chicago Press.

Dukepoo, Frank C. 1980. *The Elder American Indian.* San Diego, CA: San Diego State University, Campanile Press.

Edington, Everett, and Leonard Hays. 1978. "Difference in Family Size and Marriage Age Expectation and Aspirations of Anglo, Mexican American and Native American Rural Youth in New Mexico," *Adolescence,* 13(51):393–400.

Edwards, E. Daniel. 1978. "Destruction of American-Indian Families," *Social Work,* 23(1):74.

———. 1983. "Native American Elders: Current Issues and Social Policy Implications," in R. L. McNeely and John N. Colen (eds.), *Aging in Minority Groups.* Beverly Hills, CA: Sage, pp. 74–82.

Edwards, E. Daniel, Margie E. Edwards, and Geri M. Daines. 1980. "American Indian/Alaska Native Elderly: A Current and Vital Concern," *Journal of Gerontological Social Work,* 2(3):213–224.

Fanshel, David. 1972. *Far From Reservation: The Transcultural Adoption of American Indian Children.* Metuchen, NJ: Scarecrow.

Feagin, Joe R., and Randall Anderson. 1973. "Intertribal Attitudes Among Native American Youth," *Social Science Quarterly,* 54:117–131.

Fischler, Ronald S. 1980. "Protecting American-Indian Children," *Social Work,* 25(5):341–349.

Fox, J. R. 1960. "Therapeutic Rituals and Social Structure in Cochiti Pueblo," *Human Relations,* 13:291–303.

Garcia, Darrell W. 1973. "Far From Reservation—Transracial Adoption of American Indian Children," *Social Work,* 18(1):125.

Gibson, Geoffrey. 1972. "Kin Family Network: Overheralded Structure in Past Conceptualization of Family Functioning," *Journal of Marriage and the Family,* 34:13–24.

Goodman, James M. 1985. "The Native American," in Jesse O. McKee (ed.), *Ethnicity in Contemporary America: A Geographical Appraisal.* Dubuque, IA: Kendall/Hunt, pp. 31–53.

Guillemin, Jeanne. 1975. *Urban Renegades: The Cultural Strategy of American Indians.* New York: Columbia University Press.

Haynes, Terry L. 1977. "Some Factors Related to Contraceptive Behavior Among

Wind River Shoshone and Arapahoe Females," *Human Organization,* 36(1):72–76.
Heinrich, Albert. 1972. "Divorce as an Integrative Social Factor," *Journal of Comparative Family Studies,* 3:265–272.
Henderson, Eric. 1979. "Skilled and Unskilled Blue Collar Navajo Workers: Occupational Diversity in an American Indian Tribe," *Social Science Journal,* 16:63–80.
Howell, Norma Alice. 1970. "Potawatomi Pregnancy and Childbirth." Master's thesis, University of Kansas.
Ishisaka, H. 1978. "American Indians and Foster Care: Cultural Factors and Separation," *Child Welfare,* 57(5):299–308.
John, Robert. 1980. "The Older Americans Act and the Elderly Native American," *Journal of Minority Aging* 5:293–298.
———. 1985. "Aging in a Native American Community: Service Needs and Support Networks Among Prairie Band Potawatomi Elders." Ph.D. diss., University of Kansas.
———. 1986. "Social Policy and Planning for Aging American Indians: Provision of Services by Formal and Informal Support Networks," *American Indian Culture and Research Journal,* forthcoming.
Klatzky, Sheila R. 1972. *Patterns of Contact with Relatives.* Washington, DC: American Sociological Association.
Kroeber, Alfred L. 1939. *Cultural and Natural Areas of Native North America.* University of California Publications in American Archaeology and Ethnology, Vol. 38. Berkeley, CA: University of California Press.
Kunitz, Stephen J. 1974. "Factors Influencing Recent Navajo and Hopi Population Changes," *Human Organization,* 33(1):7–16.
Kunitz, Stephen J., and John C. Slocumb. 1976. "The Use of Surgery to Avoid Childbearing Among Navajo and Hopi Indians," *Human Biology,* 48(1):9–21.
Lefley, Harriet P. 1974. "Social and Familial Correlates of Self-Esteem Among American Indian Children," *Child Development,* 45(3):829–833.
———. 1976. "Acculturation, Child-Rearing, and Self-Esteem in Two North American Indian Tribes," *Ethos,* 385–401.
Levy, Jerrold E. 1967. "The Older American Indian," in E. Grant Youmans (ed.), *Older Rural Americans: A Sociological Perspective.* Lexington, KY: University of Kentucky Press, pp. 221–238.
Lewis, Claudia. 1970. *Indian Families of the Northwest Coast: The Impact of Change.* Chicago: University of Chicago Press.
Lewis, Ron. 1981. "Patterns of Strength of American Indian Families," in John Red Horse, August Shattuck, and Fred Hoffman (eds.), *The American Indian Family: Strengths and Stresses.* Isleta, NM: American Indian Social Research and Development Associates, pp. 101–106.
Liberty, Margot. 1975. "Population Trends Among Present-Day Omaha Indians," *Plains Anthropologist.*
Liberty, Margot, David V. Hughey, and Richard Scaglion. 1976. "Rural and Urban Omaha Indian Fertility," *Human Biology,* 48(1):59–71.
Manson, Spero M., and Audra M. Pambrun. 1979. "Social and Psychological Status of the Indian Elderly: Past Research, Current Advocacy, and Future Inquiry," in National Indian Council on Aging. *The Continuum of Life: Health*

Concerns of the Indian Elderly. Albuquerque, NM: National Indian Council on Aging, pp. 87–93.
Mercier, Joyce McDonough, and Edward A. Powers. 1984. "The Family and Friends of Rural Aged as a Natural Support System," *Journal of Community Psychology,* 12:334–346.
Metcalf, Ann. 1976. "From Schoolgirl to Mother: The Effects of Education on Navajo Women," *Social Problems,* 23:535–544.
———. 1979. "Family Reunion: Networks and Treatment in a Native American Community," *Group Psychotherapy, Psychodrama, and Sociometry,* 32:179–189.
Miller, Dorothy. 1979. "The Native American Family: The Urban Way," in Eunice Corfman (ed.), *Families Today: A Research Sampler on Families and Children.* Washington, DC: U. S. Government Printing Office, pp. 441–484.
———. 1981. "Alternative Paradigms Available for Research on American Indian Families: Implications for Research and Training," in John Red Horse, August Shattuck, and Fred Hoffman (eds.), *The American Indian Family: Strengths and Stresses.* Isleta, NM: American Indian Social Research and Development Associates, pp. 79–91.
Moroney, Robert M. 1980. *Families, Social Services, and Social Policy: The Issue of Shared Responsibility.* Washington, DC: U. S. Government Printing Office.
Munsell, Marvin R. 1972. "Functions of the Aged Among Salt River Pima," in Donald O. Cowgill and Lewelyn Holmes (eds.), *Aging and Modernization.* New York: Appleton-Century-Crofts, pp. 127–132.
Murdock, Steve H., and Donald F. Schwartz. 1978. "Family Structure and Use of Agency Services: An Examination of Patterns Among Elderly Native Americans," *Gerontologist,* 18(5):475–481.
National Indian Council on Aging. 1979. *The Continuum of Life: Health Concerns of the Indian Elderly.* Albuquerque, NM: National Indian Council on Aging.
———. 1981a. *American Indian Elderly: A National Profile.* Albuquerque, NM: National Indian Council on Aging.
———. 1981b. *Indian Elderly and Entitlement Programs: An Accessing Demonstration Project.* Albuquerque, NM: National Indian Council on Aging.
———. 1983. *Access, A Demonstration Project: Entitlement Programs for Indian Elders.* Albuquerque, NM: National Indian Council on Aging.
National Tribal Chairmen's Association. 1978. *The Indian Elder: A Forgotten American.* Phoenix, AZ: National Tribal Chairmen's Association.
Oakland, Lynne, and Robert L. Kane. 1973. "The Working Mother and Child Neglect on the Navajo Reservation," *Pediatrics,* 51(5):849–853.
Olson, Laura Katz. 1982. *The Political Economy of Aging: The State, Private Power, and Social Welfare.* New York: Columbia University Press.
Pipestem, F. Browning. 1981. "Comments on the Indian Child Welfare Act," in John Red Horse, August Shattuck, and Fred Hoffman, (eds.), *The American Indian Family: Strengths and Stresses.* Isleta, NM: American Indian Social Research and Development Associates, pp. 53–69.
Porter, Frank W., III (ed.). 1983. *Nonrecognized American Indian Tribes: An Historical and Legal Perspective.* Paper of the McNickle Center for the Study of the American Indian, No. 7. Chicago: Newberry Library.
Powers, Edward A., Patricia M. Keith, and Willis J. Goudy. 1981. "Family Net-

works of the Rural Aged," in Raymond T. Coward and William M. Smith, Jr. (eds.), *The Family in Rural Society.* Boulder, CO: Westview, pp. 199–217.

Price, John A. 1976. "North American Indian Families," in Charles H. Mindel and Robert W. Habenstein (eds.), *Ethnic Families in America: Patterns and Variations.* New York: Elsevier, pp. 248–270.

———. 1981. "North American Indian Families," in Charles H. Mindel and Robert W. Habenstein (eds.), *Ethnic Families in America: Patterns and Variations* (2nd ed.). New York: Elsevier, pp. 245–270.

Queen, Stuart A., and John B. Adams. 1952. *The Family in Various Cultures.* Philadelphia: J. B. Lippincott.

Red Horse, John G. 1980a. "Family-Structure and Value Orientation in American-Indians," *Social Casework,* 61(8):462–467.

———. 1980b. "American-Indian Elders—Unifiers of Indian Families," *Social Casework,* 61(8):490–493.

———. 1982a. "Clinical Strategies for American-Indian Families in Crisis," *Urban and Social Change Review,* 15(2):17–19.

———. 1982b. "American Indian and Alaskan Native Elders: A Policy Critique," in E. Percil Stanford and Shirley A. Lockery (eds.), *Trends and Status of Minority Aging.* San Diego, CA: San Diego State University, pp. 15–26.

Red Horse, John G. et al. 1978. "Family Behavior of Urban American-Indians," *Social Casework,* 59(2):67–72.

Red Horse, Yvonne. 1982. "A Cultural Network Model: Perspectives for Adolescent Services and Para-Professional Training," in Spero M. Manson (ed.), *New Directions in Prevention Among American Indian and Alaska Native Communities.* Portland, OR: Oregon Health Sciences University.

Rogers, C. Jean, and Teresa E. Gallion. 1978. "Characteristics of Elderly Pueblo Indians in New Mexico," *Gerontologist,* 18:482–487.

Ryan, Robert A. 1981. "Strengths of the American Indian Family: State of the Art," in John Red Horse, August Shattuck, and Fred Hoffman (eds.), *The American Indian Family: Strengths and Stresses.* Isleta, NM: American Indian Social Research and Development Associates, pp. 25–43.

Schlegel, Alice. 1973. "The Adolescent Socialization of the Hopi Girl," *Ethnology,* 449–462.

Schweitzer, Majorie M. 1983. "The Elders: Cultural Dimensions of Aging in Two American Indian Communities," in Jay Sokolovsky (ed.), *Growing Old in Different Societies: Cross-Cultural Perspectives.* Belmont, CA: Wadsworth, pp. 168–178.

Simmons, Leo W. 1945. *The Role of the Aged in Primitive Society.* New Haven, CT: Yale University Press.

———. 1960. "Aging in Preindustrial Societies," in Clark Tibbitts (ed.), *Handbook of Social Gerontology: Societal Aspects of Aging.* Chicago: University of Chicago Press, pp. 62–91.

Slaughter, E. L. 1976. *Indian Child Welfare: A Review of the Literature.* Denver: University of Denver Research Institute.

Staples, Robert, and Alfredo Mirande. 1980. "Racial and Cultural Variations Among American Families: A Decennial Review of the Literature on Minority Families," *Journal of Marriage and the Family,* 42(4):157–173.

Steele, C. Hoy. 1972. "American Indians and Urban Life: A Community Study." Ph.D. diss., University of Kansas.

Strodtbeck, Fred L. 1951. "Husband-Wife Interaction Over Revealed Differences," *American Sociological Review,* 16:468–473.
Sussman, Marvin B. 1959. "The Isolated Nuclear Family: Fact or Fiction." *Social Problems,* 6:333–340.
———. 1965. "Relationships of Adult Children With Their Parents in the United States," in Ethel Shanas and Gordon F. Streib (eds.), *Social Structure and the Family: Generational Relations.* Englewood Cliffs, NJ: Prentice-Hall, pp. 62–92.
Sweet, James A. 1974. "Differentials in the Rate of Fertility Decline: 1960–1970," *Family Planning Perspectives,* 6(2):103–107.
Tefft, Stanton K. 1967. "Anomy, Values and Culture Change Among Teen-Age Indians: An Exploratory Study," *Sociology of Education,* 40:145–157.
———. 1968. "Intergenerational Value Differentials and Family Structure Among the Wind River Shoshone," *American Anthropologist,* 70:330–333.
Troll, Lillian. 1978. "The Family of Later Life: A Decade Review," in Mildred M. Seltzer et al. (eds.), *Social Problems of the Aging: Readings.* Belmont, CA: Wadsworth, pp. 136–164.
Underhill, Ruth M. 1942. "Child Training in an Indian Tribe," *Marriage and Family Living,* 4:80–81.
———. 1965. "The Papago Family," in M. F. Nimkoff (ed.), *Comparative Family Systems.* Boston: Houghton-Mifflin, pp. 147–162.
Unger, Steven. 1977. *The Destruction of American Indian Families.* New York: Association on American Indian Affairs.
U.S. Congress. 1986. *Indian Health Care.* Washington, DC: U. S. Government Printing Office.
U.S. Department of Commerce. 1984. *American Indian Areas and Alaska Native Villages: 1980.* Washington, DC: U. S. Government Printing Office.
———. 1985. *A Statistical Profile of the American Indian, Eskimo, and Alert Populations for the United States: 1980.* Bureau of the Census, Racial Statistics Branch. Washington, DC: unpublished.
———. 1986. *American Indians, Eskimos, and Aleuts on Identified Reservations and in the Historic Areas of Oklahoma (Excluding Urbanized Areas),* part 2, sections 1 and 2. Washington, DC: U. S. Government Printing Office.
U.S. Department of Health and Human Services. 1979. *Policy Issues Concerning the Elderly Minorities.* Washington, DC: U. S. Government Printing Office.
Wagner, Jean K. 1976. "The Role of Intermarriage in the Acculturation of Selected Urban American Indian Women," *Anthropologica,* 18(2):215–229.
Ward, Russell A. 1978. "Limitations of the Family as a Supportive Institution in the Lives of the Aged," *Family Coordinator,* 27:365–373.
Wilkening, E. A., S. Guerrero, and S. Ginsberg. 1972. "Distance and Intergenerational Ties of Farm Families," *Sociological Quarterly,* 13:383–396.
Williams, Gerry C. 1980. "Warriors No More: A Study of the American Indian Elderly," in Christine L. Fry (ed.), *Aging in Culture and Society.* New York: Praeger, pp. 101–111.
Williams, Thomas Rhys. 1958. "The Structure of the Socialization Process in Papago Indian Society," *Social Forces,* 36:251–256.
Witherspoon, Gary. 1975. *Navajo Kinship and Marriage.* Chicago: University of Chicago Press.

SOCIORELIGIOUS ETHNIC MINORITIES

CHAPTER FIFTEEN

The Amish Family

Gertrude Enders Huntington

HISTORICAL BACKGROUND

The Old Order Amish are an example of an ethnoreligious group that has had great success in preserving its traditions and preventing wholesale assimilation. The primarily rural Amish, contrary to popular opinion, are probably a growing population that has managed to resist the onslaught of modern technology and major social change. Their ability to resist change is grounded in their religious commitment, which is expressed in their major social institutions.

The Old Order Amish Mennonites are direct descendants of the Swiss Anabaptists of the sixteenth century. "Anabaptist" is a historical and theological term used to designate a number of different theologies and social groups (Littell, 1964) that represent the left wing of the Reformation (Bainton, 1952). Those Anabaptist groups who survive emerged between 1525 and 1536 and are today represented by the Amish, Mennonites, and Hutterites. These churches are characterized by the maintenance of a disciplined community, pacifism, separation from the world, adult rather than infant baptism, and an emphasis on simple living.

The Amish developed between 1693 and 1697 as a dissenting conservative wing of the Swiss Mennonites. Their leader, Jacob Amman, introduced "shunning" (the avoidance of all normal social intercourse with a member who is under the ban), foot washing as a part of the communion service, communion twice instead of once a year, the excommunication of persons who attend the state church, and greater uniformity of dress and hairstyle. The Amman group, or Amish, continue to this day to abide by rules established by Jacob Amman and interpreted by each local congregation.

Although the Amish family today is an American phenomenon, its roots go back to the early days in Europe. Persecution was severe in Europe; the Amish were forbidden citizenship and thus could not own land. Therefore, they were generally unable to establish permanent, stable communities or to develop a distinctive social structure. Their livelihood, their place of residence, even their lives were subject to the whim of rulers and neighbors. Families often had to live at considerable distance from coreligionists; religious services were held irregularly and unobtrusively in the home of a church member. This mobility, isolation, and limited community interaction placed the emphasis for producing Christians directly on the family. To this day, the family has remained the smallest and strongest unit of Amish culture, the central social institution.

Anabaptist theology, which emphasized adult baptism, also supported the role of the family in child development. Protestant religious leaders such as Martin Luther and Philipp Melanchthon were suspicious of parents' ability to rear their children without the help and intervention of the state (Schwartz, 1973:102–114). In contrast, the Anabaptists never equated childrearing with schooling, nor did they believe that the child or the parent was morally subservient to some outside civil or religious authority. Childrearing was the parents' major responsibility. Menno Simons (about 1496–1561), an early leader in Holland after whom the Mennonites are named, wrote, "For this is the chief and principal care of the saints, that their children may fear God, do right, and be saved" (Simons, 1956:950). He also taught that parents were morally responsible for the condition of their children's souls. "Watch over their souls as long as they are under your care, lest you lose also your own salvation on their account" (Simons, 1956:391).

In addition to urging parents to set an unblamable example for their children and to teach, instruct, admonish, correct, and chastise their children as circumstances require, parents were also to protect their children from worldly influences and from wrong companions. "Keep them away from good-for-nothing children, from whom they hear and learn nothing but lying, cursing, swearing, fighting, and mischief" (Simons, 1956:959). Parents were to direct their children to reading and writing, that they might learn from the Scripture what God teaches. They were to instruct them to spin and to earn their bread by the labor of their hands. One example from the *Martyr's Mirror*[1] of practical instruction for child care was written by

---

[1] *The Bloody Theater,* or *Martyr's Mirror,* was first published in Dutch in 1660 and has periodically been reprinted in German and in English. It is a large book containing over 1500 pages and recounting, often with vivid details, the deaths of over 4000 men and women who *(continued)*

Jacob the Chandler shortly before he was burned at the stake (Braght, 1951:798–799):

> Furthermore, I pray you, my dear and much beloved wife, that you do the best with my children, to bring them up in the fear of God, with good instruction and chastening, while they are still young. . . . For instruction must accompany chastisement: for chastisement demands obedience, and if one is to obey, he must first be instructed. This instruction does not consist of hard words, or loud yelling; for this the children learn to imitate; but if one conducts himself properly towards them they have a good example, and learn propriety; for by the children the parents are known. And parents must not provoke their children to anger, lest they be discouraged; but must bring them up with admonition and good instruction.

During their years in Europe, the Amish lived in Switzerland, Alsace–Lorraine, the Palatine, France, Holland, Austria, Germany, and Poland. Lack of religious toleration meant that the Amish in Europe remained renters, and that families had limited choice as to where they could settle, frequently being forced to move to new locations as political situations changed. Although an effort was made to stay near members of the faith—an old Amish hymn (*Ausbund*, 1564: Hymn No. 44) quoted a martyr writing to his son: "Live, only where the believers live,"—it was impossible for the Amish to establish discrete communities. In some areas they continued for many years as a religious sect, but they never formed a self-perpetuating subculture. Today there are no people left in Europe who are distinctly Amish (Hostetler, 1955).

There is some disagreement as to when the first Amish landed in America. A 1709 letter of William Penn's pertaining to the Palatinate immigrants mentions "diverse Mennonites" (Smith, 1920:214), which could be construed as a reference to the Amish. The Amish immigrated to this continent in two major waves: The first wave from about 1727 to 1770 settled in Pennsylvania, and the second wave from 1815 to 1860 went primarily to Ohio and Indiana (Luthy, 1973:14).

The first Amish to arrive in America settled in Pennsylvania; there they formed discrete clusters, separate from the Mennonites as well as from the

---

(continued)
remained steadfast to their faith in spite of branding, burning, stoning, sessions on the rack, the severing of tongues, hands, and feet, live burials, and drowning. No one who recanted is considered a martyr, nor is one a martyr if he survived his torture. The *Martyr's Mirror* helps strengthen members "to make every preparation for steadfastness in our faith," (preface to fifth English edition, 1950) whether in the face of an inquisition, school officials, or universal conscription.

"English."[2] In contrast to their experience in Europe, the Amish immigrants to America found cheap land and religious toleration. They responded by electing to purchase farms near fellow churchmen, away from the influence of cities. This has continued to be the basis of their settlement pattern. The Ohio Amish community was started in 1808; this community in central Ohio is the largest and in many ways the most conservative of the large Amish communities. In 1839 settlers in Indiana formed what was to become the third largest Amish settlement. More than three-fourths of the Amish live in these three states. Smaller settlements are found in Illinois, Iowa, Wisconsin, Missouri, Delaware, Florida, Kansas, Kentucky, Minnesota, Oklahoma, Maryland, New York, Michigan, Tennessee, Arkansas, Montana, and Nebraska. At one time, there were Amish settlements in Oregon, North Dakota, California, Colorado, North Carolina, Georgia, Texas, New Mexico, Mississippi, Alabama, and Mexico.[3] In 1968, small Old Order Amish communities were established in Honduras and Paraguay. These communities are still in existence. However, the Honduras community has not remained typically Old Order, and that of Paraguay has only three families and one minister.

Table 1 gives the 1980 Amish population and the dates of the Amish settlers in each state. In some instances the first settlements were not successful, and present Amish population is the result of later immigrations. In other cases regular church districts were not established until a considerable time after the earliest settlement.

The Old Order Amish are a tradition-oriented, conservation branch of the Mennonite Church. The term Old Order came into usage during the last half of the 19th century when more liberal congregations separated from them. The Old Order are also known as "House Amish" because they hold their church services in their homes, or "Horse and Buggy Amish" because they do not own cars. The Old Order Amish are distinguished by prohibitions against owning automobiles, telephones, and high-line electricity. They have strict dress codes and forbid rubber-tired tractors (if tractors are used at all), central heating, and cameras. They speak a German dialect known as Pennsylvania Dutch in their homes, read the German Bible, and do not permit attendance at state schools beyond the eighth grade. In this chapter the discussion will be limited to the Old Order Amish.

---

[2]A term used for all non-Mennonites (and sometimes for all non-Amish) even those who are German speaking.

[3]Personal correspondence, December 21, 1973; interview March 10, 1980, David Luthy, Alymer, Ontario.

TABLE 1
Old Order Amish Population by State and County (1980)

STATE	DATE OF FIRST AMISH SETTLERS[a]	PRESENT SETTLEMENT[e]	DISTRICTS[b]	BAPTIZED MEMBERS (ESTIMATED[c])	TOTAL MEMBERSHIPS (ESTIMATED[d])
Ohio	1808		165	13,035	27,720
Pennsylvania	c. 1720		132	10,428	22,176
Indiana	1839		102	8058	17,136
Missouri	1856	1947	22	1738	3696
Wisconsin	1908	1925	20	1580	3360
Iowa	1840		19	1501	3192
Illinois	1829	1864	13	1027	2184
Michigan	1895		12	948	2016
New York	1833	1949	11	869	1048
Delaware	1915		6	474	1008
Tennessee	1872	1944	6	474	1008
Minnesota	c. 1890	1972	5	395	840
Kentucky	1958		5	395	840
Maryland	1772	1850	4	316	672
Kansas	1883		4	316	672
Oklahoma	1892		3	237	504
Virginia	1895	1942	1	79	168
Florida	1925		1	79	168
Arkansas[d]	1927	1976	—	—	—
Montana[d]	1903	1970	—	—	—
Nebraska[d]	1880	1975	—	—	—
Canada	1824		15	1185	2520
TOTAL			546	42,186	91,728

[a]Information supplied by David Luthy, Alymer, Ontario.

[b]J.A. Raber (1980).

[c]Data calculated using Hostetler's estimate of 79 baptized members and 168 total Amish individuals per church district (Hostetler, 1980:80–81). Cross, using data from Ohio, determined the number of baptized members to be 86 and the total membership per district to be 199 (1967:42). Smaller, less densely settled Amish communities have small church districts.

[d]Not listed in Raber (1980). Listed as having Amish community schools in *Blackboard Bulletin.* New settlements do not always have a complete church structure nor is the population as high as 79 baptized members per district.

[e]Hostetler (1980:100).

Demographic Characteristics

FERTILITY. Many people think of the Amish as a shrinking remnant whose days are numbered, but they are in actuality a growing church. Because the Amish do not proselytize, their growth depends primarily on biological increment combined with the ability to hold their children in the faith. The Old Order Amish have increased from a population of about 8200 in 1905 to 92,000 in 1980; from 43 church districts to 547 districts (Table 2). Household size varies from those married pairs who have no children to those having 15 children or more.

Studies of family size show that for completed families the average number of children born alive is about seven. This greatly exceeds the national average for white rural households. Cross (1967:108) reported the annual natural increase of the Holmes County, Ohio Amish population to be 3 percent, or a potential doubling of the population every 23 years. Assuming this growth rate to be representative and constant, it is interesting to compare the potential population growth of the Amish with the observed population growth. Taking the estimated 1920 population to be 13,900, the 1943 potential population would be 27,800, and the 1966 potential population would be 55,600. Hostetler (1980:81) gives the actual estimated total population for 1966 as 49,371. This would represent a loss to the church of possibly about 6000 individuals over a 46-year period and an observed increase of about 35,500. These estimates would indicate that the Amish are successful in perpetuating their own subculture.

Recent demographic studies of the Amish (Hostetler, E. Ericksen,

TABLE 2
Old Order Amish Population and Districts, 1905–1970

YEAR	POPULATION	NUMBER OF DISTRICTS
1905	8200	43
1920	13,900	83
1930	18,500	110
1940	25,800	154
1950	33,000	197
1960	43,000	258
1970	59,304	353
1980	91,900	547

SOURCES: Hostetler (1980:80) and Raber (1970, 1980).

J. Ericksen, and Huntington, 1977; J. Ericksen, E. Ericksen, Hostetler, and Huntington, 1979) have shown that there has been no reduction in Amish fertility over time; in fact, there may have been a slight increase in fertility. Sterility among Amish women appears to be lower than among the general American population. [Ever-married American women in the birth cohort 1922–1926 had a sterility rate of 7.5 percent while for ever-married Amish women in the birth cohort 1919–1928, it was 4.4 percent, and in the cohort 1928–1938, it was 2.6 percent (J. Ericksen, E. Ericksen, Hostetler, and Huntington, 1979:258)]. Twinning, which seems to be high, may be related to the longer reproductive history of Amish women and the larger number of children born—both of which factors seem to be related to frequency of twinning (Enders and Stern, 1948; Cross, 1967). Not only do the Amish continue to maintain a high birth rate with no indication of contraceptive practices but they are also successful in maintaining their grown children within the religious community. Detailed interviews with Amish women in Pennsylvania indicated that over 90 percent of their grown children remained Old Order Amish. [The 61 women interviewed had already produced a total of 385 grown children of whom 347 were Amish (Hostetler, E. Ericksen, J. Ericksen, and Huntington, 1977:39–40)]. An analysis of an Amish genealogy (Fisher, 1957) listing all the descendants of Christian Fisher, who was born in Pennsylvania in 1757, indicated that during the ensuing 200 years there had been no reduction in Old Order Amish fertility. However, there had been an average loss to the religious community (by individuals leaving the church) of about 22 percent (J. Ericksen, E. Ericksen, Hostetler, and Huntington, 1979:272). Given the high birth rate of the Amish, even if they sustained a loss of one-quarter of their children, they would still maintain a substantial growth rate.

The Amish have a high standard of living, good medical care, and prohibit birth control. Therefore, except for the relatively late age of marriage, their birth rate resembles that of nonindustrialized countries, while their death rate resembles that of industrialized countries. When plotted by age and sex, the Amish population forms a wide-based pyramid, with over half the Amish under 20 years of age. This is in contrast to the population pyramid of the American rural farm population, which has a relatively narrow base. Within the typical American farm population, there are a disproportionate number of old people in relation to young people. The demographic structure of the Amish makes it relatively easy for the youthful population to carry the burden of supporting the aged; there are many productive young people to care for the relatively few old people.

Divorce. The Old Order Amish are strictly monogamous. The individual's first commitment is to God; his second is to his spouse. There is no divorce, and under no circumstances may an Amishman remarry while his spouse is living. Except for widows, the head of the household is always a man. The rare unmarried farmer will have a sister or perhaps a married nephew who lives in his household and helps out.

Sexual Transgression. The Amish are strongly opposed to extramarital coitus, and any transgression must be confessed to the total membership of the church whether or not pregnancy results. The male and female have equal responsibility to confess fornication. However, after a period of punishment, during which the transgressor is under the ban, both repentant individuals are welcomed back into full church membership, and they are completely forgiven. Although pregnancy is not always considered sufficient reason to marry, if the couple decides to get married, an effort is made to have the wedding before the birth of the baby. The degree of community pressure to marry applied to a couple who has fornicated or conceived varies from one settlement to another. If the parents do not marry, the mother may keep the baby, or it may be adopted by an Amish couple.

Mate Selection. The Amish are endogamous; marriage must be "in the Lord," that is, within the church membership. Any Amish person who marries outside the church loses his membership and becomes non-Amish. Even within the Old Order Amish church there are breeding isolates resulting from preferred marriage patterns. Marriage between members of noncommuning churches is discouraged, and marriages tend to take place within one settlement or between closely related settlements. Although first-cousin marriages are forbidden, second-cousin marriages are common. The total Amish population has such a small genetic base that marriage partners are frequently as closely related as second and third cousins. Parents have considerable influence as to which group of young people within the settlement their children will "go with," for whom their children will work, and which communities they will visit. By this means young people are directed into preferred social groups and thereby into preferred marriages.

The Amish perceive the family as a religious and a social unit. Therefore, it is not surprising that Amish weddings are community affairs that fit into the general cycle of activity. The majority of weddings occur during the winter months after harvest and before spring planting—November and

December being the most popular months. In Lancaster County, Pennsylvania, over 90 percent of the weddings occur during these two months. Outside of the Lancaster County settlement, there seems to be an extension of the wedding season, with more couples being married in late winter. In Ohio, two-thirds of the weddings occur between October and January. Indiana, the least traditional settlement, has only a few more than half the weddings occurring during these four months. The variation in season of marriage may be related to the trend away from farming. Of the three communities, Indiana has the largest number of family heads engaged in nonfarming occupations. In addition to holding weddings at specific times of the year, almost all Amish weddings are on Thursday, with a few being held on Tuesday, and occasionally a second marriage may be incorporated into a Sunday church service. Thursday is the most convenient day of the week to hold an elaborate, daylong celebration, considering the prohibition against all unnecessary work on Sunday. Thursday gives the host family four days in which to "set up" for the wedding and two days to clean up afterward without infringing on Sunday.

Not only have wedding customs remained traditional, the age of marriage has also been relatively stable among the Amish for the past 50 years. (Huntington, 1956:897; J. Ericksen, E. Ericksen, Hostetler, and Huntington, 1979:257–258). The median age of first marriage for Amish women aged 45–49 in 1966 was 22.1, and 24.7 for their husbands.

SOCIAL STRUCTURE. All Amish communities are rural. Although there is a fairly wide variation in family income there are no extremes of poverty or affluence. The Amish in America have developed a distinctive social structure consisting of the settlement, the church district, the family, and the affiliation or network of communing church districts.

The settlement consists of all the Amish living in a given geographically contiguous area. A single Amish family cannot be considered to form a settlement; even a small group of Amish families is not considered to be a settlement until they organize a church district. There is a minimum size necessary for a settlement to be able to sustain itself. This size is related to the number of church officials in the settlement (there must be at least two) and to the distance from the nearest communing church district, as well as the actual number of families and the size of the families that make up the settlement. Those Amish who are isolated geographically and socially from other Amish for too long a period lose their Amish identity. The Amish realize this, and if a new settlement does not attract other Amish settlers quickly enough, it will disband. History shows that those individuals who remain where there is no organized church become absorbed into the surrounding culture (Umble, 1949).

A church district is composed of a contiguous cluster of Old Order Amish families who worship together. Typically, each church district has a bishop, two ministers, a deacon, and 25 to 35 nuclear families. The number of families is determined by the density of the Amish in the area and the size of the homes; when the group becomes too large to meet in a home or barn for the worship service, the district divides. The geographical area of a single church district is almost never settled exclusively by Amish. The area is crossed by paved roads, perhaps interrupted by a village, and is interspersed with "English" farms and homes. Although there are geographical boundaries, neither the Amish church district nor the Amish community is territorial; it is a cultural, social, and religious grouping. The community is not necessarily made up of one's neighbors but rather of one's fellow church members, who are bound together by an ideology and a way of life.

The family, rather than the individual, is the unit of the church. When one asks an Amishman how big his church district is, he always answers you by stating how many families belong, never by how many individual members there are. The *Ohio Amish Directory* lists the families in each district, with no indication as to which individuals have been baptized into the church; unmarried baptized members are not listed unless they own their own home. Growth of the church is related to number of weddings, not number of baptisms.

Due to the congregational structure and the strict rules of discipline, differences that may seem minor to the outsider often arise within the larger settlements. These differences are the basis of various affiliations. Church districts that are "in fellowship" with one another interpret the *Ordnung* (discipline) similarly and exchange ministers for Sunday services. All those churches whose ministers "help out" one another form a single affiliation. The affiliations are informal, often unknown to non-Amish, and frequently changing. The tendency is to divide into more affiliations rather than to coalesce. This functions to keep the groups small, to limit social interaction, and to protect tradition. In the central Ohio community there are at least seven different Old Order Amish affiliations that are not "in fellowship" with one another. These range along a conservative–liberal continuum from churches whose members will not ride in a private car (except to attend a funeral or go to the hospital) to churches in which young men drive cars until they actually join the church. Affiliations extend beyond settlement boundaries and, combined with kinship ties, help to bind different geographic Amish settlements together.

Kinship Relations

Kinship ties are maintained throughout the life of the individual. Excerpts from newsletters in *The Budget*, a weekly paper that goes to almost every Amish settlement, illustrate the importance of kinship ties both to the families and to the community (*The Budget*, August 7, 1973):

> The children grandchildren and great-grandchildren of Levi L. Slabach of Berlin were together for Sunday dinner at Bish. Roy L. Slabach's. All were present but three grandchildren. This was in honor of Levi's birthday which is August 6.
>
> Mother and us sisters were together at Benuel Stoltzfous, Jr. (sis. Mary). Mother Fisher is having quiltings this week and next to finish the quilts grandmother Fisher had started.

Extended families gather to celebrate birthdays and Christmas; brothers and sisters meet to work together, to help one another with church, to sew rags for woven rugs, to put up a milk house. And in the case of illness or any other stress, the extended family, the members of the church district, and other Amish neighbors rally round to help. Members of the Amish settlement are always identified by kinship groups. Husband and wife names are used together, Joe-Annie to signify Annie, the wife of Joe, or Annie-Joe meaning Joe, the husband of Annie; or the father's name is used, Menno's Annie to identify Annie, the daughter of Menno. Traditionally, the Amish children in Ohio were always given their father's first name as a middle initial to help identify them. In some settlements the initial of the mother's first name or maiden name is used for an identifying middle initial. There are generally so few last names in a given settlement that first names are used more frequently than last; thus, families are identified as "the Raymonds" and "the Aden Js" instead of "the Millers" and "the Detweilers." In the central Ohio Amish settlement 12 names account for 85 percent of the families. There are only 124 different Amish surnames found in a population of about 90,000. Therefore, it is not surprising that nicknames are also widely used to distinguish individuals: "Barefoot Sam" or "Turkey John." Individuals are always identified by their families, by their *Fruendschaft*.

Children in the Amish community schools introduce themselves by giving their father's first name. Young people quickly tell who their father and their mother are so that they can be placed genealogically. The signers of some Amish guest books are asked to indicate their date of birth and, if they are unmarried, to add their father's name. Kinship networks function to tie distant settlements together. Families visit married sons and daughters; brothers and sisters visit one another to "help out" or for a family get-together. Marriages, when outside the settlement, tend to take place between settlements that are closely related by kinship ties. Amish both publish and purchase genealogies, and family reunions are widely attended. *The Budget* has a section in the classified ads, "#23-Reunions," and in the late summer many of the columns from different communities mention reunions.

The kinship network, especially that involving parents of married children and brothers and sisters, plays a crucial role in establishing young Amish families on farms. In a study done in 1976 in Lancaster County, Pennsylvania, 76 percent of the young Amishmen who were farming had obtained their farm from relatives and the same percentage had obtained loans from family members. Seventy-four percent of the renters were renting land owned by relatives and only 10 percent were renting from non-Amish. The typical pattern is for an Amish couple to marry before obtaining a farm. For a short time the groom continues to work for wages, saving his money so he can rent a farm and, ideally, within a few years he buys his own farm. Although each nuclear family will eventually achieve economic independence, this is not expected of the newly married family. In spite of a strong community, Amish norms stress dependency on the family, especially on the extended family, for normal economic support. For catastrophic events, such as fire or unanticipated hospital expenses, the community supplements the kinship.

Family Roles

Roles are well defined in the Amish family. The man is the head of the woman (I Cor:3) as Christ is the head of the Church. Although the wife is to be subject to her husband, her first commitment is to God, and her second is to her husband. Because she has an immortal soul, she is an individual in her own right. She is not a possession of her husband, nor is she merely an extension of her spouse. Husband and wife become one flesh, a single unit separable only by God. She follows her husband, but only in that which is good. At council service before communion she decides, as an individual, if she is ready for communion. Should her husband transgress to the extent that he is placed under the ban, she, too, will shun him, as he will her in a similar situation. For the Amishman, the question of sacrificing his family for his job never comes up. The family comes first. A job is of no intrinsic importance; it is necessary because it supplies the economic basis for the family. The work of the household should provide vocational education for the children and fulfill the biblical standard, "In the sweat of thy face shalt thou eat bread." The wife's relative position is illustrated by her position in church, where she has an equal vote but not an equal voice. Farms are owned in the name of both husband and wife. Important family decisions are made jointly. Unlike the corporation wife, the Amish wife participates actively in any decision to move to a different locality. And unlike the corporation wife, the Amish farm wife makes an active contribution to the production of the household. She may help with the farm work, produce most of the salad material and vegetables consumed by her family, make more than half the clothing, help with the butchering, preserve much of the meat that they eat, and perhaps make soap, in addition to producing an average of seven children who in turn help with the farm work. Thus she has an essential role in the economic survival of the family and of the Amish community. Although Amish women appear docile and submissive, this does not mean that their contribution is not valued. Nor do they have a low self-esteem. Most Amishwomen are happy in their role and confident about the contribution they make to the family. In response to a formal interview question as to how much money she had made last year, an Amish wife would sometimes list one-half of her husband's income from the farm saying, "We're in it together. We're partners." [Abigail Mueller in Hostetler, E. Ericksen, J. Ericksen, and Huntington (1977:107).]

Parents present a united front to their children and to the community. In dealing with their children, Amish parents should be of one mind, discussing any differences privately and prayerfully. Admonitions to parents in sermons and in Amish writings are directed not to fathers as such, or to mothers alone, but to parents. Couples are never to disagree in public. The wife is expected to support her husband in all things, especially in his relationship with other people, whether it be their children, their parents, or friends and neighbors. The husband, in turn, should be considerate of his wife with respect to her physical, emotional, and spiritual well-being. The ideal is to be individuals to one another, making decisions jointly, and to be of one mind to all others.

The major role of Amish adults is childrearing. Parents of growing children have no individual rights, only responsibilities and obligations for the correct nurture of their children. They are to be examples to their children in all things, so that the children may become good Amish and eventually, through the grace of God, achieve life everlasting.

The role of the children within the family is more closely related to age than to sex. The older children are to care for and help the younger, while the younger are to obey the older in any reasonable demand. Older children do not physically punish younger children but cajole them into obeying. Although there is a division of labor by sex, children help one another and their parents as they are needed rather than strictly dividing the work by sex.

On the small, labor-intensive farms the children make a major economic contribution. Typically a child is not paid for his labor until he is 21 and if he works away from home his wages are returned to his father until he reaches that age. In turn, the parents try to set up each child in farming. Austerity must be practiced by the whole family in order to help the next generation become established economically. Children do not have a low status, although they are expected to be obedient and polite to those older than they. They are highly valued as "the only possessions we can take to heaven with us," and also, as contributors to the family, both economically and emotionally. Children function as socializing agents for the parents for as parents strive to be good examples for their children, they become better Amish themselves.

Grandparents, as parents of young married couples, have an important role in the Amish community. They are often instrumental in helping their married children get established on farms. They have a great influence as to where their children will settle. They help the young people with advice, labor, materials, and loans. Very often, the parents own the land onto which the young couple moves. The parents support their grown children with frequent visits. In Lancaster County, almost 90 percent of the parents saw all of their grown children at least once a month—in a culture in which car ownership is forbidden. Grandparents act as a buffer between the young couple and "the world." They help with labor and supply information as to where within the community the young couple can get produce they do not yet grow themselves. They teach the young family about community networks and help them interact within the community. And, as the young couple's children become old enough to help with the labor, the supportive role of the grandparents diminishes, but they continue to advise and admonish. At some stage the older couple will retire from farming, passing the farm on to one of the children and, depending on his age, the grandfather may run a small business of his own, for a few years.

Social Class and Life-style

The Amish are a small, homogeneous group within which social class has no meaning. They are exclusively rural, operating small family farms and, in some instances, working in small nonunion factories or on small carpenter crews. In relation to the outside society, these occupations would probably place them in the rural working class. Although there is considerable range in family income, and some families have a higher status than others, there are no class distinctions within the community, and lifestyle is as important as income level. No matter what the income, the need to accumulate capital to buy land for the next generation reinforces the simple living patterns prescribed by the *Ordnung.* Family farming is both the typical and the ideal occupation for a head of household with growing children. In each Amish settlement of any size there are Amishmen who own small businesses that are related to farming and the Amish way of life. Thus there will be a blacksmith, a harness maker, a buggy shop, a shop for adapting tractor-drawn farm equipment to horse-drawn, and specialized carpenters who do cabinet work and make the Amish coffins. The Amish build and remodel their own homes and barns with the help of Amish construction crews. There are Amishmen who can draw up plans, lay brick, and install plumbing. Due to the increasing cost and scarcity of land, a growing number of Amish are accepting employment in small, nonunion factories that have sprung up in Amish areas: aluminum plants, small sawmills, trailer factories, and brick yards. Farming continues to be the preferred occupation. Many types of employment are forbidden as incompatible with their way of life. Nevertheless, a growing number of Amish heads of households are working in nonfarming occupations.

The Amish life-style is distinctive and consciously maintained. In an effort to build a "church without spot or blemish" and to remain a "peculiar people," strict disciplinary codes have been developed and are observed by members and their children. Most of these rules are unwritten, vary slightly from one church district to another, and are only completely known to participants. Most of the rules are taken for granted, but those pertaining to borderline issues, about which there might possibly be some disagreement, are reviewed twice a year by all baptized members of the church district. This allows for slow, orderly change in details of their lifestyle that is necessary for group survival. Only if consensus on the rules (*Ordnung*) is achieved, and if there is a unanimous expression of peace and good will toward every fellow member, is communion celebrated. Most church districts reach this degree of integration twice a year.

The Old Order Amish style of life is characterized by separation from the world, voluntary acceptance of high social obligation, symbolized by adult baptism, the practice of exclusion and shunning of transgressing members, and a nurturing attitude in harmony with nature and maintained on a human scale. The Amish interpret separation from the world quite literally. They have a distinctive dress, somewhat similar to that worn by European peasants of several centuries ago. They speak a distinctive language—an Amish form of Pennsylvania Dutch—that separates them from outsiders. Physically, too, they prefer to have some distance between themselves and non-Amish, between their households and non-Amish households. "Be ye not unequally yoked together with unbelievers; for what fellowship hath righteousness with unrighteousness? and what communion hath light with darkness?" (II Cor. 6:14). The Amish may not be union members or form partnerships with non-Amish, for both would join the believer with the unbeliever. In spite of this created distance, the Amish are not self-righteous nor judgmental in their relations with outsiders, whom they consider to be so different that the same criterion of conduct does not apply to them as it would to a fellow Amishman. "My kingdom is not of this world; if my kingdom were of this world, then would my servants fight" (John 18:36). Observing this teaching, the Amish may not serve in the military. Formerly, if they were called, they paid fines or served prison sentences; now they perform alternative service as conscientious objectors. All forms of retaliation to hostility are forbidden. An Amishman may not physically defend himself or his family even when attacked. He may not defend himself legally even when his civil rights have been violated. He is taught to follow the New Testament teaching of the Sermon on the Mount and the biblical example of Isaac. After the warring Philistines had stopped up all the wells of his father Abraham, Isaac moved to new lands and dug new wells (Genesis, 26:15–18). The Amish take this advice, and when they cannot remain separate from the world according to their own definition of separate, they move to new locations.

The adult Amishman voluntarily accepts a high degree of social obligation. His willingness to take on this responsibility is symbolized by the rite of baptism. Prior to baptism the future communicant renounces the world, the devil, his own flesh and blood, and acknowledges Christ as the Son of God and the Lord and Savior. He accepts a personal willingness to suffer persecution or death in order to maintain the faith. In addition, he promises to abide by the *Ordnung* and not to depart from the discipline in life or death. Each young man promises to accept the duties of minister should the lot ever fall on him. Applicants are warned not to make these promises if they cannot keep them, for once made, there is no turning back. It is not unusual for young people, during the period of instruction, to drop out. Generally they join a year or two later. No one may be married in the Amish church without first being baptized.

When deemed necessary, the Amish use excommunication and shunning (*Bann und Meidung*) to enforce the discipline and to keep the church pure and separate from the world. The full church membership participates in the decision and in the ceremony, in which the erring one is rebuked before all and purged out as a leaven. An Amishman in good standing may receive no favors from an excommunicated person; he may neither buy from nor sell to him, nor may he eat at the same table with the excommunicated person. The ban applies also between husband and wife, who may neither eat at the same table nor sleep in the same bed. The *Bann und Meidung* is used both to protect the individual and to protect the church. An erring member is shunned in order to help him realize the gravity of his sin and his need to return to the church. It is also used as a necessary step in the process of forgiveness, and thus helps the individual deal with guilt. The *Bann und Meidung* serves to protect the church by removing, both from ceremonial and social participation in the community, those individuals who will not follow the *Ordnung,* thus protecting the true believers from disruptive influence and temptations to modify their lifestyle. In some communities, individuals that leave the Old Order Amish to join other Amish churches are put under a limited ban and are no longer shunned forever. These individuals generally maintain kinship ties.

The Amish have an attitude of nurturance for their land, their children, and their people. The Amish nurturing lifestyle is in harmony with nature and functions to keep "the machine out of the garden." Wendel Berry (1978:7–8) contrasts the exploiter or individual who considers land a commodity with the nurturer, who considers land a trust.

> The standard of the exploiter is efficiency; the standard of the nurturer is care. The exploiter's goal is money, profit; the nurturer's goal is health—his land's health, his own, his family's, his community's. . . . Whereas the exploiter asks of a piece of land only how much and how quickly it can be made to produce, the nurturer asks a question that is much more complex and difficult: What is its carrying capacity? (That is: How much can be taken from it without diminishing it? What can it produce *dependably* for an indefinite time?) The exploiter wishes to earn as much as possible by as little work as possible; the nurturer expects, certainly, to have a decent living from his work, but his characteristic wish is to work *as well* as possible. The competence of the exploiter is in organization; that of the nurturer is in order—a human order, that is, that accommodates itself both to other order and to mystery. The exploiter typically serves an institution or organization; the nurturer serves land, household, community, place. The exploiter thinks in terms of numbers, quantities, "hard facts"; the nurturer in terms of character, condition, quality, kind.

The prohibition against electricity holds the Amish work day to the solar day. The Amish home has neither air conditioning nor central heating, yet by modifying their daily routine, they manage to live comfortably with the changing seasons, relatively oblivious of energy crises. They do not exploit their environment, but care for it. The pea pods are put back on the garden, not thrown down a garbage disposal. There is a human scale to all of Amish life. Within the settlement distances are not too great, social groups are not too big, farms can be managed by a single family, and Amish schools have one or, at the most, two rooms. People know one another and identify with the physical environment in which they worship, live, and work. After a day visiting in a large city, an Amish farmer commented as we turned off the highway onto an unpaved road in his home county, "I know myself around here." He is the very antithesis of alienation.

By exercising a personal and a community discipline that excludes those who will not follow the dictates of the group and that stresses a voluntary commitment to a nurturing life in harmony with nature and socially separated from the outside culture, the Amish have been able to determine to a remarkable extent the style of their lives.

Family Life Cycle and the Socialization Process

The goal of the Amish family is the achievement of eternal life for each member. On an existential level, the goal is to teach children right from wrong, to be socially responsible as defined by the Amish community, to join the Amish church, and to remain faithful in the *Ordnung* until death.

In Amish society, a person passes through a series of six distinct age categories or stages of socialization as he progresses through life. Different behavior is demanded of him at each stage. The stages are: infancy, preschool children, school children, young people, adulthood, and old folks. [For a more detailed treatment of socialization, see Hostetler and Huntington (1971)]. Infancy covers the period from birth until the child walks. Children of this age are generally referred to as "babies." Preschool children are referred to as "little children;" they know how to walk but have not yet started school, which is generally entered at age 6 or 7. School children are called "scholars" by the Amish. They are fulfilling the eight years of elementary schooling required by the state. They attend either public schools or Amish schools and are between the ages of 6 and 16. Young people are in the period between school (completed at 14 to 16, depending on the state) and marriage. Adults are traditionally married. An unmarried woman, no matter what her age, is referred to as "an older girl." Old folks have all their children married or independent, and they generally live in a "Dawdy House," the grandfather house on the "home place."

INFANCY. Babies are enjoyed by the Amish; they are believed to be gentle, responsive, and secure within the home and the Amish community, but vulnerable when out in the world. Babies are not scolded or punished, and there is no such thing as a bad baby, although there may be a difficult baby. A baby may be enjoyed without fear of self-pride, for he is a gift from God and not primarily an extension of the parents. If he cries, he is in need of comfort, not discipline. It is believed that a baby can be spoiled by wrong handling, especially by nervous, tense handling, but the resultant irritability is the fault of the environment, not the baby; he remains blameless. Old Order Amish parents give generous attention to their babies' needs, both physical and social. An Amish baby is born into a family and into a community. He is never spoken of as "a little stranger" but is welcomes as a "new woodchopper" or a "little dishwasher." Each baby is greeted happily as a contribution to the security of the family and the church.

CHILDHOOD. Amish children are taught to respect authority, and respect is shown by obedience. The Amish do not strive for blind obedience but for obedience based on love and on the belief that those in authority have deep concern for one's welfare and know what is best. Most traditional Amish parents teach obedience by being firm and consistent rather than by violent confrontations or single instances of breaking the child's will. The switch is used freely but not harshly. The prevailing attitude is matter-of-fact rather than moralistic in dealing with their children. Not only is the child taught to respect and obey those in authority, but he also learns to care for those younger and less able than he, to share with others, to do what he is taught is right, and to avoid that which is wrong, to enjoy work, and to fulfill his work responsibilities pleasantly. The parents create a safe environment for their children. They live separated from the world, maintaining the boundary for their children that protects them from malevolent influence. The parent has the responsibility to punish transgressions but also the power to forgive. Punishment is used primarily to ensure the safety of the child: for his physical safety ("stay away from that nervous horse"), for his cultural safety ("be respectful to older people"), for his legal safety ("don't fish without a fishing license"), for his moral safety ("be obedient"). Rewards are used to develop the right attitudes in the child: humility, forgiveness, admission of error, sympathy, responsibility, and appreciation of work. Children are motivated primarily by concern for other people and not by fear of punishment.

Although children are primarily the responsibility of their parents, the community plays an important part in their socialization. Families attend church as a unit every other Sunday. The children sit through the long service, learning to be considerate of others, quiet, and patient. Until they are about 9 years old, the girls sit with the mothers or grandmothers, and the boys with their fathers. After the service, the children share in the community meal, and the youngest may nap on a big bed with other babies. The rest of the time the children play freely and vigorously about the house and yard, safe in the presence of many adults who care for them and guide them. If a small child suddenly feels lost, someone quickly returns him to a member of his family. The Amish child experiences the community as being composed of people like his parents, all of whom know him and direct him. He is comfortable and secure within the encompassing community. In many settlements the community also participates in the socialization of the child through the Amish "parochial" school, which supports the teaching of the home.

Throughout his childhood the Amish child spends the greatest part of his time interacting with members of his family. Unlike the typical suburban school child, the Amish child is usually in a mixed age group rather than isolated with his peers (Bronfenbrenner, 1970:96–102). The Amish child's parents and siblings play a central role in his development. Although the Amish generally consider childhood to end with the graduation of the child from the eighth grade or on his 16th birthday, they do not feel that their task as parents is even near completion. The desired end product will not be achieved until much later.

YOUNG PEOPLE. The age category known by the Amish as "young people" covers the years between 14 or 16 and marriage. It corresponds roughly to adolescence. This is the most individualistic period in the life of an Amishman or Amishwoman and is considered to be the most dangerous. If an individual is to become Amish, he must be kept within the Amish community, physically and emotionally, during his crucial adolescent years. Yet at this time the family's control of the young person is somewhat limited, the community's control is informal, and the lure of the world is most strong.

During adolescence the peer group is of supreme importance, for during these years more of the Amish young person's socialization takes place within this group than within the family or the church. If the young person's peer group remains Amish, he has a reference point, a buffer, and a support. Even though as an individual or as a member of this Amish peer group he transgresses many rules and crosses most of the boundaries between the Amish community and the world, he will eventually return to the church to become a lifelong Amishman. However, if during this stage he makes "English" friends and identifies with an alien peer group, even though he is well behaved, he will probably leave the Amish church, never to return.

A certain degree of adolescent rebellion has become institutionalized among the Amish. The Amish child is raised in a carefully protected environment by relatively authoritarian parents. However, during this stage, the young Amish person will make the two most important commitments of his life: He will decide if and when to join the church and whom to marry. Both of these commitments he must make as an individual, albeit an individual who has the help of God, the concern of his parents, and the support of the community. In order to make such important decisions, he must establish a degree of independence from his family, and to some extent from his community, in order to develop his own identity. This is done in many ways, most of them carefully institutionalized. The family relaxes some of its tight control over the young person. He goes to social gatherings of his peers rather than having all of his social life with the family. The young person is learning what it means to be Amish. He may test some of the boundaries of the Amish community, sampling the world by such means as owning a radio, having his photograph taken, attending a movie, and occasionally wearing clothes that are outside the *Ordnung*. As long as these forays into worldliness remain discreet, they are ignored by the parents and the community, for it is believed that the young person should have some idea of the world he is voluntarily rejecting. One of the reasons courtship is secretive is that it is a means of achieving privacy in a closely knit community and within a large family. The young person is protected by a degree of institutionalized blindness on the part of adults, who thereby give him freedom—within safe boundaries.

The community indirectly counteracts youthful rebelliousness by providing social activities and vocational training for the adolescents. The Sunday evening singing is an important social event in most Amish settlements. Young people generally begin attending when they have finished day school and are about 16 years old. The family that "has church" has "singing" for the young people in the evening. Generally brothers and sisters go together to the singing, although they frequently return home in couples. In some of the larger settlements there will be Saturday night singing, or the young man may visit his girlfriend in her home. Weddings, wiener roasts, and work bees, will provide occasions for the young people to gather.

Proper vocational training is essential if the young person is to become an Amish Christian. Both the young Amishman and young Amishwoman work for a number of different people during these years, learning various acceptable vocational roles and, through their jobs, gaining a knowledge of other Amish families and other Amish settlements, and sometimes even a glimpse of the world by working for "English" people. The skills the Amish need are best learned by doing, and they have worked out an informal community apprentice system that serves the needs of the individual and the culture.

The relative freedom to test the boundaries of his culture, to make mistakes, to become aware of human weakness, counterbalanced by the individual's growing ability to be economically productive, and perhaps his interest in marriage, all function to make him think seriously about joining the church. When he finally makes this commitment in his late teens or early twenties, the parents have fulfilled their moral duty to the child, to the church, and to God. However, although in a theological sense they have completed their task as parents, in practice the parent–child relationship continues. Marriage, which even more than baptism is considered the beginning of adulthood, modifies the parent–child relationship but does not basically change it.

ADULTHOOD. Marriage is the beginning of social adulthood, but full adulthood is attained with parenthood. The adult Amish are responsible for the maintenance of their culture. They produce the children, who are expected to become Amish, they raise them in such a way that they want to become Amish, and they teach them the skills and attitudes that will enable them to remain Amish. The adult Amish watch over the boundaries of their culture, participating in the selective acculturation that is necessary for their survival as "a visible church of God" in twentieth century America. Economically they must be sufficiently successful to support a large family and to help their children become economically independent after a few years of marriage. The Old Order Amish community is economically self-sufficient, and church members do not accept social security or welfare. Socially they are also self-sufficient, caring for those who are ill and old within the community. The adult Amishman or woman has no set retirement age. Retirement is voluntary, usually gradual, and related to the individual's health and the needs of his family. It generally takes place some time after the youngest child is married and has started to raise a family.

OLD FOLKS. Old folks normally signify their retirement by moving into the grandfather house adjacent to the main farmhouse. This may occur while the grandfather is still young and vigorous, but he moves to a new occupation, such as running a shoe repair shop, in order to free the land for his child. With retirement or semiretirement the role of the parents is modified, but still continues, for the old people remain physically and emotionally close to their children and grandchildren. The young farmer discusses problems of farm management and sales prices with his father; the young mother asks advice about the children. The old folks still engage in the process of helping their youngest children become established economically.

Also, the old people have an increased obligation to attend funerals and to visit the sick and bereaved. When they are ill, members of the community visit them. As long as health permits, old folks spend a considerable amount of time visiting children, nieces, nephews, and friends in different parts of the settlement and in other settlements. They form an important link in the network of informal communication that ties the larger Amish community together. They are often reliable sources of news, as well as of local history and of genealogical relationships. They exert a conservative influence as they fulfill their accepted roles of admonishing the young. As they grow older, and perhaps become senile or bedridden, they are still cared for at home, sometimes by one child, often, with the children taking turns having them in their homes. With a large number of children available, this responsibility can be more easily shared.

Typically, dying takes place in the home, the person surrounded by family and friends—not in the lonely, impersonal, mechanical environment of a hospital (*The Budget*, August 2, 1973):

> On June 19th she . . . was admitted and put under oxygen. . . . She seemed to be losing out fast, as she had to labor to breathe even with oxygen. On Fri. we pleaded to go home. So arrangements were made with an ambulance to take her home, she being under oxygen all the while.
>
> . . . At daybreak in the mornings for the last 3 mornings were her hardest and on the morning at 4:45 of the 26th of June she easily and peacefully faded away.

When death occurs, neighbors and nonrelatives relieve the family of all work responsibility, leaving the relatives free for meditation and conversation with the guests who come to see their departed friend and to talk to the bereaved family. Funerals, especially of elderly people, are large, and often 500 mourners may be present. After burial in an Amish graveyard, the mourners return to the house of the decreased for a meal. With this meal, normal relationships and responsibilities are restored. The family circle has been broken by death, but the strong belief in eternal life indicates that the break is only temporary.

CHANGE AND ADAPTATION

The rapid social changes since the Depression have broken down the isolation of the Amish. Specific threats to their community structure and family organization have been posed by (1) social security, (2) consolidation of elementary and junior high schools, (3) lengthening of the compulsory-attendance period and consequent required high school attendance, (4) conscription, and (5) scarcity of farmland. Minor, more subtle threats are the availability of motorcycles and cars, the cheapness and small size of transistor radios and phonographs, televisions blaring in every store, the ease of travel, and the use of telephones. These are all dangers inherent in our technologically sophisticated mass culture. Technological competition for land use and invasion of farmland also pose problems. In Lancaster County urban uses are pressing hard on land once available for farming. In Ohio, Amish communities have moved because of the intrusion of power plants and the risk that high power transmission lines may be strung across Amish farms, bringing onto Amish family lands noise pollution, corona discharge, the danger of electrical shock, and intrusive personnel who patrol the lines to spray herbicides and perform other maintenance chores. A specific threat to the Amish young people is variants of the Billy Graham type of religious fundamentalism. Fundamentalist radio programs are one of the means for introducing these dissident ideas into the community; local revival meetings are another. The more liberal branches of the Mennonite church also offer a ladder to those who want to climb into "higher" churches step by step, changing their life-style more than their theology.

SOCIAL SECURITY. Although the five above-mentioned specific threats to the Amish culture have been somewhat mitigated during the past few years, in every instance certain Amish bore the brunt of the encroachment by the state and paid fines, spent time in prison, and moved to other localities. The Amish do not believe in life insurance or old-age insurance. They live separate from the state, which they will support with taxes but not with their vote or with their lives. They believe that the Christian brotherhood should care for its own, and they are forbidden by the *Ordnung* to accept any form of survivors' insurance. Because they do not and will not accept social security payments from the state, they refuse to pay the social security tax to the state. After years of conflict, during which some Amish witnessed the sale of their horses and farms at public auction, the Amish were finally granted an exemption from the self-employment social security tax. This was a crucial issue for the Amish because both their family and their church structure, with the strong emphasis on social responsibility, would be weakened by reliance on outside funds.

ELEMENTARY SCHOOLING. The Amish in many settlements have responded to school consolidation and to rapid changes in the rural American culture by withdrawing further from the mainstream (see Table 3). It is not that they want to be more different from their non-Amish neighbors; it is that they do not want to change so rapidly; they want to keep the old ways. Large, modern consolidated schools are not suitable agents of socialization for the Amish child. Many of the Amish children still attend public schools. Some of these are rural schools that were not caught in the net of consolidation, some are relatively small village schools, and some are large, sprawling elementary schools. When their children attend public school,

TABLE 3

Amish Community Schools 1979–1980[a]

STATE	DATE OF FOUNDING OF OLDEST SCHOOL	NUMBER OF SCHOOLS	NUMBER OF TEACHERS	NUMBER OF PUPILS	SCHOOLS NOT REPORTING ENROLLMENT
Pennsylvania	1938	146	150	4022	
Ohio	1947	97	132	3235	
Indiana	1951	58	99	2423	
Wisconsin	1960	26	28	594	
Missouri	1950	26	29	581	
Iowa	1966	20	28	439	
New York	1949	14	17	398	3
Michigan	1960	12	14	254	1
Delaware	1925	6	10	211	
Tennessee	1975	7	7	187	
Illinois	1966	6	11	160	
Maryland	1967	4	4	135	
Kentucky	1969	3	5	130	
Minnesota	1975	8	8	44	4
Arkansas	1975	1	1	15	
Montana	1976	1	1	14	
Nebraska	1978	1	1	11	
Ontario	1953	18	24	476	—
Totals		447	561	13,293	8

[a]Amish community schools listed by state. Number of pupils given only for schools reporting enrollment (*Blackboard Bulletin* (November) 1979:11–22).

the parents attempt to isolate its influence and to counteract the disruption it may cause. Over half of the Amish children attend community schools designed, built, and staffed by members of their own church. In 1979–1980, there were 447 parochial schools with an enrollment of over 13,000 children. These schools were located in 17 states and in Canada (*Blackboard Bulletin,* November 1979). In the community schools the Amish children learn the three Rs in an environment in which they are protected from the assumptions of twentieth-century America, in which they can learn discipline, humility, simple living, and cooperation. The Amish schools emphasize shared knowledge rather than individual knowledge, the dignity of tradition rather than the importance of progress. The Amish schools do not teach religion, rather a style of living. The school's task is to cooperate with the parents to preserve the faith taught by the parents, for it is the role of the family, not of the school or even the church, to make Amish Christians of the children. The Amish family constellation will change if the school-age children cannot participate in the ongoing work of the home and farm. When the children are removed from the home for many hours each day, as is the case when they must spend long hours on the bus in addition to the hours spent in class, when the school year interferes with the agricultural season, and when the children are physically and ideologically removed from their community, they cannot be taught the skills and attitudes needed to become Amish.

COMPULSORY HIGH SCHOOL ATTENDANCE. High school attendance is no longer a problem for the Old Order Amish because the Supreme Court ruling of May 15, 1972, protects the religious freedom of the Amish by permitting Amish children who have graduated from the eighth grade to participate in community-based vocational programs in lieu of attending high school. The students spend half a day a week in school under the direction of a teacher and four-and-a-half days working in a modified apprentice system, generally under the direction of their parents. They learn technological skills in a social context as participants in the economy of the community. While working on a family farm, Amish children of high school age learn not only how to perform a task, such as how to harrow, but also when to harrow, and how to integrate harrowing into all the other work that is required of the vocation "farmer." They also learn wider community work roles by helping in threshing rings and at barn raisings, getting ready for church, and helping care for neighbors' children. Of great importance to the success of the Amish vocational training is the fact that the vocational expectations of the young people coincide with the vocational opportunities available to them.

CONSCRIPTION. Since the beginning of World War II the draft has taken young men outside of the Amish community at a most vulnerable stage in their development. The I-W program, which provided an alternative to military service, functioned in such a manner that young Amishmen spent two years outside the community, often alone in a city, perhaps wearing non-Amish clothing while at work. These measures separate the young men from community control and to a limited extent made them non-Amish. The draft was never incorporated into the Amish lifestyle. It interfered with two of the most important rites of passage among the Amish: baptism and marriage. Baptism signifies total commitment to the believing church community, physically and spiritually separated from the world. If the drafted young man were baptized before his alternative service, he could not live physically separated from the world as he was pledged to do. If he were not baptized before his service, he had not committed himself to the church community and so was more vulnerable to outside influence. Was it best for a young man to marry before, during, or after his alternative service? If he went into the world without a wife, he might form friendships with non-Amish girls, and because marriage must be with a coreligionist, such friendships were dangerous. If he had a wife, she helped protect him from worldly influences, but they started their married life with modern conveniences, electricity, and telephones, which were hard to give up when they returned to an Amish way of life. During I-W or alternative service, both the Amishmen and their wives learned non-Amish work patterns, and many received training they could never use on an Amish farm.

The most traditional Amish refused even alternative service when it required them to live in a city or to wear non-Amish garb. As one Amish father explained, "God did not mean for the Amish to take the way of I-W service. It is better for the Amish to go to prison, though it is hard. God is with them there." At the time of writing, the selective service act is still in effect and registration for selective service is required. It is not clear presently whether the draft will once again disrupt the lives of young men. Certainly the Amish community will continue to be affected by the experiences of those young men who have already spent two years outside the protective boundaries of their culture.

SCARCITY OF LAND. The Amish prohibition against contraception, their positive attitude toward high fertility, and their insistence on labor-intensive, diversified family farming as the ideal means of livelihood, coupled with the belief that all one's grown children should settle near the parents (ideally within two miles) places tremendous pressure on farmland in and near Amish communities—even if there are not competing uses for the land. The rate of growth of the Amish community has been increasing while the limits of farmland available are finite. This is especially true for the Lancaster County Amish. They constitute the oldest Amish community in the country, having settled on land along major transportation routes between the expanding urban centers of Philadelphia and Harrisburg. They must compete with factories, shopping centers, and tourism as well as with one another. The Amish in Lancaster have responded to this problem by paying increasingly high prices for their land, subdividing their farms, establishing new communities in other parts of the state (often on poorer farmland), occasionally moving to other Amish communities outside the state, and, less acceptably, leaving the Old Order to join other branches of the church that do not put such a high premium on farming. Very few of the individual families in any state who leave the Amish church are successfully engaged in labor-intensive, general farming at the time they leave. Some Amish young people never join the church, but in Lancaster, it is more typical for young Amish to join the church, marry, start a family, and then leave.

In a detailed analysis of the Lancaster Amish population conducted in 1976 (Hostetler, E. Ericksen, J. Ericksen, and Huntington, 1977) it was determined that the rate of leaving was not related to a breakdown of family ties but was more closely related to the economic success of the parents which, because it was accompanied by austere living patterns, contributes to the likelihood of the younger generation becoming established in labor-intensive, family farming (E. Ericksen, J. Ericksen, and Hostetler, 1980). Among the Lancaster Amish, heads of households who are farmers are generally more successful economically than those who have other types of employment (except for a few of the self-employed Amish businessmen). Heads of households who are farmers are considered the most successful by their fellow churchmen for they are able to practice a style of life consistent with Amish values. Among a sample of Lancaster Amish it was observed that the likelihood of leaving the Old Order Amish was five times as great for children of nonfarmers as for children of farmers. This would indicate that there is a connection between the survival and growth of the Amish subculture and the ability of the parents, and to some extent the community, to get their young adults established in farming. Lack of farmland bodes ill for the community. But as it becomes more expensive to get established on a farm, more family heads look for other types of suitable employment. Near Amish and Mennonite settlements, small factories have been built to take advantage of the cheap (nonunion), skilled, reliable labor supply. The trend from farming to nonfarming occupations may have a profound effect on the Amish culture. The Amish family and Amish patterns of childrearing are built on the concept of shared parental responsibility, on the expectation that both parents work together caring for the farm and the children, that both parents are almost always in the home and available to support one another and to guide and teach their children. For example, family devotions are led by the father, but it is difficult to have these when the father has to punch a timeclock rather than being able to adjust his farm chores to the sleeping patterns of his growing family. The authority patterns within the family change when the father is absent during most of the day. A sick baby or a fussy three-year old are minor inconveniences when both parents are available. On an Amish farm the boys spend most of the time, when they are awake and not in school, working with or under the direction of their father. In no other occupation can the father so consistently teach, instruct, admonish, and correct his children.

The social structure of the Amish community is based on the availability of brethren and sisters to gather for work bees, for barn raisings, for daylong weddings, and daylong funerals. The Amish share labor within the family, between families, and among church members whenever there is extra or special work to be done. This combination of mutual aid and social interaction keeps the community strong and of one mind. This interaction can be relatively easily achieved in a church district in which most of the household heads are farmers; it is almost impossible when most of the men work in factories or on construction crews. The traditional Amish culture is dependent on both parents working in the home, that is, being available to each other and to the children and to the community any hour of the day, on any day of the week. Although the Amish are tied to the American market system, their culture mitigates these ties and functions to isolate the Amishman by circumscribing his economic options in such a way that the Amish family-centered culture can be perpetuated both socially and physically.

OTHER AREAS OF CHANGE AND ADAPTATION. The *Ordnung* protects the Amish from the encroachment of technology, from a throwaway mentality, and from the overstimulation of the individual (Toffler, 1970). The *Ordnung* further specifically forbids members to have highline electricity, which means that all electrical conveniences, from clothes dryers to vacuum cleaners to toasters, are unavailable. All musical instruments are forbidden, and radios and television sets can come under this prohibition. Telephones connect one with the outside world and "cause women to waste time," because "you can work and talk when you are both in the same room, but neither of you can work while talking on the telephone." In addition, telephones within the home intrude into the family, disrupting meals, work, and conversation.

Cars, and to a lesser degree motorcycles, are threatening because they enable people to travel too far, too fast, and to go beyond the face-to-face community in which everyone is known and everyone is noticed. Movies are forbidden but offer little threat to the community because there is no interest in them; they are too far from the individual's experience and value system to do more than elicit passing curiosity. In many ways the Amish culture is oral rather than literary, and though they have kept out the medium, and along with it the message (McLuhan, 1962), they are not really threatened by the printed word, by radio, or even by television. Consistent with the oral tradition, the Amish stress shared knowledge and the importance of meaningful social interaction. They are so far outside the mainstream of American culture that they have little shared knowledge with the average American citizen and little reason to interact socially with him. The area in which they may be the most vulnerable is that of religious fundamentalism, for here the familiarity with the Bible gives a degree of shared knowledge that may open the way for outside influence. Although the Amish are relatively immune to changes in their world view and basic thought patterns, they are more open to change in the area of economics. They know they must survive economically in order to survive culturally, but they also believe that it is better to suffer economic and physical hardship than to lose their unique religious orientation. There is more pressure to accept telephones and electricity than to permit radios and movie attendance. Those aspects of the outside culture that can enhance Amish family life and can reinforce community ties and community economic strength are tempting and will continue to be accepted if they can be incorporated without changing the family roles or the social structure and without permitting encroachment of worldly ideas and worldly ways.

During the 250 years the Amish have been in America they have successfully obtained good farmland that would produce high yields on small acreage when cultivated intensively by a large nuclear family. Farms needed to be small and of high quality in order to be worked by one family and to support a relatively dense farming population so that the characteristic social structure, stressing strong kinship and community ties and isolation from the surrounding culture, could be established and maintained. During these 250 years the Amish have successfully resisted the lures of mass consumption and mass communication, they have maintained their emphasis on limited gratification and limited consumption, stressing economy, savings, and cash payments. While the urban villagers of Boston argue that money earned should be spent immediately to make daily life more pleasant, because "life is too short for any other way of behavior" (Gans, 1962:187), the Amish argue that "no one would want such a beautiful home here on this earth if they hoped for heavenly home after this time" (*Family Life*, June 1973:11). Life is too short to risk losing one's soul just for comfort or pleasure. "Only one life, t'will soon be past; Only what's done for Christ will last."

The Amish stress on the individual's total commitment to God, thus his responsibility to live according to the Amish *Ordnung*, has enabled the Amish culture to survive, sometimes at tremendous personal expense to the individual. In the early years of their history, some individuals were martyred, and the total group was strengthened by the payment of the few. In recent times certain individuals have lost their farms and savings; they were in a sense economically martyred, and again the total group profited by the payment of the few. The steadfastness of the Amish as individuals finally resulted in changes in the enforcement of various laws, for example, social security, high school attendance, noncertified teachers in Amish schools, and alternative forms to military service. The Amish culture will continue to change as it adjusts to economic, technological, and social changes in the surrounding culture, but as long as the Amish are able to maintain their basic cultural figuration, their unique world view, and their own social structure, they will persist even though the details of their lives change.

REFERENCES

Ausband, Das ist: Etliche schöne christliche Lieder. 1564. (1st ed.).

Bainton, Roland H. 1952. *The Reformation of the Sixteenth Century.* Boston: Beacon Press.

Berry, Wendell. 1978. *The Unsettling of America: Culture and Agriculture.* New York: Avon Books.

Blackboard Bulletin. Aylmer, Ontario: Pathway Publishing Corporation. A monthly published "in the interests of Amish Parochial schools."

Bronfenbrenner, Urie. 1970. *Two Worlds of Childhood: U.S. and U.S.S.R.* New York: Russell Sage.

Budget, The. Sugarcreek, Ohio. "A Weekly Newspaper Serving The Sugarcreek Area and Amish-Mennonite Communities Throughout The Americas."

Braght, Thieleman J. van 1951. *The Bloody Theatre or Martyr's Mirror of the Defenseless Christians Who Baptized Only Upon Confession of Faith, and Who Suffered and Died for the Testimony of Jesus, Their Savior, From the Time of Christ to the Year A.D. 1660.* Scottdale, PA: Mennonite Publishing House.

Cross, Harold E. 1967. "Genetic Studies in an Amish Isolate." Ph.D. diss., The Johns Hopkins University.

Enders, Trudy, and Curt Stern. 1948. "The Frequency of Twins, Relative to Age of Mothers, in American Populations," *Genetics* 35 (May):263–272.

Ericksen, Eugene P., Julia Ericksen, and John A. Hostetler. 1980. "The Cultivation of the Soil as a Moral Directive: Population Growth, Family Ties, and the Maintenance of Community Among the Old Order Amish," *Rural Sociology*, 44:49–68.

Ericksen, Julia, and Gary Klein. 1978. "Women's Roles and Family Production Among the Old Order Amish." Paper presented at the National Council of Family Relation, Philadelphia.

Ericksen, Julia, Eugene P. Ericksen, John A. Hostetler, and Gertrude E. Huntington. 1979. "Fertility Patterns and Trends Among the Old Order Amish," *Population Studies*, 33(2):255–276.

Family Life. Aylmer, Ontario: Pathway Publishing Corporation. A monthly "dedicated to the promotion of Christian living among the plain people, with special emphasis on the appreciation of our heritage."

Fisher, John M. 1957. *Descendants and History of Christian Fisher Family.* Privately published by Amos L. Fisher, Route 1, Ronks, PA.

Gans, Herbert J. 1962. *The Urban Villagers.* New York: Free Press.

Hostetler, John A. 1955. "Old World Extinction and New World Survival of the Amish," *Rural Sociology*, 20 (September–December):212–219.

———. 1980. *Amish Society* (3rd ed.). Baltimore, MD: Johns Hopkins Press.

Hostetler, John A., and Gertrude Enders Huntington. 1971. *Children in Amish Society: Socialization and Community Education.* New York: Holt, Rinehart and Winston.

Hostetler, John A., Eugene Ericksen, Julia Ericksen, and Gertrude Huntington. 1977. "Fertility Patterns in an American Isolate Subculture." Final report. NICHD grant no. HD-08137-01A1.

Huntington, Gertrude Enders. 1956. "Dove at the Window: A Study of an Old Order Amish Community in Ohio." Ph.D. diss., Yale University.

Littell, Franklin H. 1964. *The Origins of Sectarian Protestantism.* New York: Macmillan.

Luthy, David. 1973. "The Amish in Europe." *Family Life* (March):10–14.

———. 1974. "Old Order Amish Settlements in 1974," *Family Life* (December):13–16.

Marx, Leo. 1964. *The Machine in the Garden: Technology and the Pastoral Ideal in America.* New York: Oxford University Press.

McLuhan, Marshall. 1962. *The Gutenberg Galaxy.* Toronto: The University of Toronto Press.

Mennonite Encyclopedia. 1955. Scottdale, PA: Mennonite Publishing House; Newton, KS: Mennonite Publication Office; Hillsboro, KS: Mennonite Brethren Publishing House.

Ohio Amish Directory. Millersburg, Ohio.

Raber, J.A. (ed.). 1970, 1973, 1980. *Der Neue Amerikanische Calendar.* Baltic, OH.

Schwartz, Hillell. 1973. "Early Anabaptist Ideas About the Nature of Children," *Mennonite Quarterly Review*, 47 (April):102–114.

Simons, Menno. 1956. *The Complete Writings of Menno Simons.* Scottdale, PA: Herald Press.

Smith, C. Henry. 1920. *The Mennonites: A Brief History of Their Origin and Later Development in Both Europe and America.* Berne, IN: Mennonite Book Concern.
Toffler, Alvin. 1970. *Future Shock.* New York: Random House.
Umble, John. 1949. "Factors Explaining the Disintegration of Mennonite Communities," *Proceedings of the Seventh Annual Conference on Mennonite Cultural Problems.* North Newton, KS: Bethel College. Published under the auspices of the Council of Mennonite and Affiliated Colleges.

RECOMMENDED FILMS

The Amish: A People of Preservation. John L. Ruth, producer; Burton Buller, cinematographer; John A. Hostetler, consultant. Available through Encyclopedia Britannica, 425 N. Michigan Ave., Chicago, IL 60611, in 28-minute and 53-minute versions.

CHAPTER SIXTEEN

The Jewish American Family

Bernard Farber
Charles H. Mindel
Bernard Lazerwitz

HISTORICAL BACKGROUND

Since the days of the Exodus from Egypt, Jews have been a people on the move. Their settlements may have seemed permanent at times, but time and again political, social, or religious events have conspired to make them a nomadic people. The most remarkable characteristic of these people has been that despite the oppressions and persecutions, or perhaps because of them, Jews have retained a remarkable degree of distinct religious and cultural identity.

Judaism, a worldwide religion, embraces approximately 13 million constituents, tending to be concentrated in a few key areas throughout the world. Until the time of Hitler, the largest concentration of Jews lived in Europe. At present, approximately 46 percent of the world's Jews, or approximately 6 million, live in North America, where they now constitute a distinct subgroup among world Jewry (Schmelz and Della Pergola, 1982).

Jews in America

The settlement of Jews in America is an old one. Jews have been in America since the colonial period, though they began arriving in large numbers only 100 years ago. It has been agreed that the immigration of

Jews to America occurred in three major historical waves involving people from three national locations: Sephardic Jews originally from Spain and Portugal, German Jews from the Germanic states, and eastern European Jews largely from Poland and Russia but also from Rumania, Hungary, and Lithuania. It would be inaccurate to assume that there has been no overlap among these three waves of immigration because there was immigration from Germany at the same time as immigration from Poland and Russia. These three waves of immigration are important because they define three distinct cultural patterns that Jewish communities tended to differentiate in America.

Immigrants from the nearly destroyed Sephardic, German, and eastern European Jewish communities differed for a variety of historical, cultural, and economic reasons. Descendants of migrants from eastern Europe, who were the last to arrive, constitute by far the largest number of America's Jews, probably more than 90 percent. The Sephardic Jews and the German Jews are and have been important not for their numbers but largely because of their social position and influence.

THE SEPHARDIC JEWS. The earliest Jewish settlement in America occurred in 1654 in what was then New Amsterdam (now New York City), a colony of the Dutch West India Company. The Jews who settled there followed a circuitous route, ultimately traceable to the large medieval Jewish population of Spain and Portugal. However, the Jews were not particularly welcome in New Amsterdam. Peter Stuyvesant, the governor, resisted and argued that "none of the deceitful race be permitted to infest and trouble this new colony" (Golden and Rywell, 1950:13). However, the Dutch West India Company decided to allow the Portuguese Jews to live in New Netherlands "provided the poor among them shall not become a burden to the Company or the community but be supported by their own nation" (Golden and Rywell, 1950:14). From this beginning there continued a steady flow of immigration of Sephardic Jews and increasingly, German Jews, who numbered approximately 15,000 in 1840.

THE GERMAN JEWS. The middle of the nineteenth century, from approximately 1840 to 1880, saw a second wave of Jewish immigration, mostly German Jews. Conditions in Germany or, to be more accurate the collection of Germanic states, at mid-century were quite inhospitable to Jews and non-Jews alike. Anti-Jewish medieval laws of oppression were enacted, especially in Bavaria, that among other things, provided for heavy, discriminatory taxation, designated areas to live in, restricted occupations, and restrictions on the number of Jewish marriages. These conditions prompted many German Jewish single men to leave for America to seek opportunity. In the later part of the nineteenth century, when these laws were relaxed, immigration of these German Jews slowed down to a trickle (Glazer, 1957; Weinryb, 1958).

Many German Jewish immigrants started out as peddlers, an occupation that did not require great skill or large capital investment. They spread out all over America and gave many non-Jews their first glimpse of a Jewish face. Originally starting out with a pack carried on their back, they traversed the countryside. If they were reasonably successful, they would graduate to a horse and wagon. If they were able to accumulate a little money, they might open a dry goods store in one of the many towns and cities in which they traded. These were the origins of what later became the great clothing and department stores in America, such as Altmans, Bloomingdales, Bambergers, Gimbels, Goldblatt, Nieman-Marcus, Macy's, Mays, Maison Blanche, Stix, Baer & Fuller, and others.

The importance and influence of the German Jews is crucially linked to their spectacular financial success. Although certainly not all German Jews became wealthy, the rise of several families, many of whom started out as peddlers, had enormous implications for the status of Jews in America. They became important figures in banking and finance in a period of American history when the industrialization of America was just beginning and there was a need for large amounts of capital to feed the growing industrial base.

The German Jewish influx into America was great enough to overwhelm in number the Sephardim. By 1848, there were 50,000 Jews in America, and by 1880 there were an estimated 230,000, largely German Jews (Sklare, 1958).

EASTERN EUROPEAN JEWS. It was, however, the arrival of the Jews from eastern Europe that has had the greatest impact on Jewish American life. Beginning around 1881 and largely ending by 1930, almost 3 million Jews immigrated to America.

These individuals and families, though Jewish like their American counterparts, were in fact of another world. Whereas the Germans came from an "enlightened" modern society in which Jews were more often than not integrated into German culture, the eastern European Jews came from a milieu in which the feeling of homogeneity was strongly entrenched—a set of Jewish values and attitudes prevailed, including religious devotion and observance.

Most of the 5 million Jews of Russia and Poland had been restricted from the time of Catherine the Great to an area established for them known as the "Pale of Settlement." The Pale extended from the shores of the Baltic south to the Black Sea. Jews were generally not allowed to settle in the interior of Russia and were limited to this area. The Pale has been described, except for the Crimea, as a 313,000 square-mile, monotonously flat, sand-arid prison (Manners, 1972:30). Within this area, approximately the size of Texas, 808 *shtetlach* (townlets), each of which was perhaps two-thirds Jewish and 94 percent poor, Jews lived, survived, and "attained the highest degree of inwardness . . . the golden period in Jewish history, in the history of the Jewish soul" (Manners, 1972:31).

The concentration of Jews in these areas for hundreds of years led to the development of a culture and civilization grounded in biblical and talmudic teachings that remained to a remarkable degree unchanged until the twentieth century. Those who migrated from this society to America and elsewhere have, on the whole, become prosperous; those millions who remained, including most of the devout, were, for the most part, destroyed.

The mass migration of European Jews began in the 1880s and continued at a high level until the passage of the restrictive immigration laws in 1924. The chief instigating factors that started the massive flow were imperial Russia's governmentally inspired *pogroms* (devastation and destruction) in 1881. *Pogroms* consisted of ransacking, burning, rape, and assorted violence committed in the towns and villages of Russia. The government, driven by an overwhelming fear of revolution, used *pogroms* as a form of diversion and weapon against dissenting minorities (Manners, 1972).

Beginning in 1882, new laws, the so-called May laws, were issued by the Czar that severely restricted Jewish rights, such as they were. Thousands were forced to leave their homes, especially those who resided in interior Russia. These laws and the extensions of them left most Jews no choice but to emigrate.

Most emigrants came to America. Some went to Palestine, and some others went to other parts of Europe. Forty thousand came to the United States in 1881–1882, another 62,000 came in 1888, and by 1906 the number was up to 153,000 per year (Manners, 1972:57).

The *pogroms* and restrictive laws that forced the migration of these Jews were but the final chapter of a long process of disintegration of Jewish communities that had been going on for more than a century. Antagonisms and tensions had been developing within for a long period of time. Of more importance were the effects from the world outside the *shtetl.* Industrialization and the decline of the feudal system of relations came late to eastern Europe, but by the nineteenth century, its effects were being felt there, as well. Thus, by the time of the *pogroms* in the late nineteenth century and early twentieth century, social change, social disintegration, and demographic expansion had already come to this traditional society.

GERMAN JEWS VERSUS EASTERN EUROPEAN JEWS. The arrival of this mass of people was a mixed blessing to the already established Jews, especially to the German American Jews, who feared for their recently achieved middle-class status. However, native Jews and Americans, in general, took a compassionate though largely condescending view toward poverty-stricken immigrants (at least until 1924, when the American government, in the throes of a xenophobic isolationist wave, passed a restrictive immigration law).

Relations between the older, established Jews, primarily German American Jews, and the newly arrived eastern European Jews were nevertheless difficult. The German Jews were interested in helping the immigrants in order to "Americanize" them so they would not be a source of embarrassment. They saw the strange dress and speech and the poverty as reflecting unfavorably on themselves, feeling that the quicker they became indistinguishable from the rest of America the better. Americanization was made more difficult by the fact that the eastern European Jewish immigrants clustered together in distinct urban neighborhoods, especially in the American northeast, particularly in New York City.

The eastern European Jewish immigrants were usually Orthodox. Though the immigrants tended to be less observant and traditional than their counterparts who remained in Europe, the religious institutions established by them in America were traditional, and Orthodox recreations of the institutions that existed in eastern Europe. The immigrants did not recognize the Reform Judaism as it was practiced by the native, predominately German Jews. To them it was unacceptable. "They are Jews," declared Rabbi Dr. Issac Meyer Wise, the leading light of Reform Judaism, "We are Israelites." The Russian Jews said with equal assurance, "We are Jews. They are *goyim* (Gentiles)" (Manners, 1972:76).

One important ingredient in the continuing vigor of Orthodox Judaism in America was the immigration during the Hitler and post–World War II years of numbers of Orthodox Chassidic Jews. The Chassidic groups, organized around a particular charismatic leader (*rebbe*, or *Tzaddik*) are identified by the location in Europe from which they originated. These groups stress a communal life and close-knit group cohesion. They are generally found in the New York area, often in old neighborhoods. One group, however, the Skverer Chassidim, has established their own town, New Square, in the suburbs of New York City, in which they have attempted to recreate the traditional life of the eastern European Jew. The impact of these groups has been to bring new life into what was a disappearing branch of Judaism. The close ties of the members and the emotionalism of the religion as they practice it are attractive to many young people who have been seeking more emotion in their religious practices. Others who have not become members of Chassidic groups have borrowed much of the emotional content of this movement and put it into their own observance.

It has been estimated that today more than 90 percent of America's Jewish population are, or are descended from, immigrants from eastern Europe. Because their arrival has been relatively recent, family patterns that existed in Europe and were brought to the United States can still be expected to have an impact on present-day family life-styles. In the following paragraphs, family life in the small eastern European town—the *shtetl*—where most Jews lived is described.[1]

The *shtetl* was a poor place, a place of unpaved streets and decrepit wooden buildings. It is said that there was no "Jewish" architecture, instead the most noticeable features of the dwellings were their age and their shabbiness (Zborowski and Herzog, 1952:61). Occupationally, the Jews were generally tradesmen—dairymen, cobblers, tailors, butchers, fishmongers, peddlers, and shopkeepers.

Social Organization

The marketplace was the economic center of the *shtetl;* however, the synagogue was the heart and soul of the community. The values of the religion infiltrated all aspects of life; every detail of life was infused with some religious or ritual significance. It was impossible to escape and separate the religious from the secular.

Chief among the values of the *shtetl* and Jewish culture was the value of learning. One of the most important obligations of a devout Jew is to study and learn. To obey the commandments of the scriptures, one must know them, and one must study them to know them. Studying and learning the Torah[2] became the most important activity in which a man could involve himself—more important than earning a good living. Every *shtetl* of reasonable size would contain schools of various levels including the *cheder* for boys as young as three and four years of age. A learned young

---

[1]Much of this discussion of *shtetl* family structure comes from Landes and Zborowski (1968) and Zborowski and Herzog (1952).

[2]Torah literally refers to the Pentateuch, the five books of Moses, or the written scriptures. However, Torah has come to mean much more. It has come to include remaining portions of the Old Testament as well as the whole of the commentaries and interpretations on the Pentateuch, which was known as the oral law or the Talmud. In addition, the numerous codifications and newer commentaries that appeared during the Middle Ages such as the works of Maimonides have also come to be included under this rubric. In essence, Torah means all the religious learning and literature including and surrounding the holy scriptures.

man was considered the most highly prized future son-in-law. In fact, it was considered prestigious for a father-in-law to support his new son-in-law for the first few years of marriage if the son-in-law was bright, so that he could devote himself to full-time study.

The stratification of the *shtetl* was based in large measure on learning and the tradition of learning in one's family. *Shtetl* Jews were either *sheyneh yidn* (beautiful Jews) or *prosteh yidn* (common Jews). The position of a person in this status hierarchy was dependent, ideally, on learning, but wealth played an important part in determining the *sheyneh.* A third quality, *yikhus,* a combination of family heritage with respect to learning and wealth was also an important criteria in determining social position. A person with great *yikhus* was able to claim many ancestors of great worth particularly with respect to learning and philanthropy. To have *yikhus* was very prestigious.

Life in the *shtetl* was guided by written codes of behavior that derived from the Talmud and other religious sources. These standards ideally had the effect of regulating behavior of all Jewish residents of the *shtetl, sheyneh,* and *prosteh* alike. It is in these codes of behavior and the folklore, folksayings, and other customs that grew up around the *shtetl* that we find the unique cultural basis for Jewish family life, important aspects of which still have an impact today.

Marriage

Duties and roles for men and women were carefully detailed by traditional writings, and chief among these was the injunction that a man and woman marry. It was said, "It is not good for man to be alone."

Marriage in the *shtetl* was traditionally arranged by the parents of the young couple, frequently through the use of a matchmaker (*shadchen*). It was assumed that the "parents always want the best for their children" (Zborowski and Herzog, 1952:275), and the children went along with the match.

Because marriage was considered such an important institution, indeed a commandment (*mitzvah*), there was great pressure for marriage and families to remain united. In fact, because divorce reflected badly on one's family and stigmatized the individuals involved, it was a relatively rare occurrence. Marital stability was related to a dominant orientation in Jewish family life, *sholem bayis* (domestic harmony or peace). Only when maintaining a satisfactory family equilibrium became impossible and the *sholem bayis* was broken was divorce considered. The relative infrequency of divorce indicates that adaptations of many kinds occurred with some frequency.

Marital Roles

The injunction that a man should study, learn, and promote the book-learning tradition had important implications for the functioning of the husband in the family. The husband or father was often remote from most domestic concerns. If he was a scholar, much of the economic responsibility for the home was left to the wife. The husband's primary responsibility was in the spiritual and intellectual sphere; only the men were taught to read, speak, and write Hebrew, the sacred language; women who were literate spoke and read Yiddish.[3]

In reality, women often played a dominant role in family life and in the outside world. There was a high degree of interchangeability in family roles, and wives were trained to be ready to assume the economic burdens of supporting the family. Women often had wide latitude and opportunity for movement to conduct business or seek employment, and in time of emergency or need, women were able to partake in any number of "male" activities. It has been argued that as a consequence of their subordinate status, women were less regulated than men, and therefore they were able to partake in all activities that were not expressly forbidden to them. As a result, they quite often had greater freedom than men, who were bound up very tightly in a highly regulated way of life (Landes and Zborowski, 1968:81).

THE EASTERN EUROPEAN MOTHER. Basic to the eastern European Jewish family with its wide range of rights and obligations was parental love. Seldom demonstrated verbally or physically after the child was four or five, parental affection, especially from the mother, was felt to be an unbreakable bond. "No matter what you do, no matter what happens your mother will love you always. She may have odd and sometimes irritating ways of showing it, but in a hazardous and unstable world the belief about the mother's love is strong and unshakable" (Zborowski and Herzog, 1952:293). The Jewish mother's love was expressed by and large in two ways: "by constant and solicitous overfeeding and by unremitting solicitude about every aspect of her child's welfare" (Zborowski and Herzog, 1952:293). Both paternal and maternal love contain the notions of suffer-

[3]Yiddish, a Middle High German dialect written in Hebrew characters, was the common *mamaloshen* (mother tongue) of most eastern European Jews. Its use can be traced back 1000 years, and though Yiddish varied in form and pronunciation in different parts of western and eastern Europe, it provided a common language for Jews across all national boundaries and was a crucial factor in maintaining the unity of this branch of the Jewish people. The other major Jewish branches are the Sephardim, who spoke a dialect of Spanish written in Hebrew characters, and the Oriental Jews, who usually used Arabic.

ing and sacrifice for the sake of the children. It is said that "she kills herself" in order to bring up her children and for her husband as well, who also becomes like a child in the family. Her conduct is understood and tolerated by her children, who nostalgically idealize it when they get older; she is remembered as a "loving despot."

Affection among the *shtetl* Jews, as previously mentioned, was not expressed with kisses and caresses after a child reached four or five and, especially not in public. However, a mother was more likely to be demonstrative to her son and a father more demonstrative to his daughter. Furthermore, though much contact between members of the opposite sex was restricted by avoidance etiquette, such as between brother and sister, there is virtually no avoidance between mother and son. It has been claimed that "though marital obligations are fulfilled with the husband, the romance exists with the son" and that "when the son marries, he gives the wife a contract and the mother a divorce" (Landes and Zborowski, 1968:80–88).

The father relates to his daughter similarly to the way the mother relates to her son, only not with quite the same intensity. With his daughter, he is undemanding and indulgent. A father, however, is a distant figure for the most part, one to whom great respect is owed. He is a particularly remote, authoritarian figure for the boy whose growth into a "Jew" and a *mensch* ("whole person," or adult) was his responsibility.

FAMILY OBLIGATIONS. The *shtetl* was viewed as an extended family. At the very least, Jews consider themselves to be ultimately related as the "Children of Israel," and often, because of extensive intermarriage within the *shtetl,* they were closer than that. In any case, there were strong obligations and pressure to maintain close ties to kin. Particularly strong was the obligation to take care of elderly parents, although there is great reluctance on the part of the elderly parent, especially the father, to accept aid.

THE MODERN AMERICAN JEWISH FAMILY

Fertility

As families from all branches of world Jewry have become involved in urban, industrial societies, they have rapidly lowered their fertility levels. Indeed, the first birth-control clinic opened by Margaret Sanger was in Brownsville, a Jewish immigrant neighborhood in Brooklyn, New York.

Freedman, Whelpton, and Campbell (1959:110) report that the 83 percent of American Jewish women employing contraception start such use before their first pregnancy, whereas only 52 percent of Protestants start contraception as early in married life. Several national fertility studies (Freedman, Whelpton, and Campbell, 1959, 1961; Whelpton, Campbell, and Patterson, 1966) report that American Jews are the most successful of American major ethnic groups with regard to family planning and birth spacing. Estimates are that from about 1920 to 1940, the Jewish birth rate in America fell almost 40 percent (Seligman, 1950:42).

Reduction in the Jewish birth rate derives from not only effective use of contraceptives but also late marriage, which for Jewish women was 21.3 years of age, compared with 19.9 years of age for Protestants and 20.8 years of age for Catholics. Goldstein (1971:24) indicates that "later age of marriage has characterized Jewish women since at least 1920." For Jewish men as well, marriage has been later than it has for Protestants and Catholics. Although the high educational levels may be a factor in this tendency for Jews to marry later than other groups, it is unlikely to be the only one.

The shift from families characterized by large numbers of children in eastern Europe, North Africa, and the Middle East to families having from two to four children may have been a major factor permitting Jewish women to increase their involvement in Jewish communal life, extend and enlarge their participation in the labor force, and have less rigid sex-role work tasks within the home. Furthermore, the rapid fertility reduction characteristic of all the world's Jews who have entered to any extent in modern life seems to reflect extensive communication and decision making with regard to their husband–wife and father–mother roles within the Jewish family (Lazerwitz, 1971). Rapid fertility reduction has also permitted Jewish parents to support the educational desires of their fewer offspring and, thereby, give strong support to the rapid socioeconomic mobility that has been the outstanding achievement of American Jews (Lazerwitz, 1971).

Sergio Della Pergola (1980) estimates that American Jewish fertility at the start of the 1970s was slightly below the level needed to replace the Jewish population and was still declining. Jewish religious involvement accounts for only a minor portion of the fertility variations among younger American Jewish couples. Nevertheless, slightly more than 25 percent of American Jews do have higher fertility rates than the rest. This 25 percent consists of frequent synagogue attenders who prefer the Orthodox or Conservative denominations. At the lowest fertility rates, one finds the infrequent synagogue attenders with moderate to high occupational status. This group constitutes slightly more than 40 percent of younger American Jewish couples (Lazerwitz, 1980). Incidentally, the total Israeli Jewish fertility rate is the highest in the Jewish world. It is approximately twice as large as the total American Jewish fertility rate (Della Pergola, 1983; Schmelz, 1981).

Characteristics of American Jewish Families

Because historically European Jewish social structure and characteristics are the foundation of the American Jewish family, one is tempted to use the number of generations in the United States as a basic variable with which to analyze American Jewry. However, research by Lazerwitz (1978) and Lazerwitz and Harrison (1979) introduces a more effective and less time-bound variable—namely, denominational preference. Denominational preference incorporates historic change, gives a more accurate characterization of tomorrow's Jewry, and simultaneously describes the value stances around which Jewish families are organizing.

Orthodox Jews make up 11 percent of the adult Jewish population. They seek to carry historic Jewish religious practices, value orientations, and social roles into modern life with as few basic changes as possible. Jews preferring the Conservative denomination make up approximately 40 percent of American Jewish adults. As a whole, they seek a balance between traditional ways and the demands of modern life and are more inclined toward basic social change in Jewish life. Reform Jews constitute 30 percent of the American Jewish adult population. As a group, they have given considerable emphasis to doing what they regard as "modernizing" Judaism. For them, traditional practices depend on individual desires, and many practices have been abandoned. They also make the least Jewish educational demands on their children of the three denominational groups.

At the furthest extreme from the Orthodox are those Jews who regard themselves as "just Jewish" and have no specific denominational preference. This group constitutes 19 percent of the Jewish adult population and is, as a whole, marginal to the Jewish community and its religious practices.

It seems that denominational orientations are fairly well formed by the time young people start into their twenties. Then, the next crucial step is actually joining a synagogue of their denominational preference. The latest available national estimate (Lazerwitz, 1987) indicates that at the start of the 1980s, one-half of all adult Jews were members of synagogues.

Combining denominational preference and synagogue membership provides an informing picture of American Jewry. Because the majority of those preferring orthodoxy are synagogue members, whereas the reverse holds true among those with no denominational preferences, the information in Table 1 is in six basic categories. The five indices of this table were

TABLE 1

Percent Reaching High Levels on Various Jewish Characteristics by Denominational Preference and Actual Membership

JEWISH CHARACTERISTICS	DENOMINATIONAL PREFERENCE—MEMBERSHIP[a]					
	ORTHODOX	CONSERVATIVE		REFORM		NO DENOMINATIONAL
	MEMBERS (%)	MEMBERSHIP (%)	PREFERENCE (%)	MEMBERSHIP (%)	PREFERENCE (%)	PREFERENCE (%)
Jewish education index	70	50	35	38	14	15
Has kosher home	87	42	40	6	6	9
Religious behavior index	87	59	25	26	5	3
Jewish primary group involvement index	71	55	37	22	17	12
Jewish organizational activity index	63	49	16	43	5	7
General organizational activity index	19	32	10	50	37	20
Third U. S. generation	5	16	13	25	24	27

SOURCE: National Jewish Survey (1971).

[a]Note that Conservative Jews are more likely to be involved in Jewish social networks. Finally, the nearly equivalent activity in Jewish organizations of Conservative and Reform synagogue members, in contrast to those who merely prefer these denominations, shows a major impact of synagogue membership (York, 1979).

developed by Lazerwitz (1973, 1978) and represent amounts of Jewish education, extent of religious behavior, and the degree to which adults are involved with fellow Jews in regard to family courtship, marriage, and friendship. Jewish and general organizational activity indices measure the degree of involvement in Jewish and non-Jewish voluntary associations. Finally, "third U.S. generation" refers to those who are native-born Americans of native-born parents.

Clearly, there is a rank order, with Orthodox Jews coming first on Jewish education, kosher homes, religious behavior, primary groups, and organizational activities, then come members of Conservative synagogues. On balance, those who prefer the Conservative denomination but are not synagogue members are similar to members of Reform synagogues. Those who prefer the Reform denomination but are not synagogue members are quite similar to those who do not have a denominational preference.

There are some interesting exceptions to those patterns. For example, the retention of the kosher dietary laws by the Conservative but not the Reform denomination shows up in the differences between their adherents. Also activity in community organizations is a Reform characteristic. Even those who merely prefer the Reform denomination are considerably more active than those with no preference. On this important characteristic, too, the previous ranking relationships change. Now, Orthodox and Jews with no preference, previously at opposite extremes, share the same level of activity in community organizations.

The extent to which these denominational groups attract multigenerational American Jews conforms to the previous denominational-preference ranking scheme. The Orthodox group is least preferred by multigenerational Americans, then the Conservative and Reform groups, and then the group without a preference, at least 37 percent of whom are third-generation Americans.

These findings emphasize the diversity among American Jews. Although there might be such common features as support for Israel and aid to Soviet Jewry, it is obvious that it is not easy to speak of American Jewry as a whole. Instead, a better view would be to focus on the affinity of Jews for the various religious subdivisions of Jewry in the United States. In that way, one encounters more homogeneous components of the American Jewish community.

It is likely that among American Jews, these differences associated with their denominational outlook apply to additional life areas. One would then expect family patterns, sex roles, leisure time, and personal norms to reflect the basic value orientations that differentiate these four subdivisions of American Jewry. For example, divorce is approximately twice as prevalent among Jews brought up in homes with a low level of religious observance as among those whose parents were ritually observant. Moreover, "the lowest amount of divorce occurs among those who are most committed to the Judaic religious traditions as it is practiced today" (Brodbar-Nemzer, 1986).

Intermarriage

Marriages and conversions in the major religious and ethnic groups have been topics of major social interest for some time. Only recently, however, have reliable national data been gathered on Jewish intermarriage.

In 1971, 7 percent of married, Jewish-born adults were then in, or had been in, an intermarriage (Lazerwitz, 1981). Consistent with historical trends, in 1971, it was found that 10 percent of adult Jewish-born men were currently intermarried, but only 3 percent of adult Jewish-born women were intermarried. In the same year, 14 percent of currently married Jewish-born adults who were under 35 years of age had non-Jewish-born spouses. Among these young adults, 34 percent of the non-Jewish spouses had converted to Judaism.

By 1985, it is estimated that the overall intermarriage percentage had climbed to approximately 16 percent of married, Jewish-born adults (Lazerwitz, 1987). In the same year, it estimated that this rate was 8 percent in the New York City metropolitan area and 21 percent in the remainder of the United States.

In a study by Mayer (1980), it was found in a sample of 446 intermarried Jewish couples, that 66 percent involved a Jewish male and a non-Jewish female. However, he found an interesting trend appearing. Among those 40–49 years old, 80 percent of the out-group marrying Jews were men, and 20 percent were women. However, for those 20–29 year old, the ratio was 46 percent of out-group marriage for Jewish men and 54 percent for Jewish women—a significant shift.

What are the outcomes of intermarriage? Table 2 explores this question by contrasting religious characteristics among all currently married Jewish adults, currently married Jewish adults whose spouse has converted to Judaism, and currently married Jewish adults whose non-Jewish spouses have retained their original religious preferences. Clearly, marriages involving conversions to Judaism are much more involved in rituals than the religiously heterogeneous marriages. Only on membership in Jewish organizations do marriages with conversions attain the marginality to the Jewish community that religiously mixed marriages do.

National data (Lazerwitz, 1981) indicate that both the converts to Ju-

TABLE 2
Religious Characteristics Among Currently Married Jewish Adults

RELIGIOUS CHARACTERISTICS	ALL CURRENTLY MARRIED JEWISH ADULTS (%)	CURRENT MARRIAGES WITH CONVERSIONS INTO INTO JUDAISM (%)	CURRENT MARRIAGES THAT ARE RELIGIOUSLY MIXED (%)
Lit *Shabat* candles	36	63	4
Had only *matzahs* in home last Passover	55	22	5
Prefer Reform denomination	32	43	21
No denominational preference	13	5	63
Member of 1–2 Jewish organizations	35	11	9

SOURCE: National Jewish Survey (1971).

daism and the Christian spouses of Jews tend to have a prior history of marriage and divorce. Rosenthal (1970) reports that Jews entering a second marriage have high intermarriage rates. The national data reported in Table 2 also show that previously married Jews have a much larger intermarriage rate than Jews marrying for the first time. Work done by Bumpass and Sweet (1972) shows that first marriages in which both spouses were of the same faith had considerably lower divorce rates than those first marriages in which spouses were of different faith backgrounds.

The marriages of Jewish women who intermarry tend to break up with greater frequency than those of intermarried Jewish men. The Maller (1975) study of California divorces and the national data introduced here both show approximately equal numbers of Jewish men and women reporting terminating intermarriages, despite the fact that Jewish men intermarry more than Jewish women. However, these data may reflect the shift mentioned earlier in the sex of Jews who are marrying outside the group. The ever-increasing numbers of Jewish females marrying outside the group are now reflected in the divorce rates.

As would be expected, intermarriage rates reflect denominational orientations. In 1971, Orthodox Jews reported intermarriage rates of 3 percent, Conservative Jews reported 4 percent, Reform Jews reported 9 percent, and Jews with no denominational preference reported 17 percent (Lazerwitz and Harrison, 1979:663; see also Mayer, 1980:507). Jews now marrying or who will marry in the near future will be increasingly third-generation Americans with college degrees who are entering a second marriage and have no Jewish denominational preference. All those social categories are characterized by high intermarriage rates. Hence, the Jewish intermarriage percentage is bound to rise.

The factors that account for intermarriage are summarized in Figures 1 and 2. There is little question that, at any time, the succession of generations fosters Jewish intermarriage, but beyond that, the interpretations that seem to fit the research findings vary with the historical character of American social structure (Farber and Gordon, 1982). In those historical eras during which religious and ethnic schisms have overshadowed the values of democracy and individualism in determining personal destinies, Jewish intermarriage has been interpreted as deviance detrimental to the coherence of the Jewish community—as deriving from self-hatred (Lewin, 1948; Kardiner, 1951; Berman, 1968), hypergamy (Merton, 1941), marginality to the Jewish community (Massarik and Chenkin, 1973), and rebellion against family and community controls (Herman, 1980; Rice 1976; Spero, 1977). However, in eras in which ideals of democracy and individualism have predominated, interpretations of intermarriage as expressions of these ideals appears to be consistent with research accounts—civil rights activities (Bell, 1968:147–157; Goldstein, 1971:114–123), personal fulfillment (Cromer, 1974:164; Cohen, 1977), participation in the American mainstream (Rosenthal, 1978; Sklare, 1971), and semantic decomposition of the family as a social concept (Farber, 1973; Farber and Gordon, 1982:55–56). This ebb and flow in interpretations of Jewish

FIGURE 1 Centrifugal Influences Toward Increased Intermarriage. From Farber and Gordon (1982:53).

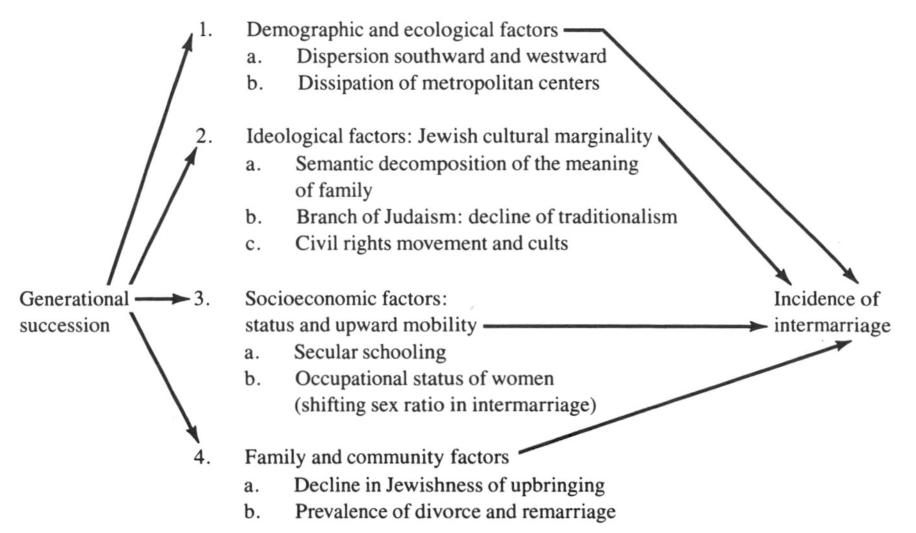

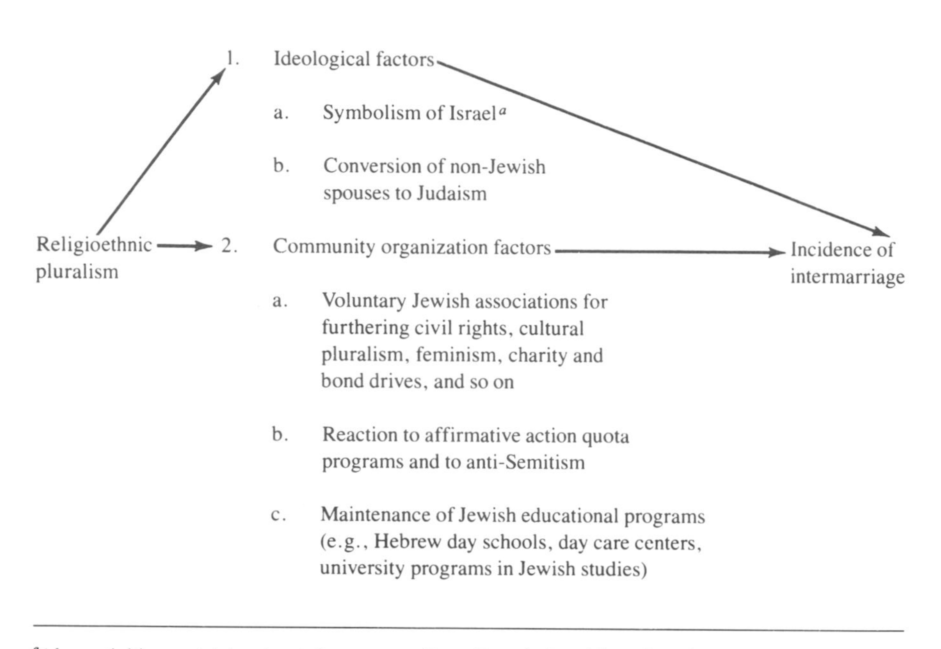

[a]Also activities pertaining to reinforcement of Israeli symbols: visits to Israel, contact with relatives who migrated to Israel, Yiddish and Israeli cultural events—theatre, music, dance—and references to Holocaust.

FIGURE 2 Centripetal Influences Toward Maintaining Endogamy. (In addition to the opposites of centrifugal factors.) From Farber and Gordon (1982:54).

intermarriage appears to reflect a continuing dialectic between the pull of special Jewish interests—the persistence and welfare of the Jewish community—and the push of divergent interests within the Jewish population (Farber, 1981). Like business cycles, it is this societal dialectic that (at least in part) makes accounting for Jewish intermarriage both difficult and important.

Family Solidarity

Writers on the American Jewish family have assumed that solidarity is a hallmark of Jewish domestic life throughout history. Brav (1940:7, 20) notes, for example, that in the Biblical period, "strong family solidarity was a matter of course," and he goes on to state that "observers of the modern scene claim to note the existence in the Jewish family of a solidarity or cohesiveness that appears to be unique in degree as well as in quality. Among Jewish writers this is generally admitted as axiomatic." Brav ends by questioning whether this assumption about Jewish family solidarity has sufficient factual support. This questioning appears to have reflected the concern of those whose family values were nourished in a European setting but who now found themselves in a society in which less emphasis was placed on family obligations.

The research findings reported by Balswick (1966:167) in his review of various studies suggest that although indices of solidarity indicate a greater cohesiveness on the part of Jewish than other families, "it seems obvious that the change has been from the closely knit European Jewish family to the less closely knit American Jewish family." Beginning with Brav's (1940) investigation, there has been little effort by researchers to distinguish between family organization of foreign-born household heads and native-born heads. Many of the findings, however, seem to refer to families of the preholocaust generation. Landis (1960) found, for example, that in families of Jewish college students in the 1950s (compared with Catholic and Protestant families), the divorce rate of the parents was lowest and the relationship of respondents to their parents was closest. W. I. Thomas's analysis of the *Bintl Brief* in the *Daily Forward* (Bressler, 1952) focused on the immigrant generation. Thomas, too, regarded "the key motif expressed in Jewish family patterns [to be] . . . an effort to preserve the solidarity of the family" (Balswich, 1966:165). Brav's own conclusion in comparing indices of solidarity among Jewish and non-Jewish families in pre–World War II Vicksburg, Mississippi, were that Jewish solidarity is not markedly stronger than that in non-Jewish families. Indeed, as the number of alternative households increases—childless, single-parent, cohabitant, mixed-marriage, and so on—levels of Jewish identification decline (Cohen, 1983).

But such concepts as solidarity or cohesiveness by which earlier writers sought to explain personal loyalties and the acceptance of familial obligations are vague, and the indicators chosen to measure them do confound various motives, pressures, and meanings. For example, merely because couples do not divorce does not suggest a high degree of solidarity, and because people live together, visit, or assist each other is not a definite indicator of personal affinity. Be that as it may, disorganizing effects of migration eventually wore off, and family cohesiveness ceased to be a primary concern; the next cohort of Jewish families no longer could make a direct comparison between the "solidarity" of the European family and the "individuality" of the Americans.

Kinship and Mobility: Diaspora Upon Diaspora

Is there a uniquely Jewish approach to kinship? To proceed to answer this question, one must first answer the following questions: How can we identify this approach? What shall we look for?

Anthropologists have used the term *collaterality* to refer to the fact that people regard some categories of relatives as genealogically closer than others. For example, in one society, a nephew may be regarded as closer than an uncle; in another, an uncle may be closer. If families possess limited resources and several relatives have an equal need for them, there must be a set of rules that tell an individual which relatives have great claim to these resources. Differences in collaterality are important because they express different modes of kinship organization—that is, different ways of figuring out which relatives have prior claim to resources and property.

Superimposed on the notion of collaterality is variation in priorities based on the personal and social qualities of particular relatives. Although these personal elements would affect the obligations one feels to them, the idea of collaterality is that underlying these personal qualities, there exists for most people a hierarchy of priorities based on kinship status itself. At times, kinship status may override any personal considerations in making decisions; at other times, the personal qualities of the relatives may be the crucial factor. The point is that people discriminate among relatives by kinship status, as well as by personal characteristics.

Kinship priorities have been found to be formalized in inheritance laws and laws defining incestuous marriage. Inheritance laws establish the order and priorities among relatives to a decedent's estate, whereas incest laws describe the relatives considered too close to marry. In Western civilization, despite great variations in economic and political systems, only a few such priority systems have emerged to accommodate intestacy and incestuous marriage laws. These systems, or models, are the Parentela Orders model (with origins in ancient Judaism and classical Greece), the Civil Law model (whose source was the Twelve Tables of early Rome), and the Canon Law model (which appeared in the twelfth-century systemization of Church Law). More recently, proposals have been made to apply genetic relatedness (i.e., shared chromosomes) to inheritance and marriage laws. For example, in decisions on inheritance, comparing claims of siblings and grandchildren of the decedent in laws of succession by choosing siblings would be appropriate for the Canon Law and Genetic models, equal claim would fit the Civil Law model, and priority of grandchildren would be consistent with the Parentela Orders model. These different models emerged to meet the specific demands on family and kinship in the particular social settings in which they originated (Farber, 1981). As described in the Mishnah and the Talmud, the Parentela Orders model places most emphasis on continuity of the family line; whereas, consistent with Church writings, the Canon Law model is least-oriented toward familial perpetuation, focusing instead on subordinating family interests to church interests.

A fifth model was identified in a study in Phoenix, Arizona. This model places its emphasis on the individual's ancestral line and classifies kin according to whether they are children, grandchildren, great-grandchildren, and so on of EGO's (i.e., the individual's) direct ancestors. Because the model is most prevalent among white Protestants of high educational and income levels (and with native-born parents and grandparents), it has been called the Standard American model (Farber, 1981:45–65).

Although people are generally unaware of the kinship priority patterns among religious groups, they tend to be overrepresented in the categories associated with their own religion. Many Catholics fall into the Canon Law category; Jews cluster around the Parentela Orders category. Moreover, one branch of Judaism is itself related to holding a Parentela Orders perspective in kinship collaterality. Persons raised in Orthodox homes show a higher inclination toward the Parentela Orders Model than do individuals from less traditional branches. In contrast, persons brought up in Reform Judaism are likely to develop Genetic or Canon Law patterns of collaterality. Nonetheless, whether one studies current affiliation or branch of upbringing, the results are similar: The more traditional the branch of Judaism, the greater the tendency to conform to the Parentela Orders model of collaterality (Farber, 1979, 1981).

What does conformity to the Parentela Orders model imply about family relationships? Regardless of religious affiliation, people who hold a Parentela Orders orientation exhibit certain characteristics in their family and kinship ties. Compared with persons who conform to other kinship perspectives, (1) their age at first marriage tends to be late; (2) they and their parents and siblings show a high degree of marital stability; (3) their fertility level tends to be above the average for their particular religious group (as does that of their parents and siblings); (4) when they marry persons of other religious backgrounds, both husband and wife adopt the same religious affiliation (their children are raised in the same religion); (5) there is a somewhat greater proclivity to live near the husband's rather than the wife's parents; but (6) residential distance is not crucial for persons with a Parentela Orders view, because even over great distances, there is intense involvement with relatives (Farber, 1981). A German study by Luschen suggests that conformity to the Parentela Orders model is related to a tendency to name children instead of spouses as primary heirs (Luschen, 1986, Tables 8 and 9).

Moreover, holding a Parentela Orders conception of collaterality is related to ethnic identity. A study of the Kansas City Jewish community found that persons with a Parentela Orders orientation tend more often than Jews with other kinship orientations to live in areas with a high Jewish concentration and maintain Jewish communal ties. They are generally nonmigrants; they tend to have Jewish friends; they are more active than their parents in Jewish matters; and they disapprove of intermarriage (Farber, 1979). The Kansas City findings relating to ethnicity are confirmed in ongoing research on Mexican Americans in Phoenix. The study shows that those Mexican Americans with a highly salient ethnic identity are overrepresented in the Parentela Orders category and have a strong family identification. Although the number of Mexican Americans falling into the Parentela Orders grouping is smaller than that generally found for Jews, the trends for the two studies are in the same direction.

Collectively, the findings of studies on collaterality support the view that Jews tend to follow an approach to family and kinship, symbolized by the Parentela Orders model, that is rooted in the Pentateuch and later Jewish writings. This approach encourages strong ties with the *mishpokhe* (extended family) despite impediments to interaction. Given this approach, Jewish family and kinship bonds provide a sharp contrast to those of other groups. For example, an investigation of kinship among people ages 21–45 living in Phoenix, Arizona, reveals that:

1. When parents and in-laws live out of state, Jewish respondents have the most frequent contact by telephone and mail; Catholics the least. The gap between Jews and Catholics is especially great when it comes to mothers-in-law. Whereas 65 percent of the Jewish respondents have frequent contact with their mothers-in-law, only 35 percent of the Catholics do.
2. For persons whose close relatives also live in the Phoenix metropolitan area, differences between Jews and other religious groups are even clearer. Among religious groups, Jewish respondents exhibit by far the greatest amount of contact with parents and brothers and sisters, and those with no religious preference show the least contact. Roughly 90 percent of the Jewish respondents have at least weekly contact with their parents, whereas only approximately one-half of those with no preference do.
3. Although the majority of Jews have known their European-born grandparents well, this is true of only a minority of Catholics and Protestants. The greater dispersion of non-Jewish families interfered with the development of close bonds with grandparents.

The religious differences in kinship patterns in Phoenix are consistent with empirical evidence derived from studies of other metropolitan areas. Research in a Chicago suburb indicated that Jewish families during the 1960s showed a greater amount of familism than Protestant and Catholic families: (1) Jewish families had more households of kin in the same metropolitan area; (2) the related households of Jewish families more often consisted of close relatives (often parents or siblings); (3) there was a greater amount of interaction among the related Jewish families; and (4) the Jewish families were more likely to give or receive assistance from these relatives. Holding migratory status statistically constant, the investigators reported that familism was more a *basis* for reluctance to migrate than a *result* of residential stability (Winch, Greer, and Blumberg, 1967).

The findings of families in other cities are comparable (Leichter and Mitchell, 1967). Lenski (1961) found, for example, that in Detroit during the 1950s, Jews, much more often than Protestants and Catholics, had relatives living in Detroit and visited with them weekly. Lenski found that Jewish respondents, more often than Christians, reported that their spouse, children, and parents influenced their religious beliefs. Croog, Lipton, and Levine (1972) found, however, that Jews did not differ from non-Jews in assistance given to relatives stricken with heart attacks. However, Wake and Sporakowski (1972) reported Jews are more willing to support aged parents.

Gordon (1959) suggests that movement to the suburbs by Jews during the 1950s did little to damage strong kinship ties. Approximately 60 percent of his respondents reported visiting with parents and other relatives as often as they did when the entire *mishpokhe* lived in the central city. Most of those who see their relatives less frequently still observe festival and holy days together. In these respects, the move to the suburbs has perhaps had a less disruptive effect than that found in England among lower-middle-class non-Jewish families (Young and Willmot, 1962). Findings reported by Gordon are, however, consistent with those that indicate that in highly industrialized societies, when relatives see one another with less frequency, feast days and holy days, for Christians as well, become special days for visiting and celebrating (Luschen et al., 1971).

A study of Jewish kinship ties in New York also shows the persistence of traditional norms. Leichter and Mitchell (1967) found that a majority of men and women each feel closer to their own relatives than to their spouse's. In general, women interact more often with their kin and have a wider variety of kinds of assistance that they exchange with relatives, much of which involves child care. Yet, men interact more often with their own relatives when matters arise pertaining to business or help in household repairs.

Until the twentieth century, Jewish communities in Europe were organized as corporate bodies (Elazar and Goldstein, 1972). The tradition of organizing formal structures has been extended in American Jewish communities to the family, as well. Mitchell (1978) reports that with the decline of Jewish neighborhoods and the dispersal of kin throughout metropolitan areas, people organize the *mishpokhe* by establishing associations of "cousins clubs" and "family circles." These associations replicate some of the functions of the organized Jewish community—sustaining family identity and solidarity (reinforcing Jewish identity and solidarity), giving to charity, planning festivities, and providing mutual assistance. Because ties to the descent group can be limited to associational obligations, these "cousins clubs" and "family circles" facilitate perpetuation of the *mishpokhe* without making excessive demands on members who have diverse professional and social commitments outside the family.

However, the very tight integration of the *mishpokhe* may have drawbacks for members. The husband's kindred may attempt to dominate his family, offering unsolicited criticism and demanding much loyalty from his wife and children. Indeed, Leichter and Mitchell (1967:177–181) found that there was greater conflict with the husband's kin than the wife's over interference in internal family matters.

In recent decades, however, dispersion of Jewish populations has occurred not only within metropolitan centers. It has also redistributed the American Jewish population throughout the country.

Table 3 presents data on trends in the distribution of the American

TABLE 3
Distribution of the Jewish Population, by Regions (1900, 1918, 1930, 1963, 1972, and 1985)

REGION	1900	1918	1930	1963	1972	1985
NORTHEAST	56.6	69.9	68.3	65.9	62.6	53.7
New England	7.4	8.6	8.4	6.7	6.8	6.8
Middle Atlantic	49.2	61.3	59.9	59.2	55.8	46.9
NORTH CENTRAL	23.7	20.2	19.6	13.7	12.2	11.4
East North Central	18.3	15.7	15.7	11.2	9.8	9.3
West North Central	5.4	4.5	3.9	2.5	2.4	2.2
SOUTH	14.2	6.9	7.6	9.1	11.8	18.4
South Atlantic	8.0	4.0	4.3	6.7	9.4	15.9
East South Central	3.3	1.3	1.4	0.8	0.7	0.8
West South Central	2.9	1.6	1.9	1.6	1.9	1.8
WEST	5.5	3.1	4.6	11.5	13.3	16.5
Mountain	2.3	0.7	1.0	0.9	1.1	2.2
Pacific	3.2	2.4	3.6	10.6	12.2	14.3
TOTAL (%)	100.0	100.0	100.0	100.0	100.0	100.0
Number (in 100s)	1053	3389	4228	5599	6115	5817

SOURCES: Data on distribution of Jewish population from *American Jewish Year Book*, 1.(1900), pp. 623–624; 21.(1919), p. 606; 33.(1931), p. 276; 65.(1964), p. 14; 74.(1973), p. 309, p. 182, 85.(1984) (cited in *American Jewish Year Book*, 1984, 85:182). Data for 1900 and 1930 cited in Goldstein (1971).

Jewish population from 1900 to 1985. The following movements seem to be occurring:

1. Prior to 1900, the existing Jewish population had spread westward and southward to the eastern north central and southern Atlantic states.
2. Immigration during the first part of the twentieth century, however, reconcentrated the bulk of the Jewish population in the Northeast. Relative to the middle Atlantic states in particular, by 1928 all other regions showed a smaller percentage of the total Jewish American population.
3. Since World War I, there has been a steady redistribution of the Jewish population, with the major losses in the northeastern and north central states.
4. Dramatic shifts occurred between 1930 and 1985 in the movement of population to the southern Atlantic and the Pacific states. For the most part, this movement represents large Jewish migrations to warmer, more salubrious climates—to Florida (particularly Miami) and to California. Writing in 1950, Seligman (1950:45) noted that Miami and Tucson, Arizona, showed "tremendously rapid growth in the last decade."

Despite the findings on the stability of kinship ties, the recent shifts in population to the south and southwest may contribute much to the decline in social relationships among family and relatives. In the Lakeville study (Sklare and Greenblum, 1967:252), there was a sharp decline in the amount of time spent with relatives from one generation to the next. Although nearly 40 percent of the respondents reported that when they had been children their parents spent more time with relatives than with friends, only 5 percent of the respondents indicated that they themselves spend more time with relatives than with friends. Moreover, whereas nearly 60 percent saw their cousins at least monthly when they were children, only 40 percent of their own children now visit with cousins.

There is also a significant decline in extended family households as families move to the suburbs or migrate to warmer climates. In their study of Providence, Rhode Island, Goldstein and Goldscheider (1968) reported that 85 percent of the Jewish households consisted of husband, wife, and their children, and a mere 8 percent held other relatives as well. The effect of generation on household composition was considerable. When age was held statistically constant, the percentage of nuclear-family households headed by third-generation persons was considerably greater than that for first-generation heads of household. Because generation is related to religious orthodoxy, one would expect to find more households augmented by relatives among the more orthodox than among the more liberal or among nominal Jewish families.

The Jewish population movement to the south and southwest has included not only young families but also the elderly. Young families may see in this migration an opportunity to live a more desirable existence away from familial obligations, only to find that their relatives, perhaps now old and retired, went their way southward and westward. It is difficult to fully assess the implications of this movement. Undoubtedly, it will act to deconcentrate the Jewish community and will most likely decompose family obligations still further.

Family Roles

Household division of labor in traditional European non-Jewish families is often associated with an ideology of patriarchal authority and the subordination of women. Yet, writers about the Jewish family generally agree that the subordination found in some European systems (e.g., the Italian) has been absent among Jews. Gordon (1959:58), for example, suggests the following:

> Historically, the entire responsibility for the support as well as the care of the family often rested on the woman's shoulders. Jewish women, through the centuries, often carried on the business or earned the family's livelihood in order that the husband might devote himself to the intensive study of Torah. Her influence with respect to her children and her husband was extraordinary.

Even among immigrant families, Gordon notes (1959:59), "there was a far greater degree of equality between husband and wife than is generally assumed. . . . The mother was the homemaker, but it was she whose personal piety and example within the home was expected to influence her children, while winning their love and veneration."

Gordon further suggests that as the Jewish families moved to the suburbs following World War II, "the wife, by virtue of her increased duties and responsibilities within the family, has become the modern matriarch of Jewish suburbia. Her ideas, opinions and values clearly dominate."

One would expect women in traditional homemaking roles to have a strong investment in their children's behavior. In a study of Westchester County, New York, concern over possible deviance in children's behavior was greatest among the more traditional groups. As one might anticipate on the basis of the Jewish-mother stereotype, "More Jewish than non-Jewish mothers reported worrying, though their children were no more impaired than those of other religious groups" (Lurie, 1974:113).

The movement by women toward increased labor-force participation (especially in professional and managerial positions) is expected to lead to a growing ambivalence toward maternal roles (see, for example, Luria, 1974). In the Phoenix study, as one might expect, the probability of finding the proverbial Jewish mother is quite high among the parents of the respondents. Only 25 percent of Jewish mothers worked during the time when the respondents were growing up—in contrast to 35 percent for non-Jewish mothers. For the respondents themselves, differences by religion disappear; regardless of religion, approximately 60 percent of the women were working. However, there is a catch: the chances of maternal employment depend in large part on the number of children in the home. Because Jewish women have very few children, one would expect even more Jewish than non-Jewish women to be employed. Because there are not, the data may well be shielding the degree of maternal involvement of Jewish women (Farber, 1981).

Traditionally, the father has had a priestly role in the household. As the link between the family and religious community, the husband was responsible for the piety, morality, and ethical standards of the family members. In the contemporary American context, the priestly status of the father is translated into his occupational dedication and his retention of achievement values for his children, especially sons (Strodtbeck, 1958). Yet, in suburban America, "few mothers or fathers accept easily the role of religious director in the family" (Seeley, Sim, and Loosely, 1956:214). In fact, in religious organizations, Jewish "women are much more in evidence than men and more frequently represent the family" (Lazerwitz, 1985). Thus, men have been shifting their social dedication from a priestly status within the family to the mundane.

Sklare (1971:87) points out that in the traditional Jewish family, a child is never considered to be truly emancipated from his or her parents. He suggests that children are seen as extensions of their parents rather than as distinct entities. One of the basic forms of exchange for parent and child is for parents to provide a basis for their children's own success in family and community, whereas the child has an obligation to supply *nakhus* (pleasure or gratification) for his parents. In providing the conditions for *nakhus,* the parent creates a lifelong obligation for the child.

The decline of the special structure of the Jewish parent–child relationship emanates, according to Sklare (1971:89), from two sources. The first source is the high level of secular educational attainment of Jews, which stresses urbanity and cosmopolitanism. The second source is the affinity of

Jews for those schools of modern psychology that "stress the reduction of dependence (whether on the part of parents or children) [and in doing so] they are necessarily critical of the structure of the Jewish family and of its special culture" (Sklare, 1971:90). Sklare thus sees an escalating estrangement that is destroying traditional family commitments.

Socialization of Children

The parent–child relationship described by Sklare (1971) of creating in the child an obligation to be successful by bringing *nakhus* to the parents makes certain assumptions about the nature of conduct. These assumptions provide a basis for the kind of socialization practices found in Jewish families. Essentially, one channels rather than shapes behavior. The person is seen not as a responding mechanism or a tabula rasa but as someone who has a drive to act that requires controls and outlets. The psychoanalytic perspective is quite congenial to this conception of socialization.

The view of socialization of children as channeling suggests that personal behavior is the outpouring of a substance (such as water or vital matter) that demands expression in its flow. One can guide the flow or dig new channels, but one cannot dam up the flow indefinitely. Punishment does not inhibit behavior but merely diverts it to other channels.

In European *shtetl,* the aim of socialization was to make each child a *mensch,* that is, one who does the appropriate things at the appropriate time and place with the appropriate persons (Zborowski and Herzog, 1952:335):

> Weeping is accepted as a normal means of expression and, on occasion, a legitimate weapon. . . . Grown men are not expected to weep as often or as freely as women and children, but for them too tears are in order during certain rituals, or as an accompaniment to pleas for help, either for themselves or for their community.

Channeling of behavior, as found in Jewish families, implies that "each year adds new responsibilities in the child's life" (Zborowski and Herzog, 1952:350) as well as fresh forms of tension release. With each special responsibility, the child is seen as becoming more of a *mensch.* "Despite the persisting, but steadily contracting, areas of indulgence, from the moment a child is able to help with the younger ones or with the family *parnosseh* (earning a living), or to go to *cheder* (religious school), it becomes a responsible and functioning member of a group" (Zborowski and

Herzog, 1952:331). Especially strong is the separation of male and female worlds in the *shtetl.* As boys and girls mature, they "become more and more aware of the rules against intermingling of sexes" (Zborowski and Herzog, 1952:352). Bit by bit, the individual assumes the "yoke of Jewishness" (*ol fun Yiddishkeit*), the discipline imposed by Judaic ritual.

The channeling of behavior in terms of division of labor seems to give rise to a heightened intensity of behavior in specific roles. Indeed, the father is not merely head of the house; he is also its "priest," responsible for its living according to ritual and Jewish law and, ideally, is dedicated to prayer and study. One is not merely a mother; one is, instead, a *Yiddished mahmeh,* with all the stereotypical nurturance, overprotection, and domineering that "Jewish mother" implies. The mother–child relationship is "complementary rather than reciprocal. Parents are donors and should not receive from children. The children can make return by passing benefits to their children" (Mandelbaum, 1958:512). In illness, a Jew does not suppress pain; instead, concerned with its symptomatic meaning, he makes the most of it, expressing its intensity at every opportunity (Zborowski, 1969:240–242). In family conflict, one is forbidden to use physical violence but may still curse, and Jewish curses contain imaginative invective in their expression—for example, "oxen should grow in your belly," or "your father's godfather should get a kick." Children are often imbued with the Protestant ethic, often to a greater extent than Protestants (Slater, 1969). Findings indicate that high-achievement motivation is related to parental praise and expression of parental pride (Rehberg, Sinclair, and Schafer, 1970). Participation thus tends to be unbalanced—perhaps even caricatured—in different spheres of the social world. Complete dedication to work, home, or piety seems to flow from the conception of socialization as the channeling of energy.

Some balance in behavior is achieved, however, through the ritualization of the rhythms. The daily prayers, the celebration of the Sabbath, and the periodic holidays during which one must turn from the tension of the workaday world, all act as regularized forms of tension release. Ritualization of tension release requires (1) the development of delayed gratification patterns because time and place of rituals are fixed, (2) the use of deflection and sublimation as socialization techniques as opposed to inhibition and negation, and (3) reliance on authority and benefice as justifying conduct rather than seeking reciprocity in all behavioral exchanges. The heavy reliance on ritual thus does not leave even tension release to chance.

The research on drinking supports this conception of child socialization. Without exception, studies of drinking patterns indicate a low rate of heavy drinking among Jews, especially in Orthodox homes (Snyder, 1958). At the same time, cross-cultural analysis of drinking shows that societies that are highly indulgent of their children in the pre-adolescent years tend to be high in drunkenness, and where there is a general pressure for obedience and responsibility in children, drunkenness tends to be low (Field, 1962). Thus, Jewish families seem to fall into the latter category, characterized by highly controlled tension release, permitting and even encouraging the ritual use of alcohol.

Psychoanalytic concepts seem appropriate to describe what happens when the channeled expression of behavior exceeds acceptable limits or when channels are blocked. Given general socialization data, it does not seem surprising that, in types of mental illness, Jews tend to have neurotic or mild or moderate symptoms of mental illness, whereas Catholic and Protestant populations are more prone to severe mental impairments (Rose and Stub, 1955:112; Srole et al., 1962:304; Roberts and Myers, 1954). Moreover, unlike Catholics and Protestants, parental religiosity is unrelated to degree of impairment among Jews (Srole et al., 1962:310). The qualitative difference between Jews, Protestants, and Catholics is expressed further in attitudes toward psychotherapy and psychoanalysis. Among psychiatrists, there is a marked tendency for Jews to hold a psychoanalytic orientation (Hollingshead and Redlich, 1958). In general, Jewish individuals are more favorably inclined toward psychotherapy as an effective mode of treatment and are more often outpatients in psychiatric services than are Catholics or Protestants (Srole et al., 1962:125–318).

As the current generation of adolescents matures, one finds a waning of the modes of socialization that have characterized earlier generations. Boroff (1961) reports that Jewish youth are losing their sense of uniqueness. He finds that the younger teenagers identify strongly with other teenagers as a generation but that older Jewish teenagers are more college-oriented than their peers. In this generation, when parents differ in attitude from friends of their children over such issues as the use of kosher meat, the children agree more often with their peers than their parents (Rosen, 1955). The youth seem to have developed a strong bond to the broad American community, with its emphasis on the insulation of youth from family influence.

Despite these shifts in patterns of socialization, however, the emphasis in the family on scholarly achievement remains high. In the Phoenix study, Jewish respondents reveal a strong relationship between kinship collaterality and emphasis on academic achievement in the teenage years. Eighty-eight percent in the Parentela Orders (i.e., the traditionally Jewish) category regarded high grades as important, compared with 82 percent in the Standard American class, 63 percent in the Civil Law group, and only 56 percent in the Genetic and Canon Law approaches to kinship (Farber, 1981). Moreover, the significance of this association is brought out by an analysis of scholastic achievement by students at Arizona State University. Those students of all religions who conformed to the Jewish kinship model tended to have the highest cumulative grade point averages (GPAs), and those persons whose pattern of answers resembled the Canon Law or Genetic models had the lowest GPAs (Farber, 1977).

American Jewry and World Jewry

It is important to realize that American Jewry is but one part, albeit the largest part, of world Jewry. Many of the characteristics that have been presented for American Jews apply in different degrees to Jews of central and eastern European background or descent who live in other countries. Many of these characteristics do not apply at all to the other major branches of world Jewry: Jews originally from Spain and Portugal who settled throughout the Mediterranean basin after the Spanish expulsion and Jews from Arabic-speaking countries—the so-called Oriental Jews. Most members of these two branches now live in Israel.

The legend of a "Jewish face" might seem to hold for American Jews. However, Israel, the gathering place of all the different branches and subgroups of world Jewry, presents such a wide variety of "Jewish faces" that one cannot determine who is Jewish by mere appearance. In today's world, it is likely that few traits of any major division of Jewry apply to most of world Jewry. Perhaps, in 50 years or more, when the current highly varied groups of world Jewry change into fewer types, especially in Israel, more widespread Jewish traits will appear. If so, it seems likely that such traits will be strongly influenced by the traditions of eastern Europe mixed in with a "strong flavor" contributed by Middle Eastern Jewry.

CHANGE AND ADAPTATION

Forecasts for the future of the American Jewish family generally fall into three groups: the pessimists, the ambivalents, and optimists. Each group has its fervent proponents, and each group establishes its case on different grounds.

The Pessimists

The pessimists view trends in Jewish family organization as mirroring those of the American middle class. According to this position, the same forces that are weakening traditional family bonds in middle-class society are destroying the Jewish family. This group sees the steady increase in mobility and migration, the continued growth of individualism, and the heightening of cosmopolitanism in American society as undermining the basis for strong family life in American society. For example, Gordon (1959:83) writes the following:

> It is my belief that, if our suburban communities continue to change internally as they have since 1950 . . . Jewish residents will inevitably feel that they are a rootless community. They will not feel "at home" or at ease within any given area. To regard the suburb in which one lives as a temporary home is to destroy the sense of permanence that all families need . . . Jewish family relations, which to date have remained excellent, may not be able to survive another decade of extreme mobility without showing signs of great stress and strain.

Focusing on the role of the family in establishing Jewish identification in children, Sklare also presents a pessimistic stance. He regards the very social and economic success of American Jews as contributing to the downfall of the traditional *mishpokhe,* which long has acted as a bedrock of Jewish community institutions. Sklare proposes (1971:89–100) the following:

> The changing significance of the family, and particularly the fairly recent declines in the frequency and intensity of interaction with the kinship group, means that identity can no longer be acquired through this traditional institution . . . American Jewry has a highly developed communal structure as well as a firmly established network of Jewish schools . . . But however significant the communal network and the school system are as building blocks, they are a kind of super-structure resting upon the foundation of the family—for it is the family that has been the prime mechanism for transmitting Jewish identity. This system of identity-formation is currently on the decline. The emerging crisis of the Jewish family in identity-formation is in part due to the newer limitations on the family as a socialization agent—limitations that affect all other Americans as well. But it is traceable to . . . the high acculturation of many Jewish parents, the diminished interaction with relatives, and the presence of Gentiles in the Jewish kinship network . . . It is the shrinking contribution of the family to Jewish identity transmission that constitutes its essential weakness.

In summary, the view of the pessimists is mainly that the American family itself is becoming ineffective as a socialization agent, and that by becoming assimilated into the mainstream of American life, the Jewish family has lost its crucial role in identity transmission.

The Ambivalent

Whereas the pessimists emphasize the decreasing differentiation between Jewish and non-Jewish family life in the American middle class, the ambivalent observers regard the survival of the Jewish family as a personal decision. The risk taken by relegating choices in social issues to personal decisions is that many individuals will choose against the perpetuation of traditional norms and values.

Liebman (1973:151–152) expresses pessimism over preference for interaction with other Jews or affiliation with formal organizations in the Jewish community to be effective in the survival of Jewish institutions. He notes, for example, that preferred association with other Jews—as ubiquitous as it is—is uncorrelated with any other index of Jewish identification. Affiliation with Jewish formal organization is of limited interest; Jewish communal organizations are experiencing difficulty in attracting talented and highly educated persons. Liebman thus expresses doubt that communal motives can be induced to strengthen Jewish identification and Jewish family life. His solution rests solely on personal decision:

> Jewish peoplehood is threatened by the growing impulse toward cosmopolitanism and universalism; in a society which increasingly stresses the primacy of conscience and individual freedom against even society's own law, *Torah* and the study of sacred texts become increasingly absurd. The very notion of sacred text is antiquarian, and there is no room for a tradition of study in a culture which affirms the values of sensation and of the individual as the final arbiter of right and wrong. It is, therefore, my strong belief that, at least until we enter a post-modern world, the Jew who wishes to remain in the United States, but who is also committed to the survival of Judaism, has no alternative but to retreat into a far more sectarian posture than has up to this time characterized American Jewish life.

The personal decision to adopt traditional Jewish norms and, by implication, Jewish family norms in particular necessarily entails the risk that a significant proportion of Jews will make this decision. Otherwise, there can be no survival of the idea of peoplehood, religious community, or communal life according to biblical injunctions. Liebman's position thus implies a faith that others will also make a "moral" decision as a resolution of personal ambivalence.

Perhaps the survival of a remnant living according to norms of Jewish family life is all that can be hoped for in modern society. Berman (1968:560) suggests the following:

> An open society where ethnic boundaries survive because they serve the individual's needs for variety, for belongingness, for continuity of identity, for authenticity—where ethnic boundaries are not prison walls—where those Jews who would rather be Gentiles and Gentiles who would rather be Jews are equally free to cross the boundary and find a more congenial ethnic home—that, in this writer's opinion, is a good society.

The Optimists

The optimists believe that modern society sustains ethnic differences by its very composition and that this persistence of ethnicity will act to sustain traditional Jewish family organization. The argument presented by Glazer and Moynihan (1974) is as follows: (1) More and more modern societies are becoming multiethnic states; (2) diverse ethnic groups occupy different and conflicting positions in modern social structures; (3) because of their opposing positions, ethnic groups become rallying points in the identification of interest groups in the society; (4) in becoming rallying points in relation to political, social, and economic interest, ethnic groups tend to stress those features that define their uniqueness; and (5) features that ethnic groups claim as unique thus tend to survive. One of the features that Jews have claimed as unique is their family life—such as the *Yiddisheh mahmeh* and the *nakhus*—hence, the optimist would see a conscious effort to sustain Jewish family norms ultimately growing out of a need to defend Jewish interests (e.g., support of Soviet Jewry, backing of Israel, opposition to quota systems in occupations).

The view expressed by Glazer and Moynihan (1974) presupposes that there will always be a series of significant issues to provide for the constant revitalization of ethnic identification. At best, however, one can expect the flow of issues as rallying points to mobilize only segments of the Jewish community, and despite the optimism of Glazer and Moynihan, people tire of mobilization. Thus, without coercive constraints, one would anticipate a general waning in voluntary mobilization. Without institutionalized factionalism, one would anticipate a slow languishing of the norms and values traditionally associated with Jewish family life.

All data show that American Jewry has continually shifted away from a traditionalist stance to one involving increasing marginality to Judaism and the organized Jewish community. By the year 2000, it is likely that the Reform denomination will be the large one, replacing the currently leading Conservative denomination. It is hard to predict the growth trend for those without denominational preferences: this category can be self-limiting. Many of those who express such Jewish marginality choose to leave the Jewish community and disappear among the vast numbers of non-Jewish Americans. As they do so, those who chose to remain Jewish and express this with a denominational preference may well become an increasing percentage of American Jewry.

It is also likely that the population exchange between American Jews and non-Jews, produced by intermarriage and conversion, will continue. If so, the religious and communal leaders of American Jewry will need to double their efforts to religiously and communally integrate those new to the Jewish community. Furthermore, American Jews will probably become increasingly like the rest of their fellow Americans, separated only by the strength of their attachment to the Jewish religion and its traditions and by a network of communal services aimed at meeting their religious, educational, and family services needs.

REFERENCES

Balswich, Jack. 1966. "Are American-Jewish Families Closely Knit?" *Jewish Social Studies,* 28:159–167.

Bell, Inge Powell. 1968. *CORE and the Strategy of Non-Violence.* New York: Random House.

Berman, Louis, 1968. *Jews and Intermarriage: A Study in Personality and Culture.* New York: Thomas Yoseloff.

Boroff, David. 1961. "Jewish Teenage Culture," *The Annals of the American Academy of Political Science,* 338:79–90.

Brav, Stanley R. 1940. *Jewish Family Solidarity, Myth or Fact?* Vicksburg, MS: Nogales Press.

Bressler, Marvin. 1952. "Selected Family Patterns in W. I. Thomas' Unfinished Study of the Bintl Brief," *American Sociological Review,* 17:563–571.

Brodbar-Nemzer, Jay Y. 1986. "Divorce and Group Commitment: The Case of the Jews," *Journal of Marriage and the Family*, 48:329–340.

Bumpass, Larry, and James Sweet. 1972. "Differentials in Marital Instability: 1970," *American Sociological Review,* 37:754–766.

Cohen, Steven M. 1977. "Socioeconomic Determinants of Intraethnic marriage and Friendship," *Social Forces,* 55:997–1010.

———. 1983. *American Modernity and Jewish Identity.* New York: Tavistock Publications.

Cromer, Gerald. 1974. "Intermarriage and Communal Survival in a London Suburb," *Jewish Journal of Sociology,* 16:155–169.

Della Pergola, Sergio. 1980. "Patterns of American Jewish Fertility," *Demography,* 17(3):261–273.
Elazar, Daniel J., and Stephen R. Goldstein. 1972. "The Legal Status of the American Jewish Community," *American Jewish Yearbook,* 73:3–94.
Farber, Bernard. 1973. *Family and Kinship in Modern Society.* Glenview, IL: Scott Foresman.
———. 1977. "Social Context, Kinship Mapping, and Family Norms," *Journal of Marriage and the Family,* 39:227–240.
Farber, Bernard, and Leonard Gordon. 1979. "Kinship Mapping Among Jews in a Midwestern City," *Social Forces,* 57:1107–1123.
———. 1981. *Conceptions of Kinship.* New York: Elsevier.
———. 1982. "Accounting for Intermarriage: Assessment of National and Community Studies," *Contemporary Jewry,* 6:47–75.
Field, Peter B. 1962. "A New Cross Cultural Study of Drunkenness," in David J. Pittman and Charles R. Snyder (eds.), *Society, Culture and Drinking Patterns.* New York: John Wiley, pp. 48–74.
Freedman, Ronald, Pascal Whelpton, and Arthur Campbell. 1959. *Family Planning Sterility, and Population Growth.* New York: McGraw-Hill.
———. 1961. "Socio-Economic Factors in Religious Differentials in Fertility," *American Sociological Review,* 26:608–614.
Glazer, Nathan. 1957. *American Judaism.* Chicago: University of Chicago Press.
Glazer, Nathan, and Daniel P. Moynihan. 1974. "Why Ethnicity?" *Commentary,* 58 (October):33–39.
Glikson, P., and S. Della Pergola (eds.). 1981. *Papers in Jewish Demography.* Jerusalem, Israel: The Hebrew University, pp. 215–238.
Golden, Harry, and Martin Rywell. 1950. *Jews in American History,* Charlotte, NC: Henry Lewis Martin.
Goldenstein, Sidney. 1971. "American Jewry, 1970," *American Jewish Year Book,* 72:3–88.
Goldenstein, Sidney, and Calvin Goldscheider. 1968. *Jewish Americans: Three Generations in a Jewish Community.* Englewood Cliffs, NJ: Prentice-Hall.
Gordon, Albert I. 1959. *Jews in Suburbia.* Boston: Beacon Press.
———. 1967. *The Nature of Conversion.* Boston: Beacon Press.
Herman, Manahem. 1980. "Manifestation of Jewish Messianic Movements and Cults," *Journal of Jewish Communal Service,* 56:91–93.
Hollingshead, A. B., and F. C. Dedlich. 1958. *Social Class and Mental Illness.* New York: John Wiley.
Kardiner, Abram, and Lionel Ovesy. 1951. *The Mark of Oppression.* New York: W. W. Norton.
Landes, Ruth, and Mark Zborowski. 1968. "The Context of Marriage: Family Life as a Field of Emotions," in H. Kent Geiger (ed.), *Comparative Perspectives on Marriage and the Family.* Boston: Little, Brown, pp. 77–102.
Landis, Judson T. 1960. "Religiousness, Family Relationships, and Family Values in Protestant, Catholic, and Jewish Families," *Marriage and Family Living,* 22:341–347.
Lazerwitz, Bernard. 1971. "Fertility Trends in Israel and Its Administered Territories," *Jewish Social Studies,* 33:172–186.

———. 1973. "Religious Identification and Its Ethnic Correlates: A Multivariate Model," *Social Forces,* 52:204–220.

———. 1978. "An Approach to the Components and Consequences of Jewish Identification," *Contemporary Jewry,* 4:3–8.

———. 1980. "Religiosity and Fertility: How Strong a Connection?" *Contemporary Jewry.*

———. 1981. "Jewish-Christian Marriages and Conversions," *Jewish Social Studies,* 43:31–46.

———. 1985. "A Revised Model of Jewish Identification." Research Report, Bar-Ilan University, Ramat-Gan, Israel.

———. 1987. "Trends in National Jewish Identification Indicators: 1971–1985," *Contemporary Jewry,* 9 (forthcoming).

Lazerwitz, Bernard, and Michael Harrison. 1979. "American Jewish Denominations: A Social and Religious Profile," *American Sociological Review,* 44:656–666.

Leichter, Hope J., and William E. Mitchell. 1967. *Kinship and Casework.* New York: Russell Sage Foundation.

Lenski, Gerhard. 1961. *The Religious Factor.* New York: Doubleday.

Lewin, Kurt. 1948. *Resolving Social Conflicts.* New York: Harper and Row.

Liebman, Charles S. 1973. "American Jewry: Identity and Affiliation," in David Sidorsky (ed.), *The Future of the Jewish Community in America.* New York: Basic Books, pp. 127–152.

Luria, Zella. 1974. "Recent Women College Graduates: A Study of Rising Expectations," *American Journal of Orthopsychiatry,* 44:109–120.

Luschen, Gunther. 1986. "Zur kontext-und interaktions-Analyse familial-verwandtschaftlicher Netzwerke." Paper presented at symposium of Change and Continuity of the Family in West Germany, Bamberg, West Germany.

Luschen, Gunther, et al. 1971. "Family Organization, Interaction, and Ritual," *Journal of Marriage and the Family,* 33:228–234.

Maller, Alan. 1975. "New Facts About Mixed Marriages," *Reconstructionist,* 34:26–29.

Mandelbaum, David G. 1958. "Change and Continuity in Jewish Life," in Marshall Sklare (ed.), *The Jews, Social Patterns of an American Group.* New York: Free Press, pp. 509–519.

Manners, Ande. 1972. *Poor Cousins.* New York: Coward, McCann and Geoghegan.

Massarik, Fred, and Albert Chenkin. 1973. "United States National Jewish Population Study: A First Report," in *American Jewish Year Book.* New York: Institute of Human Relations, pp. 264–306.

Mayer, Egon, 1980. "Processes and Outcomes in Marriages between Jews and Non-Jews," *American Behavioral Scientist,* 23:487–518.

Merton, Robert K. 1941. "Intermarriage and the Social Structure: Fact and Theory," *Psychiatry,* 4:361–374.

Mitchell, William E. 1978. *Mishpokhe.* New York: Mouton Publishers.

Rehberg, Richard A., Judie Sinclair, and Walter E. Schafer. 1970. "Adolescent Achievement Behavior, Family Authority Structure, and Parental Socialization Practices," *American Journal of Sociology,* 75:1012–1034.

Rice, B. 1976. "Messiah from Korea," *Psychology Today,* 9(8):36–47.
Roberts, B. H., and J. K. Meyers. 1954. "Religion, Natural Origin, Immigration, and Mental Illness," *American Journal of Psychiatry,* 110:759–764.
Rose, Arnold M., and Halger R. Stub. 1955. "Summary of Studies on the Incidence of Mental Disorders," in Arnold M. Rose (ed.), *Mental Health and Mental Disorders.* New York: Norton, pp. 87–116.
Rosen, Bernard C. 1955. "Conflicting Group Membership: A Study of Parent-Peer-Group Cross Pressures," *American Sociological Review,* 20:155–161.
Rosenthal, Erich. 1963. "Studies of Jewish Intermarriage in the United States," *American Jewish Year Book,* 64:3–53.
———. 1970. "Divorce and Religious Intermarriage: The Effects of Previous Marital Status Upon Subsequent Marital Behavior," *Journal of Marriage and the Family,* 32:435–440.
Schmelz, U. O. 1981. "Jewish Survival: The Demographic Factors," *American Jewish Year Book,* 81:61–117.
Schmelz, U. O., and Sergio Della Pergola. 1982. "World Jewish Population," *American Jewish Yearbook,* 82:277–290.
Seeley, John R., R. Alexander Sim, and E. W. Loosely. 1956. *Crestwood Heights, a Study of the Culture of Suburban Life.* New York: Basic Books.
Seligman, Ben B. 1950. "The American Jew: Some Demographic Features," *American Jewish Year Book,* 51:3–52.
Sklare, Marshall (ed.). 1958. *The Jews, Social Patterns of an American Group.* Glencoe, IL: Free Press.
———. 1971. *America's Jews.* New York: Random House.
Sklare, Marshall, and Joseph Greenblum. 1967. *Jewish Identity on the Suburban Frontier: A Study of Group Survival in the Open Society.* New York: Basic Books.
Slater, Mariam K. 1969. "My Son the Doctor: Aspects of Mobility Among American Jews," *American Sociological Review,* 34:359–373.
Snyder, Charles R. 1958. *Alcohol and the Jews.* New York: Free Press.
Spero, Moshe. 1977. "Cults: Some Theoretical and Practical Perspectives," *Journal of Jewish Communal Service,* 53:330–338.
Srole, Leo, Thomas S. Langer, Stanley T. Michael, Marvin K. Opler, and Thomas A. C. Rennie. 1962. *Mental Health in the Metropolis.* New York: McGraw-Hill.
Strodtbeck, Fred. 1958. "Family Interaction, Values and Achievement," in Marshall Sklare (ed.), *The Jews, Social Patterns of an American Group.* Glencoe, IL: Free Press, pp. 147–165.
U. S. Bureau of the Census. 1958. "Religion Reported by the Civilian Population of the United States: March 1957," *Current Population Reports.* Series P-20, no. 35. Washington, DC: U. S. Government Printing Office.
Wake, Sandra B., and Michael J. Sporakowski. 1972. "An Intergenerational Comparison of Attitudes Toward Supporting Aged Parents," *Journal of Marriage and the Family,* 34:42–48.
Weinryb, Bernard D. 1958. "Jewish Immigration and Accommodation to America," in Marshall Sklare (ed.), *The Jews, Social Patterns of an American Group.* Glencoe, IL: Free Press, pp. 5–25.
Whelpton, Pascal, Arthur Campbell, and John Patterson. 1966. *Fertility and Family Planning in the United States.* Princeton, NJ: Princeton University Press.
Winch, Robert F., Scott Greer, and Rae L. Blumberg. 1967. "Ethnicity and Ex-

tended Familism in an Upper-Middle-Class Suburb," *American Sociological Review,* 32:265–272.

York, Allen. 1979. "Voluntary Associations and Communal Leadership Among the Jews of the United States." Ph.D. diss., Bar Ilan University, Ramat Gan, Israel.

York, Alan, and Bernard Lazerwitz. 1986. "Religious Involvement as the Main Gateway to Voluntary Association Activity," *Contemporary Jewry,* 8.

Young, Michael, and Peter Willmot. 1962. *Family and Kinship in East London.* Baltimore: Penguin Books.

Zborowski, Mark. 1969. *People in Pain.* San Francisco: Jossey-Bass.

Zborowski, Mark, and Elizabeth Herzog. 1952. *Life Is with People: The Culture of the Shtetl.* New York: Schocken Books.

CHAPTER SEVENTEEN

The Arab American Family

Abdo A. Elkholy

HISTORICAL BACKGROUND

The Arab world, with its huge oil reserve, emerged in 1973 as an area of enormous importance to America and the Western world. It may come as a surprise for many Americans and Canadians to learn that there are sizeable Arab communities in their countries. It is also a fact that few sociological studies have been conducted on these Arab American and Arab Canadian communities and their family patterns. Although the chapter presented here does suffer from the relatively scant amount of information available on this ethnic group, I have relied on two field studies separated by 20 years, one conducted in 1957 and the other in 1977. In addition, the participant-observer technique has aided my interpretation of the statistical data gathered on these Arab communities in the United States and Canada.

Understanding the Arab Americans and their styles of family organization may enable Americans to better comprehend the Middle East. This chapter provides a spectroscopic examination of the family patterns of an old people in a new land and, by inference, a picture of an enigmatic people who may, nevertheless, through our scientific and sociological probing, provide us with the knowledge requisite to achieve an overall pattern for assimilation of Middle Eastern nations into the world community.

Arab Americans and Arab Canadians proudly mention their ancestors crossing the Atlantic from Spain and arriving in Brazil in the year 1150 AD. Before that, in the tenth century AD (according to the Arab geographer Al-Sharilf (Al-Idrisi), eight adventurous Arabs sailed from Lisbon, Portugal, trying to discover what lay beyond the sea of darkness, or the Atlantic Ocean (Audat, 1956:5–17). It is said that they landed in South America. Some historians suspect that Al-Idrisi's story inspired Columbus to try to reach the East through the West, which led to the great discovery of America. In 1955, when Italy celebrated the 500th anniversary of the birth of Columbus, there was a fair at which many of Columbus's belongings were displayed. Among them was an Arabic book, said to be the Idrisi book, in which the story of the eight adventurers was mentioned. It suffices to state that migration remains one characteristic of the Arabs because of their nomadic history. If those early migrations were initiated by personal curiosity, the late ones have been initiated by social causes.

South America captured the attraction and imagination of the early Arab emigrants, who went there in large groups to form sizable and influential ethnic communities. Perhaps the cold climate and the Europeanization of the United States and Canada made them less attractive to the early Arabs than South America, since the Arabs only started to migrate to the United States and Canada in the last quarter of the nineteenth century. One distinct religious feature dominated the early Arab emigrations of the nineteenth century: The great majority were Christians. Fear of losing their religion in the Christian, missionary-minded New World delayed the immigration of the Arab Moslems to America by about 25 years, until the start of the twentieth century (Makdisi, 1959:970). The head-start migration thus achieved by Christian Arabs increased their ratio to the Moslem Arabs up to the start of World War II by nine to one.

The Arab migration to North America resulted from two causes (Warner and Srole, 1945:105): "forces of attraction exerted by the expanding American economy and forces of expulsion exerted in the lands of emigration." Prior to 1950, only 2 percent of Arab Americans left their native land for political reasons and less than 1 percent for education in America. Driven by poverty and attracted by wealth, most of them came from the peasant sector in Greater Syria, politically recognized now as Lebanon. It is not surprising that with unfavorable demographic characteristics such as low socioeconomic and educational status, the early waves of immigrants did not fare well in the New World. One-fourth of them ended their journey in the southern states where farm labor was welcomed, and many became successful farmers in Georgia, Texas, Tennessee, Mississippi, New Mexico, and Arizona, and (in Canada) Nova Scotia, New Brunswick, Quebec, Ontario, Manitoba, Saskatchewan, and Alberta. About 50 percent of the early immigrants stayed on the east coast, in New York, New Jersey, Pennsylvania, the New England states, and Nova Scotia, New Brunswick, and Quebec. They peddled dry goods and started grocery stores. The remaining 25 percent moved to the midwestern states of Ohio, Michigan, Indiana, Illinois, Iowa, and Ontario and Manitoba to work as unskilled laborers in the railroad, steel, and auto industries in addition to dry goods peddling and grocery stores. As some pioneers recalled, they often were sponsored by successful buisnesspeople who had migrated earlier from the same region. Upon their arrival in United States or Canadian ports, immigration officials pinned name tags on them, put them on the train, and called the sponsor to announce their arrival at their destination. In most cases their passage was paid by either relatives in the old country or the sponsors, who generally assumed responsibility of finding them living quarters and providing them with employment. The sponsors were mainly dry goods wholesalers who relied on the immigrants to sell their goods from door to door. This arrangement was mutually satisfactory in the short run. The immigrant, who lacked funds and knowledge of the English language, found suitable and ready employment in a strange environment, and the wholesaler found squadrons of laborers who contributed to the prosperity of his business.

Whether Moslem or Christian, the Arabs who formed the first waves of immigrants from the last quarter of the 19th century up to World War II never intended to spend the rest of their lives in America. They only wanted to accumulate the most money possible in the shortest time and then return home. Sixty percent of those early immigrants came unmarried. Because of economic uncertainty, only 12 percent of those married came with their families (Elkholy, 1966:83).

Though attracted to America, as reported by 97 percent of a sample of the early immigrants, they were handicapped by their lack of knowledge of English: "Learning the English language was the most difficult adjustment to make" (Elkholy, 1966:84). Coming from the lower educational class and having acquired no knowledge of English prior to their emigration, those of the earlier waves found everything strange in America. The majority of the first immigrants had to cluster around pioneers in order to solve the critical linguistic handicap, which has been one of the most influential factors in erecting ethnic clusters all over the world. The less English-speaking an ethnic community in America, the more clannish it is, and the more it segregates itself from American life. Such segregation delays the process of acculturation.

The early immigration waves between 1880 and 1939 carried the Arabs to the agricultural southern states as well as to the large cities of the east coast, New England, and the midwestern states, and forced them to congregate in small as well as large communities. The second immigration waves, which started in the 1950s and are still continuing, scattered the educated elites and technicians almost randomly across the United States and Canada.

The sharp demographic contrast between the first- and second-immigration waves is the function of two dramatic episodes in the Middle East: First, the creation of Israel in 1948 resulted in the expulsion of about two million Palestinians to make room for the European and Russian Jews, who have been coming to Israel ever since. Most of those Palestinian refugees who had the chance to come to America for one reason or another remained here permanently. Some were professionals and skilled workers. The majority acquired their higher education in American and Canadian universities when scholarships were plentiful and an unprecedented expansion of higher educational institutions took place. The second dramatic episode was the Egyptian Revolution in 1952, which grew out of the Arab world's frustration over the loss of Palestine, and which instigated a series of similar military coups d'etat and revolutions in other Arab and Moslem countries and disrupted the status quo in the social structure of the entire Middle East. Those Egyptians and other Arabs with professional and financial means, who did not fare well under the military regimes, started to look around for a way out. A great proportion of them have been emigrating to America since 1952; especially after 1956 and 1967, the late arrivals, the intellectual elite of the Arab society, were highly educated and skilled (*Arab Youth,* 1975:6). Seventy-three percent were educated in the United States, Canada, or Europe. This put them in favorable bargaining positions in the expanding educational, research, and technological markets, especially since they had no linguistic barrier to restrict their mobility. They sought employment as university professors, school teachers, engineers, technicians, and physicians. Some have already acquired national fame and prominence.

Many new Arab communities sprung up over the United States and Canada during the 1950s and 1960s. From Jersey City, New Jersey, to St. Louis, Missouri, and Los Angeles, California, and from London, Ontario, to Edmonton, Alberta, the newly immigrated Arabs settled in either new concentrations or as individuals, depending on their professions. During the so-called "brain-drain" period, which labeled those two decades, 90,915 Arabs, most of them professionals, immigrated to America. Between 1962 and 1972, 68,305, or about 90 percent of the total immigrants admitted to America from seven Arab countries, were professionals. Again, the majority of them came from Egypt. Added to these 90,915, another

2,080 nonimmigrants were naturalized between 1950 and 1971. Although there is no religious census taken in America of these new waves of Arab immigrants, it is estimated that 78 percent are Moslems. High professionalism and Moslem majority characterized the second-wave immigration in contrast to the early waves prior to World War II.

To speak of this professional category as a social group or an ethnic community gives a misleading impression, for there was no single institutional organization prior to 1960 under which they could be sheltered. It was only after the creation of Israel that a number of Arab American organizations were started mainly for the purpose of defending themselves against what they considered Zionist propaganda and defamation practices. In 1952 the Federation of Islamic Associations in the United States and Canada was formed, followed by the American Arab Association in 1961, the Association of Arab American University Graduates in 1967, and the Association of Egyptian American Scholars in 1970. However, these organizations attracted only a small percentage of the Arab elites in America.

The family lifestyle of this professional category approximates that of the typical middle-class WASP family style. In the absence of distinct racial characteristics betraying their ethnic origin, the members of this professional category are fully accepted by American society. Their intention to make America a permanent home facilitated the process of adaptation. In the Elkholy study, 68 percent of the men were found to be married to American, Canadian, or European spouses whom they met on university campuses at the time they were studying. The remaining 32 percent of Arab wives of these professionals belong to the upper-middle socioeconomic class in the Arab world. They are not handicapped by linguistic barriers, compared with the previous waves of less educated wives, and thus have easy access to higher education and employment. The professional, economic, and social prosperity of this category with Arab wives made assimilation to and acceptance by the American society as easy and speedy as it was for those 68 percent Arabs with Western spouses. The average number of children is 2.27. Birth control and family planning are practiced by 87 percent of the couples. Their American-born children are typical Americans with only scant knowledge of the Arab world and its problems.

While it is difficult to identify the product of the second waves of immigration as being members of Arab communities (due to their professional commitments and their high rate of mobility), it is quite easy to find concentrated communities that are the product of the early immigration waves.

THE MODERN ARAB AMERICAN FAMILY

The structure as well as the socialization processes of the Arab family in America oscillate generally between preservation of traditional culture and acculturation, depending on a number of variables, one of which is intermarriage with Westerners. From the perspective of intergroup relations, the problem can be seen through the eyes of the ethnic minority looking toward the larger society and its various groups. The intergroup relations are affected by the stereotyped images that the minority and dominant groups develop toward each other. The stereotype, which creates social distance, is extended to the members of a given group, and thus the interaction becomes biased. Overcoming the mutually unfavorable images of East and West requires strong personal sentimental preference in the face of traditions of both the minority and dominant groups. Intermarriage is viewed here from the standpoint of the minority spouse as a strong agent of assimilation, because the spouse who belongs to the dominant culture facilitates the cultural transformation of the offspring.

The difference between assimilation and acculturation may be made clear here. Acculturation cannot occur without assimilation. When the minority members assimilate the prevailing values of the host society and prefer them over the traditional values of their cultural background, one of two things takes place: The minority community rejects the assimilated members and makes their presence in the community unwelcome, often forcing them to leave, becoming a total loss to the minority community. However, when the minority community retains its assimilated members, they become a gain to the overall community acculturation. In the first instance, the community will ultimately dissolve by the time the last member leaves or dies. In the second case, the community may remain distinct, although acculturated. Intermarriage between Arabs and Westerners is in general neither desired nor encouraged by the Arab communities in the United States and Canada. Nevertheless, there are two variations in these attitudes which are related to religion and education.

Intermarriage and Religion

Although intermarriage with Westerners is desired by neither Moslem Arab nor Christian Arab communities, it is more strongly resisted by the Moslems than by the Christians. Since it was indicated before that intermarriage facilitates the processes of both assimilation and acculturation, it is to be expected that the Christian Arab communities will be more acculturated than their Moslem counterparts. In either case the process of interreligious marriage is not always smooth. Various cultural barriers intervene, one of which is the Arab family lifestyle, which differs from the American lifestyle.

Our sample study has shown that more than 68 percent of the Moslem immigrants came to the New World unmarried. Less than 12 percent of the married immigrants came with their families. The pattern, then, was for the immigrants to come alone. Aside from the few female students who marry in the New World and decide to remain, the entire stock of the single Moslem immigrants is composed of young men. These young men are faced with a problem: Who do they marry?

Marital choice differs between the two types of immigrants. The great majority of the unmarried pioneers married within their own ethnic groups by importing their wives from the old countries. Approximately 67 percent of the late arrivals, however, married Europeans, Americans, or Canadians. Thus, despite the relatively short time span the Moslems have been in the New World, they have generally adopted a liberal attitude toward interreligious marriages. This seems to be true for both men and women, and most particularly true for Moslem immigrants coming to this country after World War II. Liberal attitudes toward intermarriage are related to education, which is related to professionalism.

Aside from the fear of diluting their communities in the long run via intermarriage, Arabs desire that their young men marry only their young women. Marrying outside the group, even when the wives are brought to the community, means that an equal number of young Arab women will either stay unmarried or marry outside, thus leading to undesirable consequences. Intermarriage always brings to the community unpredictable members whose values, customs, and habits are not in accordance with those of the community. As one member put it to the author (Elkholy, 1966):

> With our people, we can drop by at any time, day or night, whenever we feel like it. We can go to the kitchen and icebox to help ourselves with no hesitation. We feel welcome and the wives do not resent us. They are our sisters. They understand what we talk about, for there is a common theme which cannot be taught. A lot of things can be taken for granted and do not require the cautions we have whenever we visit one of our unlucky brothers who married outside. We are hesitant to eat at their homes. The wife cannot follow our conversation. She gets frustrated. We feel embarrassed and soon the atmosphere becomes boring. Some of those wives are snobbish and feel superior. I don't know whether they really feel this way or just play it that way to keep a certain distance from the rest of the community. We feel sorry for the children. They do not have the joy our children have. We also feel sorry for those foolish husbands. We suspect that they are not happy at home. They miss our food, our conversation, gossip, and our entire atmosphere.

This might be an exaggerated image reflecting attitudes of some members toward such marriages. However, such an image constrains the social relations and restricts the interactions between the community and the families of intermarriage.

A REVERSE SITUATION: AN AMERICAN WIFE. From the viewpoint of the non-Arab wife, the story might be somewhat different. The pattern of the Western family hardly coincides with that of the Arab one. The wide gulf of hard reality between the immediate family and the extended one is not easy for the Western wife to comprehend. When she has to cross that rugged gulf to the extended family pattern of her husband, she finds herself aggravated and lost in an infinite number of relationships, each of which is traditionally prescribed and requires a set of specific mutual obligations. The following case study reported to the author (Elkholy, 1966) illustrates the predicament:

> An American wife married to an Iraqi professor when interviewed tried to illustrate the sources of her agony in Iraq which led her husband to immigrate to the United States. As is often the case, she met him on the American campus where they were attending the same university. They left the States for Iraq with their 6-month old child, immediately after the husband received his Ph.D. degree. All that she knew about the Middle East came to her mind through the fantasies of the book One Thousand and One Nights, plus the Western image of the sleepy, rosy medieval conditions. She did not find Bagdad the golden city she imagined. Rather, she found in it clusters of confusion emanating from social and ecological changes. Although her husband was given a university teaching position, his salary could hardly sustain the lifestyle of their Americanized household.
>
> Her anxieties started as soon as they strove to find a suitable apartment. The landlords did not desire to rent out their nice places to natives like her husband. They preferred foreigners, perhaps to get higher rent, or to be more sure of better maintenance. Her husband, for the first time, felt discriminated against in his own country. It was some time before they acquired a suitable apartment whose rent they could afford. With one car, which they had brought with them, they could hardly manage. The heavy teaching schedule of the husband, the imposed consultations with government circles for very little reward, and the endless favors the husband had to render daily to acquaintances, friends, and relatives in getting them positions or work here and there, to write them letters of recommendation, or to call influential people in their behalf—all this hardly left any of the husband's time for her or household affairs.
>
> Managing household affairs without a car, she had to use public transportation which she found frustrating. For help, she had to rely on unreliable maids. After she had half-trained the maid, the girl would quit or was attracted elsewhere by higher wages. She found it a losing battle which, however, she could not afford to stop fighting. During the three-year period the couple spent

in Iraq, her husband hardly had time to eat dinner with her at the regular time more than a dozen times. Normal family life was quite often interrupted by unscheduled visits of demanding relatives who felt they had an indisputable right to use the house as if it were their own. The concept of hotels and restaurants was alien to them. Gradually, the social burden became unbearable. Finally, the informant said, "we had to quit and return to the States."

The experiences of the Western wife in the native land of her Arab husband are not the most pleasant. She cannot grasp or bear the burden of the complexity of kinship outside the Western world. In the West, for example, there is only one term, cousin, to denote different types of kin relationships. All of them are equal in one respect: remoteness. There are, in the Middle East, eight different categories of cousins. Each category has a definite set of mutual rights and obligations that are legally acknowledged and traditionally carried out and maintained. The following illustrates the eight different categories of cousins.

		CHILD
Father's side:	Brother of the father	1. Son of brother of the father
		2. Daughter of brother of the father
	Sister of the father	3. Son of sister of the father
		4. Daughter of sister of the father
Mother's side:	Brother of the mother	5. Son of brother of the mother
		6. Daughter of brother of the mother
	Sister of the mother	7. Son of sister of the mother
		8. Daughter of sister of the mother

When these eight categories are considered by age in relation to the child's age (i.e., younger, same age, older), the net result of the cousin categories alone adds to 24, for each category may contain persons who are older, younger, and equal in age to child. If a child died without leaving a spouse or children, his belongings are legally distributed among some of these categories, not in equal shares but according to a precise legal formula. If members of some of these categories are alive, they prevent some other categories from inheriting. By the same token, if a child survives some of these categories, he is apt to inherit a prescribed portion of their belongings. Extended kinship relations constitute the principal fabric of the social structure outside the Western world. They have the greatest functions in societies with little bureaucratic experience in which secondary institutions have not yet taken deep roots. The Western wife finds it difficult to function in this complex kinship system, which is a comfortable social world for the one reared in it, even in America.

Life-style of the Arab Family

The Arabs brought to the New World certain traditional family life-styles that are more closely adhered to by the early immigrants than by the more recent professional immigrants. Four features are identified:

1. The Arab family was traditionally patriarchal and generally oriented toward older family members. The elders had a controlling voice in family affairs including approval of marriage partners for their children. Screening of possible mates for a suitable one lay in the hands of the mother, the father making the final arrangements. Islam as well as Christianity still considers the father the head of the household, the manager of the affairs of the family.
2. Traditionally, a boy had the privilege—even right—of marrying the daughter of his father's brother. While this practice has declined, it still occasionally may be claimed as a right, or the girl and her parents may feel that she has been slighted if the cousin does not seek her in marriage.
3. Moslem women may not marry non-Moslems unless the non-Moslem becomes converted to Islam prior to marriage. This prohibition is not explicit in the Quran but is implied in the Traditions. It is felt that almost certainly the woman who marries a non-Moslem, as well as her children, will be lost to Islam.
4. Men may marry non-Moslems provided they are members of either Jewish or Christian faith—both groups being considered of the Heavenly Books and kin to the Moslems. It is anticipated that the wives will enter Islam, and their children will be reared as Moslems.

These traditional policies create many problems in the social situation of the New World and especially for American-born children of Moslems who tend to adopt the romantic-individualistic pattern of mate selection.

There are two general lifestyles of the Arab family, depending on the degree of education one or both of the Arab parents have acquired. However, those with no college education, whether Moslems or Christians, are the backbone of the Arab communities whose lifestyle is depicted here.

Through intimate contacts with their playmates and schoolmates, under the compulsory school system, second-generation members have had the chance to compare two different cultures and ways of life. The unfavorable socioeconomic conditions in the old countries at the time their parents came to America leave no doubt in the judgment of the second-generation members. They prefer the American socioeconomic and political structure over that of the old country. In fact, they consider themselves more fortunate than their parents to have been born in this country. The parents share this view. The first-generation immigrants are proud to hear their children speak English fluently—like any American or Canadian. It is also very common for the first-generation members to give their children American nicknames. In one family there are Mike, Ralph, Ronald, Fred, Dennis, Vicki, Stephen, and Churchill for outside identification, while the Arabic names are kept for the family and community identification.

The second generation plays a transitional role between the old and the new cultures and thus is often the victim of both. The members of the second generation teach the members of the first generation a great deal about the American culture. But it is hard for the first-generation members, who are dominated by a patriarchal family image, to accept the reversal of roles, which makes them pupils of their own children. This widens the cultural gap between the two generations. Most of the second-generation members, in response to the question, "About what things do you most frequently disagree with your father?", mention that their fathers are slow at making decisions and have a habit of arguing over little things. Among the common complaints against the mother are that they "interfere" in their children's personal affairs, are too absorbed in the social life of the immigrant women, and engage in too much malicious gossip in the style of the old country.

The two generations, therefore, live in two different social atmospheres with separate outlooks on life. The first-generation members are affected by the memories of their great efforts to make their way in a strange land. Looking forward, they realize that socially, as well as religiously, they have lost their offspring to America. They admit that they have gained economic wealth, but they doubt whether that wealth compensates for their loss.

Authority Relations in the Family

Most of the first-wave immigrants have had little or no formal education. The family in the old country performed many functions that, in the more complex societies, are performed by separate specialized institutions. Although the school was the formal educational institution, difficult economic conditions prevented that institution from serving as large a group as in the more economically advanced countries. The agrarian family needed the complete participation of all its members on the farm. The children simply could not be spared for formal education. Thus, the main education a child could obtain was in the tradition transmitted from one generation to another. The parents functioned in roles of vocational trainer and educator.

Since the emphasis in knowledge and wisdom was on the past, parents achieved status in the family through experiences that were associated with maturity. The traditional admiration for the aged in less literate societies derives from that association between experience and old age, accentuated in folklore. In more literate, industrialized societies, the emphasis in knowledge is on science and technology. Knowledge is not tied to the past. The machine and space era, with its emphasis on scientific achievement for the future, has shifted family status from the aged to the young. The function of traditional education in the home, to solidify the family under the control of the aged, has given way to a new concept of education.

The tradition-oriented first-wave Arab in America was puzzled by the independence and the disobedience of his children. He often expressed his disappointment about the new pattern of family relations by saying, "We lost our children in America," for they still dream of the patriarchal pattern, which they imagine (incorrectly) to be unchanged in the old country. The attitudes of the first generation puzzle the second generation, too. According to Warner and Srole (1952:125):

> Not only does the child resent the fact that his parents do not act after the American behavioral norms; not only does he resent pressure to act after the ethnic behavioral modes, but, infused with American social logics, he implicitly questions the right of his father to dominate and control his behavior.

The demand for freedom by the second generation conflicts with the desire of the first to retain control. This is the cornerstone of generational conflict. The more traditional the first-generation members, the more they demand control over the second generation, and the wider the differences become.

The progeny of the first-wave immigrants is born into two different cultures and grows up under both influences. In time the influence of his family is outweighed by the influence of the American culture. Once the children go out to play with American children, they encounter the fear and fascination of a new language. By the time they go to school, the English language is dominant. The different symbols of the English language (especially slang concerning dates, girlfriends, and boyfriends) convey lighter, easier values, which differ from the more ponderous values of their family.

Communication among generations in the family is manifested in the language both generations use at home. Linguistically, the family pattern has become heterogeneous: The first generation speaks in Arabic, while the second generation answers in English. Not only is English easier for the second-generation members, it is superior. They see the struggles of their parents to express themselves in English and use English words in Arabic constructions. Though the children laugh at their efforts, parents learn a great deal of English from their children—and much, as well, about the American way of life. The crucial point comes, as Warner (1953:126) says, when "the child, not the parent, becomes the transmitting agent of social change."

Education is, therefore, a major reason why the younger generation of the Arab community has become the catalyst for social change. The sharp educational difference among generations, especially between the first and second, is one of the factors responsible for family conflict in the Arab community. The family has become less integrated as each generation views the other from its own position and values.

Also associated with family conflict is the first generation's strong resistance to the social change introduced by the younger generation. Since the new environment continuously strengthens the value standards of the younger American- and Canadian-born generation over those of the first-wave immigrants, the latter group is frustrated in a losing battle. The unbalanced opposite forces between generations in the family relations have resulted in the father's failure to maintain tradition. "He does not know how to control the children" is the common complaint of the Arab wife against her husband. "The children," she continues, "don't listen to us. They spend most of their time out. They just come home to eat and sleep."

Arab new-generation members complain about the failure of traditional family structure to interest them and hold their loyalty. The disintegration of the traditional family structure manifests itself in numerous patterns, ranging from conversation to food. The parents' conversation is centered around persons and families taking the concrete shape of gossip. The children's conversation is centered around cars, nights, pleasures outside the home, and even general social problems. The parents continue to relish Arabic dishes, which the children do not enjoy. Very often, the housewife cooks *mijaddara* or *kebba nayya* for herself and her husband and something else for her children. A second-generation member summed up in three words the view of his generation toward their parents: "They neglect life," he said. Asked to elaborate, he replied to the author in a personal communication:

> I don't remember that my parents ever took us out to dinner, movies, or theater. They never invited any American family or accepted any American invitation. The reason is that my mother does not speak English. When I bought my car they were angry at me. I don't have complete freedom to spend my money. I work for my father. He gives me much less than what I could get

working outside. Despite this they watch what I spend as if I were spending their money. Next year I'll be 30 years old but they still deal with me as if I were a child. If I buy a new suit or spend my vacation in Florida with some American friends they cry that I'm spoiled, that I spend too much on my friends, and so on. I'm sick of this life.

The Status of the Aged

Contrary to what might be expected, when the Arab American parents retire and cease to be economically productive, they are taken care of by their American- or Canadian-born children. Usually the parents live alone in the homes they own, and their married children, if nearby, look after them. The pattern is that they spend Sundays and holidays with their parents. The old folks look forward to these occasions, when two or three generations meet. The nursing home is still an unknown institution to senior Arab Americans whose homes are social centers for an extensive network of relatives and friends. Even those who go back to retire in the old country return to the United States and Canada because they find that they miss their children, friends, and the lifestyle of the New World.

It is a Western cultural *norm* that this category of the elderly belongs in nursing homes, away from the loving, affectionate, vivacious, enthusiastic atmosphere of the younger generation. And here comes the great difference between the Western cultural norms and their counterparts in the culture of the Middle East, which are still adhered to by the Arab immigrants in the United States and Canada (Quran: Al-Isra', Sura XVII,23–24):

> And your Lord has decreed that you worship none but Him and always be kind to your parents. Whenever one or both of them attain old age, never say to them a word of contempt, nor repel them, but address them in terms of honor. And treat them with extreme humbleness and compassion, and say: "My Lord, bestow on them Your mercy for they cherished me in childhood."

The Quran is full of these moral instructions which have become an integral part of Islam and have influenced the culture of the Middle East. To cherish one's parents is second only to the worship of God. There is no ceiling to the reverence accorded the position of the mother. The Tradition states: "Paradise is under the feet of mothers." It is inconceivable of a Middle Easterner to think of sending his parents to a nursing home or similar public institution. As a matter of fact, no such institutions exist in the Middle East. Parents and grandparents are considered a valuable asset to the family, a means to blessings manifesting themselves in secular prosperity and reward in the hereafter. Senility among the aged appears to be a rare occurrence in the Middle East and could be looked upon as a Western phenomenon resulting from the feeling of worthlessness and from inactivity among the elderly.

While in the technological industrial culture of the West, the focus is on the future and changed values have given the young a higher status for their prospective accumulative achievement, the traditional agrarian culture of the Middle East reveres the past, stresses stability and continuity, and gives the aged the highest status for their accumulation of experiences. This accumulation of experiences, acquired with the passage of time, is assumed to have given the elderly wisdom beyond the grasp of the young.

Mental health is associated with self-esteem which, among other things, is the function of one's perception of one's worth. When the aged in the Western societies believe that they are useless and experience the negative attitudes of their culture as well as their families, they lose self-esteem and a sense of self-worth and start to suffer mental and psychological disintegration.

The social problems of the aged and the aging are among the awesome and bitter fruits of industrialization, technology, and modernization—all of which weakened the traditional extended family structure in which the aged were the responsibility of the younger members. Nowhere has the sociological theory of "exchange" been violated more than in the modern family, whose pattern is toward neglecting the aged rather than reciprocating the maintenance, care, and upbringing provided by them.

With the rapid medical advancement and health care programs that will ultimately prolong life expectancy, the problems of the aged and the aging will become increasingly acute. These are not merely physical or socioeconomic problems, which the modern state can handle, but rather emotional, psychological problems, which require education in the moral obligation toward the aged.

Islam, as a social system, addressed itself to these social-psychological problems and managed to form one of the more durable patterns of the family structure, which took care of its aged by equating the care of one's aged with one's worship of God.

The West might find a solution for its disintegrating family pattern in the Middle Eastern traditions of the Arab American and Arab Canadian family style.

CHANGE AND ADAPTATION

Arab Americans and Arab Canadians refer to the New World as a paradise for women and children because the Arab family has become dominated by the mother and children. This has resulted because parents attempt to provide children with opportunities they never had. Parents desire to care for their children and control every aspect of their present and future lives. It is the wife who often initiates invitations and entertainments at the home, a sharp contrast from tradition. In fact, the community affairs are to a large degree sustained and run by women.

Marriage is no longer arranged. It follows the American pattern of dating, courtship, and romantic love—a concept and experience totally alien for the older members of the community. At colleges, as well as at work, Arab boys and girls meet other young people and start dating. Arab boys generally dislike dating the Arab girls, and vice-versa, for family connections and relationships preclude any misbehavior, making for dull dates. Times of togetherness, or dates, might be interpreted by the elders in the community, especially the parents of the girl, as engagement. If marriage does not follow, ill feelings pervade the families involved. Christian Arabs and Moslem Arabs, as a rule, do not intermarry. Neither do the two Moslem sects of Sunni and Shia nor the two Christian sects of Maronites and Melkites encourage intersectarian marriage. If intermarriage takes place, it is between Arabs and non-Arabs. The Christian Arabs are more lenient in this respect than the Moslem Arabs. This is a factor contributing to the higher rate of acculturation of the Christian Arab communities in comparison to their Moslem counterparts. In the former communities, assimilation aids acculturation. In the latter, Moslem Arab girls (who are left without ethnic religious partners as a result of the tendency of the boys to date American girls) marry Americans and move outside their community. This further delays the process of acculturation among the Moslem Arab communities, which still preserve a great deal of traditional Middle Eastern values. Similar to Jews who managed to preserve traditional values on the basis of their religion, the Moslem Arabs in America have succeeded in perpetuating their religious institution around the mosque, an organization that has flourished and increased tremendously during the last two decades. Surprisingly, the mosque organization is sustained mainly by the third Moslem Arab generation, a matter that may usher in a pattern of a religiocultural revivalism similar to the pattern that occurred prior to World War II among the German Americans and the Japanese Americans. The response of Arabs in America following the creation of Israel was a revival of pride in their original culture, which they saw being deprecated by a religious minority. Here we find that religion became a tool for politics, and the mosque started to serve new functions to cater to the Sunday-oriented Moslem Arab American communities, which are gradually shifting from the traditional Friday religious activities in order to adapt to the working conditions of the American environment.

The speed and degree of assimilation of Arab Americans and Arab

Canadians and acculturation of their communities will also depend on the diplomatic and economic relations between their new countries and the Arab world, which is, after all, the homeland of their ancestors and a hidden source of their personal pride.

The accidental or intentional migration of the Arabs to the New World hardly severed their ties with their motherlands in the Middle East. Even those who married non-Arabs to constitute mixed family patterns managed to blend their family style with that of the exotic Middle East by exposure through visits, nostalgia, cultural norms, and relatives.

In contrast to the nuclear American family, the Arab family in the United States and Canada is still inclined toward the extended style. In a strange land, the psychological tendency is toward mutual support, and the family network pattern serves such needs. The inflated stories of the actual or imaginary successes of early Arab immigrants to the New World quickly spread among the relatives and friends left behind. The early immigrants paved the way and served as receiving stations to distribute newcomers to centers of economic opportunity, where the Arab communities started to take roots, to widen the circle, and attract yet more people from the homeland. During the last 15 years, as a result of the "Fifth Preference" which allows any permanent resident to bring, off quota, his spouse and/or unmarried children, and allows any citizen to bring, off quota, his parents, brothers, and sisters with their entire families, there have been more than one million additional Arabs who entered the New World to make it their permanent residence. This new wave of relocated families (not individuals) has revitalized the traditional structure of the Arab American family.

RECENT INTERNATIONAL EVENTS

Since the Arab–Israeli October War of 1973, in which the Arabs restored some of their pride and international reputation, and as a result of an embargo that demonstrated the energy dependence of the free world on Arab oil, American foreign policy became less anti-Arab. The American and Canadian media reflect a changing attitude toward the Arabs, and thus the Arab Americans and Arab Canadians are coming to feel less frustrated and more American- and Canadian-affiliated. However, cultural regression or revivalism, which awakened a sense of tradition among the Arab Americans and Arab Canadians as a self-defensive mechanism, is likely to be enhanced by the new international prestige the Arab world occupies nowadays. The oil bonanza, which spurred economic development and technological progress in the "homeland," seems likely to inspire Arab American and Arab Canadian youth to learn or perfect their Arabic and direct their professional aspirations toward the Middle East. The hitherto illiterate Arab states, for example, Kuwait, the Gulf states (United Arab Emirates), Libya, and Saudi Arabia, are launching vigorous programs in developing science, technology, education, and every aspect of their societies to catch up to the approaching twenty-first century.

There is a possibility that the recruitment of those of Arabic background who have American and Canadian technical knowledge will strengthen the Arab ethnic solidarity in the New World. A sense of self-redefinition and ethnic reidentification similar to that which swept the heart of the American Jews and revived the Jewish family lifestyle in America will emerge among the Arab Americans and Arab Canadians. The impact of the actual or exaggerated "reverse brain drain" on the Arab American family lies in the amount of inspiration developing among Arab American youth. However, it is too early to assess the psychological impact of the Middle Eastern Arab prosperity and the emerging new international image on either the Arab American personality or the Arab communities in the United States and Canada.

REFERENCES

Arab Youth. 1975. (April 7):6.

Aruri, Naseer H. 1969. "The Arab-American Community of Springfield, Massachusetts," in Hagopian and Paden (eds.), *The Arab-Americans: Studies in Assimilation.* Wilmette, IL: Medina University Press International, pp. 50–67.

Audat, Yacub. 1956. *Al-Natigun bil-dad li Amirika al-Ganubiyya.* Beirut: Dar Rihani.

Elkholy, Abdo A. 1966. *The Arab Moslems in the United States: Religion and Assimilation.* New Haven: College and University Press.

———. 1971. "The Moslems and Inter-religious Marriage in the New World," *International Journal of Sociology of the Family: Special Issue,* I(May):69–84.

Glazer, Nathan. 1954. "Ethnic Groups in America: From National Culture to Ideology," in Morroe Berger, Theodore Abel, and Charles H. Page (eds.), *Freedom and Control in Modern Society.* Princeton, NJ: Van Nostrand, pp. 158–176.

Makdisi, Nadin. 1959. "The Moslems of America," *The Christian Century* (August 26), pp. 969–971.

Warner, W. Lloyd. 1953. *American Life.* Chicago: University of Chicago Press.

Warner, W. Lloyd, and Leo Srole. 1945. *The Social System of American Ethnic Groups.* New Haven: Yale University Press.

———. 1952. *Structure of American Life.* Edinburgh: University Press.

CHAPTER EIGHTEEN

The Mormon Family

Bruce L. Campbell
Eugene E. Campbell

HISTORICAL BACKGROUND

Emergence of the Mormons as a Minority Group

Mormonism has its roots in an atmosphere of supernaturalism, millennialism,[1] and religious revivalism that characterized the "Burned-over District" of western New York during the first decades of the nineteenth century.[2] From the Pilgrims onward, America, with relative religious freedom and readily available land, has historically nurtured a variety of transplanted European, Christian–Utopian societies and these same elements proved vital in the emergence of Mormonism as an American-born religious movement. Mormons regard this constellation of social, political, spiritual, and geographical elements as proof of a divine plan to provide a fertile milieu for the restoration of the Gospel of Jesus Christ in these latter days.

The early history of Mormonism can be described as a cycle in which the Mormons created a new settlement, prospered, clashed with their non-Mormon neighbors, and then were forced to move and create a new

[1]A belief that Christ would soon establish an earthly kingdom over which he would reign for a thousand years.

[2]Allen and Leonard (1976:11) describe the Burned-over District of western New York as being intensely affected by a religious awakening "characterized by circuit-riding preachers, fiery-tongued evangelists, new-grass roots religious movements, fervent emotionalism, and the manifestations of certain physical excesses that demonstrated to new converts divine acceptance."

settlement. Each new location was, in turn, proclaimed a new Zion—a divinely chosen spot for the gathering of the faithful from all the world. This pattern was repeated in New York, Ohio, Missouri, and Illinois before they were driven by mobs out of the United States, across the western prairies, through the Rocky Mountains to the Great Basin, and then to Mexican territory. Calling themselves "the Camp of Israel," the Mormons drew an analogy between their trek through the wilderness of western America and the tempering march of the "Children of Israel" out of Egypt, through the desert, and into the "Promised Land." In the process of taming this wild, arid land, the teachings of Joseph Smith, the founder of Mormonism, were translated by Brigham Young and his followers into religious, social, political, and economic systems, forming the basis of Mormonism as we know it today. For the remaining decades of the nineteenth century, somewhat protected by their geographical isolation from the rest of the United States, the Mormons colonized much of the inter-mountain West, developing from a "near sect" to a "near nation" (O'Dea, 1957:115). Having gradually shed many of the temporal aspects of kingdom building, Mormonism seems to be evolving from an isolated "near nation" into a major world religion (Stark, 1984).

Launching an American Religion

Joseph Smith, Jr., the Mormon prophet, born in 1805, said he had a series of heavenly visions, beginning in about 1820, near Palmyra, New York. According to the Prophet Joseph, as his followers came to call him, in the first vision, God the Father and his Son, Jesus Christ, appeared to him and answered his prayer concerning which church he should join. Jesus instructed him to join none of them because His true church was no longer on the earth.

Other visions revealed the location of the Golden Plates, buried by an ancient American prophet (Mormon by name), on which were written the records and religious experiences of ancient inhabitants of America, including a visit to the American continent after His resurrection. After obtaining these plates, and some spectacle-like instruments to aid in translating them, Joseph Smith, with the help of several scribes, produced the Book of Mormon, asserted to be an inspired translation of the Golden Plates. Mormons accept this book as an important second witness to the divinity of Jesus Christ, and when it was published in 1830, it became an effective missionary tool in the hands of the young prophet and his converts.

Smith also claimed to have received heavenly instructions and authority to re-establish the true, restored Church of Christ, which he organized in 1830 at Fayette, New York. In 1838, the phrase "Latter-day Saints" was added, reflecting the belief that these were the last days before Jesus would return and establish His Kingdom.[3] Thus, Mormonism began with a strong eschatological and millennial emphasis.[4]

It may seem incredible that a movement based on such supernatural experiences should attract thousands of people, but its claim to charismatic authority[5]—revelations through a living prophet and a new scripture—seemed to satisfy the religious needs of those who had been disoriented by the religious diversity that characterized nineteenth century America. Smith also preached a brand of communitarianism that may have met some of the economic hopes of his followers.

As Mormonism began to grow, it attracted enemies, and for several decades the Mormons and their foes, including at times the government of the United States, clashed. The Mormon assumption that Jesus would someday establish this earthly kingdom was the basis for their high internal and social cohesion. Mormons believed they were chosen to be instrumental in the imminent establishment of Christs' kingdom, so they often approached their tasks with fanatical, religious zeal. Convinced they were engaged in the work of the Lord, many Mormons were willing to make great personal sacrifices to build the Kingdom of God.

This spirit of cooperation, sacrifice, and religious fervor was fundamental to their success as community builders, but it was also threatening to their more individualistically oriented neighbors on the sparsely settled American frontier (Hill, 1978). Conflict was inevitable, and in Missouri and Illinois, Mormon and non-Mormon differences escalated to armed conflict. Anti-Mormon mobs (sometimes including elements of the state militia) attacked Mormon settlements—burning homes, murdering religious leaders, raping Mormon women, and threatening the population with death and destruction if they did not change or leave. Mormons felt that government leaders at the state and national level acquiesced in these crimes.

---

[3]The official name of the Mormon church: The Church of Jesus Christ of Latter-day Saints.

[4]Eschatology is the doctrine or concept of the last days in a two-stage view of history. This evil age is to be followed by a "Golden Age" in which Christ will reign.

[5]Weber (1968) describes charismatic authority as being outside and anathetical to traditional authority. He argues that acceptance by one's followers is the only legitimization of charismatic authority. If the leader's personal charisma is rejected, he no longer has any powers. A second aspect of charismatic authority is the sense of duty the leader has to accept his own "gift of grace," or calling, to be the leader. Finally, the charismatic leader perceives following his leadership as a duty of his disciples. They can no more escape the duty to follow the leader than he can his duty to lead.

In June 1844, a series of events led to Joseph Smith's arrest at Nauvoo, Illinois, then the church's headquarters. Subsequently, Joseph and his brother Hyrum were murdered while incarcerated at nearby Carthage, Illinois. Governor Ford of Illinois tried to prevent this mob action, but Mormons perceived governmental contrivance in the plot to murder their beloved leader.

After the death of Joseph Smith, Mormon leaders concluded that they could not rely on the protections guaranteed by the Constitution and decided to leave the United States to settle somewhere in the Rocky Mountains where they would be free to practice their social and religious beliefs.

This was a fateful decision: If they remained in Illinois, either extermination or gradual assimilation seemed their likely end. In the West, however, they were able to develop for several decades unique social institutions, relatively free from outside influence. As a result, they became a unique and important ethnic group.

In February 1846, the Mormons began their epic trek west. An advance pioneer company completed its journey to the valley of the Great Salt Lake on July 24, 1847, and established the initial colony of their Great Basin kingdom in what was then Mexican territory but was ceded to America in the treaty with Mexico in February 1848.[6]

Brigham Young and the other leaders were effective colonizers; within 10 years, approximately 100 towns had been established in Utah, with outlying colonies in California, Nevada, Idaho, and Wyoming. Missionary work continued in many parts of the world, and a steady stream of converts, mainly from the British Isles and northern Europe, poured into the Great Basin, resulting in expanding colonization. By the time of Brigham Young's death in 1877, approximately 300 colonies had been established, primarily in Utah, Idaho, and Arizona.

There were many differences between the Mormons and the other Americans that might have been ignored if gold had not been discovered in California. Chosen for its isolation and apparent desolation, the valley of the Great Salt Lake was paradoxically located on the best route to the gold fields of California. Mormon theocratic political power apparently threatened federal control of the Utah territory and hence the route to California, so for several decades the government attempted to alter Mormon social,

---

[6]Approximately 38 percent of the Mormons who moved from Nauvoo to Utah from 1846 to 1850 were British-born converts to the church (May 1983). Perhaps this substantial proportion of foreign-born membership helps account for some of the anti-Mormon sentiment among non-Mormons, including local and national leaders.

economic, and political institutions. The Mormons resisted and a period of conflict ensued. Federal authorities used the Mormon practice of plural marriage as a means of diminishing Mormon political power.[7] Congress passed laws making the practice of polygamy in the territories illegal and disenfranchising Mormons who supported it. The church was even disincorporated as a legal institution. The church capitulated in 1890, ending 40 years of legal struggles with the government.

Presidential amnesty followed, but it was many years before Mormons were regarded as loyal citizens. Mormons faced a political dilemma. They loved the Constitution and were loyal to the principles of the United States, but they felt that state and federal officials had deprived them of constitutional rights to practice their religion freely. Today, many Mormons seem to solve this dilemma by adopting conservative, sometimes ultraconservative political ideas, that allow them to love and support America while they oppose a strong federal government.

THE MORMON FAMILY— HISTORICAL DEVELOPMENTS

It has been asserted that all utopian movements have experimented with the family unit. Though Mormonism was utopian in spirit, as various experiments in communal living testify, it did not begin with a fully developed theoretical or theological blueprint for changing the family. In fact, the Mormon experiment with polygamy and the subsequent emphasis on the family as a divine unit did not appear until the movement was well under way.

There was nothing especially distinctive about early Mormon families. They tended to be large, closely knit, hard-working, and religiously oriented. They reflected the social origins of the converts from Ohio, Pennsylvania, New York, upper Canada, and the manufacturing, shipping, and mining centers of Great Britain.

Ellsworth's (1951) study of Mormon origins reveals that most of the early converts were proselytized by relatives and friends and came primarily from towns and cities rather than the frontier, as has often been assumed. A considerable number of the important leaders in the church came from New England stock, including the Smiths, Brigham Young, Heber C. Kimball, and Wilford Woodruff. Most were of the working class:

---

[7]The Mormon practice of plural marriage was widely discussed and deplored in the United States. Perhaps federal authorities focused their attack on Mormon polygamy because it presented an easier target than political or economic practices.

farmers and unskilled and semiskilled laborers. A few were ministers or doctors.

The duty to gather to Zion and the unpopularity of the church often separated new converts from their families. Many sought to replace such ties within the developing structure of the church. By the middle of the Nauvoo period (1839–1846), the family was welded to the core of Mormon theology, involving concepts of (1) the eternal family, (2) celestial marriage, and eventually (3) polygamous marriage.

The Eternal Family

Many religions are pro-family, but Mormons preach that the Kingdom of God is composed of eternal, family relationships. Their high fertility roles and strongly held, pronatalist views are deeply rooted in this belief system. Allen and Leonard (1976:168) explain that the doctrine of Eternal Progression is central to the Mormon emphasis on the eternal family unit:

> Joseph Smith taught that man, far from being an enemy or mere tool of God, was actually a god in embryo. The Father had achieved godhood only by going through the same experiences man is now enduring. Having successfully met all tests, he progressed in knowledge and power to become God. In turn, he instructed his spirit children in the plan of salvation before they came to earth and promised them that if they lived faithfully in their mortal life, one day they too might become gods. This was the doctrine of eternal progression.

Mormons believe that God is the literal father of spirit beings in the same sense that earthly fathers are the procreators of physical bodies. Mormons teach that there are millions of spirit children of God who are awaiting their chance to come to earth in their continuing quest for godhood. Brigham Young (1925:305) said, "There are multitudes of pure and holy spirits waiting to take tabernacles (bodies), now what is our duty . . . to prepare tabernacles for them, to take a course that will not tend to drive those spirits into the families of the wicked, where they will be trained in wickedness, debauchery, and every species of crime. It is the duty of every righteous man and woman to prepare tabernacles for all the spirits they can."

Many Mormons assume that through their faith and works, the spirit children of God earn the right to come to certain earthly homes and that being born into a good Mormon home represents the best placement possible. Thus, becoming married and having a large family are the quintessence of obedience to God's plan of Eternal Progression.

Celestial Marriage

In the process of becoming a god, a man must enter into a "new and everlasting covenant of marriage" by which he and his wife or wives will be married for all eternity and will have the privilege and duty of procreating spirit children throughout eternity even as God procreated us. Mormons call this celestial marriage, and only faithful members of the church who can gain authorization from priesthood leaders to enter the sacred temples built for solemnizing such ordinances are so married.

To qualify for participation in temple marriage, one must be a member of the church in good standing and believe in the charismatic authority of the church. Some of the more important behavioral expectations are sexual purity, payment of tithing (10 percent of gross income paid to the church), and obedience to the Word of Wisdom, which requires abstaining from the use of tea, coffee, alcohol, and tobacco. It should probably come as no surprise that less than half of the membership of the church obey these requirements. Anything less than a temple marriage, however, is seen by many church members as failure, and entrance to the temple is one of the most effective sanctions the church has to exert control over its members.

The Extended Family

According to Mormon theology, the organizational structure of heaven is the extended family kinship network. Closely tied to this concept is the Mormon practice of extending and unifying one's family through "sealing ordinances" in the temple for members of the family who did not have the opportunity to embrace the Gospel during their lifetime. This "work for the dead," as it is called, is based on the belief that only being "born of the water and the spirit," (baptized and confirmed as a member of the church of Jesus Christ) can one gain exaltation in the Celestial World and have the opportunity to be in God's presence and "become as He is." Because most of the human race is believed to have lived and died without knowledge of the "true" church, Mormons are taught that it is their obligation to seek out the names of their dead ancestors and to act as proxy for them by going to the temple and experiencing baptism and other sacred ordinances in the name of deceased relatives. This program has resulted in the building of a score of temples in various parts of the world and the development of one of the greatest and most extensive genealogical library systems in the world. It has also resulted in extended family organizations for the promotion of genealogical research.

The Polygamous Family

The concept of eternal marriage was closely tied to the practice of polygamy, or, technically, polygyny. The practice was begun secretly by Joseph Smith and other church leaders as early as 1842 and was based on the concept that the same God who had approved the Old Testament prophets who had many wives had also revealed this principle to his modern prophet, Joseph Smith, with the command that the practice be instituted among the faithful and deserving saints. Because polygamy remained secret until the public announcement in 1852, it is difficult to describe it in accurate detail. However, there is ample evidence that Joseph Smith married a number of women before he was killed in 1844 and that Brigham Young and other leaders continued and enlarged the practice.

Because plural marriage in Nauvoo was clandestine, the church leaders denied the practice on several occasions when asked about such marriages. As late as 1850, representatives of the church in foreign lands continued to deny the doctrine and practice of polygamy. However, after the Mormons left Nauvoo and began their epic trek to the valley of the Great Salt Lake, this practice could no longer be hidden from the membership of the church, but it was not until they were established in Utah that the practice was publicly announced and defended.

Some leaders in Nauvoo refused to accept the practice as being inspired by God and asserted that Joseph Smith was a "fallen prophet." Opposition to the practice of polygamy was one of the reasons for the foundation of the Reorganized Church of Jesus Christ of Latter-day Saints in 1860.

Polygamy in Practice—An Anomic System

Characterized by an enormous diversity of marital styles (Burgess-Olson, 1975; Van Wagoner, 1985), a relative lack of norms regulating this system (Young, 1954), and the often covert nature of its practice (Quinn, 1985; Brodie, 1971; Van Wagoner, 1985), Mormon polygamy might be best described as anomic polygamy (Campbell and Campbell, 1978). When the usual norms of society are disrupted, as seems likely during the tumultuous early decades of the development of Mormonism, and new ones have not developed to replace them, a state of anomic or normlessness is said to exist (Durkhiem, 1951). Durkhiem (1951:252) claims that in a state of anomie,

> [T]he scale is upset; but a new scale cannot be immediately improvised. Time is required for the public conscience to reclassify men and things. So long as

> the social forces thus freed have not regained equilibrium, their respective values are unknown and so all regulation is lacking for a time. The limits are unknown between the possible and the impossible, what is just and unjust, legitimate claims and hopes and those which are immoderate.

During perhaps half its existence, Mormon polygamy was practiced in secret, shielding the participants from the public scrutiny usually required to ensure conformity to community standards when present (Brodie, 1971; Quin, 1985). Mormons lacked experience with polygamous practices and while they may have been groping toward some generally accepted norms (Young, 1954; Embry and Bradley, 1985), pressure from the federal government and the brief duration of the practice made the development of a mature system of plural marriage norms problematic. As a result, regulations governing courtship practices, marital interaction, economic cooperation, household arrangements, division of labor, intimate relationships, and inheritance, to mention only a few, were not well developed.

An increased divorce rate is said to be symptomatic of social anomie (Durkhiem, 1951). It is difficult to determine the exact divorce rate among Mormon polygamists. Campbell and Campbell (1978) claim that over 2,000 divorces were granted to polygamists from 1847 through 1890. Quinn (1973) indicates that less than one in five marriages of the church leaders he studied ended in broken marriages, but approximately one-half of the leaders were divorced or separated from at least one wife. Brigham Young (1858:15, December) was alarmed enough by the number of divorces occurring to declare:

> It is not right for the brethren to divorce their wives, the way they do. I am determined that if men don't stop divorcing their wives, I shall stop sealing (marrying). Men shall not abuse the gifts of God and the privileges the way they are doing. Nobody can say that I have any interest in the matter, for I charge nothing for the sealings (marriages), but I do charge for the divorcing. I want the brethren to stop divorcing their wives for it is not right.

Kunz (1980), through an analysis of genealogical records, notes that approximately 9 percent of the male polygamists had been divorced. He argues (1980), however, that a more accurate picture can be gained by calculating the rate of divorce for polygamous wives, approximately 3 percent. Both rates were higher than for Mormon monogamists; less than 1 percent (Kunz, 1980). However, the rate of marital separation reported by Kunz seems to be an underestimation of the actual rate because only the first wife was legally married; thus, when subsequent wives left the family, a legal divorce was not required (Young, 1954). If the polygamous family was the basic unit of Mormon society, the divorce rate among men seems the more accurate indicator of the effects of normlessness on that divorce rate.

However, the divorce rate alone does not paint a clear picture of the extent of normlessness among Mormon polygamists. For example, in a general conference in October 1861, Brigham Young is reported to have declared,

> Also, there was another way in which a woman could leave a man—if the woman preferred a man *higher in authority* and he is willing to take her and her husband gives her up. There is no bill of divorce required in [this] case it is right in the sight of God.

This would seem to give license to a wide variation in marital style. Limits seemed lacking.

Demographics of Polygamy

Perhaps nothing illustrates the profound Mormon ambivalence toward polygamy than the estimates of the number of members who lived this doctrine. "Perhaps the most *quoted* estimates of the incidence of Latter-day Saint polygamy is 2 percent, a figure often defensively cited by apologists who timidly indicate that 'after all, only about 2 percent of the males practiced polygamy'" (Kunz, 1980:61). The bulk of the scholarly evidence suggests that from 8 percent to 10 percent of the male population of the church entered plural marriages (Smith and Kunz, 1976). However, during the so-called Reformation, which gripped Mormons from 1856 to 1858, the percentage marrying extra wives must have been much higher. Ivins notes that, ". . . as one of the fruits of the 'Reformation', plural marriages skyrocketed to a height not before approached and never again to be reached. If our tabulation is a true index, there was sixty-five percent more of such marriages during 1856–1857 than in any two years of the experiment" (1956:231). A letter from Wilford Woodruff to George A. Smith dated April 1, 1857 illuminates this trend:

> We have had a great reformation this winter; some of the fruits are: all have confessed their sins either great or small, restored their stolen property; all have been baptized from the presidency down; all are trying to pay their tithing and nearly all are trying to get wives until there is hardly a girl 14 years old in Utah, but what is married, or just going to be. President Young has hardly time to eat, drink or sleep, in consequence of marrying the people.

From 1850 to 1890 the "Principle," as Mormons referred to plural marriage, was a central concept of the Mormon religion. Church leaders tended to have several wives and admonished others to follow their example (Quinn, 1973). The following quote from Heber C. Kimball (1858), a prominent church official, illustrates the claims made in support of polygamy.

> I would not be afraid to promise a man who is sixty years of age, if he will take the counsel of brother Brigham and his brethren, that he will renew his age. I have noticed that a man who has but one wife, and is inclined to that doctrine, soon begins to wither and dry up, while a man who goes into plurality looks fresh, young and sprightly. Why is this? Because God loves that man, and because he honors his work and word. Some of you may not believe this; but I not only believe it—I know it. For a man of God to be confined to one woman is small business; for it is as much as we can do now to keep up under the burdens we have to carry; and I do not know what we should do if we had only one wife apiece.

As pressures from the federal government increased, Mormon leaders continued to defend plural marriage with many of them (1,500–2,000) eventually going to jail or underground in support of the Principle (Allen and Leonard, 1976; Cannon, 1978). Only when it became clear that continuing to practice polygamy would result in the total destruction of Mormonism did President Wilford Woodruff issue the Manifesto in 1890 ending the practice of polygamy. The doctrine was never renounced.

What seems clear from the evidence is that despite intense pressure to take extra wives, only about 10 percent of the eligible men were willing to live the central commandment of nineteenth century Mormonism.

Ivins' (1956:233) study reveals that:

> [O]f 1,784 polygamists, 66.3% married only one extra wife, another 21.2% were three-wife men, and 6.7% went so far as to take four wives. This left a small group of polygamists of less than 6% who married five or more women. The typical polygamist, far from being the insatiable male of popular fable, was a dispassionate fellow, content to call a halt after marrying one extra wife required to assure him of his salvation.

Of those who chose to have five or more wives, Brigham Young was the most prominent. He probably had at least 27 wives, among 16 of whom he had 56 children. Heber C. Kimball, Young's first counselor, is said to have had at least 35 wives, but there were so many different arrangements that the term *wife* requires definition before totals can be determined. Recent studies support the general conclusions of Ivins' 1956 estimate (Smith and Kunz, 1976).

Foreign-born men and women were more likely to marry polygamously than those born in America (Smith and Kunz, 1980). There is some evidence that in the heavily Scandinavian sections of Utah there were more women than men, suggesting foreign-born women as a likely source of second and third wives (Mulder, 1957). But there were not enough foreign-born women to meet the demand for extra wives. This demand was met by allowing young women to marry older men. The number of males in the 30–39 age group was significantly smaller than the number of available females in the 20–29 age group (Smith and Kunz, 1976).

One of the most prominent reasons given for the institution of polygamy was the need for "righteous" men to bring as many children into this world as possible, and to do this, many wives were needed. It was also claimed that there were more women than men in the church at that time because women were more receptive to religious convictions than men. These women, from the Mormon point of view, needed protection and help on this earth, and their eternal salvation depended on their having a celestial marriage; thus it was a sacred duty for qualified men to take extra wives. This claim is subject to question because census reports of Utah Territory list more men than women in each decade.[8]

Recent research suggests that first wives in polygamous families generally had more children than either women in monogamous unions or third wives in polygamous unions, suggesting her role as first wife gave her more access to her husband and thus more power than subsequent wives (Smith and Kunz, 1976). There is some indication that second and third wives were females who survived the monogamous marriage market in that they tended to be older than first wives when they married (Smith and Kunz, 1976). It may be that second and third wives were at a competitive disadvantage to first wives in the marriage market and thus had less power in these marriages. A noted demographer agreeing with the above conclusions argues nevertheless that second and third wives were less likely candidates for monogamous marriages and, though they had fewer children than first wives, "we will find that polygamy enhanced rather than depressed aggregate fertility" (May, 1983).

All such explanations and justifications are after the fact, however, and

[8]The U. S. Census Compendium records the following statistics for the territory of Utah.

	MALE	FEMALE
1850	6,020	5,310
1860	20,178	19,947
1870	44,121	42,665
1880	74,509	69,454
1890	110,463	97,442

the official position of the Mormon church is that Joseph Smith began the practice because it was a revealed commandment of God. Religious conviction appears to be central to the acceptance of the practice.

Although Joseph Smith is credited with initiating the practice of plural marriage, it was under the leadership of Brigham Young that polygamy was publically defended and imposed on the general membership of the church. Perhaps the growth of polygamy under President Young can be understood as part of his assumption of the charismatic mantle of Joseph Smith. Weber suggests "the genuine prophet, like the genuine military leader and every true leader in this sense preaches, creates, or demands *new* obligations (1968:51)." Perhaps living the doctrine of polygamy was the new obligation demanded by Brigham Young, the second Mormon prophet.

The Mormon church now opposes the practice of plural marriage but has never renounced it as a doctrine. In 1890, Wilford Woodruff, the president of the church, issued the manifesto announcing the end of the practice of polygamy in the church. For those already married in polygamy, the manifesto created an ambiguous situation. Some men ended all contact with their plural wives, while others stopped having intimate relations with their extra wives but continued to support them financially. Many men, including President Joseph F. Smith (a relative of the founder, Joseph Smith), continued to live with their wives but took no new ones. A few married extra wives after 1890. However, having demonstrated its control over the Utah Territory, the federal government decreased its prosecution of polygamists and winked at this practice in many cases. The government seemed satisfied to let Mormon polygamy die gradually. As a generation passed, so did the practice of polygamy in the Mormon church.

However, certain persons felt that the manifesto was not God's will but political expediency, and they determined to keep the practice alive even though it meant excommunication from the church. Some claimed that church officials came to them in secret and called on them to carry on the practice of polygamy. As a result, on the fringe of the Mormon subculture, there are some persons who marry plural wives, but because of the clandestine nature of their operation, there is little reliable information on their marriage and family practices.

Although the Mormon church no longer allows the practice of polygamy in terms of cohabitation, two situations remain that are polygamous in intent. First, if a Mormon couple is married in the temple and the wife dies, the husband may marry another wife in the temple for time and eternity, which is a second celestial marriage. She is regarded as a second wife joining a polygamous eternal family unit. Second, if a man has a legal but not a temple divorce from a woman, he may marry another woman in the temple. Because Mormons see the temple ceremony as an eternal marriage, the man is in effect a polygamist. The church, however, would feel that he would be committing adultery if he tried to cohabit with his first wife while legally divorced from her.

This view of eternal marriage does have one unfortunate consequence. If a woman is married to a man for eternity and her husband dies, she may have a difficult time finding an orthodox Mormon man who will marry her. The doctrine teaches that in the eternity she would belong to her first husband, as would all of her children, even though they might be fathered by her second husband. Few orthodox Mormon men will deny themselves the right to their own wives and children in eternity. This is especially difficult for a devout young Mormon widow, for she feels she must marry an active Mormon to find happiness in a second marriage. In recent years, there seems to be some sentiment among church leaders to modify this doctrine.

However, polygamy has left its mark on the church. Those who have polygamous ancestors are often proud of this fact and see it as a mark of honor and loyalty. The practice of polygamy also seems to have increased the family orientation of the subculture and made the Mormon religion more family focused than most. However, there remains some bitterness in families that can be traced to this practice. As suggested earlier, when norms are lacking, inappropriate or unjust actions are likely to occur. In the case of Mormon polygamy, some rather strange relationships were formed, and for many years, there was a marriage underground, which resulted in secret marriages that, when exposed, resulted in resentment, anger, embarrassment, envy, jealousy, and even rejection of some marital claims as fraudulent. For example, the family of the first wife may not recognize the family of subsequent wives as legitimate heirs to the family name or fortune. Polygamy was a mixed blessing at best.

MORMONISM TRANSFORMED

Over the last century, Mormonism has been transformed from "a marginal, utopian, socially despised, and exclusive movement to an increasingly prosperous, socially respectable, and politically conservative organization of international scope" (Shepherd and Shepherd, 1984b:138). Yet, at the end of the nineteenth century, their difficulties seemed insurmountable. They were being forced to abandon some of their most characteristic practices—polygamy and building the earthly Kingdom of God, for example—at a time when their physical isolation was ending. These fundamental changes threatened this unique religious movement. Neverthe-less, today Mormonism is thriving. It is probably the most rapidly growing church in America (Stark, 1984), and Mormons are widely lauded for their health habits, strong families, religious devotion, and commitment to the work ethic (Stathis and Lythgoe, 1977). They have become the very model of conservative respectability while maintaining many of their unique beliefs and practices.

To succeed, all religions change to "accommodate to consumer preferences of modern society" and Mormonism does not seem to be an exception (Shepherd and Shepherd, 1984). A national survey commissioned by the church showed Mormon leaders that most Americans do not know much about the Bible, are not interested in denominated differences, but are interested in happiness and family life, and so church public-relations efforts and missionary themes were altered accordingly (Lythgoe, 1977). Shipps (1978:766) observes the following:

> A change in emphasis has occurred in Mormonism during the past few decades. Now the family unit rather than the priesthood quorum is the most important organization in the Church, and support for families is the central thrust of today's church program. The local ward (parish) is a community of families; ward activities . . . are planned to engender family solidarity. Home teaching and church welfare programs provide mutual support. Genealogy serves to tie in the family from past time and stress on the eternal marriage covenant takes the family into the distant future. Temple ordinances then sanctify family relations so that the entire Mormon experience can be said to uphold the integrity of the LDS family. Because the missionary message is also built on what the Church can do for families, conversion is often a family affair, and every LDS ward seems to be filled with new families being "fellow-shipped" into Mormonism.

An increased emphasis on the family appears to have been the vehicle through which Mormonism made its transformation during the last 100 years. As Shipps indicates above, religion and family life are integrated at many levels in Mormonism: the success of one is tied to the success of the other. However, many other churches have also stressed the family, so whether this family focus of modern Mormonism will be different enough to preserve the peculiar Mormon identity is not clear.

Given past persecutions and their marginal status in society, it may not be surprising that Mormons have attempted to adjust to twentieth-century America by overcompensation—being not just good citizens, but super-patriots. Their family life must be demonstrably the best. They have adopted middle-class norms and enshrined the middle-class family, so any indication of weakness in the family is often perceived as an attack on them and their church.

The Mormon Ward

The ideal Mormon ward, or parish, is much like a tribe and it is within this tribal context that Mormon family functioning must be understood. Members of the ward believe they literally descended from the same Father and thus are literally brothers and sisters, which are family terms they use when addressing each other. Convinced they are chosen by God, they accept their peculiar customs and attitudes that bind them together as the natural legacy of that choice.

There is a high level of interaction within the ward, and the claims members have on each other approach the intensity of family obligations and bonds. In their worship, they are very interdependent. As Alder notes (1978:63), "Nearly everyone who attends the ward is 'called' to serve, to speak (address the congregation), to teach, to officiate, to visit, to preside. The sacramental, pastoral and instructional functions are carried entirely by the laity because there is no paid clergy. The responsibility for the whole rests on the shoulders of all." Ward members not only worship together but also conduct business, form friendships, provide emergency aide, work on service projects, and enjoy a wide variety of recreational activities with each other, much like a large, close-knit extended family. Most ward activities are organized on the assumption of participation as a family unit.

Perhaps the most powerful worship service of the Mormon people is the Fast and Testimony meeting, which is held the first Sunday of each month and is in many ways the quintessential Mormon meeting. It is informal, family-oriented, common, intimate, revealing of diversity but unifying, and above all participatory. Each member comes to this meeting expecting that he or she may be moved by the Spirit to bear his testimony, but if he is not so moved, others surely will be. A spiritual feast is expected. These meetings serve many important functions for the individual believer as well as the congregation as a whole. Because Mormons have large families it is common to have one or more infants christened each month. Beyond the obvious function of christening the child, the performance of this ordinance has other important ramifications: (1) it powerfully reaffirms family and friendship bonds; (2) it is a powerful recognition of the father's priesthood and the role this priesthood plays in the family and the church; and (3) it often sets the tone for the Fast and Testimony meeting.

After the children are blessed, the sacrament is blessed and passed to the congregation and then the meeting is opened up to the members for the bearing of testimonies. It is common but by no means required that the parents of the newly christened infants will bear their testimonies. These testimonies often include a statement of belief in the truth of the Gospel. The eternal family bond shared with ones parents, spouse, and children is usually emphasized, as well as the delight in the new child and his or her recent departure from his Heavenly parents. Expression of love and literal brotherhood are frequently broadened to embrace the entire congregation. Other family events, such as illness, baptism, death, or mere visits, often seem to stimulate the desire to share one's testimony with others in the meeting.

Expressions of love for church leaders and others in the ward are common. Love for God and a recognition of the sacrifice made by Jesus for our sakes is usually included in each testimony. Confessions of sins or shortcomings are common as one requests forgiveness and acceptance. Members—young and old—participate, and there is usually an acknowledgement of the presence of the Holy Spirit as the meeting progresses. Thus, in the Fast and Testamony meeting, several important events occur that serve to support and strengthen the beliefs of individual members: (1) the individual experiences an emotional response to his own belief, (2) beliefs are shared, strengthing others through mutual support, (3) intimacy is refreshed in families and between members of the congretation, and (4) the individual is an active participant in a moving, shared spiritual event.

THE MORMON FAMILY TODAY

In many, perhaps most ways, the behavior in Mormon families of today resembles the stereotypical white, protestant, middle-class American family. They are unique in two important ways: (1) the level of integration between church and family and (2) their attitudes about family life. Its not so much what Mormons do as what they believe that makes them unique.

Single Cursedness: Ministering Angels

Mormons believe in the Plan of Eternal Progression through which men and women may become Gods and Godesses by obedience to God's commandments. They teach that God is married as is Jesus, and thus Celestial Marriage in a Mormon temple is an essential step toward eventual exaltation. Those who do not marry in this life are thought to become ministering angels, who, because of their lack of obedience to His plan, will remain forever in this lesser degree of glory.

It is difficult to determine just how many Mormon men and women never marry,[9] but "by doctrine, by custom, and by social pattern they should not exist" (Anderson and Johnson, 1977:2).

Men especially are exhorted to do their duty as priesthood holders and marry one of the "worthy" women in the church (Raynes and Parsons, 1983). A review of sermons by church leaders on men who remain single reveals four main themes: (1) it is the nature of men to want to remain single, (2) single men are less spiritual, or righteous, (3) single men are too worldly and materialistic, and (4) single men are defective or disabled in some way (Raynes and Johnson, 1983). Other research (Anderson and Johnson, 1977) indicates that potential homosexuality, finicky standards, and a lack of maturity and interpersonal skills are perceived as reasons some Mormon males remain single. Of course, if single men are as bad as some imply, who would want to marry one?

Single men are rarely called to high positions of leadership in the church. The positions of bishop, stake president, mission president, and the general authorities are customarily filled with married men.

Single women have not been as stigmatized as men, partly because they are perceived as victims of circumstances beyond their control such as a lack of potential worthy partners or personal unattractiveness (Raynes and Parsons, 1983). In fact, single women seem to have been called to relatively higher positions in the church than single men (Johnson, 1983; Anderson, 1983; Breecher, 1982). Women are urged to remain single unless they can marry a worthy Mormon priesthood holder, but they are promised that if they are personally worthy, marriage arrangements will be made for them in the next life.

In recent years, the church has responded to the perceived needs of singles in the church through a number of new programs. However, these programs are not meant to be long-term solutions to this problem.

MOTHER IN HEAVEN

One Mormon doctrine having important family implications is the idea of a Mother in Heaven. In her analysis, Wilcox (1980) concludes that Joseph Smith originated this concept, but the evidence is not compelling. We do know, however, that around 1845, Eliza R. Snow wrote a poem that appears is nearly all Mormon hymn books, a stanza of which reads as follows:

---

[9]In Utah in 1980 (Bahr, 1986), more than 97 percent of men and women eventually marry. Because of the heavy Mormon population, we assume that Mormons in Utah marry at this rate, but those who never marry may be greater than Mormons who do not live in Utah.

> In the heavens are parents single?
> No; the thought makes reason stare!
> Truth is reason, truth eternal
> Tells me I've a Mother there.

The context of the poem leaves no doubt that Snow is referring to a goddess, the wife of our Heavenly Father. The entire poem was later put to music and titled "O My Father." The theme of this hymn is the eternal plan of God the Father and our relationship to him, and it has become one of the most loved Mormon hymns. In 1893, the fourth president of the church, Wilford Woodruff, attributed the birth of this concept to Eliza R. Snow—a wife of Joseph Smith and later Brigham Young—saying "that hymn is a revelation, though it was given to us by a woman" (1894:299). No matter what the exact source of this teaching, the work of Eliza R. Snow must be given much of the credit for its contemporary acceptance throughout the church.

Since concepts, however, are not usually accepted unless they fill some need for believers, Wilcox (1980:15) suggests one such function in her discussion:

> The widening "theology" which is developing is more of a "folk" or at least speculative theology rather than systematic development by theologians or definitive pronouncements coming from ecclesiastical leaders of the Church. For the moment, Mother in Heaven can be almost whatever an individual Mormon envisions Her to be.

In this regard, some Mormon feminists (Johnson, 1981) have begun praying to their Mother in Heaven—perhaps sincerely, perhaps to annoy the male dominated church leadership.

One might assume that through this doctrine a new emphasis on the female side of the deity might emerge, perhaps a new appreciation for the divine potential of women, or maybe even a "feminization" of traditional patriarchal concepts, but this does not appear to have been the case. Rather than liberalizing church doctrine or challenging traditional attitudes toward women, these ideas seem to have served more conservative purposes. One insightful analysis (Herren, Lindsey, and Mason, 1984:406) of the use of this concept by church leaders concludes the following:

> From the point of view of church authorities, the Mother in Heaven seems to provide a role model for Mormon women. Patriarchy among Mormons is seen as justified by the order of Heaven. Heavenly Father plays a more prominent role in Heavenly matters than does the Mother (perhaps Mothers) of his spirit children. Thus, it should be on earth.

The very title Mother in Heaven seems to support this conclusion. Heavenly Father is also God, the Creator, and the Almighty, whereas the female deity is defined only in her relationship to her husband and children. Practically by definition, she has no other roles.

Husband and Wife—Authority and Power

The expected authority pattern in Mormon life is patriarchal. The man has the responsibility to act as leader of his family and officiates in a number of religious functions in the home. Every believing male member of the Mormon church should be ordained to the priesthood at age 12 and, from then on, should have increasing responsibilities in the church. The Mormon father who holds this priesthood (as all participating men do) performs important functions in the religious aspects of family life such as blessing and naming of children (christening), baptism, priesthood ordination of sons, some temple ordinances, the blessing of sick family members, and leading in family prayers at each meal and on other occasions. In fact, almost all of the religious ordinances that a minister or priest might perform for members of other Christian churches is performed by the Mormon father, provided he is worthy.

Because virtually all Mormon men hold the priesthood, it might mistakenly be assumed that it is common and taken for granted. However, the priesthood is the cornerstone of Mormon claims to divine authority. Mormons believe that the priesthood is the medium through which all of God's power is manifested throughout the universe. God has chosen them alone to use this power in His name. All of God's chosen leaders, such as Moses, Abraham, John the Baptist, and even Jesus himself, are said to have held the priesthood and used it to perform the works of God. Mormons teach that after the death of Jesus, the Christian church gradually became corrupt and the priesthood was lost by mankind. However, they preach that in 1829, a visit by John the Baptist and, later that same year, by Peter, James, and John restored the priesthood to earth. Allen and Leonard (1976:45) emphasize the significance of these claims:

> The importance of Joseph Smith and Oliver Cowdrey proclaiming the visit of John the Baptist and Peter, James and John cannot be minimized in understanding the rapid rise of Mormonism in the 1830's. In the midst of a period when primativism, and restoration of the ancient gospel were principle religious themes, Joseph and Oliver declared that not only were they going to restore the ancient church, but they had also been given direct divine authority to do so.

This claim of ultimate truth and divine priesthood authority continues to be an important feature in the contemporary appeal of Mormonism (Shepherd and Shepherd, 1984).

Given the importance that Mormons place on the priesthood and the fact that only men are given, it would seem to make Mormon men very powerful in their marriages. In fact, Christenson (1956) demonstrated that nearly all Mormon couples believe that patriarchal authority is a divine endowment and is necessary, in this life as well as in eternity, as a system of family government. Yet, in another article, Christopherson (1963) has concluded that "the Mormon family has always expressed democracy in its family relations to a very high and pronounced degree." A recent study (Bahr, 1977) indicates that Mormon attitudes about family power and division of labor differ from their Protestant and Catholic neighbors but that their actual behavior is not very different. In fact, they may be moving toward a wider acceptance of female participation in the provider role, while remaining traditional in the areas of child care, housekeeping, and others (Albrecht, Bahr, and Chadwick, 1979).

The explanations for this paradox—patriarchal doctrine, equalitarian practices—are several:

1. *Mormon teachings on patriarchy.* The Mormon male does not hold his authority simply because he is male, but because he is worthy to have it. Men are encouraged to seek and use the council of their wives and to avoid abusing a sacred calling by exercising "unrighteous dominion," that is, by being cruel, thoughtless, or domineering. A worthy priesthood holder should exercise loving leadership in the family.
2. *Plural marriage.* In many cases, Mormon polygamists had wives who lived in several locations, sometimes hundreds of miles apart, making their constant presence difficult, if not impossible. Therefore, their wives were often left—by default—to run the family farm or business. This may have set a pattern that made submission to patriarchal rule difficult.
3. *Work and church roles of the father.* Some Mormon men make such heavy commitments to work and church roles that they are seldom home, so their wives may be forced to assume some of his family functions.
4. *Education.* Mormons value education for men and women; educated women are less likely to assume a submissive posture in marriage.
5. *Romantic love.* Romantic love and worthiness are considered important in the selection of mates among Mormons. Consideration, re-

spect, acceptance, support, and devotion are expected in a good marriage. To allow an eternal love to die by prideful male domination would mean failure in an important priesthood role.

Status of Women

Mormon women do not hold the priesthood, and although women have leadership positions in the Relief Society (woman's organization) and other church auxiliaries, they are placed in these positions by men who are church officers. In the past, the Relief Society was rather independent, but recently, this organization has been brought more directly under the control of the church's male leadership. Although women participate in church operations, they lack the priesthood authority to exercise leadership.

Church officials proclaim the role of mother to be the equal of, although different than, the male's priesthood role. Women are urged to make motherhood a career, and women who desire other careers are cautioned that it is sinful to place a career above their God-given duty to be a mother.

The leadership of the church has reacted in an overwhelmingly negative way to the Women's Liberation Movement. The church leaders seem to see, with some justification, that the aims and goals of some parts of the Women's Liberation Movement are incompatible with their stated doctrine. The Women's Liberation Movement is seen as being against children and family and in favor of abortion, sexual freedom, and lesbianism. The movement also presents a challenge to the authority of the exclusively male priesthood in the church.

As a result, the Mormon church has responded by opposing the Equal Rights Amendment (ERA). Warenski (1978) has documented the strong stand Mormons have taken against the ERA and suggests that, to some degree, they have become captives of the far-right wing of the American political spectrum on this issue. The excommunication of Sonia Johnson in December 1979 received public attention and showed the political organization of the Mormon church to be in opposition to the ERA (Sillitoe and Swenson, 1980). The actions of the church have raised the question of whether or not a woman can be a feminist and an active, believing Mormon at the same time. The answer is not at all clear at this writing.

In the important area of women's employment outside the home, however, it appears as though Mormon women are being affected by the same social and economic forces as their other American sisters. Howard Bahr (1979:2–3) reports that

> over the past generation the labor force participation of Utah women has become increasingly like that of women nationally, and today there is no difference. Utah women are as apt as other women to work outside the home . . . Both in Utah and in the nation, the position of women relative to men with respect to higher education and to participation in high-status occupations has either remained stable or deteriorated.

Devout Mormon women face a dilemma: their religious leaders urge them to have large families, eschew a career, and follow the lead of their husbands. However, as a group, they are having fewer children and increasing their labor participation. Both trends are likely to increase their relative power in marriage. The resolution of this dilemma is likely to be an important issue in the future.

Recent research (Newell, 1981; Newell, 1985) indicates that Joseph Smith ordained some women to perform some priesthood functions and may have envisioned some priesthood role for women. However, since the prophet's death, subsequent church leaders have gradually phased out all female participation in these ordinances, and now they are performed only by male priesthood holders. Charles (1985) challenges this exclusion of women from the priesthood, citing the ordination of deaconesses in the New Testament. She encourages church leaders to re-evaluate their position, drawing a parallel to recent change in racial restrictions on priesthood membership (1985). However, there is actually almost no agitation among Mormon women in this regard because they believe church leaders are only following God's will on this important matter.

In 1979, a television documentary broadcast in Salt Lake City raised concern over the amount of depression among Mormon women (Sunstone, 1979). Subsequent research demonstrated that more than one in five of the women in Salt Lake City are depressed, but Mormon women were no more depressed than their neighbors (Spendlove, West, and Stanish, 1984). Lower levels of education, a lack of caring from one's spouse, poor physical health, and lower income were risk factors associated with higher levels of depression among Mormon women. But much concern was raised because women who are obedient to their leaders and God's commands are supposed to be happy. Other sources of strain for women in the Mormon subculture that many result in depression are (1) setting impossible standards in the role of mother and wife, sometimes referred to as the "Mother-in-Zion Syndrome" (Sunstone, 1979); (2) feeling unappreciated in both family and church roles (Bennion, 1977); and (3) being in a powerless position in the church and the family (Wheatley-Pesci, 1986).

Urban-Rural Differences

Even with intense irrigation, the semi-arid land of the West cannot support a large farming population. In 1850, more than 50 percent of Utah's population was employed in agriculture, whereas by 1960, only 5.8 percent were farmers. However, because the church promotes such practices as keeping a garden, having a year's supply of food on hand, and having large families, Mormons have been characterized as urban dwellers with rural ideals.

Smith (1959) found that urban Mormons are less orthodox in many beliefs and practices than rural Mormons. Furthermore, urban Utah Mormons conform substantially more to church practices than urban Mormons on the West Coast (Mauss, 1972a, 1972b).

Socialization

Mormons are serious about childrearing, and they focus on results rather than methods. They do what they think will produce the desired outcome and are willing to accept religious and secular advice they believe will help them to be good parents (Kunz, 1963). Thomas (1883:282) claims that "Mormon parents may be described as affectionate, inclined to establish and enforce rules, and are very concerned about their children's welfare." Research supports the importance of emotional support, acceptance from parents, and even parental control as positive elements influencing adolescent religiosity in Mormon socialization practices (Thomas and Weigert, 1971; Weigert and Thomas, 1972). Wilkenson and Tanner (1980) have identified parental religiosity—as measured by temple attendance—as the primary element in producing family affection in Mormon homes. They conclude that the pro-family messages received by active Mormons do not change the frequency of contract with the children, but it does influence the parents' attitudes and behavior, making this contact more positive and creating a climate favorable to family affection.

Mormons want their children to become "good Mormons" (Bacon, 1964) with serving a mission for the church and temple marriage as primary indicators of success. They want their children, especially boys, to be well-educated, and they are usually successful in this regard (Brinkerhoff, 1978). Unlike most religious groups, for Mormons, higher education is positively associated with higher church activity (Albrecht and Heaton, 1984). However, for most Mormons, educational achievement is clearly second in importance to missionary service and temple marriage.

To serve on a mission, a young person (usually around 19 years old) must be willing to go anywhere in the world he is called on to go, serve with enthusiasm and devotion for two years, and support himself financially. This requires a considerable financial sacrifice for the missionary and his family, not to mention postponing educational or occupational plans at this critical juncture. A missionary must also be morally worthy to be called. These goals and requirements are substantially different from the adolescent subculture with which Mormon youth have prolonged contact. Yet, despite these high standards, approximately 40 percent of the eligible young adult Mormon men serve on missions. Well over 30,000 young men are at present serving as missionaries.

We do not know the percentage of Mormons who marry in the temple, but it is clear that most missionaries marry in the temple when they return, and continue to be active, believing Mormons (Mauss, 1972b). Although the family is clearly the primary institution in this successful socialization process, the church plays an important role, also.

Of course, the obvious function of a church is to present its message to believers. However, two not so obvious factors make major contributions to the Mormon process of socialization. One important aspect of the church socialization process is that of life-long service within the ward. From an early age, Mormon children take an active role in the ward, and by adolescence, the boys, having received the priesthood at age 12, take a major role in preparing and administering the sacrament and in other duties that prepare them for missionary service and, later, other Church leadership positions. Women, because they do not hold the priesthood, do not have as many potential avenues of service as men, but Mormon women usually have several jobs in the church presenting them with substantial opportunities to serve. Through this service, Mormon men and women develop strong attachments to the church and its programs and thus are exposed to a life-long socialization process through which they grow and develop their testimonies and leadership potential.

A second and, perhaps, less noticed aspect of socialization within the ward is the informal role of mentor. It is common in organizations that informal or unintended relationships arise that greatly contribute to the success of those organizations, and this is the case in Mormon wards as well. As a young person moves through the programs of the church, he or she is exposed to many ward members in teaching or administrative offices. In their relationships, there is an expectation that an intimate friendship may occur. Most active Mormons will refer lovingly to that special person—a teacher, scout master, bishop, coach—who took a special interest in them and helped them remain in the church. These people are especially important because they set a realistic example of spirituality, church participation and leadership, family involvement, and occupational achievement. This relationship is not threatening to family authority, but many allow the young person to discuss feelings or questions with an adult who is less directly involved in their success. This mentor is often like another parent that the child chooses, and their relationship is very important in producing a devout Mormon. In premarital sex practices, drug use, religious activity, intermarriage, and many other areas, the power of this uniquely Mormon combination of family-church socialization practices will be apparent.

Drug Use

Mormons believe that God, through Joseph Smith, gave them a revelation now called the Word of Wisdom, which forbids them using alcohol, tobacco, coffee, tea, and, by extension, any other harmful drugs. Shipps (1985) claims that obedience to the Word of Wisdom serves to set the Mormon believer apart from the world and is a symbol of his personal worthiness that binds him to God's chosen people. A study of high-school seniors (Bahr and Marcos, 1986) indicates that in general, Mormon youth observe the Word of Wisdom. As shown in Table 1, Utah seniors use alcohol, tobacco, and marijuana about 50 percent less frequently than other high school seniors in the United States. This would seem to indicate that although some Mormon youth have expcrimented with these drugs,

TABLE 1
Percent of High School Seniors who Reported Using Various Drugs Ever and During the Past Month

	USA 1984		UTAH 1984	
	EVER	PAST MO.	EVER	PAST MO.
Alcohol	92.6	67.2	55.9	34.3
Cigarettes	69.7	29.3	44.2	11.8
Marijuana	54.9	25.2	33.6	16.2
Amphetamine	27.9	8.3	19.9	7.3
Barbituates	9.5	1.7	8.5	3.3
Tranquilizer	12.4	2.1	9.0	3.4
Cocaine	16.1	5.8	10.3	4.8
Heroin	1.3	0.3	1.4	1.1
Inhalants	14.4	1.9	11.3	2.7
LSD	8.0	1.5	10.5	6.0
PCP	5.0	1.0	2.6	1.2
	N=16,900		N=4,901	

SOURCES: Adapted from Bahr and Marcos. 1986. "Drug Use," in Martin, Heaton, and Bahr (eds.), *Utah in Demographic Perspective: Regional and National Contrasts.* Provo, UT: Signature Books.

the majority do not use them regularly. However, a closer examination of the data reveals that Utah seniors use hard drugs at about the same rate as the rest of the country. These rates are low, which may suggest that hard-drug use is deviant in the larger culture as well as the Mormon subculture. However, the use of alcohol and tobacco is acceptable in the larger culture, so Mormon use of these drugs is deviant in the subculture but may represent conformity to society as a whole. Thus, because these drugs are widely accepted and legally available, they may present more temptation for Mormon youth than harder drugs. Once again, however, the influence of the church can be observed in the behavior of Mormon youth.

Intermarriage

Generally, Mormons have opposed intermarriage partially because mixed marriages were assumed to be less stable and partially because they share the racial attitudes of other Americans, but mainly, they have opposed mixed religious marriages for doctrinal reasons. Most Utah marriages are racially homogamous partly because of the low concentration of minority members in the population of Utah (Gallilier and Basilick, 1979).

Apparently, certain kinds of intermarriage do have a negative impact on marital stability for Mormons. Bahr (1981) reports that Mormons who intermarry are least likely to divorce a spouse with no religious preference and most likely to divorce a Catholic spouse. Thus, although the Catholic and Mormon religions stress marital stability, marriages between Mormons and Catholics, in Utah at least, are divorce prone.

Divorce

Divorce patterns for the state of Utah and the United States as a whole are very similar. As indicated in Table 2, since 1940 the rate of divorces per

TABLE 2
Divorces per 1,000 of the Population in Utah and the United States

	UTAH	MOUNTAIN REGION	UNITED STATES
1940	2.7		2.0
1950	3.0		2.6
1960	2.4		2.2
1970	3.7	5.9	3.5
1978	5.3	7.6	5.2

SOURCES: Utah Department of Health (1976); U.S. Bureau of Census (1977, 1980).

1,000 of the population in Utah has doubled and continues to rise. The adjacent mountain states have a higher divorce rate than Utah or the rest of the nation.

There is some indication that Mormons married in the temple have fewer than average divorces (Kunz, 1964; Cannon, 1966; Cannon and Steed, 1969), but other research has not confirmed this finding (Widstoe, 1940, 1952; Bahr, 1978). However, Mormons married in the temple have much lower divorce rates than other Mormons, whether married to other Mormons or not (Christensen, 1972; Cannon and Steed, 1969).

The Mormons try very hard to produce marriages that will last eternally. To marry in the temple, the couple must receive a recommendation, which requires passing two interviews with local church leaders. These interviews focus on chastity, observance of the Word of Wisdom, agreement to pay tithing as a couple, and support for the leaders of the church. Thus, serious attempts are made to assess religious commitment and assure value compatibility between marital aspirants in the Mormon subculture in hopes of producing eternal marriages. The causes of temple marriages are not understood at this time.

Family Size, Fertility, Contraception, and Abortion

Perhaps no area of Mormon family has received more serious scrutiny by social scientists than Mormon fertility patterns. First, Mormons are proud of their large families and are willing to have this aspect of their lives studied. Second, because Mormons believe in an eternal, extended family unit as a heavenly structure, they have been leaders in genealogical research. They have collected and validated thousands of detailed family histories covering several generations in some families. These records have been made available to demographers, who are beginning to produce excellent multigenerational studies of Mormon fertility patterns (Skolnick et al., 1978). Finally, an important issue of study is how Mormon couples conform to the strongly pronatalist doctrine of the church.

There are excellent reviews of the position of the Mormon church on birth control and family size (Hastings et al., 1972; Bush, 1976a) that clearly show church opposition to birth control, voluntary sterilization, and abortion. Mormons take the biblical injunction to multiply and replenish the earth very literally and seriously. An official letter issued in 1969 seemed to allow for child spacing and consideration for the physical and mental health of women in making birth control decisions, but it also proclaimed that those who limit their family would "reap disappointment by and by." Self-control was suggested as the only acceptable means of birth control. The First Presidency of the church (Priesthood Bulletin,

1973:1) says that in some "rare cases" (rape or danger to the health of the mother) abortion may be acceptable. However, they also state that "abortion must be considered one of the most revolting practices of this day." President Kimball (1976:2–5) stated the following:

> [T]he union of the sexes, husband and wife, . . . was for the principal purpose of bringing children into the world. . . . We know of no directive from the Lord that proper sexual experiences between husbands and wives need be limited totally to the procreation of children, but we find much evidence from Adam until now that no provision was ever made by the Lord for indiscriminate sex.

If this is the ideal, how have Mormons responded to it? All surveys indicate a declining birth rate among Mormons (Bush, 1976; Hastings et al., 1972; Skolnick et al., 1978; Wise and Condie, 1975; Bowers and Hastings, 1970). On the other hand, Mormons tend to want and have more children than other Americans, including Roman Catholics (Thornton, 1979). The birth rates of Mormon leaders have followed the same general church membership, with the leaders having slightly larger families than Mormons as a whole (Thornton, 1979).

Mauss (1972b) has demonstrated that Mormons living in urban centers on the West Coast have fewer children than Salt Lake City Mormons but they still have more children than their neighbors. Converts to the church tend to have larger families than those born into the church (Merrill and Peterson, 1972), whereas orthodox Mormons have more children than their less committed brothers and sisters.

It appears that the forces of urbanization and industrialization are depressing the birth rates of both the general American population and Mormons. However, Thornton (1979) concluded that if the historical trend were to continue, it would be at least 150 years before Mormon and non-Mormon birth rates would converge.

Although there has been a dramatic increase in abortion rates in Utah, abortion remains relatively uncommon (Martin, 1986). In Utah in 1973, the abortion ratio was 4, rising to 97 in 1982, increasing almost twenty-five times. In the country as a whole, the abortion ratio went from 237 to 426 in 1982 (Martin, 1986). One can conclude that (1) the abortion ratio is relatively low in Utah, (2) Utahans are having more abortions, and (3) Utah abortion rates and those of the country at large are converging. Thus, although Mormon abortion rates are surely higher than church leaders desire, they are relatively low and reflect broad conformity to church teachings.

Mormons appear to support their leaders with regard to abortion, but on the issue of birth control, there appears to be a gap between what the church teaches and the attitudes and behavior of the members. By and large, Mormons are family members, and though they differ from non-Mormons to some degree, they practice birth control with the most effective methods available (Peterson, 1971; Hastings et al., 1972; Bush, 1976; Bowers and Hastings, 1970). For many of them, however, this discrepancy is a source of guilt and personal discomfort (Bush, 1976). Although Mormons use contraceptives, they also have a strong desire for children. Thus, their high rates of fertility are more pro-child, than anti-birth control (Heaton and Calkins, 1983).

Premarital Sex: Exhortations for Chastity

Although premarital chastity has always been important to Mormons, they seem willing to risk some premarital sex to ensure a more important goal—an eternal, love-based marriage. Given their view of heaven and the pivotal importance of a loving, eternal marriage as the basis of progression toward godhood, it is not surprising that they would create many opportunities for young people to mix socially and develop romantic-love relationships. They sponsor dances, parties, and other special activities that further courtship among the unmarried. Such gatherings are seen as a training ground for developing interpersonal skills, knowledge of the opposite sex, and the wisdom to make a good mate choice. Thus, while Mormons value premarital chastity above almost anything, they also value the sacred fundamental of free agency, or free choice, more. They do this because they believe it is the best way to produce loving, passionate, harmonious marriages that will produce an eternal commitment worthy of their most sacred ordinance—temple marriage.

However, this goal presents the risk that some will succumb to temptation and leave the church or abandon its teachings about sex. In the last two decades, the sexual revolution has presented more sexual opportunities to American youth, Mormons included. The response by the church has been to place increasing emphasis on the "law of chastity" and make their preaching more direct and explicit (Rytting and Rytting, 1982). In general, church leaders increasingly expressed opposition to abortion, pornography, homosexuality, sex education, birth control, and sex in the media from 1951 to 1979 (Rytting and Rytting, 1982). Thus, the church has responded to the sexual revolution by favoring societal limitations on sexual information and expression as well as encouraging private morality.

On the whole, they seem to have been relatively successful in this attempt. Smith (1976) has documented a slight increase in sexual compliance with church premarital standards over the last three decades. This pattern contrasts dramatically with others who have changed toward a greater acceptance and practice of premarital sex (Smith, 1976). Smith also found that inactive Mormons more often resembled the general population in sexual practices than active Mormons. It may be, as Christensen (1977) suggests, that especially among Mormon youth, premarital sex is rebellion and/or acting out behavior. Christensen (1977:4) says that Mormons

> were somewhat more promiscious once they started with premarital sex; were more apt to have engaged in their first premarital sexual experience as a result of either force or felt obligation; were more apt to have been careless or reckless in their first premarital sexual encounter, in the sense of drinking alcohol and not practicing contraception.

There is little question that the strict sexual standard set by the church is widely observed; however, this has been identified as a potential stress point in Mormon culture. Christensen (1972) finds that Mormons are more likely than others he studied to violate their own sexual standard, resulting in more guilt, hasty marriage, and perhaps more divorce later on. Thus, although Mormons have been rather successful in meeting their conservative sexual goals, the cost may be that some—having violated these standards—have become less tied to the church and its teachings.

The Elderly

Surprisingly, there is little written about the elderly in the Mormon subculture. The top leaders in the Mormon church keep their positions until death. A type of "date of rank" is important in determining who is president of the Quorum of Twelve Apostles, and the head of this quorum normally becomes president of the church when the current president dies. This seniority system is not followed elsewhere in the church, because young and middle-aged men dominate the leadership positions. It seems that the elderly, as in other churches, lose their positions and power.

Temple work, which involves participating in sacred dramas and rituals as proxy for the dead, is doctrinally important in the Mormon church and is a regular source of activity among the elderly, who have looked forward to the day when they could retire and work in the temple. Because most do not receive money for this work, it is not motivated by a desire for income. The gratification is religious and social in nature.

Many of the elderly either are not "worthy" or do not find temple work rewarding, so they do not have this outlet. It is difficult for the elderly person who has not been active in the church to be a part of it in later years.

The signs of his former "unworthy" life are all around him, and so he may not be willing to attend church. Recently, there have been some centers for the elderly appearing in Utah towns that might fill a need for many non-Mormon or inactive Mormon elderly, although active Mormons also participate in these centers.

One study of intergenerational contact in elderly Mormon families (Albrecht and Chappell, 1977:74) revealed that the Mormon pattern of intergenerational contact does not differ from the more general societal pattern and that this contact "provides no guarantee that there will be an absence of growing feelings of powerlessness and a lack of sense of meaning and purpose in life."

The church has no specific program designed to meet the needs of its elderly members and stresses the religious obligation of the family to provide for its aging members (Featherstone, 1975). If there are no family members ready or willing to care for an elderly church member, the church may provide for them, but this is not a guaranteed retirement plan.

CHANGE AND ADAPTATION

The major thrust of this chapter has been the dramatic changes the Mormon church has made in its history, which have allowed the church to move into the American mainstream while maintaining a strong identity. Like the French Canadian Americans and the Amish, there are no external barriers to assimilation of individual Mormons into the larger society. Their predominantly Anglo–Scandinavian ethnic stock, coupled with their strong adherence to middle-class norms, creates no barriers to their acceptance by other Americans. This chapter has documented the different attitudes of active and inactive Mormons. These patterns suggest that some Mormons are leaving the faith and becoming assimilated to the larger culture. However, the general trend seems to be in the opposite direction.

Leone suggests that Mormonism has a "capacity to absorb change and exists in a condition of continued renewal" (1974:763). He observes that the leaders of the church are sensitive to their followers and make Mormonism more acceptable to the membership by changing a doctrine or the emphasis on certain doctrine. For example, the church has moved from supporting polygamy as a central principle to a glorification of monogamous family life.

Dolgin (1974), having examined the belief system of Mormons, concludes that they have a strong sense of peoplehood that arises from the assumption that they hold similar beliefs. However, she reports that under an umbrella of official doctrines, individual Mormons tend to hold widely divergent views (Dolgin, 1974). Apparently, many who leave the church do so for doctrinal reasons, but other issues also influence this decision (Mauss, 1969: Seggar and Blake, 1970).

O'Dea (1972:162) felt that the issue of whether black Mormon men would be allowed into the priesthood would be a diagnostic issue about whether the church could adapt to modern realities or remain lost in the past:

> The race issue has become symbolic of the entire complex of problems involved in that challenge and the defensive attitude against the idea of change with respect to its stands surrogate for "standpatism" generally in the face of the larger challenge. The church's adequacy to handle the problems of its encounter with modernity will eventually be judged by the adequacy of its response to the problem of racial justice.

Since publication of this article in June 1978, President Kimball announced a divine revelation that blacks were to be given the priesthood. It was an electrifying event, and most Mormons who heard about the event called other Mormons they associated with to find out whether they knew. There seemed to be two general reactions: (1) they did not think this would happen in their lifetime and (2) relief—"it's about time." There was wide acceptance, and the church seems to have adapted without any problems.

However, as Mauss notes (1983:12), the future will present some strong challenges to the Mormon movement:

> New social and religious movements that, like Mormonism, survive and prosper are those that succeed in maintaining indefinitely a creative tension between two opposite strains in relation to the surrounding society: the strain toward greater assimilation and respectability on the one hand and that toward greater separations, peculiarity, and assertiveness on the other.

Just when Mormons are beginning to become part of the American mainstream, they may face an even greater challenge—becoming an important international religion (Stark, 1984). Mormonism is growing at a rapid rate despite the prejudice against it (Stark and Bainbridge, 1984). From 1960 to 1980, the population of the church more than doubled each decade (52 percent, 73 percent, and 58 percent in each decade, respectively) and it is projected that by 2080, there may be as many as 265,259,000 Mormons (Stark, 1984). Much of this increase is occurring in South America, as well as Korea and Japan. This rapid growth is not always smooth, and the somewhat jingoistic pro-Americanism of some church leaders does not play well in Latin American or Asian countries

(Tullis, 1983). To appeal to a broader world community, pressures to change some of the beliefs and practices identifiably Mormon may arise. The nature of the community spirit peculiar to Mormonism may not survive this kind of expansion. The question is, will success kill Mormonism? Shepherd and Shepherd (1984:39)

> would argue that perhaps the primary appeals of Mormonism in the modern world are not so different from what was offered by the vision of the Mormon kingdom in the nineteenth century: authoritative centralized leadership, moral certitude, a strong sense of community identification and active involvement in a transcendent cause. Like other conservative religions in modern society, Mormonism functions largely as an alternative to the confusing diversity and moral ambiguity of modern secular life.

To sustain this growth and meet the challenge associated with it, the Mormon family will need to continue to provide the church with committed men and women to serve as missionaries and devote time to the support of the church and its programs.

As church membership increases, however, this community feeling may be more difficult to maintain. Until recently, Mormons were white, middle-class Americans, usually from Utah or adjoining states. In a few minutes of conversation, newly acquainted Mormons were likely to find that they were connected through mutual friends or associates or that they held similar positions in the church. This, plus the factors previously mentioned, has traditionally promoted strong bonds between Mormons. As the church membership becomes more diverse, such bonds may become more tenuous.

REFERENCES

Albrecht, Stan L., and Bradford Chappell. 1977. "Intergenerational Contact and Alienation in Elderly Mormon Families," in Phillip R. Kunz (ed.), *The Mormon Family.* Provo, UT: Brigham Young University, pp. 62–77.

Albrecht, Stan L., Howard M. Bahr, and Bruce A. A. Chadwick. 1979. "Changing Family and Sex Roles: An Assessment of Age Differences," *Journal of Marriage and the Family,* 41:41–50.

Albrecht, Stan, and Tim Heaton. 1984. "Secularization, Higher Education, and Religiosity," *Review of Religious Research,* 26(1):43–58.

Alder, Douglas. 1978. "The Mormon Ward: Congregation or Community?" *Journal of Mormon History,* 5:61–78.

Allen, James B., and Glen M. Leonard. 1976. *The Story of the Latter-Day Saints.* Salt Lake City, UT: Deseret.

Anderson, Lavina. 1983. "Ministering Angels: Single Women in Mormon Society," *Dialogue: A Journal of Mormon Thought,* 16(3):59–72.

Anderson, Lavina, and Jeffery O. Johnson. 1977. "Endangered Species: Single Men in the Church," *Sunstone,* 2(2):2–7.

Bacon, Mary R. 1964. "Comparative Study of Expressive and Instrumental Concerns of Homemakers in Wasatch County." Unpublished paper, Brigham Young University.

Bahr, Howard. 1978. *Mormon Families in Comparative Perspective: Denominational Contrasts in Divorce, Marital Satisfaction and Other Characteristics.* Provo, UT: Brigham Young University.

———. 1979. "The Declining Destinctiveness of Utah's Working Women," Discussion Paper Series, Family Research Institute, Brigham Young University.

———. 1981. "Religious Intermarriage and Divorce in Utah and the Mountain States," *Journal for the Scientific Study of Religion,* 20(3):251–261.

Bahr, Stephen J., and Howard M. Bahr. 1977. "Religion and Family Roles: A Comparison of Catholic, Mormon and Protestant Families," in Phillip R. Kunz (ed.), *The Mormon Family.* Provo, UT: Family Research Center, Brigham Young University, pp. 45–61.

Bahr, Stephen, and Anastasios Marcos. 1986. "Drug Use," in Thomas Martin, Tim Heaton, and Stephen Bahr (eds.), *Utah in Demographic Perspective: Regional and National Contrasts.* Provo, UT: Signature Books.

Beecher, Maureen. 1982. "The Leading Sisters: A Female Hierarchy in Nineteenth Century Mormon Society," *Journal of Mormon History,* 9:25–39.

Bennion, Francine. 1977. "L.D.S. Working Mothers," *Sunstone,* 2(1):6–15.

Bowers, Donald W., and Donald W. Hastings. 1970. "Childspacing and Wife's Employment Status Among 1940–41 University of Utah Graduates," *Social Science Journal,* 7:125–136.

Brinkerhoff, Merlin. 1978. "Religion and Goal Orientations: Does Denomination Make a Difference?" 39(3):203–218.

Brodie, Fawn. 1971. *No Man Knows My History: The Life of Joseph Smith, the Mormon Prophet.* New York: Knopf.

Burgers-Olson, Vicky. 1975. "Family Structure and Dynamics in Early Utah Mormon Families, 1847–85." Ph.D. diss., Northwestern University.

Bush, Lester E. 1976. "Birth Control Among the Mormons: Introduction to an Insistent Question," *Dialogue: A Journal of Mormon Thought,* 10:12–44.

Campbell, Eugene E., and Bruce L. Campbell. 1978. "Divorce Among Mormon Polygamists: Extent and Explanations," *Utah Historical Quarterly,* 46:4–23.

Cannon, Kenneth. 1966. "Utah's Divorce Situation," *Family Perspective,* 1(1)10–16.

Cannon, Kenneth L., and Seymour Steed. 1972. "Relationship Between Occupational Level, Religious Commitment, Age of Bride at Marriage, and Divorce Rate for L.D.S. Marriages," in *Developing a Marriage Relationship.* Provo, UT: Brigham Young University Press, pp. 285–292.

Cannon, Kenneth, II. 1978. "Beyond the Manifesto: Polygamous Cohabitation among L.D.S. General Authorities after 1890," *Utah Historical Quarterly,* 46(1):24–36.

Charles, Melodie. 1985. "L.D.S. Women and Priesthood: Scriptural Precedents for Priesthood," *Dialogue: A Journal of Mormon Thought,* 18(3):15–20.

Christensen, Harold T. 1972. "Stress Points in Mormon Family Culture," *Dialogue: A Journal of Mormon Thought,* 7 (Winter):20–34.

———. 1977. "Some Next Steps in Mormon Family Research," in Phillip R. Kunz (ed.), *The Mormon Family.* Provo, UT: Family Research Center, Brigham Young University, pp. 1–12.

Christensen, Harold T., and C. F. Gregg. 1970. "Changing Sex Norms in America and Scandinavia," *Journal of Marriage and the Family,* (November):626.

Christopherson, Victor A. 1956. "An Investigation of Patriarchal Authority in the Mormon Family," *Marriage and Family Living,* 18(November):328–333.

———. 1963. "Is the Mormon Family Becoming More Democratic?" in Blaine Porter (ed.), *The Latter-Day Saint Family.* Salt Lake City, UT: Deseret, pp. 317–338.

Dolgin, Janet L. 1974. "Latter-Day Sense and Substance," in Irving I. Zaretsky and Mark P. Leone (eds.), *Religious Movements in Contemporary America.* Princeton: Princeton University Press, pp. 519–546.

Durkheim, Emile. 1951. *Suicide.* New York: Free Press.

Ellsworth, S. George. 1951. "History of Mormon Missions in the United States and Canada, 1830–1860." Unpublished paper, University of California at Berkeley.

Embry, Jessie, and Martha Bradley. 1985. "Mothers and Daughters in Polygamy," *Dialogue: A Journal of Mormon Thought,* 18(3)99–107.

Featherstone, Vaughan J. 1975. "The Savior's Program for Care of the Aged," *Conference Reports,* (October).

Galliher, John F., and Linda Basilick. 1979. "Utah's Liberal Drug Laws: Structural Foundations and Triggering Events," *Social Problems,* 26:284–297.

Goodman, Kristen, and Tim Heaton. 1986. "Divorce," in Thomas Martin, Tim Heaton, and Stephen Bahr (eds.), *Utah in Demographic Perspective: Regional and National Contrasts.* Provo, UT: Signature Books.

Hastings, Donald, Charles H. Reynolds, and Ray Canning. 1972. "Mormonism and Birth Planning: The Discrepancy Between Church Authorities' Teachings and Lay Attitudes," *Population Studies,* 26:19–28.

Heaton, Tim, and Sandra Calkins. 1983. "Family Size and Contraceptive Use Among Mormons: 1965–75," *Review of Religious Research,* 25(2):102–113.

Heoren, John, Donald B. Lindsey, and Marylee Mason. 1984. "The Mormon Concept of Mother in Heaven: A Sociological Account of its Origins and Development," *Journal for the Scientific Study of Religion,* 23(4):396–411.

Hill, Marvin S. 1978. "The Rise of the Mormon Kingdom of God," in Richard Poll (ed.), *Utah's History.* Provo, UT: Brigham Young University Press.

Ivins, Stanley. 1956. "Notes of Mormon Polygamy," *Western Humanities Review,* 10:224–239.

Johnson, Jeffery. 1983. "On the Edge: Mormonisms Single Men," *Dialogue: A Journal of Mormon Thought,* 16(3):48–58.

Johnson, Sonia. 1981. *From Housewife to Heretic.* Garden City, NY: Doubleday.

Kimball, Heber C. 1858. "Temples and Endowments," *Journal of Discourses,* 5:22.

Kimball, Spencer W. 1976. "Marriage the Proper Way," *The New Era,* (February):4–7.

Kunz, Phillip R. 1963. "Religious Influences on Parental Discipline and Achievement Demands," *Marriage and Family Living,* 24 (May):224–225.

———. 1964. "Mormon and Non-Mormon Divorce Patterns," *Journal of Marriage and the Family,* 26 (May):211–213.

———. 1980. "One Wife or Several: A Comparative Study of Late 19th Century Marriage in Utah" in Thomas Alexander and Jessie Embry (eds.), *The Mormon People: Their Character and Traditions.* Provo, Utah: Brigham Young University Press.

Lythgoe, Dennis. 1977. "Marketing the Mormon Image: An Interview with Wendell Jr. Ashton," *Dialogue: A Journal of Mormon Thought,* 10(3):15–24.

Martin, Thomas. 1986. "Abortion," in Thomas Martin, Tim Heaton, and Stephen Bahr (eds.), *Utah in Demographic Perspective: Regional and National Contrasts.* Provo, UT: Signature Books.

Mauss, Armand L. 1969. "Dimensions of Religious Diffection," *Review of Religious Research,* 10:128–135.

———. 1972a. "Moderation in All Things: Political and Social Outlooks of Modern Urban Mormons," *Dialogue: A Journal of Mormon Thought,* 7 (Spring):57–64.

———. 1972b. "Saints, Cities, and Secularism: Religious Attitudes and Behavior of Modern Urban Mormons," *Dialogue: A Journal of Mormon Thought,* 7 (Summer):8–27.

———. 1976. "Shall the Youth of Zion Falter? Mormon Youth and Sex: A Two City Comparison," *Dialogue: A Journal of Mormon Thought,* 10:82–83.

———. 1983. "The Angel and the Beehive: Our Quest for Peculiarity and Struggle with Secularization," *B. Y. U. Today,* 37(4):12–15.

May, Dean L. 1983. "A Demographic Portrait of the Mormons, 1830–1980," in Thomas G. Alexander and Jessie L. Embry (eds.), *After 150 Years: the Latter-Day Saints in Sesquicentennial Perspective."* Midvale, UT: Signature Books, pp. 39–69.

Mulder, William. 1957. *Homeward to Zion.* Minneapolis: University of Minnesota Press.

Newell, Linda. 1981. "A Gift Given: A Gift Taken," *Sunstone,* 6(5):16–25.

———. 1985. "The Historical Relationship of Mormon Women and Priesthood," *Dialogue: A Journal of Mormon Thought,* 18(3):21–32.

O'Dea, Thomas F. 1957. *The Mormons.* Chicago: University of Chicago Press.

———. 1972. "Sources of Strain in Mormon History Reconsidered," in Marvin S. Hill and James B. Allen (eds.), *Mormonism and American Culture.* New York: Harper & Row, pp. 147–167.

Peterson, Erlend D. 1971. "Attitudes Concerning Birth Control and Abortion as Related to L.D.S. Religiosity of Brigham Young University Students." Unpublished paper, Brigham Young University.

Peterson, Evan T. 1977. "Parent-Adolescent Relationships in the Mormon Family," in Phillip R. Kunz (ed.), *The Mormon Family.* Provo, UT: Brigham Young University, pp. 108–115.

Quinn, Dennis M. 1973. "Organizational Development and Social Origins of the Mormon Hierarchy, 1832–1932: A Prosopographical Study." Master's thesis, University of Utah.

Quinn, Michael. 1985. "L. D. S. Church Authority and New Plural Marriages, 1890–1904," *Dialogue: A Journal of Mormon Thought,* 18(1):9–105.

Raynes, Marybeth, and Erin Parsons. 1983. "Single Cursedness: An Overview of L.D.S. Authorities Statements about Unmarried People," *Dialogue: A Journal of Mormon Thought,* 16(3):35–45.
Rytting, Marvin, and Ann Rytting. 1982. "Exhortations for Chastity: A Content Analysis of Church Literature," *Sunstone,* 7(2):15–21.
Seggar, John F., and Reed H. Blake. 1970. "Post-Joining Non-Participation: An Exploratory Study of Convert Inactivity," *Review of Religious Research,* 11:204–209.
Shepherd, Gary, and Gordon Shepherd. 1984. "Mormon Commitment Rhetoric," *Journal for the Scientific Study of Religion,* 23(2):129–139.
Shepherd, Gordon, and Gary Shepherd. 1984b. "Mormonism in Secular Society: Changing Patterns in Official Ecclesiastical Rhetoric," 26(1):28–42.
Shipps, June. 1978. "The Mormons: Looking Forward and Outward," *The Christian Century,* (August 16–23):761–766.
———. 1985. *Mormonism: The Story of a New Religious Tradition.* Chicago: University of Illinois Press.
Sillitoe, Linda. 1980. "Church, Politics and Sonia Johnson: The Central Conundrum," *Sunstone,* 5(1):35–42.
Sillitoe, Linda, and Paul Swenson. 1980. "A Moral Issue," *Utah Holiday,* 9:18–34.
Skolnick, M., L. Bean, P. May, V. Arbon, K. De Nevhs, and P. Cartwright. 1978. "Mormon Demographic History I. Nuptiality and Fertility of Once-Married Couples," *Population Studies,* 32(1):5–19.
Smith, James, E., and Phillip R. Kunz. 1976. "Polygyny and Fertility in Nineteenth Century America," *Population Studies,* 30:30.
Smith, Wilford E. 1959. "The Urban Threat to Mormon Norms," *Rural Sociology,* 24:355–361.
Smith, Wilford. 1976. "Mormon Sex Standards on College Campuses, or Deal Us Out of the Sexual Revolution," *Dialogue: A Journal of Mormon Thought,* 10(2):76–81.
Spendlove, David, Dee West, and William Stanish. 1984. "Risk Factors and the Prevalence of Depression in Mormon Women," *Social Science Medicine,* 18(6):491–495.
Stark, Rodney. 1984. "The Rise of a New World Faith," *Review of Religious Research,* 26(1):19–27.
Stark, Rodney, and William Bainbridge. 1980. "Networks of Faith: Interpersonal Bonds and Recruitment to Cults and Sects," *American Journal of Sociology,* 85(6):1376–1395.
Stathis, Stephen, and Dennis Lythgoe. 1977. "Mormonism in the Nineteen Seventies: the Popular Perception," *Dialogue: A Journal of Mormon Thought,* 10(3):95–113.
Sunstone. 1979. "Mormon Women and Depression," *Sunstone,* 4(2):16–26.
Thomas, Darwin. 1983. "Family in the Mormon Experience," in William D'Antonio and Joan Aldous (eds.), *Families and Religious: Conflict and Change in Modern Society.* Beverly Hills: Sage Publications.
Thomas, Darwin, and Andrew Weigert. 1971. "Socialization and Adolescent Conformity to Significant Others: A Cross National Analysis," *American Sociological Review,* 36 (October):835–847.

Thornton, Arland. 1979. "Religion and Fertility: The Case of Mormonism," *Journal of Marriage and the Family,* 40:131–142.
Tullis, La Mond. 1983. "The Church Moves Outside the United States: Some Observations from South America," in Thomas Alexander and Jessie Embry (eds.), *After 150 Years: The Latter-Day Saints in Sesquicentennial Perspective.* Midvale, UT: Signature Books.
U. S. Bureau of the Census. 1976. *Statistical Abstract of the United States* (97th ed). Washington, DC: U. S. Government Printing Office, p. 71.
Utah Department of Health. 1976. *Annual Report on Marriage and Divorce.* Salt Lake City, UT.
Van Wagoner, Richard. 1985. "Mormon Polyandry in Nauvoo," *Dialogue: A Journal of Mormon Thought,* 18(3):67–83.
Warenski, Marilyn. 1978. *Patriarchs and Politics: The Plight of the Mormon Woman.* New York: McGraw-Hill.
Weber, Max. 1968. *Max Weber On Charisma and Institution Building.* Chicago: University of Chicago Press.
Weigert, Andrew, and Darwin Thomas. 1972. "Parental Support, Control and Adolescent Religiosity: An Extension of Previous Research," *Journal for the Scientific Study of Religion,* 11(4):389–393.
Wheatley-Pesci, Meg. 1985. "An Expanded Definition of Priesthood? Some Present and Future Consequences," *Dialogue: A Journal of Mormon Thought,* 18(3):33–42.
Widtsoe, John. 1952. "Does Temple Marriage Reduce Divorce?" *Improvement Era,* 55 (January):14–15.
———. 1968. "Does Temple Marriage Diminish Divorce?" *Improvement Era,* 51 (January):641–656.
Wilcox Linda. 1980. "The Mormon Concept of a Mother in Heaven," *Sunstone,* 5(5):9–15.
Wilkinson, Melvin, and William Tanner. 1980. "The Influence of Family Size, Interaction, and Religiosity on Family Affection in a Mormon Sample," *Journal of Marriage and the Family,* (May) 297–304.
Wise, Jeffery, and Spencer J. Condie. 1975. "Intergenerational Fertility Throughout Four Generations," *Social Biology,* 22:144–150.
Woodruff, Wilford. 1857. *Journal History of the Church,* April 1957.
———. 1884. "Discourse" Millennial Star 56 (April 1884):229—Delivered Oct. 8, 1893.
Young, Brigham. 1858. Journal History, Dec. 15.
———. 1861. Conference Reports, Oct. 8. (Reported by George D. Watt. Also found in the Journal of James Beck.)
———. 1925. Discourses of Brigham Young Arranged by John A. Widtsoe. Salt Lake City, UT: Deseret.
Young, Kimball. 1954. *Isn't One Wife Enough?* New York: Henry Holt.

Index

M

S